PENNIES FROM A POOR BOX

Pennies from a Poor Box

By Joseph E. Manton, C.SS.R.

Foreword By
Richard Cardinal Cushing

Second Printing

ST. PAUL EDITIONS

IMPRIMI POTEST:

    Very Rev. James T. Connolly, C.SS.R., J.C.D.

IMPRIMATUR:

    ✚ Richard Cardinal Cushing

March 19, 1962

Library of Congress Catalog Card Number: 62-14507

Copyright, 1962, by the *Daughters of St. Paul*

Printed in U.S.A. by the *Daughters of St. Paul*
50 St. Paul's Ave., Jamaica Plain, Boston 30, Mass.

FOREWORD

"Of making many books there is no end...."
So wrote the author of Ecclesiasticus two hundred years before Our Savior's birth.

Today the tireless spate of books—books—books falls into three categories. A large fraction are worthless ephemera. Another segment are cyanide capsules. And lastly, there do appear from time to time books of unassailable merit—the gold that remains in the miner's sieve when the rubble is washed through the screen. To this third category, to this select company of the blessed, I assign "Pennies from a Poor Box," the collected Catholic Hour sermons of Father Joseph Manton, C.SS.R. of the famed Mission Church Parish, Roxbury.

Let's insist—in the context of this foreword, it is an irrelevance—that Father Manton is a cherished friend. For, by a standard honestly critical and objective, "Pennies from a Poor Box" has superiorities rarely met in any writing religious or secular. Our author has given us a book which instructs, inspires, solaces and—by a wizardry uniquely Father Manton's—delights.

Born in Brooklyn, New York, Father Manton has been a priest for thirty-two years. Post-graduate studies in English at Catholic University, Washington, perfected his mastery of the spoken and the written word. At Mission Church, where he was assigned in 1939, he has been teacher, parish priest and a radio personality of national stature. The Novena Preacher at the Minor Basilica for twenty-three years, Father Manton has also presented an annual series on the National Catholic Hour every year since 1947.

In general, publishers have only a courteous but decisive refusal for the priest who submits a folder of sermons for their consideration. The publisher explains—"Priests would buy it, perhaps. But not the people. Sincerely sorry, Father, but I'd lose money." In Father Manton's case these sermons were never submitted. I practically had to subpena them for publication. I think that I know the difference between a *saleable book and that unfortunate venture—a worthy book, perhaps, but dully yawnful—foredoomed from birth for the "Reduced Price Clearances." And I am convinced that Father Manton's "Pennies from a Poor Box" is an anthology which both priests and laity will buy and read.*

To all of Father Manton's public addresses, his voice and electric presence contribute their own persuasive white magic. But, even divorced from this influence, "Pennies from a Poor Box" can stand unsupported. Like the superior pulpit eloquence of other masters, "The Best of Father Manton" is also superb literature, and, in that character, has a life of its own.

In effect: these addresses which captivated radio audiences are literature, as well as eloquence. Spoken, they thrilled and elevated. As writing, their approach is through a different avenue, the reading eye. But the echoes of even the noblest eloquence become part of the vacant air; their recollection becomes obscured or even lost totally. A good book—in a sense—is forever.

In the spirit of their sainted founder, the Congregation of the Most Holy Redeemer, familiarly and affectionately known as The Redemptorists, love the Mother of God. As Alphonsus defended and honored this Peerless Queen in his "Glories of Mary", the sons of the sainted founder have preached her fame and resisted those who sought to diminish what God has uniquely exalted.

So, in "Pennies from a Poor Box" we would expect to find—and we do find—that among the most moving eloquence in Father Manton's book are the sermons which honor God's Mother. In the apt expression and heart-deep affection of his tributes, Father Manton is a latter-day troubadour, singing the glories of our race's dearest and best—"Our Life, Our Sweetness and Our Hope."

From my heart, I congratulate Father Joseph Manton, C.SS.R. With confidence I predict for "Pennies from a Poor Box" the distinguished success its virtues merit.

†Richard Cardinal Cushing
Archbishop of Boston

CONTENTS

THROUGH CHRIST OUR LORD:
 Tears Over a City 11
 Christ and Women 17
 Carpenter and Redeemer 24

MOTHER OF GOD:
 The Real Mary 32
 Virgin Immaculate 39
 Queen of the Commonplace 46
 Mary's Apron Strings 53
 Hands That Held the Beads 61

SAINTS FOR THE AINTS:
 In Praise of St. Blaise 69
 Patron of Misfits 77
 Sawdust Halo 84
 The Mothers' Saint 91
 This Meddlesome Priest 98
 Martyr to Chastity 106

WHO IS MY NEIGHBOR?:
 The Other Law 114
 Red Stabbing Tongues 121
 Hands and Holy Water 129
 Festering Hate 134
 Honesty is the Only Policy 141

THIRD FINGER, LEFT HAND:
 The Good Ship Courtship 149
 A Perplexed Patron 156
 The Man I Marry 163
 Recipe for a Wedding Cake 171
 Out of Bounds 177

HAPPY EVEN AFTER:
 Hearts are Easily Hurt 184
 The Lock in Wedlock 191
 You Can't Marry an Angel 198
 Death is the Only Exit 205

FOCUS ON THE FAMILY:
 Mother's Day 212
 The Indispensable Woman 220
 Just Dad 227
 Family Fireworks 233
 The Young Folks at Home 240
 Mother-in-law Musings 248

THOU SHALT NOT!:
 Souls in Pawn 255
 Forest Fire 262
 And They Swallow it 269
 Sin—Original and Otherwise 277

Soiled Snow	284
In a Glass, Darkly	291
Saturday Night	298

THE PEOPLE AND THE STEEPLE:
Everybody has Trouble	307
Try Changing the Wall Paper	311
The Problem of Pain	318
Worry is Waste	324
The Winter of Life	332
The Flag of Christian Courage	339

THE STABLE AND THE STAR:
The Long "Night Before Christmas"	347
O Come All Ye Shoppers!	355
The Little Lord Jesus	363
Over to Bethlehem!	370
The Stranger in the Manger	377

NEW YEAR, NEW CHANCE:
Ring in the New!	383
Resolutions are Like Rockets	389

THE ETERNAL GOAL:
Highway to Heaven	396
Three Roads to God	403
Tribute to a Coin	410
Bronx Express	417
East Side Shrine	422

BELL, BOOK, and CANDLE:
The Bells of St. Anybody's	426
The Bulb	433
The Book Everybody Claims	440
The Box of Kitchen Matches	447

SWINGS FROM A THURIBLE:
Outstretched Hands	454
A Church is a Dull Place	461
Novena Mirror	469

SPRINKLES OF HOLY WATER:
Strange Gods Before Me	475
A Sealed Secret	482
A Funeral is a Sad Sight	490
Breathless into Heaven	498

LITTLE COLORED WINDOWS:
Man of No Mistakes	505
Catholics, Excellent and Ex	513
Keep the Door Open	520
Stumbling-Block or Stepping-Stone?	528

SHRINES ACROSS THE SEA:
The Shrine of Ireland	535
The Pride of Portugal	543
Lourdes the Incredible	551
A Visit to the Vatican	559

Through Christ Our Lord

TEARS OVER A CITY

In our parish we are the chaplains to twelve hospitals. The other evening as I came out of one of them, high up upon a hill that overlooks the city, and before I began striding down that steep ski-run of zig zag streets that drops down to the rectory, I stopped to admire the magnificent view, the brilliance and the beauty of the city's lights. There they were, spread out like a giant garden of electric flowers, green and scarlet and gold. Sometimes they all seemed to shimmer and flash in the atmosphere, and it was as though someone had laid out before you a huge tray of multi-colored gems for inspection and selection. Or the height of the hill impressed you, and it was like looking down on Fairyland from the top seat in a ferris-wheel.

But then, for some reason, I glanced up, and my eye caught the street-lamp I was standing under, the light I was closest to. And do you know—it was streaked and crusty and smudged with dirt? Yet this was one of those lights down there, one of those golden bubbles, one of those distant jewels, which were beautiful only because they were far away. I don't doubt that any one of them, if you could get close enough, would be streaked and crusty too. And I wondered if that is the difference between man and God. Man sees other men always at a deceitful distance; but God sees every man at close-range, point-blank; not merely the appearance, but the reality: just as he is!

And isn't that the reason that one afternoon, when Christ stood upon a lofty hill, and looked down upon the beautiful city of Jerusalem, He cried? This despite the fact that before Him lay a glittering spectacle; the Temple's golden dome winking back at the sun as to an older brother; the marble turrets standing like frozen fountains; the gay-tiled roofs glowing here and there amid the green trees like Oriental rugs. And yet, Christ did not catch His breath and sigh like a man who wanted to paint all this beauty into a picture, or enshrine all this loveliness in the locket of a poem. Christ just cried. Why? Wasn't it because He was seeing not merely the city but the citizens; not just houses but human hearts; not the scenery but the sin?

I wonder if Our Blessed Lord in His white robe stood up there on the hill and looked down upon our city or your city or any city, would tears come to His thoughtful eyes? As He gazes down on the distant city, the city draped with lines of electric fire, the "city smoky and populous like Hell," the city with its faint human and mechanical smell floating up to Him

—would He weep again? Well you are as good a judge of that as anyone, so stand beside Him, you, and look at it down there, the city and the lights—the dazzling rainbows of neon, the shooting sprays of color—all the flickering vigil-lights before the shrine of advertising! At Bethlehem the Heavens shone forth the glory of God, but here these man-made stars burst forth to the glory of some gasoline or some ten-cent cigar. Still, if you keep your distance from it all, and as at a museum stand back of the red velvet rope so you don't see the daubs of oil but just the whole painting, the city does make an enchanting effect. The skyline spiked with tall buildings, lighted here and there with golden squares like honeycombs; the graceful arches of the bridges; the highways coiling in and out like loops of silver braid; and over it all and around it all the lights, like strings of bright balloons hung for a festival—yes, it is all very picturesque and attractive, as long as you have eyes only for the technicolor splendor, and are willing to forget the dirt and grime, the tragedies, the sins, the souls!

But the deep, searching eyes of Our Lord would look down and see nothing but souls. And tears would glisten in those eyes because amid all this apparent beauty, this artificial glamor, look at what sin is doing to souls! Down there in the city, He sees Drunkenness lurching out of the tavern door with bulbous eyes and bleary face and beery breath, more a cartoon than a man, and staggering off to bring a little of the atmosphere of hell into some broken-hearted home. Down there in the city Christ sees flaming-faced Anger still staring and glaring at the door it has just slammed, while on the other side of the door a sobbing daughter turns desperately to the street. Down in the city, Christ sees wild-eyed Gambling, tense and sick in the stomach, throwing down its worthless cards or tearing up its useless tickets, knowing it is tearing up green dollars that should have gone for groceries. Down in the city, Christ sees Lust with its shifty eye and wandering hands, now whispering soft flatteries into a silly ear, as it turns the car out toward the dark lonely stretches of the countryside. Down in the city, Christ sees Unfaithfulness slyly slipping off its wedding ring, and hurrying to its rendezvous of broken vows; but strangely a ring still shows faintly upon that finger—a scarlet circle.

Down in the city, the Scholar is busy writing his big book, proving there is no God, and using (or abusing) the brain God gave him to do it. Down in the city, the little atheist is stamping on his soap-box and screaming that there can be no God, because God does not see fit to distinguish him out of a billion people and strike him dead this minute, as per instructions. Down in the city, the scientists in the white coats are watching their bubbling test-tubes, studying how to preserve human blood. And across the city, other scientists in white coats are pondering their tables of atomic radiation, studying how to destroy human blood. In the university, the professor is carefully bringing his class up to date on the meaning of words: what used to be pure has now become puritanical; and what used to be condemned on the stage as raw is now commended as realistic. Meanwhile, newsboys peddling their papers after school, sing out in their high young voices the slimiest scandals of the city ... and the cars purr by, and the crowds hurry along, and the electric signs blink.

There is good in the city too, of course. Like the widowed mother up there in one of those skyscrapers, on her knees in an empty office, soaking up the dirty footprints of people she has never seen, in order to buy shoes for the two youngsters she doesn't see enough. Or like all those clean young girls scattered all over the city like water-lilies on a scummy pond. Or like all those unappreciated Dads, with calloused hands and soft hearts, who work hard, say little, and love much.

Oh there is good in the city, but slow tears are sliding down the cheeks of Christ because of all the evil there, the rising, spreading, overflowing mass of evil; because the city lies under a smoky pall of sin. Does it depress you? It depressed Our Blessed Lord too. That is why He cried, yes, that is why He died. Isn't it about time that we of the city should look up to Christ and weep—weep because in the beginning God made the world a garden of goodness, and we have made it a city of sin; because we have taken the beautiful blooming tree of life, the life and innocence He gave us, and turned it into the dead ugly tree of the cross; yes, because if He hangs up there on that cross, the nails that hold Him were forged in the hot fires of our passion. Each year in the springtime, during Holy Week, the statues are draped in purple, and we know that Good Friday is near. Have you ever thought of those draped statues, huddled, indistinct, mysterious figures as the ghosts of your past sins, rising at that tragic time to haunt you and remind you of all the pain your guilty pleasure cost Him...taking you to that other hill looking down upon the city of Jerusalem, where it was not tears He shed but splashing Blood?

Yes, Our Lord looked down upon the city twice. Once, from Mount Olivet, and He weeps for it. And once, from Mount Calvary, and He bleeds for it. Shall we, like Jerusalem, forget both the tears and the blood? You, too, He says, you whom I have loved and blessed? Oh, suppose that on the black-edged day when they pushed Him out of the city and prodded Him up the hill to be crucified, He saw that the man leading the gory procession, and gleefully pointing the way was the very man whose blind eyes He had opened; and over the howling and hooting of the mob He heard the jeering voice of the man whose tongue He had loosed; and suppose as He lay flat upon the cross with outstretched hands, He looked up and knew that the arm that swung the clanging hammer was the withered arm He had made straight and strong—that is just how Our Savior still feels when we, His own, sin against Him! He is Our God who has given us all we have, made us all we are, and—well, Judas betrayed Him only once. Isn't it time that we in the city should pause, and look up to Him on the cross, and weep ourselves? Let the cross be the new rod of Moses to strike the rock of our hearts, and let those saving waters, the tears of the spirit, flow forth for the evil we have done, but by His tears and His Blood, we will not do again, so that *our* soul at least (and we are responsible for no more) will not be a grimy city of sin, but a garden of beauty like the garden through which God walked in the morning of the world, and the garden through which His Son walked and met the penitent Magdalen on the morning of the Resurrection!

Through Christ Our Lord

CHRIST AND WOMEN

This is a picture-loving age. And if the Life of Christ were published in the form of an album, every page a brilliant picture, I think most of us would be amazed how often the face gazing out of the page would be the face of a woman. From Bethlehem to Bethany, from Nazareth to Naim, from the wedding feast of Cana to the funeral procession of Calvary, the swinging boom of the camera would focus almost constantly on a *feminine* face.

Of course the frontispiece of the book would be a picture of His Blessed Mother. We all realize that. But I wonder if we realize to what an extent Christ was influenced by woman. We *would* if we remembered He had no human father; He had only a Mother. And therefore from a woman alone He took His flesh and His features, the color of His hair, the curve of His lips, the sparkle in His eye, the rich timbre of His voice. More than *that*. In the loom of her womb Mary wove the white satin flesh of Our Lord's Body, but then on the canvas of His Soul by her careful training She traced His character! So that Christ, within and without, was the product of a woman!

Riffle through the pages of this album of His life and watch the women pass. All kinds of women! Brides and widows, women buoyant with youth and women tottering with age, faces glowing with the roses of health and faces that vase the pallid lilies of sickness; some rich, some poor—but these differences made no difference to Him. Temperaments or circumstances did not matter.

Here at the house of Lazarus is Martha bending over the bubbling kettle, as she prepares Christ's evening meal; and there is her sister Mary, sitting quietly at Christ's feet, hungry only for His words. You never saw two temperaments so far apart, yet Christ was equally kind to both. And here is a beautiful girl, looking so very young and frail and pale as she lies on her funeral couch; Christ takes hold of her waxen hand, literally lifts her back to life, the daughter of Jairus. And there, by way of contrast, is the aged mother-in-law of St. Peter, her face a web of wrinkles and red with fever: Christ cured her too. Here is the blushing bride of Cana, embarrassed because her wedding feast threatens to be a failure (the wine was gone and the guests were not), but Our Lord rescues her from embarrassment. Into the stone jars gurgles the water, then blushes into crimson wine, so the bride need blush no longer. And there is that other embarrassed woman, creeping through the crowd, ashamed of her secret sickness, too embarrassed to cry out for a cure: she didn't have to. The tactful Christ healed her when she merely touched His garment. His power went through the hem of that garment as electricity goes through a wire.

Two classes of women Our Lord especially understood—mothers and sinners. When Christ met that touching funeral cortege just going out of the gates of the City of Naim, the clumsy little cart jolting out to the cemetery, the crude coffin jouncing in it, and the weeping widow trailing behind, His great Heart swelled with pity. And as if to give an eternal and universal symbol of His sympathy, to let every bereaved Mother everywhere and down the ages know that He did sympathize at the loss of a child, Christ gave this boy to His Mother! Then there was that other scene, a joyous one, when the sun hung in the West like a giant chandelier of soft-colored lights, and Our Lord, a little weary after a trying day, sat down by the roadside to rest. In a few moments the women of the village were trooping up the hill with their youngsters—they wanted Him to bless the children. But the very efficient Apostles, with all the pompous importance of petty dignitaries, formed a cordon around Him and shooed the people off. "Don't you see He is tired? Let Him alone!" What was that? Christ heard it, and said, "Suffer the little children to come unto Me!" The children came. They did not know what happened. But the mothers knew—knew that He was weary—knew that here was a thoughtful and a considerate Man. That day He blessed the children, laying His hands on their softly curved heads, but He also wrote His autograph on their mothers' hearts.

And then the Scarlet Women of His day. He was compassionate to these. The Samaritan woman whom He met by the limpid waters of the wayside well ...

she who had successively "married" six husbands, changing like transfers on a trolley, never riding to the end of the line—but Christ did not spurn her. He tried to save her. As she left Him, a picturesque figure with the jug poised gracefully on her shoulder, the water began to spill over its brim—and tears began to spill from her eyes. Then, the woman taken in adultery whom they flung in the yellow dust at His feet while they raised their arms poising their stones— He raised His hand too, but in absolution, in forgiveness. "Go, and sin no more!" And there was Mary Magdalen who had broken up her heart like a bar of chocolate and given a piece to this man and a piece to that, and in return got only scorn . . . oh in the Gospel Christ talked about the parable of the Prodigal Son, but in His life He actually practised the welcome of the Prodigal Daughters!

But it is at the Cross that women show their standing in the Life of Our Lord. That Cross was like a stake driven into the ground and sharply dividing the conduct of the men and of the women. Turn the album of Christ's Life till you come to the red-edged pages of His Passion, and you will see that in the sufferings and death of Jesus, all the cowardice and all the cruelty ooze from the hearts of men, but all the courage and the comfort bubble up from the hearts of women. Judas, a man, betrays Him; Peter, a man, denies Him; the High Priests condemn Him; Herod toys with Him; Pilate sentences Him; the soldiers torture Him; the Apostles abandon Him: all this, the magnificent contribution of men to the redemption of the world!

No wonder that at the Crucifixion, the rocks split, but the flowers held up their heads. Because at every blood-stained step of Christ, the women were courageously at His side. Before it began, the wife of Pilate pleads for His freedom. Then—look at the Stations of the Cross: at the Fourth, His Mother goes forth to meet Him; at the Sixth, Veronica braves the soldiers and bathes His brow; at the Eighth, the women of Jerusalem weep over Him. And when it is all over, when Christ is up on the observation tower of the Cross, looking over the world to count His friends, He finds only one man—and St. John was so young he was hardly a man. But the band of Holy Women are there, loyal to the end! From the womb to the tomb, the women were faithful. But from the Crib to the Cross, from Herod who slaughtered the Holy Innocents at His birth, to Herod the Younger who let this Innocent die on Calvary—the record of men is pretty much a page of blots and blood.

But if Christ owed a great deal to women, women owe a great deal more to Jesus Christ. The very hammer that was driving the nails through His flesh was at that moment pounding off the chains that held woman captive in the slavery of pagan degradation. It was Christ through His Christianity who made women cease to be a property and become a person. In pagan Rome, female slaves were kept not merely to serve the master's luncheon but also the master's lusts. His very wife your proud patrician regarded merely as an ornament he owned, a pretty possession to be shown off like a fine picture. And when he had enough of her, he could push her aside as easily as his finished dinner plate, and turn his attention to the next course. Divorce was practically as easy as that, so that there were more divorces in Rome than even in Reno. And it was the same in other pagan lands. In the Orient they thought little of drowning girl babies like kittens. In ancient Greece in the name of the gods, they celebrated the immoralities of the temple—with young girls as victims—orgies of obscenity that would hang icicles of horror on any Christian heart.

Against this background of scarlet sin, across that dark horizon of history, suddenly walks the radiant white figure of the Immaculate Virgin and the Christ-Child in her arms. When Mary walked out of the stable of Bethlehem, womanhood walked out of the stable of pagan degradation. The very day that Christ was born, that day the double standard died, and the world knew what was wrong for woman was just as wrong for man. From that day Christianity began to lift woman up out of the mire, and put her on a pedestal, surround her with the cult of chivalry, and dedicate to her the code of courtesy, of politeness, deference, gallantry—only alas! today there are women who want to leap down from their pedestal to the level of the lowest man. A man can't look up to his equal.

So I pray, God give us women who will *still* be loyal to Christ—like the women of His lifetime. Women who will not merely say "Hail Mary" with their lips, but women who will not fail Mary with their lives. Women who in their handbags may carry a little rouge, but who will also carry a little rosary, and use it! Women who may throw a cover over their typewriter over the week-end, but women who will not throw a cover over their conscience over the week-end! Women who know that profanity and dirty stories in a woman's mouth stick out like black, decaying teeth! Women who know that the strongest resolutions quickly dissolve in a solution of strong drink. Women who know that the two glories of womanhood are virginity before marriage and motherhood after it. Virginity like the engagement diamond, clear and brilliant, but also firm, resisting, unassailable. And Motherhood like the orange blossoms worn to the wedding altar; soft and tender and a pledge of future fruitfulness! May Mary—who was at once Virgin and Mother—give every woman the perpetual help to be loyal to Christ even amid the new paganism of our day.

Through Christ Our Lord

CARPENTER AND REDEEMER

When young David and his gallant band were fleeing from wicked King Saul, they hid in the caves around Bethlehem. Bethlehem was David's home town, but at that moment in the hands of the enemy. One day, sipping some stale, bitter water, David mused aloud, "I remember when I was a boy how sweet and clear and cold was the water of the well by the gate of Bethlehem. Would that I might drink some now!" That night three of his men secretly stole through the sentries of the foe, and brought back water from the well to surprise him. David lifted the gourd to his lips with a glint of anticipation in his eye, then suddenly put it down. "Shall I drink the blood of these men who have risked their lives for me?" Perhaps it was in that very cave at Bethlehem that Mary's Son was later laid in the manger. Only He did not merely *risk* His life to bring us the clear water of Baptism and Faith: He went from the four little boards of the crib to the two great planks of the cross. He gave His life. He poured out His blood in great precious rubies for our ransom. When the human race, in the person of Adam and Eve, had scornfully tossed a half-gnawed applecore into the Face of God, it was the Second Person of the Blessed Trinity who said to His Eternal Father, "Lo, here am I. Send me!" And to obtain pardon for man, this Divine Son became a Man, climbed the ladder of the cross, and re-opened the gates of Heaven.

Yet most of us think so seldom, know so little about Christ. What kind of man was this Divine Savior when His Sacred Feet pressed our old earth, and His Shoulders were hung with the shoddy garments of common humanity? Someone once figured out that all the events we know of in the life of Jesus Christ took place on just thirty-five different days. Strange is it not, that though there have been more than 700,000 days since, there has not been a day when somebody was not willing to die for Him!

Stranger still, how this Man never set His sandalled foot outside the dusty roads of His own little matchbox of a country, yet every year men willingly wave good-bye to their own great, flourishing countries and go off to bring His Name and His message even to savages jabbering in jungles at the ends of the earth! Strangest of all, that though there was no room for Him in the dingy Inn the day He was born (the Hotel Bethlehem, God help us!) yet today the swankiest hotels in the world never present a bill without a bow to His Birth, written in the top corner: A.D. 1961, (Anno Domini, Year of the Lord). Not Lord Byron or Lord Nelson or Lord Macualay, but the Lord **Jesus Christ!**

Hotels somehow bring up the picture of towels, and there is a charming tradition that on Our Lord's way to Calvary a woman named Veronica offered Him a linen towel to bathe His Bloody Face. He gave it back, and there on the cloth was His very image painted by Blood and mud and sweat.

But our Blessed Savior did not wish to survive as a symbol, even a handsome artistic Image. Symbols, images, pictures are grand in their place. Let that Divine Face shine in the jewelled windows of sun-streaming cathedrals. Let Alpine wood-carvers fashion His Sacred Head in clean white wood, or delicate fingers embroider it on convent vestments, or let craftsmen emboss it on tiny silver medals. But while we admire the Christ of Art, let us not forget the real Christ Who walked down from the mountain peaks of His Divinity into the valley of humble human things, and lived like an ordinary, commonplace man in order to come close to us, to be one of us, to be loved by us!

Whose heart would not go out to a God who was surrounded at His Birth by the straw of a stable, surrounded in His youth by the sawdust of a carpenter shop, surrounded in His manhood by the slimy fishnets and the crude peasants of Galilee, surrounded at His Death by the thieves and rabble of Calvary! For the one time you find Christ with the Three Kings of the East with their exotic gifts, or among the Doctors of the Law in the Temple, you will find Him again and again with the cripple and the leper and the beggar and the publican and the Prodigal Son and the Magdalen!

Christ was of the people, for the people, by the people. He did not pose as the aloof executive, the regal prince in the remote ivory tower. Only in stained-glass windows was there ever a dustless Christ in an immaculate robe, standing in a garden of gorgeous flowers, serenely expounding some doctrine to three or four other elegant figures paying posed and picturesque attention. More often than not, this Christ was hemmed in by crowds, shouting crowds, swarming, sweaty, ill-smelling crowds. Always, the people.

After all, even when He was scarcely born, He was encircled by earthy shepherds who had just come trooping in from the fields and the sheep. When He cured the man sick of the palsy, the crowd was so thick—in every sense—that they had to lower the stretcher from the roof. When He spoke by the seashore, they so prodded and pushed against Him, He had to step into a boat and draw off a little from the shore. And when He died that black afternoon on Calvary a mob milled around His gibbet like a lynching party.

If you orchestrated Our Lord's life you would have to weave in the common sounds of His day: the bleat of a lost sheep, the clink of a widow's mite, the groan of a saw, the creak of oarlocks, the rush of white water under a full-bellied sail. Common sounds, common sights, common food. At one time when He is with His disciples, they are nibbling at raw corn in the fields; at another there is fish broiled over the red embers on the shore of the lake.

Or do you wonder sometimes about the sound of Jesus' voice? What was it like, tenor, bass, baritone? Was it mellow, vibrant, eloquent? Judge from this! Once when He spoke only three words, "Come, follow me!", Matthew, the flinty tax-collector who had made a career of collecting taxes from his own people for the hated Romans, came out of his booth and followed this Voice even to the scarlet pool at the end, a martyr's death.

And what did this Voice talk about? Not about abstract and abstruse subtleties, but about simple things in the simple language of the simple people. He spoke of the eye of a needle and the patch on a garment; of a fatted calf and a straying lamb; of the wail of a woman in childbirth, and the shouts of joy at the happy homecoming of a returning boy. Always ordinary things, like the big copper penny with Caesar's face and name. And about ordinary characters— like the pushy people who always are out for the first places, and the sloppy housewives who clean the outside of the cup but leave specks of dried egg disgustingly on the inside.

Some statistician has gone through the Scripture with a scalpel and announced that on three occasions Our Lord wept: once for His friend, Lazarus; once over the city of Jerusalem; and once in His agony for the sins of the world. Twice He is said to have marvelled; once at the stubborn unbelief of His own people, and once at the unexpected faith of a Roman officer. On other occasions He groaned, He shuddered, He sighed. Only once He sang. That was at the Last Supper, the night before He died. But you will never find on any Gospel page that He ever hesitated or ever changed His mind. His body was a human body that hungered and thirsted and ached and bled, but His soul had the surety and the strength of Divinity. "This, indeed, was the Son of God!"

And that is the whole point with Jesus Christ, His Divinity. At least it used to be. Oh I can understand

(and pity, and pray for, because after all, Faith is a gift from the hand of Heaven) those people who sadly and sincerely say, that they cannot believe that Jesus Christ was God. That at least is their conviction, and I can respect it. But let them not be condescending and add, "But I still think Christ was a great man; He was a superb teacher, a superlative preacher, a supreme leader, in fact He was the most perfect human being that ever walked across the horizon of history." Nonsense! Just because Faith is not in the passenger list of your soul, you don't have to throw overboard Reason. Remember, He claimed to be God!

This Jesus Christ who preached three years in the countryside, and hung three hours on the cross, and lay buried three days in the tomb, was either (and I tremble even to say it) God or Fraud. He either wore under His crown of thorns the mask of the hypocrite, the hypocrite of the centuries, or He wore above it the thrice-burning halo of Godhead. There is no middle of the road. Because He said He was God. He deliberately claimed to be God. He appealed to His miracles to prove He was God. He serenely and solemnly stated He was equal to the Father, Divine. The true Christian accepts Christ as just this. A true Christian would die, as have thousands before him, for this. His life here and His eternity hereafter are founded on this. And this is not just sentiment, emotion, hearts and flowers, stained glass windows, the organ playing at twilight. It is logic. For the Christian knows that the prophets of old stood on their tall tower and foresaw and foretold Christ's coming. Daniel foretold the time, Micheas pinpointed the spot, Bethlehem, Isaias predicted the god-like circumstances of virgin birth. And when at last Christ came, in time and place and manner like a very carbon-copy of the prophecies, His miracles proceeded to write in bold, gold letters across the blue sky of all history the only rational word to describe Him: Divine!

At Cana He looked at the stone jars and, as the poet says, "The modest water saw its God and blushed, blushed into crimson wine." At Genesareth the wilder waters of the sea came rushing down on His little boat like a shaggy, plunging animal, the waves bared like gleaming white teeth. He made a gesture, and suddenly the sea fell and lay quiet as a sheet of shimmering blue silk. Not far from Nazareth when the fingers of the lepers stretched out to Him like gnarled stubs, almost like clothespins, He touched them and they became pink and pliant and throbbing with new health. By the well of Jericho when the blind man only heard the trample of many feet, and desperately aimed his voice from his perpetual night, Christ stopped, lifted the fringed curtains of those dark eyes, and light flashed, and the man born blind saw! Yes, miracles spurting like jets from a fountain; the loaves multiplied on the mountain-side, and the fish miraculously bursting the nets of the lake; the fig tree cursed, the old woman bent twenty-eight years straightened; the dead daughter of Jairus, and the dead son of the widow of Naim, both imperiously commanded back to life—the incredible wonder of His own Resurrection—these deeds that no mere man could ever do of his own power, echo back the solemn words of the Roman officer who raised his gauntleted hand beneath the cross and cried: "This indeed was the Son of God!" for these deeds were eloquent proofs that His claims to be one with God were true.

CARPENTER AND REDEEMER

And—let us never forget it—this was also the Son of Mary. Go to any art gallery in the world, even Russia. Seek and you will find in some great, golden frame, Mary, holding the Child Jesus to her heart. She is serene, saintly, lovely; and in every language they describe her in just one word, *MADONNA*, Madonna! The word is like a necklace and every letter a precious stone of each womanly virtue. Madonna! It spells all that is inspiring in womanhood.

But Mary was not just the Madonna of the blessed joys of His babyhood. From the time when the star hung like a silver lamp over the cave of Bethlehem till the hour when the golden sun, dreading what it had to watch, went dark like a black eye-patch over Calvary; from the hour when the three Kings of the East offered their gold, incense, and myrrh till that tragic hour when King Herod and his ilk brought thorns and iron spikes and sponge of vinegar—all these years between, Jesus Christ was the Son of Mary. Mary knelt closest to His crib, Mary stood closest to His cross, and at this hour Mary kneels closest to His throne. And that is why we salute her, hail her, reverence her, invoke her, Mother of Christ, and Mother of God.

Mother of God

THE REAL MARY

On the eighth of September a few years ago I met a smiling young mother coming out of church. She told me how, a few minutes before, she had led her three year old daughter to our Lady's Shrine, pointed to Mary's picture, and whispered that today was God's Mother's Birthday. Whereupon the little tot with the golden curls clapped her tiny hands, and in a thin sweet voice immediately launched into the song "Happy Birthday to you!" As she came to an uncertain finish, she took a deep breath and said, "Now we have to blow out the candles!" And she began to huff and puff at the twinkling line of vigil lights.

That youngster at least was a realist. To her this was a real birthday. She looked beyond the picture to the person. I am afraid many of us adults do not. We have all smiled at the idea of a man who could not see the forest on account of the trees. Perhaps we should weep at the men and women who actually lose sight of Mary, the Mother of God, because of their curious devotion to her. I mean that in their minds the Mother of God gradually comes to mean only a pale statue or a bright picture, a tiny medal or a great stained-glass window. But these are only symbols, only things—and the Mother of God on earth was and in heaven is *a person*.

Some of the very prayers we say are likely to make us forget this. Take the Litany of our Lady that tinkles off her titles like a string of silver bells. "Morning Star, pray for us, Gate of Heaven, pray for us, Mystical Rose, pray for us." But Mary is not a Star nor a Gate nor a Rose. These are painted words of poets. Think of Mary only in terms like these and soon she will become just a lofty, far-off vision floating in a golden mist—much too high and grand for the likes of us. Unless we remember that Mary is like ourselves, a human creature, chosen and prepared by God to be His Mother, we shall never dare to tug at her robe and ask her to carry our prayers into the presence of her Son.

Just because Our Lady lived on this earth many centuries ago, we do not have to forget that she did live here. It is bad enough that Time itself has a tendency to glamorize things that have happened in the long ago, so that any event seems so romantically different, so colorful and picturesque when viewed through the sunset of the past. For example, take the Battle of Gettysburg. Go down there today and you will see smooth stretches of well-kept grounds, stately soldiers in handsome bronze or in lordly marble—after the battle. During the battle it was nothing like that. Then it was only mud and blood, wounds and groans, dying and death. It is only long years afterward that along come the sculptors and idealize everything.

Has not something like that happened to Mary? She lived and she died; and centuries afterward came the sculptors and the painters. Especially, the painters. God help us! Maybe God help them when Mary meets them. They have given us Mary, Madonna of the Lilies, and she walks knee-deep in them without crushing a single blossom! Mary, Madonna of the Cherubs, and they come tumbling down around her like paratroopers! Mary, Madonna of the Birds, and they perch and twitter on her shoulders. It is all very pretty and very poetic, but sometimes don't you feel like asking "Where is the Mary that actually lived? Where is Mary, Madonna of the Sweeping Broom; or Mary, Madonna of the Steaming Kettle; or even Mary, Madonna of the Washtub?" After all, that is the way she really lived. You don't think she spent her days posed on a pedestal, do you, or standing in a picture frame—very gorgeous and very idle?

Remember she was the Mother of the Holy Family in an age when there were no electrical appliances to make household work easier. So her fingers knew the rhythmic upsweep of the needle hour after hour, making the family clothes. Her fingers knew the flabby feel of sticky white dough, baking the family bread. Her fingers knew the swirl of warm water in the washtub, and sometimes when she drew her dripping fingers out, rainbow soapbubbles sparkled upon them—the only jewels she ever knew.

Mary prayed, yes, but she also patched. Years of her life were spent feeding and dressing a little Boy, and putting Him to bed with a mother's kiss. And sometimes, I suppose, as a mother will, she would smile and say, "Little Son, how much do You love me?" And the little Lad, as a tot of two or three will still do today, would stretch out His tiny arms and say, "This much!" And the sun, falling on those outstretched arms would fling on the floor behind Him the black shadow of a cross; and maybe at that moment from Joseph's carpenter shop came the ringing blows of a hammer driving in nails. And Mary, thinking of the Prophecy of Simeon, snatches up her Child and sweeps Him to her breast so fiercely that His little sandal comes dangling loose—as it does in one magnificent Madonna, the Mother of Perpetual Help.

So forget the plaster-of-paris statuette by the Christmas crib, and see the real Mary, the young girl taking her first trembling step into that broken-down cattle-stall, the Bethlehem Lying-in. Then, after the star over the stable had finally flickered out, like a candle before a shrine, after the angels had fluttered away, after the shepherds had shuffled off, and Mary is alone—then you see a joyous young mother in one embrace treasuring her Child and adoring her God. Under her dark blue shawl she feels the Infant stirring warmly. She smiles down at His pink face. And her heart leaps with joy as she realizes that her blood is leaping through His veins, her features are on His face, her own eyes will look out from under His lashes. Mary, the Mother, gently lifts Him up. His tiny hand tangles for a moment in her hair; His baby breath is sweet upon her cheek. And for the first time she whispers softly the Name that hereafter would be written in silver starlight across the dark night of the world's sin—*"Jesus!"*

For Jesus was God! I have underlined the real and warm humanity of Mary only because it is a little knob that swings open a big door. Tell me that Mary is the Sister of Man and I know she can sympathize with the strivings and the failures of poor human beings. But tell me that she is also the Mother of God, and I know she can actually help us by interceding with Him. Mother of God! This is no honorary title sentimentally conferred by the Catholic Church. When our Lady became the Mother of the Divine Babe of Bethlehem, there was no Catholic Church. The Catholic Church merely found the Christ Child where the Wise Men of old had found Him—in His Mother's arms. God had chosen her Himself to be the Mother of His Son.

And because He bent over the balcony of heaven, and out of the teeming millions that were, and that were to be, selected Mary to be "full of grace" and "blessed among women"; because He asked her through the message of an angel that she, sitting there so thoughtfully at her loom, should also weave in her womb the immaculate flesh of His eternal Son; because for nine months our little Lord was closer to our Lady than a rosebud to a rose-bush—do we not do right in honoring Mary as much as poor humanity can, knowing that Divinity, God Himself, has honored her so much more?

And between the Savior Himself and His Holy Mother must not the honor flow over into love? Must there not pulse between these two a holy intimacy and a glowing affection?

If that sacred Body which for our redemption hung upon the hard Cross, once snuggled in the cradle of her soft arms; if those divine hands which took seven loaves and fed a multitude, once gratefully took from her hands a single slice of buttered bread; if those sacred feet which walked the waves as though the water were a blue-plush rug, once went scampering down the dusty lane to the village well to fetch her water; if for thirty years His goodnight kiss tenderly touched her motherly cheek—do you think our Divine Savior can forget all that? Do you think that when she raises her loving eyes and whispers a request, He could coldly turn away?

After all, since God our Father gave us the best gift He could give us, His eternal Christmas gift to the world, His own Son, through Mary—would He be loathe to give lesser gifts to us through the same immaculate hands? If God the Son came to us through Mary, would He be unwilling that we come to Him through Mary, too? Does He not understand better than we do that there are moments when we poor human beings, heart-sick and soul-sick, blotched with sin, ashamed of ourselves and afraid to raise our eyes to His dazzling Divinity—need someone like Mary, so human and yet so sinless, and, therefore, so dear to Him, to plead in our behalf? When we don't know where to turn, we turn to her. She can go to the top! Because that spotless girl who knelt in the straw of the stable, looking so pale and so pure in the light of the star, was His Mother, she can go confidently to the Throne, past the golden halos of the saints, past angels and archangels, past glittering ranks of cherubim, past seraphim that veil their faces with their wings. She can go right up to the dazzling white throne of God and whisper two words that make all heaven still with breathless awe: "My Son!"

And who will say that He will not gently bend down to hear what His Mother has to ask?

Mother of God

VIRGIN IMMACULATE

December eighth, as the whole Catholic world knows, is the Feast of Mary's Immaculate Conception. On this day in the majestic cathedral of Seville (it's an old Spanish custom) olive-skinned sacristans will be laying out vestments of silky sky-blue, and today in far off Zanzibar or Mozambique some poor missionary will perhaps sigh a little wistfully as he puts on his only set of threadbare white. And today some chaplain aboard a ship on the blue heaving Atlantic may, after an afternoon Mass, put away his utility vestments (white on one side and black on the reverse) and gaze out at the sunset, and think of a tiny sewing basket of a ship that once bobbed upon this ocean and was called, like the feast, the Immaculate Conception.

Picture that tiny ship yourself, if you have not yet pensioned off your imagination. In the West the rim of a great red sun lays a final lane of fire upon the throbbing waters, and down that scarlet sea with sails swollen and prows pointed full at the heart of the setting sun, sweep three galleons of Old Spain. Suddenly on the center ship a small cannon booms. And as the ships rise and fall on the breathing ocean, there rises and falls the old hymn of sailors on the sea—listen to it: "Salve Regina! Hail Holy Queen!"

Maybe this sounds like poetry. Actually it is history. Every sunset, after Columbus put out from Spain, whenever the weather was serene, the Admiral of the Ocean Sea reminded his little fleet it was the hour to honor Our Lady. And why shouldn't he? Was he not daring these unknown waters under her patronage? Were not those her colors, that pennant of blue and white snapping up there at the mast-head? Was not her very name emblazoned on his flagship? And not merely "Santa Maria" as the school books have it, but "Santa Maria de la Immaculada Concepcion"— Saint Mary of the Immaculate Conception! The Immaculate Conception came to America with Columbus. Not only that. The first island on which Columbus touched he called "San Salvador," Holy Savior; but the second he named "The Immaculate Conception." Was it only coincidence that all the Spanish colonies at the other end of America, like California, were eventually dedicated to the Immaculate Conception too?

And is it any wonder that the Bishops of America in solemn session assembled (1846) chose the Immaculate Conception as the official patroness of Catholic America? Were they thinking, I wonder, of the first Catholic Bishop in America? His name was John Carroll, a name as American as John Adams or Nathan Hale. The name of his cousin, Charles Carroll was written in a firm, flowing hand under the Declaration of Independence. The name of another cousin, Daniel Carroll, was on the deed donating to the American government the ground on which rises the the massive white dome of our capitol. And the name of John Carroll, the Bishop, you will find in the diary of Ben Franklin during the weeks they went to Canada together to persuade the Canadians not to line up with England against the Colonies.

True American, Bishop John Carroll had a true devotion to the Immaculate Conception. In fact a half-century before the Immaculate Conception was chosen as our country's patroness, he chose her, Mary Immaculate, for his coat of arms as a bishop. He preached his first sermon as a bishop in her honor. And when he lay dying (so deep was his humility he asked to be laid upon the floor so he might die as humbly as his Savior was born) his last words were: "At this moment one memory gives me most consolation: I have always had a tender personal devotion to Mary Immaculate; I have officially consecrated my diocese to her; and I have tried to encourage the intercession of Mary among my people."

Bishop Carroll had under his modest crozier only twenty-five priests in all America. Even then some of them were with the army. The first public Mass in Boston was said in 1788 by a Chaplain of Washington's forces in the Revolution. There were then one hundred and twenty Catholics in Boston, or about as many altar-boys and choir-boys as there are now in many a Boston Church. From the time when we had one bishop in America, we now count almost one hundred and fifty. From the time when we had a handful of priests, we now list nearly forty thousand. From the

3. *Pennies*

time when we as Catholics were one in a hundred in the population, we have become almost one in five or six. Under our Patroness we have grown like the National Shrine of the Immaculate Conception in Washington, an edifice that for years was only a promise, a basement of mosaic and marble, but recently has risen in monumental majesty.

For a national patron, England has St. George; France, St. Dennis; Ireland, St. Patrick; Germany, St. Boniface; Spain, St. James; Italy, Sts. Peter and Paul. How fortunate we are to have the very Mother of God, Mary Immaculate! Did even the early Catholic explorers reason that America was a virgin frontier and so rated a Virgin Patroness? Did the Catholics in the early Colonies figure that as America had been conceived in liberty in a world darkened by the tyranny of kings, she deserved a Patroness who had been conceived in unspotted innocence in a world darkened by the larger tyranny of sin? Did they think of Betsy Ross and the flag of red, white and blue, and then remember how Mary had stood beneath the flagstaff of the Cross with its red wounds, its white Body, its glinting blue spikes?

When Our Lady appeared to St. Bernadette, the peasant girl of the Pyrenees, in the rocky grotto of Lourdes she wore a robe of radiant white, and round her waist a sash of blue. Blue and white—as long back as monks bent their hooded heads over parchment, to blazon paintings like tiny stained-glass windows on the margins of Bibles and Missals, blue and white have been the traditional colors of Our Lady. By the mercy of God, blue and white are in our American flag. Take them out and you have only red. All red. Like the total red of Communism. Red only for the red of Communism. Red only for the red fire that burned so savagely in Spain that a man could find his way around Spanish cities at night by the light of blazing churches; red for the bright blood of thousands of priests and nuns that has stamped its sticky seal of martyrdom on so many prison courtyards. Hammer and sickle! Hammer that built the gallows for the Church of God. and the sickle that cut down like golden grain the rights of man. The Iron Curtain! Well, what kind of curtain should a country which is only a concentration camp have? Who believes that the Iron Curtain is there to keep undesirables out, when everyone knows its chief purpose is to keep the Russian people in? And if they can't get out, doesn't that make Russia the world's largest prison?

Once a nation rejects the Divine, it rejects also the human, and tends to become inhuman. Once it throws into the ash barrel its respect for God as the Father, how could it have any consideration for the children, mankind? On the other hand no one ever loved God more than His Mother, Mary Immaculate, and our country's Patroness. May her colors in our flag (and her virtues in our lives) never allow the red of human strength, human power, to run wild over the other colors, Mary's colors,—so that forgetting the inherent right of God we forget also the inherited rights of man!

However on this feast we honor not Mary's virtues in general but her one dazzling distinction, her Immaculate Conception. By the way, sometimes even Catholics confuse the Immaculate Conception with the Virgin Birth, though they are as different as a flower and a fruit. The Immaculate Conception refers to Mary's soul; the Virgin Birth refers to Mary's body.

The Immaculate Conception means that the physical conception of the infant Mary, through her parents Joachim and Anne, took place in the normal human manner. But in that normal physical conception, the soul of Mary was preserved by God from the stain of original sin, the universal brand of our fallen race. And this soul without stain, is the Immaculate Conception. The Virgin Birth on the other hand means that Mary, now grown to be the maiden of Nazareth, in turn conceived her Son, Jesus, but without the agency of any human father. Her Body, intact as a Virgin, still gave birth as a virginal Mother. In the Immaculate Conception of Mary, God was preparing for Christmas, which was the Virgin Birth of Jesus. Eve, the first woman, had brought sin into the world in the garden of Paradise. Mary, the Christmas Eve, brought the Savior into the world in the poverty of a stable. That is why God made her immaculate from the beginning—to be His Stainless Mother, stainless even in her very Conception.

In this she stands apart from all other creatures. Just as there are many waterfalls, but only one Niagara; many mountains, but only one Everest; many diamonds, but only one Kohinoor, there have been in human history all sorts of lofty geniuses and anointed kings and towering saints—but only one Mary, one human being whose soul was never for a single moment marked with mankind's original sin. It was a Protestant poet, Wordsworth, who phrased it so well: "(Mary) Our tainted nature's solitary boast!"

It was a convert to the Catholic Church who left us a memorable example of love for America and love for the First Lady of the Land, Our Patroness, Mary Immaculate. Mention the word Molokai and everybody thinks of that grim, grey-cliffed island rising out of the sea, where the victims of leprosy were hurriedly unloaded, and where Father Damien lived and died among them as apostle and martyr. When Father Damien was so stricken with the disease that he could not walk, one day they wheeled him down to the beach, where he saw a gaunt, bearded man wade in from the longboat that would not come any nearer to this infected shore. This was Brother Joseph Dutton, born in the hills of Vermont, former officer in the American Army, and the forgotten hero of Molokai. He buried Father Damien, and stayed there working among the lepers for the love of Our Lady for forty-four years. But he never forgot America. Every day the Stars and Stripes streamed above his little cabin. Somehow the President, then Theodore Roosevelt, heard of him, and when the American Fleet was on tour in those waters, he ordered it to steam past Molokai in tribute to Captain or Brother Joseph Dutton. And when the long grey line of ships had passed into the sunset, Dutton, as he did each dusk, slowly lowered the flag, and with the soft folds resting lightly on his shoulder, he faced toward America, the land he loved, and said his short silent prayer to Our Lady, its Patroness, for the land his heart had never left at all.

On our Patronal Feast we too say and pray "God Bless America" and we thank Him for our double blessing: we have the True Faith, and we have it in the most favored country on the face of the earth!

Mother of God

QUEEN OF
THE COMMONPLACE

The preacher in the pulpit in a sense has a captive audience. True, they can get up and walk out but, they generally don't. But the man behind a microphone can be flipped far into outer space by the mere flick of a dial. So in hopes of soothing itching fingers, all the speaking experts implore the radio preacher to begin with an arresting, ear-catching sentence. It always reminds me of the high school boy who had the same idea and so began his composition. "Hades!" (only he spelled Hades differently) "Hades!" growled the Duchess, as she lit another cigar."

I'm afraid all I can say by way of introduction is that I've been looking at this week's calendar, and noticing that Tuesday is the Feast of Our Lady's Purification, and wondering if you sometimes get the same thoughts about all these feasts of Our Lady

QUEEN OF THE COMMONPLACE

47

as I do. Well, it's an easy error and it needs continual correction. I mean, don't you sometimes think to yourself, "Mary has so many feasts!" (That is true; they just about sprinkle the calendar like holly-berries.) "So, Mary must have led a crowded, colorful, thrilling life!" (That is wrong.)

Certainly her feasts move along the avenue of the church-year like a bright procession of gorgeous floats, the Annunciation, the Visitation, the Presentation, the Immaculate Conception, the Assumption, and all the rest. But notice this. The last two feasts I mentioned, the Immaculate Conception in December and the Assumption in August, on the calendar have not six months between them. But in the life of Our Lady they were separated by more than sixty years! A crowded, colorful life? It is we who do the crowding—crowding the events of a long life-time into twelve short months. A colorful life? On the calendar Mary's life may seem a gay parade of festivals, but in her kitchen as she lived it, it was just a run of routine days, monotonous months, commonplace years.

And why not? In all things save sin, was not Mary one of ourselves? The soft airs of spring were gentle upon her face. Winter winds chilled her. The summer sun bronzed her brow. Wasn't her home like any of the other little stone houses in the village, a spinning wheel by the hearth, brown-crusted bread in the oven, a jaunty plume of blue smoke curling from the chimney? It was between the fireplace and the well, between the loom and the broom that Mary passed her humdrum, uneventful hours—her life!

If you wanted a colorful, dramatic patron among the woman saints, you would be well advised to skip this house-wife of Nazareth. I would tell you to take St. Joan of Arc, really a glamorous figure in her silver armor, on her stately white charger, under the silken banner of France, leading an army into battle! Or take St. Catherine of Sienna, the counsellor of Popes and Kings, actually going back and forth across Europe making peace between enemy camps! Or take St. Elizabeth of Hungary, a glittering queen living her life of hidden sainthood amid the rustle of brocades and the flash of jewels. Yes, take them all, but never forget that the highest saint in heaven is still a simple mother, a quiet home-body whose world was bounded by walls and windows.

But is not this the very reason why she should be our patroness? In the indifferent glance of the world are we too not just ordinary people? Our names do not stream in black banners across newspaper headlines. Our deeds do not spurt out in blue flashes from a telegraph key, news of the moment! Our successes do not gleam in white bulbs over theatre lobbies. No, we are ordinary people leading ordinary lives. Tuesday is just a dull echo of Monday; and Thursday is a faint carbon-copy of Wednesday. We walk in the unexciting footprints of our yesterdays.

So, like Mary we live a commonplace life. But why then can't we take the one additional step and like Mary live that commonplace life for God? Don't you see that every time Mary tossed a stick of wood into the crackling red fireplace, she could say to herself, "I am warming this room for God!" Every time she laid the earthenware plates on the supper table, she could think, "I'm setting this table for God!" And a glance out the window showed her Jesus and Joseph trudging up the road from the carpenter shop ready to sit down to a workingman's meal. An ordinary, commonplace life? Absolutely. But an ordinary, commonplace life lived for God!

Can we do that? Can we glorify our monotony, dedicate our routine? The answer should be as simple as the five fingers on our hand, five words that consecrate a day to God: "All for Thee, my God!" Say this after your morning prayers, and it means that everything you do that day you are offering to God as a prayer. And whether you are an operator at a switchboard, or a teacher at a blackboard, or a housewife at an ironing-board; whether you run a typewriter or run a truck; whether you fill teeth or fill gas tanks, the good God will accept it as a prayer. He knows that we cannot be always praying, but isn't it a tragedy to let all the rest of the time go wasted as regards gaining merit for Heaven?

How many hours do you give to God in a week? I mean directly, specifically to God. Count your Sunday Mass, morning and evening prayers, rosaries, and you do better than average if you give Him three hours. Three hours out of one hundred and sixty-eight useless for eternity. At the end of a life of seventy years what a pathetic little pile of merit for Heaven, compared to the massive mountain of life lived, and work done, but useless for eternity!

But say a little prayer each morning, and mean it, and it will in a way turn a cooking range or a carpenter's lathe into an altar. Repeat it during the day. Don't go round, of course, mumbling "All for Thee, my God! All for Thee, my God!" like a broken record. You may go mad, north-north-west. But before the more important actions of the day, renew it; say it again.

However we ought to point out that before such drab actions can be burnished into a prayer, there are two conditions. But they are conditions and not catches. The first is that we must not be in the state of mortal sin. Naturally. From filthy fingers God does not accept offerings. The second condition is that the work itself be not a sin. Otherwise you have the absurd situation of a man heaving a brick through a jeweler's window, scooping up bracelets and brooches and rings the while he piously murmurs, "All for Thee, my God!"

No. Actions that are bad, automatically rule themselves out. Actions that are good, automatically register themselves for our eternal reward. What I am pleading for is the vast majority of actions that lie in between, the thousands of "neutral" actions, all the way from baking a cake to filling out an income-tax report. Ah, what a super-natural good intention you would have to make there!

Somewhere I have read that the most gorgeous sunset is the result of our central sun pouring its golden beams on millions of tiny particles of common dust hanging in the atmosphere, giving us the purples and pinks, the orange and scarlet that turn the western sky into an autumn hillside of color. Just so, one central golden good intention shining upon all the thousands of tiny, grimy, insignificant, workaday items in our ordinary day transforms them into a spectacle of splendor in the eyes of God!

If I may illustrate with a modern parable. Once upon twenty years ago, there lived in Dublin a humble workman. And every morning on his way to work he would drop into his parish church and say a few prayers. On his way out he would stop for a moment before a marble statue in the back of the church. It was a statue of Christ the Worker, sitting down after a hard day's work, His weary hands crossed on His lap. The man in the Dublin overalls would put his hands into the Hands of Christ, say just a few words, pick up his lunch-box and go hurrying out.

Day after day, like that, and year after year. And one day, just before he was due to retire from his job, the old worker collapsed at his bench in the foundry. They brought him to the hospital, gave him the Last Rites, and had just finished the prayers for the dying, when the grey haired old fellow looked at the flickering candle and smiled. "So this is the day," he whispered, "the day when all the lights go out. Because for me they will all go out, the bright lights in the stores and theatres, the blue lights in the foundry, the soft lights of home. And into the dark I can carry only this one light, this blessed candle, the light of faith. When I think how long I lived under those other lights, and how hard I worked, and how the grave is only a few feet wide, but you can't bring anything across. You can't take it with you. . . ."

And then he spoke faster so that the candle-flame danced. "I don't care. Every day for thirty years I have put my work into His Hands, and offered it to Him as a prayer. You can't take it with you? I have sent it on ahead! And it will be waiting for me, in the vaults of Heaven."

Somebody put the candle into his pale fingers. And he seemed like a traveller in the olden days who had come to the end of his journey, and now at the inn took his candle and was going upstairs, up to his well-deserved rest, eternal rest. And that's the way the Foundryman of Dublin went to meet the Carpenter of Nazareth.

In this little talk I have spoken to you perhaps two thousand words. Forget them all, but never forget five of them. Use them every day of your life, "All for Thee, My God!"

Mother of God

MARY'S APRON STRINGS

Suppose you said to a world-traveller, "Look, *you* have hopscotched across all the lines of latitude and longitude that map-makers have drawn on the face of the globe. Do you have any favorite spots? Or—let me ask this—what would you say is the world's finest river?"

And the bronzed explorer of far-away places might look off in the general direction of Madagascar and murmur, "I really don't know. You see, every outstanding river has its own particular glory. But do you know what I would like to see? A river that combines the special beauties of them all! For this dream river's length, I'd take the long winding stretch of the Amazon, coiling across a whole continent. For its width, the broad majestic sweep of the Mississippi. For its color, the blue of the Danube where the Danube is blue as melted sky. For its banks, the climbing green hills and the many-towered castles of the picturesque Rhine. And at its end, as a crown and climax, the rushing white rapids and the roaring falls of the Niagara... Ah, that would be a river!"

What that *would* be among rivers, do you know the Rosary really *is* among prayers? For, it too is a combination of the best.

Run through them rapidly. What is the first prayer of the beads? The Apostles' Creed: "I believe in God, the Father Almighty; I believe in Jesus Christ His Only Son Our Lord; I believe in the Holy Catholic Church; I believe in the Resurrection of the body."

Each phrase is a fundamental truth, a great block of granite, and all are cemented together by the blood of martyred men, and together they form the very foundation of the cathedral of the Catholic doctrine!

And the next prayer of the beads? The Our Father; words that first trembled upon the lips of a God, Our Divine Lord Himself! Can the fountain of prayer leap higher than that? And then, the Hail Mary. "Hail Mary, full of Grace, the Lord is with thee"... when an Archangel came coasting down the skies to a workman's cottage in Nazareth, and with celestial courtesy saluted an unknown maid as the Mother of God.

The next words were spoken by the Mother of John the Baptist, St. Elizabeth, when she looked up and saw Mary framed in the doorway of that little house up in the hills, and impulsively cried out, "Blessed art thou among women, and blessed is the fruit of thy womb!"

The next part, the "Holy Mary", is the swelling, soaring greeting of the whole Church, that acknowledges Mary's high place, and invokes her heavenly power. But put them all together. Words of the twelve Apostles, words of Our Lord Jesus Christ, words of an Archangel, words of a Saint, words of the inspired Church—put them together and you do not have half the rosary! You have only the words, the bones, the outward structure. The heart and soul of the rosary is the meditation.

Meditation is a frightening word, so put it this way. In the rosary, the words are the beads, but through the beads there runs a chain. Call it a chain of thought. As we say the words, we are supposed to think. Think of what? Not of the words of each Hail Mary. That might be feasible for the first five or even fifteen Hail Marys, but by the time you got to the thirty-seventh, your head would be spinning, like a weather-vane, south-southeast.

No, we are not expected to, in fact, we are not supposed to try to concentrate on the meaning of the words of the Hail Mary. These are only a physical tribute of our lips and a measure of the time. Call it, if you want, a kind of musical accompaniment to our pious thoughts. It is something like a man singing at a piano. His hands are on the keys, his voice is on the notes, but his mind (if he is an artist) is on the theme, the spirit of the piece. And just so, our fingers slip along the beads, our lips whisper the words, but our mind and heart are on the mystery of the decade.

Now *there* are two more words, which, like stained-glass windows, are religiously beautiful but don't let in much light: mystery and decade. Decade is a Greek word for ten, and means a series of ten beads or Hail Marys. There are, of course, five of these decades in a rosary, whose theme can be Joyful, or Sorrowful, or Glorious. Each decade is dedicated to a certain mystery, only mystery here means an event, an episode in the life of Jesus or Mary. And this is what we should fix our mind upon, this colorful happening, this hour of trial or triumph, this black or golden day in their lives, while we murmur the Hail Marys as a kind of orchestral background.

But, it is best to learn by doing. Today for example is Sunday, and on Sunday we say the Five Glorious Mysteries. So we announce, "The First Glorious Mystery, the Resurrection of Our Lord from the dead," and we begin our first decade: "Our Father Who art in Heaven..." and our mind zooms off the earth like a plane and we see before us the grey tomb of Christ, the pink and silver Easter dawn, the sentries pacing back and forth. We can see the glint of the rising sun on their helmets, we can hear the clank of their swords against the armor. And suddenly the earth trembles, shakes, quakes! The soldiers are flung on their faces; spears and shields go clattering all about. And out of the tomb bursts Christ in His swirling white robe almost like the white plume of a spurting fountain. He rises, glorious, victorious, the wounds in His palms sparkling as though He held handfuls of stars!

And we think, "Dear Lord, if ever I am walled up in the tomb of cold hatred for a fellow-man; if ever I am shut up in the spiritual death and corruption and foulness of a bad habit, oh may I—even if it takes a moral earthquake, a very shaking of my life—come out into the clean sunshine of Thy grace!" And by now we are saying "Glory be to the Father and to the Son"—finishing the decade, and ready to begin the second decade, "The Ascension of Our Savior into Heaven."

Say the rosary like this, and can anyone claim that the repetition of the Hail Marys is boring or monotonous? Why, it is like strolling through an art gallery, each mystery, each decade like a pause before a fascinating painting. The wonderful thing is that though you are living in the twentieth century, your beads take you back to the first. You are a contemporary of Our Lord and Our Lady. You follow the pageant of their lives. Now you are looking at them against a background that is the straw-littered floor of the Stable of Bethlehem; now it is the Temple of Jerusalem with its golden dome and marble turrets; now it is the sullen, black Good Friday sky and the Body on the cross white as a slender candle held up against it.

Of course, I grant that the more religious books you read, the more Catholic magazines you leaf through, the more pamphlets you pick up, the more sermons you hear, then the broader will be your spiritual knowledge, and the more colorful, stirring, and appealing your rosary. Even so, if we only do our best (and what man can do more?) the rosary still will be a profitable prayer.

I like to remember the incident of the young mother rocking serenely on the white porch of a little summer hotel. And in the field alongside, her little daughter, blond and blue-eyed and at the magic age of four, was picking wild-flowers, under the mother's watchful eye. Finally she finished, and came running back with her bouquet. Have you any idea what little fists can do to flowers? These were crumpled, shaggy, soiled, tattered, oh a sorry little bundle! But you should have seen the shining look in the mother's eyes, when the little hand thrust them out to her and said, "Mommy, I picked these all for you!"

Do you think our Mother Mary is any different? Rosary really means wreath of roses. True, when we finish, our rosary may be a forlorn, droopy thing, but if the hands of love offer it, Mary will take it with her warmest smile. Our lips and our minds said a terrible rosary, but she heard our hearts.

A rosary is a pocket-chapel where we can get in touch with Heaven no matter how far we are from a church. When sorrow strikes, get out the beads and you will find that as your fingers travel over them, you will be following Christ over the cobblestones on the way to Calvary. At the end you, too, will come to a little cross, but the memory and the merit of His big cross will help you to carry yours! When temptation rises up before you, temptation that is so strong, and you know yourself to be so weak, go to the beads! Goliath was strong, too, a human tower of glittering armor. But David, the shepherd boy, with a sling and a few smooth stones from the brook, felled him like a tree, because the might of the Almighty was behind him. Your smooth stones are the beads, and no temptation can ever conquer you if you sincerely want to lay it low, for behind your stones, your beads, is the power of God's own Mother!

Even when you are only worried, agitated, confused, go to the beads; there is no tranquillizer like them on any drugstore shelf. The restful repetition of the prayers, the peaceful pondering of the holy scenes in the mysteries, lay a calm upon the soul like the quiet of a cathedral window in the sunset. I think of Pasteur (the scientist who gave his name to Pasteurized milk) kneeling behind one of the huge pillars of Notre Dame and letting his beads slip through his chemical-stained fingers before he hurried off to the microscopes and test-tubes of his laboratory. I think of Joyce Kilmer and his poet's ink-stained fingers saying his beads every morning in that little church in the very midst of New York's wicked Tenderloin which bore the ironic and gallant name of The Holy Innocents. I think of Matt Talbott, the ex-drunk who bounced from the gutter to the stars, waiting for the doors of that Dublin church to open each morning, and then the beads inching through his hard, sand-paper fingers, so in-worn with honest grime and grease that no soap could ever gouge it out.

These people knew that a rosary wasn't just a dainty circle of colorful beads that you twirl round and round during Sunday Mass while your eyes go wandering round the incredible hats. The rosary is not a bright clicking toy that you toss to the baby when you can't find his rattle. The rosary is not that thing you bought at a mission two years ago and—where is it now? Probably in the bureau drawer lost in a pile of cufflinks. More's the pity because the rosary, if you say it right, is the best there is in prayers!

If you want a devotion that is not new-fangled, but stamped like old silver with the seal of the centuries; if you want a devotion that is freighted with rich indulgences: if you want a devotion that is as attractive as the life of Our Lord and Our Lady in technicolor; if you want a devotion that is convenient (you can say the beads in eight minutes, and say them a decade now, a decade later)—if you want a devotion that can be said any time and any place, then the rosary is for you!

Get the rosary habit; try to say it every day! For if you hold on to the beads, you will be like a child holding on to your Mother Mary's apron strings. You can never stray far away. She will use the beads to draw you gently back!

Mother of God

HANDS THAT HELD THE BEADS

The Beads, of course, are at home in any hands but we may as well start at the top. I am thinking of hands old and white, yes, white as milk, and the thin blue veins in them like the blue streaks in marble, and those hands hung from the cream-colored cassock of a Pope, Pope Pius the Ninth who lived a century ago. One day, in that simpler age when Popes could walk alone, Pius the Ninth was on his way from one wing of the Vatican to another and enroute he passed through the Vatican Art Gallery. And there—even in those days—was the inevitable knot of tourists gaping up at the glowing masterpieces and the Grecian marbles, and gurgling their *ohs* and *ahs* of admiration. The Pontiff paused and smiled. "Do you like them?" he asked. "Like them? Holy Father, they are magnificent!" "Would you like to see *the* treasure of the Vatican?" "Would we!"

Pius the Ninth shrugged his old shoulders and smiled. "I am a simple man, and to me the most precious treasure in all these gilded halls is right here." And he opened his palm, and there lay a little coil of black rosary that he had been saying on his way through the lofty corridors. Pius the Ninth was not wearing the pious mask of pretension. He *was* pious, and he remembered how often when his shoulders were stooped with the worries of the world, he would slip into his private chapel and let these beads slowly slip through his fingers, and somehow power (as from the hem of Christ's garment) came into his soul. Do our beads mean half so much to us? They could; they should; and they would, if we said them with half as much fervor! The beads are like anything else. We get out of them what we put into them.

From the Vatican to the Varsity may seem a long leap, but the rosary can make it in a stride. By varsity, I mean a football team, and more specifically Notre Dame, and even more particularly its one-time coach, Knute Rockne. Incidentally, Rockne, a non-Catholic, literally followed his team into the Catholic Church. Early Saturday morning before a big game, unable to sleep he would be restlessly roving the hotel lobby. He noticed his boys slipping out in groups of threes and fours. Where were they headed? He followed them. They were going to the Communion Rail. He followed them to the Baptismal Font as a convert.

You men will remember that Rockne was the coach who took football off the ground and launched it in the air by means of the guided missile of the forward pass. Fittingly, he went to his death in a plane tragedy, sailing through the air like one of his own forward passes, his soul caught safe in the arms of God beyond the goal line of eternity. When they tenderly lifted his body from that sad air-liner wreck (and you can read this in his biography by his widow Bonnie) they found his beads wrapped around his hand, the chain snapped by the impact. Mark you, this is not something snipped from the lives of the saints. It is not a fragment from a medieval legend. This is a twentieth-century football coach on his way to the west coast quietly saying his beads. Would you have been saying your beads? Would you even have had a rosary with you? Never forget if you are knocked unconscious in an accident, the beads in your purse or on your person will shout like twenty trumpets: "I am a Catholic. Get me a priest!"

Perhaps you think that the mangled fingers of Rockne were the most pathetic that ever held the beads, but for that I nominate the hands of a black-robed Jesuit missionary among the Indians. You can picture him preaching to them as they squatted in a stolid copper circle around him. He seemed to be making progress, but one day they suddenly turned against him. Now he was no longer their priest but their prisoner. I do not dare list the barbaric tortures they inflicted upon him. But I will tell you this: despite all their mocking taunts and all their white-fanged cruelty, they could not lower the flag of his courage one inch! They themselves marvelled at his great heroic heart.

Where did he get that superhuman courage? Not from the altar: he could not say Mass; not from his Breviary: he had no book. But they did notice that inside the little wooden stockade where they kept him caged like an animal, he said and re-said his beads. Well, they would soon fix that. A brave snatched the rosary from his hands and flung it into the crackling fire. Did that stop the missionary? He went on saying his rosary, ticking off the Hail Mary's on his thin, tapering fingers. The Indians would fix that, too. A brave (God save the mark!) took a tomahawk and hacked his fingers off. Did that stop the missionary? He went on mumbling, groaning the Hail Mary's on those poor scarlet stubs till an enraged tomahawk sent his soul to its tremendous reward!

The point is that *we* can say the rosary so comfortably—in church, or at home, or walking along the street, or riding in a bus. Nobody need know. When we say the rosary in private we don't have to open our mouth like a yawning alligator, or a hippopotamus absorbing his breakfast cereal. We don't have to make a noise like those dear pious old souls who pray "Ps-st! ps-st! ps-st!" like a distressed steam radiator sighing for a plumber. When we say the beads in private there should be no sound at all, and only the slightest perceptible movement of the lips.

Pius the Ninth was an Italian; Knute Rockne was Scandinavian; the missionary was French; and Daniel O'Connell—well, Daniel O'Connell was not born in Bulgaria. If you saw him saying the beads in church I think you might look twice, because the beads dangled from a pure white glove. When O'Connell was a young man he had accepted a challenge to a duel, and slain his opponent, and thereafter, to show his everlasting remorse and repentance, he never approached the altar rail but that his hand was gloved in immaculate white.

HANDS THAT HELD THE BEADS

But O'Connell said his beads in other places besides church. One day in the corridor of the House of Commons he was pacing up and down, head bowed and hands clasped behind his back, apparently in deep thought. Suddenly a fellow-Irishman came bolting out of the chamber, saw O'Connell, and stopped dead. "Glory be to God, O'Connell, what are you doing out here? Don't you know that your country's fate is at stake in there?" And O'Connell looked at him and said quietly, "Maybe I'm doing more for Ireland out here than the pack of you in there. Listen." And he jingled his beads behind his back. "Do you hear them? Ah, they only tinkle, but in a few minutes O'Connell will go in there and thunder, and it will be the Mother of God herself who will put the words in his mouth."

Or go from the House of Parliament in London to the Sistine Chapel in Rome. Today's tourists, who after the first few days walk past masterpieces as though they were billboards, certainly never notice one detail in Michelangelo's wall-to-wall painting of the Last Judgment. There, a sinner is plunging into the flaming abyss of hell, but the Madonna is bending over from the heights of Heaven, flinging out her rosary to him like a lifeline, and the sinner's hands are desperately clutching the frail, miraculously powerful beads.

It is a colorful, swirling scene, the projection of a powerful imagination. But I am more impressed with the quiet fact that Michelangelo himself—who perhaps could make canvas glow and marble breathe like no other artist in all the studios of time—this genius of the centuries, each day after he had scrubbed from his hands the streaking paint or the powdery marble-dust, would take into those strong, inspired fingers a string of simple beads and pray his rosary. I wonder was it this regular round of the beads, day after day, that helped him live an almost austere life in that scarlet and gold age of the Renaissance when the sensual paganism of the old Rome started to take over the new one?

Rome somehow brings up Naples, and a Neapolitan nobleman named Alfonso de Liguori. As a brilliant young lawyer, Alfonso had scored golden successes in many courtrooms, but one day came the moment of truth when he saw how fame and failure may be only a comma apart in the intricacies of human law, and he murmured, "World, I know you now. Courts, you will never see me more!" He knelt before Our Lady's Shrine and there hung up his nobleman's dress sword.

Did he miss its cheery tinkle at his side? I only know that later when he founded his "order" of Redemptorist priests, he saw to it that there hung at the left side of the uniform or cassock a new weapon, a long fifteen decade rosary that clicks merrily at every step. If we Redemptorists (if I may interject a local commercial) are tenderly attached to the beads, perhaps it is because the beads are literally attached to us.

Why should a jewelled sword and its silver sheath stir its artistic poker in the fires of memory so that I see there now a policeman's club? In my Brooklyn boyhood, the cop on the beat was the common natural enemy, for no more good reason than that, for example, by which a boy of eleven also knows he is supposed to hate girls. But this officer we did respect and even liked. Not only was he, by our standards, fair, but you see we had noticed (with that peculiar sharp sight of children that dismays magicians) that while his left hand held the loop of a twirling night stick, his right hand held the little black loop of a pair of beads. We used to call him "Hail Mary" Finnegan. I suppose that in a crisis that called for vigorous action, he would obey the Scriptural warrant and not let his left hand know what his right was doing.

This much is sure. Whether you are policeman or painter, football coach or Indian missionary, the rosary is at home in any hands. Stylish hands with elegantly slender fingers and nails laquered like strawberries. Domestic hands that are raw and red from soapy water and scrubbing brush. Craftsman's hands ingrained with black from honest machinery grime. Hospital hands stained with iodine, or office hands stained with ink. The beads, like an umbrella handle, fit any hand. The important question of the moment is, are they at home in our hands?

In the normal course of events, someone someday will force the beads into our dead hands. That day an undertaker's assistant (he may be painstaking, he may be bored, he may be humming) will drape a rosary round the bloodless white icicles of our cold dead fingers. And it will mean absolutely nothing! Oh, it may be a tiny delicate touch of consolation for the bereaved, but it will not mean a thing to the deceased. If they put a revolver in our dead hands, would Almighty God punish us as a murderer? Well, why then, if they put a rosary in our hands should He reward us as a pray-er? I have been to wakes, and I have seen people laid out, and I have noticed with a start the beads in *their* hands, and believe me, it looked about as much in place as a Sunday School pin on Khrushchev. I have sometimes wondered what would happen, if life came back to one of these people and he found himself holding a rosary? I think he would be so surprised he would drop dead again.

It is not when our hands are cold in death; it is now when they are tingling with life, vibrant with health, maybe prone to passion—it is now that we need the beads in our fingers! You can say a rosary each day in about eight minutes. Surround your life with the loop of the beads. It will keep a great deal of trouble and temptation out, and bring a great many special graces in!

Saints for the Aints

IN PRAISE OF ST. BLAISE

When I originally selected that title, "In Praise of Saint Blaise" I thought I might excavate a few solid facts about him and give you what I had never heard myself—a little sermon about a saint whose Feast Day fills our churches but about whose life so many of us know so little. However, I have sad news. When you go to the books about St. Blaise you come away with nothing but armfuls of legend. After you have snipped off all the frilly lace which sentimental tradition has sewed on his life you have only a few square inches of fact. Namely, that somewhere about the fourth century, Blaise, a Bishop of Armenia, was martyred for the faith, and his festival was kept on February third. Church historians look down their learned noses with scorn in one eye and amusement in the other at the famous fishbone story that perpetuates his fame. According to this, when a boy had a bone stuck in his throat and was turning blue, who should happen along but Bishop Blaise, who blessed the lad, and out popped the bone! But this is still the remote reason, at least as far as I have been able to find out, why on February third Catholics will crowd the altar-rails for the Blessing of the Throats. In this ceremony the priest will say over every person, "Through the intercession of St. Blaise, Bishop and Martyr, may the Lord deliver thee from all throat troubles and every other evil". And each person as he tilts his chin and feels the crossed candles touch his neck will breathe a little prayer that St. Blaise will ward off from him everything from laryngitis and tonsilitis and the common cold all the way to cancer.

There is of course absolutely nothing wrong in this, but don't you think St. Blaise himself would feel more flattered if we asked not merely that our throats should be healthy, but also that they should be wholesome and clean—that is, free not only from "chronic respiratory infections" but from conversational indecency? With many throats the danger is pretty remote of the man choking and turning blue, but out of too many throats pour blue stories. Blue? Well the color isn't too definite. In fact, sometimes they are called off-color stories. But generally they let it go by labeling them just plain dirty.

Isn't it strange that everyone refers to them as dirty stories? Catholics, Protestants, Jews, atheists with no religion whatever, all call them dirty stories, as if admitting there was no argument about it. Like dirty water they are just foul and unclean. And yet there is a type of girl who might tell her mother that at the party so-and-so told some stories "that weren't so nice." But isn't it a pity that we even have to mention dirty stories or double-meaning remarks or immodest talk or suggestive allusions in the same breath as girls or women? Isn't it a little sickening to know that the plague has infected even them? Not, mind you, that there is in God's Bureau of Weights and Measurements a double standard, a different one for men and for women. Sin is sin no matter who commits it. And yet even Nature herself, don't you think, seems to have made women more refined, more delicate, more sensitive; and if you were to hear a dirty story from a woman's lips it must give you the same shock as if you bent over to admire a blossom and suddenly behind it a snake uncoiled and reared its poisonous head.

But custom cocains delicate feelings till they are numb, so that today these dirty stories buzz back and forth between desks in offices like flies shuttling back and forth between garbage cans. They crawl like spiders from bench to bench in factories. And sometimes at bridge parties they are dealt out as casually as the cards. Just why any member of the fair sex should relish or tolerate or encourage such foul allusions in her presence is something of a major mystery. Can any girl actually think it a graceful compliment if anyone tries to tell her a dirty story? This is the very height, the very top of the chimney in black insult, because by the very telling the talker practically says, "Look, there are lots of people to whom I wouldn't tell this story. I'd feel embarrassed, low, cheap, out of place. But you—you don't matter. You're just like the rest of us; dirt is part of your diet and you love it."

It is to marvel how people who want to be decent let the people who ladle out the dirty stories get away with it in the thin and tissuey name of politeness. We don't want to hurt their feelings—after they have jigged and stamped and jumped all over ours! Why should we fear to offend offensive people? If the gentle Christ drove the cashiers out of the temple with knotted whips, and if the same Christ said that it is what comes out of a man's mouth that defiles a man—must we stand by patiently and sweetly as the muddy flood of filthy stories rises round us? You wouldn't let anyone fling a sack of refuse over your living room floor, would you? Then why allow anyone to scatter moral refuse across the floor of your mind? Or to place indecent statuettes in the cabinet of your memory?

There is an ancient rebuttal to all this, but I never could accept it. To me it never quite rang true. That defense is, "But, Father, aren't you exaggerating all this? These dirty stories, I admit, are not pretty. But they don't affect me. They just go in one ear and out the other." That is what is hard to believe. If they just go in one ear and out the other, why let them go in at all? Or do they go in one ear and out the other because there is nothing in between to stop them? Unfortunately, whether there is an intellectual vacuum there, or whether there is a sixteen cylinder brain, it is pretty hard to believe that there is no impression made, no effect at all! I would like to offer two reasons why I doubt it.

The first is this. A dredging machine on a mudscow scooping up mud has its own particular rattle and squish and oozy gulp, and a dirty joke has its own particular kind of laugh. You are not a priest very long till you find that out. You may be going over to the hall to direct a play or some such affair and you come upon a group that is unaware that you are approaching. You don't do anything to conceal your coming; they just don't notice. And then suddenly you hear this strange loud laugh, a sort of bursting guffaw, something about it primitive and raw. Then they see you right in their midst and silence comes down upon the crowd like a stovelid. A strained silence with everybody embarrassed. But they don't have to tell you what's been going on, the kind of humor they've been sniggering at. They've already told you—by their laugh. What made the laugh different? You call this not making an impression? If it were decent humor the laugh would be clear and merry and innocent, but if it is sex with a new twist, that is something else again. Where there is dirt in the story, there is gravel in the laugh.

And about that going in one ear and out the other, let me tell you a little incident by way of parable.

It sounds like something out of Ripley but once I knew an ear specialist who practiced in Erie, Pa., and whose name was even Doctor Heard. (He's dead now, Lord rest him!) But this particular day I ran into him and he was shaking his head over a case he had had that morning. Seems that several days before, a young lad had been mowing his lawn and an insect had flown into the boy's ear. Well, this does happen now and then, but generally the frightened insect takes the nearest escalator and is very happy to come right out. But this particular insect got frightened or something and chose the boy's inner ear as a kind of incubator in which to lay its eggs. With the heat of the boy's body the eggs hatched, and in a few days the boy was almost insane with torture. When the doctor went in, he found the inner ear writhing with tiny crawling grubs.

Isn't that a picture of the dirty story? It may enter your ear all alone, but once in, it may breed many unchaste imaginings, improper desires, indecent daydreams, perhaps unclean deeds. Why not? Whatever goes into the human brain, that is what will come out of the brain by way of thoughts—and acts. A magician may take a black silk-hat, put into it a green scarf, and pull out a white rabbit—but we know that it is all a trick. You cannot do that with your mind. You cannot put unclean stories into the human mind and expect to bring clean thoughts out. Every man's skull is his own little theatre, and if he rents his films from Dirty Stories, Incorporated, those are the pictures that his mind's eye is going to see!

Only humorists who cannot be funny try to make up for it by being filthy—because they are not really humorists. They have minds that are tethered to one theme, and no matter how they move about they never get away from it.

They would make you believe that God created the world not in six days but in sex. They would have you regard a relation that is personal and sacred as merely animal and casual. They frame their cynical regard of the marriage bond into a slimy anecdote which may arouse in the listener first blatant laughter, later on (with enough stories) develop into an amused tolerance, and then go on to secret approval, and finally even become the accepted pattern of conduct! Do not ideas have an impact? And does not repetition have its effect like a hammer which, blow after blow, drives in the nail?

IN PRAISE OF ST. BLAISE

And what a tragic misuse it all is of the precious gift of speech! Not long ago I was called to the hospital to attend a boy who had just been placed on the D.L.—the "Dangerous" List. He was a clean-cut looking lad, about ten years old, with bright blue eyes and curly hair. When I bent over and spoke to him he just looked at me. He strained as if trying to speak but nothing came out. I went into the corridor and asked the nurse. She said, "Lockjaw. And he's dying." For confession all he could do was answer my simple questions by shaking his head yes or no. After I had anointed him and said some prayers aloud, I had to leave him, but as I walked down the hospital steps I could not help thinking. Here was this wholesome, innocent boy and he could not move his lips even to whisper, "My Jesus, mercy," and at that very hour all over the city, in barrooms and factories and restaurants and cars, hundreds were abusing the precious gift of speech with smutty stories and vile talk!

On my way home I chanced to pass a doorway where a policeman was indignantly telling off the housewife because the garbage can in the yard was without a lid.

"Lady," he said, "don't you know there's a law that all garbage cans have to be covered! Spreads disease! City Ordinance!" I felt like praying that Almighty God would make a law that all mouths that spread moral contagion should be forever covered.

Animals have throats, but they have no speech. May the blessing of St. Blaise be not merely upon our throats for health, but also for holiness so that we may speak only as befits men and women who are the children of God and the brothers and sisters of Jesus Christ!

Saints for the Aints

PATRON OF MISFITS

Any pious gambler would give you heavy odds that you never heard of a Jesuit priest named Noel Chabanel. And there is no particular reason that you *should* know him, because if ever a man were a big round zero on the world's score-board, this was he. A total loss—except for one tiny detail. A few years ago, in St. Peter's at Rome, with silver trumpets blaring, they canonized Noel Chabanel as a saint. Saint Noel: you could even call him St. Christmas, for that's what it means.

Did you ask what is he patron of? As far as I know, of nothing, unless they declare him the friend and patron and shining example for misfits, for all the little square people in the world who are wriggling uncomfortably in round holes. You see, in the beginning Father Noel Chabanel flourished in his native

France like the elegant champagne grapes of that countryside. Then he was the cultured Jesuit priest, the brilliant young college professor, a clerical gentleman polished to his fingertips. But one day transfer orders arrived, and he closed the classroom door on his orderly academic world, and opened the tent-flap of an Indian wigwam among the Hurons in Ontario, Canada.

Perhaps when he had dreamed of all this in faraway France, with his imagination unfolding like a travel-folder, he saw himself planting the standard of the cross, like a spiritual Columbus, on a new frontier of the faith—he, the blackrobe missionary in a colorful, romantic, tingling adventure! Now he was there, and the whole thing appalled him. To live in a smoky, smelly tepee, with dirty savages and dirtier dogs; to squirm and scratch from lice and fleas; to eat greasy chunks of meat—he hated to think what—out of crusty pots; the food nauseated him, the vermin tortured him, the hunger and hardship weakened him, and the danger of death, always lurking about, secretly terrified him.

To add to his humiliation, he just could not learn their barbaric language. He, the master of French and Italian and Spanish, and so proficient in Latin and Greek and even Hebrew, now was a blank, stumbling moron. He was used to neat dictionaries, logical grammars—but the Hurons only sprayed him with grunts, and the great professor never got beyond the kindergarten. Besides, the Indians just didn't like this palest of palefaces.

There were some blackrobes, huge men with booming voices and vibrant personalities, whom they rather admired, but on Chabanel they only smiled, as if he were a little bug that had fallen on its back and was making ridiculous efforts to right itself.

Five years of this, of utter loneliness, of wincing revulsion, of absolute failure, during which he did not make one single convert—not one Confession and Communion—and do you know what this man did? Then, when the going was toughest and the night was darkest, he dropped to his knees, held up his crucifix like a sword, and took a solemn vow to stay there, never to leave this hopeless mission! The months passed, Indian scowls seemed to grow blacker; and one day at the very bottom of his fruitless, futile life, a tomahawk was raised stealthily behind him, and he was mercifully dead before he knew it. They picked up his body, and flung it from the steep bank into the dark, rushing river. Nobody ever recovered it. Not one trace of it ever turned up. You will never see a relic of the martyr, St. Noel Chabanel. He was just thirty seven years old.

If ever a life looked worthless and wasted, like wine poured out upon sand, this was it. On the tape measure of achievement, it does not reach a half inch. Isn't it so like that soft echo which rides the winds of the past, off the Galilean sea, "Master, we have labored all the night, and taken nothing"? So this poor fellow tried, and tried, and then he died; he failed miserably, and that was all there was to it. Say rather that would have been all, except that this man had tried and died for God! A failure—if you will—but to me somehow he appeals more than those headline saints who succeeded, who left behind them the golden halo of shining accomplishment, and little black armies of devoted followers to continue their work.

The world itself smiles approvingly on success, even when it is success in the strange field of religion. But this man died a lonely failure, went down with banners trailing in the dust, down to a nameless grave, down in the grim heroism of bloody defeat.

But for this reason—for on the cash register of results he rang up a hollow "No Sale"—is not Noel Chabanel even more like his Master, Christ, the pale young Savior spread out on a black cross, a blood-smeared Corpse, a tragic, sagging Figure; the cross itself a bitter monument to failure, the exclamation point at the end of a dreamer's life?

They buried Christ in the tomb, and sealed it with a huge stone, but then God moved the stone as easily as you might turn a page, and lo! it was the beginning of a new chapter called Christianity. Out of failure, success! as if to show that God is not impressed by what we achieve. After all, He, being Almighty, can do anything. What He looks for is our good will, our best effort, our never turning back! That was all that Noel Chabanel gave Him—it was all he had to give—, but if later on, the Faith burst into flower on this continent, it was because of the damp, blood-stained soil where a failure, a nobody, died and prepared the ground. In God's eyes, Chabanel was not a zero but a hero!

To each of us (for aren't we all just little, undistinguished people trying to do our best?) this saint's story is like an encouraging pat on the shoulder from the fatherly hand of God. It reminds us that the world's thermometer of values registers one way, but God's is altogether different, like Fahrenheit and Centigrade. Could be, a man might be a headline in his home-town paper, and so simonized with success that he blinds the underlings about him, and so influential he throws his weight around like an All-American-tackle—but somehow God is not impressed at all. On the other hand our successful friend has been much too busy ever to have bothered about God. Sometimes, when his conscience begins to growl like a bristling watchdog, he reassures it softly, and it stretches out again for another long sleep. Then one fine day (and it seemed so unfair, because there was no entry in his appointment book that afternoon about dying) a finger touched him sharply on the arm (the left arm—he felt it like a stab in his heart) and a voice he hardly heard whispered, "Almighty God would like to see you in His office, now." Everyone said it was a most impressive funeral.

Underneath all this, coincidence had slipped in a sheet of carbon-paper, because that same afternoon a certain mother died too. Time had been touching her up for the last act, so there were streaks of grey in her hair, but in all her years of life and despite the fact that they both worked in the same building, she had never even seen the aforesaid Mr. Big. Hours after he left his office, she used to come in, an aproned figure behind a swishing mop, soaking up the footprints of big business, a silent silhouette in a midnight skyscraper. Because she had been a widow these past five years, and because her two girls were still in High School, and because her whole life was spun around them like a sheltering cocoon, she worked for them, prayed for them, every day slipping into church for a few earnest words with God. She never knew a single soul in the gilded worlds of business or politics or society. But when she died, it turned out that God *knew her* and welcomed her into Heaven like a Queen.

Just one of the saints that nobody knows; the unpretentious men and women who wear their halos carefully tucked in under their hats; men and women whose biographies have no bloodstained pages of shuddering penances; men and women who never saw a vision or ever thought of a miracle; no, just men and women who followed the monotonous car-track existtence of a routine life, who doggedly kept the Commandments, humbly received the Sacraments, kept on saying their prayers, perhaps sometimes stumbled and fell and struggled again to their feet, and eventually died in the grace of God, and saved their souls, and in the simplest sense became saints!

And each of them an individual personality. I suppose it is the prim, stiff statues that have given us the impression that the saints were all alike. Well, it is a wise saint who would know himself on a pedestal. Because the statues are so similar, and the saints were so different. Some of them were tall and thin, like window-poles. Some of them were short and broad like book-cases. Some were twitchy and some were dreamy. They were the same only in this: they were human beings.

But they were not born saints. Ah, that would be a soft, plush, reassuring philosophy: that men are like seeds; some will be radishes and some will be roses. Plant where you will, nurture them as you like, they will come up what they are! Nonsense! Deep down we are not different! All men are cut from the same bolt of cloth; there is only a snip of the shears between us. We make our lives an altar-cloth or a dust-cloth. We! There is no secret to sanctity. There has not been a new Sacrament in two thousand years, or a new temptation! The same catechism that we learned, the saints learned, only they lived it. The same Lord that we have, they had, only they loved Him. There is one thing about the saints though; they never set out to change the world. They just wanted to change themselves. And one of the latest among them, Pope Pius X, once said to a group of Cardinals who were moaning about the sad state of civilization, "Gentlemen, I have an infallible means of reforming the world." And when they leaned forward he whispered: "Let each of us begin with himself."

How true! Some people can be holy in church, but when it comes to living with other people they are holy terrors. Whoever claimed sanctity was sending your fingers galloping round and round a rosary like a runner doing his laps round a track? Or that holiness consisted in lighting a lot of vigil lights like a pious pyromaniac, a kind of theological arson? Or attending three different Novenas a week like a juggler keeping three colored balls in the air at once? Or having more holy pictures and statues than you can shake a feather duster at?

Men and women have become saints without any of these, but nobody ever became a saint without saying or at least meaning many times the hardest little sentence in the English language: "Thy will be done!" Sin does not bow and whisper, "Thy will be done!" It throws back its head and shouts, "My will be done!" The man who slobbers up drink till his words come out as obscurely as wads of wet paper, still says very distinctly, "My will be done!" The devout woman who holds on to a grudge just as tightly as she holds on to her prayerbook... she may read one thing, but she is saying another, "My will be done!"

It comes down to this. A saint is someone who puts self second and God first. God *always* first. That's the major difference between a saint and an ain't.

Saints for the Aints

SAWDUST HALO

If you asked this bearded gentleman to sit for his portrait, he might snort gruffly or smile deprecatingly or raise an eyebrow in puzzlement, but even if he did pose, it would be a hard picture to paint. Granted that you have a palette with colors that would do for most saints: here is bright gold for golden eloquence, but this saint never preached a sermon. Here is soft green for miracles, like the delicate green miracle of each new spring, but this saint never performed a miracle. Here is rich scarlet for blood bravely poured out, but this man was no martyr. Here is plain black, like black on white for famous quotations, some sage counsel that he has left us, but there is not one simple, single word that you can quote and whisper, "He said this."

And yet, look at that sign in front of his shop. Oh, it isn't much as signs go. Not one of our neon jobs dancing with colored fire, like the Fourth of July caught in a glass tube. This sign is a mere wooden board, worn and weather-beaten, creaking in the wind. But look at what it says! "Joseph and Son, Carpenters".

I know St. Joseph was only His foster-father, but do *you* know what that means? It means that for years upon years St. Joseph lived closer to Christ, than any other saint in Heaven (except Mary of course) ever dreamed; sat at the same table, slept under the same roof, worked at the same bench. That sign says that inside this carpenter shop is the gentle, quiet man who taught the Maker of the universe how to make chairs and tables. It means that inside is the craftsman who had the King of Kings for his helper. It means that inside is the great, fatherly man whom the boy Jesus called Dad.

The bread Joseph put on the Holy Family table— let's not forget!—was not miracle bread. There was no such thing there as multiplication of loaves. When an Angel appears, it is to wake him up, as the head of the family, and tell him to get going into Egypt with the Child and His Mother because Herod is hot on the trail. But the Gospels never mention any radiant angel suddenly hovering in the doorway of the shop and waving a wand over that overdue job for a rich and cranky customer. Such a predicament just meant more work. But even under the guttering candle-light it was enough to know that the hours he put in and the splinters he took out, the blisters and the callouses, the decades of his beads of sweat, were all for Jesus and Mary.

If you really want to know the rank of St. Joseph, turn to the Bible. But first understand the spirit of the Bible, how it does not braid bright adjectives, or paint words with the rouge of rhetoric, or send off every sentence with the feather in its cap and a gold chain jingling round its neck. As a rule the Scripture is as simple as stone. On Good Friday you may hear a sermon that turns Calvary into Technicolor with splashing Blood and silver tears. The Bible says simply, "They crucified Him". And that is the way it was with St. Joseph. All the Bible says about him is, he was a "just man". But in the Bible's sense "just" means holy, and (as far as human nature can reach it) perfect. "Just" is a jeweler's tray sparkling with the gem of each virtue. "Just" is posing behind a man's head the golden halo of sainthood.

Ask Almighty God Himself what He thinks of St. Joseph. He will not answer you literally, but if we can judge by what happened, once Almighty God bent over the balcony of Heaven and saw all men who would ever live go swinging past His Throne: Moses, the meekest of men, was there; and Solomon, the wisest; and Job, the most patient; patriarchs like Jacob, prophets like John the Baptist, Apostles like Peter; but think of it!—God let them all go by, and His finger touched this man! Of all men He chose as the protector of His Son Jesus, and as the Spouse of Mary, this humble, humdrum, commonplace carpenter, Joseph!

Ask the Church what she thinks of St. Joseph. And she would reply that in twenty centuries she has seen all sorts of saints. Saints who were martyrs, saints who were virgins, saints who were abbots, saints who were kings. But when it came to choosing from among the countless figures in the dazzling Court of Heaven a guardian for the three hundred million of the Church's world-wide family, she went back to the

Guardian of the Holy Family of Three, to St. Joseph. As if she had said, you Irish may honor your St. Patrick, and you Germans your St. Boniface, and you French your Joan of Arc, and you Italians your St. Anthony; and so on—but when it comes to the official Patron of the whole universal Church, there is no one but St. Joseph!

Ask the Popes what they think of St. Joseph, and you find Pius IX has in a way spoken for them all. You may have heard how a celebrated artist came to him one day with the preliminary sketch of a huge painting. It was to portray Pius IX solemnly proclaiming the doctrine of the Immaculate Conception. "See, Holy Father, you will be in the foreground, reading the parchment. Around you will spread the Bishops and Cardinals in their robes, like a red sunset. Up above in pearly clouds of glory will be Our Lord and Our Lady and angels and archangels." "Yes", said the Pope, "but where is St. Joseph?" "Oh, er, St. Joseph. We'll put St. Joseph over here." And the artist pointed to a corner of the picture where tiny cherubim were tumbling down like paratroopers. The Pope laid his strong finger on the center of the picture. "You will put St. Joseph here," he said quietly. "Next to Jesus and Mary. That is where he was on earth, and that is where he is in Heaven."

It's an old yarn, but there are those of us who love it because it cuts through all the pink glamor to the grey rocky facts. After all, in color how can St. Joseph compete with the exciting, dramatic saints, like Bernard of the crusade, or Thomas Aquinas of the racing pen, or St. John Chrysostom of the golden tongue, or St. Jeanne d'Arc of the silver armor, or St. Theresa of the shower of roses, or St. Dominic of the Rosary, or St. Peter of the Keys—poor St. Joseph with his hammer and saw and sandpaper and pot of varnish!

What did it matter? Was St. Joseph not "The Saint who loved a little Boy, and guarded Him with care, and earned for Him His Daily Bread, the clothes He used to wear."

If about the round table of Heaven, Saints took to reminiscing, Joseph would merely smile (he was that kind of quiet man) but he would be remembering the days when the Christ-Child's tiny fingers were clasped about his neck, and the little Head nestled content on his manly shoulder. The days when the Lad toddled through the carpenter-shop with sawdust sprinkling His small sandals, and curly golden shavings falling into His curly golden hair. The days when St. Joseph had whittled a toy-boat for the Boy who had not yet seen the clean green sea of Galilee. The days when Joseph and Mary with the Child between them had strolled in the sweet evening air, like a stained glass window walking down the village street. Maybe St. Joseph has left no miracles, no relics, no quotes, but he has his memories! And how should we measure a man, by what he did, or by what he was?

And the other saints know it. You hear of an actor who is called an actor's actor; a ball-player who is called a ball-player's ball-player. No razzle-dazzle; makes the hard ones look easy; not too much color; does nothing but quietly win ball games. In his own league St. Joseph is a saint's saint. Read their biographies and find how many saints chose St. Joseph as a special patron. St. Theresa (that is the older St. Theresa, if that is a chivalrous distinction to make) besides being a genuine mystic, was a hard-headed executive who went up and down Spain founding new Convents, reforming old ones, and practically revamping the whole Carmelite Order. To her, St. Joseph was an anchor, a solid, non-sentimental devotion, a substitute for popcorn piety. And she goes on to add, with a confidence that makes us blink, "I do not remember ever having asked St. Joseph for anything and having been refused." Do you think the trick is, a Saint would know just what to ask? Maybe we should pray in this fashion: "Dear St. Joseph, I am a pretty poor chunk of timber, cross-grained with stubbornness, knotty with this or that bad habit, splintery with a thousand little defects. But you are skillful enough to plane me off and polish me down and make me something worthwhile for God. Please do it."

It is always easier to pray to St. Joseph than to preach about him. Do you know that for centuries the Church almost deliberately ignored him in the portrait-gallery of her heroes? She figured that if too much emphasis were placed on St. Joseph at the cradle of Christianity, the common people would begin to associate him with Mary as the physical father of Jesus. So the spotlight of oratory and poetry and painting and devotion circled the Madonna and the Child, while Joseph was lost in the shadows. But now at last he is coming into his own, Foster-Father of Jesus, saint without glamor, saint of the calloused hands, saint with a halo of sawdust!

I like to think of St. Joseph in heaven as an older man, retired, but like many such men, still loving to putter around his celestial carpenter shop. Only now he spends his time turning out not tables and chairs but jobs for those who pray to him for employment.

5. *Pennies*

Now he can take that yellow sawdust and turn it into gold-dust for those who come to him in desperate financial need. Now he hears the prayers of mothers for sons who have gone astray; presses down his carpenter's rule, draws his straight line, and brings them back to it—to the straight and narrow. Now he sees someone lying in the pit of an evil habit, and in no time at all he can hammer together a ladder and bring him up rung by rung, up out of the dirt! Now he can take a marriage that is about to split wide open, and with his magic carpenter's glue bind it together as good as new. He can even make a splint for a broken heart!

In any trouble, go to Joseph!

As a Boy, Our Lord went there Himself!

Saints for the Aints

THE MOTHERS' SAINT

Some call him St. Gerard (almost rhyming with Herod); some call him St. Gerard (hit the last syllable hard!); but few, it seems, call him in vain. If you want to fix him historically, just remember he lived at the same time as George Washington. If you want to pinpoint him geographically, unroll the map of Italy and let your magnifying glass circle the tiny town of Muro, near Naples. If you want to picture him physically, see on the television screen of your imagination a young man, thin and white as a stalk of celery, and with a rattling cough that sounded like gravel drumming on the rough box at a grave.

Education? St. Gerard had two years on the benches of a country school. Yet he lived to lecture to seminarians, and to illuminate mysteries of faith with the clear white light of a wisdom that made doctors of theology blink. As a boy his first odd-job was guiding a broom in a Bishop's palace; he finished guiding a Bishop, as the latter's spiritual director, and this though he never became a priest, but remained a simple brother.

And doesn't it open another door on the democracy of the Catholic Church that this young man, Gerard Majella, living in the lowest ranks of the peasants, was raised to the highest honors of the altar, a canonized saint? The elegant nobles of his day, with their velvet cloaks, jeweled swords, perfumed handkerchiefs, now moulder forgotten in their marble tombs, while every year the Church reverently remembers this man—from whom they would have turned away with the twitch of an aristocratic nostril. It is always like that. Many men whom we call great are merely prominent. In the scales of eternity to be great is only to be good.

When he was about seventeen, Gerard decided he wanted to do the menial tasks in some monastery, a laborer working for the Lord. So, timidly he tapped at the door of the Capuchins. The Superior took one look at this frail lad, thin as a flute and pale as a candle, and smiled, "No, we aren't buying any invalids today." So Gerard hiked off to the house of the Redemptorist Fathers. "What is your trade?" this Superior asked. "I am a tailor. At least I have been an apprentice for three years." "Well," said the Superior good-humoredly, "Tailor, stick to your thread and tape. If there is one man out in the world who can get to Heaven through the eye of a needle, it is a good, God-fearing tailor."

So Gerard went back to sitting cross-legged like a Turk in the dingy tailor shop, giving every extra penny he earned to the poor. But one day, when he was nineteen, a band of Redemptorist priests came to his town to preach a mission. They stayed three weeks, and Gerard was so stirred by these trumpets of God, so impressed by the solemnity of the message and by the sincerity of the messengers, that he knew he must become a Redemptorist. The head of the mission band sensed what was happening, and he told Gerard's mother: "I am afraid that when we leave here in our farewell procession, Gerard will trail after us. So at that time by some pretext or other, get him into his room, and turn the key. Then he'll forget all about us." Which is just what the mother did; but St. Gerard —ah you know the saints are such dull people—merely eloped to his vocation. Melodramatically he lowered himself from his attic room down a twisting rope of bed-linen, and caught up with the missionaries a few villages farther on. So the chief missionary shrugged his shoulders and wrote the most unflattering letter of introduction ever penned. It was addressed to the Rector of the nearest Redemptorist Monastery and it read: "I am sending you a useless brother." Do you wonder who wrote with such brutal bluntness, and who was the man who read, with perhaps a smile or perhaps a scowl? All I know is that you can search the calendar of the saints and not find the name of either.

But when Gerard became a Redemptorist brother, strange things started to happen. In fact, miracles began to spurt out of him like colored fire from a Roman candle. Breath-taking wonders! He was Aladdin with a Sanctuary lamp. In an age of miracles, he was known as "The Wonder-Worker." But in a sense, the greatest wonder was Gerard's daily work. He may have been emaciated, but he labored like a lumberjack. Whether his hands were dipped in garden dirt or baker's dough or kitchen dishwater; whether he was sewing patches on coats, or decorating the altars in the Church, St. Gerard did every task well. He was like one of these pocketknives with a half dozen different attachments.

Add to his work a spirit of prayer that rose up like a perpetual fountain, a spirit of penance that trained and disciplined his body like a drill-sergeant, a spirit of charity among the poor that remembered only misery and forgot sleep; and you can surmise why at a mere twenty-nine the young man with the chalky face and the deep, blazing eyes died of tuberculosis... what you might call a dry martyr. On the small headstone that juts out of a Redemptorist grave there is not room for an epitaph, but only a name and a date. Yet who can forget, (once he has heard) the tiny card so crudely lettered that Gerard had tacked on the door inside his sick-room: "Here is done what God wills, as God wills, and as long as God wills it." Program and epitaph for a hero! It's a whole lot harder to be a saint on the horizontal.

After Gerard's death came an amazing twist. Slowly his fame began to roll first across Italy, then across Catholic Europe, as the saint to be invoked in cases of childbirth. But why should a celibate brother have any celestial influence in the delicate realm of maternity? I wonder is it a grim reward from God because of that incident which once threw an ugly shadow over Gerard's name? A woman had run to St. Alphonsus, the founder of the Redemptorists, and whispered that this young brother had been unchaste with a certain girl who had since moved to another part of the country. Tricky circumstances—the inevitable coincidences—closed around Gerard like a web. The rule of the Order (which certainly was not meant for serious matters like this) forbade a subject to defend himself. St. Alphonsus, shocked and shaken, strongly forbade Gerard to receive Holy Communion, and was about to drum him out of the Order when the venomous gossiper took suddenly ill, and feeling she was about to die, before a roomful of people gasped out that the whole story was a scarlet lie. Maybe then and there the Lord who hides diamonds in the dirt decided to recompense Gerard for this grimy trial by giving him a brilliant power of intercession on behalf of mothers and babies.

Maybe it was that. Or perhaps it was simply because St. Gerard loved the Virgin Mary, Mother of God, with a love that leaped up like a pure flame; or because Gerard was so devoted to the Christ-child that he tried to keep the spirit of Christmas every day, that an understanding God allows this celibate saint to spend his Heaven strewing miracles in the realm of nature's greatest miracle, the birth of a baby, and the ordeal of a mother. Time and again I have heard priests tell how prayers to St. Gerard have baffled the gloomy predictions of the doctors, blown away complications like cobwebs, and tenderly placed a healthy child in a mother's happy arms. Or where there were no children before, (and sometimes a childless marriage can be a bleak desert) devotion to St. Gerard has suddenly made the emptiness bloom into the gay garden of a family. In other cases the disappointment of a mis-carriage has turned inside out into the joy of a baby-carriage. Not long ago a doctor, who had delivered more than three thousand babies, told me he was summoned on a maternity case where the situation was desperate. From what he had learned over the phone from the other physician, he feared the worst. So on the way up in the hospital elevator, he lifted a silent prayer to his silent partner, St. Gerard. He was not in the delivery room two minutes when suddenly the whole situation changed. "And," he said, "the ironic feature is that I got the credit. I am convinced it was St. Gerard. I have seen it too often." Then he smiled. "I don't want to pun, but when you pray to St. Gerard, he delivers."

That is why the news is going quietly from hospital to hospital, like a sacristan quietly lighting candle after candle at a Shrine, that St. Gerard has extraordinary power in difficulties of childbirth, and is the "Mother's Saint." After all, who deserves more a special patron and protector than she who, though she may groan through the pangs and pains of maternity, struggles up out of the valley wearing a weak but radiant smile as she feels snuggled in the hollow of her arm, a new life, flesh of her flesh and bone of her bone,—something, someone so helpless and weak and sweet and adorable and alive and her very own!

It is all very well to remind a young expectant mother that she should not worry. That is the cold fact but the girl at the threshold of maternity is not a cold creature and often despite herself she will show concern. Tell her about St. Gerard. Tell her to say a small, fervent prayer each day in his honor. And then on that glorious day when she lies in that strange room where the mystery of life renews itself, and down the frail bridge that swings between eternity and time, a tiny traveller makes his way, there will stand at her side all the help of Heaven, shepherded there by the spirit of St. Gerard—who in God's mysterious Providence, protects mothers-to-be, and hears the helpless unborn who sigh, "Pray for us now, and at the hour of our birth. Amen."

Saints for the Aints

THIS MEDDLESOME PRIEST

Would you think it a tale of arrogance if I told you today about a saint who, while he was alive, presumed to name a church after himself? Put like that, it does sound as though the man had an ego the size of an elephant, but like the back-country motorist who told the judge he thought the red and green traffic lights were Christmas decorations, it has its explanation. Way back in twelfth-century England, the Archbishop of Canterbury (Roman Catholic of course —the other variety was then undreamed) bore the strange name, Thomas a Becket. One day when he was blessing a new chapel, the people of the village requested that he himself choose the patron saint after whom the little church should be named. Thomas quietly pushed aside this little dish of sweet flattery and said, "Suppose we call it after the next martyr." And it seems that for a while they did—called it clumsily, prophetically, "The Church of the Next Martyr." And then just four days after Christmas, the Archbishop's purple was dyed martyr's red, and overnight the church's name became to people wide-eyed and wet-eyed "St. Thomas a Becket."

But who in a Christian country, would want to murder the Archbishop? Here the scarlet threads get tangled and snarled, but eventually they lead back to the throne of the King. The main trouble with Henry the Second was that he could not brook even God the First. Among men he fancied himself an eagle among sparrows. Impulsive, aggressive, blustery, he would sweep a desk clean of papers and books and ink-bottles with one furious gesture. He never could forget that the British crown on his thinning red hair made him the mightiest monarch in Christendom, in the day when kings were never jokers, and their scepters had not been whittled down to a mere symbolic stick.

In the other corner, as the ring announcers have it, loomed a king-size foe, for Thomas a Becket was a great oak of a man with long black hair, piercing eyes, and a voice, they say, like a church bell. The poor loved him because his purse opened easily and his inherited wealth poured out. The common people admired him because they remembered the young warrior who had ridden under the king's banner, and fought saddle-to-saddle against the king's enemies, hacking helmets and routing the field. His friends marvelled that this hard-riding, sword-swinging, full-blooded soldier should now be just as much at home bent over musty books in his candlelit library.

To surprise them still more, Thomas a Becket now had the bare circle of tonsure cropped in the center of his handsome black head, like a silver half-dollar, and entered the service of the Church as a clerk or cleric. But, once he reached the order of deacon, he deliberately advanced no farther. At this juncture, King Henry the Second who liked the notion of a man who could double in steel, whether it was broadsword or pen-nib, asked him to become his Chancellor, then a sort of executive officer in charge of honors and patronage. Thomas accepted, but in this new post he won no popularity poll. When Bribery clinked its persuasive gold, it found that the new Chancellor had a stone ear. When the time came for promoting minor officials he draped the cape of advancement only round those shoulders he thought worthy. When he went on to wear the white flower of an unblemished life in the silken corruption and pagan looseness of the royal court, they shuffled uneasily in his silent presence. They hated and they feared. Not entirely a lovable character. Stern, just, fair. You think of his face in terms of one of those granite carvings of the Presidents, cut out of the mountain, a profile in rock.

Then the Archbishop of Canterbury died. Now, at that period in history this prelate was by office the first lord of the realm; in rank he was second only to the King. And now the King said to Thomas a Becket, "You are a cleric, a deacon. You shall be the Archbishop of Canterbury, the primate of all England." Thomas shook his head. "You put the crozier of Canterbury into my hands, and your crown may splinter against it." The King laughed. He felt he could control an Archbishop of Canterbury or any place else. "Besides, you and I are friends."

"We are friends now, but should you as King strike away any right of the Church, I would fight it to the death. Has your majesty considered that?" His Majesty winked and smiled and purred, "I think we can get along."

So it came about that Thomas a Becket was ordained priest and shortly after consecrated bishop, and took over England's chief See at Canterbury. But oh, what a change was there, my masters! What a tearing out of the old page and beginning of a new! For look you, off came the rich velvet cape of the gentleman cleric, the plum colored robe and the jingling golden chain, and on went the coarse common gown of a monk. Under that (though few knew it) bristled and twitched a penitential hair-shirt. Wine and meat he banished from his table, and gave himself to fasting, praying, and overseeing his diocese, and to preaching even in the remotest hamlets.

Do you think this was only a passing fad of fervor that came over him and as quickly left him, like a shower in the springtime when the sky is one moment weeping grey and the next blazing gold? No—the steel of his old sword, tried and true, had become the metal of his priestly soul. No paper flower of pretty piety, this man. For seven years he rose in the dawn, scourged himself with leather lashes, lived as meagerly as any hermit in the desert, till his great frame grew gaunt, and his deep eyes seemed black hollows, but the flame in his heart leaped ever higher toward God. Thomas a Becket had an extraordinary mission. For it he must make extraordinary preparations.

Meanwhile the King, Henry the Second, decided to move in upon the authority of the Church. Enough of this remote control by the Vatican over English churches and English priests. The Cross must know its place: footstool to the crown! "Spiritual or temporal, clergy or laity, prelate or prince, you shall have no appeal," he thundered, "above me, the King! Let the Pope rule in Rome; here I make the laws." And the King looking out at the great council at Northampton saw that Thomas a Becket stood there, not with the Archbishop's Cross before him as was the custom, but gripping it in his own hand, almost like his old sword. Quietly, with the slow serenity of truth, the Archbishop pointed out that the Pope claimed no power in matters temporal; and in matters spiritual he could not surrender power. "And," he finished, "whoever attempts to take that spiritual power by force, to rape the bride of Christ, will find Thomas a Becket in his path!"

Now the royal friendship, as Thomas had warned, swung around like the wind and blew raw and cold; became in fact an icy hate. Complications spiralled up, and one day the King turned scornfully to his courtiers and mused aloud: "Is there not one knight in all my kingdom to rid me of this meddlesome priest?"

That afternoon four courtiers leaped into the saddle and galloped for Canterbury. It was just before New Year's, and in the winter dusk the wind howled and slapped the snow like castanets against the tall cathedral windows. The Archbishop was within. Now, outside by the steps, the unholy four dismounted. There were wild shouts and the clanging of arms. One of the monks bolted the great oak door. "No", roared the Archbishop, "this is a cathedral. Would you make it a fortress?" And then more gently, "If you are afraid, drop back." And they all did, save one cleric named Grim.

Meanwhile, with swords drawn, the weird quartet clattered down the center aisle while the Archbishop stood in the gloom near one of the great pillars. He seemed like a thin straight pillar himself, the large eyes in the pale face staring ahead. Suddenly a torch burned a yellow hole in the dark and a voice cried, "Where is the traitor?.... Where is the Archbishop?" Stepping out from the shadow of the column Thomas said, "I am the Archbishop, but no traitor. What will you have?" "Your life!" And the sword struck him a glancing blow, sending his biretta flying from his head. He tottered to his knees, swayed toward the altar, and murmured, "To you, Jesus, Mary, I commend my soul." The next sword swung in a shining arc, struck his head, and as the poor prelate lay face down, dead, his blood, in thin red lines, slowly crawled across the white marble floor.

An hour later the people knew. A blaze of candles flickered in the cathedral. A strange, unseasonable thunderstorm growled overhead. Peasants and tradesmen knelt beside the gashed body and dipped little cloths into the blood for relics and heirlooms, and whispered in awe or cried out in trembling tribute: "Saint Thomas! Is he not surely now a saint?" Within an hour the common people had canonized him: within a week the shocking news of murder in the Cathedral had reached every fireside in the land; within a year Canterbury was on its way to becoming the most revered shrine in England. And one of the first pilgrims to kneel at the martyr's tomb, barefoot and clad in sackcloth, was the King, Henry the Second—how sincerely who can say?

That was eight hundred years ago. But it was not eight hundred years ago to Thomas a Becket when he refused to hide in that chill December dusk. To him it was now, the golden present, and life was just as sweet to him then as it is to us this living hour, and death just as sharp as we would find it, if it struck us down this minute. He was not thinking that History would tip-toe into the scene and paint the picture in mellow oils for posterity: all he knew was that he was doing the original in his own bright blood. It was no consolation to him—how could he foresee?—that for centuries the Canterbury pilgrims to the sweet tune of tinkling bridles would come riding to his tomb as a national shrine and even a landmark of literature. He only knew, like any martyr, that one moment he had life, and the next he freely gave it up.

From this distance, *why* he died may seem trivial, or at least involved, but fundamentally it was a simple thing. The things of Caesar must not encroach on the things of Christ! Sometimes we call it totalitarianism or dictatorship: these are nothing but new labels pasted on the same old bottle. To make the Church just another department of the State has been the aim of every tyrant who ever gathered all the reins of power into one pair of hands. Henry the Second merely led the parade; after him came such men as Hitler and Stalin and Tito and the rest. Alongside Thomas a Becket have dared to stand men like Cardinal Mindszenty and Stepinac and Wyzynski, and all the obscure, unknown little men in China or Russia or Siberia or Hungary or any of the Satellite states, men who have heroically taken their place on the side of God, when the government had on its side the tanks, the prisons, the whips, the concentration camps, and the unmarked graves!

Between Canterbury and the Iron Curtain the only difference is time. The question is the same:

Caesar or God? And the answer has to be a spiritual Declaration of Independence. For those who have made it and have paid for it with life or liberty; for the Christian underground in the new catacombs; for these we should pray daily, but oh how easy we forget! But blood is thicker than water—especially the Blood of Christ, the Blood that makes these gallant Catholics our brothers! CARE packages? By all means! But most of all, Prayer packages! At least we can pray!

Saints for the Aints

MARTYR TO CHASTITY

Like most other visitors to Rome, we had shuffled reverently through the Catacombs, kissed the glass-smooth foot of Peter's bronze statue, marvelled at the majesty and the splendor of the four major basilicas, smiled at the colorful line of contemporary wash waving at the ancient Forum, frowned disappointedly at the narrow, muddy Tiber, climbed down into the Mammertine Prison and climbed up the Holy Stairs—but on this particular shimmering, simmering afternoon we boarded the wheezing old bus for a destination that the travel ads would probably advertise as "off the beaten path."

The radiator cap pointed southward, and soon we were out of the city rolling along the Old Appian Way that glides like a snake between crumbling ruins and tombs, and then on to the New Appian Way that lies there like a straight grey bayonet piercing the flat and monotonous Roman plain. Of course after you have been riding a bus for a month or more across Europe, much of the scenery is bound to seem monotonous. When we started, a thatched roof or an ivied castle had us pressing our nose against the window, but later on a river would almost have to loop the loop to draw a raised eyebrow.

The one time you could always be sure of a reaction, the one sight that always touched silence, was an American military cemetery. At Florence, at Belleau Wood, and now near Nettuno it was always the same. This latter was the cemetery of the Anzio Beachhead, where the blue Mediterranean had been so sadly reddened with young American blood. Now more than seven thousand white marble crosses stand here like a ghostly army at eternal attention. As we walked up and down the grim rows, and then paused to say a prayer together, war never seemed more horrible. Here you realized that when the bombs plow the earth and blood irrigates the furrows, lines of death-crosses are the tragic harvest. This was the spot where you really wanted to kneel down and pray for peace.

These young men were martyrs to war, but our destination was the resting place of a young girl who was a martyr to chastity. Her name was St. Maria Goretti, and tomorrow would be her first official feast day as a saint, and soon we found ourselves marching up the steps to her parish church, which isn't too far from the cemetery, in the town of Nettuno. Except in Venice we never saw a church so near the water. A bride could stand upon those church steps and toss her bouquet into the wavelets of the Mediterranean gently lapping the sand. Within, the church was unique too, because the walls and ceiling were done in a very unusual combination of brown and blue. But this was the eve of the great feast, so the huge scarlet drapes hung from the pillars, and over the sanctuary was suspended a great gilded crown. Inside the altar-rail and directly beneath the crown you started at seeing a burial casket of clear crystal. It rested on a stand of dull ornamented silver and the floor all around was scattered with a shower of flower-petals. In the casket you saw the wax figure of a young girl with dark hair and a long white dress.

Within this life-like image are the bones of the girl who used to come to this town each week to sell her basket of eggs, and who was murdered just sixty years ago while defending her virginity. We asked the old monk in the sacristy if this was an exact likeness of St. Maria Goretti, and he shrugged his shoulders. If you mean was it made from an actual photograph, no. After all, cameras were not exactly common in the villages of Italy in 1902, and as a matter of fact, she never had her picture taken. But this image was made from sketches approved by her mother and her family. The long white dress, trimmed with lace, could have been just like her own, because in those days children were rather old when they received their First Holy Communion. As a matter of fact, Maria, a tall girl for her twelve years had just made her First Communion at the end of May. Then she received twice in June, and was looking forward to receiving again on the first Sunday in July—when it happened—and on that day she received the Last Sacraments, and Christ Himself received her into Heaven.

The bearded monk assured us that the scene of the martyrdom was only ten miles away, and we would be foolish to come this far and not go on to see Maria's home. Besides, Maria Goretti had been canonized only a few months before and it would be interesting to contrast where a saint lived with where she was canonized. This young girl had been declared a saint in the presence of three hundred thousand people, as the Pope stood on the balcony of St. Peter's. That very morning we had been to St. Peter's, and it was easy to imagine the canonization Mass—one of the most gorgeous and solemn spectacles in all the world, with the silver trumpets blaring high above the twisting pillars, and the winding procession of prelates in purple and scarlet, and the white-robed Pontiff borne on the swaying throne, and the crashing harmonies of the choir, and the breathless moment when the veil flutters down and the likeness of the new saint is revealed, and His Holiness Himself intoned the first prayer for her intercession. To the stranger it may all seem like extravagant pomp and ceremony, but the saving glory of the situation is that the elaborate ceremony is hoisted as a background of honor for somebody who was generally a nobody, ordinary, obscure, perhaps unknown even in the next town.

That is the fine democracy of the Catholic Church. To be a saint you don't need a big bank balance or any blue blood or assorted university degrees or influence in high places. In fact you can live all your life in a place as unpretentious as the home of Maria Goretti. She didn't even know how to read or write. She only knew how to live and how to die. We were talking about this as we got back into our bus and took off with much racket and roar for the shrine

—if you want to call it that—of her house. It wasn't by any means a pleasant ride. This was not the Italy we had travelled down from the north, with soft rolling hills, fluttering vineyards, squat rows of olive trees, little streams lying like satin bookmarks across the green page of the land. Here the road was more like a dry canal that bumped along from shell-hole to shell-hole while the sun beat down fiercely and the white dust of the road powdered your clothes and choked your throat, while swarms of tiny flies circled your head. Those ten miles we were almost authentic pilgrims.

Fifty years ago, during St. Maria Goretti's life, in these dreaded marshes the mosquitoes all but flew in formation, and malaria was the perpetual plague. The Count who owned the land used to buy coffins wholesale, and Maria's father unloading a new batch, predicted that one of these would be for him. It was too, and thereafter Maria, the child of poverty, had to walk this road each week bringing her pigeons or eggs to the market at Nettuno. They say that people would see her walking along and would ask, "Who is that beautiful young girl? She walks like a princess!" The truth is of course she was the daughter of the poorest peasant roundabout. She never spent a day in school, but there was about her not only a startling beauty, but a natural refinement, a grace and charm that stood out strangely in these remote swamplands.

When we got to her house, we found that the war had not completely spared this either. It is an old two-story stone affair, and the front was pocked and scarred from shrapnel. A stone stairway runs diagonally right up the side wall of the house to the second floor where the Goretti's lived. It seemed strange and mysterious climbing those stairs, and then stepping inside. Talk about simplicity. The floor was rough red bricks, like a village sidewalk. The walls were whitewashed like a cellar. There was a business-like open fireplace, a kitchen table, two rickety kitchen chairs, and a couple of pots and pans hanging from hooks on the wall.

On that blistering July day in 1902 Maria was sitting just inside the top of those stairs—what we would call baby-sitting, because she was taking care of her tiny sister, Teresa. Maria's widowed mother had to work in the fields with the other people of the neighborhood. One of these workers was Alessandro Serenelli. As a matter of fact he lived downstairs in the Goretti house. Serenelli was only nineteen, but two years spent amid water-front dives had already soiled his youth. Now returned to the farm, he began to notice how Maria the child was growing into girlhood, and lust began to burn in his grimy heart. Twice in the last two weeks he had whispered his unclean proposals to her, and when she had turned pale with horror, he had threatened, "If you tell your mother about this, I will kill you." Maria told her mother but with the threat of death hanging over her daughter's head the mother frowned and said, "Let me think this over."

The very next day young Serenelli made his move. Nobody noticed him slipping away from the workers in the field. The first thing Maria heard was his springing step hurrying up the outside stone stairs. She was knitting in a corner, the baby was playing on the floor, and suddenly he stood there filling the doorway.

It is best to draw a merciful curtain over the too vivid details, and state simply that he attempted to seduce her at the point of a knife; that she said she would rather die than sin; that he stabbed her fourteen times, and ran away.

Maria managed to drag herself to the door and groan. The little baby began to cry. Somebody heard the commotion, came running up. They did what they could by way of first aid, gently lifted her into a farm-wagon, and brought her to the little hospital at Nettuno. The doctors worked swiftly, but from the beginning there was little hope. Now the priest came in with Viaticum. It was after midnight so it was Sunday, the Sunday she had been looking forward to for her fourth Communion. As she lay there making her silent thanksgiving, the long lashes over her eyes like shadows, the pale figure might have been another St. Agnes in the twentieth century. Then she slowly opened those eyes to the priest's question which had come as an afterthought. "Do you," he asked, "for the love of God, do you forgive Serenelli?" There was no hesitation. She knew that "Chastity without charity shall be chained in hell." "Of course I forgive him, and I pray that he is sorry for his sin, so that God can forgive him too." Then she turned to her mother. "Mamma, don't cry. I'm all right." And with a thin smile playing round her bloodless lips she died.

In every age God raises up appropriate leaders, and youth in our day needs an inspiring patron like Maria Goretti. Sin—that some commit for pleasure, and some for flattery, and some for money, and some just to be modern—she would not do, not with a knife at her throat, to save her life. It wasn't a sudden decision. The lips that then had boldly said no to sin, had

MARIA GORETTI, MARTYR TO CHASTITY

been speaking every day to God in prayer. In her little home the family supper was always followed by the family rosary. Maria's mother said, "I taught the babies to pray as soon as they could talk. Otherwise little children will be only like little animals." Isn't it true in adult life too, in a sadder sense? We must pray or we will fall; we will forget that we are human children of God and sink to the level of beasts.

There are people who think that purity is a pallid, frigid, timid thing, frosty and lifeless as an icicle. The truth is that purity is white, but it is white-hot like a pure flame. It is not that it lacks love, but that it loves God above all else. As the Pope phrased it in the canonization ceremony, "Maria Goretti was no pale weakling but a valiant heroine. She had no fear of the assassin's dagger; the only thing she feared was sin."

Too many young people today think that modesty and self-control, about which they hear so often, are only like the bars on a jail, keeping them shut off from happiness. Oh if they only knew, these are not steel bars on a jail but handrails on a bridge, that treacherous bridge that swings between adolescence and maturity! And only those who have fallen off and lie there bruised and broken know how necessary modesty and self-control are!

The last thing we saw in Maria's house was a little picture of the Madonna over her bed. Every Saturday Maria used to gather some flowers in the field and arrange them near her picture. That Saturday she never got to the fields. But Our Lady was not without flowers. She had a gleaming lily, stained with blood. And Maria didn't need the picture. She was in Heaven with the person, Our Lady Herself!

Who Is My Neighbor?

THE OTHER LAW

The other day I was visiting a Rectory and there on the wall hung a very gaunt and impressive crucifix—though, to tell the truth, I was even more impressed by the two lovely paintings of Our Lady that hung on either side. The picture on the left portrayed Mary kneeling in prayer, eyes modestly cast down, hands devoutly folded, while a very courtly Archangel was announcing to her that soon her Cousin Elizabeth would give birth to John the Baptist. Now the other painting showed the reaction, the response. There was Mary hurrying over the rolling green hills of Galilee, her white robe fluttering like a sail on the waves, as she hurried to help Elizabeth in her imminent confinement. Somehow to me these two pictures, flanking the Cross of Christ like wings on a stage, seem to catch the spirit of the whole drama of Christianity. For—isn't it true?—the first picture shows religion at prayer; the second, religion in practice. The service of God in the Temple, and the service of neighbor in town!

We need both but more easily forget the second. And when Christianity falters (it never can fail) the reason will never shine in the sharp bayonets of persecution. The Church patiently buries her persecutors, and makes each tombstone an altarstone over which she sings the Te Deum of her new deliverance. Nor will the reason be the false doctrines of Communism, which is only the contemporary heresy, and which eventually will go into the musty files of finished business with Arianism or Nazism. Arianism—once half the Christian world was Arian; how many can even define it now? No—when Christianity falters, there is only one reason—Christians! You know there are people, and if you hinted they were half-pagan, they would boil you with an incredulous glare; but as a matter of cold, objective fact, they are only half-Christian. They practice only fifty percent of God's law. Oh, let the church bells tumble about in their towers and ring the call to prayer, the law of the love of God, and they answer eagerly. But let the doorbell ring—somebody in need or in trouble—(the law of the love of neighbor) and somehow they can't seem to hear!

Put them in a quiet prayerful church, especially at sunset when every stained-glass window blazes like a flowergarden, and the soft candle-light mellows the pale and peaceful statues, and perhaps a rosary rustles leisurely through their fingers, and they love it! But this is only half of religion: religion under the steeple. The other half is the harder half: religion out there among the people. Surely, it is considerably easier to live piously and righteously among the statues and stained-glass windows! Why, *there* is no trouble at all——no irritations, no complications, no obligations.

But remember God made the people. God loves the people. God died for the people. He didn't die for any statue or stained-glass window, or for any rosary even though fashioned from olive wood and brought all the way from Jerusalem or Lourdes or Rome. Why, the sorriest, the most soiled and tattered wreck of humanity that shambles along a city street is more precious in the eye of God than the most glorious statue of the Madonna executed by the most famous artist and exhibited in the world's greatest museum. Because the only purpose of the painting is to lift up the minds and hearts of human beings to the love of God, and (for His Sake) to the love of neighbor!

That is why it has always struck me as a bit strange (maybe your experience is different) that I have never seen in any rectory or in any church a picture or a statue of a certain Scriptural figure who stands very high in the litany of practical charity. Maybe he is not the champion, or even the challenger, but only a candidate; still his particular deed was very dear to the Heart of Christ. We don't even know his name, but History has always called him the Good Samaritan, and admirers for short have called him just Good Sam. Anyway, here he is loping along on horseback over the sloping road that dips down from Jerusalem toward Jericho; and suddenly, there in the bushes beside the road, he sees a groaning Jew, beaten up, bleeding, robbed by bandits, helpless and pitiful. ... The marvelous thing about the story is that the Samaritan did something; did it promptly; did it himself.

If you don't think that was pretty extraordinary, just remember that a priest and a Levite, who had possibly just come from the Temple at Jerusalem, passed by—as coldly as icebergs in the Labrador current. But the Samaritan stopped. And notice too the easy and obvious things the Good Samaritan didn't do. He didn't wring his hands in pity and murmur, "Poor fellow! How I pity you! My heart goes out to you!" He didn't stroke his beard and mutter, "I wonder who this chap is, and how did it all happen?" He didn't unload a quantity of that very free and futile product, good advice, and say very cheerfully, "Come now, my man, you must learn to help yourself. On your feet with you! You can if you try, you know." He didn't wrinkle his brow and begin to wonder, "If I were the one in this mess, would anybody stop and help me?" He didn't get official and formal and shake his head and say, "This situation is horrible. Of course when I get to Jericho I shall report it immediately to the proper agency." He didn't put his hands on his hips and get I-told-you-so-ish and say, "Well, after all, if a man is going to travel this road alone and in the dead of night, what can he expect? He's inviting assault and robbery!"

No—the marvel of the whole story is that the Good Samaritan saw a man in trouble. He did something immediately. He did it personally. He did it effectively.

And furthermore—he did it for someone who meant nothing to him at all. There was no human attraction in the case. He wasn't playing the gallant knight to a beautiful young damsel in distress. He was a Samaritan, before anybody ever heard of a "Good Samaritan"; and the man bleeding in the bushes was a Jew. Probably the closest modern parallel to the feeling between the Jew and the Samaritan in Palestine, was the feeling of a few years ago between the Irishmen of St. Patrick in the South of Ireland and the Orangemen of Ulster in the North. The Jews despised the Samaritans for "selling out" to the Romans. They looked down on the Samaritans as half-breeds. They hated the Samaritans as heretics. But the Good Samaritan never thought of these things. All he knew was that there in trouble was his brother in the great family of humanity, his brother because they were both children of God—so, like a brother he helped him!

And oh, notice this, because here is where most charity stops dead. People will make the highest resolves, the noblest promises—to themselves or to others—and then, then they run flush against the realization that this is going to cost them something, cost them in some way or other, and they draw back. They didn't think the water was going to be so cold. But not the Good Samaritan! And it cost him, too. It cost him time and trouble, to begin with. It interrupted and delayed his journey. Very possibly it made him miss an important appointment. Possibly it meant explanations to his wife who was waiting with fire in her eye and thunder on her tongue. It cost him physical effort. He had to bandage up the poor fellow as best he could, heft him up on the horse, and himself trudge along on foot all the way to the inn. It cost the oil and wine he poured into the wound. It cost him money to the innkeeper.... And that's the last we see of the Good Samaritan as he goes riding down the road of history, an obscure, humble figure without benefit of press agent, who never even turns around in his saddle to show his face. I wonder how many of us will ever catch up with him, Christians or Catholics though we be?

Who was it that said God had divided man into men so that they might help one another? Yet you will find people who bubble and gush, for example, about their love for the Mother of God, but who never dream of giving any practical help to some other poor mother who really needs it. If there is sickness in that mother's home, they never think to drop around to help straighten out the house or stir up a meal. They will dress an Infant of Prague in rich silken robes, but they would never get the idea to manoeuvre in a very tactful and delicate way to outfit one of the children for First Communion, or send one of them away to summer camp. Children? Listen to some good church people prating of their tender and vibrant love for the Child Jesus, and you might be impressed; but you soon find out that He is the only child they do tolerate and that at a pious and poetic distance. Every other child is apparently just a brat, brats to be shooed away from playing in front of their door; and the youngsters scatter like a flock of sparrows! That is all they are, little grey sparrows hopping around the city streets. Still not one of these sparrows falls, but He knows it and loves it.

Didn't Our Blessed Lord say, "Whatsoever you do to the least of My brethren, you do to Me?" There is the difficulty: to recognize God behind the masks of men. But we have to do it. Because when He appeals to us for help, He won't send a special Star of Bethlehem pointing its finger of fire to the spot where we are to do our bit of good. Charity done for Christ doesn't need celestial fireworks and a full heavenly choir. No, Our Blessed Lord will always stand in the shadows, and under the guise of some poor creature, even as He hid that Christmas Eve under Mary's ample robe. Someone else always knocks at the door *for* Him, as at the Inn of Bethlehem. If that door had not slammed and shuddered in His face, to this day men would have beaten a path to it, the most famous Shrine in the world! As it is, it is only the sad symbol of Christ unrecognized, Christ turned away!

In these matters you cannot go wrong in following the Saints. Yet here is something fairly startling from the life of one of them. One Holy Thursday morning, Blessed Angela of Foligno, with her girl companion, went to the Cathedral. They heard Holy Mass, received Communion, made their thanksgiving, and then Blessed Angela nudged her companion. "Come on," she whispered, "it's all over here. Now let's go out and find Christ among the poor and the sick and the needy." Our Blessed Lord is still out there among them. So, hands clasped in prayer? By all means! But don't forget to unclasp them and reach them out to any neighbor in need! The body you help may be anybody's, but the soul you save will be your own!

Who Is My Neighbor?

RED STABBING TONGUES

Our Blessed Lord once said, "Behold the lilies of the field!" and went on to draw a parable. I would ask you to have a look at the lilies of Easter, and draw a parable in another field. Did you notice how the trumpet-shape of an Easter Lily looks like the horn of an old-fashioned gramaphone? Or how the cup of an Easter Tulip looks like the mouthpiece of an old-fashioned telephone? Or how any bed of Easter flowers stirred by the breeze looks like a group of brightly bonnetted heads nodding and whispering together? Like a good, old-fashioned gossip session! Only the results of gossip are never so pretty—or so good.

Time was when gossiping was a back-fence affair, done to the hanging out of wash or the feeding of chickens. Now it is the telephone wires that run along the back fence, and the gossiping is done very comfortably from an easy chair. And of course, you will find plenty of gossip where there aren't any back fences—in hospitals and hotels, in tenements and housing projects. In fact in the center courtyard of a very large housing development in New York City there is, or there used to be, a pointed piece of statuary. It shows a person (I'm sorry, it happens to be a woman) with her stone eyes staring at one of the windows, and her lips parted so you can almost hear her saying, "Did you hear that b-z-z-z?" And the other figure (I'm sorry again) has *her* ear poised like an attachment on a vacuum cleaner to suck in all "the dirt." The listener's hands are held high in horror as though she were saying, "No-o-o!!" meaning "Yes, yes, go on!" And her lips seem to be saying "Don't tell me!" meaning, "Tell me more!" On the base of the statue, as though that were necessary, are carved the words: THE GOSSIPS. And every man who sees it, smiles and thinks, "Well, there's one sculptor who knows his business!"

But gossiping is by no means confined to women. Go to the locker rooms of golf clubs, go to the Directors' rooms of big corporations, and you will hear gossip. Only the men call it constructive criticism. Go to a wedding, and before the bride in her gown of ivory satin has reached the front of the church, the tongue of gossip is liable to be rattling like a telegraph key in the back of the church. Go to a wake, and the people on this side of the room are liable to be talking about the people on that side of the room, and the only one out of range is the corpse. They have, we hope, that decency. You will hear them gossiping on the sand at beach parties, and gossiping over the sandwiches at bridge parties. It is a kind of National Game.

Game? Yes, it is like one of those games where you flick a metal spinner to point out where you move. So in gossip, the conversation, like that little arrow, goes round and round, skimming over this topic and lightly touching that, and finally stops at and goes through the heart of some absent person. Target for tonight! Or it is like a game of cards where, in order to win, you have to go higher or trump. One by one the juicy bits of scandal are flung down till someone who has been playing it close to the vest triumphantly says, "Yes, but did you hear *this*?" and of course wins. It is like a jig-saw puzzle in reverse, where piece by piece we take our neighbor apart.

But why call gossip a game? There are games of skill and games of chance but in gossip the players need no skill and the victim has no chance. Why even in the Dictator countries a man gets at least the semblance of a hearing. Maybe they only go through the motions—the motions of a mock trial—but at least they make their charges in the presence of the accused. But when the Supreme Court of Gossip in solemn conclave assembles, the case is called, the evidence heard, the verdict reached, the sentence passed; and the poor culprit does not even know there has been a trial! But his reputation hangs there helpless and scarred like a dartboard. And since cowardice is the badge of all their tribe, what better symbol for the gossiper than the dart itself, which is a sharp needle with a wooden head and flaunting a couple of white feathers?

Now and then though, and it gives you joy just to think of it, the victim suddenly appears unannounced and unexpected right in the circle of the little red stabbing tongues. If ever you encounter a scene like that, polish your spectacles because you are bound to see some of the finest acting in America. Broadway stars could humbly watch and gratefully pick up a few pointers. Here is the drama of hypocrisy polished like bright steel, but with the touch of a button, the sharp sword slides back into the casual cane. I remember once I had the good fortune to have a front seat at such a performance, only to be exact I was standing at a bus stop, energetically minding my own business, but I couldn't help hearing the group next to me. They were doing a terrific job, especially Mrs. Slash (call her that after her tongue)—a terrific job on well let's call *her* Mrs. Hash because that was the state of her reputation at the moment. Anyway, at that moment doesn't the door of the beauty parlor open and who should flounce out with innocent eyes right into the midst of her own autopsy but the aforesaid Mrs. Hash!

This, I said to myself, should be good. I was all eyes and the rest of me was ears, but what happened? Did Mrs. Slash blush or bite her lip, or drop her eyes, or murmur that she had an appointment with the dentist and scurry away? She did not! Have I a lot to learn! Without flickering an eyelash Mrs. Slash flashed on a smile like a neon sign. "My dear!" she exclaimed "you are looking so well!" She should have said "so well grilled." Then actually she put her arms half around Mrs. Hash. The arms should have been ice tongs. But you see that is civilization and society. In the jungle if you don't like someone, you burble a war-whoop and hurl the whistling spear. But in society, you smile, and smile, and when the victim's back is turned the poisoned arrows fly!

Poke around the roots of this weed of malicious gossip and you will find that it thrives best in certain soils. Vanity is a fertile field: I mean some people peddle scandal because they want an audience. More than anything else in the world they want to talk; to dominate the conversation; to have every chair inch forward in their direction, and every ear tilted toward their wagging tongue like teacups toward the spout of the tea-pot. And out pour the stories, hot and strong. A good deal of gossip also sprouts from the rotten ground of envy. Let somebody else have more brains or more beauty, more popularity or more money, or even more virtue, and the green eyes of jealousy start staring to find the flaws.

There are folks like that: they cannot see a clean shining window but they want to hurl a brick. They cannot see somebody above them but they want to pull the upstart down. Just try to sound the praises of someone and see. "Oh, yes, he's clever enough and ambitious, but ..." That *but*! "Why yes she is attractive and pleasant but ..." They have more "buts" than a goat and the target is generally the lid of the garbage can. Good just doesn't appeal to them.

Did you ever pass a stretch of lawn, smooth and green as a billiard table, and then a couple of weeks later pass the same place and see twisting trails of humped-up grass and dirt? What got into it anyway? I'll tell you what! Somewhere underneath a mole is at work—a mole that has no use for clean fresh air, a mole that can't stand golden sunlight, a mole that sees no beauty in flowers, but spends its life pushing its snoot through the dark depths and throwing up dirt!

But the mole ruins the lawn in front of the house, while the malicious gossiper can ruin the lives of people in the home!

I say malicious gossip, because gossip is like larceny, it can be grand and it can be petty. It is true we should do neither, but while petty gossip is not exactly high up on the spiral of Christian perfection, it is not the bottom of the cistern of iniquity either. To criticize a lady's hat because it looks like a lampshade trimmed with stuffed canaries, or to find fault with a man because he talks so much that he won't even give the echoes a break, may not be charitable but on the other hand you would not brand it malicious. In the first place these are little things, and in the second they are obvious. Everybody knows about them. But malice puts its heavy foot forward when the faults are serious and comparatively secret. To whisper it about that a man is a crook, or that a girl is loose and easy, or that a doctor is careless, or that a public official is corrupt—this is what you call streaking the black brush of gossip across a reputation.

But perhaps you say that the charge is true. In that case you have the right to bring your information to two groups of people: those who might suffer from the fault, and those who have the obligation to stop it. Suppose late one night Mrs. Telescope Eyes draws back her curtain (it's worn at that spot) and sees the young girl across the street being helped into her house quite the worse for liquor. Fortunately there is a meeting of the bridge club the next afternoon, and when the fire of conversation burns low, Mrs. T. decides to throw on a log that will really crackle. "My dears, you should have seen young Millicent last night. Carried in like a bag of salt. Positively petrified!" Of course the group may eat it up and prefer this minced and shredded reputation even to the cute sandwiches, but it is still entirely and absolutely wrong. Whoever may have a right to know about the affair, it is certainly not this circle of gloaters who knit and nod and smile around the guillotine. Or should we call them the mob under the cross at the crucifixion of a character?

If we must talk, why not speak to the only One Who knows the whole story—why not talk to God and confine our whispering to a charitable prayer?

Who Is My Neighbor?

HANDS AND HOLY WATER

The Angels of Christmas have whirred away, trailing a wake of golden light and golden song, but in proper time other angels will come coasting down the skies to render their shining service to Our Blessed Lord. Angels will come to minister to Him after He has fasted forty days in the desert. Angels will be there to fling back the stone of the tomb, and fold the winding-sheet at His Resurrection. Angels will draw the clouds about Him and pilot Him home as He surges upward in the Ascension. They are all in the Gospels.

And so is that Angel at the pool of Bethsaida or (as some call it) Bethesda. In Maryland there is a huge Naval Hospital called Bethesda. Very appropriate name for a Naval Hospital, isn't it, because at the original Bethesda an angel stirred the waters, and the sick plunging into them, were cured. I thought of that last month, in reverse, in a certain church. Because just

HANDS AND HOLY WATER

inside the entrance stood two marble angels with gracefully folded wings, each holding a tiny pool of Holy Water. Only here, unlike Bethsaida, the worshipper stirred the water; each Angel just held his pool and held his peace.

If angels ever were grounded, these were they. Not only that. Angel literally means (if I remember my distant Greek) a messenger. Yet it seemed to me, as I watched the people come in, that this was the charm and the appeal of that particular pair of angels, that they carried no messages, told no tales, spread no word. In dips your hand; with beads of water glittering on your finger-tips you cross yourself, and pass on. And the Holy Water Font says nothing.

Can't you imagine on Sunday morning in any large city church the strange and varied procession that curls up to the Holy Water Font, stops at it and passes on? All sorts of hands skim the little pool. Dedicated hands that perhaps have just come off duty, nursing the sick. Guilty hands that last night like Pilate have crucified Christ by scarlet sin, and now like Pilate dip their fingers into the water, fling off the sparkling drops to make show of innocence, as though protesting that they are just as good as anybody else.

Dainty, delicate hands flick into the basin, fingers fragile and feminine, but fingers that were strong enough to drag a man away from his sturdiest resolution and to push him to the brink of Hell,—yes, into it, should he suddenly die. Hands that one day may themselves reach straining out of those fires for just such a small pool of cooling water. And all the while the Holy Water Font says nothing.

They keep marching into church, and the parade pivots slightly and pauses momentarily there as the hands glide in and out of the water in the scalloped shell held out by the Angel. Here are fingers plunging in now, bright with long, laquered nails, blazing with a rainbow of rings, and the wearer wearing a dress best described as indescribable. She is an old friend of the Holy Water Font. Every Sunday she shows up in order to show off; goes into competition with the High Altar as the center of attraction. But the Holy Water Font says nothing.

Now a hand plumps in that is more familiar with fire-water than with holy water; a hand that tosses down with grimacing gulps his children's future; a hand that has more than once fallen heavily on a helpless wife. But the Holy Water Font says nothing... The circles are still running around in the quiet pool when there plops in the flabby hand of a loafer. It is not merely that he does not have a job. He does not want a job. His kind survive only because other people are willing to take over the responsibilities that he blows away like smoke from a cigarette. Then (but mind you I am just pointing out the characters; most of the people that stop to cross themselves at the font are good, God-fearing Catholics living honest lives, loving their home and hoping for heaven) but then comes the smooth hand of a politician whose conscience has three different speeds and a reverse. His hand is so smooth because it has been greased so often with that invisible "honest" graft, and even at the Holy Water Font he greets those about him with a wide, wooden smile like the opening in a ballot box. But the Holy Water Font says nothing.

A moment afterward a young man strolls in, jaunty and brash, and when his hand snaps into the Holy Water, it is a wonder it doesn't cloud over into a mud-puddle. At least the girl he escorted home last night would think it should... But now a hand dips in, wearing a thick wedding-band. And nobody could be more faithful to her wedding vows. But the poor fellow who took the vows with her, and is just as faithful, he often dreads to come home at all. Oh, she will be there; no question of that. But she will be there squawking like a parrot, or rumbling and grumbling like a coalshute, or pointedly silent like thirty seconds to Zero Hour—and he wonders did he take this woman for his lawful or his awful wife.

They are almost all into Mass now; and anyway maybe you are wondering why in the world I have had the effrontery to make myself the Grand Marshal of the parade of other people's faults. I assure you it was not to make easy listening; but to score (if possible) a hard point. You perhaps recognized the types as they passed by; the hands that brushed in and out of the water. So does the Holy Water Font, and all the while it says nothing. It minds its own business. It keeps its secrets. It simply stands and serves. It does not bend toward the nearest Station of the Cross and whisper, "Did you see that fur coat that just passed? Well she..." or "That's So-and-so going down the aisle now. They say that he...".

Nothing like that. Nothing but silence. All sorts of hands darting in and out, but over the Holy Water Font might be carved, "No comment". And the lesson for us is not that we should not talk about people in church, though in some churches you would think that each Sunday morning was a new Pentecost and the Holy Ghost had descended again with the gift of tongues. But that is on the way out rather than on the way in. The lesson of the Holy Water Font is, that we should not talk about the faults of people anywhere. Not in the backyard or in the bus, not over the bridge table or at the bar, not around the television or on the telephone. And not because it is impolite but because it is wrong. Not because it is not in gracious accord with Emily Post, but because it offends Almighty God.

It is often astonishing how people who are straitlaced and pious and solemn and who certainly have no keen sense of humor, do have a very keen sense of rumor. They can smell the thinnest wisp of scandal at four thousand yards. How can you explain it, that the very tongue that is a crimson cushion for the Sacred Host in the morning does not feel the slightest remorse about curling like a python around somebody's character in the afternoon? It is a fifty-fifty proposition: God in the morning, gossip the rest of the day.

It is amazing how you can be a fairly good Christian (?) and yet develop on the moral retina a definite blind spot that sees no evil in skewering three or four reputations like a shish-ka-bab. It is a curious inconsistency in the pattern of, "You know I wouldn't say anything about her if it wasn't good, and brother, is this good!" And then the deluge.

But no remorse. You know why? Because (and she will tell you with all the injured dignity of a Roman Senator) that what she said was true. So what? If it is true but secret, we still have no right to reveal it, to revel in it, to gloat over it. The picture rises way back in my memory, probably from some book of travel, of a corpse floating down the Ganges and two crows perched on it, pecking and chattering. A foul picture, but on the other hand is it not a fair picture of a pair of gossips feasting on some helpless human being who is down?

These are the days when our thoughts beam down like the light of a star to the Madonna of the Stable, Mary, the Virgin Mother whose breast is the brightest, cleanest throne in all the world for the Little King of Christmas. Well, can you imagine Mary when she finally got home to Nazareth, traipsing about the town, rag-picking for shreds of grimy scandal about her neighbors? Can you imagine her at the spinning wheel in the little cottage, spinning yarn and at the same time spinning unsavory yarns about the folks up the road? Ripping out stitches and ripping up characters? "That old woman? Oh, she's the drunken hag!" ... "That young slut? She's the loose one!" The words freeze in our mouth. Such a Mary would not be a Mary at all! But Mary who "kept all these things in her heart"—she is our Mother, is she not? And should not children take after their Mother? Then, this Wednesday in her memory, when the midnight bells tumble and clang in their slender towers, ringing out the old, ringing in the new, think how the great brazen tongues are always under control—the tug of a rope, the push of a button—and let's keep our little tongues under control too!

In fact, you won't have to crick your neck toward the church tower. New Year's Morning on your way out of Mass, as your fingers dip into the Holy Water, take a little tip from it too; take a little wisdom as well as a little water from the Holy Water Font that sees so much, yet says so little; meets everybody and leaves everybody with a blessing, because it knows that other people's faults are none of its—*its*? None of our business either!

Who Is My Neighbor?

FESTERING HATE

At a banquet one evening in his honor, an admirer gave Thackeray—you remember he was the novelist whose pen was the very sword of satire—an elegant statuette. It was like one of our modern Hummel figurines, and it portrayed St. George slaying the dragon. Thackeray took it with a polite word of thanks, and then said in an incisive aside, as though he were thinking aloud: "You know, each of us has his own personal dragon, his own monster fault. And we had better kill it before it kills us!"

Isn't this true even of people who secretly think themselves rather pious? Each of us not only has his major fault, his strongest weakness, but if we are honest, and sharply examine our character, like a fisherman going over his net, we shall probably find one particular spot where it is always tearing, our weak spot. It can be anything from dishonesty to drink, but for the moment let us consider the faults against what Our Blessed Lord called half the whole Christian law, the love of one's neighbor.

How is it that people can hold the rosary beads so devoutly in one hand and in the other hold so grimly to some ancient grudge? Apparently they see no contradiction. Do they need spiritual bifocals? And speaking of eyes, there are people who all but roll their eyes in an ecstasy of prayer, and yet will give some neighbor a hard stony stare, a look like a spike, sharp enough to hang a picture. Why? Is virtue for God, and venom for the people across the street, or next door, or upstairs? They say very airily, "Oh, there is no love lost between us." But they are wrong, fearfully wrong. Somewhere between them the love for one another that Christ came on earth to proclaim has been completely lost!

To the eye of Heaven this poor earth must sometimes look like a land where little volcanos of spite, and big ones of enmity are exploding all over the place. Look at the Business World. Do you not find sullen bitterness and scowling hate in what sometimes seems a chrome-plated, fluorescent-lighted, air-conditioned jungle? One man moves up one desk, and another man begins to see red even under his green eye shade. From then on, envy sits down to its favorite meal, which is eating out its own heart, and the indigestion that follows is the heartburn of hate!

Or, look in the Home. In one of those domestic civil wars where a grown son or daughter secedes from the family circle, and in the fury and thunder of the fight, stamps out, slams the door, goes out into the night—in every sense out into the night—and from then on, for perhaps a lifetime, parent and child are standing on opposite shores of the bitter grey waters of Lake Malice.

From then on, in the eyes of the one, the other can do no good. From then on, one fixed idea fills the picture-tube of his mind. This person is bad and I hate him ... or her. How bitter, how unreasonable can you get? When Napoleon was banished to St. Helena, he was sitting down to breakfast one morning with his little household, when the Governor of the tiny island entered the room. This high officer for all his gold braid was really Napoleon's jailer, and Napoleon loathed him. When he had left, Napoleon pointed to a cup of coffee. "Throw it out!" he ordered. "That man was near it!"

You see how intense, how insane, hatred can become? And how long it can stay. Maybe it was five or ten years ago that an angry scene first exploded between two friends, but in that bitter hour the friendship came crashing down like the falling of a tree. But years after, the memory is still there like a stump, just as ugly, just as stubborn. Sometimes people even give the impression that they are secretly proud of their unchristian feud. They love to go over what she said and what I said, and so on. It is like a garrulous old guide in some European town pointing out the ancient cannon-balls in the city wall. He is proud they are studded there like raisins in a cake. You give them a passing glance, and thank God they did no more harm than this, and forget them.

But rancor writes its diary on granite. *They* (the grudge-bearers) won't forget! In Heidelberg around the turn of the century any student who had been slashed on the face in a duel would go to one of the medical students and have the wound treated in such a way that it would stay open and form a livid scar, something to remind him of his enemy, something to avenge!

But how can a Catholic man or woman be happy if their secret vow is to get even with someone? How can life possibly be sweet if he is constantly pouring bitterness into it, if he sees with the eyes of rancor, listens with cold suspicion, and thinks with dull hatred? He is always plotting to teach so-and-so a lesson, to bring him down from his high horse, to make him eat crow, to show him who is top-dog, and so on through the zoo of primitive revenge. The incident must never be allowed to die! Keep it alive, a kind of pilot light on the stove of hatred, always ready to be turned up in full flaming, searing force!

But what sensible person wants to live in a funeral parlor with a corpse, a dead quarrel, always there in the background, an embittered, embalmed, but unburied memory, the dead past left there to foul the sweet air? I do not want to wave the jester's bells of a pun but I have observed that nothing makes a man so odd as the sworn resolve to get even. That old ugly little quarrel sits on his back like a hideous dwarf and steers him like a beast ... but never steers him toward peace of conscience or happiness of heart. There is only one solution: throw him off!

I am not saying that if someone wronged you long ago that the mere passage of time has made it right and *therefore* you should forgive and forget. If it was wrong, it was wrong. God does not tell us to forgive those that did not trespass against us, but those that did. I am not asking you to admire an evil deed or an evil man. We forgive not for his sake (or for her sake) but for God's sake; or to be blunt about it, even for our sake, because one day we shall want to be forgiven at that Supreme Court of the Last Judgment, the Court from which there is no appeal. Surely, we do not think that we are utterly without fault ourselves, without any smudge of guilt, we the blameless ones, we the immaculate ones, we the gleaming lilies looking scornfully down on the surrounding dirt? It takes humility to forgive, and humility (as St. Teresa of Avila said long ago) is truth. On the other hand, if you trace the bitter black river of unforgiving hate back to its source, you will always find it on some high stubborn, stony hill of pride.

Somebody wrote a poem once about this forgiveness in Our Lady. Did you know that according to tradition she first made the Stations of the Cross in reverse? That is, on the day He died, Mary in the gathering dusk slowly retraced her steps from the Tomb, along the road where He had written His autograph on this old earth with a dragging cross, back to the very balcony where Pilate had snapped the rod of the judgment and sent Him off to die. That, incidentally, is why you also can make the Stations of the Cross beginning with the fourteenth and going back to the first, and gain all the indulgences. Anyway, according to a touching fancy in this poem, as Mary made her way along the road, with here and there a tell-tale dab of blood upon a stone, she saw a woman plodding toward her, head down and shoulders shaking with great sobs. For one heartbreaking moment they looked at each other, recognized each other, and the next instant Mary had taken her in her arms. The Mother of Jesus was comforting the mother of Judas! Yes, that is just the way it would have happened. What else? Can we even imagine Mary touching the Cross sticky with Her Son's fresh crimson Blood and vowing vengeance? But do we not claim to be children of Mary? Then will we not take after our Mother? For that matter are we not first of all disciples of Christ? Or are we Christians only when it is convenient, and cave men when Christianity comes in our way?

It is easy to check whether you love both Jesus and Mary sincerely and even to the point of sacrifice. Our civilization has not yet reached that El Dorado in electronics where a collection can be taken up by radio. Yet today I am going to ask you to make a contribution, now, from where you are, even while you are listening. No ushers will pass before you, but the Mother of God herself. There will be no long-handled basket but only Her appealing hands. You need not open your wallet or your purse but only your heart. As in all collections, some can give only a little, some can give a lot: but all can give. But this collection is only for old currency. Give the tattered bills of old enmities, the battered coins of ancient grudges, even the counterfeits of make-believe friendships, those surface politenesses which are really hidden hates. Before you snap off this radio program, pour them all in, get rid of them, stand up free! Let there be no Grand Canyon of hate between you and Heaven. Do it now, for common sense alone tells you that the first step toward inner happiness is to throw up the shades on brooding bitterness and let in the light! Get off the road of revenge. That way lies madness, and sadness, and sin!

In South America on the border between Chile and the Argentine soars the majestic statue called

"Christ of the Andes." For decades these two countries had screamed hate at each other in flights of whistling shells and hissing bullets. Now there is friendship. In that strangest of all peace treaties they agreed to melt down their cannons of war and from the metal rear this mutual towering statue of the Prince of Peace. Their grievances are buried beneath His holy feet.

If two Christian nations can do this, why cannot two Christian people? Or if not two, cannot at least one—meaning you? Can you not be the first to forgive, to greet, to throw the first plank across the chasm, to begin the new bridge of friendship? There is only one argument anyone can give against taking the first step toward forgiveness and reconciliation, and that is this: it is hard. But didn't Our Blessed Lord have just this in mind when He said: "The Kingdom of Heaven suffereth violence, and the violent bear it away!" Violence toward ourselves, toward our faults! If you tear up the thorn bush of hatred you have to expect to get your fingers scratched. No one else can do it for you, and there are no gloves that you can put on a sensitive personality. It may hurt. But forgiveness is a virtue, like honesty, sobriety, purity; and like them it has a definite cost in the coin of self-control and sacrifice. But oh, the approving smile of God is worth it, and your own deep joy. Joy? I think the word is lightheartedness, because once you have dropped the burden of an ancient grudge, an old score, even a recent bitterness, there is more room in your heart for the sunny, weightless gold of true happiness and inner peace!

Who Is My Neighbor?

HONESTY IS THE ONLY POLICY

It's just a little more than a hundred years ago that a poor widow and her young son were living in one of those rickety shacks on the outskirts of a midwestern town. Times were pretty hard, and money scarce enough, so when the widow gave her boy a tightly folded dollar bill she told him to squeeze it in his hand till he got to the store. He was to buy flour and butter and sugar and tea and bacon—well, after all this was a hundred years ago and a dollar was bigger then—in every sense. The youngster went hiking off to the store, brought back his bag of groceries, dumped them on the kitchen table. When the mother totaled up the crude sales slip it came to ninety cents, so she said to the boy, "Where is the dime?" The boy insisted there was no dime; the store-keeper had charged him exactly one dollar. That evening as mother and son sat down to supper in strained silence, (the mother was all grim suspicion and the boy all injured innocence) there was a knock at the door. A gaunt, rangy young man stood slightly stooped in the doorway. "Beg pardon, ma'am," he said, "I'm the new storekeeper in town, and when I reckoned up today's business, I found I had overcharged somebody ten cents. I figured it must have been the boy here, so this dime belongs to you." He smiled and started down the road on the long mile back into town. Mother and son stood watching him as the tall figure blended into the dusk. Suddenly the mother called, "Say, what's your name?" And out of the gloom the voice came back, "Lincoln. Abe Lincoln." "Ah," she said almost to herself, "Honest Abe!"

This week America will celebrate Lincoln's birthday, and while not even the Republicans would go as far as to canonize him as a saint, the occasion offers a very appropriate moment for some considerations on a virtue which men formerly wore as prominently as Lincoln sideburns and whiskers, but whose absence now looks barefaced and smooth in the other direction. The accent is on the smooth. The emphasis is on the sad fact that in many levels of life we are losing our sense of honor and of honesty. I am not referring to the situation that there is a big boom in the building of jails. The text of this little talk is not, "Stop Thief!" No, nothing quite so blunt and brutal as that. As a matter of fact it is quite the opposite. Some of you may remember at the old-time missions that when the missionary wanted to encourage the people to fill up the front pews first, he would jokingly announce that tomorrow night the last six benches would be reserved only for horse-thieves, hijackers, safe-crackers, and hold-up men. My point today is to remind you that we can shatter into splinters the Commandment "Thou shalt not steal" without ever wearing a mask, or pointing a gun, or sliding our fingers into a bulging pocket.

In fact, we can break that Commandment by doing nothing—when we should be doing something. For example by not doing the job for which we are being paid. That isn't very complicated: we get our salary; we are supposed to give our services. The employer is supposed to give a decent day's wage, and the employee is supposed to do a decent day's work. In many instances labor has made magnificent strides in getting its rights; but in many instances it is now time for right to step in and get its labor!

In this matter of honesty we can also do wrong by doing nothing in the case of deliberately unpaid bills. Several years ago I remember broaching this subject to a doctor. I brought it up, because I knew him and admired him. I don't mean just for his professional competence but for his conscientiousness, and the amazing amount of charity work he performed. Well, he told me that when he mailed out his bills, only five percent of the patients paid at once. About fifty percent would remit within six months. The other forty-five percent might eventually remit or might just omit. When I thought how hard he worked, and how he had practically no home life at all, I guess indignation was strong on my face, because he said, "Listen, don't you be putting this into a sermon!" (The way people get suspicious of me ... as if I ever would!) "Besides," he added, "the people in your parish are pretty poor. And the poor always pay. It's among the people with the check books that you have to check off most of your losses."

I happened to be impressed by this incident of the doctor, but whether it is the butcher or the baker or the furniture maker, if it is a just debt we have a duty to meet it. Anybody can understand how some business reverse or (put into plainer English) losing a job can sweep away a man's ability to pay till he gets on his feet again. But who will solve the brazen mystery of the crowd that goes on living in present luxury while ignoring their past liabilities? The people who have plenty of money for liquor and shows and dazzling new outfits and bets on horses and dogs, the while they keep their bills in the deep-freeze and keep their consciences cocained; the people who buy on the installment plan but stall on the paying plan—should not such people have a try at looking their obligations, their responsibility right in the eye? Perhaps that dentist was a bit too precipitous who laid down his last tool and immediately said to the patient, "Well, there's your new bridge. Now come across!" but the general principle still stands up, namely, that where possible, prompt payment is not just a favor to be desired but a duty to be met.

So you see the Commandment that forbids us to steal forbids much more than brazen stealing. Such stealing is admittedly the black bull's-eye on this target, but there are several close circles all around it. One of these circles, and close to the center, would be not returning borrowed money—a fairly obvious wrong, don't you think? I heard of one of these chronic, incurable borrowers who approached his dear friend, a saloon-keeper, for the loan of ten dollars. The saloon-keeper could have been sarcastic and said, "Like all other times?" But instead he went over to the cash register, punched it, took five dollars out of the till and laid it on the marble bar. "Thanks—" said the borrower, "but, but you know I asked you for ten dollars." "I know," said the saloon-keeper wearily. "You lose five. I lose five. We're even."

There is nothing so fatal to friendship as floating a loan till the loans become a fleet. But the point is that we cannot borrow and blithely forget. The borrowed money is still his, not ours, and should go back as surely as the swallows go back to Capistrano...and if possible as swiftly.

Do you remember that lilting, airy tune, "Whistle while you work"? With some folks it might be rendered, "Chisel while you work!" We hinted before at the "workers" who arrive late, leave early and dawdle or loaf in between. But there are other tributaries to the same dishonest stream. For example, that matter of expense accounts. Some expense accounts are not merely padded; they are upholstered. And it is wrong! Or a girl may be employed, let us say, in a drug store, and each week she nonchalantly drops into her purse a bottle of perfume or lotion or what have you. It becomes part of her take-home pay. She takes it home all right, but it isn't her pay. It's loot and it's wrong. Or a man may be in charge of some garage or a machine shop or a repair place for some big concern or even for the city, and he finds out that a friend of his needs a certain drill. "You need a drill? I'll get you a drill!" You—what right have you to give out or give away drills? Some people are so generous with other people's property—and it is wrong.

The more you look at it, the more you are impressed that on the map of morality,—stealing is a very big state and covers a lot of territory, like Texas. How about, for another instance, unjust insurance claims? Just because your left front fender was dented last week, you have no right to include the right rear door which has been sprung since last summer! And speaking of Texas and the "Panhandle," how about the Charity Chiselers who would appall St. Vincent de Paul himself. To them Charity or Welfare is a big dumb cow that is to be milked for all it's worth from every outlet. Last Christmas I met a very irate Judge who had been informed by investigators that this particular "poor woman" had contrived to receive from various sources twelve different Christmas baskets. She must have been reading the Bible about the twelve baskets the Apostles filled after the miracle. What burned the Judge up was that he had expansively contributed one basket himself. The tragedy in a case like this is that it chills the generosity of would-be donors and severely hurts the really deserving cases.

A more recent face in the rogues gallery of what the G.I.'s used to call "moonlight requisition" is the souvenir collector. He walks into a smart restaurant with a few boon companions and he manages to walk out with a few oyster forks, or whatever his sense of devilment suggests. At a hotel he pays for a room and takes a couple of towels. After all, he figures, they expect it. They may expect it, but they don't like it! "Oh, lots of people do it." Listen: elections are decided by numbers. Morality, never. Crowds have nothing to do with Commandments.

To discuss stealing and omit graft would be like naming great sculptors and overlooking Michaelangelo. And that illustration is not so far-fetched as it may seem, because once in a Catechism Class when I referred to one of his statues in a story I asked, "By the way who was this Michaelangelo?" and one little red-haired urchin said, "Wasn't he the greatest chiseler that ever lived?" So the transition to graft is made licitly and vividly. And here there is only one thing to emphasize, namely, that graft is a true, lineal, fullblooded member of the Stealing family. But can you convince some Catholics of this? In that particular field of moral vision they have a definite blind spot. It is so strange, yes, and shocking, because in all the other departments they are models of conduct. Their sexual morality may be as chaste as snow. Their family life is probably the mirror of virtue. Their word of honor is as good as a sealed bond. But give them a chance at graft and their hand plunges into the public till right up to the elbow. Sometimes of course even they, who for a conscience have a seismograph where only earthquakes register, may feel slight stirrings of guilt, but they console themselves that this is "honest graft." Honest graft is about as logical and true as cool fire. If at Christmas you give the mailman a gift in the spirit of the season, that present, as far as he is concerned, is honest but it is not graft. As far as you are concerned it is no more than a practical smile of appreciation and approval for duty well done. But if you give a policeman a bundle of green that isn't holly because he overlooks the fact that the lending library you run offers service not only in books but also in bookies, that is graft with a capital Gr. You are paying him not to do his duty.

So, to conclude, if ever you are tempted to any kind of dishonesty, no matter how glittering or attractive, try to think of just these two words: double trouble. Because in the first place you will have to tell it in confession; and in the second place you will have to give it back anyway. You end up twice as bad as when you started. From way back Satan (who tempts us to steal) has always been a swindler himself. When he flips the coin it is always, "Heads I win, tails you lose." Then there's the devil to pay—in confession and restitution.

Third Finger, Left Hand

THE GOOD SHIP COURTSHIP

About a week before Christmas the romper set suddenly stop being jet-propelled imps, and become incredibly well-behaved little angels. When this happens, your eye-brows go up in the gentle cynicism of the parent who realizes that the crafty youngsters are being good just for the present: Christmas present, that is.

Well, let the rippling curtain of time fall to denote a lapse of fifteen or twenty years. The rompers are now grown all the way to Bermuda shorts, but the same spruce young adults are again playing the role of being glossily perfect. Only this time it is not Christmas. It is Courtship. They are in love with someone, and they want that someone to see only their loveliest side. A period like this can produce the finest acting in Shakespeare's famous stages of man. Pity it never gets an Oscar. But then it doesn't want an Oscar; it wants a ring—or a bride.

THIRD FINGER, LEFT HAND

The good ship courtship has three decks. It should be Catholic, cautious, and clean. By Catholic we mean there would never be any mixed marriages if there were no mixed courtships. But we tried to treat that topic in another talk. By cautious courtship we mean the reverse of that bitter proverb, "Marry in haste; repent at leisure." The casualty list of the Second World War had their sad columns of Dead, Wounded, Missing in Action; but you never saw published the frightening numbers of *marriages* that foundered in the wake of that war. On the desk of every Catholic Chancery in the country the postman poured his little blizzard of letters with the same monotonous message: a petition that the marriage be annulled. Look back at the history of such a marriage and what do you find? So often this: boy and girl both very young; a chance meeting at a USO dance; a couple of dates; a correspondence courtship; a whirlwind wedding; a furlough honeymoon; and when these two comparative strangers met after the war they found they could not endure each other; and one more digit went down in the long grim column of divorce statistics. The marriage looked so sparkling-bright as it left the church, like a shimmering new car rolling out of the show-room; but now before the ashtrays were filled, it was being towed away, a wreck, crumpled like a paper cup.

"Marry in haste; repent at leisure" is more than a proverb; it is practically a promise. How can young people believe that an acquaintance of four months is strong enough foundation for a marriage that should last forty years? Is twelve or eighteen months too long for a girl to get to know the boy to whom she is giving herself for life? (Of course they may be married seventeen years and the boy will still be finding out things he never knew about the girl: but that is one of life's little mysteries whose answer lies hidden in the lovely depth of woman's unfathomable nature.) Anyway, a good rule for a boy or a girl is a cautious courtship of one or two years, with eyes wide open, and not too much stardust in them. Then you won't be falling into a tender trap that soon stops being tender. You won't be hurling yourself with panting passion into a lifelong mistake, to be opened only by the cold Key of Death. Leap year is only one of four, but every year should be "Look before you leap!" year.

The third deck on the Courtship stands for a courtship that is clean. Who was it that overheard one New England spinster saying to her sister, "My dear, the trouble with matrimony is that it breaks down the natural barrier between the sexes." That is not the trouble with matrimony; that is the triumph of matrimony. The trouble is when the barrier drops before matrimony—during courtship, for instance. Engaged people are not married people; therefore, they do not have the privileges of married people. Bluntly put, they have no right to indulge in any action to arouse passion. The passions in themselves are good; God put them there. Why? As a drive to the procreation of children. Now the proper care of children implies permanent parents. But the idea of permanent parents implies marriage. That is why passion or sex outside of marriage is wrong.

And yet courtship by its nature sends two young people out together into what you might call a necessary danger of sin. It is necessary because how else can the two know each other unless they are frequently with each other? It is a danger, because if they are attracted to each other, in him burns the masculine urge to possess, and in her the feminine yearning to yield. And in both the corruption of original sin: the beast which is always only caged, never killed. Here they dare not follow appetite or instinct, for it leads into a forbidden kingdom to which only marriage has the moral passport. They cannot plead love, because true love would never want to leave the beloved in mortal sin. Lust, yes, because lust would overthrow any barrier to satisfy its hot desire. Love loves a person; lust craves only a body. Lust pants only for its own pleasure. Love considers the true happiness of the other.

Undoubtedly, courtship drops the two young lovers into a dangerous spot, like parachutists who find themselves behind the enemies' lines with perils all about them. Or maybe a better comparison might be the priest who goes into the contagious wards at the hospital. He has a right to be there, but he also has the obligation to employ the necessary safeguards against infection, like mask and gown and so on. Well, the chief safeguard in courtship is to be alone in a crowd. In other words to be with each other, but be chaperoned by the passing world.

Would it be clearer if I pointed out there is a deep wide difference between driving in the park, and parking in the drive? In one of the suburbs of that vast empire we call Greater Boston, there is a Catholic Church with a large grey expanse of a parking lot. But some parishoners (wanting to be closer to God no doubt) persisted in leaving their cars right at the church entrance, and, naturally, blocking it. So the Pastor with a twinkle in his eye and a can of yellow paint in his hand painted another Golden Rule: Thou

Shalt Not Park. It looked like another commandment. It *is* an excellent commandment for company-keeping.

You can pray, you can go to Holy Communion, you can ask God's grace. And He will give it to you, especially if you ask through Our Lady. But grace may do no good if we deliberately enter the occasion of sin. Grace often means God's help, not to conquer a temptation, but to avoid the situation altogether in the first place. If passion is fire, God does not give us an asbestos suit to survive in the midst of flames. He gives us a fire-escape to get out beforehand. If you park deliberately, doesn't it look as though you don't want God's help? By the way, wherever you park, even though it be a dark and lonely spot on the edge of nowhere, do you know there is always a parking meter there? And into it you put a coin all right, one of the pieces of silver of Judas, the price of the betrayal of Christ, a coin crusted red with His Precious Blood. When you drive home don't you think less of each other? Don't you wonder if you can trust each other? Because impurity before marriage is the best training for infidelity after it. At any event to be happy with guilt in your heart is as hard as to see with a cinder in your eye. At times it may be a rugged battle, but a clean courtship is the one surest to reach the port of a happy marriage.

May I here interject a grimy bit of realism? Suppose something has happened. Suppose, as the ancient but not honorable phrase has it, the girl is "in trouble." Suppose there is a prospect of a teething ring without benefit of a wedding ring. This is the biggest bomb that ever drops into a family circle, so look out! Snarling astonishment, wounded family pride, furious anger explode like a package of shells. "She is a disgrace. She has let us down! She and her pious devotions—a pious fraud!"

It is a black hour for any family, but let it only be an hour! If we are Christians let us act like Christ, and forgive and forget. Kindness! Then add more kindness. Then multiply by still more kindness. What else? Would you dare suggest abortion? Save face but lose a soul—and a body? Or condemn and nag and drive away—what is this but being a Christian Pharisee?

Certainly what she did was wrong. *Was* wrong. The deed is done; now let the family close around her in a protective circle, keeping their own sacred secret, like swords raised up around a wounded queen, so that the slashing tongue of gossip, the snickering sneer of a neighborhood can never come near her. If Mary Magdalen and Mary of Egypt and Margaret of Cortona could pass from scarlet women into golden saints, from a career of sin to a cleansed and shining sanctity, should not a girl who falls perhaps once, be helped to carry her burden, a precious burden now, and be reminded that the mercy of God is so great it will forgive even the righteous who lift scornful noses in the air!

Incidentally, what about the young man, the father of the baby? Should he marry the girl? Chivalry leaps forward and replies with a ringing yes: what else? Be what the novels used to call a cad? Can a gentleman act otherwise? Sometimes he should act otherwise. Figure it out. He certainly did wrong by fathering the child. But he would be doing another wrong by marrying the girl merely for that reason. You do not correct one mistake by adding another.

You say he has an obligation to the girl. Rather he has an obligation to the child, to make provision for its birth and rearing. But he cannot have an obligation to marry this girl, because marriage must always be a free contract, or it is no marriage at all. It may be a curious way to say it, but nobody can ever commit a sin so great that the penalty is marriage; that is, that a man should be bound over to someone for the rest of his natural life because of something he did in his premarriage past.

So in the eyes of the Church he never has to marry her. Should he marry her? Only if they had both really intended to get married before the baby entered the picture. If this is the case, let them marry sooner than they intended, if they wish; but the baby should be a reason only for advancing the marriage, never for advising it. So much so, that if he does not love the girl, and did not intend to marry her before, he should not do so now. I am not wiping his slate free of guilt and holding up his strong arm as that of a victor. I am simply repeating, marriage can never be a penalty. In the Sacrament of Confession you can never get as a penance another sacrament, Matrimony.

But why do we even speak of this? Those who steer by the Star of the Sea, Our Blessed Lady, will be far from such danger. May she be at your side to guide the good ship Courtship cautiously, between rocks of tragic mistakes; and cleanly, through the clear waters of purity, to the haven and (as far as humanly possible) the heaven of a happy marriage.

Third Finger, Left Hand

A PERPLEXED PATRON

Maybe your experience is different, but I have never seen a statue raised to this particular saint, nor even a tiny medal struck in his honor. To this day down the highway of history he comes with the cloak of mystery held high before his face. He is so obscure a saint that on the calendar of the Church he rates the very simplest rank of feast that she can give. His background is so vague that about the only things we know about him are that he lived in the third century, died in a pool of blood, a martyr, and was buried outside Rome. The mystery is that in our own twentieth century when the memory of far more prominent saints has withered brown with the passing years, the memory of this undistinguished man keeps strangely green. But I doubt he would be flattered if he knew why, or how.

If you, by a clap of your hands, could resurrect him this very day (because the fourteenth of February is his feast-day) and transport him by stratoliner across the sea to any city in America, you would have on your hands a very bewildered saint. As he trails his long white Roman robe past the candy-store windows with their large red hearts of shining pasteboard, and the drug-store windows with their little red greeting cards edged with paper-lace, and the flaring red signs everywhere: "Don't Forget St. Valentine's Day!" "Won't You Be My Valentine?", your poor perplexed saint, the original Valentine, might shake his holy head and wonder if they had not confused Valentine with Valentino.

You understand there is nothing wrong with mailing Valentine cards or giving Valentine candy. What is wrong is that they should be called Valentine cards or candy in the first place. You can slog up and down the dreary columns of encyclopediae and come away with not one simple, solid reason why St. Valentine should be associated with romance at all. Oh, some allege that in warmer climes it is around his feast-day that the birds begin to mate. This is about as logical as the case of poor St. Philip on a certain tropical island. Here, many years ago, they had a tremendous hurricane on the feast of St. Philip. To this day they always refer to it as St. Philip's hurricane. He takes the rap. With even less reason St. Valentine has somehow become part of the legend of love, and takes his place with June and moon, balconies and serenades, covered bridges and diamond rings, as one of the standard props on the stage of the sighing heart.

If it were a pure, continent Christian love, it would still be a mistake. But by and large the love they want St. Valentine to endorse, almost like a testimonial in a commercial, is love gone pagan. Better if they called it not St. Valentine's Day, but Cupid's Day and Cupid's candy and Cupid's greeting cards, after the fleshy little god whose only principle is pleasure. "Won't you be my Valentine?" This should mean won't you be my fine noble Christian Saint? There are many who would think twice before they asked for that. "Won't you be my Christian martyr?" But a martyr is one who stands for conscience and right. Many would prefer someone who would not be quite so stubborn and stuffy about conscience in circumstances that call for a soft and passionate surrender.

Look again at that heart-shaped box of candy in the window. It is red, and red is traditionally the color of love. But this is not the true deep red of lasting loyalty. This is the bold flaming red of hot passion. The box too is shaped like a heart, and the heart is traditionally the emblem of love. But this is a hollow heart, crammed only with creams and caramels which, like the stolen sweets of lust, are soon consumed and leave the heart empty indeed. It is no longer a "Sweetheart." The box too at first glance seems to be bound firmly (as true love should be) because there it is, tied with a ribbon and a big bow. But look a moment, and it turns out that the big bow is only a fluffy ornament on top and doesn't bind the box at all. In just the same way it is only a light fancy that joins pagan love together, and when that goes they fall apart like an empty box of candy.

If I were a Communist and wanted to ruin our country, I would advocate light and loose love on every side. Isn't that one more reason the Communists have for hating the Catholic Church? We do not claim that the Catholic Church is the last sanctuary of pure womanhood, or high morals, but do you know of any other voice raised more strongly and more steadily in support of chaste courtship and permanent marriage? All decent people should be alarmed at the pagan standards that youth is sopping up on every side, from the trashy paper-back books in the corner drug-store to the learned lecture halls in some universities. Listen. The professor of Biology is pontificating: "You girls may wear a coat made from the fur of one animal, a hat made with the feathers of another, and shoes from the hide of a third. But don't forget: you yourself inside make the fourth animal. You are animal, so why fight it?" I wonder if the Professor pauses to ponder that the difference between man and the monkey is still the monkey-wrench? The class files into another room. And the Professor of Psychology is droning on: "Free will? Nonsense! Stimuli and reflexes, nerves and responses, you are only a bundle of instincts. Free will is a high, flattering idea but it just doesn't stand up." I wonder what would happen if you stole the professor's wallet on the way out and maintained you couldn't help it, you had to do it, a compulsion; after all you had no free will. But the bell rings, and in a little while the class settles itself before the Professor of Sociology: "Of course when you decide to choose a mate you will have to get a marriage license to comply with the law, but as students of human society you should know that marriage is an outworn tribal custom edging toward extinction. Soon it will go the way of the cave and the stone hatchet."

Then some of these very teachers who may be old and cold and academic and theoretic, these professors profess to be shocked when the young people carry their liberal lectures out of the classroom into life, into the park or the parked car. Well, what do you think is going to happen if you break up old decencies like dry wood and toss them on the impetuous fires of flaming youth?

Furthermore, this gospel of pagan love, where pleasure is enthroned and conscience is entombed, this devil's gospel is preached from other pulpits than university desks. Is it too much to say that the "modern" attitude toward love stands somewhere between a wink and a whistle? Take the gospel of love according to St. Cinema and recall how frequently in the movies, marriage is a flippant, frivolous affair played for laughs. Or, if they are young it is a sudden adolescent thrill; and if they are older it is a sophisticated interlude, with at least one of them wearing the degree "D.G." meaning Divorce Granted, or possibly Damaged Goods, but how often on the screen do you see marriage emphasized as a final, life-long contract, not to speak of a sacred Sacrament?

Take the newspapers and love, and you know as well as I do that a chorus girl's scandal will be smeared over page one while the golden wedding of some sterling citizen is lucky if it gets ten lines near the obituaries. Take love and contemporary fiction. They tell me that today's author, this drug-store Dickens, thinks nothing of sending the heroine off on a week-end with one arm around the "hero" and the other snapping its fingers at stodgy, long-haired convention. Take love and Tin Pan Alley. Listen to some of these modern songs and you wonder if they didn't take both morals and music from the felines on the backyard fence, a long piercing wail of desire. Would you ever suspect from all this that love could be sweet and wholesome and possibly shy and certainly clean and good?

Oh it is a soft, sticky, sickening goo that the world will slap on your mind if you go to it for standards of conduct! But in so delicate a field, in so sacred a human relationship, should we go for our standards to the films of Hollywood, or the scandals of the newspapers, or the divorce courts of Reno, or the beauty contests of Atlantic City, or the brassy songs of Broadway, or to the Commandments of God and the glorious ideals of Christ?

Certainly it is natural for a man to love a maid, but certainly it is not natural, not the nature of man, that his love be no higher than the beasts! Human love is human and therefore it must be guided by reason, subject to conscience, worthy of creatures who are children of God. For the good of the race the married have rights and privileges. The unmarried do not. No matter what a leering world hints.

Pontius Pilate sent Christ to crucifixion by washing his hands. Youth can do the same thing today by dirtying its hands. Oh, the phoney philosophy of the world will guarantee to dye your conscience a white gold the way the beauty parlors do hair. It is a synthetic rinse. Alibis like: "Well, that is my weakness," or "If you love somebody, what can you do?" Or "God will understand." Aren't they ever afraid He will understand that they broke His laws like peanut-shells, or put His commandments out of the way like a floor-lamp that got in the way at a party?

Certainly at times it is hard to be pure. But do you know of anything in life really worthwhile that isn't hard? Perhaps that is just why Our Blessed Lord on the cross allowed a soldier to open His side so that we might see the great red valentine of His own crimson bleeding Heart, a Heart not pierced by a tiny Cupid's arrow but with a long cruel spear; a Heart not fringed with dainty paper-lace, but circled, as St. Margaret Mary saw it in a vision, with a wreath of sharp thorns. He wanted to remind us that if we want to keep our hearts clean and good they too must be surrounded by the thorns of hard things; the thorns of self-respect and self-restraint; the thorns of decency and modesty; the thorns of will-power and (what is more important) won't power!

After all, Valentine means "Strong!"

Third Finger, Left Hand

THE MAN I MARRY

It is almost an axiom among preachers that if you want your audience to stop coughing, just start talking about marriage. Well, I don't think that what I have to say on that subject will make any serious inroads on the cough drop industry, but since this Sunday finds every Catholic pulpit ringing with the Gospel of the Wedding Feast of Cana, it certainly would be in tune with the time to discuss if not the main fabric of matrimony at least some of the fringes. I would like to direct my questions (as they say in the TV panels) to those, who in the prim Victorian phrase, are beginning to keep company, and also (so that I'll have somebody who will agree with me) to their mothers and fathers.

If anyone sniffingly suggests that this is scarcely the proper field for a priest I can only smilingly remind him that it used to be a legend on Newspaper

Row that all the gooey, sentimental, pastel-tinted prose that dripped and drooled into the advice to the lovelorn columns, was usually battered out of a typewriter by a bald-headed, pot-bellied, hard-boiled newspaper man, sweating in his shirt-sleeves and smoking a big black cigar. Admittedly, a priest in a black robe would be almost as strange a counsellor in this department, except for one thing. When you have passed the thirty year mark in the priesthood and have seen enough of courtships that were supposed to be divine, end up in a courthouse and divorce, you gradually pile up opinions—no, convictions —about what makes for a dependable partner in married life and what does not. So, if this little talk is only coaching from the sidelines, isn't it still true, in bowling for example, that actually the pin-boy at the other end of the alley has the best view of just where the ball skidded off its course and what was wrong with the delivery—precisely because he is off at a distance and can see down a clear lane?

At any rate I say these things with deep sincerity and kindness, not to hurt but to help. And I am going to address myself, for the sake of simplicity and clarity, to just one branch of the partnership, the girls; with the understanding that merely by changing the focus of the binoculars the boys can see the same view and apply it, with minor reservations, to themselves.

All right, let's begin by agreeing on this: when you decide to marry, by all means give him your heart. But first use your head to decide just who is going to get your heart. Only when your head is as cool as dry ice, can you let your heart go on fire. Otherwise, if the emotion that throbs so strongly within you is not carefully guided toward the right man, your life will be like a car with a powerful engine and a faulty steering-wheel, and could easily be headed for a wreck.

So, what should you look for in a partner? Good looks? A smooth dresser? A car? A bright line? A plushy bank account? If you anchor your hopes in any one of these, a few short years may find your happy marriage broken loose and tossing in rough seas. Because, don't you see these things are only things, and may vanish almost overnight? Never marry a man for the sake of things. Of course there is no objection to marching down the middle aisle with a handsome man whose handsome jacket is buttoned over a handsome wallet (a slight bulge you will tolerantly excuse)—provided you are genuinely in love with the man and not with his wavy hair (long may it wave, but you never can be sure) or in love merely with his trim profile (which may soon increase by a couple of mezzanine chins) or his wallet (which may soon decrease and slenderize till it becomes an imaginary line like the equator).

The important thing is to love and marry a man, a personality, not just a set of circumstances, because as a rule the man himself will not change, while the circumstances very easily may. That is why it is important to get a man of principle rather than of profile. Those excessively good looks that attract your eye now, may break your heart later when other adventurous and envious feminine eyes notice his chiseled features. Good looks are fine if he is also a good man. Not that I am suggesting that you select a husband from a freak show, but I do mean that the girl who is happily married ten years after the cutting of the wedding cake, is the girl who chose a boy not so much for his external attractions (which can be just as gay and promising and flimsy as the dust-jacket of a book, and no measure whatever of the worth of the contents) but for his character, his sense of duty, his disposition, his responsibility, his simple and solid dependability. The question therefore you want to ask yourself is not, "Isn't he a glorious dancer?" or "Doesn't he look divine in a tux?" but "Can I live with him forever after and be happy?" Not happy like the fairy tales, but reasonably happy like human beings. That patent for perfect happiness is still held only by Heaven.

Besides looking into the future and asking yourself that Golden Wedding question, it is also a pretty good idea to ask your mother what she thinks of the boy. Superman in the comic-strip had an x-ray eye that could look right through a wall, but often a mother has an x-ray eye than can look right through a would-be son-in-law. Call it intuition, call it experience, mothers are pretty keen in this regard. Of course if the mother objects to the first boy, rejects the second, vetoes the third, and wants to have the fourth arrested, such a mother is not opposed to her daughter marrying any particular boy. She is just against her daughter marrying, and as such she should be piously, affectionately, effectively disregarded. But that is the exception, and normally if a mother turns thumbs-down on a boy, the girl should think twice of putting her finger out for the ring. She might end up wearing it in her nose.

No girl would dream of buying a dress simply because it looked good in a store window. Many a man too may look wonderful posing there behind the plate-glass window of his best behavior, under the flattering fluorescent light of your shining eyes. But if you would see him as he really is, see him in his natural habitat, his home grounds, his home. You can bank on him there to be off his guard. You can study him almost like a fish in an aquarium. You can see how he reacts to homey situations. Is he lazy, sarcastic, selfish, temperamental? He will reveal it there! You might even consult a few local experts. The boyfriend's brother or sister might unwittingly babble out more revealing commentary on his true character in a few minutes of casual conversation than you could dredge up in a few months of company-keeping.

Does all this sound sly and tricky and frightfully cold-blooded? I realize it. And some of you dimpled dreamers may scornfully call it romance by slide-rule and marriage by the Bureau of Standards. Well, don't forget you are not signing up for a month, or enlisting for a few years; you are taking him for life, and if possible you want a life-time guarantee.

Suppose you were entering a convent. Before you could take even temporary vows in a religious order, you would have to spend at least a year in a Novitiate, where you are shown the religious life at its worst. I mean at its strictest; no exemptions, no exceptions, no distractions, no dispensations—just the rigid rule. But the fact is, the rest of your life as a Nun will never be as hard, as austere as that. But before marriage vows it is just the opposite. Each partner tries to show the other partner the best side. Everything is sweetness and light and courtesy and admiration and flattery and generosity and all the rest. The rough times come later. One of the jobs of courtship is to foresee the worst while you are seeing only the best.

For example if now he is a heavy drinker (and I didn't say drunkard, I said heavy drinker) do yourself a favor and forget him. If you built a new home on a swamp would you expect the swamp to dry up just because you built your home there? Well, you have just about as much chance of drying up a heavy drinker by marrying him as you would of drying up a swamp by living there. It is much more likely that he'll just slide down deeper and, like the swamp, drag your home with him. If long ago a priest put too much salt on this man's tongue when he was baptized as a baby, and he has been thirsty ever since, don't try to cure him with another Sacrament, Matrimony. M-R-S before your name may seem an impressive degree, but at that price it would be better to keep your own name and let him find help through that magnificent organization, Alcoholics Anonymous.

It is hanging neon lights around the obvious to remind you that marrying a gambler is a bad bet. The impulse to gamble runs through some men's blood like the corpuscles. I am talking now of course not about rare and minor gambling, but gambling that effects the family groceries. Some of the saddest tales that a rectory parlor hears tremble on the tongue of some poor wife whose only rival is a horse. Stay away from a rabid gambler. If he has heavy inclinations in this direction and you still insist on taking him "for better or for worse," you can be pretty sure that he is a bettor whom you are taking "for worse."

As to the matter of age, it is only common sense to pass up a boy who is considerably younger than you are. Otherwise some day he may want to rhumba and by that time you may be rheumatic. They say the ideal is when the boy is three or four years older than the girl, but this is an ideal and not an essential.

I have been mentioning boy, boy—but please marry a man! Steer clear of those young fellows who, when they marry, want all the privileges of marriage and all the freedom of bachelors. Make sure that your man puts his home before any club or lodge or game or hobby. After all, you want to marry a hubby not a hobby. And, oh, make certain that he loves children! The sphere of a husband is not recreation but creation. Marriage is not a gadabout existence but a life centered inside the golden circle of the wedding ring.

If all this time you are anxious to throw the ultimate inevitable question, "But how can I be *sure* that so-and-so is the man for me?" let me admit that you never can. You see there are two extremes. If you wait for the perfect man, the knight in shining armor and without any fault to come along and sweep you off, you may just wait, and wait ... On the other hand it is much better not to be married than to be married to misery, or to wed just for the sake of being married. Only the Mounties *have* to get their man. I am begging you, if you have grave doubts about his character, let him go! Otherwise you will become so infatuated with his surface charms, so blind to his serious faults, so emotionally involved, so used to his company, so afraid of calling things off for fear of what people may say, so panic-stricken that no other man may come your way, that you'll go ahead and marry him anyway, smiling defiantly in spite of your own secret misgivings, and hoping desperately that somehow everything will turn out wonderfully. But it won't!

And isn't it better to break off an engagement now than to break up a marriage later? Some day you will see that fellow again, after years and years, and you will look after him as he passes down the other side of the street, and you will take a deep breath and say, "Mother of God, there goes a mistake I almost made!"

If all this sounds as gloomy as a Chinese gong, it isn't meant to, honestly. My purpose is to slow you up enough to make you think and pray, so that through Our Lady's intercession, your wedding bells will ring with a silvery joy that will still last even to your golden jubilee!

Third Finger, Left Hand

RECIPE FOR

A WEDDING CAKE

Perhaps a rectory kitchen, (Catholic, that is,) is the last place you would look for the recipe of a reasonably happy marriage. I mention "a reasonably happy marriage" because anyone who is looking for perfect happiness on this burnt-out star, this second-class planet, is ringing the wrong doorbell, and had better search for the name of Saint Peter on a pearly gate. I mentioned "recipe" for a marriage because a marriage is like a wedding cake. If the baker does not pour into the batter the right ingredients (and they had better be the best flour, finest eggs, generous sugar, and the rest) he cannot expect that rich monument of pastry the occasion deserves. And in just the same way, if you do not pour into your married life the right qualities of heart and soul and in generous quantities, you cannot rightfully expect a married life that will be both sweet and solid. In this respect, marriage is like money in the bank; you get out just what you put in—plus now and then a wonderful little dividend or interest.

First of all, a successful marriage is dotted with small compromises the way the streets of a thriving, bustling town are sprinkled with *STOP* signs. You want to do something; then you think of its effect on the other party, and you stop! There are no *STOP* signs on a desert or in an abandoned quarry. There are no other people to consider. But marriage begins with a procession down the aisle; it continues with concessions all through life. At Christmas (you must have noticed) if you bring a decent-sized tree into your living-room, you generally have to rearrange your furniture. Perhaps the TV set has to come out of that corner; or the coffee-table must be moved from North East to South West. But, if you bring another person into your life (as you do in marriage) you have to rearrange much more, not your living-room but your whole pattern of life. That is why when a man becomes a groom, he often has to wave a gallant farewell to his favorite game. But the person who really loves, does this willingly, because love consists not in seeking to make yourself happy (that is selfishness) but in making another happy: that is love!

Of course there will be grey days and heartaches and snubs and slights, but most of them are just little thorns on that scraggy bush of poor human nature. They are not deliberate arrows dipped in the venom of malice. Do you remember what the old Scotch widow said about her man? "Ah", she said, "Husbands are a lot like teeth. They cause you a good deal of trouble when you are getting them, and they hurt sometimes when you have them, but oh, they leave a big blank when they are gone!"

Granted that a husband brings faults into a home the way a little boy (and isn't he one?) tracks mud across the kitchen floor, it is seldom done with cold and deep intent. For that reason a wife who sees herself solely as a martyr is usually overplaying the part. There are exceptions, of course, exceptions that stand out like Eiffel Towers. And these wives deserve sympathy just as truly as the husband deserves Siberia. But how about the husband whose faults do not cry to Heaven for vengeance, though his wife may often scream in that direction? Yes, she has her grievances, and she lives on them the way a dog lives on bones. Sometimes, like a dog, she may bury the grievance for a while, and seem to forget it, but don't worry, she'll dig it up a couple of weeks later and start all over.

For this pouting, self-pitying tribe, Soap Operas were born. They identify themselves with the heroine, the unappreciated, neglected wife of the story. Their eyes glitter as they hear the bubbly voice of the announcer ask, "Will Stella leave Stanley for Stephen? Will she step off the drab cinder-path of her monotonous marriage? Will she follow this fascinating stranger, this gay-plumed bird who whistles so alluringly from the tree of forbidden fruit? Will—listen tomorrow and see how Portia chases Life!"

And the little wife who is listening to the little radio as she launders doesn't need one of these newfangled steam irons to moisten the clothes. Her tears drop in front of the iron and take care of the job. After all, she broods, her husband is not at all like young

Doctor Mercurochrome. Her husband thinks the romantic leading men in the movies are fluffy phonies. She thinks she is just being taken for granted.

Many a wife would not mind so much if she was sure her husband really loved her. Meanwhile the husband is totally unconcerned, absolutely unaware "What do you mean, I don't love you?" he asks, in honest amazement, "I sure do! I told you I did the day I proposed to you." It may have been fifteen or twenty years ago, of course, but for a man that is enough. To him it is a fact, like the price of fish. But he forgets that to a woman it is something tied up with dozens of frills and the pink rosettes of warm tenderness.

Some years ago a housewife was interviewed on television. "What was the happiest day in your life?" Her face lit up like Aurora Borealis, and she said, "The day I was married." Then they led her off-stage and brought the husband on. Neither knew the other was there. They asked him, "What was the happiest day of your life?" A long pause. That was his first mistake; he stopped to think. "I guess the day I first wore long pants." "Oh no," the interviewer said, "This day you acquired something real special." "Oh sure, she was a honey all right—my own first car!" "No—this day there was a big crowd around—" "You mean the day I joined the Elks?" Anyway, he finally stumbled on the day he was married. The point is that this man was happily married, but he took that for granted. And that is why men can forget anniversaries and birthdays with no meanness or malice whatever. But not even that is a reason why they should. Sentiment may not come easy to a man, but a few crumbs of it may go further with a woman than all the groceries of a mere good provider. Who was it that said, "Try praising your wife, even if it does frighten her at first."

The mind of a man and the mind of a woman are two different pieces of mental machinery altogether. A man argues to something the way he climbs a stairway, step by step, logically. A woman is just as likely to take a pole-vault to her conclusion. (The marvel is she is so often right!) So let the man remember he has married a woman, not another man. Sure, they have two different natures, but they are like the blades of a scissors which have to be going in opposite directions to do the job. Sometimes the husband may be out of sorts, gloomy, surly, down. That is the very time for the wife to be serene and sunny; like those two little figurines in the tiny weather houses that indicate rain or fair. When one is in, the other is out—they balance each other. The important thing is for one of them to stay calm.

Every marriage is a union bound by a triple cord. Marriage is first a union of bodies. Didn't God Himself call it, "Two in one flesh"? Sex is good in itself, but not just for itself—that would be merely the sex of animals; and the very fact of this sermon proves we are not mere animals. Marriage is also the union of two hearts, which means that—well, a poet might say they are like two blossoms twined on a vine, breathing perfumed sighs to each other, but practical experience would settle for two pledged people who stand shoulder to shoulder, facing the problems of life, instead of toe to toe fighting each other about them. Thirdly, and most important, a Christian marriage is a union of two souls which have been forever united by the special, mutual Sacrament of Matrimony.

Why is Matrimony special and mutual? Because in Baptism, for example, it is the priest who baptizes the baby. In Confirmation it is the Bishop who confirms the child. But in Matrimony it is the bride and groom who, by their mutual solemn vows, confer on each other the Sacrament. The priest? The priest is merely like the best man and the maid of honor: he is only an official witness, essential, but only a chief witness to their sacred pact.

But his presence there reminds the bride and groom that in the eyes of the Church the golden ring of marriage is just as much a Sacrament as the golden chalice of Ordination. And with that Sacrament of marriage goes a supply of very special graces that God puts away for the married couple almost like meat in a deep-freeze, so they can draw from that supply of grace in time of need. After the honeymoon is over, and the stardust falls from their eyes, comes the cold light of reality, the inevitable disillusions, the unforeseen complications, the fly in the ointment, or maybe even the centipede in the marmalade. Nobody marries perfection. You may court an angel or a saint; you may woo one, but you never wed one. You find you have married a very human being. And that is just where the special grace of the Sacrament of Matrimony, if you fervently ask for it in any matrimonial crisis, will give you balance, and courage, and joyful strength.

There may never be in the wind-tunnel of this world, (God's testing ground), a perfect marriage. But a happy one can often be had for the asking—when the asking is prayer that rises like a perpetual fountain from an unselfish heart.

Third Finger, Left Hand

OUT OF BOUNDS

I was thinking a couple of Sundays ago when we heard that Gospel about the marriage feast of Cana, how naive I was as a young priest about the process of courtship. In those days I took it for granted that it was the man who pursued the girl, proposed to her, and finally got her reluctant consent. Wasn't I innocent, though? I was under the impression that the girl was always demure, and rather unsuspecting, and almost taken by surprise when he popped—or cooed—the question. Of course, now I know. I know that the shoe is on the other foot, or at least the looping lariat is in the other hand. Now I know that once the girl has finished her window-shopping for a husband, and has made her decision, the poor fellow selected hasn't a chance in the world. Perhaps I began to suspect the truth when in wedding after wedding as I asked the groom, "Do you take this woman" and so on, I noticed how he trembled, and often stuttered like a telegraph key. But the bride—the bride would be as cool as a detective booking a prisoner. "Do you take this man?" "Do I take him?" (she seemed to look) "Haven't I had him on my line for the last two years? Do I take him? What else?"

So, on this playful premise, that it is the girl who first secretly makes the decision and then quietly plots her campaign, I should like to remind Catholic girls that there is one class of men who are not a lawful military objective. On their brows you should read, printed in invisible letters, "O.B." meaning "Out of Bounds." Who are they? Non-Catholics. On the other hand if it really is the man who goes after the girl (of course he will always think he does) let him read the same letters on the forehead of every non-Catholic girl, "O.B."—"Out of Bounds." And lest any non-Catholic, boy or girl, be listening and be tempted to take offense at what sounds like downright discrimination, let me show my absolute impartiality by offering the very same advice to them: If you want a happy marriage there is one class of people to avoid, and that is Catholics. Steer clear of them! If you are not a Catholic and you marry a Catholic, you are getting into a boat with someone who rows altogether differently from you. Chances are it will be choppy going, and may easily end with one pulling against the other and a capsizing. *Any* marriage can sprout a couple of disagreements a day, but disagreements over religion are always the bitterest of all. Because they go deepest, into the heart, into the conscience, into the reason of life, into the world to come. Marriage should be a union, not merely physical but also spiritual. But how can it be if each partner lives in his secret soul, on the *other* side of the Grand Canyon of religion?

Put it this way. Milk is a wholesome food. Mustard too has its own excellent place on the table. But when the two are mixed together, you get a natural emetic, guaranteed to turn the stomach upside down. So, a Catholic and a Catholic in marriage is fine. Non-Catholic and non-Catholic, splendid. But Catholic and non-Catholic—so often you get an upset marriage, a mixture which just doesn't blend. Yes, there are exceptions. And if you happen to be one of the exceptions, I congratulate you, because you *deserve* congratulations. God bless you, and may you always have the wind at your back! But because *you* took a treacherous road and survived it successfully, we can't take down the *Danger* sign. There are still too many wrecks along the side, and new ones crashing off every day. As a Catholic priest I must cry the warning that the Catholic Church does not want you to take the chance. In certain circumstances she will yield, but in her eyes are the tears of a mother who says "Yes" when her heart sobs "No."

Do you think for one moment that the Church would oppose these so-called mixed marriages if they really worked out? Look at it from this angle. The Catholic Church, going all the way back through the Popes to St. Peter, believes it is the one true church founded by Jesus Christ. Therefore, it has a solemn obligation to bring as many people as possible into the true fold. For that reason, year after year the Church sends missionaries to out-of-way places like Madagascar and Zanzibar, Iceland and India, the frost-glittering world of the North and the palm-fringed isles of tropical seas. An expensive proposition, mind you, with the going rough, the obstacles tough, and the progress slow! Now wouldn't the Catholic Church be a fool if at the same time she neglected a foolproof means of getting more Catholics, right under her nose? I mean the Apostolate of Mixed Marriages. I mean why not encourage Catholic girls to marry non-Catholic men, raise children, and since the non-Catholic in a mixed marriage signs promises that the children will be reared in the true Catholic faith, why here you have a perpetual fountain of guaranteed new Catholics! Because these Catholics could in turn marry other non-Catholics, and so on! Why in a few generations can you imagine the superb progress the Catholic Church would make! How our numbers would grow and *grow!* A magnificent plan—with only one disturbing drawback. IT DOES NOT WORK!

Cold, stubborn figures and hard, sad facts puncturn this rainbow soap-bubble—the way that mixed marriages are *supposed* to turn out. A council of German Bishops once declared that every year the Catholic Church *loses* through mixed marriages as many souls as missionaries convert. It has been estimated that in seven out of every ten mixed marriages the children are lost to the Catholic Church. More than that: the Catholic party herself is often swept away from the faith by the downstream pull of such a family's religious indifference. Why? Because a family founded on the unnatural compound of *mixed* religions easily crumbles into *no* religion.

Weirdly enough, sometimes you will find the most pointed proof of this carved on the tombstones in Southern cemeteries, Protestant cemeteries. Maybe it was because my father and mother, Lord rest them, were born in Ireland, that as I traced the old names in one such graveyard I could scarcely believe my eyes. Names like Regan and Ryan and Meagher and Murphy. Murphy! Glory be to God, how did *Murphy* ever get there? He didn't go scholastic and re-examine the credentials of Catholicity. Much more likely he simply married a non-Catholic, cut his moorings, and drifted off. But come out of the cemetery and go into the divorce courts. And where one of the parties in a case is a Catholic, so often, so very, very often the other party is a non-Catholic. Sometime ago I read where a Chicago lawyer made a study of five hundred divorce cases in which one party was a Catholic. Almost invariably the rift first started with religion. Certainly! The difference was there the day they married. The pressure of the years only widened it and finally popped them apart.

And yet you find starry-eyed youngsters soulfully discussing whether their wedding should be a single or a double ring ceremony, and blithely ignoring the fundamental importance of having one or two religions in their married life. It makes you wish that the starry eyes would see the clouds ahead. At that moment, of course, during courtship, all the clouds are tinted a lovely pink, and the difference in the boy's and girl's religion is something purely academic. It will never affect their practical daily lives. Won't it though? It will affect their lives every week of the year and all year long, from Sunday morning's Mass till Saturday night's confession. Sunday morning—which church will they attend? Shall Mamma go to her Catholic Mass, and Daddy to his Methodist prayer-meeting? But what will the children think? Oh, Mamma likes tea, Daddy prefers coffee. Mamma goes to the Catholic Church, Daddy to the Protestant—what's the difference? And after a while in many cases, Mamma stops going to her church, and Daddy to his, and the children go to no church.

Or take Monday morning. The Catholic mother, let us suppose, knows that if it is possible she has an obligation to send the children to a Catholic parochial school. The non-Catholic father has signed promises that his children would be brought up in the Catholic faith. But (and that "But" rises ten feet high) is it unknown that promises made in the rosy days of romance are coldly overruled in the realistic days later? Things that looked one way in the happy hour when the wedding rice was tossed in gleeful handfuls, now look different in the years when the rice is monotonously boiled.

And speaking of boiled rice, what about Friday dinner? What shall it be—two little separate meals, meat and fish, or just one big sizzling quarrel? And how about Saturday night confession? If the non-Catholic husband uses contraceptives and the Catholic wife allows this practice, the absolving hand of the priest is hand-cuffed, unable to give her absolution. She may have to choose between her husband and her Faith. Her husband, who stood at her side when they pronounced their marriage vows, now stands between her and the Communion Rail. Marriage vows? He as a non-Catholic may think that Birth Control is not an abuse of nature in the marriage relation. That doesn't help her; she knows it is. He as a non-Catholic may believe that Divorce is a fire-escape which a marriage ought to have, if he gets "fed up" with the union. She knows that they are married until death do them part. He may get a divorce and saunter off and marry another; she knows that she can be no man's wife again until she is first a widow.

Tell this to a Catholic girl, and here is the answer you get. (I know it by heart, because I have been getting it for over thirty years.) "Father, you are right, perfectly right—in *general*. But you do not know the man *I* am marrying. Our marriage is going to be different." The strange thing is, *every one* of them thinks *her* marriage is going to be the exception. The tragic thing is when they come back, applying in vain for an annulment, and you think: "And hers was supposed to be different!"

This is not saying anything against the non-Catholic party. In intelligence, in courtesy, in disposition, in acting according to his lights, in virtue, he may be far superior to the Catholic. But marriage by its very nature demands complete unity for complete success. It is hard enough to lead a good married life in these neo-pagan days even when your partner is of the same religious conviction. But when pilot and co-pilot differ as to where they are going or how they can best get there, it is immeasurably harder. Why take such a fearful chance? And statistics show it *is* fearful! What Catholic girl would want to be responsible for her children lost to the church, and *their* children, and *their* children? And how about herself? God grant that the flowers she carries as the bride of a mixed marriage may not be the flowers for the funeral of her faith!

Happy Even After

HEARTS ARE EASILY HURT

If you are a curate in a large parish, you find yourself stopping off at a great many wakes, but amid the sad whispers and the head-shaking whimpers, two things continue to fascinate me. One is, that as a rule, the corpse looks so much more attractive than when I saw him on his death-bed. And it isn't merely that death has been dressed up in its Sunday best, and corruption has been gaily smeared over with cosmetics, and the whole thing framed in fragrant flowers. No. Generally on the countenance of the dead man lies the serenity of a sunset. The hectic, bustling day is over, and peace falls as soft as the velvet dusk.

On the other hand, there is anything but peace written on the moist and almost crumpled page of his widow's face. (I say widow, I should say survivor, because it works the same way no matter which of them goes first.) The survivor steers you over into a corner and murmurs in a self-scourging tone, "Oh, if I had only been a little kinder to him!" or "Oh, if I had only been more understanding of her!" But it always comes down to this: the person who looks down on the silent stony face lying in the rippled white silk of the casket is conscience-stricken because she (or he) so often hurt the other party's feelings.

Most weddings could take a tip from most wakes and learn that while romance seeks pleasure for itself, true and deep love never wants to cause the other person any pain. Here marriage is not so much a matter of finding the right person as of being the right person. In mere business the smooth code of success suavely insists that within reason the customer is always right. Within reason should not love, the noblest and most generous of emotions, grant as much to the beloved? If self is not second after the one you have chosen from all the world, what shrewd and measuring kind of love is this?

Benjamin Disraeli was one of Britain's most brilliant Prime Ministers, the Churchill of his day, a statesman, an author, a swift high-powered brain. He was married to a woman who made no pretence to an education at all, and who used to say that she never could remember who came first, the Greeks or the Romans. But every night when Parliament was in midnight session, she would wait up for her husband, every light in the house blazing to welcome him and a hot dinner waiting to nourish him. But this devotion was not all one-sided by any means. When Queen Victoria wanted to reward Disraeli with a peerage and a title, he answered, "You do me great honor, Your Majesty, but it would please me far more if instead you would bestow this honor upon my dear wife." And in fact upon her silvery hair Queen Victoria placed the coronet as she became Lady Beaconsfield. When she died even Disraeli's enemies were touched. They knew that in her grave he had buried his heart. They knew it was no pretense when this old man used blackedged letterpaper for the rest of his life.

Don't these pages from the diary of a happy marriage throw a spotlight on the old adage, that when God created woman He did not take her from man's head, as though she should stand above him like a commanding empress; nor from man's feet as though she should cringe beneath him like a slave; but from man's side so that she should be alongside him, his companion, his treasure, closest to his heart! In any language, in any dialect, a marriage proposal knows only one phrase: "I love you." I love you—not, I love myself. If that love is there, no marriage will ever break from the outside, no matter how many regiments of marching troubles bear down against it. Whether it is her in-laws or his business reverses, or trouble from any quarter at all, no matter how dark the sky and rough the sea, if genuine love is holding the helm, meaning "I love you, I put you before any other creature in the whole world," a devoted husband and wife will run out the black storm not only safely but with a kind of fierce joy.

But the modern world is a conspiracy against young couples in this: it hides the hardships that may happen, and hints that married life is only an extended honeymoon. For this is marriage as it charms and infatuates in the silky pages of modern fiction; this is marriage as it glitters with technicolor elegance in the modern movie (where the bride has a cinemascope train like the wake of an ocean liner). This is marriage as it quivers and swoons in the syrupy modern song; this is the gospel of marriage that is preached up and down the land and in the air by Tin-pan Alley and drooling magazines.

It is all as far from reality as orange blossoms from applesauce. No wonder the June bride can become disillusioned by July, and the groom disgruntled, and both dismayed when they find they cannot live in romantic splendor like the little figures on top of the wedding cake, but have to climb down to the hard ground of ordinary life where the sudden smoke rises from unsuccessful cooking and short-circuited tempers, the very real world of bills and budgets and trying relatives and all the rest.

And meanwhile the whole smooth, enameled advertising world is hinting that you cannot possibly be happy in your young home unless you have this or that new mechanical gimmick—and have it in two-tones, three speeds, four dimensions, and five months to pay. All the emphasis of happiness is on things, not people. It is the paganism of possession whose god is the gadget. According to its chrome-plated creed nobody was ever deeply content until the invention of the electric coffee percolator. It reaches the height of something or other in the tens of thousands of tiny bottles that send men off each day to fight the battle of life sprayed with reassuring deodorants. Which makes you wonder, how did Washington ever stand Jefferson?

Anyway, wedding presents with automatic starters and disposal units never yet made a happy marriage. The wedding itself may be a romantic festival with beribboned gifts and jolly songs, but the marriage itself is a job. And a successful job requires intelligence and work and patience and a sacrificial sense of duty. Nobody stumbles on a happy marriage. You patiently climb the steep heights to it. It may mean closing your eyes to this, closing your ears to that, closing your mouth to the other thing. And curiously, it will probably be the little things that will irritate you, like the grains of sand in oysters on the half shell.

When Thomas Merton, the convert and author of "Seven Storey Mountain", left his blasé and sophisticated set of gilded worldlings to become a Trappist Monk, he said it wasn't the austere, severe monastic life he minded. It was not the hard cot, the long fasts, the midnight meditations that tried him. These he had known about, these he had anticipated, these he had freely and fervently chosen. But the little things almost threw him. The saintly monk next to him in chapel who sniffled and snuffled utterly unconscious of Emily Post; the monk in back who at the oddest moment would shift his false teeth with an indelicate click—things like this set his own teeth on edge and put his virtue (if not his vocation) on trial.

Who needs to be told that in marriage, life is lived in even closer scope; and a half-dozen times a day you can screech the nail down the window-pane of the other party's feelings? You can just forget, or you can refuse to be considerate. And that is how two good people can enter marriage as virgins and leave it at death forty years later as martyrs, each having spent a lifetime quietly torturing the other. Aren't you sensitive about some things? Why not presume that she is, or he is, too? This will mean constantly thinking of someone else, but then, is not marriage a generous total giving? The ceremony says, "I take this woman," "I take this man" but it also means—I give myself. The highwayman snarls, "Your money or your life." A successful marriage speaks sweeter but it demands more. It says, "Your money and your life." Like growing old, you have to give all your time to it. And even then you need—shall we call it—outside help?

You remember things went wrong at the very start of that marriage at Cana. The little group of musicians were playing merrily, their heads nodding to the happy rhythm. The guests were all chatter and chuckles and cheery toasts. The waiters were weaving in and out among the tables filling the goblets with red bubbling wine. But now in the back of the hall stood the steward, his arms folded grimly, his head shaking as each waiter came up with his empty jug. "No more wine. No more."

You remember how Our Blessed Lord, at the prayer of His Mother, saved the day, the wedding day. But did you ever wonder how they happened to be there? Happened? *They had been invited.* And they still accept invitations. Not so much to the wedding day as to your married life. You invite Jesus and Mary by prayer, by asking their help not to turn water into wine but to turn tears into joy. If you devoutly ask, they will see you through, not with mink stoles or theatre tickets but with courage and contentment, and a happiness that grows like a hardy flower in the heart, though outside the bitter winds blow. You can take the troubles from outside if inside there is love.

Do you know the prayer I pray for the bride and groom as I see them start smiling down the aisle, arms clasped, hearts linked, the principle figures in the world's favorite picture, two young people in love: the sturdy oak and the lovely blossom, the baritone and the soprano, the bread-winner and the homemaker, the pilot and the co-pilot, the violin and the bow? Dear Lord, send them happiness like an old wedding ring, solid and genuine and strong. Let the wedding march follow them at least faintly through life—oh, a few little human discords now and then, but lost in the general swell of mutual harmony! Let other bridesmaids take over and walk invisibly by their sides: gentle Patience, clear-eyed Trust, tender Devotion, sweet and staunch Loyalty. Let Thy fingertips, O Lord, scatter upon them the rice of a thousand blessings, but chiefly this, that each will be resolved never to hurt the other's feelings, because then their home, no matter how humble, will be a little suburb of Heaven.

Happy Even After

THE LOCK IN WEDLOCK

In tiny mission chapel and towering metropolitan cathedral this Sunday morning, Catholic priests have been reading the Gospel where our Lord goes to a wedding. I don't remember reading that He ever went to a divorce. In fact some of His statements, like "Two in one flesh" and "Let no man put asunder" give you the impression that in wedlock He put the accent strongly on the lock. Late confirmation of the wisdom of this comes from the most unexpected of sources. Maybe you too have read how Russia has done a neat, clicking, right-about-face in this matter of easy divorce. And maybe you remember when in Russia all you needed for a divorce was a wife and a postcard. Now in the Soviet Union it is as hard to get a divorce as it is to get a deep-freeze. Because it has slowly dawned on the dull bureaucratic mind that a nation is made up of families the way a wall is made up of bricks, and if the bricks begin to break up, your wall is about as solid and cohesive as a jigsaw puzzle.

Yet while godless and backward Russia begins to tighten the bolts on shaky marriages, some bright strong American minds continue to think it liberal and progressive to give away easy divorces like Superman badges, so that America can become the undisputed champion in the league of the broken home. I use the general term broken home because you have to remember that for every official divorce there is probably an equal number of separations and desertions. These cases do not go down in the books as divorce cases, but they cut just as deeply into human hearts as tragedies. Unhappiness doesn't have to be official. The worst of it is that the weather report for tomorrow's marriages is stormier than today's. At least the joyless experts who make a study of statistics, and then shinny out on a limb waving their predictions, are morbidly confident that in fifty years, one marriage out of every two will be popping out of the toaster a charred and ruined reject.

By that time America will really be "the land of the free." But let the twenty-first century pick up its own pieces. Why is it that even now the bridal gown is so often changed for the divorce suit? According to the records it seems most bad marriages drift on the rocks when they have just about cleared the harbor; that is, in the third, fourth, and fifth year. You might expect the cause to be anything from in-laws to sex, but if you listen to the young casualties themselves, they will tell you most often that they were disappointed with marriage itself: disillusioned.

Marriage was not the mirage that their flushed and feverish early love had painted so hopefully on the horizon. In those days they had wondered how they could ever have lived in the wasted days before they had known each other...before this wonderful, splendid, utterly darling creature had suddenly given a new meaning to life, and made the world glorious and vibrant overnight, and existence itself a joy, and even pouring rain a pleasure if they were walking through it together, and a long wearisome trainride worth every boring minute of it if the beloved was waiting at the other end! But almost before the pelted rice is out of the hair and the stardust out of the eyes, each begins to see that the angel married, has some very peculiar angles. The cover girl is never the same glamorous creature in the rest of the book. There are plenty of dull chapters, plenty of irritating footnotes, and plenty of unexpected pictures of kimono and curlers shuffling round a breakfast table. On the other hand, Prince Charming is never quite the courtly personage he was when he was courting. Quite possibly he leaves a trail of ashes, clothes, and faults all over the house. So what? Isn't all this the history of practically every marriage that ever walked down the magnificent aisle of organ music and orange blossoms, out into the hard, cold, shocking world of reality?

But in former days they must have had the maturity to face it. Maybe now it is Momism that doesn't let the American boy grow up on his own, hardened, self-reliant, and prepared for set-backs. Maybe with the girl it is the foolish romances, as sweet and unsubstantial as cotton candy, in movies and magazines that makes the future bride imagine even a mop in technicolor. Does it take so much maturity to realize that marriage, like the year, has its own different seasons, and it cannot always be spring? But for those who have the common sense to see this, the wisdom to accept it, the courage to face it, the loyalty to see it through... there are joys and rewards and compensations in every season of married life!

Of course married life presumes love. And love means simply that you think so much of the other person that self is always second. In life together, once self swaggers into the picture, from either side, romance becomes rivalry, and the soft voice learns to hiss. They often forget that before you can love anyone deeply, you have to know that person deeply. That is why a swift, whirlwind courtship often ends like a whirlwind... with the ruin of two lives and the wreckage of a young home in its impetuous wake. If courtship were merely a physical affair, like kissing and petting, then almost any young man might marry any young girl, each convinced that this would be a good deal and a grand game. But the whole purpose of courtship is not to know the other party physically, but to know the other person mentally and temperamentally, to see if your individual traits of character, your likes and dislikes will orchestrate together without too many jangling discords. The more observing you are while you keep company before marriage, the less chance you take of parting company after marriage. And if you do not spend about a year sizing up your beloved's faults and virtues and moods and disposition, the cold figures of case histories imply you are not likely to spend many years united in marriage.

How about finances and marriage, or matrimony and the matter of money? A study has been made of that question too, and it seems that most authorities agree that essentially the husband's income has nothing to do with the happiness of the marriage. Whether the man of the house is a laborer or a lawyer, whether he goes to work in overalls toting a dinner pail, or in a pin-striped business suit jauntily swinging a brief case, these circumstances are only like the picture frame, sometimes plain, sometimes gilded, but have nothing to do with the inner picture, the marriage itself. I like that finding; it scores heavily for real love. In fact the only exception is this: when times are more prosperous, divorces are more numerous. I guess hard knocks tend to hammer people together, while the soft warm breeze of luxury is apt to blow them apart.

But if insurance could be taken out against the break-up of a home, do you know which home would be the poorest risk and therefore would have to pay the highest premium? The home in which for some years the husband and wife each morning leave the house together for their respective jobs. Granted that there are exceptional cases, normally when the wife works she is in danger of undermining her marriage by three separate tunnels. First, the working wife comes flouncing home flourishing her own pay-check, always a silent, threatening weapon of independence, whereas if she would do her work for him at home, and he at his job for her, they would grow like two branches on one bough, bound by interdependence. Secondly, if all day long she mingles with other men in the business world, she may glide into dangerous friendships, especially if the sea is running a little rough in her own domestic world. And thirdly, she will be channelling the major portion of her time and energy outside, so that only a slender trickle will dribble into the home. Can anyone doubt that such a home is sure to suffer ... in its care, its importance, its very spirit?

Naturally—or unnaturally!—if there are no children, there may not be much home to take care of. For that reason a miniature empty cradle ought to be the class-pin of the divorced, because the chances are ten to one that if the married couple multiply (that is, beget offspring) they will not divide (that is, get a divorce). Curious thing about children: they may tear a house apart, but somehow they keep a home together.

May I say here in a sympathetic parenthesis that in those marriages where God in His wisdom withholds the gift of children, He generally compensates by giving husband and wife an even greater mutual love? And such a wife in many ways is God's gift to a parish, because without such a one to give to parish projects her leisure and her enthusiasm, where would many of our parish activities be?

Some divorces ought to wear as their class-pin a yellow triangle. Yellow because of being a traitor to their marriage vows; triangle because the triangle (for example the husband, the wife, and the other woman) is the arch-enemy of the family circle. Is it any wonder that one survey claimed that the real cause for most divorces during the war years and immediately after was adultery? But then you cannot even plead with this. All you can do is pity and pray for it.

At the moment, the most monumental mockery in the English language are those five monosyllables, "Till Death do us part." By the way, I saw Death a couple of weeks ago. He wore a double-breasted grey suit, clipped grey mustache, thinning grey hair, and eyeglasses. He was getting into a cab and he had just thrown away a cigar. I have the solemn word of at least a hundred people that he was Death, because they had vowed to be husband and wife "till death do us part." Well, he parted them—in a courtroom. He must be Death.

He, this judge—is this Death? Not as God meant it, in raising marriage to the dignity of a Sacrament. Not as Nature meant it, because the baby looking up so helplessly from its crib, the boy at school, the youth in adolescence, yes and the wife who walked down her wedding aisle longing to be loved forever (even after she had given her youth and beauty to the bearing and raising of these children) she as well as they needs someone to cherish her and leave her *never!*

In any marriage there will be flaws and faults, on both sides. And if love is blind, it should not have the cataracts removed right after the wedding. It must learn to overlook and to understand; to readjust and to compromise; to realize that the marriage ceremony is a contract, but from then on the job begins! And like any job, it entails hard work, changes, disappointment, courage. Above all it is a contract for life, because if either party keeps open a back-door of escape, divorce, then when things get rugged, the temptation will be to slip through that exit, give up the job, skip off. Nail that door of divorce shut! This is the post you have sworn to hold till death, and if you pray, Our Lord Himself, even if it takes another miracle as at the marriage of Cana, will turn your tears into the wine of joy!

Happy Even After

YOU CAN'T

MARRY AN ANGEL

They say that marriages are made in heaven but sometimes something seems to happen to them from the time they leave the angels and the time they wind up at the attorneys. I do not now refer to the marriages of these moderns who walk out of a marriage as casually as they would walk out of a movie if they found *that* boring and dull; these moderns who take their "contract" seriously only at the cardtable, but airily ignore the contract they made at the wedding altar; these moderns who, to their marriage vows today solemnly say "I do," and a year later to those vows lightly say "Adieu."

On the contrary, today we are discussing the solid, average married couples who stand by their bond (even if it is a bond and not a bargain) but at the same time are in some measure unhappy. They are vaguely or definitely discontented. Well, perhaps they expected too much of marriage. Perhaps somewhere they had read that husband and wife, like violin and bow, make one instrument of sweet and melting melody—only in their case it is more often the jarring clash of a couple of cymbals. Perhaps in rose bowers on soft summer nights, when the sky wore a veil netted with stars, they had dreamed of marriage—at least their marriage—as a state of perfect and perpetual bliss. They forgot that in the Catechism this is the definition of Heaven, not of Matrimony.

The simple truth is that nobody is happy all the time. All of us are happy and unhappy by turns. Single people are not forever skipping through the stars of ecstatic joy. Neither are married people. Neither is anybody. Every life is a little plot of flowers and brambles; a path of sunshine and mud-puddles; a mine where the occasional diamonds of brilliant happiness are surrounded by tons and tons of monotonous clay.

Despite the fact that most movies end on that optimistic note, a marriage is seldom a lifelong romance. Romance and marriage are about as different as a recruiting poster and the army. You know, the recruiting poster is all glamour, novelty, appeal, color, excitement, promise, while the army is—well, just the army. I hope it is not unpatriotic to suggest that an army post rarely matches an army poster. It is the same in other fields. To many of us, Christmas Eve is a more exciting time than Christmas. Wherever anticipation is the architect, he draws up such glorious plans that prosaic old actuality, the builder, shakes his head and simply cannot follow them.

Now, if a bridal pair went to Niagara Falls on their honeymoon, they certainly would be enchanted with the tissuey white bridal veil of the Falls, the bridesmaid pinks and blues of the rainbow spray, the thundering wedding march of the symphonic waters, and so on. But if the honeymooners strolled far enough up the river, they would find that the rest of it was pretty ordinary and undistinguished, and flat, and monotonous, and routine. But it is just here that boats are sailed, and barges towed, and fish caught, and ice cut, and life lived! It is as unreasonable to expect a married life to be an unbroken series of thrills and joys, as it is to expect a river to be an unbroken series of Niagara Falls.

Only an adolescent thinks of marriage as a state of sugary sweetness, moonlight and poetry, all framed within the lacy borders of a sighing valentine. Adults will look ahead to its grim realities as a life-time job, and not to any honeymoon standards of delirious happiness. There will, please God, be many, many joys. There is more genuine entertainment in the unpredictable antics of *your* little child toddling across the floor and discovering the world, than there is in any other floor show. There is more genuine fun in the very serious statements of *your* child, at that age when he is perhaps missing one of his first teeth after trying to shift gears on a lollypop, than in all the canned corn of professional comedians. But, both before the children come and after, there will be plenty of chances for disagreement, misunderstanding, friction, sudden flareups or sullen smoulderings. And unless the sea of matrimony is not to be the old story of first friendship, then courtship, and finally battleship, that sea of matrimony must become a whole ocean of patience and tolerance, compromise and concession, a submerging of one's own tastes and whims and conveniences for the common good.

Certainly, there will be disappointments. But you don't solve the problems by dissolving the partnership. By its nature marriage is not perfect, but it is permanent. A marriage *license is never a money-back guarantee*. It is a Last Will and Testament in which you bequeathe yourself to another forever. It is a vow in which you pledge to walk arm-in-arm with another along the road of life, no matter what lies beyond each new bend. It is a declaration of love so deep that it says and means "to the end of time." Like the wedding ring, the gleam and the polish of love may dull away with the years, but underneath it is still just as good, still just as solid, still all gold.

If you could ask a couple who have made a success out of their marriage, what is the secret, the answer would come back that there is no secret, except that they *made* a success out of it. How does anyone make a success anywhere? How does a student get good grades in school? How does a man get a promotion in his job? How does a gardener grow a flower-bed bright as a stained-glass window? The normal answer is by working at it. For a successful marriage, too, you have to work at it—after the wedding. You work at being less selfish, at being more patient, at cultivating gentleness and self-control, at smiling through the dark times and being content when the going is rough.

Content! Some young folks are a bit stunned at where they have to start, in making their home. "Be it ever so humble"—but they never imagined it would be *this* humble. It takes them a little while to realize (they always knew, but never realized) that they just cannot begin their home on the same standard of comfort where their fathers and mothers left off. Sometimes when the girl threatens to go home to mother's, perhaps she just misses mother's home.

Besides the economic difficulty, there may be also the emotional one. Marriage is a merger of two different personalities. Now it is a hard enough job to throw up a bridge between two opposite shores, but it is a still harder job to build a permanent bridge of understanding and harmony between two opposite temperaments, two utterly different dispositions. After all, by the time you marry your partner, that partner is pretty well set in his traits and his character. The concrete has hardened; and frankly, there is precious little you can do about it. As the school girl wrote in her eighth grade composition, "We get our parents at so late an age that it is impossible to change their habits." And the same applies, probably with compound interest, to husbands and wives. You do not marry something like a bouquet that you can take apart and rearrange as you would like to see it. You marry someone who is more like a book, already bound and the pages numbered. Often the best you can do is thank God for the good qualities there, and pray God about the bad ones.

However, here is one suggestion, and who knows, perhaps a solution, from of all places, the Department of Agriculture! Somewhere I read of a man who wrote to that Bureau for advice about the dandelions that sprinkled his lawn. In a protracted correspondence the Department of Agriculture sent him letter after letter, mentioning various ways of getting rid of them, but the stubborn little dandelions just stayed. Finally he wrote, "I have tried every method you advised without success. Have you anything further to suggest about the dandelions?" And the answer came back, "We suggest you learn to love them." If it is asking too much for you to learn to *love* your partner's faults, at least learn to overlook them. Perhaps *you* have a few dandelions of your own; even one or the other cactus. And there you can surely make headway, because correcting faults is like tying a necktie or a bow; we can always do it easier on ourselves than on anybody else.

Just for the rare luxury of the experience, every one of us should now and then own up to the fact that we, and not the other party, were at fault. Elocutionists may say that the hardest words in the English language to pronounce are: "If Peter Piper picked a peck of pickled peppers," and so on, or something like that. Not at all! The hardest words in English to pronounce are: "I was wrong," because you have to say them not with the tongue and teeth, but with the conscience and the heart. That is why, when one of the parties in a marriage flies off the handle like an axe-head, the noble party is the one who, right or wrong, first buries the hatchet—and not in the other party's skull either. For, if we do not take the first step toward reconciliation what are we but ersatz Christians or church-going pagans?

Surely, if even one party is determined that there will be no quarrel, then there can be no quarrel. Not even the heavy-weight champion of the world can have a fight alone. It always takes two. Naturally there will be times when one party's nerves are jangled and out of tune and off-key, but that is precisely the time when the other party has to hold the melody, sweet and sure, so that the other can get back. If both get off, it will be bedlam. They say that at the Battle of New Orleans, Andrew Jackson stopped the British bullets with bales of cotton. On the same principle, the soft answer is still the best defense against wrath. But the softest answer is that whispered to God in prayer. With His Divine help and our own determined self-control, family friction can be reduced to a fraction.

Happy Even After

DEATH IS THE ONLY EXIT

Sometimes they write (on tinted, fragrant stationery) but more frequently they come to the rectory parlor. They possibly have gone to college; at any rate, they generally exude culture almost like a cheap and too obtrusive perfume. This type is rather young and often stylish, and after pingponging some small talk to the priest about the weather or the traffic, she flutters her eyelashes (generally native, sometimes imported) in a just-beween-us-two manner and says very softly, "Father, I know our Church does not permit divorce, but . . ." (and here she sounds as though she were encouraging a timid fellow-conspirator) "but how about an annulment for my marriage?"

The way they whisper it you would think that an annulment were a bootleg divorce, an under-the-counter "out". After all, some call it jam, some call it jelly; some call it a tram, some a trolley. And non-

Catholics call it a divorce, but Catholics call it an annulment. Simple as that, they would like you to believe. They darkly hint that, talk as we may or, better, keep quiet as we may, an annulment is the secret magic key that opens the lock of wedlock and lets the Catholic go free, free as a bird and not tagged with the tell-tale metal ring of divorce.

Of course it is all rubbish. And off the smouldering rubbish of ignorance, rises the weird, blind smog of error. But if this is what some Catholics believe, can you blame non-Catholics? As the Church marches through history, many of her institutions and beliefs, rolling by like picturesque floats, are jibed at and derided, but most taunting stones are slung at her concept of marriage. And in the whole field of marriage nothing is so calculated to flick the shutter of a hostile eye in a knowing wink as the mere mention of the word annulment. Isn't it a cozy back-door, a handy fire-escape, an emergency exit whereby you can slip out of a marriage you decide is intolerable, and still have the nodding blessing of an understanding Church?

So far the innuendos, the insinuations, the presumptions. Now let us look at the facts. In the first place the difference between an annulment and a divorce is not just a matter of words, like the difference between a taxi and a cab, or a book and a volume. It is the difference between Hamlet's to be or not to be. It is the difference between a marriage that really is a valid marriage, and a mirage that only looks like a marriage.

Annulment does not mean that a marriage is made null and void, it means that it is officially pronounced null and void, but it *was* null and void from the beginning, and always would have been, even if nobody had ever noticed it.

Let's focus the white spotlight of comparison on an annulment in a completely different field, politics. It may illuminate the meaning of annulment and at the same time make clear that the Church enjoys no monopoly in this kind of thinking. Suppose a man should run for the United States Senate, be elected, serve there awhile, and then someone reveals that this document or that has been forged, and the Senator never was a United States citizen. The Courts would immediately declare his rank as Senator null and void. That would be an annulment. They do not say we are divorcing you from your status as Senator. They are saying, you never were a Senator in the first place. You failed to meet one essential requirement for the office, according to law. It does not matter that you were addressed as Senator, or that you voted as Senator, or that you served on committees with other Senators. Actually your election was invalid. You never were a Senator.

Now, transfer that to marriage. Suppose Mr. Jones marries Miss Brown in a large Catholic Church with a big wedding, with a file of pastel-tinted bridesmaids and a glorious recessional like a royal coronation. It comes to light, alas, that a few years before, the same Mr. Jones had married Miss Green in a little wedding at a little Catholic church, perhaps in Australia. Here is where an annulment steps on the stage like a sheriff waving the proof of the first marriage, and officially declaring the second annulled. In other words, Mr. Jones and Miss Brown merely went through the motions of getting married. And all the ceremony and pageantry from vested priest to stirring organ could not make it a marriage. One of the essentials was missing: one of the partners was not single and free.

When the horrified bride (so-called) discovers this, the Church does not say, "I grant you a divorce from Mr. Jones." The Church says "I declare, after examining the evidence, that you never were married to Mr. Jones." This, and only this, is an annulment.

At the opposite extreme lies the case of David Dimples, star of the cinema, sometimes spelled with an s. David, you may remember, married Blondie Bleach before a Justice of the Peace. Now David was a Catholic, so that marriage in the eyes of the Church was no marriage at all. This may seem autocratic, imperious, and sweeping as a snow-plow. But here is the way the Church reasons. Point one: Marriage is a Sacrament. Point two: the Church has the right to make laws for the Sacraments. Point three: the Church has made a law to this effect that for a Catholic, the marriage must be performed in the presence of a priest and two witnesses, the priest because it is a Sacrament, the witnesses because it is a contract. Therefore in the eyes of the Catholic Church, David Dimples just was not married. And that is why, when David a couple of years later finds his love for Blondie Bleach fading, and divorces her, he can slip his new ring on the finger of Second Choice in the Catholic Church.

Whereupon the cynic with the built-in sneer says, "I told you so. You see how easy it is." But it isn't easy at all. When David Dimples went through that first civil ceremony, he merely made his union with the first woman respectable. He did not make it right.

DEATH IS THE ONLY EXIT

He was living in sin. If he had lived with her without having had a civil ceremony, he would have been able to be married in the Catholic Church too. As far as the Church was concerned, that ceremony made no difference in his status whatever.

The grounds for annulment are not spacious grounds at all. In fact, as most hopeful applicants heart-brokenly discover, the grounds are not much bigger than a grave—"Till Death do us part." Otherwise, rare are the reasons to justify the issuance of a decree of nullity. Force is one. For example if a gun gleamed behind a curtain aimed at the bridegroom's heart, and he were told, "You marry her or else. This is either going to be your wedding or your funeral." Well, obviously great force or great fear takes away free will, and nobody can make a contract, least of all a marriage contract, without free will. Or if one of the parties is proven to have been at the time of the marriage too young before the law, that marriage is invalid and can be annulled. And there are a few more general headings, but each case must be individually investigated. You could no more decide your case from a talk like this than you could normally diagnose your illness from a popular handbook of medicine.

The important thing to remember about a marriage annulment is that there has to be a grave defect according to the law and mind of the Church, something seriously wrong with the marriage contract, *at the moment it was made.* To repeat: the decree of annulment does not make the marriage null and void. It simply declares officially that the marriage had been null and void from the beginning. Therefore, if your complaint is something that happened after the marriage was performed, it cannot be offered as evidence

10. *Pennies*

for an annulment. As a matter of fact, what happens afterward is taken care of and consented to in the marriage contract,—"for better or for worse."

That contract is like a deed for property in the Hall of Records. That deed establishes ownership of such and such land. The land may be only unprofitable rock or marsh or it may gush fabulous oil; but what happens after you purchase the land, whether it yields wealth or woe, never can go back and affect the original deed. What happens to the land later has no effect on the title.

It is the same with matrimony. If the original title or contract is valid, anything that happens later, that is, after the marriage, can never be a reason for an annulment. Drunkenness may stagger through the marriage; adultery may defile it; desertion may leave it abandoned. A wife may deserve our deepest sympathy and a husband a horse-whipping. It is regrettable, it is criminal, it is damnable. But it offers no ground for annulment, because it is something bad that happened after a good and valid contract.

In cases like this the priest needs to wear not a biretta but a brass helmet, for the abuse comes clattering down on him like a landslide. And he has to take it because if he pulls the lever on his own coal-chute and buries them under black and bitter invective, if the priest points out that it is they who plunge into a hasty marriage and then come whining for a release, he is letting go the only thin thread by which he may draw them back to God—patient sympathy and encouraging kindness. "But, Father, in the sixteen months we have been married he has divided his time between bottles, bets, and blonds. These get his salary. I don't. Am I supposed to stay with him and put up with this for the rest of my life? Father, I'm young. I can support myself. I can easily find happiness with another man. Am I supposed to pay for his sins with a life of loneliness and frustration and heartbreak? Do you mean to tell me the Church sentences me to live with a man who delights in making my life a hell?"

You see how the priest is made to look like a tyrant? But the priest has nothing to do with the situation. As a matter of ironic fact he may have a sister in the same spot. The blame does not lie even at the doorstep of the Church. It belongs (if we dare say it) on those sacred shoulders that once swayed under a cross, Jesus Christ . . . and on the pair that pronounced the marriage vows.

For it was Christ who decreed, "What God hath joined, let no man put asunder" and it was the marriage couple who sealed their contract with "Till death do us part." And once that marriage contract is validly made and the nuptial vows exchanged, no priest, no Pope, no judge, no king can put it asunder.

Does that mean that an innocent woman would have to spend the rest of her life under the same roof with a man who is just a human beast? Neither Christ nor His Church demands that. A separation can be obtained, of course, but not the right to remarry. This is the teaching of the Catholic Church, not because we like it that way, but because we believe this is the law of Christ as written in the Scriptures. Strictly speaking, we believe that the Catholic Church has nothing to do with it. It is the doctrine of Jesus Christ, and the Catholic Church only follows it.

Focus on the Family

MOTHER'S DAY

Toward the end of the Second World War, the magazines blazed with bright, optimistic ads promising us the most amazing post-war gadgets. Somehow you gathered the impression that after the boom of the last big gun, Science would wave its magic wand and turn the average home into a wonderland of marvelous devices. Somehow you came to believe that it would not be long to the day when you luxuriously rose from a "down of angel wing" mattress to the soothing chimes of a gentle alarm clock that all but coughed politely before it woke you, and when you snapped on the recessed wall-cabinet TV, you would get not merely your favorite television program, but out of the back of the machine into an awaiting glass gurgles a stream of golden, vitamin-rich orange juice. From the side, pops out a crisp copy of the morning paper, and from a slot underneath, a pair of vitamin pills carefully sealed in cellophane. I'm afraid you will have to see about the coffee yourself.

It all sounded like the morning after Arabian Nights, but there is no harm hoping that some day Science will catch up with its boasting young brother, Advertising. In the meantime, we call attention to this. Gadgets and gimmicks can make a model house. But it takes a Mother to make a model home. Nobody ever learned to say his night prayers kneeling at the side of a de luxe refrigerator. Nobody ever came running home from his first day of school to throw his arms around an electric squeezer. Nobody who was all worried and disturbed over something, ever looked up for the answer to a brand new electric mixer. He was mixed up already.

The most important thing in any home is still the Mother. And this is her Day. Of course the idea of honoring Mother was in the Commandments long before it ever got into the calendar. Sometimes I think we emphasize the "day" too much. For a whole year of work and worries and wrinkles, poor Mother gets one day of candy, cards, and carnations. And inside these is quietly hidden a contract to keep on working for the next three hundred and sixty-four days. Somebody ought to write a poem on " 'Twas the Day after Mother's Day"—and the family was just finishing the chocolates they had so generously given to Mother, and the flowers that they had arranged so tastefully in the tall vase yesterday in her honor were now pleading for Mother to change the water . . . and so on. Has possibilities.

Not Mother's Day but a Mother's day. . . . A Mother's day is one that begins pretty close to the dawn and goes on deep into the dark. A Mother's day that starts helping the man off to work and hustling the children off to school. A Mother's day that is merely interrupted by preparing breakfast and lunch and dinner. A Mother's day that ends when the rest are in bed; and when her hand is on the light, her thoughts are perhaps on the eldest who is still out. Even when her work is finished, her worry is not.

A Mother's day is spent in a mother's world. It is a world of monotonous martyrdom ... the world of pots and pans and dirty dishes; the world of washing and ironing and folding and putting away; the world of medicine bottles and measles and mumps. It is a narrow world, too, bounded on the north by the kitchen stove, on the south by the clothesline, and it stretches east and west the magnificent distance between the super market and the sink. If "all the world's a stage," Mother's world is a stage where she plays many parts in one costume. Now she is a Queen whose scepter is a broom, and now she is a Judge whose court is a porch of quarrelling youngsters. Without benefit of double billing, she is cook and nurse, laundress and seamstress, and maker of beds, and duster of furniture and official scrubber of floors. In *her* world there is no five o'clock whistle to listen for, when she can drop her mop and forget everything till tomorrow morning. Her average day runs about sixteen hours in which she may get sixteen complaints, and not one compliment. The last time she had a real vacation she was single, and the next time she may be dead. You could not get a coolie to take her job, and she would not exchange it with a Queen. Nobody can explain this, except that in the purest sense *this* is love.

A Mother's day? Think of a Mother's life! She wonders about us before we come; she works for us as long as we are with her; she worries about us whenever we are away. She gives her very blood to our making, her milk to our nursing, her sweat to our rearing, her tears to our straying.

It does not matter to her that when we are young we cause her work and break her back, and when we are old we cause her worry and break her heart—because she loves us. Fathers are wonderful, too, as witness the Father of the Prodigal Son. But witness, too, that in that touching story there is no mention of any mother, as if Our Lord wished to intimate that if the boy had known a mother's love, he would never have left his home for the harlots and the husks. The bond between father and child is the bond of pride and joy, but the bond between mother and child is the bond of love and suffering. When a father tucks his baby in his arm—almost like a football—he is complacently happy; but if the baby starts to cry the father usually stretches out his arms and says, "Here, Mother, you take him!" Strangely enough, it works just the opposite with the Mother. Automatically, as soon as she hears the child cry, her arms go out . . . not to get rid of him, but to take him. When the child is in trouble, that is the time the mother wants the child most. She risks her life bearing us, and she spends her life bearing with us.

To the rest of the world we may be pretty small print, but to Mother we are a headline across the front page. We always were. Take that twelve year old boy riding by on his bike. To the neighbors he is only a rather wild lad with scuffed shoes that hate polish, and disobedient hair that won't lie down, and a face that doesn't mind either freckles or dirt. He runs to fires but loafs on errands. He picks up warts but forgets gloves and caps. He has the mysterious gift of coming home with wet feet on a dry day, and making any manufacturer's claim about durable material look slightly ridiculous. He likes nothing better than to emit a sudden ear-splitting whistle.

To the man behind the soda fountain down at the corner drug-store, the boy may be just a fifteen cent customer, and a slow and sloppy one at that. To the teacher he may be a tepid seventy, much better with bubble gum than with fractions. To the preacher he may be, as he squirms in his pew, the first patent on perpetual motion. To everybody else, this boy, as long as he is somebody else's boy, may be a nuisance, a problem, or a plague—but to his Mother, he is the reason why the world goes around and the sun shines and the robins sing. And it will always be that way. If some day the boy grows up and breaks a law instead of a window, and his former friends begin to develop faulty memories and a tendency to walk on the other side of the street—he can be sure that if all the world is against him, there is a Mother with him still.

You might think that this would make us appreciate what a Mother is. Yet the uncomfortable truth is that too many of us, while we have our Mother, we take her for granted; and by the time we really come to know all she has done for us, and what she has meant to us, she goes and does the only really harsh thing a good Mother ever does—she dies and leaves us.

Much as a child depends on its Mother, it still does not realize what a Mother is; and as a matter of fact it *cannot* realize. In its own tiny mind the child perhaps sees its Mother as a radiant creature sur-

MOTHER'S DAY

rounded by a wonderful golden light in which float cookies and kisses, story books, and evening prayers, and bandages to bind up little bruises. I heard a story once though of a boy who did come to realize what his Mother meant.

The boy's name was Bobby. Bobby's father was a businessman of some sort and the boy found out that on the first day of each month, his father sent out bills, and got money back in return. Bobby pondered this awhile, and decided to try it himself, perhaps with improvements. So one morning, Bobby's Mother came down to breakfast, and found two surprises. One was Bobby, down there already, and the other was a piece of white paper under her cup and saucer. She picked the paper up and read it silently. It said:

What Mother Owes Bobby:

For going to store last week	.15
For practicing on the violin	.20
For eating spinach twice	.25
For being a good boy (he was not so sure of that so he let her off with)	.05
Total of what Mother owes Bobby	.65

Mother folded the paper, and began to give extraordinary attention to stirring her coffee. Noontime came and Bobby, who boylike had already forgotten the incident, burst into the house, tossed his cap on a chair and dashed for the table. But look—there on his plate was a gleaming half-dollar, a dime, and a nickle. Boy! Why hadn't he thought of this before? But—he looked again. There under his plate was a piece of white paper, the same paper, only reversed. And this time it read:

What Bobby Owes Mother:

For feeding and clothing him for ten years	Nothing
For staying up nights when he had whooping cough and virus	Nothing
For giving him toys each Birthday and Christmas	Nothing
For just being a Mother to him	Nothing
Total of what Bobby owes Mother	Nothing

The youngster's silver did not seem to shine so bright now. He took the coins, pressed them into his Mother's palm, and said with a sniffle that was neighbor to a tear, "Gee, Mom, I never thought of it like that." And he finished with an impulsive kiss.

Too many children grow up without realizing what they owe to Mother. Some of them, forgetting that they came into this world through a Mother as across a threshold, even treat her like a door mat, all but trampling her down as they stride on to their own lives and careers. Others still love her, but from a distance; how seldom they return to see her! No wonder such a Mother, looking at a robin fluttering over her nest of little ones in an ecstasy of joy, whispered, "Don't love them too much, mother-bird. Don't put your heart in the nest. For the day is coming too soon when your brood will find their wings and leave you—alone!"

But today at least many of us come back. On the second Sunday of May all the roads of the land lead to Mother. Maybe she has changed a little with the years. Maybe she has not the face or the figure of a Hollywood star, nor the gown and jewels of a society leader, nor the education of college Dean, nor the crisp efficiency of a business woman. Maybe her face is wrinkled, and her hands are rough and her shoulders stooped. But she still is beautiful to God and to all who love her. The glowing bloom of her fresh young years, when she was as a pink rose, is gone; but she is still a rose, only now the rose is white. She has her faults, perhaps, like anyone human, but all things considered, a golden halo would fit more gracefully round her grey hair than round the heads of the rest of us.

Holy Mary, Mother of God, pray for our Mothers! You who knew the warm joy of softly swaying the Christ-Child in the cradle of your arms; you who guided in their first faltering steps those toddling Feet that one day would walk surely over the fluid blue carpet of the rolling sea; you who felt round your neck the clasp of little pink Fingers that one day would be spread out in red agony against a cross— sweet Mother Mary, Mother of God, be a good Mother, in bright joy or black sorrow to the mothers of us all!

Focus on the Family

THE INDISPENSABLE WOMAN

About fifty years ago, O. Henry said that all the Christmas stories had been written. In the same sense, we can say that all the Mother's Day sermons have been preached. Yet, though no man can really add anything new, it is a sweet pleasure for us to stand reverently before the old shrine, and salute humanity's closest approach to Heaven—a good Mother. Some may urge that, after all, Mother's Day is only a recent artificial flower in the plastic vase of convention. That may be true for the "Day," but the spirit of the day is as natural as the clinging arms of a child. Not only that, it is a spirit that has its roots deep in religion: to be exact, in the Fourth Commandment. In fact, we can trapeze from the Commandments over to the Creed: "born of the Virgin Mary." If on the 25th of December we recall that the Great God became a Little Child, on the second

Sunday of May we should remember that in that bleak stable of Bethlehem He found what all the glittering Courts of Heaven could not give Him... a Mother. When Jesus, the Divine, was born of Mary, the human, then Motherhood received its highest compliment!

Some sophisticated observer may curl his lip and sneer that our modern dedication of Mother's Day is nothing but a huge cake baked with "the dough" of Big Business and spread between layers with a smeary filling of sentimentality. It is true that somehow Mother's picture has found its way into the gilded frame of commercialism, complete to the price-tag; but can't a man forget the extravagant frame, and have eyes only for the extraordinary face within? About sentimentality, it may even be true that an over-sweet sentimentality has tried—God help us—to touch up that face, sometimes adding wrinkles and sometimes rouge, but every honest man will go on seeing and loving only the picture of Mother that he carries in the locket of his heart. It may not be Whistler's Mother—as austere and stylized as a statue. It will not be the teary creature on the song-book cover, with the lavender dress and the snowy shawl, fumbling a prop letter in her frail ivory fingers. More likely his picture will be closer to an energetic woman bustling around a busy kitchen, wearing an ample apron and flat shoes, but in that simple setting, Love shines like diamonds from her eyes. Looking back now, he knows that his Mother was Self-Sacrifice with a smudge on its cheek, Wisdom with a wisp or two of straggling hair, and Sanctity under the halo of a dustcap. She was the financier who never heard of a budget, yet mysteriously made both ends meet like a magician. She was a first-aid attendant who never heard of a manual, but somehow could do just as well with a twist of bandage and a kiss. She was a hotel-chef at her old-fashioned oven; a priest at the children's bed-time prayers; and after that an unabashed teller of tall tales that made little eyes grow bigger and bigger, till the eyelids got tired with the strain and then slowly fell like the curtain at a play. Another day was done.

For the epitaph of every real Mother you could carve this simple sentence: "She lived for others." Notice, she not only gives us our life, but from then on she lives her life for us. Her motherhood is not something merely physical, in the womb. It is deeper, in the heart. I mean a real Mother. But from those who are Mothers only technically, that is physically, but who alas at the same time are sacrileges against the Sacrament of Motherhood—from these, deliver us, O Lord! If they are mothers, they are mothers only in the sense that Judas was an Apostle, and Pontius Pilate a Judge. Some of them are drunkards, and some are lazy, and some are domineering tyrants, and some have given their hearts into another man's hands. No matter what, the lives of such have localized like a boil in one ugly spot: Self. And in the dictionary of genuine Motherhood, self is the very last word on the last page.

But there is this consolation. To balance these unworthy Mothers, these third-rate stones cracked and full of flaws, we have what you might call beautiful synthetic gems, women who may not be Mothers by nature but certainly approach it by dedication and devotion. I am thinking of those maiden aunts who once were vivacious young girls, but father died, and

Mother became an invalid, and after that they spent the best years of their lives mothering their own Mother. I am thinking of those wives who longed for children, and when the cradle stayed empty they determined to fill their hearts, and became magnificent Mothers to the children they adopted I am thinking of all those kindly women who have to find their children in nieces and nephews, but to these they are Santa Claus at Christmas, Lady Bountiful on Birthdays, and Fairy Godmother all through the year, finding their happiness in bringing happiness to the youngsters. I am thinking of those other women who have nothing to give to other people's children but their lives, like the consecrated nun in the classroom, who spends hundreds and hundreds of hours each year amid freckles and curls and lisps, and who knew about bubble-gum long before the parents ever heard of it. Does not some of the golden glory of Motherhood's shining candle fall upon such as these?

Still, today the doorbells ring, and the telegrams are delivered, and the carnations bloom in buttonholes, to honor Mother in the ordinary sense—that extraordinary being who is the purest tabernacle of human love. There is a phrase, and you hear it a great deal, about the indispensable man. Mother is really the indispensable woman. A Mother who perhaps groans through the pangs of childbirth, but then wears a weak but shining smile, because she feels snuggled in the hollow of her arms, a new life, a tiny traveller who has safely made his way across the frail bridge of birth, a child woven of her own flesh and blood and bone, so small and sweet and lovable and her very own! A Mother who went on to weary her feet carrying us when our little feet were too weak to carry ourselves! A Mother who went without sleep many a night trying to bring sleep to us! A Mother who later on was always there setting the table when we were hungry, bending over our bed when we were sick, picking us up when we fell, cheering us when we were sad, forgiving us when we were bad, and more than once standing between us and the towering form of an angry father. Oh, a Mother is a candlestick with a hundred different golden lights, a fountain with a hundred different silver spurts, and we need them all!

Now, everything in life is designed for a purpose. A thermometer is made to register temperatures; a lawnmower, to cut grass; but a Mother's heart must have been made by God for sacrifice. In each pilgrimage to the altar of Motherhood she leaves upon it something of her youth and beauty. However there are compensations. Perhaps she is not now the radiant figure that once walked down the wedding aisle. But she sees that flowerlike grace living again in youthful Irene. Perhaps at the end of the day her eyes are dull and work-weary. But she sees her own youth dancing again in Michael's merry eyes.

There is comfort too, the way they depend upon her, like the little girl who was skipping along at her Mother's side, and suddenly tripped on a stone, and then got up and said, "Mommy, why don't you look where I'm going?" There is humor in their childish subterfuges, like the little lad who said, "Mom, if this house was burning down, you know who I'd save first? Yes, if this room was on fire, I'd rush in and save you! . . . Mom, kin I have a dime?" There is immeasurable and unspeakable sorrow in their early death, like a flower torn up from its roots in the Mother's heart;

like that little first grader who came running home from school on St. Valentine's Day with a Valentine in his hand. He had colored the red heart himself, and was so anxious to get home to show it that he didn't see the oncoming car. When they picked him up, the paper heart was even a brighter red, but you could still read the scrawled title: "To Mom." Ah, when the bony fingers of death knock at a family's door, nobody feels—nobody can feel—the loss like Mother. She is losing something of herself.

But, praise God, most children live; only as we grow up, our Mother grows old. As we grow stronger, she grows weaker. She has brought us safely to maturity, and now her life begins to slow down like the propeller of a plane that has landed, revolving faintly before it finally stops. But then, when the snow of years and work and worry has whitened her hair, and perhaps has melted in tears through the deep lines on her loving face, and when her soul is a little weary of living and a bit homesick for heaven—surely we cannot look to her for help then! Then it is up to us to help her, to take her arm as she walks down the descending slope of life toward the sunset, and never leave her abandoned and alone!

But one day Mother dies, and we are alone. Yet who will say that we do not need a Mother still? Don't we need a Mother even more in the strong and headstrong days of manhood and womanhood, than we did in the faltering footsteps of childhood? Because now it may be a question not of breaking windows but of breaking Commandments; not of falling in a puddle with clean white suit, but of sprawling a clean soul in the mud-puddle of impurity; not of running home with a skinned knee, but of crawling home with a broken heart; not of fearing a whipping from an angry father, but of facing the Judgment of an Angry Lord—ah, God knows we still need a Mother! God knows? God knew, and so dying on the Cross, He gave us His Own: "Son, Behold Thy Mother!"

In Her, in Mary, we always have a Mother! Only slip off the years like a soiled and worn cloak, and kneel at her knee like a child! Whisper to her all those troubles of adult life that nobody sees, and nobody knows, and nobody ever suspects! Lift up your face, and even if it is dirty with sin she will look behind the dirt and see only the child she loves! Mother of God, for many of us our earthly Mother is gone; oh be our Mother still!

Focus on the Family

JUST DAD

If ever a saint needed a press agent, if ever a saint has come down the broad boulevard of the past, not marching down the center under the bright lights, but shyly shrinking in the shadows—that saint is Joseph. The lives of many saints have been spectacular fountains; St. Joseph's was a deep and quiet well. In the average "History of the World" he would be fortunate to rate a footnote. You see, he worked no miracles, wrote no Gospel, spoke not a single sentence that has survived. In Bethlehem he managed to keep out of the spotlight even when the spotlight was a star. In Nazareth, to all the other workmen of that tiny town, to the man who grew purple grapes up on the hill and the man who raised black olives down in the valley, to the shepherds and the potters and the village blacksmith, Joseph was just the village carpenter. Any day they could see him through the big open door of his shop, brawny arms and leather apron, whining saw and swishing plane, making the tables that held their frugal meals and the cradles that held their chubby babies. Any twilight they could see him, when the great red sunset came down over the clustered houses like a gorgeous awning, as he tossed aside his work apron, swung his cloak about him, shuffled out through the sawdust and shavings, and went striding up the road to the small cottage where the earthenware plates stood on the supper table, and Mary stood at the window watching. And every day the door would open and a little Boy would come running down the road to meet him. In view of Joseph's closeness to Jesus, it is a bit strange to realize that if you go through the galleries of Christian art you will find one hundred Madonnas to one Joseph. Read through the Canon of the Mass and you will come across strange saints' names that possibly you never heard before, like Chrysogonus and Felicitas and Perpetua, but no Joseph. The toiling Saint who coined his perspiration into pennies to support the Holy Family has become the Forgotten Man. But is not that just what happens to almost any father in any family?

Poets have braided together miles and miles of flowery lines about mother. Musicians have sat down at jangling pianos and tinkled off teary tunes on mother-love. Artists have copied her in her rocker, the soft hair like spun silver, the quiet, dignified dress, the caressing shawl, the frail, pale fingers—ah a really good mother deserves every bit of bunting that they can hang out in her honor!

But do not all these salutes to mother emphasize the obscurity of the man in the background? In picture or song or story how much tribute is ever given to father? Cartoonists may dedicate to him a comic strip, like "Bringing up Father." Department stores toward mid-June may suddenly start loving him from the bottom of their bulging stock-rooms up to the top of their clanging cash registers ... you might call this, "Ringing up Father." But on the whole he gets about as much attention and appreciation as we give to the water we drink or the air we breathe. It is the old human tendency to take the important for granted.

Yet these are the men—these fathers of families—who, more than anyone else, have made America. Some of them are miners working deep in the earth with a lamp in their caps and a pick in their hands. Some are linemen perched high on telephone poles, and with their wires and pliers weaving the miraculous net of communication. Some are architects bending over blueprints, sketching the skyscraper of tomorrow. Some are riveters with clattering drills, making blueprint lines come true in girders of steel. But all these men, lawyers or laborers, butchers or bakers or electric light men, are the sturdy pillars that support the achievements of America. Their breath is the smoke of mighty factories, their heartbeat is the pounding throb of giant dynamos, their voice is the roar of rumbling traffic, their medals—their medals are mostly spots of grease on overalls, or bloodstains on an operating gown. And yet we pay no special attention to these men, as we pay no special attention to the flagpole that holds up the flag. The Father of Our Country was a distinguished general and is a well-remembered hero. But the fathers of our country are just undistinguished millions of unappreciated men—often unappreciated even in their own families.

In the average family the father is treated pretty much like the furnace. (I do not mean you have to shake him down if you want something. Or that you have to watch him or he will go out. But, in passing let us admit here that there are drunken and unfaithful fathers, and let us pray that these prodigal fathers may quickly return to the merciful Son of God!) I mean that the average father, like the average furnace, is very much in the background. You see, the furnace serves obscurely. You never show if off before visitors. You come to take it for granted. You take what it gives but pay it no great heed—until something goes wrong with it. Then, if the furnace begins to flare up, everybody gets excited and a little scared. Well, if that is the only way Dad, too, can ever attract attention, I don't know whether you could blame him too much for occasionally blowing off a little steam. At least it reminds you he is there.

I suppose one reason why a father is seldom appreciated in his family is because none of them sees him at work. Oh, mother works hard, too, very hard, but—almost all her work is done under the eyes of the children. They see, they know, and in their limited way they appreciate. But Dad—why often he is up and out of the house before the children are out of bed. At lunch he is far away, eating from a dinner-pail or snatching a bite at a restaurant counter. They don't see the sweat pouring off him at his job, or the worries piling up on his desk, the disappointments, the pressure of a dead-line, the frustration of a dead-end, the personality clashes, and the rest.

And consider this. Mother does her work in an atmosphere of love, the home. Yes, the children can be irritating and noisy, and adorable nuisances, but even when they get in mother's hair they are still deep in mother's heart. They love her, and she would die for them. But Dad—he has to do his work in a world that is hardbitten and heartless, cold and cruel, where the only code is tooth and claw, where if you slip they trample over you to a higher job.

And, ironically enough, the more years the father spends out there working for them, the more patronizing his growing children become toward him. Well, maybe if you were to take your Dad out to dinner in a smart hotel, where the silverware is laid out on either side of the plate like an array of dentist instruments, perhaps he would not know which fork spearheaded each course, but never forget he was putting food on your plate when you could not be trusted with any fork. Maybe at a modern dance, Dad would be hopelessly out of place—not knowing a rhumba from a conga or a samba—but never forget he was putting shoes on your feet when your only dance was a toddling two-step and a tumble, then another two steps and another tumble. And if you have attained a higher education than he ever had, the chances are you climbed up to it over his bent back as he toiled through the years.

But to some young folks Dad is just old-fashioned, and to others—well, they just forget. He is something like an engineer on a train. The train comes roaring into the station; the passengers pour out. They never dream of even glancing up at the man who brought them swiftly and safely in. Isn't it pretty much the same with Dad and his grown children? There he is in the cab up there, grimy and tired after bringing them up the steep grades and round the dangerous curves—but they step out of the train jaunty and smart and eager, without even a wave to the man who brought them in. The important thing is they have arrived; they must hurry on; they have a date with destiny... their career, their life!

True, if you buy a ticket on a train, at the end of a journey you don't have to shake hands and congratulate the engineer. But if you think any grown son or daughter who turns over to Dad part of the pay envelope each week is doing enough...! Enough? Do you really believe that can ever pay for the hardships and the heartaches, the sweat and the sacrifice, the golden years he left behind on the road—why nothing can begin to pay for that but realizing it, appreciating it, and loving him for it!

For heaven's sake, don't go up to your Dad now and begin to tell him what a grand old fellow he really is. Because I'm afraid he would look at you quizzically from under his bushy brows and remove his pipe, and mutter to himself, "Either she has a hot fever or she is out for a little cold cash." No—don't say it with words. Say it with your whole attitude, your thoughtfulness, your kindness, your affection. Let your whole life say, "Our father, who art on earth, and who givest us our daily bread, forgive our trespass in taking you for granted!"

Focus on the Family

FAMILY FIREWORKS

Ever since the Holy Family was gathered in the Stable on that bleakest and brightest of all Christmas Days, Christmas has been essentially a family feast. New Year's may be for visiting; but behind the soft curtains and around the cheery fireside America loves to spend Christmas at home. By this time almost all the world has contributed to making this family celebration the warm and picturesque event that it is. We took jolly old Santa Claus on lend-lease from Holland. We transplanted the gay and glittering Christmas Tree from Germany. We borrowed the stockings hung over the fireplace from France. Ireland lit the Christmas candles in our windows. England piled the Christmas cards in the postman's bag. The angels over Judea gave us the Christmas carols; and the tiny crib with its colorful statuettes we owe to Italy and St. Francis.

11. *Pennies*

In some parts of the world, like the Virgin Islands and Brazil, Christmas is a bang-bang affair with the accent on fireworks. They welcome Christ at Christmas the way we welcome the Fourth of July. I still think that a flaming poinsettia has it all over a fiery pinwheel. In fact I think that the very best welcome we could give the Newborn King might be to abolish altogether *fireworks in the family.* And we could begin that welcome right now and without any fear of rushing the season, because *this* welcome, this preparation for Christmas is fundamentally an interior preparation of the soul.

By family fireworks I mean episodes like this. Somebody mislays Dad's battered slippers or his odorous pipe or his evening paper, and zoom! he goes up in the air like a sky-rocket, exploding in a burst of wrath that fairly drips fire. Christmas may be coming but it is no longer Silent Night. Or, a couple of sisters along the sidelines, who feel that "Peace on Earth, Good Will to Men" does not include women, begin to bicker and quarrel, and this word leads to that, and tit for tat, till the whole thing sounds like the spit-spat of a couple of fire-crackers. By way of background obligato, some families have among them a voice that never would be mistaken for one of the Herald Angels. It is a dusty, discontented voice, and in the way of fireworks resembles most one of those firecrackers that has been broken in the middle like a cigarette, and therefore doesn't go off with an honest little bang but just hisses out. Just so, this big brother doesn't explode. He merely sits there hissing through his teeth, and grumbling "Have we got *that* for supper again?"

Similarly, in these pre-Christmas days you would think that anything like the bark of small fire-arms is hardly the proper welcome for the Prince of Peace. Yet you will find in some homes individuals whose temper works on a hair-trigger mechanism. These are the cap-pistols, the touchy people. A mere touch—the least fancied offence—and they go off, and the air all around them is blue—and not just smoke either. Of course they will tell you that you must understand them; they really don't mean anything by it. Well, maybe it is only a blank cartridge, but just the same the sudden sharp blast makes everybody nervous, if not actually scared. The trouble with these touchy, unpredictable people is they have to be labelled like medicine bottles—with directions just how they are to be taken. They are like landing fields: you have to have a weather report before you go in. No wonder Santa Claus sneaks down the chimney and first takes a look around.

Other homes are not content with Christmas candles; they also have Roman Candles. These are the naggers; and a nagger is a person who gives a new meaning to the old adage, "There's no place like home!" because when she is on the job there certainly isn't. In the arsenal of family fireworks, the nagger is the Roman Candle because complaints and abuse pour out of her in spurt after spurt of hot flame. And when at last you think it is all over—your mistake! It isn't. Somehow there always seems to be just one more shot left in the Roman Candle, and there always *is* one more last word in the nagger.

Then there are families which, left to themselves, might give the New-Born Christ the perfect welcome of a happy and harmonious fire-side. *If left to them-*

selves—but that is leaving out the in-laws (maybe we should call them outlaws.) You see, sometimes a husband or a wife will have a set of little hidden grievances lined up like a string of firecrackers. But nothing much happens until some meddling in-law comes along and plays the punk. Please do not think I am descending to slang. I am staying very technical, even pyrotechnical if you will. But this rash, intruding in-law is very like a piece of punk in that she is all burned up about somebody else's business, proceeds to ignite husband against wife or wife against husband, and then when the snap and crackle of the battle is on, she withdraws, glowing with delight at the fireworks she has started.

Other families, if the Christ-Child chose to come to them at Christmastime, would welcome Him with a Silent Night that was not at all a Holy Night. This situation is very much like a big jumbo firecracker that doesn't go off. You know it has been lit; you fear the fuse is smouldering; but nothing happens. Yet the very silence is dangerous; you are afraid to go too near because it may explode in your very face. In a family, this is the ominous silence of hate. It could be two brothers or two sisters who refuse to speak. But over the whole house hangs that strained silence, that tense vacuum, that secretly burning bitterness. This is the worst of all, and who doubts that to this the Little Christ would prefer His Stable, and the company of the gentle beasts and the warm-hearted shepherds?

Well, what is the *answer* to these un-Christmas-like backgrounds for the Christmas Feast? Are you just thinking, "Gee, I wish so-and-so at home were here now! Does this fit her!" I am afraid that like an umbrella it may fit any of us. The best answer

FAMILY FIREWORKS

might be a question. Am I one of these sky-rockets that go up in the air in flaming anger, or one of these touchy little cap-pistols, or an endless Roman Candle nagger who would fight an echo for the last word? Am I? There is nothing like a little humility to make a big change in a home. If the Stable of Bethlehem was a cave, I suppose the Shepherds had to stoop in order to get in. Anyone who wants to come close to Christ has to stoop a little. The proud, whose noses are elevated like an anti-aircraft gun, cannot see their own faults. They cannot see the entrance to the cave either. They stay outside.

Besides, the Holy Family in Bethlehem's bleak Stable was a Family, not just three individuals under the same roof. And a family—any family—is no place for independence, but rather for interdependence. Its feast is *not* the Fourth of July, but Christmas. A family is no place for these people who are always asserting their rights. "I want my rights! That's all I ask—justice!" You do—well, just how far do you want justice? All the way up? Up to the Throne of God? I think most of us would settle for a little mercy there. The family is no place for a dictator who is all temper, nor for a prima-donna who is all temperament. After all, the only fireworks over the Stable was a Star. A Star that helped bring others nearer to Our Lord.

On greeting cards they usually paint the Christmas Star as a tiny golden burst of flashing rays, so that at first glance you might mistake it for a Fourth of July sparkler. And that should be the pattern for family fireworks. There will of course always be some domestic misunderstandings, some minor clashes. Where people's lives run so closely side by side, there is bound to be occasional jostling, bumping, stepping on sensitive toes, and occasionally a head-on collision. But if these family tiffs *must* be, let them be like the Fourth of July sparkler: a little heat, a tiny flare-up, a few sparks, and it is soon over and no harm done.

The point I am trying to make in all this is, that as Christ stands on the threshold of your home ready to come in for Christmas, it is much more important to do your part in the preparation of the family rather than in the mere decoration of the home. Hang your heart with holly, not merely the house. Kind words in the family are better than Christmas candles in the window, which after all give most of their cheer to passers-by. *Emptying* a narrow soul of petty spites and jealousies is much more in the true Christmas spirit than filling a conventional stocking. The family tree comes before the Christmas Tree and if some of the branches are a bit snarled and tangled, this is the season to straighten them out. Family feuds have spoiled more Christmas dinners than the choicest of foods ever made.

Some people may think that in these pre-Christmas musings I have read you the Gospel of Christmas according to Charles Dickens rather than according to Jesus Christ. But this *is* the Gospel of Christ. I grant it is not the lofty—and vague— spirituality of the stratosphere. It is more the homespun spirituality of the sidewalk and the stairs and the living-room. It emphasizes the little things that hurt Our Little Lord—like the pricking of the straws, not the piercing of the nails. It concentrates on the home because Charity begins at home. And Charity in that sense never meant a dime clanked into a beggar's cup nor a philanthropic check flourished off for some fund. That word Charity originally meant in English—as it still does in Latin—love.

It can of course, and should, express itself in gifts, particularly in the approaching joyous season. But some Christmas gifts are only an external formality, very much like the popcorn and the peppermint canes hung on the Christmas Tree. Real Christmas gifts are like the flowers and fruit of a cherry tree: they spring from deep within. Aren't the best gifts those of the heart? Therefore these days when we are smuggling our mysterious bundles into secret hiding places, we should remember that while a year's supply of scented soap may be a very welcome gift, a year's supply of consideration, thoughtfulness, tenderness, charity, will be more welcome still! A year's subscription to this magazine or that may be ideal, but a year's subscription to life as lived by a kindly, considerate, loving member of the family would be appreciated even more!

It is all for the sake of the Little Stranger in the Manger. It is a new kind of Christmas welcome—a real one. Because between the inner peace of your conscience washed sweet and clean, and the outer peace of love for those around you, the true spirit of Christmas will swing and ring in your heart like a merry bell!

Focus on the Family

THE YOUNG FOLKS AT HOME

Today in many a family the major problem is the minors, those slender saplings of young manhood and those frail blossoms of young womanhood whom we conveniently classify as "the teenagers." These young people represent life just poured out and still bubbling and fizzing; and only a man through whose veins crawls cold vinegar instead of warm blood would deny that youth has a special right to recreation. The difficulty seems to be that too often youth's recreational activities are passive, and too seldom its recreational headquarters is the home!

Home? The magazines still feature flamboyant, technicolor pages of "How to Make Your Home Attractive", but some people just don't want to stay home as long as the other places stay open. As the young society matron said, with just the slightest lift of her delicately curved eye-brows, "Home? I was born in a hospital. I was educated at Boarding School and College. I was married in a City Hall; I live in a hotel; I shall be buried from a funeral parlor—what is this *home*?" Even in poorer and saner circles, home threatens to fade into the twilight of fine and forgotten things. The housing shortage after the Second World War, for all its pity, was not half so tragic as the shortage of homes. No wonder that for recreation, the center of gravity, or rather the center of gaiety, seems to be shifting from the home to the joint with the juke box.

Gone are the days—and from a better land, I know—when the young folks would gather round the family piano and sing singable songs or play hilarious games in the parlor. Parlor? Nowadays they call it the Living Room, but very little living is done there anymore. Now you could call it the leaving room; on the way out. After the evening meal it is likely to be as empty as a politician's promise. And you will find parents who have not the vaguest notion where the young teenager is going when she gleefully slams the door. Who her companions are, what she intends to do, when she will return—these are minor matters blown away as casually as smoke from a cigarette.

And this, mind you, by parents who take a deep interest in their children, but alas the interest is mostly physical. Their children shall never lack for vitamins, but as for virtue—alas, that is presumed, like a radio in a car. Actually they pay more attention to the youngsters' carrots than to their character. I wonder if this is not one of the many woeful heritages of wars, first the need, then the tendency to leave young people too much on their own. It started in the days of the woman welder in her slacks and goggles, laying steel plates on the deck of a ship instead of being in a housedress and laying dinner plates on a family table. When it was necessary to build a battling America of copper and steel, we allowed another America of flesh and blood, a more precious one too, the living, breathing America of our children, to suffer through serious neglect.

The remedy—and it is plain to read on the prescription pad of common sense—is that now parents must strive to make the home not just the headquarters but the heart of their children's life. It won't be easy. Listening to the giddy chatter with their friends may give you an earache, and wincing at the peril to your furniture may give you a headache, and picking up after them may give you a backache, but won't it be worth it if later on it saves you a heartache?

However, there is another angle to the recreation of youth. Outside of rock'n roll (and if that is a dance, so is St. Vitus)—have you never noticed that so many of the diversions of the young are not youthfully active but lazily passive? I mean that in too many instances the young people do not entertain themselves but prefer to be entertained by others. This, of course, is a product of our modern age where so many of the things we want can be done for us. For instance, if you want to wish a friend a happy

THE YOUNG FOLKS AT HOME

birthday, you do not have to riffle through a rack of greeting cards, buy a stamp, poise your pen and stare out the window wondering just what you will say. You need merely pick up the phone and a uniformed boy will appear on the spot and warble your greetings for you.

In a sense this same sort of thing has percolated down to the recreation of youth. If *they* want music and song, instead of trying to sing themselves, they merely twiddle a radio dial and languidly listen to some pair of teary tonsils and a voice like a melancholy moo. If they want entertainment, instead of making the fun themselves, they slump in a chair and dully stare at shadows on a TV screen. If they have a half hour on their hands to kill, though only the Lord knows why the poor half-hour should be murdered, they seldom have an absorbing hobby, so they idly flip over the pages of a picture magazine with their brain in neutral.

Now it is bad enough that these recreations should be idly passive and characterized by the empty stare of a cow, but it is worse when you realize that these same diversions, like cows, can stray over the borderline and trample the delicate flowers of youthful modesty. Take some of the picture magazines, for instance. In the front pages it may feature news of the week, which is perfectly all right; but in the back it is liable to feature nudes of the week, which is absolutely all wrong. Take recreational reading. Some of your best selling best-sellers are only mud sandwiches between covers. Dirt? Nowadays you cannot tell from the product whether it came from a publishing house or a real estate company. And too often you will find the dirtiest books in the daintiest of fingers. Take the motion pictures. We are given some magnificent movies, but we are given too many that are scanty in costume, suggestive in situation and daring in dialogue. In 1849 California was a place where miners got gold out of dirt by using a kind of screen. A century later, Hollywood, California, is still a place where they get gold out of dirt; only they keep the gold, send us the dirt, and use a different kind of screen.

Radio and television should be the cleanest of the entertainment media because you do not go forth and seek them out: you turn a knob and as it were invite the people on the program into your living room, your family circle. But who has not heard comedians who have sniped at purity not with double-barrel guns but with double-meaning gags?

You say all these are only little things? Yes, they are little things—little termites boring away ever so gradually but ever so surely at the pillars of purity on which rests the American home! Nothing which constantly affects a nation's morals is a little thing. Nothing which constantly influences impressionable youth is a little thing. Nothing which provokes widespread adulation and imitation is a little thing. I wonder if we oldsters realize how things which may bounce harmlessly off the armor-plate of hard-boiled adults, can easily pierce and fester in the soft, warm imagination of youngsters? I wonder if we realize that delinquency (just a big word for a child gone wrong) is *never* a sudden and swift drop into evil, but a gradual one-step-at-a-time affair; a *little* step but downward; a *slight* influence, but bad. It seems to me that unless there is sane supervision of these passive entertainments by the parents, such recreation will chip away at the very ideals the parents are trying to build.

How about the active recreations? As paramount in popularity among the social diversions, the teenagers would nominate dancing. And there are people who fervidly maintain that this dancing, however cramped in space or acrobatic in style, should still be centered in the home. This is a minority opinion not shared by the people living on the floor below. The sad truth is that many homes are no more able to provide youth with the facilities for such recreation than they are to provide youth with facilities for education. We need schools; we also need clubs. Is it not true that if we had more parish social clubs with juke-boxes and dancing and soft-drinks, we should have less young people going giggling after fun into doubtful and shadowy places? Of course in parish dances, the danger is never at the dance. This, to be sure, is carefully supervised. But for the parents, the danger lies, and the anxiety lies awake, wondering about "After the ball is over," and "I'll take you home, Kathleen."

The best way to insure that Kathleen does not come home by way of Australia, delayed by a little spin, a little gin and who knows what sin, is obviously for the mothers to insist on a return at a reasonable hour. Naturally there will be a protest; naturally your Geraldine will whine that her girl friends, Barbara and Patricia, have no such tyrannical and childish curfew to obey. "All the other mothers allow their daughters to stay out; everybody does it." And the mother who demurs is made to feel she is a Mrs. Hitler. You notice the whole argument is based on numbers. The teen-ager shudders at the prospect of being different or alone. I have known a group of mothers who met this united front of the bobby-sox brigade by uniting themselves. First, telephones tinkled between four or five houses; polite inquiries were exchanged; and it turned out that each of the mothers had wanted her youngster home at an early hour, but had never insisted because she had always felt she stood alone. Now each of the united mothers can say, "Look at Barbara, look at Patricia—they have to be home early." Quite a telling point!

Outside one of the largest night clubs in New York a ten foot sign shrieks: "Nowhere in the world can you enjoy so glorious an evening at so moderate a cost!" Those words would look better on a ten-inch wall-motto hanging in the place where they are true: the home. Let us put the emphasis on good times there. Even in an atomic world, our first concern should be our family. In fact, if we make our family better, we do something practical toward the making of a better world. There is a grand simplicity about good times at home that mellows and betters us far above commercialized amusement. It makes the family a more wholesome family, and that is a practical contribution to a pretty dizzy world.

You probably have heard about the lad who was quite the genius at putting together jig-saw puzzles. This particular Sunday morning he asked his father for a new one. The Dad happened to be reading the Sunday Supplement, and there was a map of the world in colors. He tore it into small pieces, handed them to Junior and said, "Here, put this together. This will jig-saw puzzle you." Do you know that boy was back in an amazingly short time with every piece in place? The father said, "Say—what did you do, buy another paper?" "No, Dad," said the boy. "You see when you were tearing up that map of the world I noticed that on the other side was a full-page picture of a family group. So—I first went to work on the family. And I found out that when I had the family straightened out, the world had taken care of itself." It will, too.

Focus on the Family

MOTHER-IN-LAW MUSINGS

In a wedding the bride marches down the aisle on the arm of one man and out on the arm of another. Apart from this temporary escort service that he gives his daughter to the altar-rail, and the wincing expenses he totals up after the party is over, the father of the bride (like that of the groom) is a fairly remote and wispy figure in the marriage pageant. The mother has no place in the ceremony at all. But sometimes her disturbing shadow falls across all the radiant gaiety. Thank God, only sometimes, but the "sometimes" should be never.

It happens when, for example, a daughter has been supporting her mother. That is the daughter's duty. Then, she meets the boy of her dreams and wants to get married. This is the daughter's right. The boy and she are perfectly willing to go on helping mother, but the mother cannot bear to let the girl go. After all, for five years the girl has been almost her personal slave. If the daughter brings the boy to the house, the mother not only gives him an Admiral Byrd sub-Zero reception; she gives him a look as though she were trying to recall, "Now, in what Post Office did I see his picture?"

Why is she opposed to the young man? Because he is a drunkard? No. Because he is a ne'er-do-well? No. Because he is a shady character, possibly a criminal? No. The only thing she really has against him is that he is a man; a man who threatens to destroy Mother's little monopoly on a devoted daughter. So what happens? They have to keep company on the sly, which isn't good. And as the years go on (I said years) the man gets disgusted, the girl gets grey, and the marriage gets a burial permit in the sad cemetery of tragic romances. For mothers like these we don't keep Mother's Day; we keep Bastille Day.

Sometimes it is her son that the possessive mother tethers with the silken threads of love. He may break away, but she doesn't like it. Not long ago I met a very upset young mother in the back of the church, before a novena service. "What's wrong?" I asked. "Oh Father, I just turned to dip my finger into the Holy Water Font, and my three year old disappeared right under my eyes." "Well," I said, "the child is around somewhere. What did the youngster look like?" "He is blond and he is wearing a blue sailor suit." So I went over and told an usher that if he noticed a particularly small sailor floating around to anchor him. I started to look about myself, but the next thing I knew, there was the happy mother marching down the side aisle, the little boy's hand in her glove, like a velvet vise—he wasn't slipping away any more! As I passed, I whispered, "Where was he?" She whispered back, "With another woman!" It seems that while the lad was prowling round the church, some sensible lady noticed he was alone, figured he was lost, and wisely took him to the back of the church, and waited for someone to claim him.

Somehow I could not help seeing another scene twenty years hence, when the blond young man would go gaily off with another woman to the chime of wedding bells. I wonder will the mother be upset and angry then, too? Angry because she has lost something precious. Will she follow the wedding march out of the church as though it were a funeral march? Obviously, she will have to make an adjustment. Every mother whose son becomes a husband has to. She has to realize that once the young couple have soldered their lives together with the silver rivets of "I do ... I do," her relationship to her child has changed. Of course the girl was not good enough for her boy (what girl could be?) but once her finger flashes his gold ring, the back seat suddenly becomes Mother's seat, while the young wife takes her proper place up front alongside her husband. It is hard, but it is the inexorable law of nature and of God.

At this a good mother will sigh a little, maybe secretly cry a little, but will not try any back seat driving. She knows that a mother's strange and sublime vocation is to give and to give all her life long. Even her children are not hers forever. She has seen the boy wear a score of pair of shoes in his life, from baby booties to almost landing barges, and finally in one pair he walks away from her to lead his own life with somebody else. She has brought him along from toddling weakness to towering strength; and now with that unique holiness which makes a good mother's heart a fragrant altar from which one sacrifice after another ascends like incense—having spent her life sacrificing for him, she now sacrifices him himself!

Unfortunately there is another type of mother. They used to say that it takes two to make a marriage; a single girl and an anxious mother. Far more deadly is the interfering mother who breaks marriages. She wants to pretend even after the marriage that nothing has changed; that her baby boy is still her baby boy, while this girl—oh, she is nice enough and means well enough, but of course no one can really come between me and my son. He would never let anyone. Why, he would die for me! Yes, he would. But if he could give his life for only one of you two, he should give it for his wife. She must be forever first in his duty and in his devotion. The Sacrament of Matrimony cannot evict the Fourth Commandment, but it does take precedence in the home.

It is always sad when people do not recognize that things have changed, and go on acting as though they had not. Pity the poor old opera star, the slightly mildewed soprano, standing unsteadily in the arch of the grand piano, the once rich golden voice now a thin brassy quaver, standing on her tonsil's tip-toes and desperately reaching for a high C and hitting only a thin radio beep—oh, why doesn't that old fool know, that, like the old grey mare, she isn't what she used to be? And do you know who says this? Maybe out there in the audience, the very mother who doesn't know things have changed with her, too, she who is still trying to run the life of her son, her married son, run his life and his wife and home and family, by remote control perhaps, but oh, such power steering!

In driving if the car skids a bit, the theory is to steer the car gently in the direction of the skid. But in a marriage if something goes a bit wrong, the interfering brand of mother-in-law wants to whip the wheel completely around in the opposite direction. What the girl did was wrong, and this is right! Poor mother, so reluctant to release her boy forever, so resentful that another woman should take him away—so that secretly (or sometimes openly) she opposes the girl in almost every step. At the wedding reception such a mother-in-law should wear a tiny pin of crossed swords to symbolize that she is pledged to fighting the wife; to contradiction every inch of the way. Do you recall the woman St. Francis de Sales used to speak about? When she drowned they searched for her body upstream even though the current swept fiercely down. They felt that even her corpse would manage to contradict the river.

Mind you, what the mother offers in way of advice may be logical, prudent, wise, in fact the only common sense course. But giving the best advice can be the worst procedure, because when you open it, the music box seems to play "You should have thought of this yourself, you sweet little fool." There is always castor-oil hidden somewhere in the orange juice. Besides, what sharp eyes you have, mother! Meet an optician socially and he instinctively notes whether your glasses are crooked or not; meet a dentist at a dance, and I suppose he does not look soulfully into your eyes but clinically at your eye-teeth. I know I have attended a barber on a sick call, and when I finished and turned to go, he said, "By the way, who gave you that haircut?" Each to his own business; and for so long that boy has been his mother's business that actually she probably does understand him better than does his bride. It makes no difference. When you turn over a business, how often does the new firm let you continue to run it?

Interference has its place—in football; never in somebody else's family. Of course there will be domestic problems. Practically every new home, every young family is going to tilt perilously on a rough sea of bills, sickness, temper, worry, weariness, children, misunderstandings—but if there is genuine love in those two hearts and the grace of God in those two souls, they will weather the high-running waves even with a kind of eager zest! When the man grows discouraged (as men are prone to) the wise woman will reassure him into confidence bright as a new coin. When the woman feels lonely (as women are likely to) the alert man will give her the attention, the appreciation, the companionship she instinctively craves. But it is always best for even the best of mothers to stay outside that closed, small, sacred circle of the wedding ring.

In this connection a flip lip might be tempted to quip that St. Joseph was distinguished among other things for this: that he had a Saint for a mother-in-law: good St. Anne. I, for one, doubt that St. Joseph was unique in this. Do we forget that every mother-in-law was first a mother, with (let us hope) a mother's normal good sense and better than average virtue? Actually the majority of mothers, when their son or daughter founds a home, have the wisdom to stay on the sidelines and do not try to referee the game, much less get into the scrimmages. They may and do help the new household, of course. In fact the babysitting concession of America is about equally divided between bobby-soxers and grandmothers; only the grandmothers do it for nothing. In other words, the average mother goes right on sacrificing herself even unto the second generation.

She is not a mother-in-law; she is a mother-in-love, in love with a whole new family. She is no longer the jealous spotlight, fiercely concentrating her rays upon her darling, holding him (or her) in a small white circle of possession. Now she is more like the sunset, her love spreading out like a beautiful fan, broad, mellow, serene, betokening the happy close to life's troubled day.

Thou Shalt Not!

SOULS IN PAWN

In this modern age when undertakers have become morticians, and barbers tonsorial artists, and street cleaners sanitary engineers, it is reassuring to remember that a pawn-shop is still a pawn-shop. The painted wooden Indian no longer stands sentinel before the cigar stores. The huge shoe that used to swing in the wind outside the cobbler's door is now likely to be a pink neon sign proclaiming "Ye Bootie Shoppe." But, at least it is nice to recall that, almost alone in a changing world, the three balls still gleam above the pawn shop—the gilded shamrock glittering over the city street.

I bring up this matter of pawn-shops because December 6 happens to be the Feast of the Saint who is the patron of pawn-shops, at least in an indirect way. His name is St. Nicholas. Now everybody knows that through the friction of use and the erosion of time, St. Nicholas has become Saint Niklaus, and finally Santa Claus; though the original St. Nicholas, a kindly old Bishop of southern Italy, would have blinked gentle astonishment at the notion of chauffering chimney-minded reindeer on a gusty Christmas Eve. However, he did have the habit of leaving presents with something of a flourish. Once he tossed three purses of gold into a poor man's window so that the three daughters would have a dowry and could enter into honorable marriage. Well, the story got around, and naturally it grew, and by the time it reached Lombardy in the North, the Bishop had heaved into the window three bulging bags of gold. Who should then adopt St. Nicholas as their patron—he was dead by now—but the money lenders of Lombardy! And over their banking houses blossomed the three golden balls which the cynical interpret as "two to one you won't get it back."

But there is a very sober side to a pawn-shop. Every pawn-shop window is a pathetic little history of humanity—of human vanities and hobbies and treasures and failures. Behind the black-grilled gates folded across the front, somebody's happiness is there in jail, waiting to be bailed out. Look at the windows: watches and fishing rods and cameras and diamond rings; pearl-handled revolvers and blue-barrelled rifles; binoculars that however powerful still could see no hope in the future; the inevitable mandolin that once knew merry tinkling nights; in fact musical instruments enough to equip a little orchestra. You wonder what the window would look like if all the owners took their places behind the weird collection. And inside the shop perhaps a man with a black coat and a cold appraising eye, and a faint, carved smile like the smile of the king in a pack of cards.

Every now and then they pick up a dead vagrant in the Bowery of New York or the South End of Boston, and in his pocket perhaps nothing but a couple of pawn tickets. You can read the story there. He gave up something valuable, maybe a handsome ring; and now all that is left is a soiled bit of paper. Oh, there was something else, there were the few dollars he got, but they slipped through his fingers like water—water or something stronger. But isn't this the very process of sin? In a way, the Devil is a Pawn-broker. He takes your soul, your innocence, your clean conscience, sparkling and clear as a white diamond, and he gives you some sensual pleasure that is gone like the flare of a match, and you have nothing but a soiled memory, a little stub of remorse that never lets you forget that you have given up something precious, and you will never be really happy till you get it back—*because it belongs to you!*

Some patrons of the pawn-shop redeem their little diamond regularly—say once a month. They have it for a few days and then, after a wild time, they go on the rocks and their diamond goes in hock. So it goes with their little treasure month after month; in and out, in and out. But most of the time it is in the pawn-broker's safe, and they carry nothing with them but a nagging reminder. There are people like that, too, on the street of life, with souls in pawn. They don't really own their own soul. If possession is nine-tenths of the law, nine-tenths of the time it is in possession of the Devil. I mean people who come

12. *Pennies*

not to grated doors of the pawn shop, but to the grilled screen of the confessional, perhaps every couple of months, and redeem their shining innocence, their peace of conscience, their soul. But a few days later, they have pawned it for pleasure, and the rest of the month they do not have it—have nothing but a guilty conscience to remind them that their soul is in the Devil's keeping.

However, underline this difference heavily. If you leave anything in a pawn-shop, say even an overcoat, your Uncle there will take better care of it than you would. It will be hung very neatly, securely locked against thieves, carefully stored away so that it will never become a Blueplate Special for moths. You'll get your pawned overcoat back in a superb condition. But it isn't like that in the Devil's Pawn-shop. The more often your soul goes over the counter of sin, and the longer it stays in that musty, mouldering vault of bad habits, the more it deteriorates; the thinner, the weaker, the more flimsy and sleazy it becomes. And when you really need it, it just won't stand up.

If you were to ask what is the best season for the pawn-shop, I would tell you that in times of depression, pawn-brokers are never depressed. It is the same with the soul. In periods of personal depression, or discouragement, people will slink into the little shop of sin, who in a happier hour would briskly pass it by. Self-pity is the side door of sin. It isn't all lit up on the front like Glamorous Temptation, but it gets us in just the same. When we are down in spirits, our only hope is to go up in spirit to God. If something has got us down, the best thing is to go down farther—on our knees. It may not settle our problem, but it will settle our soul. And when we stand up, we shall be better able to stand up to our trouble.

If depression is the pawn-shop's best season, Monday is its busiest day. Ask the pay envelope—the pay envelope that was so fat on Friday night, but over the week-end went through some strenuous reducing exercises. Too much dice or cards, dogs or horses, Scotch or Rye—this was the dumb-bell reducing routine that took the bulge off the little bankroll. And by the same token, isn't the soul weakest over the week-end? Aren't more souls sold out, more sin committed, innocence bartered, self-respect surrendered, ideals given up, resolutions broken, promises forgotten, and commandments shattered *over the week-end?* Wouldn't it be better if we all took a tip from experience and were doubly careful on doubly dangerous days? This is not a sour indictment of wholesome recreation. Real religion flourishes under the bright banner of Joy. But like mushrooms and toadstools, there is often a deadly difference between pleasure and happiness. It simply means we have to pick our recreations carefully, especially over the week-end.

Theoretically, every article in a pawn-shop is waiting to be *redeemed*. Did you ever wonder what happens to the unredeemed articles? After a certain time they are disposed of at public auction, almost like a little General Judgment. But first the owner has to be warned. He is given a chance to salvage what he has given over. God acts in pretty much the same way with people who have given over their souls to sin, people whose souls are in pawn. He gives His own warning. Sometimes it is death tapping on the shoulder and beckoning away someone who only yesterday strode briskly at our side. Sometimes it is a spell of sickness flinging us on our back and letting us see how different the world looks when viewed from the horizontal. But always it whispers, "This life is only a bridge between a brief here and an eternal hereafter. How foolish to concentrate on the bridge and forget the goal!"

But what good would be the warning—that souls in sin, souls in pawn, must be redeemed before that Final Auction, if we do not have the means to redeem them? True enough, of course we have not. But across the scarlet horizon of the world of sin, out of the merciful bosom of God there walks toward us His only Son, whose very name is "The Redeemer." The prophets of old stood in their high towers and with straining eyes looked for and longed for His coming. That is what the very word "Advent" means; and during that sacred season we rehearse their vigil, our own eyes fixed on the golden speck of the oncoming Christmas Star. He is coming—our Redeemer —who counts not the cost of the Redemption.

Judas Iscariot was to ask cynically, "How much for a God?" And they counted out thirty clinking pieces of silver. If Jesus Christ had been asked by His Heavenly Father, "How much for man?" How much will You pay to *redeem* him?" Our Saviour would have answered, "I will give every drop of My Blood." And He did—poured out His Blood like rubies from the Cross. And now through Christ's redemptive

Blood the Sinner receives the price (the grace of true sorrow and purpose of amendment) to buy back his soul from Satan.

Shall we still go on treating Christ as though He were worth only thirty pieces of silver—selling Him and our soul over the counter of sin? We can best answer that by treasuring our soul as it deserves. There is no jewel in any pawn-shop in the world one tenth so precious. A pure soul is the pearl of great price that one day will buy heaven!

Thou Shalt Not!

FOREST FIRE

As all the Christian world knows, next Wednesday is called Ash Wednesday. That evening in every Catholic Church you can hear a strong and stirring sermon, and watch a grim and symbolic ceremony as the priest dips his thumb into the powdery grey ashes and traces a smudgy cross on every forehead, young and old, smooth and wrinkled, as they kneel at the altar rail. But Sunday must come before Wednesday, and fire before ashes, so this Sunday suppose we first turn our thoughts to the fire. What makes me turn my thoughts in that direction is that recently I happened to see a forest fire, and I don't think I'll ever forget it. Once Moses heard the Voice of God coming from a burning bush. Today may that Voice still speak to us out of the mental picture of a thousand blazing trees, brush and bush and timber all aflame like a red exploding sunset!

FOREST FIRE

If you could view a forest fire at a safe distance, I think that your first reaction, shameful and ironic though it seems, would be breathless admiration. As sheer spectacle a forest fire is one of the most gorgeous sights in the world. Picture a riotous army of marching fire, marching to the cheering roar of the wind, marching to the crackle of burning branches like the crackle of drunken rifles, marching to the hissing of sparks that go streaking up like tracer bullets and then hover overhead like giant swarms of golden bees, marching like an army waving a hundred bright banners, crimson and gold and blue and orange, marching columns of flame, huffing, puffing, roaring, screeching, a rainbow in a whirlwind—I tell you it is something to make you catch your breath in wonder and admiration and awe!

But all the time you know that behind this fearful beauty lies Death. Tomorrow where once life teemed and hummed and throbbed will stand but smoking ruins; where once waved green and stately trees will lie only squat, blackened stumps; and where once nestled a lovely home, only a charred chimney like a headstone over a grave. Isn't it all like the illustrated story of sin? Let us admit it: sin too has its beauty, at least its fascination, its glamor, its colorful allure. If it did not, we should not be attracted toward it. But never forget, under this gay charm, this sinister beauty lurks death, moral death, complete spiritual ruin.

Do you know that if a man could see his soul after he had committed a serious sin, that soul would look like a charred, ruined wasteland, with every good deed he had ever performed crumbled to the ground? One mortal sin, which seems so attractive before you commit it, sweeps through your life like a forest fire through a harvest field, and lays low every good action of your whole life as though it had never been done! Does this seem too harsh on God's part? But don't we act the same way ourselves? Suppose a soldier should perform so gallantly on the field of action that in one battle he was awarded the Silver Star, and in another the Distinguished Service Cross, and in a third the Medal of Honor—but suppose he should later turn traitor and go over to the enemy, why every military honor or privilege or pension accruing from these previous decorations would immediately be cancelled, and there might even be a price on his head! Just so— a serious sin is a treason against the Almighty, and wipes out all our claims upon Him, but so great is the goodness of our Gracious God that if we crawl back to Him in repentance, all those good deeds of the past that sin tumbled down are miraculously rebuilt!

But, how does a forest fire start? There are a dozen different ways. Perhaps the torch of a wild-eyed fire-bug, or a cigarette flipped thoughtlessly from a passing car, or a camp fire carelessly put out. Put out? Except that the fire was playing dead till all had left, and then it went to work! But sometimes a fire suddenly seems to spring up out of nowhere; I mean nobody had been near the spot for a week. Then they theorize as to the cause, and sometimes the theory is quite plausible. Imagine for example a large bottle, like a milk bottle or a beer bottle, broken up and lying among the dry leaves at the edge of a wood. All day long the sun beats down on the bottom of the bottle (and it is as thick as a magnifying glass) so that this heat is concentrated, focused on one little spot—on the leaves under the glass which are dry and crinkly as paper. And after a while that first leaf is burning hot, and a thin wisp of smoke goes curling up, and a spark leaps to the next leaf and the next, and soon the whole lonely hillside, fanned by the wind, is a red, roaring furnace!

Sin starts like that too. Because any sin begins with the concentration of our thought, the focusing of our brain-power on some imagination, some mental picture. It may be a picture of revenge, and under it your vengeance smolders, and the more you think about the wrong you have suffered, the more your hate leaps up and the more burned up you become about it... something against the Fifth Commandment. Or it may be a sensual or sexual imagination, and the more you gloat on it, the hotter burns your lust—something against the Sixth Commandment. Or it might be something you want, something you desire for yourself, something you are going to get even though you have to do it dishonestly—something against the Seventh Commandment. No matter what it is, it is your fiery imagination playing upon your fallen nature, which is tinder drier than fallen leaves— and before you know it, your passions are on fire and out of control.

But how is a forest fire stopped? The best way is a shift in the wind. This of course in the physical order we cannot manage, but in the moral order we can. When temptation starts to flame we can sweep it out with a gust of good wholesome thoughts. May I suggest just one, as broad and sweeping as the very wind? It is this. Everything in this life has a fluttering little price-tag tied to it. The tag may be little but the price may be big. Over-eat, and you will get sick; over-drink and you will get sick; commit any serious sin and you pay the penalty, even though the penalty is only a secret remorse and self-disgust. So before you reach for any sin on the Devil's bright counter, take a good look at the price-tag. If you do, you will know that the sin is not worth the cost.

And if you should find yourself hesitating, anticipating the pleasure of sin, trifling with temptation, wondering whether you should go ahead—remember that in those moments you are as it were jingling the very coins of Judas in your palm. You are toying with the thirty pieces of silver, looking at the gleam of them, while outside Jesus is waiting and wondering whether you are going to send Him again to Calvary! What else does St. Paul mean when he talks about sin that crucifies Christ yet again?

There is another way of stopping a forest fire. It is laying out a big barren lane or a trench which the fire cannot leap. But sometimes there is standing, right in the way of this operation, somebody's home, a home round which memories cling and hearts are twined. But for the sake of a greater good, to save the little town, to save lives, it must go, and the dynamite booms! Maybe in our lives too there is some person to whom we are closely but wrongfully attached, some place to which we feel strongly but wrongly drawn, some shameful pattern of action we have woven into our very lives—but it must be dynamited out! It may seem to us we are losing half our life, but we are saving all our soul! For with forest fires or with serious sin, compromise means tragedy.

There is still one final way: fighting fire with fire. Right in the face of the onrolling flames the firefighters will sometimes start a counter-fire. Then when the two fires meet, their red flames tangle like the bloody spears of two ancient armies. But it does the trick. The marching fire is stopped.

Sometimes too, when the vivid fires of passion stir within a man, the only thing that will stop him is the thought of another fire; looking down into the red crater of Hell. Is anything worth the risk of that everlasting fire? Of course if a man doesn't believe in Hell, it is no motive at all. But why is it that so many people will fondly believe in Heaven but reject with horror the very idea of Hell? There is not one more splinter of proof for the existence of Heaven than there is for Hell. But there is all the proof we need for both of them, the solemn word of God. And when the gentle Jesus, not once, but again and again, so there could be no mistake, reminds us of that everlasting fire, it should stop the sinner in his tracks! If he thinks about it, it will.

But let me emphasize this. The fear of the fires of hell should be only an emergency motive in some great moral crisis. To serve God only through fear is to serve like a slave and to be tempted to rebel. There is another fire we must set blazing in our hearts, the fire of love for Our Divine Lord. Is this hard, when you ponder how much He loves us? Figure it out. The soldier who falls on a foreign field knows at least that he dies as a patriot hero for the sake of a great country. The man who gives his life defending a woman's honor has at least the consolation that he dies for decency and virtue. The detective who crumples under a gangster's bullets goes down knowing that after all he is a martyr to duty. But Our Blessed Lord did not die for such glorious causes as duty or decency or patriotism. He died for the likes of you and me, for us the undependable, the lukewarm, the up-and-downers, the in-and-outers, the back-sliders, the lazy, the lustful, the thankless, the selfish, the spineless puppets of sin. He died for us! Oh how great must be *His* love that gave its life, since there is so little to love in our lives!

But should not that very realization start a fierce fire of love for Our Lord in our hearts? It had better, or we are doomed. The stronger fire will always conquer. We have to love God more than we love sin—otherwise Sin will be our Master, and God will be only an occasional Boarder in our heart, maybe at Easter Communion or around the Christmas Holidays. What a pity for anyone to try to serve God without really, fervently, fiercely loving God! What a tragedy to go through the mere motions of religion, like being so particular this Wednesday about getting the Blessed Ashes, and living every day as though there were no everlasting fire!

No wonder that in the famous picture of Our Mother of Perpetual Help, Mary is not looking at the Christ Child in her arms, but instead her sad eyes are fixed directly on us, as if to say, "What are you doing to Him? Are you preparing a Cross for Him, a crucifixion?" Oh Mary, pray for us sinners! The gray ashes of penance soon blow away, the flames of hell seem far off, but enkindle in our hearts, Sweet Mother Mary, a personal flaming love for Christ Our Lord . . . because when the heart really loves, it does not want to hurt!

Thou Shalt Not!

AND THEY SWALLOW IT

There is (or there used to be) an unadvertised exhibit in one of the side corridors of the Children's Hospital in Boston. On the wall hung two large picture frames, and behind the glass gleamed an alarming array, in orderly rows, of all the little objects that curious toddlers had casually swallowed and which deft surgeons had fished out of their throats or gullets or even lungs. Each indigestible item—and there must have been almost four hundred—was neatly mounted on its own card, bearing the youngster's name, and the precise date on which he had become bored with cornflakes and decided to switch to carpet tacks or collar buttons. One sweeping glance over that collection of grim trophies makes you marvel how mothers stay sane. All the things that can happen to a child! From now on I shall never see a penny in tiny, sticky fingers without the urge to take it away and substitute a half-dollar. An expensive precaution I grant; but pennies, and nickels, and dimes and quarters they swallow. I saw the evidence. And not only these. The extra-curricular diet of young America shows unlimited imagination. They go for money, and they go for medals. They toss down straight pins, safety pins, even fraternity pins. They gulp rusty screws and picture hooks. Buttons? There they were: shirt buttons, cuff buttons, even a faded Roosevelt campaign button. I stopped looking when I saw one of those little tin keys that goes with a can of sardines. I have a job swallowing a dry pill.

Now, the average Airedale or Boston Bull wouldn't eat these things. They have a protective instinct. But little children are the most beautiful and wonderful and helpless and senseless creatures on the face of the earth. As we grow older of course, we grow wiser—or do we? The truth is that some adults are more thoughtless and more reckless still. Look at what they swallow! And I don't mean the deadly poison or the sleeping pills of the deranged suicide. I mean what some people will swallow mentally, or morally; and no stomach pump or bronchoscope can ever reach it.

Yes, take morality. Or immorality. To get rid of that distressed feeling of guilt, they gratefully swallow some sugar-coated sophistry like, "After all, man is merely an animal, and after all, these things are only natural." But wait a minute. Let's break this thing in two and look at it closer, Man merely an animal? He is the strangest kind of mere animal you ever saw. He is the kind of animal who, when he wants a dwelling, does not burrow a hole under a tree, but builds cottages, mansions, skyscrapers, and the silhouetted spires of majestic cathedrals. He is the kind of animal who, when he wants music, does not point a wet snoot at the moon and howl (though I admit that some crooners may weaken my argument here considerably) but he produces glorious melodies, marches, symphonies that lift up the spirit like surges of the sea. Man is the only animal that speaks and writes and thinks and prays and reads and invents; and to say that a man is only an animal, in the sense that an alley-cat is only an animal, is like saying that the back of a freshly painted red barn and a masterpiece by Michelangelo are both paintings. They are, but what a Grand Canyon of difference swings between them! An animal is only an animal. Man is an animal plus, and it is the plus that makes the difference. Look at that huge plus sign of the Cross on which Christ died—died for mankind, not for the Bronx Zoo or the Circus Menagerie, and you know there is a difference!

And "these things", like premarital liberties for example, or sophisticated adulteries are not "natural". What does natural mean? "According to the nature of the subject": in this case according to the nature of man. But the body is not the whole nature of man; it is only half his nature; in fact only the inferior half. Try to cash a check which is only half legal. In the same sense, sin is an action which is only half natural, because man is a body, yes, but a body guided by reason, responsible to a conscience, subject to the moral law, illumined by a human soul—and will anyone pretend that indecency is natural to these—to the whole man? But they swallow it!

I pity, too, those young people who swallow the modern novel, the highly-spiced fiction that makes perfumed and silken sin something magnificent, glorious and brave. According to this gilded lie, virtue is timid and stodgy and dull. It is mouse-like and milk-toastish. But sin is strong and adventurous, glamorous and colorful! Strong? It doesnt take any strength to fall. It takes strength to stand up. It doesn't take any strength to be a "Yes-man" to the Devil. Any dead fish can go down stream with the current. It does take strength and power, will-power and won't power, to say "I am the Captain of my soul!" and not this sleek, smooth-tongued tempter!

And sin is colorful? Well, there they have something. Because the trembling weakness before it is the color of yellow jello; and the act itself is the color of mud; and the regret that follows it, when passions' embers are cold, is the color of the grey ashes of remorse; and the punishment that awaits it, if it be not repented, is the color of the red fires of hell. Sin may be colorful, all right, but so is the first stage of a black eye. But they swallow it!

In some pretentious circles there is another fallacy that goes down gullible gullets as easily as fruit juice. Namely, "It's about time we changed our moral code to fit a changing world." The idea seems to be that since sex liberties and sex indulgences are increasing, let's relax our sex standards. But that is like saying, "Here in our city we have an alarming increase of cases where drivers break the speed limit and race through red lights. So, as a solution, why not raise the speed limit to seventy miles an hour, and take down the red lights?" In other words, instead of putting the law in force, put it in moth balls. And if anyone doubts that a lowered sex morality is more harmful to a people than are traffic violations, let him look at some of the matrimonial driftwood washed up in the divorce courts, or let him seriously ask what standards he would want set for his own sons and daughters. But they swallow it!

Then there is that other tidbit of logic, which slides down like a lozenge, and which is the favorite of the literary or the entertainment world. "We just give the public what it wants." This observation is generally accompanied by the pleasing jingling of profits in the pocket. Many years ago the editor of a sensational and risque publication summed up his case neatly and frankly. His defense ran something like this: "I'm like the attendant who throws the horsemeat and the garbage to the animals at the Zoo. They seem to like it, and I get paid for it. Of course, when I go home, I eat something different myself. Why, I *couldn't* read, I couldn't stomach the kind of trash I publish. But there are a lot of people who pounce on it, and I—I just give 'em what they want."

You don't have to be a private eye to see that such reasoning justifies anything from prostitution to peddling narcotics. They too are gloriously dedicated to supplying a demand. But no one has a right to give the public, or any portion of the public, what it wants, just because it wants it. If something is obviously against the moral law, we simply have no right to want it or demand it. In these matters you do not step up to the polls and register your choice. You don't count noses, you go all the way back to Moses, and the Ten Commandments of God. Democracy is fine for politics; it is futile in morality. Because, like it or not, Almighty God is an Autocrat, a benevolent Autocrat Who has made the moral law for our good. We obey, or else.

But if it has the sweet taste of an alibi, some people will swallow anything. Like that other bit of honeyed hokum, "To the pure, all things are pure." Sounds even pious, doesn't it? Lofty and clean, like mountain air! And like any good epigram it has the ring of finality, like a pistolshot; only this time Shelley fired a blank cartridge: nice sound but no sense. You might just as well say, "To the honest all things are honest", especially blackmail and burglary. Can't they see it isn't what *you* are that makes things pure or honest; it is the things you *do* that make you pure or honest. In other words it is the liquor in the bottle that dictates the label, not the label that decides what is in the bottle.

Of course—to get away from the abstract—what they are slyly hinting at is that the human body is the handiwork of God. Without a doubt. But unfortunately for us there was only one brief period in history when humanity was pure enough to view it that way. This was before Adam and Eve sinned, incidentally not sexually but by an act of disobedience which amounted to rebellion. And once man rebelled against God, from that moment man's passions rebelled against man. From that moment by a kind of "moral law of gravity" we tended downward; we felt the pulling attraction of sin, especially in the sexual field: concupiscence or lust.

That is why they could sew the label "Original Sin" in every garment that we wear. This is why, too, a man can read a murder mystery with blood on every rug and a corpse in every room, and feel not the slightest impulse to close his fingers round a knife and run his neighbor through; but he cannot read or see the equivalent in the sphere of sex and remain entirely undisturbed. Your eyes don't have to be twin mud-puddles to see impurity where there is impurity; they just have to be normal human eyes in a normally sensitive human body and with a normal conscience that knows it is responsible to moral law. Of course if a man's conscience is a seismograph that only an earthquake can jolt, its reaction has probably been dulled by familiarity with sin. He has got so used to ignoring the alarm-clock that it doesn't wake him any more.

Much of this free-wheeling philosophy goes back to another weird opinion which they swallow with apparent relief: "After all it can't be so wrong, if everybody does it." Everybody? Everybody is a big word. Everybody is a lot of people—in fact all people. No! Everybody doesn't do it. Not everybody! And suppose everybody did. Who is this everybody anyway? Do the Commandments read, "I am the Lord Thy Everybody . . .?" Did Everybody die for us on the cross? When we stand before the Judgment Seat, will Everybody be our Judge? Everybody! Wrong would still be wrong if everybody did it, and right would still be right if nobody did it! Are we to drop down to the level of the lowest around us? What did Christ call us as His Church? A little salt that keeps a great amount of meat from corruption, a little yeast that makes the whole mass of the dough to rise! That is our job—not to sink down to the level of others, but to bring them up to the high plane of Christian purity!

During the Civil War, when battles were fought with more of a flourish than they are today, a young color-bearer led the charge waving the regimental flag. In his impulsive daring, he found himself far ahead of his regiment. He dropped into a shell-hole, and soon a messenger crept up, gasping: "The Colonel says, 'Bring the colors back to the regiment!'" Without thinking, the boy blurted out, "Tell the Colonel to bring the regiment up to the colors!" And there are our colors, hanging up there from the flagstaff of the cross, bright red Blood, candle-white Corpse, glinting blue spikes. Let's go up to the standard of Christ!

Thou Shalt Not!

SIN—ORIGINAL

AND OTHERWISE

When a sleepy-eyed man bends over in the morning, and yawningly ties his shoe-lace with a few swift flourishes, the last thing on his mind is his hands. He is merely tying his shoes; he ties them every morning. So what? Well, if he had hooks instead of hands, he would realize. But he goes on during the day, pulling open this door, pushing shut that drawer, picking up a postage stamp, flicking a bit of lint off his coat, twisting the cap on a bottle of ink or olives, and wherever his thoughts may be, they are not on his fingertips. Yet that unappreciated hand of his, that tool of a thousand tasks, with its fleshy cushions and its sinewy little cables, its springs and levers, its joints and sockets, its webbing and hinges and smooth over-all upholstery is a miniature masterpiece of engineering whose patent is held only by God. The thumb alone (dear alike to Little Jack Horner and hitchhikers) is so constructed that it serves as a base and grip for any of the other fingers. Other mammals have nothing like this. Without it man could never hold civilization—as he does—in the palm of his hand.

But granted that the hand has a hundred uses, he would be stark mad who would use his fingers to re-arrange the red hot coals in a fire-place. Nature itself would tell you with a blistering hiss that this is not their purpose. Everything in life has its appointed purpose, and if you ignore it, or defy it, you pay. Who would be fool enough to use his fountain pen to drive a nail? The nail wouldn't budge, and the pen would shatter into bits. By the same token, a dark-room is made to develop film and a hot-house is made to develop flowers. Bathe your darkroom with light and you will get no pictures. Hang your hot-house with black curtains and you will get no petals. You are charging head on against the very nature and purpose of the thing, and there can be only one result: ruin.

Now what is true of things is just as true of man. As human beings, we must act according to our nature and our purpose, but remember, it must be according to our whole nature and our ultimate purpose. And what is that whole nature? Well, man is a combination. Just as water is made up of hydrogen and oxygen, man is made up of body and soul. You must always consider the whole man. If you considered only the soul, you might refuse to eat anything, and you would end up as a suicide, but not as a saint. On the other hand, if you thought only of your body, you might reason: "God gave me a palate to enjoy tastes. And there is no taste on earth like Scotch and soda, so the more Scotch and soda I toss down, the more I shall be showing my appreciation for that superb gift of God, the delicate tastebuds of the human tongue!"

The difficulty is that too many tumblers of Scotch and soda sloshed down, soon begin to break like waves over the human brain and wash away the very pillars of reason. Part of the man enjoys it, but the whole man suffers. The man who saunters up to his favorite bar as a steady customer and tilts so many glasses that he lurches out the door as a very unsteady customer, who can't walk straight or talk straight or think straight, has betrayed part of his nature. The proof of the pudding is eighty-six per cent.

He has pampered his palate and capsized his reason. In other words, he has acted against his *whole* nature, which is a human body directed by intellect and reason and conscience and soul. He has acted like a man who would use an American flag as a floor-mop. Such a man might argue, "Oh, the flag and the floor-mop are both the same kind of cloth." But the Stars and Stripes on one make it a very special kind of cloth. And in the same way man is a body, but the image of God within him makes him a very special kind of body, a creature with a purpose in life and a destiny hereafter that soars far beyond eating and drinking or anything merely physical.

For example it is exactly the same in the more delicate realm of sex. God is not a towering Roman candle shooting off indiscriminate fiery "Thou shalt not's" in all directions. Nothing is ever just wrong; it is always wrong for a reason. What is forbidden is forbidden because it runs counter to the nature and purpose of man as God made him. Why is the solitary abuse of sex a serious sin? Because from the beginning, long before Noah ever marched them two by two into the Ark, God made them male and female. He arranged that if sex is to achieve its natural purpose, it requires a *union* of both sexes. Why is that union wrong outside marriage? Because normally it is only in marriage, in a family, that the child resulting from the union can be assured of the rearing, the care and the love it deserves. Why is Birth Control wrong? Because it throws into action the powers of generation, and then deliberately prevents them from achieving their purpose. But don't eyeglasses also interfere with nature? Yes, in the sense that they help nature to do its job better. But Birth Control is like opening the eye to see and then clapping a black patch over it so it can't. Why are sexual liberties, like passionate kissing or touching, wrong for young people before they are married? Because the whole nature and purpose of the passions is to stimulate people toward the fulfillment of those passions in the marriage act. That is why God put the passions there. But if you have no right to the marriage act, you have no right to start the machinery in motion.

So God isn't always blowing the whistle on us like a basketball referee with the hiccups and with no justification. If there is a ruling against something, you can be certain there is also a solid, logical reason behind the ruling. And one overall reason that many moderns overlook is original sin, though it does stand out like an ugly diabolical gargoyle on the cathedral

SIN—ORIGINAL AND OTHERWISE

of mankind. Original sin is the ancient, but scarcely honorable page in the diary of man which bemoans his first fall from grace, and oh, what a fall was there, my brothers! Then not only Adam and Eve, but you and I and all the world fell and we rose from it with a definite spiritual limp.

Or, to put it another way, there is this difference between man as he was created and as he is now—the difference between the rich shimmering model of a new car, and a second-hand job after a collision, whose steering gear is treacherous and whose brakes won't hold. That is why we cannot be guided by the gospel of mere nature, or that smooth sophistry "To the pure all things are pure." Our car is no longer under perfect control. Of course, they will maintain, for example, these modern pagans with the antiseptic minds, that if God created the human body as something good—well, why cannot we admire it, without benefit of draping; as it is; just as we admire the gay flowers in a garden that God created too. The answer is that once we could. The answer is in the flowers (and the birds and the bees) of another garden. To Adam and Eve as God created them, all things were pure, and every passion was under perfect control, and there was not even a word for shame. But once our first parents rebelled against God in the Garden of Eden, their passions rebelled against them, and since then, our passions against us. The dropping of an atom bomb may well turn out to have been the second most damnable day in the history of the human race. The first was the eating of the forbidden fruit. Since that first sin of rebellion against his Maker, man has been tilted in the direction of evil. Did not

Ovid, most pagan of the poets, admit: "I praise the better things; I do the base." Didn't St. Paul mutter, almost in disgust: "Those things that I do not want to do, I do; and those I want to do, I do not."

Any explanation of the world that leaves out original sin is describing the dust-bowl without mentioning the dust. Any attempt to be good without reckoning with original sin is to forget that moral saboteur, the enemy within. Because in every human heart there hides like a dark conspirator, a built-in attraction toward evil, always ready to betray us, a kind of moral force of gravity always dragging us down. Argument is no match for it, not at the critical moment. That is why it is good to ponder in a serene moment like this, that any serious sin is another thankless outrage against Our Beloved Savior, Who atoned for the Garden of Eden in the Garden of Gethsemane.

But even before that, any serious sin is a direct violation of the nature and purpose of man, because by it man debases his God-given human nature into vile and awful use, almost as though he were using a consecrated chalice as a cuspidor—oh, it is fine to philosophize and ponder these things and pile up the arguments now—but when the sermon is over, when the scenery is no longer cardboard, when the play is life and the chips are down and some real temptation suddenly spreads before you like an inviting limpid pool, and you are teetering and swaying on the edge, and you feel you are being drawn in, at that moment don't look to logic, look to the Lord! Alone you just can't win. With His help you can always win. And if it be a temptation against chastity, ask the help you need through Mary, the Virgin Immaculate. She shines above this old world like a white star hanging above a slimy swamp. But she is more than an inspiration. She is an Intercessor. Because Mary is a human mother, she sympathizes with us. Because Mary is the Mother of God, she can assist us. When any passion pounds at the door of your heart, call for help, and call in the name of Mary!

Thou Shalt Not!

SOILED SNOW

Our memory plays us curious tricks, and from one of its dusty trap-doors, a phrase popped up the other day that I had long forgotten. Maybe in your part of the country it is common, but I cannot remember ever having heard the term since I was a boy on the sidewalks of Brooklyn too many years ago. As soon as the first snow came, we would pack it down on the sidewalk in a long, narrow path, and pour water over it till it glistened into ice. Then taking a quick run and standing up straight, we would go flying along our little shoe-leather ski-run. Only we called it—I wonder if they still do—a sliding pond. But generally our whistling speed was cut bluntly short. Some crabbed and crusty ambassador of safety (though we didn't call him exactly that) would come grumbling out of his house and heave a pail of crunching cinders and ashes on the icy strip, and in every sense we were stopped. It was no mystery to us that the Church used ashes at the beginning of Lent. Ashes always meant the end of fun. But though I early recognized ashes as an emblem of penance, it has only been recently that snow has stood out as a sad symbol of sin.

Such a notion may jolt your poetic soul. After all, snow is something delicate and lovely and clean. But isn't sin too always something good that is misused? Look upon the starry flakes as they flutter down, and snow is beautiful, attractive. It is like soft lace curtains blowing in the wind. The streaking white lines are the dancing shuttle of winter weaving next spring's apple blossoms. What silversmith could ever hammer out the intricate design of the snowflake that falls so casually upon your sleeve? But sin has seeming beauty too; at least, it's attractive, alluring, fascinating... otherwise, why would people be drawn to it? *But don't let it fool you!* Wait a little while and see what happens to your attractive snow! There it oozes on the city street, grey around the edges, the surface blackened with soot, and before long the once sparkling track of white is only a mass of foul dirty slush. Didn't Shakespeare say something about "lilies that fester smell worse than weeds"? If you could see a soul in the state of grace, you would see a white radiance like the snowy purity of an Alpine peak. If you could see a soul fallen into unrepented serious sin, you would, I think, see something like the grimy slush that sprays and spatters you when a heedless car whizzes past. Dirty snow and sin are each the defilement of something that once was high and clean and good.

And sin and snow are alike in this too: they know no favorites. Amid the shabby city tenements, laced with the zig-zag black ladders of the fire-escapes, the snow swirls against the drab window-panes of the poor. Out in the comfortably spaced suburbs, it drums like fingertips against the softly lighted windows of the well-to-do. It falls on the man in the frayed and greasy overcoat and upon the lady in the fabulous mink. Sin is the same. There is not a man or woman on earth who has not felt the clammy touch of sin in some degree. Perhaps the marvel is that God, seeing sin so blanketing the earth like snow, lodged in high places and nestling in low, still does not turn His Face away in disgust and let all creation drop back into the black void from which He drew it forth.

It is very disarming, however, and cutely deceiving, this snow. As it flutters down quietly, sifting, drifting, it seems so soft, so gentle, so tender Every strand of sharp, sturdy trees gradually becomes a cotton-grove, tufted with soft whiteness. Though the tree trunks be gnarled and twisted and scarred, the snow bandages them with tender white flannel . . . so gently. But isn't sin like that too? How many sins are committed through softness, through sympathy, through sentiment! *But don't let it fool you!* Look at your soft caressing snow, on the young trees especially. See that grove of young pines, notice the branches, how the tender snow has dragged them down. Once so upright, reaching for the sky, now pressed so low. Isn't sin like that too? It may disarm and deceive you with its gentle approach, its softness, but before you know it, it drags you down to the dirt, loads you with guilt, weighs you down with remorse. But here is the difference. It is not an easy thing to shake off sin, and grow straight again as though nothing had ever happened. Far, far better to realize the danger before than to regret it later! Who was it that said so satirically: "There is no substitute for experience, except being eighteen years old"?

And here is another angle about this many-sided snow. When first it falls, tiny tumbling wisps, flakes light and airy as moth wings, you ignore it. You shoulder your way through the frail white whirl contemptuously; you scuffle your feet through the first marshmallow inch as though it were not there. But isn't sin too a very gradual process, a little-by-little, step-by-step affair? At first, trifles that don't seem to amount to much. Little meaningless things. Little perhaps, but not meaningless. Little glances, little liberties, a little toying with possibilities, a little experimenting with danger.... *But don't let it fool you!* Look at your little insignificant flakes of snow now! Suddenly they have roared into a blizzard, a wild uncontrolled storm whose icy fingers tear down the wires with blinding flash of electric blue. Now the feeble flurries are a whole white wasteland. The roads are clogged. Communication stops dead. And isn't this the very blueprint and the buildup of sin? A mild, insidious beginning, gradually rising, whipping to a storm of passion, and you are not snowbound but sinbound, and the wires between you and God are down, and your soul is in the dark and the loneliness and the cold.

It is sad because we are so easily misled and swindled, but even so we should never be discouraged. The other day after a storm I saw a lineman go clanking up a telephone pole with his spikes, perch trimly on the cross-bar, and set skilfully about splicing a broken wire. I always look upon such a man with a special interest and even affection because that is what my father used to do. But that day I saw more than a lineman on a pole. I thought I saw the pole of the Cross, and the cross-bar where Christ the Lineman hangs, even to the spikes; only these spikes are not on His Feet but *in* them, as He hangs there, repairing that long-distance line between Heaven and earth, restoring communication between the sinner and God!

Maybe if more often we lifted our eyes to Him, maybe if we would more often close our ears to the false promises of the devil who is a liar from the beginning, and a "line-man" in another sense—but when will we learn to tell the false from the true? When you see snow upon a cliff, cold and solid and sparkling, you might think it were gleaming white marble built into the very ribs of the hills. It's like a first impression of sin. When first you have it, you think this is wonderful, this is what I have wanted, this is the happiness I craved, this is mine! *But don't let it fool you!* Take another look at the massive snow on the mountain side. Oh, it is glittering all right, because the sun is hitting it with a million blazing arrows, and the next thing you know it will start to go to pieces. The first trickling drops, the thaw, the running rivulets, the final bursting flood! In sin, too, you may think you have happiness fixed in your grip; then you find that all you have had was pleasure that melted right through your fingers. The thaw of sin is often tears, blinding and bitter. Yet to many a Magdalen these have been the pearls of great price that have bought pardon and Paradise.

SOILED SNOW

I grant you there are other people without regrets and without remorse, people who seem to ride sin like a gay carousel, snatching at the brass ring of every new temptation, apparently feeling no slightest twinge of moral guilt. Why? Long habit keeps their conscience under a local anaesthetic; their soul is numb to any sense of sin. Yes, and they are all the more to be pitied! I always think they are like that drummer boy of Napoleon on the retreat from Moscow. The tattered regiment came tramping through crunching snow, slogging along mile after mile, stumbling and shivering in the sub-zero blasts. And the drummer lad was tired, so tired. When he stumbled the next time, he didn't get up. He just lay down in the snow at the side of the road. His companions pleaded with him to stand up, to keep moving. He just smiled and said he felt all right. And they marched on, and he pitied *them*. He didn't feel so cold now—in fact, he didn't feel anything. But the next morning a few lonely stragglers wandered past and shook their heads at the youthful corpse that still looked so serene, content, while the hail beat its slow rattle on the drum at his side.

In its way, isn't this scene a tolerable parallel to the man who is so sunk in sin he doesn't feel guilt any more? He too lies perfectly comfortable amid his sins, his conscience frozen... there is no wincing, no pain... everything is snug and wonderful, only suddenly in that state he dies. He had turned off and silenced conscience, like an alarm clock, but suddenly he wakes to the Voice of God, pronouncing judgment! The sinner who has shattered all the commandments and who realizes that his soul is all grimy blots and slimy stains and who is terrified at the thought of standing before his Maker, can at least do something—he can repent and reform and make his peace with God. But the man whose soul is a long black list of insults against the Almighty, sordid sins against every virtue, and who has long since ceased to worry about it—he is like a man dying without feeling in a snowbank. He doesn't even know he is dying. He fears no danger, and that is the greatest danger of all!

Dear God, we are all sinners, every one of us. But at least, give us the courage (and the common sense) to admit it, to confess it, to repair it, to try to change it! We too can be transfigured from the ugliness of sin if only we lift our eyes to the Savior Whose Face shines like the sun and whose garments are white as snow!

Thou Shalt Not!

IN A GLASS, DARKLY

Up our way the windows of the department stores are already draped with the radiant white of the Annual Linen Sale like an indoor January snowstorm. This is a surer sign than the last burning, crackling Christmas Tree that the holidays are really over. The point of this post-holiday homily is to remark and regret that for some people (and for more this year than last because it is increasing all the time)—for some people the holidays went down with one stupendous gurgle, almost like a sinking ship, only with them it wasn't water—but fire-water.

Preceding the festive season (for these people it isn't the Holy Season, but just the holly season) magazine ads glow like a lit-up jukebox with technicolor testimony to the convivial warmth of bottles blazing with the heraldry of red roses, golden crowns, white feathers. Nothing is ever said there (though I think something should be said here) of the thorns that may lurk under the roses, the hang-over headaches that can groan under too many crowns, and the cowardice that sometimes shows behind the white feather.

But—and let us make this distinction at once and put it down in sharp italics—what is wrong is *not* the *use* of liquor, but the *abuse*. You have only to look at that vivid vignette in the Gospels where the Savior Himself in the midst of the wedding banquet changed water into wine, to realize that the normal, moderate, temperate use of alcoholic beverages is perfectly all right. But you have only to look at the increasing, intemperate, immoderate, abnormal consumption of liquor to know that the latter is all wrong. Orators sometimes appeal to "sober statistics." That is not exactly the appropriate word here, but there are few people (except perhaps those that get stiff at bars or silly at parties) who would not concede that heavy drinking is coming on with staggering strides.

It is true that perhaps a priest does not get a balanced view. It is true he sees so much of the sickening effects of the abuse of drink in his parish rounds (because these are the families he has to visit and help) that he doesn't get a fair picture. But he cannot forget what he has seen—and this is the point—he is seeing it more often now than ever before. And it is the impression in this corner (because I cannot of course speak for other priests) that if a man wants to dig his grave financially, or physically, or morally, he could not choose a better tool than a corkscrew.

Sometimes on a lovely Sunday afternoon, traffic will jam up at some avenue entering the city. Policemen will tell you, sometimes profanely, that "This congested bridge" or "That narrow street"—is the whole trouble. It's the bottle-neck! In the same way, when you find a home where the children are in tatters, and the mother is a broken-hearted martyr, and the home itself like a tiny suburb of hell—trace back the cause, and you will find it too is a bottle-neck. A brown bottle-neck!

Take the man, if you can call him that, who presides over such a home. Respectability, responsibility, integrity, even security—what do they mean to him? Put them all in one scale of the balance, and in the other put a whiskey bottle. Does anyone doubt which one he will dive for, almost die for? Because he is half-sponge and half-jellyfish. These are not just abusive words flung out like tracer-bullets. I think that in zoology there is a close relation between a sponge and a jellyfish. I know that in life a drunkard is a sponge when it comes to absorbing liquor, but a jellyfish without backbone when it comes to saying "No."

Twenty years ago in a certain city I knew a fine handsome hulk of a man. I'm ashamed to tell you his nationality. He had six of the most beautiful children I have ever seen. And many an evening they cowered in the doorway of a neighboring tenement, as Daddy came swaggering up the stoop wildly drunk, shouting out that he had just seen two antelopes with yo-yos. Yes, they were afraid of him, but most of all they were ashamed. And shame in the heart of a child burns like a hot coal.

He lost his job, because it is quite a trick to hold a bottle and a job at once. He began to throw things about at home, and was sent to jail for thirty days.

I visited him there, brought him cigarettes, helped get him out for Christmas. I'll never forget that Christmas Eve afternoon. We had got a tree for the family, and gifts for the children from a Welfare Society, and there he knelt, trimming the tree, the children around him, the first snow sifting down outside like a lace curtain. It was like a storybook. I went back to Church to hear confessions with bells ringing in my heart. And I found out that just one half-hour later, he clapped on his hat, walked out to the nearest tavern, and was carried in dead drunk late that night!

Is there any moral to it? I don't know. Sometimes I think such a man would be better dead than just dead drunk. Sometimes I think it has gone so far that only a miracle in reverse—Our Blessed Lord changing the wine into water—could do any good. But at least we can warn the perhaps unsuspecting young. Maybe I look very simple, but you would be surprised how often a girl will come up and tentatively begin to tell me all about her boyfriend... how handsome he is and how courteous and how ambitious and how clever, and maybe that he has wavy hair and three dimples. And then it comes out. It seems he has only one fault. Every six or eight weeks he drinks far too much. And the girl hurries on to say, "But, Father, this shouldn't prevent our marriage, should it? After all, only once every two months—I could put up with that. I should marry him, shouldn't I?" And her eyelashes go up like an awning in expectation. I don't think she gets the answer she wants. My answer is, "Girl, for your own sake, for your future family's sake, for God's sake—

don't risk marrying a sponge! If you throw a wedding ring into a puddle, it won't dry up the puddle. The ring will be lost and stained in the puddle!"

Aside from the personal unhappiness that often pops out with the cork, consider the abuse of liquor and Sin. There are critics of English literature who think that our language has no lovelier lines than those used by the poet (Crashaw, I think) to describe the very miracle of the changing of the water into wine at Cana. He says, "The modest water saw its God, and blushed"—blushed into crimson wine. And well might the wine blush red! Red for all the future abuse of liquor! Red for the red and purple-veined noses of drunkards which burn (if it be not blasphemous to say so) like sanctuary lights before their god, because of such St. Paul says, "Their god is their belly." Red for the red ink of bills and debts piled up in the drunkard's home. Red for the red blood spilled in bar-room brawls—and there is no more pathetic sight on this old earth than a human being lying there, perhaps dying there, in a drunken stupor, his glassy eyes staring upward like the eyes of a dead fish.

The wine blushed red. Red for the red traffic lights through which heavy-drinking drivers heedlessly speed. Red for the red tail-lights when they come to a stop in a lonely lane. When they drive, they are a menace to life and limb; and when they park, they are a menace to morality. Red for the red blushes of the young girl who first finds out that it is not "Wine, woman, and song"—but wine, woman, and wrong! Don't these girls realize that alcohol blurs the brain like a fog, unleashes passions like a wild beast, snaps will-power like a toothpick? And that in some circumstances a little liquor is too much! Otherwise, why is it that later on when people bring their sad story to a rectory parlor they so often end, "That's all, Father, except—except it never would have happened, if I hadn't been drinking."

With God or His Church there is no double standard, but even more revolting than a man "under the influence" as the kindly phrase has it, is a tipsy, maudlin woman. I can imagine a type of man who might want to pass an evening with a painted, fragile toy of a girl who could lift cocktail after cocktail with him, and who might even be a switch drinker—that is, when her right arm got tired she turned to the left. But I can't imagine any man choosing such a creature to be the Queen of his home, and the Mother of his children. Can you imagine a grandfather with curling white mustachios dandling his great-grandson on his knee and saying, "Why sure I knew your great-grandmother when she was a young lady! What did she look like? Oh, I can see her now. The gold in her hair, the stars in her eyes, the roses in her cheeks, the bottle at her lips—and the words coming out mumbling and stumbling as she sat there on the sofa loaded with giggle-water!"

You may faintly smile, but it is never a joke when a woman's drinking hurts her home. Not too long ago I gave a Novena, and there was a Petition Box, and one of the petitions was scrawled in the wide, looping hand of a boy, (they get about two words to the line) and the note said, "Dear Father, I am a boy and I would like you to pray for my mother, as she drinks a lot. I am making this Novena for her. She is a good mother when she does not drink, and us children need her. Hoping this Novena will change her. Hoping it will." And with all the simplicity of a boy, he signed his name. I checked up quietly in the parish school, and sure enough, there was such a boy. Seventh Grade.

Isn't that sermon enough? I pray Our Blessed Lord, through the powerful intercession of His Mother, who saw them push a sponge of vinegar into His Holy Face when He hung on the cross (and He took it in reparation for the abuse of drink)—oh, if there is anyone out there who is abusing drink, give him the grace to cut it down, or if necessary, to cut it out! Hoping this plea will change him! Hoping it will!

Thou Shalt Not!

SATURDAY NIGHT

During the last quarter-century or so, we Americans have raised up Saturday as a kind of carved altar to the cult of leisure and dedicated it to the goddess of good times. Sometimes the altar in this new religion of Saturday recreation takes the form of a portable grill in the backyard where the incense smoke solemnly spirals up from charcoal steaks. Sometimes it is a gaudy umbrella at the beach. Sometimes, on rainy Saturdays, it may be a television screen and a couple of tall, clinking glasses. In any event, by Friday afternoon many Americans begin to behave like bored tourists on a voyage, sick of the sameness of the sea, and now eagerly looking forward to the change and the challenge of the approaching, exciting port.

And this is good. Any break is a godsend in a world where so much work is monotonous, mechanical, routine: the mailman toting the same old bag up and down the same old streets; the milkman hearing the same clink of endless bottles; the telephone operator facing the same switchboard with the same snaky cords and their blinking eyes; the mother making the same beds, washing the same dishes... but come to think of it, for her, Saturday often means she is busier than ever because on Saturday the little angels (slightly shop-worn) are home from school, and mother, besides borrowing a few arms from an obliging octopus to do her usual tasks, must also referee a series of unpredictable intramural massacres. Anyway, for all those who can get it, Saturday leisure is a wonderful little island of sweet and serene relaxation amid the rushing white waters of a hectic and hyped-up world.

But, notice, we are praising Saturday and relaxation, not Saturday night and dissipation. What a black eye is to a normal face—a puffy, smeary scar, discolored like a purple clam—a dissipated Saturday night is to the rest of the week: something ugly, and horrible, and pathetic. Did it ever occur to you that Saturday is named after a pagan Roman god? Or that Saturday is also related to Saturn the planet, the one that is surrounded by rings like a beer ad, for after all isn't Saturday the moistest night of the week? And more to the point still, Saturday is basically related to the Saturnalia, that period of wildest revelry in the time of pagan Rome when every restraint of decency was snapped like a rope of rose petals, when toasts were drunk and drunks were toasted, when they called for madder music and stronger wine, and when for a few frenzied days Rome became a marble jungle.

Today we do not have the Saturnalia. We do have Saturday night. The classic lute and the poetic lyre have melted away in favor of the hot trumpet, the sexy saxophone, and the yawping jukebox. The wine is seldom mere wine, but the imagination reels (and that is truly the right word) at the river of firewater that coils across our continent on Saturday night. Yes, firewater; fire to inflame the passions and water to drown the conscience. And if this seems a mite exaggerated, laying it on a bit thick, is it not but plain, unrouged fact that more liquor is tossed down on Saturday nights; more men walk on uncertain legs, circling homewards over sidewalks that seem to pitch and roll like the deck of a ship, on Saturday nights; more men drive home with a glazed look in their eye like a zombie, and breath on their lips like a brewery, that not even St. Christopher can stand—that's why he gets out, on Saturday nights.

Is it not true that more wives wait at home worrying, on Saturday nights; more children dread the lurching foot on the stairs, on Saturday nights? Are not more voices raised in anger, more tears poured out, more homes broken on Saturday nights? Yes and more money spent—money that should go for groceries—goes gurgling down the alcoholic drain on Saturday night! If Sunday is the Lord's Day, then Saturday night is the Devil's night.

There are no longer Roman Saturnalia, no; no dancers in loose garments with vine-leaves in their hair go pirouetting between the pillars of the temple. But in many a smoky, beery, rock-and-roll joint there are young people tossing their torsos in all directions in the kind of dance that suggests that the dancers have just dropped down after dangling up there

SATURDAY NIGHT

among the coconuts. There are no two-wheeled chariots swaying past the Forum, but convertibles do go whizzing round corners on two wheels. Does anyone doubt that hospital emergency entrances are busiest on Saturday nights? Or that there are more tragic cases, on Saturday night, of the girl who slowly climbs the stairs to her room, sits down on the edge of the bed, alone with her regrets, her remorse, her shame, her fear, and wishing to God she never had yielded! Friday, in Robinson Crusoe's story, was first a footprint on the sand. To such a girl the memory of that Saturday will always be a footprint in the mud.

Meanwhile, across the town the drunkards have toppled into bed and are snoring out blasts of alcoholic fumes. The next day is Sunday, but for them the Lord's Day is a lost day. For when, ironically, are most Sunday Masses missed? Really on Saturday nights! It is then that they render themselves too sick or too soggy or too foggy or too groggy or—just too lazy to derrick themselves out of bed and get to church. And the pity of the whole sad situation is that this neon-lit, gin-swilling, zulu-dancing, sordid love-making world, that lays a stupor on the mind and a stain on the soul, takes place on Mary's Day!

Saturday *is* Mary's Day. Go back a thousand years and look over St. Bernard's white-robed shoulder as his quill scratches briskly across the parchment. Read what he writes: "For a long time now the Church has kept Saturday in honor of Our Lady because on the first Holy Saturday when Our Saviour was in the tomb and the Apostles were in flight, Mary remained steadfast and true. She never doubted that He would rise. On that bleak Saturday we can almost say that Mary was the Church. And therefore on each Saturday we honor Mary in a special way."

On many Saturdays of the year the priest recites the office of Our Lady. On Saturday evenings in most seminaries the students in cassock and surplice lift their ringing young voices in Our Lady's silvery litany. In most monasteries Saturday is just like Friday: not a morsel of meat is eaten, in salute to the agony Our Lady endured when she stood beneath the cross and, heartbroken and helpless, saw Her Son's bright Blood patter down, drop by drop, like red autumn leaves from the gaunt tree of the Cross.

There are, of course, many ways to pay tribute to someone. We can christen a ship in a man's honor, or dedicate a bridge, or raise a monument, or even plant a tree. But surely the lowest form of showing honor is not to dishonor. In other words the very least we can do in praise of Mary is not to profane her day.

I am quite well aware that for the vast majority of those who listen to a talk like this, the average Saturday night, far from being an orgy, is likely to be as subdued as the siesta hour in a sanatorium. The closest some of us come to painting the town red on Saturday is when we drop a bottle of catsup on the sidewalk on our way home from the supermarket. But, by the law of averages, there will be a few in whose diary there *is* one day of the week whose page is smudged with blots of sin and smeared with tears of remorse above all the other days—and that day is Saturday. Generally these will be the younger people.

If life, as Scripture says, is a warfare for us all, then for the young, Saturday night can be a minefield

SATURDAY NIGHT

studded with hidden moral dangers beneath the casual surface of recreation or relaxation or "a date." If life for all of us is a highway, where we have to hold the road or become moral wrecks, then for the young, Saturday night can be a steep curve, slippery when wet, especially when the wet pours out of a bottle.

Which reminds me that in our part of the country at this time of the year, Saturday is often dedicated to a week-end of skiing. Now, skiing for those young enough to sit down suddenly without doing damage to anything but their dignity, is a delightful sport. But some young people are not content with skiing, but add to it whiskey-ing, and then you have to fear not only broken bones but broken commandments. A man does not have to be a research chemist to know that when you add alcohol to youth, good resolves tend to settle like sediment in the bottom of the glass, and unlawful desires bubble eagerly to the top.

In an earlier and earthier America, Saturday night was sacred to the weekly bath-tub. Blessed are those young people who today set apart some time on Saturday for the spiritual bath of confession. You leave it clean and you stay clean. You may go out later that Saturday night, but you know the difference between fun and filth. To any priest the most sparkling sight in the world is young people at the Communion Rail on Sunday morning, their fresh faces brightening the very sanctuary, and their clean presence quietly implying a Saturday date that was not defiled. "Saturday's heroes"—remember the phrase? They were supposed to be the football stars, the gridiron greats for three pennant-waving hours. They made the passes, they sometimes sprawled in the mud.

Maybe the real Saturday heroes are those who did not make passes, or fall in the mud, and whose goal line was not crossed by the Devil.

Anyway, if you find yourself weakest over the week-end, remember that the Saturnalia were for the pagan Romans, but our Saturday is dedicated to the Immaculate Mother of God. So spend it, that Sunday morning will find you among the faithful who come marching along the quiet streets, marching toward the chiming churchbells, marching toward the uplifted spire and its saving cross, marching eventually even to the altar rail where the priest waits with the golden ciborium and the snow-white Host. You have spent Saturday, Mary's Day, with no reproach, and she leads you on the Lord's Day to Her Son, Jesus, and every grace.

The People and the Steeple

EVERYBODY HAS TROUBLE

There is one sacred picture that shines in almost every Catholic Church. It may gleam in oils, or it may glow in a stained-glass window, but generally it will be there. It is The Holy Family, that Trinity of the Fireside: first, the Virgin Mother so tender and fair; then St. Joseph bearded and strong; and standing between them, the Boy Christ looking very straight and handsome in His fine white robe. In the shrine of our own heart too we have this picture, and there we think of The Holy Family as surrounded by the golden frame of perfect happiness, and protected under glass so that no slightest smudge of the world's trouble can ever mar their serene bliss. And it is all so wrong.

The Holy Family was a *holy* family, but it was not a happy family; that is, not if you take as your standard of happiness the smiling faces of the family grouped around the new car in the magazine ads! Remember, this was the Family so persecuted that it had to leave town and hide out in Egypt; the Family where the Boy was lost for days in a big city and the Mother broken-hearted with worry; the Family where the Foster-father died, and left the Widow and Son alone; the Family where the grown Son was arrested as a criminal and executed on a Cross. Would anyone call this the life of a happy family? Yet this was the life of God's own family when His Sacred Feet pressed our poor earth.

We take the pointer and trace these shadowy lines in the picture of the Holy Family to console other families, because so many people say to the priest, "Why should this happen to *our* family?" But, if they would only look around, they would find that the same thing, or something as bad or perhaps even worse, is happening to almost every family. Every family may not have shares in General Motors or General Foods or General Electric, but practically every family somewhere along the line inherits a big block of stock in General Trouble.

You take that big house on the hill, the one where the brass knocker glitters so bright, and the drapes hang so rich, and everything seems so smooth and flawless. You don't know, do you, that the older daughter is running around with a divorced man, and that behind those very proper curtains the mother is crushed and often crying? Or, take the house next door. Two sisters live there and the rooms are filled with expensive furniture, but they will always be empty of happiness till the wayward brother, the black sheep, one day comes home leaving his past behind him!

Why, you could go to every house on the street, not like the postman who never gets farther than the front door, but like the priest who gets into the heart of the home; and you will find that Trouble has a master key to practically every door. That two-family house on the corner now, (I mean the people downstairs)—they are constantly uneasy and embarrassed because they never know when Jack—that's the drinking son—is liable to come lurching up the steps, swinging his arms, singing a song, and suddenly shouting that he had just seen an elephant with a halo. But the people upstairs are more sympathetic than you might think. The cross is carved over their door too, for every few weeks finds them making a sentimental journey to a distant hospital where their daughter is mentally ill.

The family on the opposite corner—but that is just their trouble, it is not really a family. Two of the finest people God ever made, and a silver jubilee of married life behind them, but their rooms never rang with the silvery laughter of a child. No children, no grandchildren: it must be pretty lonely sometimes, don't you think? On the other hand in the big grey house just across from them, you will find a string of children; healthy, attractive, radiant youngsters. But the mother and father are not the same loving, trusting people who joined hands over the first gurgling cradle. Just recently doubt has begun to smolder in bitter eyes, and love has begun to die. The reason? A damnable, unfounded suspicion! One of these days even the children will vaguely be aware that something is wrong. And all the brilliant parlor lamps in the world will not brighten the shadow that darkens the home, till humble trust and the old love return!

So you could take a bundle of tags—call them trouble tags if you will—and tie one on almost every door of the parish. Tie a green one on this door, because their trouble is debt and their need is money. Tie a yellow one here for sickness, the case of a helpless invalid and all the care and sacrifice which this demands and which only love can lighten. For this door, a red tag for sullen hatred, a case of bad blood between two brothers, and like a spreading bloodstain it spreads to the rest of the family. *This* door does not seem to need a tag? But don't be too sure. Sometimes when everything appears to run so smoothly, it is not because the trouble is smaller, but because it is deeper.

Even the families of the saints had their troubles, and in the big family-size package, too. St. Elizabeth had a husband who was insanely jealous and hypocritically unfaithful. St. Thomas Aquinas had a couple of brothers who sent into his room a lewd woman to tempt him. Possibly she was an old flame of one of the brothers. But St. Thomas fixed her. He seized a blazing fagot from the fire, and with this new flame drove the old flame out. The parents of St. Rose of Lima did not understand their daughter at all. They meant well but they certainly made things uncomfortable for her. St. Bernadette's family were poor as church-mice. St. Lucy's folks were pagans. The father of the Little Flower became blind and eventually, due to brain deterioration, lost his reason. St. Lazarus had a sister who, in her early days, every time she flounced down the street started tongues buzzing and heads shaking. You might have heard her name, Mary Magdalen.

I bring up these witnesses because I have a conviction, not only that every family has troubles, but that troubles actually weld a family together. It is luxury and money and good times that separate the family, but sweat and tears keep them together like a binding cement. Look at a colorful cathedral window in the glory of noon, and you see a pageant of glass, deep scarlet, cool green, mellow gold. But look more closely and you notice that through the colors run heavy, black lines of lead. It is these dark lines that give to the window its very design, its figures, its meaning. More than that. Take those dark lines away and your window would fall apart, a shower of meaningless clattering glass. So it is with a family. It is the dark and heavy lines of trial and trouble that hold the family together. Out of mutual sorrow grows mutual love and mutual help.

But here's the rub. On the mountain peaks of great crises, family devotion is often beautiful and generous. But most of life is lived down in the valley of the ten thousand little grasses of commonplace events. If Sheila undergoes an emergency operation, and needs a transfusion, her sister Joyce hurries to the hospital, eager to give blood. But the very day before, when all Sheila wanted was not Joyce's blood, but merely to borrow her blouse, why the house all but exploded! Again, too many of the little kindnesses, those bright little ball-bearings that make life run smoothly, we reserve for strangers. Eighteen year old Tom is snarling at his sixteen year old sister: "Sis, of all the impossible people, you certainly..." The phone rings and he picks it up and says gruffly, "Yes", and then, "Why, hello, hel-lo," practically cooing into it. You know it isn't another member of his family, and probably not a top-sergeant either. I am not advocating syrupy insincerity, but I am wondering if our family does not deserve our best self.

When God in His Wisdom lays a cross on the family shoulder, some members are no help at all because they are used to going through life with a chip on their shoulder: their own aggressive, self interest. Like Jeanette the Jealous who sees life through the green glasses of envy and is always bemoaning that she never gets her just deserts. (She never does, either.) Or Susie the Stubborn who says with tight lips, "I have made up my mind," and her tones are like a key clicking in a lock. That settles it—even though she is wrong, as she often is. Or Pete the Impetuous who would rather fight than be lonesome: and he is never lonesome. Or Mike the Moody who today is riding high on the crest of elation, and everything is wonderful—but alas, tomorrow he is way, way down in the depths. He ought to wear a weather vane instead of a hat so you could tell how he is feeling. Or Willie the Weigher who is always weighing out how much each member contributes to the family budget. His secret sorrow is that the mint does not issue a coin smaller than a penny, so his calculations can be even more exact.

From the likes of these in our home, deliver us O Lord! Give us in their stead a family whose family ties are like the ropes of Alpine climbers, so bound together that if one falls, all the rest dig in and help to draw him up. And when heart-breaking sorrow comes to our home, as to every home in this vale of tears it must, may we, O Blessed Savior, not fly into Thy face in rebellion, but fly into Thy arms for comfort and courage and peace!

The People and the Steeple

TRY CHANGING THE WALL PAPER

All day long yesterday the radio and television were wishing you a Happy New Year. I do too—from my heart—but I would also like to suggest to some of us, including myself, a strange program to help really make this new year happy. During these hours you hear a great deal about turning over a new leaf. My advice is slightly different. It is "Change the Wall Paper." *You* make the weather in the country of your mind.

Do you remember those dear dim days almost beyond recall when you could sweep your eyes critically around a vacant apartment and decide: "I rather like this. Yes, I think I'll take it. But of course you will change that wall paper. Positively repulsive! I'll let you know the pattern I prefer." Nowadays in this post-war shortage you are content if the apartment has walls, never mind the wall paper, even though the design be skulls and bones bobbing in a sea of blood.

On the other hand if you are decorating your own home, and the need for wall paper is indicated, selecting the kind can be an eye-sparkling adventure, because while walls provide only shelter for the body, wall paper can be a lift and a spectacle to the spirit. Choose the right gay pattern and you have a perpetual banquet laid out for the eye, a stimulating climate for the soul. Look at the choice of colors—all the way from lemon to lavender, from prize-fighter's-eye purple to dandruff off-white. If you like motion, you have your choice of swans poising their necks like white periscopes above the lake, or peacocks sweeping tails of emeralds and amethysts across the lawn. At dinner you can eat your baked ham within a blazing rose-garden, then move into the living room and watch television surrounded by Japanese pagodas and temple bells.

There may be one drawback. Few of us have the roll of money we would need to get exactly the rolls of wall paper we would like. Anyway, there's something far more important, and far easier. For, if we cannot always choose the wall paper for our livingroom, we can always choose the wall paper for our life. We can surround ourselves with high, clean thoughts, with noble principles, with a wholesome Christ-like attitude.

I know this sounds foggy and vague, but by way of contrast, picture and pity the man, for example, whose life is hedged about by the jungle green of jealousy. He lives in a negative world of sour wishes. He spends hours brooding how other men get ahead, fiercely wishing he could drag them back. And all that this internal churning does, is hold *him* back. Jealousy is the most stupid of all sins: it bares its teeth toward other people's success, but it eats only its own heart. Why live in the dismal den of an attitude like that? Choose your own wall paper... but don't make it Envy Green!

There are other people, dreary, teary people, who seem to favor, when it comes to a color, solid unbroken black, sometimes set off by a nice depressing border of the blues. Well, let's be fair about it. Life has dealt them a hard blow. So it has to many of us. But if we cannot change the situation, the wall, we can at least change the wall paper, our attitude toward the situation. Suppose there is some grim tragedy in your home, or some disappointment in business, or in school, or even in love. What good will it do to keep it before your eyes all day long like a wall paper design of crepes and headstones, and do nothing but feel the pain and wince over and over again? Must you keep this trouble on each of the four walls all around you, never out of your sight? Don't you know that sadness is the Devil's secret weapon? He knows that the heart that serves God best is the heart that loves God like a fire roaring in the grate, so naturally he is always ready to drop a sopping wet blanket of gloom over it. Sorrow is part of every life, but we can endure it better if we do not make it a chronic, weeping wall, but see upon it the golden pattern of God's great hand, taking our little one and leading us along.

I think it was Daniel O'Connell who remarked about someone that even when he smiled it was as cold as the glint of winter sun on the silver nameplate of a coffin. You can scowl through life, you can develop a face with a built-in frown, plus an automatic snarl or whine. But you won't be the better Catholic for it, and you'll change or be changed before you get into Heaven with it. Besides, the hardest, steepest approach to Heaven is the road of discouragement. And you know something? It isn't the troubles that break the heart, it's the brooding over them! I am not trying to tell you to toss all your troubles into a cast-iron chest and then sit on the lid and laugh. But if you *can* push them in, and kneel on the lid and pray, the chances are far better it will stay shut and you can face life freer. Not that anybody can whistle his troubles away: that is absurd. But if you have ever rowed a boat you know how tough a pull it is when some swimmer grips the boat and is towed, dragged through the water behind you. But stop the boat, take him aboard, and you hardly know he's there! With the human heart, too, the load is always lighter when you suddenly decide to take it in, accept it, live with it. Just another way of saying, that you can live with your problems better if you hang on the walls of your mind the bright hopeful pattern of Christian acceptance and optimism.

For a young married couple who are just moving into a home, I have a suggestion in the way of wall paper for at least one room. I doubt whether the design I propose will make any interior decorator throw her lorgnette into the air and cheer, but it might prevent the newlyweds from ping-ponging some first bitter words. In a calmer, coyer, less sophisticated age (when Victoria was on the throne and embroidered mottoes on the walls) some pastors often gave the bridal couple a present of a pair of teddy bears for the mantelpiece. One of the bears would be marked Bear, and the other Forbear. I would suggest stencilling a series of these right along the wall. Then when quarrels came, and a pair of angry eyes glared like headlights, they might flash upon one little bruin pleading "Bear"—take it, bear it—and the other brown fellow coaxing "forbear"—don't throw the sewing machine at him—and at least life would be less fury and more fun. Ah, that invisible wall paper is a wonderful fabric if you glance at it when you need it—especially when you feel like tossing a hand-grenade of temper at someone you love. Bear and forbear, or you both will get hurt in the explosion.

Somewhere I heard of a chap who had his whole apartment, upholstery and all, done over in leopard skin, because his fountain pen leaked. That was carrying precaution to the very end of the road, but to avert another kind of accident it might be a good idea to have the walls of our brains, the house of our thoughts, covered with black and white checks. Check and double check. After we looked on that for a while we might try to be *sure* before we serenely sit in judgment on our neighbors. After a few early mistakes we might slowly learn that "seems" is not always "is." Not everyone who walks unsteadily, has opened a bottle and thrown the cork away. Not everyone who is late just doesn't care—there may be an excellent reason, and before you bang your gavel and deliver sentence, perhaps you had better check. Not every article broken or lost deserves the pointed finger and the crushing indictment of rank negligence. Perhaps you had better check and double check. Not every one of your friends who passes you by without a greeting is giving you five pounds of cold shoulder. Her eyes may have been upon you, but her thoughts were miles away. The truth is she never really did see you. And so on. Not every beautiful woman or handsome man is vain and arrogant. Not every rich man made his money without letting his right hand know what his left was doing. Whenever you feel that sweeping, heady rush of pole-vaulting to a rash judgment, just wink at that checkerboard wall paper and check first!

These days the kitchen is likely to see as much service as any room in the house. So, as a final suggestion (though I doubt whether the wall paper firms will feature any of these perfectly free proposals) I would recommend a series of alternate panels. In the first, a pair of hands drying a plate, and in the next those same hands clasped in prayer. That's right, it is the old Gospel of Martha and Mary in the same one person. Because you *can* serve your family and serve God at the same time. Even the dishes become a devotion if you offer them up. And maybe you had better, because all work seems boring and unbearable and wasted unless every now and then we slip in a prayer and send the work up to God. "My whole life, my round of work is so dull!" you hear people groan. And the world answers, "Sprinkle it with variety and a change; spice it with hobbies and recreation!" Not enough. Spiritualize it with frequent little prayers, small and bright like sequins. Even the drabbest task offered to God, automatically takes on the radiance and the grandeur of something significant, worthwhile, important!

So choose your own wall paper, at least in the house of your heart! This year hang it with the symbols of Christian faith and hope and kindness and holy joy! And notice how much happier you will become. Life is a mirror; it will reflect back whatever you show to it. Life is a cave; it will echo back louder whatever you say to it. So, make it the cave of Bethlehem—ringing with a modern, practical echo of God's own love for all men!

The People and the Steeple

THE PROBLEM OF PAIN

On the third of May the Church celebrates the feast of the Finding of the Cross of Christ. In some of us that statement might provoke the grim thought that *we* have no difficulty in finding our cross, and when we find it there is no cause for celebration. So today let us try to lift up a tiny corner of that heavy black curtain of suffering and see if any good at all lies behind it. But please believe this: The farthest thing from my mind is merely to lecture you on patience; rather we are thinking the problem out together. Otherwise the priest who stands in the pulpit or behind a microphone or at a bedside and counsels courage and optimism is in the hollow but hollering position of a prize-fighter's manager. The poor fighter may be slumped on his stool about the eighth round, his eyes black and blue, his nose trickling red, his cheeks puffed, his body battered, but the manager is patting him on the back and chattering, "Go in there and fight! He can't beat us!" Whereupon the bell rings and the manager with the brave talk steps briskly out of the ring. And the poor fighter is in there alone, murmuring, "Us?"

This, I hope isn't our situation. I am just trying to blow the dust off a few principles that hold for me as well as for you, and which we are all liable to forget. And the first is that from every eye some tears must fall: suffering in some form or other is inevitable. Life is like the keyboard of a piano...first a white key, then a black. Bright days, dark days. A note of glittering joy, then a deep melancholy minor, yet somehow they blend into the perfect song. Who was it that said we just have to take the bitter with the better? We must remember that this human nature of ours limped out of the Garden of Eden a wounded veteran, subject to future twinges and aches, both physical and moral. For instance, the very fact that we have teeth (which is good) means that sooner or later we are in for a toothache (which is bad). God never claimed that this earth was to be a mountain-peak of joy. We ourselves call it in the prayers after Mass "this valley of tears." So don't be disappointed if it isn't the vestibule of heaven; it is only the rugged testing-ground outside, with plenty of bumps on the roads. How hard we hit them depends on our moral and spiritual springs.

All this may seem like hanging neon lights around the obvious, yet you would be surprised how many people feel cheated if their piety and devotion do not protect them from the scars of life. They bristle, sullen and hurt, when hardships and headaches dare to plant their thorn-bushes in the garden of the righteous. They might not admit it in so many words, but they feel that their religion ought to act like a sort of spiritual vaccination and keep them immune from trouble. The proof is that when trouble does come, their faith falters. Let disaster come into their life, and doubt comes into their heart. Their whole faith has been pinned on the absence of sorrow or misfortune. But you never can pin your faith on the absence of something. It has to be pinned, like Christ, to a Cross, the Cross which stands there like a signpost on a road and reads simply, "God's Will is this way." But there is infinite consolation in the memory that God's own Son, the day He trudged back to Heaven, took this very road of suffering. His Blood-Stained Footsteps are there before us, and if like the servant of good King Wenceslaus we set our feet in our Master's Footprints, His Own warmth and strength and courage will flow into us from that hallowed ground.

So let's put aside the notion that faith, or religion, is a guarantee against trouble. No, it is rather a guide and a help during it. Faith is not an escalator to bring us up the steep hill of life, but more like a staff to lean on while we do the climbing. Religion is not a magic charm to keep the world we live in away from us. Some people apparently would want an ocean but no seasickness, breezes but no gales, rain but no rheumatism or postponed ball games, sunshine but no sunburn or scorched lawns, fire that broiled a steak beautifully but never burned down a house, soil that shot up towering wheat but simultaneously withered the weeds. No, the laws of nature work for the general good, and we cannot expect the Almighty to step in, throw a switch, and stop the machinery to avoid our individual harm. It is a great, wide, wonderful world—for the exercise of virtues—and for that reason, difficulties and hardships and sickness and death lie ahead on everyman's road, and there is no detour around them.

As to the evils that come to us from human nature, from the perversity of men, of course God could have arranged things differently. He could have made a world without drunkards or adulterers or perjurers or thieves. This is saying He could have made a world without free will, where the whole human race would have been a regiment of goose-stepping, mechanical, iron puppets marching on the straight and narrow path because they simply could not swing off in any other direction. God could have, but He did not; and it is no use to ask why not. Nobody audits the Books of God. He chose instead to honor us with free will, with the power to choose between good and evil, so that He could reward us with an incredible Heaven.

In the world as it is, the best that Faith can do even for a saint is, not to deliver him from the backlash of nature or the malice of men, but to give him the spirit and the weapons to meet his particular trials. Like the suburban gardener who may have insects attacking his plants, but he also has a spray to fight them; there are weeds that crash the garden party but he has a tool to root them out; there come dry spells that powder the earth, but he has his hose to dampen it down. So intelligent men and women look to Faith, not for freedom from troubles, but for courage to cope with them under the banner of their Captain Christ. And when we are most *down*, then especially we should look up—to Him! In a sense we shall be like a deep-sea diver. Maybe we are beyond our depth. Maybe the water around us is so murky we cannot see our way. But as long as our air-line is clean, as long as we keep contact with Him watching up there, we are safe!

The rub is that many of us look down at our trouble all the time. Did you ever see one of those jet-black silhouettes that they sometimes give away as ads? It may be the face of Washington or Lincoln, but the idea is that if you stare at it long enough, intently enough, you will see it even on a blank wall,— the same black image. So it is with us; look on the dark side of things and you will see your trouble everywhere. It will be like Macbeth's dagger hovering before your eyes wherever you turn. Isn't it better to look up, to lift up your eyes and your heart to the God of all consolation?

Maybe you are old and lie today on the cross of a sick-bed, with the thorns of a burning headache jabbing your brow, or the crippling nails of arthritis twisting hands and feet till the whole tortured figure is a living crucifix—what can I tell you but that such suffering *bravely borne* is a greater glory before God than the most majestic and gorgeous Cathedral ever to stand against the sky? It is the bell that is struck that gives the melody; the candle that wastes away that gives the light. And it is the human soul in suffering patiently borne that offers the greatest prayer to God.

Or perhaps you are young, and your life only yesterday seemed a garden of roses like Eden, and almost overnight it has become a garden of agony like Gethsemane, because someone you trusted and loved, betrayed you—perhaps even with a kiss. But remember —we don't have the blueprints of our future lives. God does! He knows what He is doing. Sometimes Christ the Carpenter has to hammer us down so that we fit snugly into place. Sometimes He is like a Jeweler who has to grind the gem to give it the polish He wants. Sometimes He is like a Life Guard who must knock us out—in order to save us.

Or possibly you are a Father or Mother, and death has left an empty chair in your house and a dull aching emptiness in your hearts. And as you move slowly around the house, your eyes fall on his picture there on the piano, his prized autographed baseball here on the mantle, a jacket hanging in the closet—oh it is like having your own stations of the cross hung in your own home. You can become bitter about it and shake your fist at Heaven in rebellion. Or you can clasp your fingers and bow your head in prayerful resignation. You can be like the gravel path, which, when it is trodden upon, becomes hard and glinty; or like the Oriental rug which under pressure becomes softer and richer every day. You can ask the oldest question in the world, "Why should this happen to me?" Do you know the answer to that question? There isn't any answer. Unless it is the oldest answer: God (because He is God) knows best. We have to put our little hand in His Big Hand; and trust, like any child with any father, that He knows where He is going.

Or maybe the answer is this. Germany used to give its heroes the Iron Cross, and France gives the War Cross, and England the Victorian Cross, and America the Distinguished Service Cross. Who can say but that God gives His heroes and heroines—just the Cross!—a splinter of the Sacred Wood conferred by His own Bleeding Hand; because anyone who is really close to Christ must, sooner or later, share His Cross!

The People and the Steeple

WORRY IS WASTE

In recent years the Church has established the feast of St. Joseph, the Worker. Oh, he has another Feast on the Nineteenth of March; but, in the first place, that date always falls within the lean days of Lent; and in the second, the Nineteenth of March is pretty well overshadowed by the great green Seventeenth. Around that time every preacher practically says, "Er-r good St. Joseph, would you mind standing aside for a moment while we pin a few sentimental medals on St. Patrick?" I don't suppose St. Joseph minds very much either, because since he never stood "front and center" in the spotlight and fanfare when he was living, he probably will not miss them too much now that he is dead. But at least the Church is resolved to make amends, so each First of May she sets aside another feast day and dedicates it to St. Joseph, the man who worked, not the man who worried. And therein lies a lesson for us all!

Isn't it a pity that though St. Joseph is one of the really towering figures on the skyline of Faith, the mists of the centuries have so enveloped him that we know very little about him? Oh, you read this and you read that, but it is mostly rainbow imaginings blown from the bubblepipes of pious writers. Precious little that is authentic. Nowadays, when a prominent man goes to his reward (or to his punishment) newspapermen scurry to their paper morgues, take out Mr. Dead's folder bulging with clippings, and swiftly compile his obituary. But if you go to the filing cabinet of history, you will find St. Joseph's folder very slim. If the word "Gospel" means "Good News", St. Joseph broke into the news on only four occasions; and ironically enough each time it was bad news for him, at least he was in trouble. That in itself should draw us commonplace people close to him, because isn't that the way it is with us? The only time the ordinary good man gets his name in print is when his house burns down, or he is robbed, or the undertaker suavely requests not to send flowers.

But take St. Joseph and *his* troubles. Here he is at Nazareth, pacing up and down his little carpenter shop, perplexed at the mysterious pregnancy of Mary. At Bethlehem the inn door slams in his face, and he trudges on to hang up a lantern in the broken down cattle stall where the Boy had to be born. In the flight toward the frontier of Egypt, he is just one step ahead of Herod's Storm-troopers, their swords still dripping with the blood of the Holy Innocents. And at the Gates of Jerusalem he begins his distracted, frantic search for the Lost Child which lasted three agonizing days.

Enough worry for one man, don't you think? Yet tradition has always painted St. Joseph as the serene Saint. In Christian Art you will see picture after picture of the Christ-Child curled against His Mother's Breast, and St. Joseph standing by, ruggedly handsome with his distinguished beard, staff in hand and eyes thoughtfully focused on the road ahead. Trouble might be lurking just beyond the bend, but you would never guess it from those calm eyes and that unclouded brow. St. Joseph never saw an American dime, but he lived its little motto: "In God we trust."

St. Joseph is the Saint who would not worry. His carpenter mind would have seen worry as a colony of spiritual termites: though a man's heart be of solid oak, worry will gnaw it away! Worry may not be listed among the Seven Capital Sins, nor included among the thundering "Thou Shalt not's" of the Ten Commandments, but it is still one of the sharpest arrows in the devil's quiver, and once he can lodge it in a man, the victim thinks of nothing else. It is pretty hard to get interested in doing good, or even in being good, when some worry is bothering you like a cinder in your eye.

Let me say that I have the greatest sympathy for people who are prone to worry. For one reason, I have done my own share. And for another you cannot be a priest in a busy parish, and day after day come face to face with the problems of the people, many of them bewildering, heart-breaking problems—why you would have a temperament and a disposition like a deep-freeze if you were not touched to the very depths of your being! But in spite of all this, I still insist worry is absolutely wrong. It only drills holes in the one bucket that will put out the fire: Christian courage!

Mark you, I am talking about worry, not reasonable thinking, not prudent planning. We should think; we must plan. But worry is useless thinking. Maybe we can explain it better with—of all things—a lemon. You squeeze a lemon and you get what the advertisements call rivulets of rich, golden, tangy lemon juice. But keep squeezing beyond that point, and you get that tart, bitter acid in the skin. Anybody can see it in lemons. Why can't we see it in life—see that there can be such a thing as too much thinking, brooding, and no good come of it at all?

Trouble is trouble, but worry sets out to make five thousand extra carbons! Call it anxiety or call it agitation, call it fretting or call it fear, worry is the victrola needle of the mind caught in the groove of a cracked record, going round and round, over the same ground, whimpering out the same whining tune, and getting nowhere. It is worry that can concentrate on a little cough and convince people they have consumption, or that sees in every little sore the possible beginning of cancer; in fact it can build up an ant-hill of trouble into the Alps. Worry has worn out more carpets with people striding back and forth like a sentry; has put more creaks into rockers as they go from a canter to a gallop; has wrinkled more foreheads till they look like washboards; has plowed and harrowed more hearts—and some doctors believe that worry is at the core of many an ulcer. (Now, I suppose, the people who have been worrying, will start worrying whether they may not have an ulcer too.)

But even these things might be tolerated on the debit side, if the credit side of the ledger could show that worry was right there with the production and the profits. But it isn't! Can you show me one house that worry ever built? One sickness it ever cured? One bill it ever paid? Yes, even one soul it ever saved? Take the smartest man you know—all right, take yourself—that merely means that when you are worrying, a pair of very sharp scissors in your brain is clicking and clicking at empty air, closing in on nothing. This is particularly true of those people who are always worrying whether the sins they confessed are really forgiven. If the Psalmist can call God "angry", I imagine this constant clicking at least gets on God's nerves, and it is no compliment to His Mercy either. Some people complain that they cannot forget their past sins. But God never promised forgetfulness. He promised forgiveness. What matter if the bills still exist as long as they are stamped paid?

In any area, spiritual or material, worry is a complete waste of mental energy. All the effort is channelled into discouragement and alarm. It is just the opposite of the old steam locomotive. In a locomotive all the steam, the energy, went into the boiler, and the locomotive got somewhere; but in the worrier all the energy, the steam goes into the whistle. And he (or she) just stands still and quivers and screams!

But when you have said that worry is utterly useless, you have fired only one barrel. The other one is that worry is incisively harmful. And the damage does not lie there like an open wound, but rather festers underneath. If you were to stroll into a factory, and glance around at the throbbing machines, the whirling wheels, the whirring belts, you would probably figure that the wear and tear on all that speeding machinery must be terrific. And yet it is not the constant revolutions that wear out the equipment, it is the constant friction. Theoretically, without the friction they could go forever. In the same way, it is not work that will wear a man down half so much as worry. It grinds like an emery wheel, and frays away the very heart, and peace, and happiness, and even hope. Filling your mind with little worries is like filling your shoes with little pebbles—what can you do but go limping through life?

All right, some of the worries are not little. Perhaps they are king-size problems, major fears. But isn't that still just what they are—fears? This terrible blow may fall. Now, I can see a man drawing an advance on his paycheck, but who in his sane mind wants to draw an advance on trouble? Especially since, unlike the chunk out of the pay-check, this anticipation will not lessen the evil when it comes. It lessens only our strength to meet it. We worry so long and so intensely that a certain blow is going to strike us that when it does fall, we crumple up and go down flat on our faces. Why? Because we have already gone down before it a hundred times in imagination, and the real thing is only the one hundred and first. No wonder we are battered down by one punch. We have weakened ourselves shadow-boxing in an empty ring. You don't train for trouble by worrying about trouble.

Suppose I were to say to myself, "Let's see. In the course of my life I'll probably fall down the stairs once anyway. Well, may as well start getting used to it!" Worry is falling down those stairs mentally, and the bumps really hurt! Shakespeare said the same thing much more elegantly and eloquently when he wrote: "Cowards die many times before their death.

15. *Pennies*

The valiant taste of death but once." And anyone who has ever kept a diary knows that the proper entry for each December 31st should be: "Dear Diary, I have had many fears and worries this year. But, thank God most of them never happened."

The situation seems to simmer down to this: If there is a problem or a hardship, we should think it over, see it from different angles, and come to what decision we can. After that, it is only useless, repetitious worry. It is like one of those brads or tiny nails that go into the making of your shoe. The nail goes into the first layer of leather—good. Into the second—fine. That's what it is made for: to hold the two layers together. But if it goes any farther, it goes into your foot. Worry is useless thinking gone so far that it hurts.

Some of you may be thinking, "This is all very well, but what has worry to do with St. Joseph?" A very good question, and I think the answer is this: Worry has really nothing to do with St. Joseph, because St. Joseph *would have nothing to do* with worry! Each evening when he came up the road from his little carpenter shop, and the tiny Fingers of the Christ-Child clutched his big hand as they walked together, St. Joseph knew Who was really leading whom! That is the way he walked through life, his hand in the Hand of God. He would do his best, and for the rest—trust in his Savior! Worrying was sawing that produced nothing but sawdust ... or crosses that a man should not be carrying at all. There is your example and patron when worry starts pinching your face into a frown. If St. Anthony is fairly successful in scouting the lost American pocketbook, and St. Christopher somehow manages to hold the car on the road even when the driver's Guardian Angel is out of breath,

St. Joseph is the reassuring Saint for troubled minds, a very lighthouse of silent strength and sure direction for the worriers. Wasn't it the older St. Teresa who said that she could not recall ever having asked St. Joseph for anything and being refused? But notice especially his influence on her mind, that calm confidence, that majesty of self-control, summed up in St. Teresa's book-mark:

> "Let nothing disturb thee...
> Nothing affright thee...
> All things are passing...
> Only God is enduring...
> God alone suffices..."

So, if our courage has been lying like a forgotten flag in a dark closet of our heart, riddled not by battle but by the moth-grubs of worry, let us take it out, shake it out, lift it high in the streaming sunlight of our confidence in God, and march on in the footsteps of St. Joseph, the Man who threw his care upon the Lord!

The People and the Steeple

THE WINTER OF LIFE

Modern Paganism attacks life at both ends. It is more difficult to be born now because of Birth Control, and easier to die because of Euthanasia. And when Paganism thus slams the front door against the Child timidly trying to enter the world, and pushes the old man, before his time, out the back door, the rooting section of Paganism lifts its old cheer, "Survival of the Strong!" On the other hand, Christianity has always quietly consecrated itself to the help and protection of the weak, whether they be in their first or second childhood. To that end it has its orphan asylums for the young and its homes for the aged—but some social workers tell us that today, when it comes to taking care of their own old father or mother, many young people, otherwise almost pious, have calluses on their hearts.

Well, it's true we of today dwell in a distant valley of time, but there still comes rumbling down from Mount Sinai the thunder of the Fourth Commandment: "Honor thy father and thy mother!" We learned that in grade school. And even though at times we grumbled and balked, we still could see it was reasonable. To obey, well that was O.K., but when the lesson droned on that we were supposed to support our parents in their old age, to provide them with food and clothing and shelter and medicine and spiritual assistance—why that went over our heads like a cloud. We were wondering what Mom would have ready for lunch. Our busy and bustling mother didn't seem to need any help. Not then. Maybe she does need it now. And the obligation to support our parents which we took so lightly when we were nine, still binds heavily whether we are twenty-nine or thirty-nine.

After all, they provided for you for many years when you could not provide for yourself. Why shouldn't you do as much for them now? Maybe they are a care, and tie you down. Don't you think you were a care, and tied them down, when you were young? Perhaps they are cranky or crochety on occasion; so were you, unless as a child you were the angelic exception. Maybe they upset your routine a little; you used to upset their whole house. And do you know, their whole life faced toward you, toward welcoming you into the world and making you comfortable when you came? Don't you think you could do a little toward making their life comfortable as they get ready to leave?

I don't imagine it is easy to be old. I remember once hearing a young girl pouting and whining because she thought her home supervision was too strict. It wasn't, actually. But the girl flared up and said, "The trouble with you, Mother, is you don't want me to have a good time!" "Good time!" said the mother. "Sit down, Citronella. You talk about me keeping you from good times. Did you ever think about the good times you keep me from? You know, it would be a whole lot easier to forget all about you. Some day you are going to learn that being a mother is a whole lot harder than being a daughter. It's work, and it's worry."

And sometimes I wonder if being a grandmother may not be even harder than being a mother. Oh not from the score of work or worry, but because of neglect and suffering. After all, to be a grown woman, and an older woman, in a younger woman's house—say, your daughter-in-law—and to be definitely secondary and always in the background, don't you think that hurts? To feel as you grow older more like a boarder and less like a relative; to be a mother-*in-law* but not *in-love*—oh, if there is one word I would gladly rip out of the dictionary, it is that word, mother-in-law! Doesn't it seem to imply and to insinuate an unwelcome meddling stranger? Well, on second thought, maybe some of them do meddle. Maybe at the marriage ceremony, we should have something like the solemn cutting of an apron string, to symbolize that henceforth just as man and wife are joined, mother and son must part,—in the sense, that henceforth the best mother in the world has to be a distinct second in the life of her married son. The girl he chose was not good enough for him, of course—what girl would be? But, once he has "thrown himself away," and has given his hand and heart to the girl of his choice, a real mother never interferes.

THE WINTER OF LIFE

Some mothers are so determined not to interfere that they deliberately live alone. Some prefer it because, though they reared a noisy brood of their own, now when they are no longer cushioned by youth, they wince at the shrill voices and stamping feet of the grandchildren. There are many old mothers like this, living in little rooms, all alone. Well in this situation, do you think it is enough if a son or daughter mail them a few dollars every month? Surely they deserve more than mere support. They are not old police horses turned out to pasture. They are mothers. They are hungry for other things than food—hungry for a little affection, a little visit, a little remembrance, a little love. And mark you, all this is not sentimental charity. This is our solemn, bounden duty. It is the adult part of the Fourth Commandment!

I don't think I have to add that it holds for fathers too. Yet, personally, I have come across a case where they forced an old Dad to take his meals *in the cellar*. In that house they treated the dog better than Dad. Oh it must be the very worst feeling in the world to realize that somebody you live with thinks you are a burden, and will be relieved and happy when you do the decent thing and die. I think that God will see to it that we are treated when we are old, pretty much as we treated others. And it's not too long away. Every old person we see is the first rough proofs of our own picture a few years hence. Every baby carriage coming along the sidewalk says, "Get out of my way! Here I come!"

Do you remember the story of the sturdy Bavarian peasant who got disgusted with his father because the trembling old man, carrying his plate away from the table after dinner, had broken two plates in the last month? Don't ask me why he had to carry the plate away; the farmer wanted him to carry it and not break it. So this day when the old man dropped it, the farmer swore at him, and went out into a nearby forest, and began to carve a plate out of wood. Seems his own little son had tagged along after him, and got interested and asked his Dad what he was making. "I'm making a plate that that clumsy old grandfather of yours won't be able to break!" The boy watched his father whittling away, and then he said, "Daddy, be sure you make that plate good and strong, because then when you are old, I can give it to you!" Daddy almost cut his finger when he heard that. He looked at the boy, looked into space, tossed the plate back into the woods, and said, "Come on, son, let's see how Grandpa's doing."

Practically the last words Our Blessed Lord preached from the pulpit of the cross was when He rolled His blood-rimmed eyes toward Mary and said to St. John, "Son, behold thy Mother!" as if to say, "Be good to her, take care of her, when I am gone." The eyes of Christ still look lovingly on those who are good to their parents *before* they are gone! For example, often it is a daughter who gives up her own motherhood to take care of her mother. And in return the world is pretty cruel toward her, pinning on her the label of old maid, as though she were only a remnant left there on the bargain counter of life after the rush was over . . . a spinster . . . an old maid. They forget that once she was a young blooming maid with an old fading mother. They forget that when her generation walked up the aisle to the pulsing boom of the Wedding March, she wasn't left behind: she stayed behind. Yes, she is a spinster, maybe now and then

THE WINTER OF LIFE

she spins dreams of what might have been; but all the time she is spinning out of herself care and comfort for an old parent who needs it.

And for the young and vigorous that isn't always easy. Most people love old folks at a romantic distance. They think of the sad beauty of an old face, the gleaming silver of the hair, the gentle manners of a by-gone day. Meaning they like old age in charming little poems or in character actors in the movies. But that's like liking a snowstorm through a comfortable picture window. To live with the foibles, crotchets and eccentricities of the old is quite another matter: all the way from a hand cupped suspiciously to the ear, to a noisy way of taking soup as though there were an outboard motor on the spoon.

Especially it isn't easy when the old person is an invalid, so confined by walls and window-panes that she is restless; so crippled by pain she is cranky; so helpless to do anything herself that she wants everything done at once and perfectly! Show me the girl, the daughter who cares for a parent like that; a girl who spends all day patiently answering each petulant call, and who is all honey to an invalid who is sometimes all hornet; who takes her mother's thin arm as she hobbles down toward the sunset, when she might have slipped her arm into some man's and headed toward the sunrise of a new life of her own—a girl whose brothers and sisters are married off and have their families, a girl who perhaps is just pitied as Aunt Peg or Aunt Sue—well, I don't think God pities her. I think He loves her dearly and will reward her richly!

Maybe she is not a saint; maybe her picture is only on a piano instead of up in a stained glass window; maybe her name is in a letter box instead of in a litany, but she belongs to those martyrs not of blood, but of blood-relationship, who do not lay down their lives but who give them up! That God who loves old people like old books, old books that were tossed around so much in their time they are battered and faded and falling to pieces, and are now on the shelf, ignored; that God Who loves them, these precious first editions, and sends His angels to collect them for Heaven, He will write high in His own Book of Life, the Catalogue of Heaven, those who appreciated and valued and cared for this treasure they had, their own old mother or father!

The People and the Steeple

THE FLAG OF CHRISTIAN COURAGE

When I was in the Seminary many years ago, three or four of us used to meet every week in the Lower Chapel and practice speaking. We would preach to one another and thereby strengthen our voices, and we would listen to one another and thereby strengthen our patience. Being very young we wrote pretty flamboyantly, and every sentence pranced along flaring its adjectives like jockey silks. Being very young too, we walked among the mountain peaks of high ideals, not knowing much at all about "this valley of tears," the world of reality where people lived and loved, and had their headaches and their heartaches, and worked and suffered and died.

All this came back to me a couple of weeks ago when I opened an old book, and out fluttered one of those forgotten youthful sermons. Reading it now was like finding a picture of yourself as an altar boy. Apparently the Feast of Christ the King had just been added, like a new campaign ribbon, to the calendar of the Church, and this particular sermon was a salute to that occasion. Talk about rhetoric and decoration: every paragraph was painted like the Book of Kells. It was more like a stained-glass window than a sermon. It had Christ, the King, up there on an Ivory Throne, amid the waving of purple banners and the blaring of silver trumpets, and all the races of mankind like different-colored rivers, came streaming past the Throne to pay Him homage. Prominent in the picture was a Crusader, blood upon his armor and a broken sword in his hand, a warrior for Christ the King! An early Christian too, a smile wreathing his lips, going gaily forth to meet the bounding lions, a martyr for Christ the King! Not to mention the foreign missionary, courageous blackrobe amid the green palms and the brown natives of a tropical island, holding aloft his cross, a courier of Christ the King! And of course, a saintly nun, immaculate lily growing in the garden of the cloister, the princess of Christ the King!

In a way, I suppose, it was all beautiful and true, but again as remote as a stained-glass window to the people kneeling down there in the pews. You see, in the Seminary we lived on a little island of innocence in the midst of the rough and bitter waters of the world. We were barricaded behind bookcases. Our skyline was steeple and tower and dome and the rolling ridges of distant hills. We read no newspapers. We saw no secular magazines. We heard no radio. Being members of a Religious order, we went home once in six years, for not quite four days, after we were ordained. So the world outside was almost only a sad rumor. Sin was something in the textbooks. Suffering was something in the Lives of the Saints.

I am not saying that this was a bad preparation for a future priest. I think it was good. As a matter of fact, it was just an elaboration of the forty days Christ spent on the mountain-top in meditation and prayer, communing with His Heavenly Father before He Himself came down to preach. But it is still true that when we came out and at the first step stubbed our toe against hard reality, we winced with the shock. Well, you got over the shock, but you would never preach a sermon like that on Christ the King again. He was still your King, only now you knew Him better—and His followers. Henceforth to you His crown would be thorns, and His throne a cross, and in His Hands not a scepter but a nail and a wound. And His heroes and heroines would not be dramatic figures in picturesque costume. They would be, and they are, the little people in the small print whom the world never hears about; heroic but unsung; not the crusaders in their castles, but the common people in their kitchens; not shouting dramatically, "Long live Christ the King!" but whispering, and perhaps even sobbing those hard, hard words, "Thy Will be done!"

For instance, the other day I met a postman coming down the street, whistling like the very spirit of spring. We stopped and chatted for a moment, and I turned into the gate of the house he had just left. Would you believe it, already some tears glistened on the letter he had delivered two minutes before? I saw them when that mother handed me the letter.

Alas, it brought the details of how her boy had been killed in Korea. And as I tried to console her, I saw the postman on the other side of the street now, ringing doorbells and dropping letters, his brown bag jouncing against his side. Oh, that bag carried some good news no doubt, but it bulged with more than its share of bad. Bills that cannot be paid, taxes that cannot be met, this envelope with a crushing hospital report, and that one a failure at school, and another one regrets that there is no position available at present, but if in the future—

Every postman's bag is heavy with heartaches, life's little unknown tragedies delivered right to the door. Every rectory parlor echoes the same sad stories day after day. Every votive candle burning before a shrine tells the same tales in the language of light and shadow. When you see a candle burning like that before a shrine, never think it is just a pious decoration. Every holy candle waving in the dusk is like a little golden flag waving over a battlefield where some soul is hard-pressed in the fight. Every bright candle is a blazing flare leaping up from a sinking ship. Every nervous flame is a moving tongue of fire calling, "Help! Help!"

Sometimes the trouble is so overwhelming, the situation so apparently hopeless, and we so helpless, that we just feel like burying our head in our arms and almost crying. With some people, especially at the first impact of sorrow, this is understandable. But to stay that way for a long time, to be always despondent, in chronic despair—where is the virtue of Fortitude (as the theologians call it) or plain Christian Courage? Whom do you think Our Lord loves the more, the sniffling, pouting self-pitier, or the person who quietly takes it on the chin, or even on both chins? Once, the test of Christian Courage was pouring out one's own blood; now the test may be not shedding tears. Peculiar thing here: each of us thinks that his trouble is greater than anybody else's. If you ever feel that way, a good rebuttal is a walk through the nearest hospital. If after that you don't come running down the hospital steps, thanking God that you can run, your sense of values is off-center. None of us has any monopoly on trouble. There is plenty to go around. There always has been. And besides the obvious one of prayer, the only antidote is Fortitude, Courage!

And yet sometimes people will light a candle (as we mentioned before) and then go back to their pew, and as they gaze at the sweet, serene face of the Madonna, a bitter rebellious feeling wants to break through their lips: "Mother of God, it is well enough for you to be so primly pious up there, sheltered and quietly happy in your Shrine! But you don't know what it is to be responsible for a struggling family, to provide for them day after day—do you remember that you must eat before you can pray?" Does she remember? How could she forget? We forget, for example, her flight into Egypt when the Holy Family were refugees, and Joseph trying to get a job in a foreign country and not knowing a word of the language! Don't you think those days needed courage flying like a flag?

Or a young man might kneel before Our Lady's picture and try to choke back the thoughts that rise within him, "Forgive me, dear Mary, but I don't think you know what it's all about. Oh it's easy for you to be so immaculate and chaste and saintly there in your picture frame. But I don't live in a picture frame. I live out in the world. How can you know what it means to try to be good when everything around seems bad, to keep a clean tongue in your mouth when so many tongues about you are dripping with slime, to hold on to those Ten Commandments till your hands are raw and bleeding, when so many others have let go, and are boasting of their freedom, and taunting you with being too strict—oh, it isn't easy serving God out past the church doors!" And Mary listens sympathetically, but there is a far away look in her eyes. She is still thinking of her sojourn as a young mother in Egypt—Egypt where there were no Ten Commandments, and where god was an obscene carving multiplied a hundred times over, and where vice was a virtue, and men and women went singing merrily down the road to hell—only there was no hell, because when you died, your body became a mummy, and your soul went drifting off into a beetle or a bee. Don't you think that to live for God in an atmosphere of utter paganism took the highest kind of courage?

Nobody who ever served God ever served Him long, without courage! Courage sat in the prow of Pere Marquette's canoe as it swerved round each new bend of the river as he dared to bring the faith to hostile Indians. Courage steadied the fingers of Father Damien as he wound his bandages round the leprous sores of the walking ghosts on the grey island of Molokai. Courage filtered through the tiny barred window in the Tower of London as St. Thomas More knelt for the last time on the stone floor beside his bed, before he laid his head on the hard pillow of the headsman's block.

But these are headline figures and we were talking about the postman's bag and ordinary people and the tragedies and the courage in little lives. Often it takes more courage to meet disaster in your own living room than it does for some national hero in his hour of crisis. Because in your ordeal there is no dramatic setting to remind you that everyone is looking; no electric excitement to make you forget danger and lift you above yourself; no thought of thundering applause when it is all over. Nobody but yourself or your family will ever know.

Who is courageous? I will tell you. Courageous is the mother who keeps the home going despite a husband who is a drunkard, a sodden, useless thing, like a cork fallen into a whiskey bottle. Courageous is the man who on his job silently swallows insults and abuse, not because he is afraid of the boss, but because he needs that job for his family. Courageous are those who sincerely go on striving to serve God, though they sometimes fall, even though the world hangs round their neck the sign "Hypocrite." Courageous are those who go on praying when no answer comes back and their prayers seem to go into a dark, empty tunnel, and Heaven seems to be a wall of brass; because in God's own way, in God's own day, the answer will come!

Courageous is the wife who enters marriage as a virgin and remains in it as a martyr for the sake of her little ones, and in spite of a husband who even taunts her to her face about another woman. No matter where such a wife lives, whether it is the slums or the suburbs, the address is Calvary, and Christ the King recognizes the vinegar and the gall, and the kiss of a Judas that mocks and betrays.

Courageous are those people who have come to know how bereavement can empty the heart of happiness overnight like an empty cup, but comfort and resignation are slow to trickle in—people who may have lost a loved one in cruel circumstances but do not therefore lose faith! People who have humbly stretched out their arms to embrace the *cross*, and find that their arms are around the *Crucified Himself*... for only from His wounds can come a transfusion of the courage they need!

The Stable and the Star

THE LONG "NIGHT BEFORE CHRISTMAS"

If you were compiling a dictionary of new words and phrases—say those that had minted fresh and sharp in the last thirty years—you would probably sprinkle Volume A with combinations like air-craft carrier, atom-bomb, Alcoholics Anonymous, anti-histamine and so on; but if you included "Season of Advent", many moderns would find it the newest or at least the most mysterious phrase of all—the only one they did not understand. Ironically Advent is older than the oldest dictionary, but it is a religious term, which sometimes means it is the clergy's well-kept secret.

How should a modern know? After all, religion is not splashed across billboards like cigarettes. On the television screen the Church can hardly compete with the incessant golden bubble of the sparkling brew or the slick quick click of the razor. And newspapers which will keep you precisely posted on who slugged whom in which swanky saloon, can still leave you a religious illiterate. Walk down the Main Street of modern life and the gay, dancing signs leap at you with announcements about everything except God. I suppose that even if a prophet came into the world with a flaming message, the world would tag him as just another press-agent, and wonder just what was "the angle."

Well, even if we live in the midst of the world, we don't have to live like the world. Each of us can be a rich, green island of Faith, not just a reef of rocky, barren materialism. Let the world keep its month of December with so many shopping days till Christmas. As Christians we should thoughtfully and prayerfully keep the season of Advent. "Season of Advent"—tear the phrase apart like a sandwich and what does it mean? Literally, the coming; specifically the coming of Christ.

In the film of history, Advent is a flashback to the weariness, the dreariness, the emptiness of the world before the coming of the Savior. But the Church does not merely point to that shadowy twilight of paganism, to the prophets and patriarchs standing on their watchtowers and straining for a glimpse of the crimson dawn of Redemption.

"No," the Church whispers, "Let's pretend—pretend that the darkness is still hooped over us now; pretend that the Star of Bethlehem has not yet begun to swing across the midnight sky; pretend there never has been a Christmas, and we are on tip-toe looking toward the first Christmas. The world is waiting for the sunrise. Heaven is not yet open; Christ has not been born. There is no Christianity!"

THE LONG "NIGHT BEFORE CHRISTMAS"

How fitting it is that the four weeks of Advent come during this time of the year, the time of the darkest days and the longest nights, because Advent is a call to remember that long dark night of the world which we toss off with a couple of letters: B.C. or Before Christ. Before the first Christmas. In Advent we long for Him again, yearn for Him once more. Now when you sigh for something there is always a tinge of sadness (because you do not have it) and that is why these mornings when the priest marches to the altar of Holy Mass he is draped in vestments of violet, a sad shade, the wistful color of the longing of Advent for its Redeemer.

Not so of course with the brisk world outside the church doors. There, red and green blaze on the billboards, blink in the neon-signs, shimmer and glow in the store windows. So much red and green it makes the town look like a giant salad of tomato and lettuce. But give the world credit: at least it prepares for its Christmas. Do you know that many of these brilliant holiday decorations were designed sometime around the Fourth of July? In one sense, many people who do not even believe in Christ make the most of Christmas; sometimes even the most out of Christmas too.

God prepared the world for the first Christmas through the prophets. Each one as from a high peak peered into the future and foretold some feature of the most important birth in all the annals of time. Isaias predicted the miraculous manner—how a Virgin would conceive and bring forth a Child and His name would be called Emmanuel, or God with us. Daniel revealed the time—the Child would be born when seventy weeks of years should pass after the edict for the destruction of the Temple. Micheas pin-pointed the spot: "And Thou, Bethlehem of Juda, thou art the least of the towns of Juda, but out of Thee shall come the Leader who will rule my people, Israel." Can't we at least prepare by remembering during these days that the heart of the first Christmas is not in a store but in a stable: the Baby whose bassinet was a bundle of straw but whose lullaby was an angel-song lilted under the stars!

How? Well, I don't want to scare you off by telling you to meditate. But why not (and it really is the same thing) why not pick out some particular character or some special incident connected with that first Christmas, and see it all happen again, vividly, in the little theatre of your own mind? For example, it really started with a census. Try to imagine, to see that census. Here at the head of it, just as real as Dr. Gallup, is a Roman official named Quirinus. He is supervising the registration in Palestine for the Emperor, Caesar Augustus. In Nazareth little knots of people cluster round the proclamation, posted there by the village well, and swear softly. Some snarl their open hate. Here is the State pounding at the doors of their homes and interfering with their private lives! Here are these busybodies in far-off Rome telling them to be off by a certain date and register in the city of their forefathers! But in one little cottage, Mary and Joseph look at each other with understanding eyes. Was it not written in the ancient scrolls that the Savior would be born in Bethlehem, and God would see that He would be; though it took a census of the whole Roman world, including this Jewish colony, to bring it about! Bethlehem was the town of the forefathers of Joseph. So imperial Caesar proclaiming his census was, for all his royal purple, only a Western Union boy

THE LONG "NIGHT BEFORE CHRISTMAS"
351

in blue with a telegram for Mary and Joseph to get going toward Bethlehem. Caesar decided he would count all the subjects under his scepter; he would feed these statistics to his fat vanity. He would show the world what a mighty Emperor he was! But, as we view it from the box-seat of history, little Caesar was only like the dummy of the ventriloquist, the puppet on the knee of Almighty God who pulls the string, and moves the mouth, and proclaims the census that will bring Mary and Joseph from Nazareth, where they would normally be, to Bethlehem where the Scriptures had foretold the Child would be born.

The point is that in our own life, when injustice or tragedy seems to be the order of the day, a reflection on something like this will remind us that Almighty God can write straight with crooked lines, that on the mountain-top of eternity He has the clear, far-seeing view, and that what now seems so wrong can turn out exactly right—like Caesar's inconvenient and egotistic census.

So you could take any episode connected with the coming of Christ and let it unreel in color in the film-booth of your brain. See Joseph and Mary trudging the few narrow streets of Bethlehem, knocking at door after door. At this door: "Sorry, no room!" (angrily). At this one: "Sorry, no room." (apologetically). At this one: "Sorry, no room." (Matter of fact and in a hurry). And reflect: Our Divine Lord is still knocking at doors in the twentieth century, at the doors of human hearts, and much of the time there is no room. But He still pleads.

You would think He would get tired, like any man. But He is God, and God never gives up! Even though you slam the door in His Face, some time or other He will be back, humbly asking to be admitted into your heart. The trouble is you never know which is the last time; the next time the knock comes from the bony fingers of Death. And you follow his silent figure not to the radiant presence of a Savior but to the grim presence of a Judge. Fruitful is that Advent that reminds us not only that on one historic day Our Lord came to us, but that on another historic day (for us) we shall go to Him! His Birth and our death.

Now and then, when the material preparation for Christmas, the shopping and the crowds and the confusion, the swollen feet and the vibrating nerves and the short tempers, all make you feel as though you you were being strangled with ropes of tinsel, then try thinking about good old St. Joseph. Possibly I am prejudiced, but I admit that while for many saints of the shadowy past I have only a kind of remote respect, for St. Joseph I have a deep personal affection. And in a mythical museum I for one would walk past the scepter of Solomon, the sling of David, the sword of Richard the Lion-Hearted, the quill of Shakespeare, to spend a little more time looking at the staff of St. Joseph that thumped along the Bethlehem road.

Poor Joseph! It was the worst time of the year for weather, and the road wasn't much more than a wide rut. Getting ready for Christmas for him meant only responsibility and heart-scalding disappointment. And despite his efforts, the best he could come up with was a stable. Under the flickering lantern that he hung from a roof-beam, the whole thing looked like a pathetic mistake. But God doesn't make mistakes. He, the Eternal, wanted to be born here—in timeless surroundings. A garage and a tractor, for example, are twentieth century equipment and atmosphere. Who knows what a few centuries hence will bring? But the Almighty, who belongs to all ages, knew that as long as men farmed their food from the earth, each new generation of men would easily understand the first Christmas scene, and their eyes shine with recognition as they beheld the stable, ever ancient, ever new, with the familiar "props" of animals. God foresaw that even the men who split the atom would be familiar with the music of milk splashing into dairy pails.

And the stable was the only way the world would remember. "This shall be a sign unto you" the Christmas angels carolled to the astounded shepherds. What was the sign? Not the star; that was only the lighting effect. Not the angels; they were only the chorus. But "this shall be a sign unto you. You shall find an infant wrapped in swaddling clothes"—sure, they all were. But here was the difference, the sign: "lying in a manger." Here was something more startling than a golden cradle in a royal palace. The star standing over a stable—this the world could never forget.

And it was Joseph who brought it about. Joseph who had done his best, and when his best looked like miserable failure, it turned out this was the very way God wanted it to be, and the only way the world would remember. For every year its eyes would turn with amazement toward a stable, and its heart would kneel with pity by a straw-filled crib.

It doesn't matter much which particular star of the Christmas constellation you gaze at through the telescope of quiet thought. Only now and then, from now to Christmas, meditate on some of them—Mary or Joseph, the Inn or the Stable, the Shepherds or the Kings. The whole idea is that if Christmas is primarily a religious celebration, why should it not have a religious preparation? And the best way to begin a happy Christmas is to begin at the beginning; to set out in spirit on the Bethlehem road; to take your place alongside Joseph as he leads the little grey donkey that carries Mary on its glossy back, while she in turn carries the Christmas Child beneath her virginal heart.

On the map the road dips down from Nazareth to Bethlehem almost due South some sixty miles. But on the calendar it passes only four milestones, the four Sundays of Advent. In a way it is like a Christmas Club. Each week you put in a little thought about the Savior to come, a little prayer of preparation, a little word of welcome and at the end you pick up your due reward, a heart aglow with deep Christmas happiness, because amid so much pre-holiday hoopla and so much neon-lighted nonsense, you still never lost sight of the very heart of Christmas, the birth of Jesus Christ!

The Stable and the Star

O COME ALL YE SHOPPERS

I hope it is only a repulsive rumor that next Fall the first ball of the World's Series will be thrown out by Santa Claus while a brilliant score-board flashes how many shopping days till Christmas. Well, some of us wouldn't be surprised if Santa Claus turned up in late August sporting red and white Bermuda shorts and cranking a hurdy-gurdy that trilled and burbled: "Come All Ye Shoppers, Cash Down or Credit" with clanging cash register effects and shivering cymbals.

This is the season when you get weary of herald angels who come whirring up from their home base on Madison Avenue and carol commercial jingles from T.V. skies; weary of shepherds who come running down from merchandise hills with good tidings of great bargains. And you wonder if the Star of Bethlehem has become so dim that it has faded to only a soft spotlight on the cosmetics counter. When all this has come to pass, you know that you are in the holy season of Advent—no, excuse me, the hollering season of Advertising, of course.

The month before Christmas is no longer what it always was in Christian tradition, a penitential preparation for the coming of Christ. Now it is just a jolly, glamorized anticipation of "the holidays". Instead of remembering the spiritual darkness that hooded the world before the Birth of Our Redeemer, we have a carnival of commerce in colored lights. No sooner has the Thanksgiving turkey been demolished to a fragrant memory (and sometimes before that!) than all the store-windows suddenly blaze with pyramids of Christmas presents; the magazine ads explode over the pages like fountains of fireworks; holly-covered catalogues (the prayerbooks of big business) slump the poor postman's shoulder; crowds of shoppers prowl and growl (in the spirit of the season) around the counters; and Silent Night is blasting out of a loud speaker.

No wonder John the Baptist, the prophet of Advent, called himself a voice crying in the wilderness. How amid all this hectic hoopla can any voice be heard announcing the coming of Christ? But that *is* the message of Advent. John the Baptist never flashed those eyes that glittered like swordpoints to plead: "Do your Christmas Shopping Early", but "Make the crooked ways straight. Level down those hills of hatred between you and your fellowman. Fill up those valleys, at least those ditches of spiritual sloth. Not because there are only X many shopping days to Christmas, but because the Kingdom of God is at hand!"

Thus spoke John the Baptist, not as a shopkeeper, nor as a shopper, but almost as a surveyor. From the point where the Star of Bethlehem hung like a golden plumb line to where the future Cross of Calvary rose like a measuring rod, he was laying out the straight and narrow path which every one who follows the Prince of Peace must pursue; the road of being good. Advent reminds us to get back on that road if we have wandered off. This is altogether different from the Christmas spirit, because Christmas, in the expansive sentiments of the seasons, is the time for *doing* good. But the best preparation for doing good is being good. And that can be a far grimmer proposition—even the difference between philanthropist and saint.

But who is to remind us of all that now? Who even hints that the pre-Christmas season ought to be a period of prayerful preparation for the coming of the Babe of Bethlehem? Bethlehem? Near the city of London there stands a mental hospital named Bethlehem—because, like the cave in the hillside, it was refuge and a shelter for the wanderer. But through the long erosion of a slurring pronunciation the name Bethlehem became Bedlam. That is the origin of our word Bedlam today. And isn't it a closer description of our present preparation for Christmas? Don't we approach nearer to Bedlam than to the Silent Night of Bethlehem? Silent Night! Look at a list of some of the so-called Christmas hits of recent years. They are not hits; they are blows, at the very spirit of Christmas. When disc jockeys turn herald angels they sprinkle the Christmas air with such lofty lyrics as "Mama did the Mambo while Santa did the Samba under the Guided Mistle-toe." Or some such drivel. This is the hushed expectant silence in the purple dawn before the rising of the Sun of Justice? This is Yule drool!

To compensate for the likes of that, let me say in fairness that the heart of our town, which is Boston Common, has become a miniature Bethlehem. Shepherds and flocks, camels and kings, stable and star, Mary and Joseph, Infant and Crib—all these stand out in picturesque splendor under the illuminated trees that shimmer like torches of soft blue light while choirs in overcoats and fur jackets send "The First Noel" pealing over the public address system. Really, it stirs you; something heart-warming to hear and to see. So when I spoke at a children's novena service, I took it as an enthusiastic theme. Then, as you do with children, I asked questions. And did I get my dimpled, blue-eyed, shrill-voiced come-uppance! Oh, they had seen the Common all right, and it was pretty, but in some ways it was all wrong! Now I began to get my suspicions, for every half-dozen benches or so there sat a Nun. And you know Nuns: they can keep a perfectly straight face; give you no clue whatever. I have sometimes thought that if they went in for cards instead of holy pictures, they would make the finest poker players in the world. Anyway, I began to suspect the children had heard this from someone else. Do you know what they told me? That all these decorations around town, including crib and candles and carols, are out there at the wrong time, for the wrong reason, and in the wrong way!

It came out, (sometimes lisping and whistling through missing front teeth) that it was not Christmas *yet*. It was Advent. And nobody—but nobody—starts celebrating a birthday a whole month before the day. Don't we have to admit that the youngsters have something there? All the fiery-colored festoons of lights draping the store-fronts, the little bands tootling "Little Town of Bethlehem", even a miniature Bethlehem come alive on Boston Common is (when you figure it out) preposterously premature. Or (to speak English) rushing the season. And besides: of all the seasons of the church year, Advent comes closest in spirit to Lent. Really a time of penance. Why Christmas Eve itself is canonically a fast-day!

Only *then* comes Christmas. Then let our joy burst forth with the suddenness of an angel song splitting the Silent Night. Then let the celebration begin! And then let the festivities continue till Twelfth Night. Didn't Shakespeare, child of a Catholic tradition, who knew that Christmas deserved a long, flowing celebration (namely, twelve full days) write his play "Twelfth Night" as a rollicking climax that would ring down the curtain on one Christmas season?

But *now* what happens? We begin Christmas practically at Thanksgiving, and Christmas ends on the night of December twenty-fifth as suddenly as a blown fuse. The very next day in some of the biggest store windows the gay decorations have gone with the snows of yester-year; but to make up for that, the linen sales are piling up in the windows like a fresh blizzard. By the way, doesn't this draw up the shade and let in a little light on the second objection that my young friends of the snow-suit set were making... that is, that the Christmas decorations were up there for the wrong reason? Boston Common, for example, with all its Bethlehem motif is very literally a stone's throw, or an advertising man's pitch, from the bright lights of business, just across the street. And all the decorations in the stores—what is the motive behind them? Not the Birth of the Savior but the booming of sales. It doesn't lead to a crib but to a counter. It doesn't stem from an old Christmas custom but from new Christmas customers.

As to preparing for Christmas the wrong way, the youngsters mentioned several things. Like the music. Well you have to admit (as I hinted before) that some so-called Christmas records, novelty numbers with a tom-tom beat, are about as congruous to Christmas as a conga line shuffling down a cathedral aisle. Or run your eye over a display rack of Christmas greeting cards. It reminds me of an exhibition of paintings we had in a park here one summer. They were mostly what is called modern art. I honestly believe that if a sudden windstorm had whipped off the cardboard titles from the paintings, nobody could have pinned the right titles back on the right pictures. So with many Christmas cards. Take the printing off and they would do just as well for an invitation to the christening of an ocean liner. To me it has always seemed as simple as this: a Christmas card without Christ makes about as much sense as a rice pudding without rice.

Or take the verbal greetings that you will soon hear over the radio or simpering on the television screen, those weasel words: "Happy Holiday!" Was there ever a greeting so anemic, so pussy-footing, so broad? "Happy Holiday" is like a shower cap. It can be stretched to fit the head of any day. Washington's Birthday, the Fourth of July, Labor Day—they are all happy holidays. But Christmas is a very special holiday, the Birthday of Our Lord Jesus Christ; so let us acknowledge it or be silent. His friends Our Savior loved; His enemies He forgave; but the luke-warm in-betweeners even *He* could not stand, and said

O COME ALL YE SHOPPERS

(pardon the bluntness of Scripture) He would vomit them out of His mouth.

Not to speak of (the children didn't bring up this) the weirdest of all ways to welcome the Holy Christ Child: the Christmas office party, where decent reserve is often drowned in alcohol, and where tragedy is written in lipstick scarlet. I wonder if that little boy who was learning the Our Father did not have something when he prayed, "And forgive us our Christmases..."

That is the dark side of the picture. But since it is not a perfect world, and since we should be thankful even for small favors, perhaps we should rejoice that each year the Christian concept of Christmas is actually gaining. Each year more people are getting disgusted with the wilder office parties, so this abuse is gradually gurgling down the drain. Each year more millions of greeting cards go to market with a religious theme, to offset those creations that ignore the Creator, and don't even give God a nod. Each year the stores are stressing more the sacred aspect of the time so that their very windows sometimes glow like stained-glass windows with the story of the New-born Babe. Each year we are gaining, so be glad! And we are making such progress in putting Christ back into Christmas, who knows but that someday we may even go one step further and take Christmas out of Advent?

Anyway Advent is not the occasion to play District Attorney to other people's consciences and cross-question them about a pagan preparation for the great Christian feast. It is a season for us ourselves to turn away for a few minutes each day from the color-splashed bazaars of merchandise, and peer into the dark tunnel of time where the Star of Bethlehem is silently sweeping toward us like the great white headlight of a locomotive! Ever nearer, nearer! The shadow has almost crept round on the sun-dial of history to the hour; the wrinkled finger of prophecy is pointing out the place; the Redeemer and Redemption are due. Not silver-ware sales, not fountain-pen bargains, not new ideas for gift-wrapping, but Christ Our Savior is at hand!

So, if you do not want to leave Christ off your Christmas List, or slam the door (like the innkeeper) against Our Lady, homeless and heavy-laden, or look upon December 25th only as "the day there are so many shopping days until," then give the tiny caravan on the Bethlehem Road a daily thought. And when that constellation of stars we call the Northern Cross, which each night marches majestically across the Advent skies, stands bolt upright on the horizon as it does on Christmas Eve, like a cross of diamonds lifted to salute the entrance of the Savior of the world, you too will lift your heart to Him in joyous welcome. You will be one of the precious few that are dear to His Heart, because you have spent Advent not merely getting ready for Christmas—*you* were preparing for Christ!

The Stable and the Star

THE LITTLE LORD JESUS

In the Basilica of Bethlehem on December twenty-fifth, during the Solemn Midnight Mass, the Deacon will solemnly carry the Book of the Gospels across the sanctuary, and reverently take his stand upon a silver star that is countersunk in the marble floor, and there on the very spot where once lay the straw-filled Crib, will chant the Christmas story—there on the very center spot of all the world!

Will the crib and the Christ-Child be the center of our Christmas too?

Some years ago the art world was shocked by a cultural sacrilege. It seems that a wealthy connoisseur had bought a painting by Murillo, which portrayed with all the radiance of the master, a Baby Christ surrounded by a flutter of adoring cherubs. But somehow, between the place of purchase and the site of delivery, a mad artist had broken into the consignment, cut out the incredibly sweet face of the Infant and painted in its place a simpering tenth-rate substitute. Later on, whenever the art connoiseur was showing guests through his private gallery, he would pause at this picture and say, "You have heard of the tragedy of Calvary? Well, this is the tragedy of Christmas!"

Isn't it still the tragedy of Christmas for many that in the gilded frame of gay celebration the Christ Child has been cut out and replaced by a cheap, garish, vulgar counterfeit? He is, as in the Murillo, out of the picture! The accent is on merry, not on Christmas. The Babe of Bethlehem is smothered under the bright blanket of "the holidays".

Let *us* at least recall instead that, one night when the world was very dark God hung out a new, comforting Star; one night when the world was very lonely, He gave it His own Son. Oh, it had been a drab world and a dull night for the shepherds there, as they stood on the hunch-backed hill blowing out frosty breath like clouds of incense smoke. Then all at once, like some one ripping the paper off a package, the sky opened and rank upon rank of choiring angels burst into song, and the glory of God was about them, and the light like a golden finger pointed to the last place Heaven should be interested in: a stable. The very words "Christmas Cave" remind you it is the spot where opposites meet: for this Child was both Man and God, and the breast that suckled Him belonged to both Virgin and Mother, and the people on their knees were both princes and peasants, shepherds and kings—everything as far apart as a stable and a star! Opposites, yes, for meanwhile, in faraway Rome, Caesar snored while down the silver stairway of the stars came the Infinite, to become an Infant; there, between the four rough boards of a cattle crib, on a heap of straw, under a glimmering lantern, the Almighty was born. "Oh," cries St. Alphonsus, "who would ever have thought of it if God had not thought of it and done it!"

God gets around to the unlikeliest of places, doesn't He? Here was this hole in the hillside, only a temporary stable for animals, an emergency shelter for passing shepherds. Birthplace of the Savior of the world! Yet notice this: Mary made it do. Can't you almost hear her consoling poor, disconsolate Joseph as he flashed the pale lantern around the place. "Why, it is just what we need; privacy and quiet; and it's snug against wind and weather. And look at that little manger—it even looks like a cradle!" ... So much of life still consists in getting along with a sad situation, taking the thorn with the rose, putting up with something grim that God for some reason of His own wants, as He wanted to be born in that unlikely and unfitting stable. At Christmas you have to begin by putting rebellion out of your heart if you want to let happiness in.

Put away rebellion, and put on humility. We often say, "God's ways are not our ways", but do we really believe it? Look again at where the King of Kings chose to find His royal cradle and you will believe it! Doesn't the choice of Bethlehem for a birthplace look like the Almighty's silent snub to the swaggering big cities that were so proud of their sword of power, of their goldpieces of wealth, of their shelves of learning, but who heard this talk of a Redeemer with a sour and superior smile? So God walked around them and slipped into a stable where

He knew His first callers would be shepherds, the poor. Speaking no language but a baby's faint cry, having as His companions only dumb cattle and not much brighter peasants, no retinue, no glamor, no speeches, no flags; only humility, poverty, yes, and a towering love! For He went from the cave of Bethlehem to the cottage of Nazareth, to the cross of Calvary, just to live and die for the likes of us! Crouch in the mouth of that cave and gaze out and you murmur "Greater love than this no man hath than that He lay Himself down at Birth in a manger!"

But alas! do we not so dress up Bethlehem in our imagination that we hardly realize the swoop that God made from the heights to the depths that first Christmas Day? How we prettify the stable, romanticize the shepherds, then paint it all on a gay Christmas card, sprinkle it with sparkling crystals, perhaps even pad it with silk or satin, and then write across it, "Merry Christmas!" Somewhere along the line the little town of Bethlehem has blossomed into a Radio City. But, mark you, the stable where Christ was born was not a handsome barn converted by a wealthy eccentric and done over in knotty pine so that a man could "rough it" in luxury. The first Christmas stable was a stable, and never was meant as a roof for a man, not to speak of a baby, not to speak of God!

And the shepherds. On our greeting cards they cluster about the crib, a troop of well-washed, picturesque fellows, as gaily costumed as the extras in an opera. Please! They had not been anticipating this call from the skies; they were not dressed for the occasion; they were just earthy peasants running down from the hills, clumping into the stable with muddy boots and matted beards and dirty hands and rough voices—not at all the class of people you would invite to a classy christening. The whole point is that God knew that these would be the people who would come, and He wanted it that way! You have to stoop to get into a cave and the proud never make it.

It is the same way with those boisterous, roaring characters (like the people in the Inn) that turn Christmas into nothing but noise, nothing but the clatter of riot and revelry, and never a deep quiet thought. Has it never occurred to them—no, of course it wouldn't—that the most popular of all carols is "Silent Night?" Sometimes the best of us forget (though spiritual writers have been stressing it for centuries) that the stable of Bethlehem, as it stands out on the page of Scripture, is a tableau of complete silence. No single word is spoken—by anyone. The Infant of course does not speak; as a matter of fact the word infant is a Latin word that literally means unable to speak. Mary says nothing—only her heart beats faster as she bends over in breathless adoration. Joseph is silent—probably busy with a half-dozen details. The shepherds may have chattered excitedly on the way, but once arrived, their mouths hang open with astonishment. Inside that abandoned cave at the dead of night the heart of Christmas is a hushed and holy silence, a speechless wonder that this could be: that the Lord of the world and of all vast plunging space would make Himself small as a new-born Child!

It is marvel enough that God should come from the jewelled halls of heaven to a dark rocky grotto, but the marvel grows so bright it all but strikes us blind when we realize that God became—like any clumsy, hard-breathing shepherd there—a man! Occasionally in the newspaper you see a photo of a King on a good-will tour surrounded by some local group, say coal miners, with their grimy faces, and lamps on their caps, and picks on their weary shoulders; or maybe the King is standing in the center of a circle of thin, pinch-faced orphans. Oh yes, the good King poses with them, has his picture taken among them. But then he goes away; into the big shimmering car, and the tail-lights blink good-bye. He does not become a coal miner. He does not become an orphan. The great blazing marvel of Christmas is that the One Omnipotent God, Creator of star beyond star, did in His little crib become someone just like you and me, a man. Do you see now why we say He came down to us?

Down to us ... down to everyone of us! To the tired salesgirl with the aching feet and the frayed temper; to the backward child with the dull eyes and the slow tongue; to the rich man who cleaned up in the stock market and to the poor man who cleans up in the stockyards; to the elegant lady with the crimson nails presiding at the silver tea-urn, and to the dumpy woman with the red hands plunging her scrubbing brush into the bucket; to the saintly souls in cloistered convents and to the drifting derelicts along Skid Row; to the cosy family in the fire-lit living room, and to the prodigal son (or wayward daughter) in a lonely furnished room; to those who have and to those who have not; to those who should know better and to those who do not; to these, yes (and oh deepest of all mysteries) even down to me, way down to me, the traitor, the ungrateful, He comes! And His coming is Christmas.

Do you notice, by the way, that everyone clustered in the glory of the first Christmas had to leave something to get there? Joseph and Mary had to leave the vine-covered little cottage of Nazareth that to them was "home sweet home." The Little Lord Jesus Himself had to leave the glittering courts and the angelic hosts of Heaven. The shepherds had to leave their sheep in the bleak unguarded hills. The Three Kings had to leave country and family and friends. It has been that way ever since. If you want to come close to Christ at Christmas (not like the revellers in the inn) you have to leave something. Very often it is simply sin. Anything else is welcome at His crib, and His little Hand is raised to bless it—ragged poverty, stammering ignorance, ill-formed ugliness, tottering sickness. Let these come in and be welcome and feel at home, for the eyes of the Christ Child see only souls! But sin, no!

How will my soul look to His clear eyes this Christmas? What a mockery if a Catholic should mail a hundred cards, buy a half-dozen presents, loop the front of his home with necklaces of colored lights, call "Merry Christmas" to friends and neighbors—and all the while his soul is like a stable of mortal sin! The Sweet Babe of Bethlehem spent one Christmas in a stable; please, no more! Give Him a white Christmas, with the Hosts of Holy Communion falling like snowflakes on reverent tongues, and One of Them on yours, because your soul has been cleaned and garnished, and the Little Lord Jesus is come to be your Guest! This is keeping Christmas as we should keep it today.

The Stable and the Star

OVER TO BETHLEHEM!

This Child was not only new. He was news! Only, instead of news-boys shouting it on the street corners, angels sang it in the skies. It was the front page of the Gospel—and that word "Gospel," if you break it in half, "Good-Spel"—is the sturdy old Saxon way of saying "Good News." His Birthday was the best news, the greatest headline of history. But when the story broke, like most *Extras* it took the town completely by surprise.

Early that evening there was plenty of stir and bustle in sleepy little Bethlehem. This was the eve of the big census, so the narrow streets never throbbed with so much excitement. It was like a family reunion. In the cottages, housewives were humming happily as they flung the best spread over the best bed, because that rich relative from Jerusalem was due any minute now. In the inn, the smug proprieter was rubbing his oily hands and bowing distinguished guests to their special quarters. In the census booths, the clerks smoothed out the longest parchments, ready for the largest registration ever. Oh, there was plenty of eager preparation all around! Too bad they were preparing for everything but the one thing that mattered, the one thing that was to outlive that night and put Bethlehem with a star on the map of the world. Everybody was expecting somebody. Nobody was expecting Christ. Little wonder a gulp comes into your throat when you hear that Gospel line: "He came unto his own, and his own received him not."

But why must this same blunder happen every Christmas? *This Christmas!* Why must some of us go on making Bethlehem's mistake all over again? There they were all business at the census booths, and all pleasure at the inn, so the Great Event went over their heads like a Star. But nowadays too, don't we have a Christmas which in some quarters is too commercial, in other quarters too convivial, and in both the Little Christ left shivering out in the cold? For some people "Silent Night, Holy Night," still rings out loudest on the tinkling xylophone of the cash-register while the Birth of the Savior rings up an unresponsive "No sale!"

There are other people who will spend Christmas with the innkeeper. Like Uncle Egg-Nog who is already dreaming of a "tight" Christmas, whose "many happy returns" will be hiccups; and who filled with Christmas spirits, may well wind up *under* the tree. True, Christmas is a Feast, and therefore calls for celebration, but not for dissipation, not for sodden drunkenness, and not—incidentally—for the indecent excesses of some pre-Christmas parties in otherwise staid offices. What a weird way to welcome the coming of the Son of God! Isn't this almost like crucifying Christ on a Christmas tree, and crowning Him with a sharp-edged holly wreath?

No wonder then that the first Christmas went walking with saddened heart past the inn, and went on to the shepherds. A little group of God-fearing men, humble and wholesome, they stood on that midnight hill, leaning drowsily on their staffs, drawing their cloaks closer about them against the tingling night-air. A dull, routine job. Every night a carbon copy of the night before. You looked down and saw the purple slope of the hill; you looked around and saw the white blotches of dozing sheep; you looked up and saw the far-off silver pattern of the stars. This was the last outpost of obscurity. Nothing ever happened here. Nothing *could* happen—when suddenly all around them a thousand stars seem to melt into one glittering brightness! The frosty air quivers with glorious music. The voice of an Archangel trumpets forth: "Fear not! I bring you good tidings of great joy! For this day is born to you a Savior!" The next moment, when the angels have wheeled away, and when all that beauty has passed like the turning of a page, the stunned shepherds stare into one another's eyes, grip one another by the arm, and whisper, "Let us go over to Bethlehem and see this wonder that the Lord hath made!"

So they go over to Bethlehem, and come clumping into the shadowy stable. That lantern swinging from a rafter is a dim, misty affair after the dazzling glory of the miraculous skies. But they grope their way through the half-gloom, and the next moment they see—they see what a hundred gaudy holy pictures and a thousand artificial cribs have made us take for granted, have robbed of its freshness and wonder, have dulled and deadened the impact of a scene that should make us draw a quick breath of astonishment and awe! They see, in the last place in the world you would expect to find it, stirring feebly in the straw of a cattle-crib, bundled in soft swaddling clothes, a Baby! On one side a radiant young Mother bends over the manger, in her eyes a light like diamonds, but on her cheek a tear, as though love and adoration and joy had filled up her very spirit and now are over-flowing from her eyes. On the other side St. Joseph stands as though he felt a little in the way, and somewhat bewildered. When an impulse comes to take the Infant up in his arms, another impulse tells him he should rather get down on his knees. *Because this Child is God!*

Now Mary notices her visitors, shepherds who had left their flocks and come running to the Lamb of God. With a graceful gesture, the Maiden Mother lifts the Infant up and turns toward them. It is the first Benediction. Sticks of golden straw still cling to the white swaddling clothes like the golden rays of a monstrance, and the frosty breath of the huge ox floats up like clouds of incense. And in the straw, seraphs and shepherds, the holiest and the lowliest, kneel together.

Of all the impressive places where the Little Christ could have been cradled, He chose this! This place and these people! Not Rome with its imperial pomp and its helmeted legions, not Athens with its fine-spun philosophies and its marble art, not Alexandria with its noisy harbor and its haggling bazaars, but this! A little manger in an abandoned stable on the outskirts of an obscure town in the remote province of a pocket-handkerchief kingdom! The poorest shepherd there did not have a humbler birth. And the next morning He was just another Name on the census list... just another Boy. You have often heard how Abraham Lincoln, who was born in a log cabin, said "God must love the common people. He made so many of them." On Christmas morning we gaze at our Blessed Lord born in a stable, and we murmur, "Yes, He must have loved them, because He became one of them Himself."

That is why Christmas will always be the Feast of the common man, the festival of God's esteem for the obscure, ordinary little people. So if nobody pays much attention to you, if there is no room for you in the inn with the important ones, if you are just another name on the census list, just another undistinguished nobody—then Christmas is especially *your* day. It is still the day when Christ with the neat irony of God goes past the proud Herods, and the over-learned Pharisees, and the carousing revellers, and is born again among the modern shepherds—the ordinary simple people, the humble of heart, the wholesome of life, the quietly and sincerely devout.

When the Almighty took that star and streaked it like a piece of golden chalk down the blackboard of the midnight sky, and pointed to the Child in the Crib, He was teaching us the lesson of every Christmas to come. Things would change of course. Things have changed. This Christmas the heavens do not echo the carols of shining spirits; instead, thanks to the radio and television, the heavens will ring with the carols of men. The wings of archangels do not beat rhythmically over Judean Hills as they call out the first Christmas greetings; instead the outspread wings of the air-mail will coast across the sky, carrying sacks of Christmas cards. Shepherds will not stand ankle-deep in the straw of a stable, but cab drivers and engineers and nurses and housewives will kneel in orderly pews. You see, everything has changed. The only thing left of the original Christmas is Christ.

And Christ is not a thing. He is a Person! So the bright beam of the Christmas Star must focus on that one Person, not on many things. Don't spend too much time wondering whether those slippers you are sending Aunt Harriet are quite big enough—or are they too big, and will she feel insulted? Or worrying whether Grandma will really care for that pink bed-jacket, or will she perhaps promptly exchange it for an album of progressive jazz? Or pondering just what toys you can give Junior which will delight him and at the same time not disturb you. Trouble with this sort of thing is that they are only *things,* and the Little Christ Child somehow gets lost in the red ribbons and the crinkly holiday wrappings. After all it is *His* Birthday, isn't it? Give Him a thought! Give Him your chief thought! Wouldn't the Shepherds have been amazed if someone suggested that they turn their backs on the Crib, bow courteously to one another, and give one another gifts—say, a pair of sandals or a scarf? Wouldn't they have said, "But what about Him? *This is His day!"*

It is still His Day. At least when we give our presents, let us give them in His name, in His spirit. Then we shall not be tying up perfume or gloves or neckties or fountain pens, but tenderness, thoughtfulness, love. And gratitude—gratitude to God Who became one of us. Gratitude for humanity's most thrilling hour, the highest compliment mankind ever received. The cynic talks about resigning from the human race, and the Almighty elects to join it! *This* is Christmas! The rest is mostly crepe paper. He lies there in the Little Crib, and there I lay my heart.

The Stable and the Star

THE STRANGER

IN THE MANGER

Miss Suzanne Somebody, Bright Young Thing, just loved Christmas. It was so Christmasy. Still, after shopping, she was glad to flutter home in the Christmas Eve dusk, all a-twitter with the Christmas spirit, but somewhat tired from the Christmas rush. She threw her bundles into one deep chair and herself into another. She ripped the crinkly Christmas wrapping from a carton of cigarettes, lit one, snapped on the radio, and picked up a magazine with a Christmas Snow-Girl cover. Idly her fingers flipped through the ads, red and green ads that carolled of Cabinet Models with that Christmas Tone, Fruit Cake with that Christmas Taste, Coffee with that Christmas Tang. She paused only once: where Christmas Diamonds inside a holly-wreath were billed as "Yule Jewels with that Star of Bethlehem gleam." Then she hurried on, through the Christmas Vacuum Cleaners and the

Christmas Oil Burners till she found what she was looking for: Recipe for a Christmas Cocktail.

But something would not let her concentrate. Out of the radio came ringing the sweet clear voice of a boy soprano.... "Adeste Fideles... Jesum Infantem... Bethlehem." She scowled. Churchy stuff. Her scarlet fingernails tweaked the radio knob as though she had the choir boy by the ear. "For heavens' sake," she grumbled, "don't the stations know that these are the holidays? Hey, tomorrow is Christmas!"

As if in answer the radio blared, "take pride in presenting Ziggy Zulu and his Zanies who will now shatter the chandelier with their special Christmas arrangement of that galloping Christmas hit, 'In my Christmas Stocking I want only You.'"

Suzanne smiled at the dial. She settled back in her chair, cozy and content. Once more she felt so Christmasy.

Poor Suzanne, she was not celebrating Christmas. She was just celebrating the twenty-fifth of December. But these days aren't we all a little in danger of letting Christ slip out of the focus of Christmas? In danger of forgetting the Holy Day because of the holiday? In danger of forgetting a certain dim little stable in favor of the dazzling stores? In danger of losing the Star of Bethlehem in the neon glow of the gift bazaars? In danger of thinking of Christmas in terms of Something wrapped in holiday ribbons lying on a department store counter, instead of Someone wrapped in swaddling clothes, lying in a manger?

Mind you, the trimmings of Christmas—like the brown turkey in the oven or the green wreath on the window or the gift package under the tree—are good, and grand—provided we remember they are only trimmings, and we do not lose sight of the central fact: "This day is born to you a Savior Who is Christ the Lord!" Wouldn't it be tragic if in our home amid all the rollicking merriment, the Little Boy Whose Birthday it is, is left outside in the cold, peering wistfully in the window, forgotten at His Own Feast?

Forget Him? Logic should not and love would not. *Because He started it all!* Because Christmas was one Child's Birthday, now millions of other children in fuzzy pajamas patter down the stairs and hug their little presents with squeals of delight. Because two pilgrims and a donkey went plodding along the backwoods road from Nazareth to Bethlehem, a hundred thousand travellers line up before ticket windows. Because some nameless shepherds, standing on a nameless hill, suddenly heard singing in the skies, we find ourselves twenty centuries later humming Christmas Carols as we leaf through a telephone directory. Because Three Kings from the mysterious East, stepped into a stable with their gorgeous robes and royal gifts, aunts and uncles in modern overcoats come with armfuls of presents not by camel but by car. And because (till later on when the Kings came) one Boy had a bleak time of it at Bethlehem that first Christmas in what was half a stable and half a cellar, hard-boiled newspaper editors are running appeals to make this Christmas a little brighter for the thin and sparrow-like children of the slums.

Ah, it is hard to believe, isn't it, that one little manger should hold so much goodness! So much that the straws in it, like straws in the wind, have blown clear across the world—the lovely gestures and customs of Christmas! But even these are not worth a straw, unless we keep them in memory of the Divine Child Whose coming started and hallowed them all. So amid all the evergreens and the holly-berries, the gifts and the greetings and the gay home-comings, don't lose sight of Christ on account of Christmas! He is only a little Boy, and the Child Who was once lost in the temple can still be lost in the tinsel.

Gifts, greetings, homecomings! You wonder vaguely how can Christ be brought into these. It sounds like excessive piety or exaggerated poetry. But here is what I mean. Take the gifts. Isn't it a fact that many of us in giving presents do not celebrate the Feast of Christmas at all? That's right: we really celebrate the day after Christmas, the Feast of St. Stephen. You know—"Even Stephen." We give a pair of slippers and we get a pair of gloves. *You* send a waffle-iron and *they* send an electric clock. These are hardly gifts; they are practically gambles or investments where you win a little, lose a little. Fine spirit behind them, you understand, but if you want to thrill to the Spirit of Christmas in its truest sense, did you ever try giving where there isn't a chance in the world of getting? Where you are honestly playing Santa Claus to someone who really needs it, and not just playing tit for tat with someone who had better come across too, or next Christmas his name will be stricken off the list! This year, if you can afford it, pick out a hard-up family, or an invalid, or a worthwhile cause or a poor youngster, in other words the people for whom, like Christ, there is no room in the holiday inn. Your name may go off somebody's list, but it will go on God's.

Now about Christmas travel and homecomings. Ever since that first Christmas when God came into the world, and the angels swept across the skies, and the shepherds raced breathlessly down from the hills, and the Wise Men of the East came riding in on tall loping camels—Christmastide has been a time for travel. Today the means of transportation have changed, but the tradition of travel lives on. Some in cars or buses streaking along the highways; some in streamlined trains, snaking around sweeping curves of glistening tracks; some in planes so high that the last grey clouds of Christmas Eve seem to hang like woolly stockings before the red fireplace of the sunset; some, in more rugged regions, in a whistling sleigh where the horse's hoofs go clopping over the wooden bridge toward the lighted farmhouse which spells home. Yes, everyone who can make it, goes home for Christmas, to the fireside and the folks. But the soul has its fireside too, and that is the Flaming Heart of Christ. "Thou hast made our hearts for Thee, O God, and they shall not rest till they rest in Thee." If in any serious moral sense we are away from God, Christmas is the time to come home. The first Christmas His tiny arms welcomed the Shepherds; this Christmas His bigger, broader arms are out to welcome the lost sheep, the black ones, and the oxford greys. The first Christmas He greeted the Wise Men from the desert. This Christmas He is still waiting for the learned who have lost their way in the dry scholarly desert where theories shift from day to day like the sands, and where Truth holds her secret like the Sphinx. Not all the Wise Men have yet arrived at Bethlehem.

Finally, about the Christmas greetings. It is the strangest thing. You take the sourest, gloomiest, meanest man you know. He may have a face like a Vermont winter and his tight lips may be padlocked in a perpetual frown, but come Christmas and something magic touches them and they spring open—not for his usual grumpy "Good Morning," but for a warm (at least for him) "Merry Christmas!" They say "the whole world is Irish on the 17th of March;" well, the whole world is almost human on the 25th of December. For one brief day they remember that God thought so much of men He became one Himself. But alas, let the Christmas clock boom midnight, and the spirit of Christmas (which literally is out of this world) rushes off to catch the last Reindeer Express for its trip back to heaven. Our hearts crawl back into their hard shell for another year. The twenty-four hour truce with mankind is over. The grim, sullen fight for self is on again. After all, the important party is Number One.

Yes! And Number One is God—the God who became one of us to teach us to love all! Christmas made Him little; it ought to make us big—and keep us that way. He did not vanish after Christmas. He stayed—from the Crib to the Cross. He did not glorify one day on the calendar. He began a whole new calendar—from B.C. to A.D. So, let's not make Christmas a day, but a doctrine: that every man is my brother, because his little Brother—and mine—is in the Christmas Crib!

New Year, New Chance

RING IN THE NEW!

Tradition has always painted the stable of Bethlehem with a couple of animals stamping in their stalls. But that is almost all you can say about the ox and the ass: apparently they were there. The heavens glittered, the angels sang, the shepherds adored; the book of the past, closed with a dusty thud; the Hope of the Ages was laid in a manger—and it got no more response from the animals than the blink of a vacant eye or the swish of a restless tail. So close to Christmas, yet so far from Christ. Their stupid and staring brown eyes could not see the Infant for the hay; on the Feast of Christmas they were interested only in the feast.

Poor beasts, perhaps God sent them there as a symbol. For, New Year's, too, is close to Christmas, but for many, its spirit is far from Christ. In anybody's life New Year's should be a milestone; but some by the scandal they give make it a millstone round their necks. It is a new-born year, but they cannot see the Infant on account of the Inn—the modern inns, which, like Bethlehem's, turn Silent Night into Strident Night, and amid all their riot and revelry completely miss the whole point.

Celebration is all right as long as it does not become hellabration. But in too many night clubs and hotels they will welcome the New Year pretty much as the natives must hail a new chief in the Isle of Pago-Pago. There will be music—well, it squeaks and squawks out of horns, and quivers and shivers on strings—so let us call it music. There will be dancing—at least there will be unsteady gentlemen in full-dress swaying with daringly gowned ladies in almost half-dress—call it dancing. Later there will be paper hats perched like pink dunce-caps on their reeling heads, and paper streamers draped over their deafened ears, and thin-stemmed glasses trembling in their fingers. Since this is the end of the Old Year, you might suspect the glass might be an hour glass, but if so, the last grain of sand has swollen into an olive. And amid the clanging of cowbells and the tooting of horns and the brackety-brack of noise-makers, at the stroke of twelve, the cry "Happy New Year!" is broadcast over the country on a national hiccup.

This is supposed to be the sophisticated way of welcoming a God-given New Year. The cash registers won't tell just how many hundreds of thousands of dollars are spent for the privilege of smelling like the village winepress and acting like the village fool. You may think, "A sadder and wiser man he woke the morrow morn," but generally he does not wake till the morrow afternoon and then, with a head spinning like a cocktail shaker, and with the drums of last night's orchestra beating out a return engagement in his poor throbbing head.

Is it not a shameless gesture, a mocking sneer toward God, to take the first fruits of the New Year that He gives and drown them in excessive drink or trample them in pagan revelry? After all, only God can give us time. Men can present us with a clock or a calendar, but these do not make the minutes or the months; they only measure them. Time is like thread reeling off a spool, spun by the hand of God; we have to seize it as it comes, and weave it into a worth-while pattern. You never know when Death, with one snip of the shears, is going to cut the thread and send us to God for the inspection and judgment of our life work.

Now of course, we can do with time whatever we wish. Time is only raw material. Every year is like a freshly-picked puffball of cotton. That lump of cotton, plus a little black dye will make a dark mask for a highwayman who kills. The same cotton, plus a little bleaching, could make a white mask for a surgeon who cures. God gives us time in the rough, but at the end of each day He always wants to know what we have done with it. The first returns of the New Year from some precincts will be pretty sad. Like new-fallen snow soiled into muddy slush, the first hours of this "Year of our Lord" will be dedicated to the devil!

But the sophisticates who look forward to a fashionable orgy in the Imbecile Room of the Hotel Cover-Charge, where more than the walls will be plastered and more than the chandeliers will be high, are not precisely the type of people who listen to a talk like this, so why waste time in slapping their erring wrists? Instead, why not a pat on the back for the many, many people who are really trying to do what is right, and still at the end of the year tend to be discouraged. Because besides the giggle-water group who look upon New Year's too lightly, there are those despondent souls who at New Year's look upon themselves too darkly.

Possibly too many pulpits at New Year's encourage discouragement. Why should New Year's be the accepted occasion when the preacher is supposed to wear his extra-long face, say about twenty inches, and shake a long, bony finger, and solemnly drone on in tones that sound like gravel falling on a casket, all about and only about the long black litany of our misdeeds that are writ forever in the closed book of the year just finished? Didn't we do a few good things too? But of course, if you bring these in, it spoils the preacher's doomsday effect, like a line of blue-birds suddenly starting to sing on a cursed and withered branch.

It is true we have all made mistakes in the past year. The memory of these ought to be a steadying and sobering influence on our future. It should make us lift our heavy foot off the gas, and pay more attention to the curves in the road. But it should not shake our confidence! Otherwise a man might say to himself, "Sure—I've messed up my past. At times I have fallen so low that my feet have all but touched hell. Oh, what's the use?" There certainly is no use at all in "blowing off" like that. You are only blowing taps over the grave of your hopes—and only your sins should be buried, not your hopes! Hold up those hopes like a banner, and go back to the fight! Courage, like truth, may now and then lose a battle, but it always wins the war, even the war against the world, the flesh, and the devil.

Otherwise—well, sin in a way is like sickness. Once a sick man turns his face to the wall and thinks, "I'll never get well," very likely he never will. And once a man says morally "I can't lick this thing," the Devil wires ahead for reservations under that name, and goes after another prospect. There are many gradual staircases into hell, but there is only one swift toboggan slide, and that is discouragement, despondency, despair. So never mind the long and morbid autopsy on the year that is dead. Turn away from that, and turn your face to the first small cries of the infant year, just born, and pleading for your interest. You cannot be a failure while he is around. This New Year is a vote of confidence in you from Almighty God. It shows He still believes in you; He is giving you time. And He does not want you to spend the golden present brooding over the tarnished past.

In other words, you cannot feed this baby year on a formula of spilt milk and tears. Strange thing, by the way, about these people who are always worrying about their past sins, and always wondering whether God has really forgiven them. Because often the last person they are actually concerned about is— God. If you could see their souls, I am afraid they would be like a two-colored cordial. The first layer is Wounded Pride, a deep humiliating chagrin—oh, to think that *they* should have done these terrible things! The other layer is Selfish Fear—oh, to think that they will be held responsible in eternity for all that! The fact that they offended God may not even get inside the frame of the picture. They are unhappy only because in the joy-ride their shining moral fender has been pretty badly scraped, and they will also have to pay a future fine. If only they would just be sorry that their conduct has injured God, and then He could generously forgive and then they could safely forget.

So, take a good look at the new calendar, and assure yourself that New Year's Day is not Memorial Day, and should not find you wandering dolefully through the cemetery of bygone sins. New Year's is a new start! It is the Land of Beginning Again. It is the command, "Forward march!" with eyes front. For what man can go forward if he insists on looking backward? He will only step into every hidden hole and every mudpuddle in the road. Or, put it this way: it is only by drawing away from the dirt and looking up that a lily becomes a lily. Mary Magdalen could tell you that.

Tell yourself—and of course mean it—that this year you are going places, for God! Last year perhaps your soul rode in a Ferris Wheel. As soon as you were way up on top, sitting pretty and proud in your lofty virtue, suddenly you found yourself dropping down to the very bottom. Then you got disgusted, slowly struggled to the top again, once more felt the exhilaration of being good, and the next thing you knew you felt yourself slipping downward once more. In all honesty we have to admit that this Ferris Wheel routine got us nowhere. All the motions, but no progress. This year, too, we may have ups and downs, but it will be like the prow of a little ship: maybe up and down, but always going forward!

I wish each one of you, saintly nun and struggling sinner, a really Happy New Year—happy because it will bring you closer to the New-born Christ.

New Year, New Chance

RESOLUTIONS

ARE LIKE ROCKETS

Christmas is just over, but somehow it seems a long time ago. Looking back now, doesn't it strike you that like most things human, the joy was mostly in the anticipation? Once the day itself dawns, once the flower is plucked, it begins to fade and die. And now everything is over but the cleaning up. Mother is murmuring to herself, "This house looks a perfect fright!" But really, Mother, it is a picturesque little earthquake, and presents a state of charming disarray with the floor littered with open gift boxes and bright red ribbon and greeting cards and toys. Toys.... Watch your step, Dad, because one careless stride and your foot will be on a tiny fire-engine, and the next moment your two feet may be in mid-air, and you'll have a touch of black and blue added to the usual Christmas colors of red and green. But you can smile a little grimly yourself that the youngsters have not gotten off entirely unscarred either. The situation is reversed from this time Christmas Eve. Now the candy boxes are empty and the youngsters are full; only the boxes still look fairly comfortable. But perhaps you yourself are just a bit drowsy. And the thought comes to you with a shudder that tomorrow morning the icy jingle of that alarm clock will splinter your dreams and wake you to the horrible reality that work is beginning all over again.

You will not like it; but you will go. Because you realize what would happen if you quit. So there's no need to talk about that. But, if we can do it without much grinding of gears, I would like to shift to the subject of people who quit in a more important and even tragic sphere. I mean people who quit on the one job the Almighty had in mind when He sent us here on earth; the job where no one must shirk and from which no one can transfer; the job where there are no executives and no minor employees. The job of saving one's soul. The job not of earning a good living, but of living a good life.

And today—even today—somebody, somewhere is going to quit. Today after weeks and months and maybe years of trying, somebody is going to give up. Today somebody is going to scream, at least mentally, "I can't hold on any longer!"—lose his grip and fall—maybe into sin, maybe into despair, maybe into hell.

You are thinking to yourself, "These are strange thoughts, and we still gathered round the Christmas Crib." I know, but look past the Crib a little, just toward the horizon of next week. I see tall blue shadows showing across the desert. I hear the silvery tinkle of shaking bells as the camels come springing on. I realize the Crib is not yet complete. But in a few days, on the

Feast of Little Christmas, our feast of the Epiphany, three new figures, come from afar, will kneel in the straw. This is the feast that shouts down the valleys of time like a thousand trumpets, "Never quit!" Because it is the Feast of three strangers who kept following the Star till they came to Christ!

They say a word to the wise is sufficient. This is a word from the wise, from Three Wise Men to any of us who may be tempted to be foolish and quit. They would tell you their journey wasn't easy, but it was worth it. Over mountains they came, and through deserts, and across rivers, and past cities, always following the Star. Some people smiled at them, and some sneered. Some shook their heads in amazement. Some held their sides in laughter. Some winked, and some asked sarcastic questions. What did it matter to the Wise Men? Because beyond this mockery, yes and those mountains, beyond the sneers and the sands, they saw the Star! And they never stopped till the Star stopped and hung like a lamp over the Cradle of God. Tradition has baptized them with musical Oriental names, but never mind the names. Call them what they proved themselves to be: the Patron Saints of Perseverance!

Perseverance itself is likely to be a vague, fuzzy Fifth Avenue sort of word for a commonplace, kitchen kind of idea: "Don't quit!" I know that it is very easy to say. And I certainly am not trying to tell you it is easy to do. As a matter of fact that very word "perseverance" implies just the opposite. Originally it was a wedding of two Latin words: *per*, meaning through; and *severa*, meaning hard. So perseverance literally means "through hard things"—because that is when you need perseverance—when the weakling whimpers and the quitter quits—when the going gets rough. You don't persevere through a delicious Christmas dinner or through a Florida vacation. The only time you can really talk about persevering is when the urge is overwhelming to quit—and you don't.

This rugged old world is so full of hard things that no worthwhile goal is ever reached without perseverance, without throttling that temptation to give it all up, without an iron resolution that has to go on like a revolving iron chain. It is that way even in the material world. In any honest success story the first dozen chapters are up-hill, and without benefit of ski-tow or escalator. When Benjamin Disraeli rose to make his first speech in the House of Commons, his voice squeaked like a tin whistle, and his ridiculously big words flapped round his sentences like overlong sleeves. Everybody started to laugh. There were rude cries, "Sit down!"

Disraeli stood there for one moment, silent. There may not have been any thunder in his voice, but lightning flashed from his eyes. He raised his arms and in the strange quiet he all but whispered. "I will sit down—now. But I promise you that the day will come when you will rush to hear me. You will rush!" And they did. For this same Disraeli, the young dude in the canary-colored jacket, had determined that one day he would become Prime Minister, and he did! Grant that he had talent, grant he had industry, but behind both lay the driving dynamo of perseverance!

Perhaps there were other factors, like luck and influence. Perhaps in the present jangling commercial world in which you live a great many doors to success are marked "Pull"—and the right "pull" will get you in. But I am not talking about that. I am assuring you that the Gate of Heaven is marked only "Push," and only push, determination, resolution will get you in. Nobody is the brother-in-law of God.

Hell, on the other hand, they say is paved with good intentions. No! It is paved with intentions that were not quite good enough; intentions that never developed the muscles of resolutions. Some people think they make a resolution. They only make a wish. When they close the door against sin, it is like a swinging door that flies open at the first touch of the next temptation. Other people compromise with sin: "I'll do it just this one last time, and then no more." The door *they* close is a revolving door, and the first thing they know the same old sin is around again. A real resolution is like the door that is slammed and bolted and barred.

We are approaching the season when cartoonists go to their dusty files for the musty jokes on resolutions. "Let me see—Newlywed's Biscuits—ah, here—New Year's Resolutions." And the less talented comedians will hurl the old custard-pie sentences at the equally ancient targets. Never mind. "I firmly resolve" still has the power to take a sinner and make him a saint. Of course the resolution may have to be renewed. Long before our so-called Space Age you can find yellowed copies of Sunday Supplements vividly picturing a cruise to the moon on a "rocketship." The idea behind it was that when one rocket-motor was just on the point of expiring, it automatically ignited another, and so on. I am not sure that this will ever get us to the moon. But I do know that the power and drive of renewed and repeated resolutions will get us to heaven. And in a very literal sense God will give the quitter hell.

It isn't that God expects us to reach great heights of virtue. But we won't reach anywhere unless we keep trying. I always like that old story about the traveller whom the monks of St. Bernard found on a snowy Alpine slope—frozen in death, his face toward the summit, and his knee bent as though about to take one more step. And as they carried him to his grave, one of the monks unconsciously preached his eulogy. "He never got to the top. But he never quit. He died *climbing!*"

So, don't quit! You, worn little mother, with your worn little beads, keep praying for that boy who has turned his back on God. Some day he will turn and stretch out his hands for help, and the loop of your beads will catch him like a lifeline—perhaps even after you are gone!

And you, whose marriage has proved a sad disillusionment, and who are nervously thinking of a divorce—don't quit! Your wedding ring has not been all sweetness like a coffee-ring; nor all fun like a circus ring; but it is not a loose-leaf ring either, to be snapped open and one partner rejected and another inserted. The little two-paged book, the contract, is *bound* by the *bonds* of matrimony. Your consolation and encouragement is that *your* page is clean, and God understands and He will reward!

And you, young man, who sometimes kneel in the shadowy church uneasy and ashamed, half-afraid to raise your eyes to the white altar, feeling that vile sin has tramped its muddy boots over the altar of your soul—do you think there is any stain so black or so deep that the Blood of God cannot wash it away? Don't quit! Yesterday a fellow just like you quit. He doesn't know it yet, but as of yesterday and into eternity, he is the saddest kind of fool, a damned fool. You, be wise! Follow the Star, and it will lead you *out* of the stable!

And you, young girl, who sometimes wonder whether in this smart, shallow, wisecracking world it really pays to be good; in this cheap new edition of the old paganism, where petting is considered petty, where the chaste are seldom chased after, and where purity is a quality looked for in soap or oleomargerine. No matter, you still are right, and they are wrong, and in their hearts they know it! Stay up there, a shining unsmirched star and one day you will brighten the life of the man that deserves you!

So for us all, each in his own rugged spot, *a new resolve*, and then, what we can only wish to one another, God in His Goodness will really give:

A Happy New Year!

The Eternal Goal

HIGHWAY TO HEAVEN

Since last we met, the Church celebrated a feast which, come to think of it, I have never heard a Catholic layman mention—the Feast of Epiphany. Mostly it is called the Feast of the Three Kings, and at any Christmas Crib last week these colorful gentlemen had dismounted and parked their picturesque camels close by. This little talk is not going to be about either the camels or the kings, except that on Epiphany night I was thinking about camels as means of transportation. And I tell you these long-legged, swaying beasts, loping rhythmically, padding silently across the desert, seemed to have their points.

You see, from ten at night till six in the morning the thoroughfare that runs in front of our rectory is Big Truck Boulevard. And that night they were whizzing by so steadily, booming so heavily under the window that I just couldn't get to sleep. Of course no preacher should ever get insomnia: all he has to do is get up and read some of his old sermons. But for this I was too lazy, and since it was impossible to quiet the trucks, and unchristian to curse them, I just lay there thinking about them, and the first thing you know it seemed they were preaching a sermon to me!

Here they were, cargo camels twentieth century style, these trucks, huge battleships of the road, grey or green or brilliant red, outlined with amber bulbs, rumbling along with all sorts of loads, milk or oil or furniture; pair after pair of headlights like shining yellow eyes, zooming on through the night with a sullen roar, riding eventually into the pink dawn, then with a change of riders, highballing along other highways under blue skies and into a far-off flaming sunset... I guess if you look hard enough you can see adventure and romance even in hubcaps and grease.

Curious thing, though, about a truck: The bigger part of it (almost like in a human being) they call the body. But the other part, the more important part, is the cab. Almost like the soul. Because there, in the cab, is what you might call its principle of life, the motor—what makes the truck go, and without which the truck would be as motionless as a corpse. And in that cab turns your steering wheel, like free will. You can drive right, drive left, even drive off the road—but you take the consequences. Isn't that what free will means? And right beyond the steering wheel glows the speedometer, just as plain as conscience itself, always registering and constantly reminding you when you are overstepping bounds.

When a truck starts to climb a hill it seems almost human the way it grinds and grunts and inches slowly up, like a man with bent head and drooping shoulders plodding up the slope of trouble. "For the heart of a man is a heavy load for a man to bear alone." But how simple and easy it is for truck or man to go roaring downhill! It may take a man sixty years to become a saint, but he can land at the bottom of Skid Row in only six months. It all depends on who is in control, the soul or the body. Put the truck on as high a hill as you like. Then, up in the cab, shut off the motor and release the brake. The body of the truck, always eager to throw its weight around, will exert its pressure and force the whole vehicle down, faster and faster. It is no different in a man's moral life. The body, left to itself and all brakes off, has a natural inclination to go downhill; and if you let it, the end must be a wild careening ride and a shattered moral wreck.

Nobody knows this better than the fellow who thought he knew how far he could go, how far he could let his emotions or desires coast along before it would be really dangerous and out of control. Just let passion get rolling a little bit and it picks up fearful momentum. And the only sure way of stopping it is never to let it get started. You are not a beast; you are a man; and the control should be in the cab, in the human soul with its conscience and its will-power and its moral code. Oh the pity of it that when you counsel modesty and purity to young people they think these are the steel bars of a jail shutting them off from happiness. They may be steel bars, all right, but they are the steel handrails on a bridge, that perilous bridge that swings between youth and maturity, and only those know how necessary they are who have fallen off and lie at the bottom, bruised and broken. Or, to get back to trucks, aren't some trucks, simply marked "Flammable"?

Most trucking jobs are long hauls over the highway toward the horizon, and you could hardly get a better picture, a sharper modern parable of a man journeying toward eternity than the driver in the cab of his truck as he rolls along the grey stretch of road toward his far-off, unseen destination. The little sign on the windshield says, "No Riders," and in the cab of his own soul every man rides alone. You, and nobody else, has the responsibility for *you*. And every driver has basically the same obligation. It doesn't matter what kind of cargo the truck is carrying, whether it is Christmas trees or brand new cars—the idea is always to get to your destination and bring what they expect. Isn't it the same way on the highway of life? Whether you are the conductor of a subway car or the conductor of a symphony orchestra, the whole idea is so to do your work, so to live your life that you will be doing what God wants and eventually reach your journey's end, Heaven.

Ask the average truck driver what are his thoughts as he sits behind the wheel, and you find the one constant overpowering thought is just to get where he is going. What he passes along the way is of minor consideration. Enchanting scenery, eye-catching bill-boards, famous landmarks—these he goes wheeling past with hardly a glance. They are on his route, but he is on his way! His eyes are focused on the road, his thoughts fixed on the goal. All the rest is trivial. The only thing that matters is, reach the right address and deliver the goods, intact and unspoiled. Wouldn't it be wonderful if we could be like that in our lives, passing through this world but making our main concern the end of it all, God and Heaven and Salvation? All right then, by the same yardstick wouldn't we be pitifully foolish to let something along the road so distract us, take up our attention, fascinate us—something like money or sex or hate or ambition or any mere creature—so that before we know it, our eyes have wandered off the road, and maybe at that very moment we go hurtling off the sharp wild curve of sudden death into the wrong eternity?

Sometimes for a truck driver, danger leaps up from the very opposite source. I mean he is looking at the road so long and so steadily that after a while he doesn't really see the road. They call it highway hypnosis. Here's a competent driver with a good night's sleep behind him on an open highway with a perfect view and no mechanical trouble, and he suddenly goes crashing off the road to disaster. The best explanation seems to be that the grey monotony of the road lulled him, hypnotized him, drugged him into a kind of trance, and before he knew it, the wheel loosened in his grip—just for a couple of moments—and he went roaring to destruction.

It's sad, but aren't there plenty of people like that spiritually? Year after year they stolidly, languidly follow the road of life, hardly realizing what it is all about. Day in, day out they drift along the same dull round of duties, automatically, mechanically, almost in a daze. Their eyes are blank, their soul is numb, their heart is wooden, their spirit dried-up, dead. Theirs? This is a danger to any of us! From time to time we all have to stir ourselves, rouse ourselves, make ourselves sharply aware that we are on the road to eternity, that we carry a precious cargo (our very salvation), and that there are dangers all about us! Remind ourselves that life is more than typing letters or driving nails or cooking meals or filling gas tanks! We are the children of God, on the way home to Our Father Who is in Heaven—and all these material things are but as steps on the stairs as we go up to Him! Life is a prosaic, boring journey only to those that forget God is the goal!

And, like the truck drivers, we had better take no chances along the way. It may surprise you to know that the most cautious of all drivers (except perhaps the men who pilot the school-bus) are the broad-shouldered boys behind the big steering-wheel of a truck. Haven't you ever noticed, for example, how on a dark afternoon or a foggy morning a truck will drone along all lit up like a theatre marquee? They take no chances. Haven't you often heard how a truck driver who feels himself growing drowsy will immediately pull over to the side of the road for a few minutes of exercise or even sleep? They take no chances. If it is a question of a risky road or a longer road, they unhesitatingly swing off on the longer. They take no chances. Certain roads they have to keep off altogether: "Trucks Not Allowed." And it might be well for us if mentally we pictured certain books or plays or places as marked with the warning sign, "Decent People Not Allowed." The trucks are forbidden because with their tonnage they would ruin certain thoroughfares. We ought to keep off the dirt roads of literature and entertainment because they can ruin us—or at least spatter us with mire, or in some moral mud-hole bog us down.

I have heard from salesmen who drive long hours to cover their broad territories that truck drivers are not only the most careful drivers on the road, but also the most courteous and considerate. Many a motorist broken down in the middle of nowhere with nothing but bleak miles of highway stretching away on either side, has found in the truck driver a huge grimy angel who somehow got him started again. When you are lost, a truck driver really seems willing to show you the way. When bright beams meet on a midnight road, the truck (which could play the role of bully) as a rule is the first to click the switch and dim the lights. And, if there is any danger ahead or any trouble (even if the trouble is a state trooper!) the truck will always blink you a warning.

Isn't it all a heart-warming, practical, modern example of kindness to our neighbor as we move along the road of life, and meet opportunities for doing good every day? Doesn't it accent the fact that in this breathless age we have plenty of intellectual brilliance and industrial genius and executive skill—only the men tend to become like their own machines, polished, efficient, impersonal as steel, without heart or soul? We have too many clever people; what we need are kind people, good people. And the truck driver is the modern Good Samaritan of the road!

So we close as we began. We turn from the trucks to the camels, with the thought that times have changed. The Three Wise Men who rode them were drawn to Christ by the splendor of a Star, like converts who are attracted by the sparkling genius of some priest, but nowadays most converts are first drawn to religion by the simple kindness of some human heart on fire with love of God and radiating that warmth among men!

The Eternal Goal

THREE ROADS TO GOD

Probably because it is a blowy, snowy winter here in Boston, my thoughts go winging back (like the wiser birds before me) to the mellow sun and the gentle airs of last summer. Especially the other night, preaching in a frosty-windowed church, when the radiators began to bang and clang as though some communistic janitor deep down in the cellar was trying to jam the Voice of God, I thought how wonderful it was last August to stand in a rugged pulpit of rock and preach to an outdoor congregation in a rustic setting where the only competition was the background twittering of the birds. To see two or three thousand people gathered in a great green aisle whose pillars were towering trees, whose walls were the four winds, whose ceiling was the soft blue canopy of summer sky, whose illumination this particular afternoon was the dull bronze lamp of a setting sun, and to hear those voices ringing in vibrant prayer and swelling hymn—the sight then and the memory now sends a wave of emotion over a man, thrills him, fills him with spiritual exaltation!

Even as I say this, I fear the Catholic fear that I may be interpreted as rattling the tambourine in favor of the majestic cathedral of the forest, the rising blue incense clouds of autumn smoke, and all that sort of real estate religion. Not at all, not at all! I suppose we have all met breathless, bubbling people who lyrically insist that they can worship God far better high on a wind-swept hill than squeezed in the stale pews of a stuffy church. It makes you remember the old priest that Gladys Stern, the Jewish convert-novelist, mentions in the story of her conversion. "On the hilltop is it," he would ask, "is *that* where you love to worship God? And tell me, do you do *much* mountaineering?" Can't you almost see the gentle mockery glinting in his eye?

And anyway I wonder how often these "cathedral of nature" boys buckle on their overshoes and worship the Creator in a roaring blizzard? He is there after all in the sleet or the heat or the fog as well as in the technicolor sunset that marches off with massed banners. Those who protest they adore God best without benefit of steeple often are merely enthusiastic over a pretty landscape and fair weather, and God gets a nod only as the stage manager who arranged a rather striking set. Would they ever have thought of Him in a dismal rain? This is postcard piety!

For that matter, every Catholic priest every day of his life recites after Mass a crackling litany of the elements, praising the Lord in everything from frost to lightning. We do this, but at the same time we don't leave the more important thing undone. We Catholics hold that this world is an orderly place, and so we have books in libraries, money in banks, operating rooms in hospitals, and altars in churches. God Himself favored the fixed and definite place. He had His Mount Sinai, crowned with fearful smoke and bright flame; and the Burning Bush from which He spoke to Moses; and the Pool of Bethsaida where the water was stirred and the sick were cured. Bethlehem itself was pin-pointed on the map, and in it one definite stable where the altar was a manger and the sanctuary light was a star. Why, man's natural instinct alone suggests that there should be a special spot, a definite place for the practice of religion, in other words a church, a meeting place of man with God, and God with man. Such a church no more stands between a man and His God than a cup stands between a man and his coffee. And as long as we first honor God in His official place, the church, on His official day, Sunday, we can also honor Him Monday at sunset or Thursday at dawn, on a snowy spike of mountain or a dimpled blue lake.

Come to think of it, there are three major highways over which we can send our homage to God. The first way, as we just intimated, is by assembling as His creatures in His dedicated temple, the church, to pay our collective formal tribute to Him as our Creator. And as the ironic saying goes, we Catholics are "humbly proud" that on Sunday morning, hour after hour, Mass after Mass, our churches fill and empty, fill and empty with streams of people pouring in and out, as they hear that soft whisper that rides down the centuries: "This is My Body. This is My Blood. Do this in memory of Me!" True, not all Catholics stir themselves and push off to church on Sunday morning. Would that they did! Would that every church in the U.S.A., of whatever creed, were bulging its walls with Sunday worshippers! But so often the chime of church bells is drowned out by the rustle of the Sunday paper, and Christ cannot compete with the comics! But the Catholic who on Sunday mornings rather prefers being horizontal to being holy had better realize that there are no honorary members in the Catholic Church. One day he may be carried into one of them, but that could be only a formality. But by that time, his soul's fate will have been eternally decided, decided by the Christ Who said: "Unless you confess Me *before men,* I will deny you before My Father."

A second but secondary way of honoring God, a definitely subordinate way, is appreciating His work in creation. There is no question about it: Nature is a fascinating book and on every page there flourishes the signature of God. Whether you stare up through a telescope or squint down through a microscope, you catch your breath, either at the vast majesty of the world or the perfect detail of its miniatures. A little while ago I spent an evening in a doctor's home where television (the pictures on the wall of our twentieth-century caves) was pointedly absent. But he did have the latest in binocular microscopes so I took a soda straw, siphoned a drop of water from a slimy puddle in the roadway, fixed it on a slide and peered at it. And what I saw, as far as I was concerned, no television show could touch. That tiny droplet was like a lake darting with fantastic creatures that a sober man never sees at all. I particularly recall one weird monster, in scale long as a crocodile, who seemed to be latching on to bits of food with his curled tail and at the same time sweeping other fragments into his mouth with his long hairy claws. Here was one scummy drop, and it was like a swamp crawling with its own midget dinosaurs!

Then, you could lift your eye from the microscope and stroll out to the porch and look up at the stars. There's that big bright bead in Orion, the star with the curious name of Betelgeuse, and you remember reading that it is a star so vast that if it had men and women in proportion to our six footers, they would go striding about more than ten miles tall!

No wonder the impulse in a thinking man is to gaze at creation on his knees. Probably the poets do it best, souls with eager, appreciative eyes, seeing in Nature the art gallery of God. Like that strange, bearded convert Francis Thompson: to other men it might be only another setting sun; to him it was the great golden monstrance of the sun being put away in the cloud-curtained tabernacle of the West. And then Night, the black-robed sacristan, lights the stars like candles round the casket of the deceased Day. Such poets "see His Blood upon the rose;" they see another Calvary in the scarlet of a sunset sky.

It is beautiful all right, but if you are not a poet, you never recognize it until your head is banged against it. On the trail of natural beauty, which certainly leads to God, most of us are only stumbling clod-hoppers and hardly see the clues scattered under our very feet. We see our roses and our rainbows, but because God never gives a commercial, we never think of the sponsor. And that is why there is a third way of paying honor to God, apart from in His Home (the Church), or in His Garden which is Nature, and that is in His Family, which is our fellowmen. Those who knew St. Francis de Sales used to ask, "How can he love God *more,* he so loves man?" Didn't the very pagans murmur in awe about the first Christians, "See how they *love one another!*" Hasn't many a cynic remarked that the world would change almost overnight if only Christians really lived as followers of Christ? And didn't St. John who wrote the loftiest of the gospels, reduce his teachings as an old man to a half dozen words, "My little children, love one another." Didn't Our Blessed Lord Himself solemnly say, "Whatsoever you do to *these,* the least of My brethren, you do *unto Me*"? The trouble is we are willing to accept that as true enough, but we actually treat it as something remote from everyday life. Something written on curling parchment in the first century, a pious motto for a medieval stained glass window, yes. But how close do we ever come to putting it into actual practice in the gasoline-stained streets of the twentieth century?

Just take that reference to gas. The auto is of course only one tiny tile in the mosaic of modern life, but so common among us it is almost a symbol of our civilization. Well, in that particular department (call it car-Christianity if you want) how do we treat other human beings? What is it that gets into some people when they get behind a wheel? Whatever it is, it is not Christian charity, it is not consideration for their fellowmen. The very man who would apologize politely if walking along the street he so much as brushed your elbow—put him in a car and his eyes harden and his mouth goes grim, and nobody's getting an inch *on him!* Suddenly the world becomes a jungle, a two-toned jungle with chrome, and headlights that glare like tiger eyes. It may be that the power in the motor goes to his head—possibly there is plenty of room there—and when a petty mind gets intoxicated with a powerful motor, he begins to imagine he is Napoleon on wheels. All that horse-power suddenly becomes mule-power, stubborn and stupid, selfish, arrogant, spiteful, muttering, fuming mad! It is true there weren't any motor cars parked under the Sermon on the Mount, or any convertibles at Calvary, but isn't it our job as Christians to apply the old unchangeable morals to the ever-changing times? To be men of God even in a mechanical world?

May Mary, the Mother of Our Savior, who adored God in the Temple at Jerusalem, and acknowledged His works in the gorgeous tapestry of nature from Palestine to Egypt, and who was devoted to her neighbor from the wedding feast of Cana (where she was practically the waitress providing the wine) to the child-bed of Elizabeth (where she was probably the nurse)—may she inspire us to honor the Triune God in all three ways; honoring Him in church, in nature, and in our fellowman!

The Eternal Goal

TRIBUTE TO A COIN

When I was a youngster (and the current first-graders guess that was about eighty years ago) the very pinnacle of happiness was having a penny. Of course in those days you could buy things with a penny, like a pencil, or a pen-nib, or a whistle, or a strip of pink shoe-button candy. And if you can remember that, how is your rheumatism? Many a time though, before we bought anything, we would lovingly study our penny. Ah, when you gazed at the copper-colored profile and the feathered head-dress, you held the whole Wild West—war-dances, wigwams, wampum, right in the palm of your sticky hand. If we had known then that the face on the penny was actually a paleface, we would have felt cheated, and if we found out that it was the face of a girl, the daughter of the engraver, we would have been clean disgusted.

TRIBUTE TO A COIN

I have never been a collector of coins but when you think of it, isn't every old coin a piece of the past? When you have it in your fingers, aren't you holding the hand of history across the gulf of a thousand years? A thousand? Why there are in existence today coins that once swung jauntily in the handbag of Caesar's wife. In fact the Roman coin that blinks up at you from some musty museum-shelf may be the very penny that lay in the palm of Our Blessed Lord when He asked, "Whose image and inscription is this?" Have you ever noticed how coins clinked through His life in the Gospel: the widow's mite, the hirer who gave to every man a penny, the thirty pieces of silver that jingled in the money-belt of Judas and that after a while sounded like the faint clanking of a hammer driving in nails?

Some coins are round, some square, some oval. Some are gold, some silver, some copper, or bronze, or any metal. But they all have one thing in common. They are stamped with the seal of a government. That gives them their special value. They had a value before, the value of the particular metal, but now the official seal of the state makes the original metal more valuable still. And, to shift gears into the spiritual, isn't this the precise situation with a human soul? It has from the outset a worth of its own: it has memory, it has intelligence, it has free will. Then at Baptism the Church comes and stamps that soul with its sacred seal, and the value of that soul leaps higher far. Now it is a Child of God, now it is a coin worth enough to purchase Heaven. It bears and wears the stamp of a great power, God's Holy Church and its Founder Jesus Christ. And if coins have individual names, like francs and pesos and shillings and sovereigns, this new coin freshly minted from the font of Baptism is a Christian. When you think you are a nobody, think of that!

To mutilate a coin, to destroy the image on its metal, to bore a hole through it, to deface the coin in any way at all, is a crime against the government. What then shall we say of the act of defacing, defiling a human soul, blackening it and battering it perhaps with the hot hammer of passion? *Now* it is not a coin valuable enough to purchase an eternity of happiness in Heaven. Now it is worthless, and if it were called in at this moment, would be fit only to be melted down in the fires of Hell. When you are tempted to sin, look at your little coin and think of that.

The ordinary coin is a precise job of engraving. Did you ever notice how sharp and clear-cut the image is? That did not come there easily. It was not sprayed on lightly. It was stamped on, driven in—at tremendous pressure. For example, the head of Lincoln on the ordinary cent is stamped into the copper under a pressure of forty tons. The head of Liberty on the silver dollar is put there under a pressure of one hundred and seventy tons. And, as with coins, so with character, so with people: the more pressure, that is the more suffering, the higher the value—if they can take it. The hard stamp of hard knocks, adversity, trouble, leaves us either bitter or better. If we are the real metal, we *can* take it. If we are "phonies", we crumble.

Come to think of it, how do you tell a counterfeit coin? Don't you fling it down on the counter or on the sidewalk? I wonder if God does not sometimes do the same with us, fling us down, away from Him, to see if there comes back the true ring of courage, or the dull plop of a lead quarter, the whimper of the quitter.... Look at your coin, and think of *that* when some misfortune sends you sprawling.

The counterfeit is always soft, and so is the cream-puff Catholic. A little too showy, a little too sweet, yet he sours so easily! Not only in time of hardship, but in the trying climate of temptation. Put him on the spot that calls for red-blooded moral courage and he feebly waves the white feather of the coward. And it does take courage to roll out of bed on a snowy, blowy Sunday morning and hike off to Mass. It sometimes takes even more courage when the weather is balmy and the crowd is going fishing or golfing. It takes courage to walk away from a ring of foul-story-tellers who pour out their evil like men emptying their garbage pails into a common dump. It may even take a smidgeon of courage to tip your hat when you pass a church. But, what is this to the monumental courage of the martyrs, or to a man like Father Damien. He gave his life to the living dead, the lepers on the gaunt, grey island of Molokai. One morning, as he was preparing his breakfast, he accidentally spilled some boiling water on the toe of his sandalled foot. Instinctively he cringed, and then the reality smote him. Gingerly, deliberately he poured a little more scalding water. He felt nothing. The next Sunday he got up in his crude pulpit, looked at his congregation and began, "We lepers...".

Ah, there was a gold-piece stamped deep and clear with the image of the King, Christ the King! When you stand at the cross-roads of some great sacrifice, and wonder if you can make it, think of that!

Another thing a coin whispers to you, if you will listen, is not to judge by appearances. In coins or in people, things are sometimes not what they seem. For instance you can lay a quarter on a counter, ask for a pack of cigarettes, and be politely told, "Four cents more, please." But that particular quarter, because of the year of its mintage or some obscure detail, may be worth dozens of cartons of cigarettes! Or for a penny stamp you might put down a Roman penny, and be told "One cent please, American money." But this does not prove your Roman coin is worthless. It proves only that the clerk did not know value when he saw it.

It is the same way with people. You can't be sure of their true value just by what is stamped on the surface, just by their appearance. In the eyes of God, and He knows values, they may be priceless. And at a certain future auction that we generally call General Judgment, these coins that looked so worn and scarred, these people who seemed so undistinguished, unimpressive, unimportant, God will pick up and say "These are priceless!" Because God, the Expert, can discern greatness of soul even when it walks in rags.

By the way, isn't it consoling to realize that there is Someone Who knows the good things about you that others don't even dream—like all the times anger stood on the end of your tongue like a diver poised on a springboard, and you hauled it back; all the times when temptation tugged at your elbow and cooed into your ear and you flung it far with a prayer; all the times you just trudged on and trusted in God when you wanted to give up—isn't it comforting that at least God knows these good things about you, that He sees the value in the despised and battered old coin? When you are down, feeling low as the ocean's floor, think of that!

Our great grandfathers used to put pennies on dead men's eyes to keep them closed, because, I suppose, it was uncomfortable to look at the bulging, staring eyes of death. It is always easier to contemplate money than mortal dissolution. But concentrating on money does not prevent death or judgment or eternity; it just puts it in the background. For that matter, you can hold up a half-dollar to your eye and blot out the vision of the sun; but the sun is still very much there. What a pity that so many in America spend their lives scheming for money, slaving for money, some like Judas even betraying Christ for money! Once Christ seized a knotted cord, threw over the tables, lashed the money-changers out of the Temple. Now ironically the tables have been turned, and money has set up its tables in the hearts of men and is driving out Christ!

Perhaps you tell me money is necessary; and it is. Or that it can do much good; and it can. Or that even the Church needs it, and it does. I know families that would give more attention to the things of God, if they didn't have to worry about the grocer. But I also feel that a great many men would have a better family life, if they lowered the bar of their financial ambition two or three notches. I think of what Robert Louis Stevenson used to mutter, "A hand to get money, a safe to keep it—dear God, man, is this all?" Do we as Catholics realize that the Hail Mary the rich man murmurs on his death bed will do him more good for all eternity than the hundred thousand dollars he leaves behind? Behind is right; because when they bury you, they never toss in the bank book! It is the prayers you said and the Masses you heard and the Communions you received that will make you a millionaire in Heaven, where merit is money!

An English newspaper ran a contest once asking for the best definition of money. The winning answer ran something like this: "Money is something that can buy you anything but happiness, and pay your fare to every place but Heaven." It comes down to this: put first things first. Seek ye first (as Our Lord said) the Kingdom of Heaven, and you will not go bankrupt to Hell. You will not have to worry about that grimmest of all coins. You will not have to "pay to the last farthing."

The Eternal Goal

BRONX EXPRESS

I was in New York last week to preach a little sermon, and while I was riding the subway I remembered how they would tell us Brooklynites that the subway was built so that we could get back and forth to Brooklyn without being seen. Then for five years I was stationed in the Bronx and the subway was my limousine. I used to think how Our Lord never lived in an ivory tower but was almost always in the middle of a crowd, and a subway car is a crowd on wheels, a Noah's Ark of unassorted humans, the United Nations (every color and shape and size and language) *so closely united* by the five o'clock rush. On the first Pentecost, a mixed crowd like this was the rainbow mob that listened to St. Peter. To whom or to what are they listening now?

Not much. Here was this long train, this huge black snake with the glaring green eyes, slithering under the earth, swishing its steel tail around curves, a machine-age monster that made men seem insignificant. Here were the men, hundreds of them, little black ants crammed into these boxes on wheels, rolled to their work in the morning, and back again at night. Some have their noses in newspapers, but it's like an ether cone and they are in a dull anesthesia. Others are staring blankly at the colored ads around the car, ads that preach polish for your nails, lotion for your hands, cream for your cheeks, drops for your eyes, rinses for your hair, and hope, if you have no hair. What a difference, you think, between that glamour gallery of gods and goddesses in the advertising heaven up there, and the real people slumping in the seats, crumpled people, weary people, listless, bored, almost every face a sour vacuum.

And yet these are the people that God made to know Him, to love Him, to serve Him; the souls for whose redemption Our Savior paid out the last ruby of His heavy-dripping Blood. Do they ever think of Him? Or are they so busy making a living that they forget the purpose of life? Are they so intent on rushing here and there that they never get one yard closer to God? Are they so concerned with catching this local or that express that they never think of the last stop, the end of the line, where there is no more changing, but *you are there*—forever?

On one platform I had to ask a man whether a certain train went to such and such a subway station. He smiled and shrugged his shoulders. "Honest, Father, I haven't the slightest idea. I just come to this station, and then go back. What lies beyond—I just never thought about." Are we all like that, I wonder? Are we so grooved in our routine, riding back and forth on the same stretch of work-a-day track, the same dull daily duties, that we never give a deliberate thought to what lies ahead, the hereafter? In New York there is a subway shuttle that runs all day and all night between Grand Central, which you might call the center of business, and Times Square, the bright lights section, which you might call the center of entertainment. What a pity for a man to spend his whole life shuttling back and forth between business and pleasure, and never giving a thought to getting his ticket and his baggage for the long, long trip to eternity!

Oh, sometimes he may think about it, when he is sick, pressed down on the flat of his back, and suddenly how different life looks from the horizontal! It's like in the subway when the train lurches to a sudden stop between stations, and the lights go out, and the little dim bulbs over the doors peep on, and he is a little nervous and he wonders is it a wreck, or a fire, or what? But then the motor starts, the train grinds on, the lights blaze brightly, and he goes back to his paper—and it's all forgotten. So, when a man becomes seriously sick, when the lights of this world grow misty, when he is in the tunnel between life and death, and death seems so terrifyingly close, and judgment so awfully stern, and eternity so incredibly long—but the next thing you know, the lights of health glow brilliant again, and he is on his feet, and (as it were) moving along the old tracks, and following the same crowd.

Follow the crowd! On the subway platform the sign says, "Follow the green lights!" and under the string of emerald bulbs on the ceiling you push along like plodding cattle. At the platform the heaving crowd can lift you right up like a wave and drop you into a train you had no intention of taking—as once happened to me. Even inside you find you are still following the crowd—your head nods in rhythm with your neighbors', your hand sways in unison on the strap, you lurch when they do—you are just another little berry shaken up in a basket of berries.

But isn't it that way upstairs above the subway too? Follow the crowd! Read the same best-sellers, sing the same hit tunes, wear the same new styles, take in the same movies! Don't ask are the books clean or the songs noble or the styles modest or the movies decent. Don't wonder if the crowd left to itself is liable to be earthy and pagan and low. You're just supposed to follow the crowd.

And isn't the average Catholic, once he steps outside his church, lost in the crowd? What sets him apart? A K of C pin? A scapular medal? Perhaps, but can he be told apart by his life?

Wouldn't it be wonderful if it really happened like this:

Scene One: the office. Someone has just told a vile story, and at the water cooler a newcomer on the office staff says in a low voice to another, "Say, what's the matter with Bill over there. I noticed that during that story he did not laugh at all. His face was stiff as a stone wall; just went on working as though he wasn't interested." "Yeah, I know. You see, Bill's a Catholic, and Catholics don't go for that sort of thing. Didn't you know?" Is that the way it happens in life?

Scene Two: the beach. Molly is whispering to Polly: "Look at Dolly's bathing suit. I love the shade but isn't it conservative?" "Yes, but then Dolly's a

Catholic, and you know how Catholic girls feel about modesty. They wouldn't buy a daring suit." Is that the way it happens in real life?

Scene Three: a smoke-filled room. "Look, if we want this deal to go through, we have to reach a politician. Somebody who can get us clearance. And naturally we'll have to lay some of the long green on his outstretched helping hand. Now how about McMackmick?" "McMackmick? Are you crazy? He's one of the untouchables. You ought to know that. He's a Catholic, and Catholics believe that graft is just slang for stealing. We have to approach someone who isn't a Catholic." Is that the way it happens in life?

If it doesn't, it should, and some day God will want to know why it didn't. In the subway headquarters there hangs a huge electric board. A man constantly sits before it, eyes on it all the time. On that diagram of moving lights he can watch every train on every track. If a red light is passed, he knows what train did it, where, and when. God is watching too, watching the way we run our lives, whether we obey the signal lights of His Commandments. And some day He is going to call us into His office and ask some very pointed questions. Wouldn't it be tragic if we who in our lives had known so many people (and forgot Him), worked for so many bosses (and never really served Him) spent so much time riding the subway of our routine daily life, in the end missed the boat for a happy eternity!

The Eternal Goal

EAST SIDE SHRINE

I came upstairs from the subway and dropped into the little church on the lower East Side where I used to preach a little Novena several summertimes ago. I remember the side door of the church would be open and as you preached you saw to your right the high grey cliffs that were the back of the tenements, the network of white clotheslines, the black fire-escapes zigzagging down the walls. If it was a bright day the clotheslines blazed with flamboyant color, fluttering like pennants strung out on a ship. You could hear the whimper of the pulleys as the clothes were dragged in, and sometimes it rose to a shrill scream. It used to make me think of Judgment. How we are all out there on the line waiting, and someday the Hand of God is going to reach out and draw us in, and we never know just where we are, or whether we are next, and when our turn comes, shall we in our mind scream with terror? Not if we come into God's presence (like the clothes) washed—by His Sacraments, and clean and fresh and sweet from the sunlight of His Grace!

I'm glad I never saw the fire-escapes used as fire-escapes, though they were used for almost everything else. As they criss-crossed down the building like a shabby old shoe-lace, you thought of the horror of fire, and the more you think of that the more careful you are going to be about fire, and the less chance there will be that you ever need a fire-escape. I wonder if that is why God made Hell? To scare us into Heaven, if we wouldn't go there any other way? But all the saints have agreed that the man who goes down into Hell in spirit when he is alive, is the least likely to go down into Hell in fact when he is dead. At any rate if in the back of your mind you have the memory of Hell, it will be a built-in fire-escape from hot temptation now, and from an exceedingly warm and non-air-conditioned hereafter.

Sometimes you would see in the front of the tenement, way up on the fourth or fifth floor, a window-box. Just a pathetic little box of dirt, a few struggling leaves, maybe a couple of wan flowers, perhaps a faint flush of geraniums... way up there above the dusty swarming sidewalks. And that little window-box whispered the yearning of someone in the hot grey grimy streets for the cool groves and the green fields of the country. It was more than just a box of dirt. It was almost a box of dreams. It was a longing for clean air and blue sky and bright flowers—a sigh for the spacious suburbs. It was hope on a window-sill.

Spiritually, don't we need something like this? If we ought to have a fire-escape—the thought of Hell—in the rear of our souls, we ought to have a window-box in front: the thought, the reminder, the promise of Heaven! When this obstacle race of life becomes unbearable, when pain flings us down on a mattress of braided thorns; or when even going out to Mass on a wintry Sunday morning seems to call for heroism—then take a peek at your little window-box. Remember that you are not doing all this for nothing, that there is a reward to come, that the fringed eyelashes closing in death are not the final curtain, but that upon the solemn word of God, the gates of Heaven will swing open before us, happiness without a flaw, and without an end!

That teeming street on the East Side where the air hung thick as smoke, and the sky seemed only a square of skylight, and the children hopped about the street like thin nervous sparrows, was certainly a far cry from the white cottage up in the hills of Judea where Elizabeth had greeted Mary "Blessed art thou among women, and blessed is the fruit of thy womb..." and Mary had humbly reflected, "All generations shall call me blessed." If you had been the third person in that far-off room so long ago, would you ever have imagined that twenty centuries later, amid the crowded tenements of a then undreamed city, New York; on a continent then still undiscovered, America; in a language yet unspoken, English; strangely dressed people there would be fulfilling that very prophecy! For out of the open windows you could catch a snatch now and then of the radio rosary, "Blessed art thou among women, and blessed is the fruit of thy womb..." And as a mother leaned out the window and called her children in to supper, the name "Mary, Mary" rang out over the sidewalks of New York. And a couple of hours later streams of these mothers and fathers, perhaps not gilt-edged with wealth but solid gold in their faith, came pouring into church to kneel before a lighted shrine and listen to my ragged sermon. Meanwhile Shakespeare was right: there are sermons in stones, even when the stones are the cobblestones of New York or the concrete walls of her subways, and if you listen with your heart, you will hear them!

Bell, Book, and Candle

THE BELLS OF ST. ANYBODY'S

Last night at a half-hour before midnight, high up in the twin spires that soar above our majestic Basilica, called the Mission Church, the huge bells began to ring. "Ring out the old, ring in the new! Ring happy bells across the snow! The year is going, let him go! Ring out the false, ring in the true!" Down on the street I could see some people standing around and looking up, standing a bit unsteadily one or two of them perhaps, and looking up with surprise in their eyes, and with cricks in their necks, and a great crooning hum in their ears; and I was glad that the churchbells, so generally taken for granted, were having their brief hour of popular glory.

Come to think of it, I never heard a sermon on churchbells. Possibly the preachers feel that from its lofty pulpit of the belfry, and with its brazen throat and its aggressive twanging tongue, any churchbell, should be able to speak for itself. Give it enough rope, and it will clang itself. I say "it," but in the two giant towers above our church loom thirteen bells, like Christ and His Twelve Apostles gathered in the Upper Room above the city . . . and like the Apostles their booming voices fling the message of God to every point of the compass. In fact at more than two hundred feet in the air they hang poised up there more like the herald angels calling out the good news of Christ, not to Bethlehem but to Boston.

In that image, however, you might have to regard some of the bells as archangels, because a few of the big bassos weigh a ton or two, while the slimmest tenor scales down to a round four hundred pounds, which is a bit robust even for opera. Speaking of tonnage, it is a massive bit of irony that the hugest churchbell under heaven has been sleeping these many years in Moscow. Some day, please God, religion will rise from its tomb there, and the Russian air will ring with exultant Alleluias. In the meantime, the next largest bell swings above Germany's cathedral of Cologne. So high in the graceful spire it hangs, you might almost suppose it an ear-ring on a tall, stately Empress, till you learn its weight: a massive twenty-seven tons. But it is not so much the weight that impresses as the fact that this giant bell was molded entirely from melted-down cannon. Wouldn't it be a glorious world if we could take all our dented old quarrels, fling them on a scrap pile, and melt them into one harmonious prayer—from many foolish fighting people to the One Great God of Peace!

Those that make them say bells are as different as people. When a bell is cast, for example, nobody can predict with certainty just how it will sound. Temperametal, you might say. And for that very reason, because they are as individual as people, churchbells are christened practically like babies. First the bell is washed (not just sprinkled, mind you) with holy water. Then, like a child at the font, it is anointed with sacred oil. After that its wide-open throat (how like an outraged, protesting infant) is incensed with fragrant smoke as a symbol of rising prayer, and the Bishop continues in Latin: "May this bell be hallowed in the name of the Father and of the Son and of the Holy Ghost, and to the heavenly honor of St. Such and Such." In our particular carillon, for instance, the chief bell is named Our Lady of Perpetual Help, and the others St. Joseph, St. Patrick (remember this is Boston) down to the Patroness of music, St. Cecelia. Some bells have inscribed on the gleaming metal not only the baptismal name but a sonorous Latin motto, like: "The Lord I praise, the dead I mourn, the people I call." And one bell, possibly the Vice-President in charge of the eleven-thirty Mass, pointedly reads: "The laggards I hasten."

During the Middle Ages the privilege and the duty of ringing churchbells was confined to those clerics who had reached that rung on the ladder of holy orders known as porter or doorkeeper. I have a misty memory of a spring twilight in the Seminary Chapel many years ago when we received that rank in the hierarchy (or the lower archy) and then in order to exercise it, softly and ceremoniously tinkled a tiny bell. Now, of course, that particular dignity is like a precious stone encrusted in the old gold of tradition, kept in the safety deposit box of the past, but no longer worn abroad. Now, anyone rings the churchbells. We used to do it even as altarboys in Brooklyn in a great dusty room of rattling ropes on which we loved to swing back and forth and up and down, flushed with excitement. Give a man a horse he can ride, and give an altar boy a bell he can ring—and he has Heaven on the half-shell before him. But the Brother Sacristan, who always stood by, used to scare us by telling of a half-drunk sexton he had known who had been hanged with just such a rope as it twisted accidentally round his throat, and the bells with their big iron mouths (as the brother told it) went on laughing till they tired and stopped, and someone discovered the dangling figure who had rung for his own funeral.

Nowadays in many churches electricity has put the bells under a man's thumb, and the mere push of a button sets them swinging and ringing, dancing puppets on the ends of invisible wires. But I still love to see men pulling at the big ropes which in a way are pulling in the people. The hunt for souls is on, and these are the men holding the leashes of the hounds of Heaven baying up there in the sky. Or shut your eyes and forget the men, and listen to the lofty music, now mellow and gentle and sprinkling the golden notes like holy water; then the crashing hammer clanging against the bell's solid crown in a great crescendo, and strumming off in lingering overtones. Swinging, tossing, turning handsprings, the carillon of bells is like a troupe of tumblers—Our Lady's Jugglers—performing against the sky. Or are they artists that raise up a stained glass window in sound? Alas, that it fades the moment it is finished!

It is a pity too that the bells, hung so high, so seldom touch the swirling activity on the streets below.

For example, we talk and write and sing of "wedding bells." But for myself, I have never heard bells ringing for a wedding in my life. We speak of bells tolling in full-dress sorrow at a funeral. "Never send to know for whom the bell tolls; it tolls for thee." Ah, in our large parish Death is so familiar a guest he has no need to ring the bell. He knows his way too well. So, in this teeming city parish, where both brides and burials leave the arched doors like ferries at a busy slip, you get neither the wedding bells dancing and clapping for joy, or the funeral knell that almost humanly moans and groans. I suppose they still toll that way at country funerals as some quiet neighbor slips so quietly into his humble space in the shadowy churchyard. Nowadays in the city, amid the strange requiem of impatient auto-horns, he is whizzed away through miles of busy streets to a distant machine-dug hole surrounded by a shaggy rug of artificial grass.

I sometimes wonder if the big Bell, standing up there in his tower like a sentinel on the battlements above the sleeping city, I wonder does he ever dream of days gone by when the bell was really king? The old days when the first goal of a stealthy enemy, scaling a town's midnight walls, was to seize the bell-tower, for then no alarm could be sounded—much as modern invaders might first take over radio and television stations. The old days when curfew had nothing to do with teen-age crime or called ball games, but the curfew bell meant literally what it said, "Cover your fires"—and turn in for the night. The old days when the bell was the community's central clock, as it always was in the vast, thriving monasteries, and when the bell clanged from the chapel-spire, hooded monks in fields and roads far apart laid down shovels and rakes and trowels and shears, and came striding in to common prayer or the common table.

But in history's musty house of bells there is still one fresh room that crotchety Time has not yet closed off. Even in this atomic age, "at morn, at noon, at twilight dim", the Angelus is Mary's hymn. It is rung at twilight dim because in the velvet darkness of the Holy Night Our Blessed Lord was born; it is rung at noon because at noon when the sun was high Christ hung high upon the cross, though red as a sunset; it is rung in the early morn because in the pink and silver dawn that first Easter, Our Savior rose, glorious and victorious, from the tomb.

It is called the Angelus Bell because its accompanying prayer reminds us that the Angel of the Lord announced unto Mary (as you can read in St. Luke) that she, the Virgin, would conceive the Son of God. Even non-Catholic poets like Edgar Allan Poe, Robert Southey, Sir Walter Scott, have snared in the golden web of verse the appealing beauty of the Angelus bell swinging in its tower and a world pausing to pray. But how hollow, how sad if the bell in the steeple seems to call out: "I ring ... you pray!" if the people below pay it no more heed than a plane droning across the empty sky! Is this another casualty of our so-called progress, of our vaunted civilization, another one of those little green plants of devotion that die so easily amid the fumes and the grime and the soot of the black-edged city? Pity the dictator's land where the Angelus bell cannot ring its triple reminder of how God once became Man. But pity, in a way, even more the land where people are to busy to notice it, even when it rings. Whenever you hear the Angelus Bell, lift up your heart to God and bring down God's blessing on your work!

I have always thought that the saddest bell of all is the so-called Sinners' Bell. Every night during a Redemptorist Mission, the bright, shining service of Benediction is suddenly broken off, and up in the tower the great bell tolls, deep and slow, while prayers are said for those people of the parish who should be there making the Mission and are not. You hear that slow, terrible bong and you shudder, because it cries in every language under Heaven that something is fearfully wrong. Somehow you almost hear the grim, final sound of a hammer ringing against the spikes of a cross. Or the funeral knell of a lost soul. Christ is calling, and so many shrug their shoulders and walk away. If they only knew that for some of them it is the bell on the locomotive of the last train out before the Enemy takes over the city. The next call will be Judgment.

And so it swings and rings, the church bell, now speaking deep and stern like an angry father, now rollicking light and mellow like a tumbling cherub; today ringing under the golden arrows of the sun, tomorrow in and out through the silver shuttle of the rain; ringing above all the little bells of earth, the whirring alarm-clocks, the tingling telephones, the piercing doorbells; ringing high above all the bells of this life because it speaks to you of the life above and beyond! Sometimes saying more than it seems to say, sometimes starting that tiny bell called conscience tinkling in a man's startled soul. No wonder they call the church bell, Vox Dei—the Voice of God. "Today —if you hear His voice—harden not your heart!"

Bell, Book, and Candle

THE BULB

In the movies one camera trick always good for a smile is to make the diver return to the diving board backwards, in a weird incredible arc. There he is where he started, and more marvelous still, perfectly dry. Well, I sometimes think that if I could reverse not a camera but the calendar so that it would bring me back to standing in my first pulpit, back up from more than thirty years thrashing around, sometimes over my head and sometimes not, I would make one important change. If I could begin my priestly life all over, I should try to give little talks that would teach. More and more I am convinced that people do not serve God because they do not love Him. And they do not love Him because they do not know Him. And they do not know Him because they have not been told—or they do not understand.

This was rammed into my slow brain, like a thumb-tack into a bulletin board, a few months ago when I gave a series of talks in a rural Catholic church where perhaps forty percent of the audience was non-Catholic. Of course when you advert to it, you realize that the ancestors of practically every Protestant were Catholics, and that the original Catholics were Jews—so to that extent we all do have a common kinship. However, with such an audience I was very careful to explain everything as I went along, and it seemed everybody was interested in the explanations. Thundering threats or blistering denunciations, moans and challenges or pleas might have gone past them like birds past a steeple, but explanations seemed to encircle everyone's interest like a quoit.

Apparently a good deal of it was news even to the Catholics. Not really of course. Once upon a time they had droned out these very facts from the dog-eared pages of a frowsy Catechism. Once they could rattle off religious definitions like coal rushing down a chute. When you are young, you have a memory like a trailer-truck: you can pack in everything. But your understanding, your intelligence is a motor that hasn't really got started, and meantime Time is a thief who silently steals your load. This is true not merely of Catechism and religion. It is true of everything. Once we knew the exports of Eucador, the mysteries of cube root, the remote causes of the Civil War... would we like to take an exam now? The years lay their layer of dust over once bright and shining facts. Things unused lay forgotten in the cobwebby attic of the mind.

So, today let's blow a little dust off a topic which is as ordinary in the Catholic Church as aircraft carriers are in the Navy. I mean the idea of Sacraments. It is easy to see where the word comes from: sacred, sacraments—they both flower from the same root, and a sacrament, from its very name, is a sacred thing. Maybe now you recall the Catechism definition that you used to sing out with rocking-horse rhythm: "A sacrament is an outward sign instituted by Christ to give grace." I'm afraid most of us as children might just as well have been chanting a phrase of Siamese sing-song for all we really understood. And I'm afraid that most grown-up Catholics today would shy away from a wager that they could not give a clear and precise explanation of just what a Sacrament is and what it does. They just have never thought it out. Never underestimate the intelligence of the people, but never overestimate their information.

For a little light on the subject of a Sacrament, suppose we turn to a very ordinary object, an electric bulb, an ordinary 40 or 60 watt bulb. A lad of seven could tell you that the whole idea of an electric bulb is to give light. He could tell you too that you could hold a bulb in your hand all day and it would not emit a single gleam. Ask him why. "Because it's not attached!" In other words the bulb, in order to do its job or fulfill its purpose, (to give light) needs electricity pouring into it and pulsing through it. Which is the same as saying it needs the help of a power outside itself!

Now, man is like that bulb. His purpose, the only reason God made him, is to know God and to serve Him; to know Him by the light of Faith and to burn out in His service. But, like the bulb, man cannot fulfill his function by himself. He too needs the help of a higher, outside power. The bulb needs electricity;

man needs Grace, which here merely means the help of God. And one of the two chief supply-sources of Grace is the Sacraments. That's why we say a Sacrament is an outward sign instituted by Christ *to give grace.*

But let's lay the bulb on the shelf for a moment, and turn our attention to the button. Remember we said a Sacrament is an outward sign. Suppose you are now at the threshold of a dark room. Your hands grope along the wall. You feel beneath your fingers a button, or a tiny switch. That button or switch is a sign of electricity. But notice it is not merely a sign, like a placard saying this room has been wired for electricity. It is (this button on the wall) not only a sign of electricity but such a sign that if you use it, it will produce electricity. And that is just what a Sacrament is! It is an outward *sign* of interior, spiritual grace, and at the same time it *produces* that grace.

Just take the first Sacrament, Baptism. Our Lord, instituting Baptism said, "Go into the whole world and preach the gospel to every creature, baptizing them in the name of the Father and of the Son and of the Holy Ghost." *Baptize* of course is merely the Greek word for wash. So the priest pours the water over the brow of the baby and says, "I baptize thee (that is, I wash thee) in the name of the Father" and so on. But the point is, the child who is being washed is generally glistening clean before the priest pours one drop of water. If anyone does not need his forehead washed, it is that child. So the washing, the Baptism, is only a sign, a symbol. But it is such a sign that when the water is poured over the child's brow, the stain of original sin is washed off the child's soul.

At this point Common Sense, which perhaps has been loitering in the last rank of the little group around the baptismal font, makes its way to the front and almost peevishly wants to know how this can be. How can a cup of water rippling over a few pink inches of baby skin, cleanse a stain which is on the youngster's soul? Well, do you remember how Our Blessed Savior in an instant cured a man who was blind? While the poor fellow stood there in his tattered rags, gripping his staff and staring stonily ahead, and the villagers who had known him as blind from birth leaned forward like an audience at the climax of a play, Our Lord stooped down, scooped up a dab of common clay, touched it to the blank, bulging eyes, and commanded him to wash in the pool of Siloe. He went, he washed, and he saw.

How did that happen? Do you think for a moment that light bubbled up in the dark pools of those sightless eyes because of the water or the clay? Then there would have been no more blind men in Judea. They needed but to bend down and pick up some clay, or dip their heads in the pool of Siloe. No, it wasn't the clay nor the water, but the power of the Divine Christ working through the clay and the water like electricity through a wire. And in Baptism, it is not the magic of the water or the words, but the power of that same Jesus Christ working through them, that same Son of God who touched lepers' fingers, scaly stubs like rotting twigs, and they became whole and smooth and tingling alive; that same Christ who by a word and a gesture made the shaggy savage sea, baring its cruel white teeth in an oncoming wave, lie down like a drowsy dog before a winter fire; that same Christ who planted the banner of His Divine Power on bread when He multiplied it, on water when He transformed it, on sickness when He cured it, on the future when He foretold it, in death when He conquered it ... that is the capital on which the check of every Sacrament is drawn, the Divine Power of Jesus Christ!

Every Sacrament is a gracious gesture on the part of our most considerate Savior toward human nature. He knew that we were not angels, but physical creatures with a body and sight and hearing and touch and taste, so He used physical things like bread and water and wine and oil as the outward signs of the graces He was giving us. So we have water in the Sacrament of Baptism, bread in Holy Communion, oil in Extreme Unction. In the first Olympics the athletes used to rub oil into their muscles for strength. So oil, as you can read in the epistle of St. James, became the external sign of the inward grace, the strength of soul that Extreme Unction imparts to the sick.

It is true we cannot see grace. For that matter we cannot see electricity either. You can show me an avenue of brilliantly illuminated shops, the *effect* of electricity, and I can show you a glittering litany of saints, the effect of grace. If you then ask, "Why do not Sacraments have the same effect on me?", I suggest that for a moment we forget the bulb, and the button, and now examine the wire that runs between them. If that wire is imperfect, worn, frayed, some of the current is going to flow off, and the light in the bulb will be dim and misty. Yes, and if when we receive the Sacrament of Holy Communion (for instance) our attitude is careless, our disposition dull, our whole approach casual, indifferent, routine—then we are going to lose much of the grace of the Sacrament. "Fill my heart with grace" we say, and we bring to the altar-rail a thimble, when we could bring a barrel!

It is good to understand about the Sacraments, but it is better to use them. Steep is the stairway going up to God, and of ourselves we grow weak and weary. But there are two banisters all the way up: Prayer and the Sacraments. Cling to them, lean on them, never let go of them, and one day you will triumphantly arrive at Heaven's gate!

Bell, Book, and Candle

THE BOOK

EVERYBODY CLAIMS

I suppose it happens to every priest, if he lives long enough, and last week it happened to me. The middle-aged man in the brown overcoat had one arm looped grimly around the lamp post, but he still swayed gently like a sailor on a mast. He pointed a wobbly finger at my Roman collar, and demanded, "Are you a Catholic Priest?" I could sense from the tone that he was not a Catholic, and (believe it or not) this was a pleasant switch. That Roman collar on streets and subways and buses always attracts its share of moist and militant Catholics, so it was a welcome change to be the target of heretical hiccups. "Are you?", he demanded. I nodded yes. "Then don't expect me to call you 'Father.' I read my Bible, and the Bible says (and he pounded the words with beery emphasis) 'Call no man Father upon the earth.' " I was going to ask him what he had called his own Dad when he was a boy. (Did he say "My male parent"?) But I could see he was too far gone in his cups to argue about sources.

Did you ever meet people who can spray Bible texts in all directions, like a garden hose, but are honestly amazed when you remind them that the Bible was not originally written in English? For one person who can glibly quote St. Matthew, how many have even heard of Aramaic, the language in which St. Matthew wrote?

One of the Reformers maintained, of course, that any servant girl, in fact, even his own nine-year-old daughter, could interpret the Bible. Well, yes, in the sense that they could plunge in, and come sputtering out with an "interpretation." But, would the little girl's and the servant girl's interpretation be the same? And if not, which would have the true meaning? Go further than that. Take so simple a matter as Baptism, and set before three sincere, godly men the text that enjoins Baptism, and then ask, "Does this mean infants are to be baptized too?" One may answer with some spirit, "Certainly. Infants are human beings. They have souls. Of course, baptize them." But the second may demur: "I don't think so. After all, the the baby hasn't the faintest notion of what is going on." And the third may merely shrug his shoulders, thereby saying in every language known to man, "What difference does it make? Is it that important? Do as you like."

Interpreting the Bible like this is like setting the same sheet of music on forty music-stands, only every musician ends up playing a different song. So each reader who throws open a New Testament, automatically becomes his own Pope, frames his own faith, chooses a la carte his own personal beliefs, differing perhaps violently from his neighbor's, but each contradiction goes proudly marching along, bravely holding up its banner as *The Truth of Christ*. Have you ever thought what a mocking scene this spreads before the searching eye of the atheist? Every separate booth in the Christian Fair cries out that it alone has the genuine truth, and offers to quote Scripture to prove it! It might make the atheist laugh, or it might make him cry; but it is shocking to the point of scandal, "scandal" in the Scriptural sense of a rock in the road over which a man stumbles and falls.

Wouldn't you think that Christ Himself would have foreseen this chorus of chaos? Didn't He know that every human institution must have some official body to interpret its constitution and laws and so determine what is true and right? Should not the Scriptures too have their own Supreme Court, guided by Him? Or are only the things of God reduced to a guess, and His Sacred Words become only tailors' dummies on which to drape, one after another, the loud, sensational opinions of men? The mere existence of some two hundred varieties of Christianity in the United States alone, should be proof aplenty that you cannot roll your own with texts as you can with tobacco, or use Bible quotations as an Erector Set to assemble your own personal religion. In this situation Peter becomes not the rock on which Christ said He built His Church, but a pile of pebbles. Truth is never reversible like a top-coat. It is only one. The opposite may be honest, sincere, earnest error. But it is error.

So, out of "the Bible alone" stream forth all these faiths, like different ornaments *on* the same Christmas Tree but not springing *from* the tree. The Bible alone can never be a satisfactory standard of faith or test of truth. It must have as its official and divinely guided interpreter, its Supreme Court, the Church that Christ founded to preach His Gospel. When I say this I remember immediately that there are people who energetically believe that the Catholic Church is somehow opposed to the Bible. The Church opposed to the Bible? You might as well say that a librarian was opposed to his books, or a carpenter to his tools, or a miller to his flour. Maybe this fiction got its sprinting start (and poor, plodding truth can never hope to overtake it) from the fact that once the Church chained Bibles. But I have seen Telephone Directories chained for the same reason: not that they would not be used, but so they could not be stolen, and would be there to be used! Again, so many people have the impression that the founder of one of the non-Catholic Churches battered down the stony dam of Papal opposition, and thus allowed Bibles to pour across Germany in a bright powerful stream. But how many people know that when this future founder was still a Catholic seminarian, there were, even then, fifteen editions of the Bible in German? The real river that was starting to flow was printer's ink.

And by that very fact don't you see that if the true Church had had to depend for its foundation or its spread only on the Bible or on Bible-reading, then it would have had to patiently await the invention of printing and of paper, and its chief Apostle would not be Peter nor Paul so much as Gutenburg, and the poor Lord would have been fourteen hundred years premature! Because before that, if you wanted to be a Bible Christian you had to be first, very wealthy, because even in the thirteenth century a Bible cost more than a house, since every word had to be laboriously copied on parchment. In the second place, you had to be quite learned, because for century after century not one man in ten could spell his way through a psalm. In the third place, in the first ages of Christianity you would have to have been a wide traveller even to encounter all the parts of the Scriptures, because the different sections were scattered in different places.

Do you know that Christianity was more than three hundred years old before all the parts of the New Testament were assembled in one authentic volume? It was sixty years old before all the books of the New Testament had even been written. It was twenty years old before *any* of the books had been written. It was the Church that came first. The Scriptures only followed.

Did it ever strike you that Our Blessed Lord never wrote a single word—except what He traced in the sand? Our Lord when He walked the earth never commanded His disciples to put one word on paper or parchment; but He did say, "*Preach* the Gospel to every creature." "Go and teach all nations." He never said: "If any man will not read the Scriptures" but He did say "If any man will not *hear the church*, let him be to thee as the heathen and the publican."

For that matter, leave out the Church, and how do you know that the Bible *is* the word of God? Because of its majestically marching sentences and its luminously beautiful prose? But what about the Old Testament where you get page after page of dry law and dusty genealogy? Because of its message, lofty and clean and stimulating, soaring off the page like an Alpine peak? But in the Old Testament you will slosh through verses vile as mud-puddles. Because it (let's turn to the New Testament, our main consideration anyway)—because it was written by Our Lord's chosen band of Apostles? Then you must reject the Gospel of Mark and of Luke, and the Acts. Not one-half of the Apostles ever wrote a single surviving sentence. And some of those that did write, wrote only because particular circumstances compelled them to write: they were in prison or far away on a journey. And it shows in the result. Because the New Testament, far from being a crisp, clear, methodical textbook of Christianity, is more like a tangled chain of parables and persons, miracles and sermons, and casual day-by-day happenings. Our Lord never took time out to dictate His Autobiography. There was no press-tent on Calvary, and not one of the wire services sent a man to cover the Resurrection.

Everybody knows that Bible is the Greek word for book. It is *the* Book of all ages. But you cannot live just by the book ... even that Book. For example most Christians connect the Lord's Day with Sunday. Why? It's not in the Bible. From some authority bigger than the Bible? That's right. And that's why when some man strides up to you (as they have to me) flourishing a copy of the New Testament and says, "This is the word of God. All I need is between these two covers. I don't want any church telling me ...", ask him gently where he got that New Testament. He might tell you he got it from some hotel—but ask him where did the first one come from? Or does he believe that right after Our Lord ascended into Heaven, the Holy Ghost Publishing Company somewhere up there started its presses rolling, the pages were gilt-edged with the gold of sunrise and bound in the soft down of angel's wings, and sped on their way by seraph air-express into the outstretched arms of the waiting Apostles? Not quite so dramatic as that. A couple of hundred years after the death of Christ, the present Epistles and Gospels were floating about in different sections of the Christian world, together with others you probably never heard of (like the Gospel of St. Bartholomew and the Epistle of St. Clement). So it was not till almost the fifth century that the Church—the only Church then in existence—examined these documents one by one, accepted this, rejected that, and that is how you got your New Testament.

But if that Church was *not* the one true infallible Church of Christ, how do you know that the Scriptures she certified are really the word of God? On the other hand, if this Church did have the Divine guidance and authority to do this, must she not be the True Church—and since Truth is one—the only True Church? During this week, when we commemorate the conversion of **St. Paul, may** many straying souls find their way back **to the Faith of their Fathers**!

Bell, Book, and Candle

THE BOX OF

KITCHEN MATCHES

A few months back I saw, in a rectory parlor, the strangest little altar. It was about three feet long and a couple of feet high, with steps and tabernacle and spires—all the majesty of soaring Gothic in cute miniature. From the other side of the room the little altar gleamed with a curious black-and-white effect that became clear when you got up close. The whole thing was made of matchsticks, common kitchen matches, first ignited, then extinguished, then varnished, and finally fitted together to form this dazzling model altar. I asked one of the priests about it. "Oh, that. Made by one of the lifers in the prison. He did it in honor of St. Jude."

I thought how symbolic it was, this altar of charred matches, like the prisoner's own wasted, burned-out life, now (like the altar) turned towards God. It seemed to say that as long as we live, there is never total failure. You *can* do something with the pieces. And St. Jude is supposed to be the patron of the impossible. He was an Apostle, and when you thought of it the Apostles were something like ordinary wooden matches. For example the first thing to be noticed about a match is that you *don't* notice it. There is nothing prominent or conspicuous about a match. In a little pile of all kinds of tiny pieces of wood, like lollypop sticks and roast-beef skewers and toothpicks and slivers, an ordinary wooden match would not stand out particularly. It would be lost in the pile. And yet, there is something about a match that sets it entirely apart. Something in its head! Stored fire! So it was with the Apostles, too. When they were tugging at their heavy nets on the sea, or plodding along the dusty road toward the Temple's golden dome, they looked like any other group of Galilean peasants. They would be lost in a crowd. And yet there *was* something different about them. Something in their heads, stored fire, the fire that came from the hovering tongues of fire at Pentecost, the fire that was to light the candles of the Christian faith on the altars of the civilized world!

I wonder is there anything really different about us, their spiritual descendants? We dress and look and seem like everyone else. What sets us apart from modern pagans, on the sidewalks or in the shops or in our homes? Do we stand out as children of Christ's True Church? I don't mean distinguished by a dainty medal dangling from the throat, nor a Holy Name pin glinting in the lapel—should we not be known by the cleanness of our speech, the purity of our lives, the integrity of our word, kindness to our neighbor, unbroken fidelity to Mass and the Sacraments? If only we Catholics really lived as Catholics, we couldn't handle the procession of converts into the Church!

Then there is this feature about a match. It never shows what it really is or what it really has within it, till it meets resistance, till it comes head on against opposition. Then when it strikes something hard in its way, suddenly with a little rush and roar, all its powers leap up in a glorious fighting flame! So with the Apostles too. When our Lord in their midst was scattering brilliant miracles the way a fountain tosses off glittering rainbow droplets, the Apostles showed no particular heroism or zeal. It was only after Christ was crucified, and the Jewish synagogues and the Roman Empire rose up against the spread of Christianity like a stone wall that the Apostles rushed against it, like a match literally losing their heads, but breaking into sparks that set the world on fire with the new, true Faith of Christ!

And—we ask ourselves in a theatrical aside—how do *we* act in time of opposition? When misfortune breaks through the line of our careful plans and throws us with shuddering tackle, when a sudden sharp reverse in business strips our financial gears, when overnight the world lies before us without sun or birds or flowers, as empty and dark and lifeless as a crater in the moon, and life is only a frame with the picture ripped out, how do we react? I don't mean our very first reaction. That is understandable. But a sturdy ship soon steadies itself. But if we continue to brood within ourselves and whimper to others and murmur against God, where is our faith—we who are the children of the martyrs, the sons and daughters of those pioneers of Christ on whose banner rippled the hardest of all heroic mottoes, "Thy will be done!" This we must remember: Faith never was an escalator to carry a man in comfort up the steep hill of life. It is but a staff on which he leans while he does the climbing himself.

There's something else about a match. For the greater part of its life it stays a dull, undistinguished bit of wood. But at the last it has its breathless moment of glory. Then, when it is giving its all, when it is sacrificing everything it has, when it is dying—a brave, struggling flame—then it is most beautiful. In that magnificent moment it becomes a blossom of flame blowing on a stem, a little golden pennant rippling from its tiny staff, even almost like the blazing halo round a martyr's head as he burns at the stake.

But wasn't it that way with the Apostles too? When they were living they never achieved so much as when they laid down their lives. Pascal says that we more easily believe those who are willing to have their throats cut in testimony that they speak the truth. When the Apostles were preaching, many people listened with their mind in neutral: maybe so, maybe not. But when they saw the Apostles shed their willing blood in the name of Jesus, like a red seal encrusted on the truth, then people began to examine and to embrace this Christian Faith. In their lives the Apostles were only stolid, plodding peasants, but in their deaths they flared forth as martyrs, men with a message, saints whose impact on the world would ring long after the blow that struck them down, like the lingering hum of a great bell.

But this heroic sunset is not the usual pattern of life. As a rule, death is only the carbon copy of how we have lived. And a sinner who sets the alarm of his conscience to wake up and repent at the final hour will generally be dead and judged when it rings. But I once knew a notorious ne'er-do-well whose final few months were a sermon to the whole neighborhood. I suppose as he wove his reeling, drunken way so often along the street and home to his patient sister, he must have scandalized a multitude. But in August a dread disease flung him on his bed, wasted him away, whittled him down like a white stick. In those dying months his face seemed to grow almost transparent (as though there were a lamp inside it) and the real man began to show through. By the gentle patience of his suffering, by the solid granite of his faith, by the almost gay buoyancy of his spirit, by the simple fervor of his prayers, by the appreciation he showed for the slightest service, by his constant consideration for others . . . well, I think no cathedral has ever rung with such a sermon as he preached from his inching deathbed. He died on the feast of All Saints and I wonder if like another great Sinner, the Good Thief, he did not use the cross of his dying as a ladder to climb into Heaven. His end was his crowning.

There is a further feature about a match to make a man think, and it is this: every match swings over a wide, wild gulf of different possibilities. You can take a match and with it light the sparkling candles of a holy shrine. Or you can take that same match and set fire at midnight to a cottage where people lie in their dreaming beds. But wasn't it the same with the Apostles? In every Apostle there burned a spark of—call it passion—that could have flared into blazing hatred of Christ, or of warm, shining love. Every

Apostle could have been a traitor like Judas who sold Christ to the Cross, or a quiet hero like John who stood beneath the Cross, loyal to the last.

Isn't that true of any man? Let them talk of heredity, apologetically mention environment, learnedly discourse about glands—deep down *we* know that in the main *we* are responsible for our actions. In that sense, I am the Captain of my soul. Breezes may blow, but I can set my sails to meet them. Under the flag of free-will I steer my own course for good or evil, for Heaven or Hell. In God's eyes, everyman's life, be he apostle or upholsterer, is a blank check. You yourself fill out how much it is worth; you fill out to whom you want to pay your soul!

One final point. A match does not exist for itself. I mean you do not frame a match and hang it on a wall, like a picture, for people to admire. You do not set it on a shelf to tick independently away like a clock. No, a match is always directed toward something else. You light it to look for something you have lost in the dark, or to start a fire against the cold, or even to light a cigarette for your comfort and pleasure. Its very nature is to bring its flame to something other than itself. And wasn't that the way it was with the Apostles? They never lived narrow, self-centered lives, like a nut in its shell. From the day of the first Pentecost when the tongues of fire hovered over their heads, each curling flame as scarlet as a bishop's skullcap, they flung open the doors that had barred them in, and strode out to *serve others*, each to light the fire of faith, each one burning down and crumpling over (like a match) as he brought the great news of the Gospel to some who had been in the dark.

Doesn't this hold for us too? A man is never closer to Christ than when out of Christian kindness he is doing something for others. Who was it that said that God had divided man into men so that they could help one another? The selfless man who lives to do good is the happy man. Like the sacristan's taper igniting candle after candle on the altar, the more he gives of himself the brighter it is around him. That is why the noblest professions in the world are those that are concerned directly with helping others, like nurses or teachers. For that matter, what is the true glory of motherhood? Not just child-bearing, or childbirth, but a love for the child that knows no limit, and sacrifices for the child that never stop. And isn't it one of the good Lord's little jokes that the people who give away happiness, are the very ones who have the most themselves? The stagnant pond gets covered with scum, but the fountain that flings itself away stays wholesome and bright.

In other words, take a tip from a match and an example from the Apostles, bring light where there is darkness, warmth where there is cold: a light not hid under a bushel-basket of self, but a tiny, generous image of Christ, the Light of the World!

Swings from a Thurible

OUTSTRETCHED HANDS

If Heaven had a Complaint Department, perhaps the busiest window would be "Unanswered Prayers." At least I think that the question people put most often to priests is: "Why aren't my prayers heard?" And the priest who in his time has perhaps preached with rich and rolling eloquence on "Ask and ye shall receive" almost feels that now he is supposed to find God an "out." As though "Ask and ye shall receive" were a handsomely illuminated script or document like a contract or a deed or an insurance policy, and now the priest smugly points to the fine print underneath and suavely explains, "I'm afraid you overlooked this" or "Your particular case is definitely excluded here." There is no such trickery in the Trinity. God needs no defense, because He is God, and that means all-good.

True, this would be easier to see if the answer to every prayer came out as promptly and precisely as a piece of pie at the automat—or like that rather recent incident in London. A young Catholic lawyer had his shingle hanging out but no clients hurrying in. He was depressed almost to desperation. Then he got an idea. He left his office and went down to a little chapel at Moorfield and prayed fervently, almost fiercely, before the picture of Saint Thomas More, who in his day had been the most brilliant lawyer in the realm, in fact the Lord High Chancellor. When the young lawyer got back to his chambers, there was a note scribbled on the telephone pad by the man in the next office. A client would be in at eleven. The client turned out to be a very important person, and thereafter was so pleased with the young lawyer's work that he introduced him to several prominent friends and started him on a very promising legal career. By one of those eyebrow-raising, "let me get that again" coincidences, the client's name was Mr. Thomas More.

Oh, if prayers were always answered as dramatically as that, or even if they were dramatically left unanswered, and we could see why... For example, if you prayed to catch a certain train (and you missed it) or if you prayed to make a certain plane (and had to hitch-hike forty miles on a winter road, as happened to me, and missed it by one minute)—if then the next morning you read in the paper how the train was wrecked or the plane had crashed... then we could see why our prayer was not answered, and be grateful! But as a rule, the mountain peak of God's design and providence is not so sharply clear. Often it is hidden in the clouds, dark swirling mists through which human eyes cannot peer.

But way back fifteen centuries ago, one of the dazzling luminaries of theology, Saint Augustine, dropped some realistic pointed hints why some of our prayers are not heard. The way he phrased it, it has almost the ring of a college yell: "Mali mala male petimus." In a kind of free-wheeling translation, that would mean that some of us ask for wrong things, some in a wrong way, and some while kneeling on the very ground of wrong-doing.

The wrong things?

Now, nobody in his right mind would brazenly pray for what is downright sinful. But often our faith is so thin we just annoy God asking for trifles, the small change of temporal things, hardly ever asking the great gold of grace and salvation itself. We pray "Deliver us from all evil." But don't you know that in the eyes of God there is on this whole earth only one real evil—and it is not poverty, it is not pain, it is not disappointment. It is sin. Because only sin can clang against us the gates of Heaven and keep us from God forever.

How ironically there stands against that, the prayer of a woman amply dressed in flowery chintz like a slipcover and upholstered almost like a sofa, who now at breakfast between her fourth and fifth jelly-doughnut, breathes (with a little difficulty) a petulant prayer to God to take off a few pounds from her tonnage. Or a high-school boy blowing the thick dust off his chemistry book, and saying a panicky prayer that somehow the Lord will see him through tomorrow's exam with flying colors and bubbling test-tubes!

It is perfectly proper to pray for God's help in our particular need, but it is good to remember that God is not a traffic cop who suddenly holds up his hand in the middle of the street-corner and stops all the normal course of things, holding back, you may say, the laws of nature while our petition goes screaming through with motorcycle escort! Our prayer should be not so much for exceptions or exemptions to the general rule, but rather strength to bear the order of things as God has established them.

I remember once in the springtime seeing a sobbing mother kneeling on the green cushion of a grave, her hands clasped upon the tombstone as though it was a pew in church. She had prayed there like that, she told me later, till she had buried the black devil of bitterness that had darkened her heart ever since her boy had been plucked away in the bright bloom of his youth. Before this she had tried everything to forget—tried taking a trip, tried plunging into her work, tried listening to the sympathy and the counsel of her friends. But until she got down on her knees and turned to God in prayer—really prayed—nothing helped. But prayer had flung up the gloomy blinds of grief and let in the golden sunlight of God's own comfort.

As to asking the wrong way—I suppose the father of a family never lived who did not at one time or other grumble that the only time his children recognized his existence was when they wanted something. "Dad, may I have the car tonight?" When the "bite" is on and the hand is out, then Dad suddenly assumes in the family a stature of importance. But wouldn't this make any normal sensitive Dad glumly wonder if he were really the father of a family, or just the disbursing agent of a little corporation? Well, how do you think Our Father in Heaven feels if the only language we ever speak to Him is the prayer of "Gimme" or "Please"? If we didn't need something, would we ever notice Him?

It must be far from flattering to the too-tolerant Almighty. Honestly, I think some people must really picture God as a sort of super-clerk in glistening white, behind a long, long soda fountain with all kinds of chrome levers and porcelain taps. This one is marked Jobs; that one, Boy Friend; the next one Health, then Exams—and so on. And as soon as our order comes in, He is supposed to spurt that particular syrup into the glass and hand it over—quick. And if He doesn't do it immediately, we get a little impatient in our prayers, a little irritated, and there is a kind of pious pounding on the marble counter—"What's holding things up, anyway?" Look: we cannot turn the Deity into a delivery boy—but oh, how some of us try!

As regards asking against a background of wrong-doing, tonight in more than one home across America, some boy will put out his hand across the table and whine, "Mom, kin I have some more?"—more anything from an ear of corn to a piece of cake. And when the mother sees that hand stretched out, grimy, smudgy, just plain dirty, she will glare, "Willie, where did you get those hands? How dare you come to the table like that? Now leave at once and don't ask for one more thing until you have washed!" How many of us larger people are in a larger sense stretching out toward God dirty hands, hands filthy with sin, and asking Him to fill them with some favor? Should we not first clean up before we dare speak up?

Ponder the parable of the second-story man who has just smashed a window and ransacked a home. Now he is climbing down the ladder. Suddenly a rung snaps, and he plunges to the ground, breaking a leg. All at once there is the owner of the house looking down from an upper window... so what does the culprit do? He calls up, "Mr. Owner, first of all I want you to get me the best doctor in town. I'd also appreciate a little help with my hospital bills. And by the way, I could stand a new ladder." You think this is a fantastic, grotesque exaggeration—but think again: haven't we all done something like that to the Man Upstairs—shattered not God's windows but His commandments, invaded His dominion, robbed Him of His due honor, torn virtue apart—by our sins and more sins? Are we in any position to ask anything except Mercy? And if we do ask for anything else, should it not be with deepest humility and broken-hearted sorrow?

We think that what we ask for is for our good, but the road of life takes some strange curves. Remember the ten lepers in the Gospel? Here they were with their blotched and horrible masks of faces, following Our Lord, hoarsely pleading to be healed. So He heard their prayers. But the very moment their leprous fingers, numb and dead as twigs on a tree, began to feel the ruddy vibrant pulse of health, they all—all but one—forgot the Christ that cured them. Ten lepers sick, sought out the Lord, clung to Him, prayed to Him. Ten lepers cured—nine of them never even went back to say "Thanks!" Perhaps instead they took the first muddy path back to sin. Isn't it better to crawl into Heaven, even as a leper?

God the Father looks not at the particular request, but at the over-all picture. Isn't that what every good father does? Isn't there many a boy going to bed tonight with an upset stomach because some short-sighted, indulgent father (or mother) gave the child all the chocolates he wanted—in other words, gave him just what he asked for? Our Father in Heaven is too wise and too loving ever to do that with us, His children. The wisdom we lack, He has. Where we are blind, He sees. But a little poem, whose author I cannot find, mirrors that thought clear as a Holy Water font:

> I know not by what methods rare—
> But this I know: God answers prayer!
> I know that He has given His word
> Which tells us prayer is always heard
> And will be answered, soon or late...
> And so I pray, and calmly wait.
>
> I know not if the blessing sought
> Will come in just the way I thought;
> I leave my prayer with Him alone
> Whose Will is wiser than my own,
> Assured that He will grant my quest
> Or send some answer far more blest!

Swings from a Thurible

A CHURCH IS A DULL PLACE

A Novena Service I know has so grown with the years that now they need a bus despatcher and traffic cop to keep the black streams of cars and people from clogging up before the church doors. Well, the other Wednesday night Big Boy Blue (the traffic policeman) said to the frailer fellow in blue (the bus despatcher), "You know Sandy, there's plenty of action out here, waving on these lanes of taxis and trucks and buses and all kinds of cars, and those drivers who ought to be in baby-carriages, and the life I save two or three times every Wednesday night is my own—but as I was saying, at least it's some excitement. But inside that big church it must be awfully dull. I'm not saying, mind you, it isn't good for people to go there and the Lord knows I'd probably do better going oftener myself, but all the same I took a peek in there last week and it's a fearfully quiet affair. Not absolutely silent of course because the crowd says some prayers out loud together, and they sing two or three hymns, and there's a man in the pulpit dressed in black and white like a domino and not much bigger, and he gives a bit of a sermon. But the whole atmosphere is pretty tame. Never any excitement at all. Whatever happens in church?"

Well, officer, maybe we don't have many three-car wrecks down the middle aisle, and perhaps we can't boast of a cocktail bar at the Holy Water Font, and it is pretty rare that international spies meet stealthily under the Seventh Station of the Cross to exchange notes in code . . . But even while the traffic officer was pitying the lack of glamor in the big grey church, some pretty important things were happening inside those stained-glass windows and under the twin spires. If he only knew it, decisions were being made in there as dramatic and drastic as pulling the switch on the main line of a man's life and sending off a whole train of years in a completely new direction!

For example that night the officer never noticed an attractive young lady way up in the fourth bench, right near the Shrine. She was praying, not just fervently, but almost fiercely. Her face was tensely pale, but once it seemed to blush scarlet with shame, almost like the red altar-light flickering across the white marble. Her lips moved in a silent plea to Heaven, and as she nervously clasped and unclasped her slender folded hands, three gold bracelets tinkled elegantly on her wrist. Out of the corner of her eye she glanced down on them, and she thought to herself scornfully, "These are not bracelets. They are handcuffs. Handcuffs to him and to sin. But tonight, please God,

A CHURCH IS A DULL PLACE

please, Oh God! I break them! Mary, Mother of Jesus, Our Mother of Perpetual Help, help a prodigal daughter!"

An hour later, at the other end of the city, an older man in a flashy car scowled at his watch for the last time, swore under his breath, pressed the starter and drove angrily away. The seat at his side was empty. And he would never have dreamed of looking in a church-pew before a candle-lit Shrine.

No. Not much happens in a church. At least nothing you can see. The people there are as quiet and undistinguished as chessmen on a board. But all the time a game is playing, and the stakes can be as high as Heaven and Hell. This is why here, in this unspectacular silence, changes are made and lives pulled inside out like a stocking, and people go out altogether different than they came in. The traffic officer wouldn't particularly have noticed, in these pews polka-dotted with people, a young fellow in the third bench from the rear. A trim, clean-looking chap, and to the college authorities just another student in his sophomore year. But to the lad himself he was a man standing perplexedly at the cross-roads of life. Every Wednesday evening for two years now he had knelt there, and besides the usual Novena prayers he had repeated another one over and over to himself. It was a strange prayer on the lips of a clear-eyed youth with 20-20 vision, because it was the prayer of the blind man squatting against the wall of Jericho when Christ and the crowd went shuffling by: "Lord, that I may see!" And tonight at least he thought he did see. The mist lifted. The way was clear. He had made up his mind. He was going to take the path to the priesthood. A whole life turned round that night, like a whole world turning round on its axis. Souls still unborn would some day feel the sublime impact of that decision!

Meanwhile outside, the traffic cop was disgustedly holding up a smart convertible and an equally smart driver who was trying to make a U-turn. But who would suspect that the young fellow in the third last pew had just made a U-turn with his life and had headed back the opposite way (where God was calling him) right under the officer's nose?

So sometimes something does happen in church, if you don't expect golden trumpets and purple banners and gorgeous spectacles, but if you could just see things as the Lord does, as He looks down from the choir-loft of Heaven. At that very moment you would have seen a grey-haired man sitting half way down the side aisle at the end of a bench, as though ready to leave at a moment's notice. The way he looked at the altar, so uneasily, so diffidently made him seem like a man who feared he had rung the wrong doorbell and would not be welcomed in. As a matter of fact, it was the first time he had been inside a church for twenty-three years. Just what had brought him there tonight he himself was not sure. But as he sat there and looked shyly around, the marching columns of the bygone years tramped past him in a review— because this was the church of his childhood, the only church he ever knew, and suddenly his past began to stand up before him like a pageant of colors on a stage. There he was in white, a sturdy little chap, at this very Communion Rail making his First Communion. And there he was a couple of years later, at the altar itself, so proud in the red cassock of an altar-boy. And then, in that very sanctuary, in a dark blue suit (they wore knickers in those days) receiving that rolled-up diploma, not much bigger than a windowshade, at his grammar school graduation. And then (how quickly those ten years sped by) he was marching down this middle aisle in the formal black coat and the striped trousers of a bridegroom. And after that, every month in suits of grey or brown or blue among the First Friday Communion crowds . . .

Then, that quarrel with the priest. A just judge might have decided that the priest was right in the matter, but not in the manner. And a priest is very foolish to win an argument except almost apologetically. He must win, as it were, with his hat in his hand, or in the ancient phrase he will win an argument and lose a soul. This man was lost till now. (And lest you think his case is only a pink bon-bon of the imagination, let me assure you it is a hard solid fact.) But all these years somehow he had never missed saying his three Hail Mary's each morning and night to the Mother of God, though she seemed far away. And lately, in fact for the past year, he had been saying his beads each night before going to bed. And tonight he had wandered into the church of her Shrine. It was gradual, you see, like the rescue of people from a sinking ship. First the Coast Guard shoots out a thin white line—so frail it doesn't seem to promise much. But as the survivors drag it in, it gradually thickens into a stalwart rope to be made fast. And finally comes the bosun's chair to ride them over the waves to safety. Just so, the strong line of God's grace that began with the little inspiration to slip into this church was now ready to carry this man back to God . . . .

Outside, the traffic cop was too busy watching the lights flash green and red, so he never could see the little white bulb suddenly gleam over the confessional door to indicate a penitent had just gone in. It wasn't very exciting to be sure, but if angels could do handsprings in heaven, they might have been that happy over a wanderer who had at last come home.

A bit later, when he came out of the confessional he all but collided with a young lady who was a little too gayly attired and too brightly made up. You might guess she was the giddy, frivolous, chorus-girl type, except that in church you never can tell whose soul lives in the spiritual slums and whose dwells in the suburbs. Anyway she went clicking down the aisle on high twinkling heels, but *he* was so happy he thought he was walking on air.

Meanwhile, at one of the side altars in the sanctuary knelt another man. He wasn't a stranger to church, but he was a stranger in this particular church. His face wore the grim set look of someone who has prayed his heart out and there still was no hope, and life was hollow and his soul was numb. His faraway look was fixed absently on a little white flower that was drooping out of the vase on the altar, but his thoughts were on his little boy, like that flower pale and frail and drooping toward death in the nearby hospital. Leukemia, and the lad was only five. The little fellow, he thought, was like that small vigil light feebly sputtering out before that statue. It couldn't be long now. Maybe even tonight. But why, he asked with a sudden rebellion, why must God take this innocent one and let so many villains live, their fast artificial lives flaming brightly like the candles on the tables of night clubs....

Just then the Brother Sacristan glided out in his black robe, dipping his long taper into that tiny dying light, carried the flame over to the main altar and, in preparation for the Benediction, lit the tall white candle next to the Tabernacle, closest to Christ. And slowly, like angry waves steadying down to a smooth shimmering sea, peace came over that father's soul. Because he was reminded that from the end of one life, God could make the beginning of another.

He could take a life from this world and carry it to a world far better and brighter! Had not the Lord promised it in His Gospel? Had He not proven it in His own Resurrection? For all eternity the boy was certain of happiness in the Arms of God. But I, thought the father, I am not—not certain yet. So from that very day (and this is no fairy tale) from that day he began to receive Holy Communion every day of his life. He could have walked out of that church cynical and bitter, into a life of sullen rebellion and shattered commandments. Instead he took the outstretched Wounded Hand of Christ. It all happened in a short space in church, but just at that time the fire engines went roaring past, bells clanging and sirens screeching, so the traffic cop had his hands full—of real excitement. A few minutes later the apparatus crawled back. The fire was a false alarm. So was the excitement. But the man in church was not.

No—you never can tell who may be kneeling next to you at a church service like this. You never know what purpose or what problem lies beneath the mask of another human face. I have known a chief of detectives dropping in regularly to ask the guidance of God on his hard cases. I have no doubt that more than one thief has knelt here like a very statue of devotion, though meanwhile swivelling his eyes about to see whether some lady in her piety would not be careless of her purse. This does not mean that the next time you go to Mass or to a Novena you should glare with cold distrust at the people on your right and left, but I assure you that such thievery has happened in church more than once, especially with those shoulder bags that hang behind you and that must have been designed by pickpockets.

Which reminds me that various things have been left in our church, even a Poor Box stolen from another church, emptied, and left in ours with the significant motto still clearly saying "God loves a cheerful giver." Then there was that stylish, stately lady, panic on her aristocratic face, praying so nervously that she twisted and tugged at her expensive rosary till the chain snapped. But her prayer was heard; she got the grace she pleaded for. Because afterwards in the pew somebody found the broken string of rosary beads and a package she had pulled out of her purse and left there, because she had changed her mind, and didn't trust herself even to throw them away. She left the bottle of sleeping pills and suicide behind her.

Yes, it's pretty quiet in church, and maybe nothing very exciting happens there. But all sorts of people wander in, all kinds of brooks run into this mysterious sea. And no matter how muddy the brooks may be, the sea is so big (big as the mercy of God) it is always deep enough and clean enough to receive them all. And the Star of that Sea, with a name that embraces them all, is Mary, Mother of God and Mother of Perpetual Help.

Swings from a Thurible

NOVENA MIRROR

Spiritually our time has been called the Age of Novenas. Every priest wishes to Heaven it were known as the Age of the Mass. Between a Novena service and the Sacrifice of the Mass there is no more comparison than between a devotional vigil light flickering away at a shrine, and the great crimson sanctuary lamp blazing forth the Presence of God at the Main Altar. But people like Novenas, partly I think because they participate more actively in the service, and partly because they are praying for some particular personal intention. This is not bad; it is merely the lesser of two goods. So we encourage people to make Novenas, but we should also remind them that a novena is not just spiritual confectionery or a spiritual toy like a kind of pious yo-yo. And since this is January, the month of inventory, what could be a better time for taking stock on our Novena (whichever one it may be) and us?

Say to yourself: "See here, I've been making this 'Perpetual' Novena for some time now. What has it done for me?" I don't mean what has it done for that arthritis which we hoped to get rid of, nor for that apartment which we hoped to get hold of, nor that annoying neighbor we wanted God to inspire to move, nor for that diamond ring we wanted God to inspire a certain somebody to give us ... but what has the Novena done for me, myself, my character, my life, my soul?

In preaching a weekly Novena for many years, you encounter some weird requests, even to the blessing of sweepstake tickets with the sugared inducement that in event of a win you would get half. I remember during the war one woman told me she was making that Novena to get butter. All right, but the first purpose of every Novena should be to get better; that is to glorify God and to make ourselves better—I mean to become better in thought and word and deed in the eyes of God. Otherwise our Novena is in danger of dropping to a mere game of Gimme, or becoming a spiritual charm bracelet, or a religious cosmetic, a kind of powder-and-paint deftly applied to the soul.

Maybe that powder and paint idea is not too bad, with this observation: that while the illustration is lifted out of the life of the ladies, the application fits just as snugly into the lives of men. Suppose then, it is Monday or Tuesday or Wednesday evening, and Noreen Novena is prettying up before hurrying off to church. In her left hand she holds a compact, like an artist's palette, and begins a little exterior decorating. This of course is perfectly all right, though sometimes I think the Novena preacher, booming the attendance, is misunderstood when he asks his congregation to bring a new face to the services. Anyway Noreen here goes on making minor repairs or even extensive alterations at the point where God left off, and as she smiles into the compact's little mirror, she suddenly becomes confidential with it. "You know, little mirror, I was just thinking. Here I've been taking you to the Novena in my handbag for the past two years. And you know something? I haven't changed a bit!" "Right!" retorts the mirror. All mirrors reflect; this one does its reflecting out loud. "You haven't changed. The same old faults, worn into your soul like stale powder into that puff. The same old toying with dangerous occasions of sin. And don't try to tell me otherwise. Sure, you brought me to church every Monday, but you brought me other places too—where you were not quite so archangelic. Now do you remember when..."

"Humph!" She tosses her shoulders indignantly and swishes her hair as though shaking off some insect buzzing around her. Is she hearing things? Anyway, she goes on to crayon her lips into a dainty Cupid's bow in a shade that was probably advertised as "Sunset in the Sierras" but which sometimes turns out like Firebox on the Corner. But not this time. "Well," murmurs the mirror, "not so bad! Some of your faces should be in Museums. You are very skilled at making-up. But why is it you never think of *making-up* with those people with whom you have quarrelled? You don't go in for that kind of making-up do you? No, but you go to your Novena ever Monday and with your pretty painted lips shout your prayers, but it would take a chisel to pry open those lips and say a Christian word to so and so, or so and so. When you pass them it is warpaint you are wearing, and your nose suddenly tilts up like a giant telescope. Oh, *you* are in the right and they are in the wrong! But, is Christianity a law court? You are not supposed to greet them for their sake because they are right and so it is only just; nor for your sake because you are right, but you feel generous; but for God's sake, no matter who is right or who is wrong, because He wants it!"

Miss Noreen Novena doesn't like this rebuke one bit, and bang! she slaps the powder-puff so hard against her nose that a little white cloud of powder-dust drifts off like smoke from a cannon. "Ah... there's another thing I've been noticing lately," says the mirror. "That atom-bomb temper. In church aren't you the sweet one, so gentle and so devout! At the Novena, Noreen is a little lamb. But at home, Noreen can be a pretty little panther, snarling, snapping, surly, selfish..."

But before the mirror could finish, Noreen clicked the compact shut, and went clacking off on her high heels (and probably her high horse) to the Novena. The stained-glass windows wouldn't be so gabby.

Honestly, though, isn't there something in what the mirror said? What is the difference between standing before a little mirror and putting on your cheek a dab of rouge and a pat of powder, and kneeling before a little shrine and just putting on your soul a little patch of prayer and a little snatch of hymn—if that is all the Novena means! In both cases isn't it all on the surface, only superficial? Don't they both effect a mere temporary change, a passing glow? Isn't it true that neither of them gets inside to produce a permanent improvement?

No Novena or Sodality or Devotion is meant to be a mere spiritual bon-bon, wrapped in attractive tinfoil. Rather that weekly half-hour should be more like a tiny cake of yeast dropped in among all the other hours of the week and raising them to a higher level. But it never will, unless we go to the Novena not just praying for the goods of this world, but also to be good in this world.

Several years ago a Pastor told me that a Lady-lecturer in his parish hall had said among other things that some people were like Christmas trees and some were like apple trees. Who she was, how she developed it I don't know, but I do think that this divides the people who go to a Novena sharply and vividly. Take a Christmas tree for example. It goes big for glamor; it is all razzle-dazzle; it loves to stand there with its gaudy ornaments and necklace of colored bulbs, the center of attraction It doesn't do anything. It just stands there. It doesn't give anything; it just gets. It expects you to lay presents at its feet. It isn't a strong tree: a little push, and over it goes; it has no roots. And is it not true, in a few days the needles start turning brown and falling off, and the tree is flung out as a fire-hazard?

Now the apple tree is different. No show-off, no splurge of artificial razzle-dazzle. It stands there quietly, naturally; and it is always giving: in the spring, frail white blossoms like orchard snows for poet or painter; in the summer, cool sheltering shade for the wayfarer; in the fall, luscious mellow fruits. It is a strong tree. When a storm comes, it may bend and shudder and groan—but its roots are firm and it does not fall. And always it is growing!

So at every church service there are Christmas tree people, and apple tree people. The Christmas tree crowd are all a-flutter over the externals, the color, the lights, the music, the incense—God help us even the sermon. Like the Christmas Tree, they expect some favor to be laid at their feet. Like the Christmas Tree, they are not strong; the first push of temptation and down they go. They are not true; as soon as the Novena service is out, their piety fades and falls away like the needles, and they are in the world and of the world and ready for the ways of the world.

The apple tree people are different. They don't bother too much with the externals of the Novena. It doesn't particularly matter to them which priest gives the sermon, because they are not devoted to any particular "Father" but to the Mother of God. When temptation stirs them, they may for a moment waver, but their resolution grips the ground like deep roots, and they don't go down. And above all, they go on bearing virtuous fruit—more frequent confessions, more fervent Communions, more numerous visits to Our Blessed Lord and also, more constant and more intelligent assistance at the Holy Sacrifice of the Mass.

Anyway, what better time than the beginning of the year to take an inventory of our church-going? Especially when we lift our eyes to that other tree, the gaunt tree of the cross, holding its dark, stark branches against the somber Good Friday sky, and dripping slow splashes of Blood like sad red petals from the last rose of summer. Shorn of the foliage of all smaller matters, the cross stands there as simple and straight as a sign-post. And it says: "Seek ye first the Kingdom of Heaven, and all these things shall be added unto you!"

Sprinkles of Holy Water

STRANGE GODS BEFORE ME

One night thirteen men sat down to supper. The next day two of them, Jesus and Judas, were dead. This was the origin of the absurd superstition about number thirteen. Because of a mere coincidence, that poor number has limped through history like a leper, ringing its outcast bell and hoarsely warning everyone to keep away. You may have read of the hotel in the Mid-West where if you discover to your consternation that there are thirteen people in your dinner party, the management will graciously provide you with a dummy figure attired in faultless evening dress. Naturally his name is Louis the Fourteenth. I suppose that if some item on your bill should amount to thirteen dollars, the hotel would be willing even to change it to a felicitous fourteen.

A couple of years ago I was a minor casualty in a major Catholic Hospital, and during that delightful period of convalescence when I was once more vertical and could prowl the corridors, I noticed there was not one sick room marked thirteen. On one floor they ran 210, 211, 212, 214. On the next, 311, 312, 314, and so on. Here, you must admit, is another very wise reason for forbidding children to visit a hospital. The school teaches them to count 211, 212, 213, 214. But in hospital-mathematics, thirteen suddenly submerges like a submarine. The child might wonder whether in the hospital, arithmetic itself were not a little sick.

Of course the nuns in charge shake discouraged bonnets and protest, "It is not our fault. It is the patients. The pressure comes from them." Apparently when a patient is being wheeled into a room, one thing he dislikes is looking up and seeing a number-plate on the door blink down on him with the ominous, sinister, never-to-be-mentioned thirteen. For the same reason (if you can call it reason) there are tall buildings, twenty stories high, that still do not have a thirteenth floor. And it has finally dawned on me why on the popular overnight boats that used to ply between Boston and New York, I never had any difficulty getting a room, no matter how late I applied. I used to get number thirteen, used to ask for it. It was quiet, comfortable, cheap, and always available!

Thirteen! But the Thirteen Colonies did rather nicely don't you think?

However thirteen is only the grand marshal in this parade of fantastic freaks called superstition. "Never walk under a ladder!"; well, not if there is danger of a bucket of white lead plopping on your head. "Break a mirror and you will have seven years hard luck!" Break a mirror and you break your back picking up the pieces, that's all. "Don't let a black cat cross your path!" No and if one should, just whirl around and hurry right home! "Carry a rabbit's foot for good luck." But it wasn't such good luck for the rabbit who once owned four of them, was it? "Don't light three on a match!" I wonder what brilliant young match company executive dreamed up that gimmick to step up sales?

Of course we, in our superior fashion, smile at these silly practices. Or do we? Perhaps if they bob up on the sea of conversation, we take pot-shots at them as mockingly as anyone else. They are perfectly ridiculous, they are echoes from the jungle, they are shadows from the dark ages, they are as phony as witch-doctors and as pathetic as a charm bracelet rattling with human teeth.

So in conversation, in theory, we scorn them. But how about when it comes to acting ourselves? I remember I could always get room thirteen on the boat. I remember the hard-boiled hospital superintendent who said with a kind of twisted smile, "People are funny, Father. But they never will admit it." Is that the way it is? We pooh-pooh all superstition in public, but when it comes to our own private life, we secretly shelter a lurking fear that there may be something in it. After all we might as well play safe, there's nothing to lose and you never can tell. In other words, (plain words) when we are alone and superstition shakes its Halloween mask, we play the coward.

In such an offence, it is true that Conscience in its roll of District Attorney would not attempt to indict you for serious sin. But it is just as true that you are dethroning your God-given mature common sense and for the moment placing on the dunce-stool of your mind a childish folly unworthy of a thinking man. And sin is not completely out of the picture, either. As a matter of fact superstition is wrong, precisely because it pushes God out of the picture and presumes to take His place. For doesn't its frightening voice whisper that this four-leaf green clover, this scared and scurrying black cat, this amputated white rabbit's foot, this shattered mirror, will actually influence your future? By some mysterious power within it, it will brighten or darken events to come, for good or for ill. But the only Hand that throws the switch of the future is God. Only the one All-knowing and Almighty God; nobody or nothing else. Because if anything else could, it would be independent of God, above God, greater than God. It would be God. We talk so freely and so glibly of our luck, of good luck and of bad luck. There is no luck. Whatever happens, happens only because God wants it to happen or because God (having given free will) at least permits it to happen. And no insignificant creature can trip the straight and lordly strides of the Creator.

So the sin of superstition is that it gives to some ridiculous object the power that belongs only to God. "I am the Lord Thy God. Thou shalt not have strange gods before Me!"

In olden times the Jews bowed down before a golden calf. Nowadays millions of Americans press their foreheads to the dust before a similar idol: astrology, fortune telling, and the like. And if you do not think this is a golden idol, just reflect that the annual take is over one hundred million dollars! So much does the great and gullible American public, whose godfather was Barnum, hand over each year to the multitude of mysterious prophets for profit, who learnedly read palms, cards, stars, crystal-balls, tea leaves, almost anything, *for* anything from a half-dollar up. To these practitioners it is an "abstruse science"; to the ordinary envious by-stander this is too modest; it also must be a fine art to separate so much money from so many people. And it seems to be growing. Along with the comics and cross-word puzzle and the obituaries and the stock-market, many papers are running a regular column for those who pin their hopes on horoscopes.

Tell your fortune! It seems just as logical to predict a man's future from the egg-stains on his vest as from the tea leaves in his cup. In both cases part of him goes to the cleaners anyway. And haven't you often wondered why these people who have a private knothole into the future do not use their top-secret and advance information to invest in a few good stocks on the market, or a few good steeds on the track, and so *accumulate* a fortune instead of merely telling one?

It should be comforting to know that acts of superstition are practically always saved from being grave sins by the unflattering fact that we do not think. We do not realize what we are doing. This is handy because some superstitions have their roots even in religion. Like that one of thirteen at the table, or Friday the thirteenth, or knocking wood. In medieval Europe the peasant on his way to the fields might bow his head in prayer before some wayside cross. Then he would reverently touch the carved wooden figure and make the sign of the cross on himself. But suppose that day while in the fields some sudden danger threatened him, maybe a wild animal, maybe a crackling lightening storm. He was far from his roadside crucifix so he reached out and touched the nearest object of wood, crossed himself, and said his prayer again. Now, centuries later and without knowing why, his descendants are solemnly knocking on wood to fend off disaster. They might just as well scratch their heads; in fact it might amount to the same thing.

Then there is the chain prayer. Not long ago I found one in the last pew of our church, a greasy typewritten page containing some sort of prayer and the dire warning that you must say this prayer eleven times for eleven days before eleven a.m., otherwise eleven terrible misfortunes would befall you, topple on your helpless head, I suppose, like eleven coconuts out of a tree. Give a moron a typewriter and he will compose a chain prayer. People who circulate chain prayers almost deserve to be sentenced to chain gangs. By deliberately breaking a chain prayer and becoming a missing link, you prove that you are not a duplicating monkey but an independent man.

Then St. Alphonsus tells us of bandits he encountered who would light their votive lamps at a Shrine of Our Lady and pray devoutly that she would send rich travellers into their hands. We would never do that. But some of us can be as inconsistent. There are nominal Catholics who devoutly wear Our Lady's scapular medal over a heart scabby with sins, brazenly pretending that as long as they hold on to the medal, they can also hold on to the sins, and some how Our Lady will sneak them in through the service entrance of Heaven. Aren't they afraid they may end up in the incinerator?

And what about those Catholics who put the Sacramentals above the Sacraments, who would never dream of going without a smudge of ashes on Ash Wednesday, or a sprig of Palm on Palm Sunday, or a blessing of the throat on St. Blaise's Day, or a St. Christopher Medal in their car, and at the same time go on missing Mass, missing Easter Duty—*this is religion?* This is a superstition clumsily wearing the mask of religion!

Religion is like a mountain whose head is crowned with snow but whose heart burns with volcanic fires. There must be cold sense in a man's head before there can be true ardor and fervor in his heart. Superstition is unworthy of man and insulting to God. Serve God because He is great. Serve Him joyfully because He is good. Serve Him only because He alone is God!

Sprinkles of Holy Water

A SEALED SECRET

It is a happy thought that all along the religious front, at least here in the United States, bigotry is on the way out. The frayed banners of hate, dragged along by men who hated merely because their fathers hated, are fast disappearing over the hill. But while the wars of prejudice were on, the Catholic Church probably made the best target of all because its teachings never were vague and drifting like clouds, but always straight and pointed like cathedral spires. Everybody knew just where She stood and just what She stood for. This is a great advantage now when the new generations carry not torches to destroy but flashlights to examine. Bigotry is dying for want of darkness, because it cannot live in the light. As a result you seldom hear those old stock charges that used to show up again and again, like horses on a merry-go-round, flashing their big harmless teeth, galloping up and down to the canned music of the same old slanders, and like the carousel cavalry all the time getting nowhere.

For example, in intelligent circles you never hear it whispered nowadays that Catholics adore statues of the Virgin Mary, because nowadays people know we do not adore a statue of Our Blessed Lady any more than we adore the Statue of Liberty.

We honor both because they stand for something beyond the statue. Again, these days you never hear people murmuring what a pity it is that nuns (I mean the contemplative nuns) should have to stay inside those big somber walls, because nowadays people know that the door of a convent, like the door of any other home, opens easily from the inside, and the walls are there not to keep the nuns in but to keep the world out.

And so on through the wax museum of stock charges against the Church, the ancient errors and the moldy myths. They gather no customers but only dust, because knowledge is on the march out in the open air and people can find out for themselves the living truth. But did it ever strike you that in the cathedral of the church there is one stained-glass window at which, so far as I am aware, no stone was ever flung? This is all the more surprising because it concerns a religious practice which is peculiarly Catholic and particularly mysterious. I mean Confession, and specifically what we call the Seal of Confession. Because even the people who attacked the Church, sometimes splitting hairs and sometimes splitting heads (and this happened on both sides) still even the enemies of the Church tacitly admit that whatever sins are whispered in the sacred silence of the confessional fall like gravel into a grave, and never again see the light of day.

This obligation to silence on the part of the priest is called the Seal of Confession. But if the Church be a purely human establishment, a mere world-wide organization like some international oil company, doesn't it almost touch the miraculous that with all the millions of confessions heard, these secrets are always sacred, the seal of the confession always inviolable, the sins as safe as though they were confided to the dead? You can trace back the river of the Church's history, back even to where its first springs bubbled up at the rock of Peter, and though you will find some stretches where the stream was muddy, you will never find any period where the people ever lost confidence in their priest or feared a leakage from the confessional! Does not the answer seem to be that the same Divine Lord Who gave the power to forgive sins to His Apostles (and through His Apostles to their successors, the priests, because He founded His Church not for just the lifetime of the Apostles but for all time) that Divine Lord Who fits the burden to the back, gives His priests not only the power to forgive the sin but also the grace to keep the secret?

Of course to be frank (and what's the good of being anything else?) in the vast majority of cases there is no need of any special grace to keep the penitent's secret, because in the average church the priest does not know who the penitent is. The confessional is as dark as a closet; there is a screen between the priest and the penitent; the priest's head is averted;

so as a rule the penitent is only a voice whispering out of the blackness. The priest will not remember this confession any more than you would expect a letter-carrier to recall an individual letter out of the thousands he delivers, or a telephone operator to remember a call she has put through. The case of conscience before him now gets all the confessor's attention and help; then it is lost in the pile and forgotten.

But suppose the priest does recognize the penitent, as in the case of a penitent who chooses this priest as his regular confessor, or the case, say, of a G.I. who kneels beside a chaplain seated upon a soapbox in a field somewhere in Korea.... It may interest you to know with what a wall of steel the Church protects the confession in any circumstances. In the first place of course the priest is not allowed to reveal to anybody any sin that you have mentioned in confession. It doesn't matter whether the sin is terrible or whether it is tiny, or whether it is only a temptation. It doesn't matter whether you are still alive or whether you are fifty years dead. Not the smallest detail, not the slightest hint about anything you have confessed, even though refusing to do so were to cost him his life. In the second place once the confession is over he is not allowed to refer to what you have confessed, even with you privately, unless you request his advice and give him permission to discuss it. Thirdly, no matter what sins you confess, no matter what you tell him, the priest may not change his attitude toward you—not in the faintest degree. In other words he may not use any knowledge acquired in the confessional, because what he knows only from confession he does not know at all.

Let us imagine, for example—and a rather bizarre example it is—that you happen to confess that while you were taking off your toupee it fell to the floor and you swore in vast anger. The next time the priest sees you he can't say to himself, "So, he has a toupee, has he? Now imagine that! I wonder just where it begins", and start to stare at you curiously. Or suppose the grocer comes to confession and tells the priest, among other things, that every month he pads the Rectory bill by an extra ten dollars. May the priest change grocers? Not on your seal of confession! Or suppose the sexton confesses to the pastor that he has been stealing money from the pastor's desk which is always unlocked. May the pastor then fire him? He not only may not fire him, he may not even begin to lock the desk. What he knows only from confession he does not know at all.

Or take this example. A gang of men are plotting to murder the priest by luring him to a dark deserted spot on a fake sick-call. But that afternoon one of them becomes conscience stricken, goes to confession and tells everything to the priest. "And," he says, "'one of the gang just saw me coming in here now. If you don't answer the sick-call tonight, or if you tell the police, they'll know I was here and they will surely kill me as a stool-pigeon." In such a case, if the man there will not let the priest use this information (and he won't) the priest will have to go—even to his death. Because what he knows only from the confessional he does not know at all. So, when the sick-call comes in, to him it is a real, ordinary sick-call.

Just as a priest cannot use his confessional knowledge to protect himself, neither can he use it even to prevent sin or sacrilege in another. Take the case of an engaged couple who have committed a sin against chastity. The young man enters the confessional, tells the sin, says that he and the girl-friend feel very low about the whole thing, have decided to come to confession, clear it all up, and from here on live clean and pure. "So, I'm here now, Father and she's coming in next." But when the girl comes in, she says nothing at all about that sin. Well, can the priest say to her, "E-r, isn't there something perhaps that you forgot?" He can say nothing. Even though she is making a bad confession, he may not break the seal of another confession to prevent it. What he knows only from the confessional, he does not know at all.

More than that. Suppose on Sunday morning the priest hears confessions before his Mass, and this particular morning he has to refuse absolution to a married man because the latter will not promise to give up immoral conduct with, let us say, his secretary. But then at Communion time, when the priest goes to the rail to distribute Communion, there is the man at the rail, kneeling calmly alongside his wife! Even though the priest knows that this man is in the state of mortal sin, unrepentant and unabsolved, he cannot pass him by. He must cooperate in a sacrilege. He has to give this man Holy Communion even though it means placing the Body of Christ in the stable of a filthy soul. What he knows only from confession, he does not know at all.

Now it is obvious from all this that in certain circumstances this unbreakable silence, this seal of confession, could work very much to the harm of the priest. It is evident that he could be framed as the culprit of some crime and then silenced as to telling what actually happened. You say well, if a man goes to confession just to seal the priest's lips, that is not a real confession, and the priest would not be bound by the seal of confession. Absolutely true. But how is the priest to know the man's purpose? And he may not guess. He must know. If the priest doubts that the penitent is sincere, or if he will not do what the priest counsels, then the priest may refuse him absolution. But as long as the man tells his sins apparently for the purpose of getting absolution, it is enough to silence the priest.

For example, in 1889 a French priest named Father Dumoulin was sent to a penal colony for life after a conviction for murder. Only when the real criminal was dying did the latter call the police and show them the loot and reveal how he had planted the evidence in the Rectory, and had made the whole crime point to the priest. He told how he had then gone to confession to Father Dumoulin, gave the impression he was heartbroken, promised to make amends ... and disappeared. He had not only sealed the priest's lips; he had sealed up the priest's life on a convict island.

In 1927 a Mexican priest named Father Correa was cold-bloodedly killed by a bullet from an army officer's revolver because he would not reveal the confessions of some Mexican soldiers when the officer wanted the information as evidence. The patron of confessors, St. John Nepomucene, according to tradition was summoned one day by Wenceslaus, the suspicious and brutish King of Bohemia, and ordered to disclose the confession of the Queen. Naturally he refused. The King threatened "It's either her confession or your life." That night they trussed up Father John Nepomucene hand and foot, and tossed him from the bridge at Prague into the dark waters of the Moldau. Confessor and confession both went down, but the secret of the seal of confession was safe under the black sliding waters. And that is what every Catholic knows: that when he goes to confession he is like a man standing at the stern of a ship at midnight and dropping his sins like stones into a deep, dark, silent ocean . . . sins that will henceforth be forever hidden from the gaze of men, forever buried in the mercy of God.

Sprinkles of Holy Water

A FUNERAL IS A SAD SIGHT

It must have been a grim and tragic day even in Nazareth when Death first stopped his black chariot outside that humble cottage and silently stole one of the Family away. That was the day when Mary's tear-dimmed eyes blinked and twitched and then stared at the corpse of Joseph as he lay there in the marble dignity of death. Only sometimes I wonder if in the mercy of God those cold carved lips for just one fleeting moment did not seem to soften into a smile, as if to whisper, "Do not weep too much for me. I have only gone a little ahead over that shadowy bridge to the Eternal Shore. It is just a brief parting, a temporary separation, and then a reunion forever!"

You see bereavement happened even to the Holy Family. And it happens to every family that one day the somber hand of death hangs upon our door that sinister crepe bouquet that silently announces that for a few days Death is a boarder in this house. It isn't a pleasant thought. Like making a will or buying a plot in the cemetery, everybody shrinks from it. And a preacher who wanted just to be popular would be well-advised to walk on the other side of the street from the drawn shades of the wake house.

Choose a cheery topic. Talk about the holly wreath in a Christmas window and Happiness, Joy! And still, I believe that ordinary people are realistic and want this problem of bereavement met and solved rather than by-passed or side-stepped. So, if Death comes as the Unbidden Guest into our family circle, what should be our attitude?

In the first place nobody, least of all Our Blessed Lord, expects you to meet death in your midst with the granite composure of the Great Stone Face. Is not the parchment of the Bible itself damp not only with the Blood of the Savior but also with His Tears? Do not those Gospels contain the very human note that when He heard of the death of Lazarus, His Friend, "Jesus wept"? It is only the iron-browed barbarian, the machine-age pagan, the super-man without humanity who holds that grief or pity or sympathy is watery weakness. The truth, the Gospel truth, is that a man can be a valiant Christian hero and still let the tears drip from a broken heart.

But, as in so many other departments of life, it is the excess which is wrong. The river flowing between its banks is good; but the river rising to a flood and bursting out of bounds is bad. Or to be practical (and what's the use of being anything else?) these carryings-on you sometimes see around a casket or an open grave, this wailing and screaming and hysterical wringing of hands—are these a suitable final tribute to the deceased? Isn't it more like shaking our fist in the Face of the Almighty? It doesn't show more love for the departed dear one but less trust in the Providence of God.

It isn't sorrow for the dead who are gone, so much as it is sorrow for ourselves who are here. And especially when the period of mourning stretches on month after month like an endless gloomy tunnel, when the soul won't come out into sunlight but sulks and broods in a secret rebellion against God—doesn't this kind of sorrow come pretty close to being a big empty square of selfishness framed with a little thin black border of bereavement? The simple, blunt truth is that such a person feels not grief for the loved one but pity for himself . . . or herself.

About this rebellion against God. Will you tell me why it is that if a hearse rolls up to their door some people feel that their religion has double-crossed them? This, they think, should never have happened. They feel as though all the prayers they had said were like dollars deposited in a bank, and now suddenly the bank goes broke. They look upon themselves as the victim of a spiritual swindle. But why? Why? Is there anything in the Catholic Faith, or for that matter in my Christian Faith, which guarantees, no, which even hints that if we serve God well, our life will be a snug, serene harbor sheltered from all the storms that blow? God never made such a promise. The Apostles never preached it. The Catechism never taught it. The terms have always been (and a creature has to take the Creator on *His* terms): to know, love, and serve God in this world and be happy with Him *in the next*. Every man's life is like the chalice that the priest offers up at the altar, and which we should silently offer in the pews. In that chalice glows the red wine of joy, but into it too at every Mass are poured a few trickling teardrops of water, because the life we offer to God in harmony with His will is bound to be a mingling of happiness and sorrow.

Still, if that sorrow comes from the loss of a dear one, be consoled, and lift up your heart, because over every Christian grave the silver trumpets of courage should sing! Why? Because this bereavement is not an absolute, final loss. If Death were the blunt end of a Dead-End Street; if Death were the tiny black period at the end of the sentence of life, with no new page to follow, then every grave would be no more than a king-sized ash-tray, and every headstone a monument to futile despair. But Death is not just an end. It is also a beginning. Death is not a wall. Death is a door. For this we have the word of Truth itself, Almighty God, set down in His Sacred Scriptures and proved by His stupendous miracles. For this we have the earthquaking example of His Own Son, Who rose from the Dead not only as a proof of His Divinity but as a pledge of our immortality.

That is why the empty chair of a child can whisper to a broken-hearted parent of a new throne occupied in Heaven, and of a representative of that family in the shining court of Christ the King! At the first stunning impact of loss it will not be easy to think like this, and anybody can understand and make allowances for the sudden overwhelming grief that lays us low. But, if we don't want to stay down, the only answer is to look up! Earth has no sorrow that Heaven cannot heal. When Christ was literally sweating Blood in Gethsemane, and turned to His Heavenly Father for help, suddenly there was an Angel to comfort Him. The same God, our Father too, never sends us into a Garden of Agony but He also sends an Angel to bring us courage and comfort!

Sometimes our very grief is like an Angel that takes our hand and leads us back to God. How many times it has happened that a man all his life has just gone through the motions of religion, till some heavy sorrow really presses him to his knees and opens his lips in the first prayer that ever burst up from the very bottom of his heart! Isn't it because we never really come close to Christ till we come close to the Cross, to suffering? Nicodemus never had the courage to serve Christ in the open till He saw Him nailed to the cross. Thomas the Apostle recognized the risen Christ by the wounds of the cross in His Hands and Feet and Side. Sometimes it takes a cross of lilies or roses, propped up near a casket, to remind us that we have really forgotten Him and have been living as though He were only the answer to a question in a childhood catechism.

I have heard that over the spot where someone lies buried, the grass grows greener and the flowers brighter. About that I do not know. But I do know that over the grave of a loved one, if accepted with Christian resignation, the spiritual harvest waves tallest and richest, so that (and I dare to say it) even bereavement may be a blessing. How many cases there have been, and every veteran priest has seen them, where a dead mother or father, or sister or brother, or husband or wife, has done almost more good for the bereaved than they had done when alive. Not only by their prayers, though it is their precious prayers which Heaven honors as currency for the purchase of special graces and helps for us. But the phantom fingertips of the departed reach out to us even in more vivid fashion. How often when we are tempted to do wrong their memory rises up as a reproach; when we are dispirited, as an inspiration! And this, mind you, for some strange reason more forcefully than when they walked beside us in the noonday of their life.

In a way it is something like those tiny guideposts along the highway. Drive along the road in bright daylight and you scarcely notice these narrow sticks with their little built-in reflectors. They just look like a row of ordinary sticks, not strong enough for a fence, and although they outline the road you can see that anyway. So you don't pay them much attention, and you rather take them for granted. But when the dark comes down, and the road is black, and the headlights throw their beams ahead, immediately these sticks leap to life, stand out as clear, illuminated guides, glittering reflectors, showing the way and helping us to stay on the road! And so it is not till the dark night of death comes down and we turn the loving light of memory on our own that we appreciate their worth. In the darkness of death they show up best and influence us most. In this connection isn't it ironically true that the promises that are best kept are the promises that have been made to the dead?

Because they are not really dead. There is no death. When the body composes itself in the sleep of the middle aisle, and the six candles stand about it, their golden flames flickering like little hands waving good-bye, the black-chasubled priest at the altar is singing the Preface whose message soars up like an eagle spiralling toward the sun: "Eternal God we thank Thee... that the undoubted sadness of this present death finds consolation in the promise of a future life... because for Thy faithful, life is not taken away, but only changed... so that when the house of this bodily existence is destroyed, an eternal dwelling is prepared beyond the stars..."

"I am the Resurrection and the Life! He that believeth in Me shall live!" In His care, Who died on the cross to prove His Love and burst forth from the tomb to prove His Power, we leave the dead who have died in the Lord. Will you then, you who have perhaps recently lost a loved one, and who still miss him and mourn him, and maybe are inclined to be bitter, will you go on staying unhappy and begrudging him to God? When you weigh all things, would you really call him back, if you could? And if you did, wouldn't it be simple selfishness? Imagine the Angel of Death (so often the Angel of Deliverance) with snowy robe and silver wings standing by your dear one's coffin and whispering to him your thoughts: "She wants you back. Back from the glory of Heaven to the grime of earth, back from salvation to struggle, back from an examination that has been passed to the chance of failure, back from happiness forever to a brief, soiled sordid world—"Oh, think" (whispers the Angel) "think what this poor earth is, compared to the great shining world to which his soul has winged its flight, and would you, if you really love him, would you utter the wish that would bring him back?"

No—we answer—knowing that even if his body is planted in the furrow of the grave like a seed, he will one day bloom to new beauty; and if his casket sinks beneath the rim of the grave like a setting sun, he will rise to a new and brighter day; and if he now lies asleep in death, he will wake to the splendor of the Resurrection! Ah, it is sad only for us. But for him, after the aching toil, at last the welcome rest; after the bleeding fight the blessed, eternal peace; after this passing world, an imperishable Heaven with Jesus and Mary!

Sprinkles of Holy Water

BREATHLESS INTO HEAVEN

Today let us consider the case of Mike Machine Gun, gambler, gangster and Catholic. The name of course is pure fiction, but the circumstances are solid fact. And it happens often enough in every American city to make most Catholics want to cross to the other side of the street in order to avoid being hooked and thrown by the question marks of their non-Catholic friends.

Strangely enough the major trouble begins when Mike Machine Gun comes to his end. Not that he didn't cause trouble enough in his day—and his night. Behind him lies a rolling road of drunken parties, a twisted trail of broken hearts and empty bottles, the sad wreckage of other men's homes and business and lives. But comes the day when Mike Machine Gun suddenly crumples over the wheel of his cream-colored convertible, mowed down by the bullets of a rival mob. However, thanks to a natty steel vest he has been thoughtfully wearing, he is not killed outright. But Mike is dying. He knows he is dying. And Mike remembers he is a Catholic. Maybe the last time he was inside a Catholic Church he was in the Seventh Grade, but he feels he is a Catholic. He always said he was a Catholic. He had always planned that he would die as a Catholic; though, to tell the truth, he had not planned on doing it so soon. Anyway, in his agony he groans for a priest. So in the white hospital room, as the black-clad priest with the purple stole round his neck bends over the bed, Mike Machine Gun hoarsely whispers his confession, his brutal story of shattered commandments and stained lives—the autobiography of a minor Beelzebub. Then the priest solemnly pronounces the absolution. With cool, moist thumb he anoints the eyes and ears and lips; administers the last rites. And Mike Machine Gun, in the middle of a panting, half-remembered prayer, goes into a shuddering convulsion, and then lies very still.

That evening the newspapers flare it—and the newscasts blare it—the story of this man about town who has suddenly left town for good. Mike Machine Gun, gambler and gangster, died at Mercy Hospital early this afternoon. He received the last rites of the Catholic Church. He will be buried with a Requiem Mass from St. Mary's Church on Tuesday at ten.

People read this, and their eyebrows go up like trunk-lids. Heads shake, tongues cluck, and there are deep sighs of scandal. Not only non-Catholics, mind you; Catholics too. Why, the whole affair cheapens religion!—implying that a case like this hurts the Church's social prestige, or pulls down its batting average. It reduces all standards to elastic;—meaning, if you have enough pull, the rules will stretch. It turns the hard, persevering virtue of earnest Christians into a farce. Because if this swaggering rake can lead a life like that, bowling down the ten commandments like ten-pins; walking arm in arm with the very devil all his days, till Death like a conductor shouts, "All aboard!" and then just hops on the train for Heaven as it is actually rolling out of the station—then what is the sense and where is the percentage in trying and striving to be good all your life? Why not choose what you fancy from every bright counter of sin, and then just when the bill is about to come in, when the end is near—humbly and shyly declare bankruptcy, that is, go to confession; and presto, everything is cleared away and straightened out and the slate is absolutely empty. You've had your fun; and now, after all this, Heaven too! If Mike Machine Gun can get away with it, why can't other people?

That is just what I'd like you to remember. Other people do. I don't say they actually "get away with it." I don't admit that Mike Machine Gun "gets away with it." But at least notice that the case of Mike Machine Gun is no unique, towering exception in the pattern or the policy of the Church. The only thing exceptional about his case is the publicity. Why, in every hospital in the land, in almost every week of the year, the very same procedure is being followed with sinners whose names don't happen to be up in neon lights. Other men and other women, who have eaten every forbidden fruit in the devil's orchard, who have never said "no" to an impulse for forty years, who have lived and laughed and sinned under the bright lights of pleasure ... but now when the darkness of death suddenly falls around them, and the noiseless gate of eternity slowly swings open before them, and fear clutches at their heart, they turn to God too. Maybe it is just terror of the unknown ahead of them, maybe it is really disillusionment and dissatisfaction with the past behind them, maybe it is a sudden awakening and sorrow for sin. Anyway they send for a priest, and he comes. He hurries to the death-bed of life-long sinners every day of the week, but they are obscure people, so nobody pays any attention because nobody cares. But because Mike Machine Gun has lived his life under the television lights of prominence and notoriety, when *he* dies this way everybody notices and everybody wonders. They know the hero so they ask, "What's the story?" There is no story. The Catholic Church has not done a quick shuffle with her doctrine just to favor a prominent gangster. The only thing different in Mike Machine Gun's case is the size of the electric bulb. He just happened to die under a spotlight, that's all ... the white glare of publicity picked him up receiving the Sacraments, but any other Catholic properly disposed would have received the same Sacraments!

Put it another way. Is there any man who dares say when another man may not return to God; or, from this point on, it is too late, and you must stay on the dead-end street of despair? That was the thought of Judas, not of Jesus. With Him, as long as there is life, there is hope. The sinner may be dyed-in-the-wool, but as long as he is not dead, he is a prospect for Paradise. And why should anyone be scandalized that there are great sinners in the church, when if there were not, Christ would stand branded as a liar? Didn't He compare His church to a net containing all kinds of fish, both good and bad; to a field where the wheat and the weeds would grow up side by side? And, by the way, didn't He Himself take the outstretched hand of a dying criminal, and draw him up to Heaven? We call him the Good Thief, but we forget that up until a few minutes before he died, he was a felon and a public enemy, dying the death of a murderer. His life was finished. Like a letter, it was written, folded, inserted in the envelope, about to be sealed. But now when it comes to sending it off, at the last moment he writes as the address not Hell but Heaven. He had sinned; he was sorry; and at his side the Savior whispers, "This very day thou shalt be with me in Paradise!"

Granted that this Good Thief's faith may have been exceptional, and his sorrow extraordinary, does it not still prove that with God all things are possible? If not, then when a headstrong boy leaves home, takes the trail of the prodigal son, hugs to his heart the husks of sin—if in spite of all this, he cannot somehow be saved in the end, then let all you good mothers who pray each night for your straying boy, get up off your knees, and give up your praying! That perhaps shocks you. But aren't you forgetting that Mike Machine Gun's mother may have worn out her knees and cried out her eyes, praying that he would come back to God? Will you deny to her boy what you would want for your own?

So let's not be harsh and judge the death-bed repentance of Mike Machine Gun. But even more, let's not be foolish and imitate it. Suppose he did have a Funeral Mass, and a glittering funeral, with a bronze casket now instead of a steel vest, and celebrities for pall-bearers, and the longest line of limousines winding out to the cemetery. People have left before, are leaving every day with great pomp—for hell. About him specifically, we do not know, and until Judgment Day never shall.

All you can say about any death-bed repentance is that it is possible. A theologian or a philosopher would defend that to the last ditch; but only a fool would want to risk it for himself. Because normally, doesn't a death-bed repentance seem like eating the apple of life and then generously flinging God the core? Flipping at the feet of God a cigarette stub, after the years you should have given Him have gone up in smoke? On his death-bed, is the sinner really abandoning sin, or is the ability to sin abandoning *him?* "I detest all my sins"—oh what a miracle of grace he needs, to detest what all his life he has loved! "I firmly resolve to sin no more"—but if at that moment the nurse came in with ten more years of life on a tray, would he go back to sin for another nine and 99/100 years? God knows and God judges.

And suppose the man grown grey in sin does have true sorrow in the end. But suppose too that in that same hospital, at that moment, in the very room next to him, there dies a holy nun, grown old in the service of God, a life of sacrifice and service behind her—do you think that both souls will go streaking off together to the same joys of Heaven? I'm afraid that Mike Machine Gun's train would have a rather long stop-over on a very uncomfortable side-track called Purgatory.

However, let's be charitable, and not judge death-bed conversions. But above all let's be wise and not bank on one. It isn't easy when you are old and your muscles are stiff to do a somersault or a back-flip—especially from sin to virtue. And if we could, how do we know we shall have the chance? The God who always promises forgiveness, never promises even tomorrow to ask for it. And people who figure on coming back to God at the eleventh hour, generally die at half-past ten.

Little Colored Windows

MAN OF NO MISTAKES

Most Americans in this enlightened age are willing to concede that the Pope of Rome is at least a venerable figure dedicated to the service of God (as he sees it) and to the good of mankind (ditto). In fact the present Holy Father, John the Twenty-third, with his genial smile and unpretentious manner, has achieved something of a warm and sunny miracle in the sometime glacier field of public relations.

But if many people like the Pope, many more do not like the Papacy. They mistrust it. They resent it. They don't understand it; sometimes they even fear it as a sinister, mysterious Power that should not be there. And if there is one Papal claim apt to make some good church-going people bristle, and bring their Christian blood to a fervent boil, it is the mere mention of that proud, sweeping, god-like word, infallibility.

I bring up the subject now because on February twenty-second, the day we dedicate to the first head and Father of our Country, we Catholics keep a feast in honor of St. Peter, the first Head and Holy Father of the Church. On the calendar it is called the Feast of St. Peter's Chair. But since even Catholics do not canonize furniture, obviously we have to sandpaper the phrase down and see what lies underneath; get down, as it were, to the grain. Well, the Greek word for chair is our English word cathedral, and it stands for the throne of a bishop as the seat of ecclesiastical authority. Now, on the list of the Apostles you always find one Apostle leading all the rest, namely, Peter. You find it was to Peter personally that Our Lord (the Good Shepherd) said "Feed my lambs; feed my sheep." You find it was to Peter only that the words were addressed, "Thou art Peter (the Rock) and on this Rock I will build my Church." How then can anyone doubt that Jesus Christ made Peter the Prince of the Apostles and the Head of the Church, the Man in Charge? But this Church was not to exist only for the one generation of the Apostles any more than it was for one city like Jerusalem. It was to plant its cross on each succeeding peak of the mountain range of time. It was to bestride continents and oceans till Gabriel took up his trumpet. Therefore it would always need a head, and that head in any century would be the legitimate successor of St. Peter. But St. Peter's official Chair, his cathedral, was finally established by him in Rome, so the Bishop of Rome would always be the successor of St. Peter, and the head of the Church founded by Jesus Christ.

But where, we may legitimately ask, does the infallibility come in? If I admit that John the Twenty-third, having been elected the present Bishop of Rome, has the right to wear the Tiara of the Papacy does that make him something that doesn't exist, an infallible human being? Does it give him the right to emboss on his coat of arms a pencil with no eraser on top? You can see how such a towering claim could induce in some quarters much agitation. After all, even Einstein could make a mistake adding up a bridge score. Even Paderewski probably plunked a few sour notes in his day. Even the world's best doctors have made diagnoses they would like to forget. Even geniuses have been monumentally wrong, even saints have sinned—is not then this infallibility too big a bird to nest in the brain of any mere man? Do we claim it seriously? We not only claim it seriously, we mean it literally.

But please notice this particular brand of infallibility, far from being an arrogant, sweeping, unrestricted domain, is actually a tiny territory, rigorously bounded on four stubborn sides.

Point one. Infallibility certainly does not mean that the Pope cannot commit sin. He can, and being human, presumably does. Like any other man he kneels in confession, receives absolution, and performs the enjoined penance. It is even possible that a Pope could die in mortal sin and be eternally damned. Infallibility has no more to do with sin than it has with synthetics. Many of the Popes have walked the high trail of sainthood, but even those who wore the tiara without any encircling halo have never been charged by hostile historians with teaching false doctrine. Even in the few cases when the Pope's personal moral weathervane whirled wildly, his doctrinal compass never veered one degree from true North.

Point two. The Pope's area of infallibility is comparatively modest. He sticks to religion. He does not make the weird mistake of presuming that prestige in one field gives a man the right to give off with pronouncements all over the place. When some seventh-rate scientist climbs into the pulpit and proclaims what is religious truth and what is the moral law, he often presents the sadly humorous incongruity of a skin-diver shuffling his flippers in an attempted tap-dance. He is pathetically out of his element. Of course such savants never claim they are infallible; but the implication is that if you do not agree with them you are somewhat south of a moron.

Unlike these wandering stars, the Pope stays in the orbit of his specialty: teaching what is true in faith and morals. Or at least his right to infallibility stays there. Leo the Thirteenth was a pioneer, and an expert in the rights of Labor. Pius the Eleventh had been an expert mountain climber and wrote authoritative articles on scaling inaccessible peaks. But either one of these experts could conceivably be caught far off base in discussing the Matterhorn or the matter of strikes. You see, infallibility does not attach to the genius of the individual; it rests, like a stone in a ring, in the office. The power is in the keys, not in the grip of the holder, and the keys of St. Peter open only two locks, faith and morals.

Point three. Don't ever get the idea that even in the narrow field of faith or morals the Pope can launch out in his own and teach something absolutely new. He is no Columbus discovering continents or even islands of religion hitherto unknown. He never can be a Pasteur in a religious laboratory producing new Sacraments or Commandments or Articles of the Creed. When the last Apostle died, the treasure chest of Christian belief was shut like the lid of a trunk. And unlike cigarettes or toothpaste or shaving soap, nothing new can be added. The most the Pope can do is to clarify or interpret what the Scriptures or Tradition has said. That is, he can define the Church's teaching and what logically follows from it, like a man drawing out one by one the tubes of a telescope. It is the same instrument, just extended, and so one doctrine may be drawn from another and you get a clearer view.

Point four. Even when the Pope makes a statement about faith or morals he still can make a mistake. Suppose His Holiness preaches a sermon to a churchful of eager pilgrims. He could, in the full flight of flowery oratory, take off into a beautiful little heresy, that is, some technical theological error.

Or consider his messages to the world, which are so flatteringly front-paged by the press. They are decanted from the mellow wisdom of a learned man, himself advised by learned men, fed from listening posts all over the civilized globe—yet any paragraph could be grandly and majestically wrong.

So, hemmed in by all these restrictions, does not the infallibility of the Pope shrink almost from an ocean to a well? Is it not a far more modest endowment than most people dream? Actually, it narrows down to this. The Pope is infallible in only one situation: when, having investigated Scripture and Tradition, and invited wise counsel, and invoked the Holy Spirit, then as the successor of St. Peter and as the Head of the Church he speaks officially and formally to the whole Church on some matter of faith or morals, then he speaks, as the phrase has it, *ex cathedra;* that is, from the chair or throne, in the cathedral. At this particular time only does the good Lord guarantee to guard him against all error, and guide him in the truth. And how often do you suppose this happens? Not every morning or evening or even every Sunday edition. With the exception of the canonization of saints, most Popes never make an infallible pronouncement in their whole reign. With others it might happen once, once in a lifetime. Rarely more.

Now why do Catholics, who otherwise appear to be fairly normal people, acquiesce to this weird teaching that makes another man, prey and heir to human ills and weaknesses like themselves, infallible? Why do honest people outside the Church dismiss the very idea with withering scorn, and brand it "intellectual slavery." Well, the way we Catholics look at it is, that we are only the intellectual slaves of God, because the Pope is only the instrument of God, the hook on which the Lord hangs His lantern.

Others proudly maintain that they do not want pat answers, ready-to-take-home solutions of religion. They prefer to be adventuring pioneers of the spirit, pressing their faces ever toward the unknown. This makes us wonder do they really want truth or do they just want freedom? They want most of all to decide *personally* what the Word of God, the Bible, means. But isn't this like saying, down with one Pope and up with a hundred million popes, as many popes as there are people, each free to hold what he fancies; to cast his vote for two Sacraments or for six; to let his judicial gavel drop with a decisive bang in favor of divorce but against confession; to run down the Christian menu and order a la carte to his individual taste? True, every man must follow his own conscience, but just look at what this freewheeling theology, this walking down the uncertain road of mere human wisdom, has produced—the sad scene of two hundred different varieties of "authentic" Christianity in the U. S. alone! Could any Catholic seriously believe Our Blessed Lord came upon earth to establish *this*?

There are Christian Churches where a preacher can look down from his pulpit and suspect that no two listeners under that roof hold the same entire Creed. After all, the Scriptures are not so easy to understand as ABC's, and if everybody gets into the act (or into the Acts) the streets of the City of God must go wild with spiritual anarchy. Christ founded one Church—not churches—and for unity there has to be authority. There has to be an external guide to save people from inner delusion.

If a Divine Lord founded a Church, it cannot be a democratic institution because you just don't get democratic with the Divinity. He did not found a debating society. We obey or we take the consequences. We believe that Christ is Divine, that He established a Church, that the Pope is His living representative, the lawful successor of that Peter to whom Our Blessed Savior solemnly said, "Thou art Peter—the Rock—and on this Rock I will build my Church, and the gates of Hell shall not prevail against it." But if that Head of the Church, Peter, or any succeeding Head, (because the Church was to last till the end of time) if any Pope could lead the Church into error, into false doctrine, then the gates of Hell would prevail, and our Lord—if I dare say it—would be unmasked as a liar!

"Behold I am with you all days," Jesus solemnly assured His Church. But if He is with the Church and that Church can still officially teach false doctrines—is not the presence of Christ in it a meaningless mockery? You know that if you launch a ship without a rudder it will go round in circles. Christ knew that if you launch a merely human church, men and women, and leave them to themselves in the sea of faith and morals, without a rudder, without a helmsman, they too will go round in circles. There has to be someone at the wheel and he has to be under the guidance of God! If you believe Christ was God and founded a Church that was to teach the truth in faith and morals and teach it forever, teach it undiluted and undefiled, then infallibility is not an imperious, arrogant claim but a downright necessity! You find the root of it in Sacred Scripture, but you find the reason for it in common sense.

Little Colored Windows

CATHOLICS,

EXCELLENT AND EX

The jewelry ads, if nothing else, remind us that the graduation season is again upon us, and in the next few days across every college campus in America the annual academic procession with its bright hoods and rippling robes will wind along like a stately river. Somehow it takes you back—or it does me anyhow—to a smaller academic procession when the flowing robes were worn by only three Wise Men, and the lamp of learning was a golden Star, and the central Figure was not the President of a University but the President of the Universe. If that traditional phrase, "The Three Wise Men" means anything, it means that Christianity began by attracting the best brains of the hour; and ever since that day, learning has had its place of honor in the Church. "Bell, book, and candle"—thus Shakespeare used to capsulize religion—but always uniting the bell and the candle was the book.

LITTLE COLORED WINDOWS

Sooner or later really learned men find their way to religion. It is the fool that curls his lips and scoffs; the wise man bends his knees and prays. Of all the weird creatures in the side-show tents of this earth, the most laughable and yet the most pitiable, the most inflated and the least informed, the most eager to demand the floor and the most deserving of the door, is the sophomoric student who has read a book, or has heard a couple of lectures, and now feels he can airily relegate religion to the attic. He is just bursting with brand new liberal views! He doesn't know it but these liberal discoveries were discussed and dissected and put in labelled bottles on the shelves of theology back in the days when monks were writing the rebuttal on parchment. Certainly it seems new if some glib Tom, Dick or Harry prints it on slick paper in the twentieth century, if you are not aware that St. Thomas Aquinas was anticipating that point in the thirteenth. A little knowledge may be a dangerous thing, but more often it's just a shame.

By and large, deeply learned men are likely to be deeply religious men. Old Father History will stroke his silken white beard and assure you that through the centuries the torch of true knowledge has illuminated the cross like a holy candle. It is only false science, like Hitler's fantastic theory of a master-race, that has been a fire-brand seeking to char and consume the cross. After all, religion and learning are twin sons of the same God; why should they not march along shoulder to shoulder? Why should not the same names be written twice, side by side—once on Fame's golden scroll, and again on the Church's Baptismal Register—the names of men who were both prominent in their chosen field, and pious in their cherished faith? Astronomers like Copernicus, who was a Cathedral Canon; poets like Dante; explorers like Columbus and Magellan. Mendel, the biologist who blazed the trail in studies of heredity, was the Abbot of a monastery. Stenson, the first name in modern geology, was a Bishop. Lavoisier, the father of modern chemistry, was a devout communicant.

When you glance across the dashboard of your car and read the "amps", you are recalling a Catholic pioneer in electricity, Ampere. When you check the voltage, you are recalling the Catholic scientist, Volta. When you flick on the car's radio, you utilize the invention of another Catholic scientist, Marconi, who incidentally got his inspiration for wireless while pacing the cloister of a Cathedral, and who dedicated his first broadcast to the Mother of God. And the mat under your accelerator might be synthetic rubber invented by Father Nieuwland of Notre Dame.

So, too in music. Written in golden notes are Catholic names like Mozart and Palestrina. In art, the Michelangelos and the Raphaels; the Murillos and Correggios and Da Vincis. In the more practical field of preventive medicine a man as brilliant in the laboratory as he was pious in the church, Pasteur. And Fallopio of the fallopian tubes, Galvani of the galvanized electric current, and so on, and on.

But down the broad aisle of the church you see marching not only the brilliant men of a bygone day, carrying their plumed hats and swishing their gay cloaks, but still they come, modern men of letters and art and science with their fedoras and brief-cases and double-breasted overcoats. You can believe in God, Grace, the Mass and the Sacraments, and still be several degrees above a moron. Or would you call G.K. Chesterton a dumb plodding peasant? Was John L. Stoddard, the world-traveler and lecturer, a narrow-minded know-nothing? Was Ronald Knox who translated the Bible from the Greek a relic of medieval superstition and ignorance? And Sigrid Unset the novelist, and Sir Esme Howard the ambassador, and Eric Gill the sculptor, and John Moody the financial authority, and Joyce Kilmer the poet, and Carlton Hayes the historian, and Jacques Maritain the philosopher—these people read a book, too! In fact among them they wrote shelves of books. And they are, everyone of them, converts to the Catholic Faith! As in the very first church, there was room for the unlettered shepherds who tended their sheep, and for the Wise Men who held the sheepskin of learning, so the true Church will always attract the very simple and the very smart; the simple who sense the Truth, and the wise people who reason to it.

Obviously not all the bright people, the sixteen-cylinder brains, are Catholics. Faith is still a gift, and for some God does not hang up the Wise Man's Star, its beam pointing to the Church like a golden finger, pointing out the Way and the Truth. For others God has held aloft faint glimmerings of the True Church, but they failed to investigate. These men may have minds like great white searchlights in their own particular fields. They may be lighthouses along the dark coast of knowledge. They may know literature, and thrill to the lilting measures of great poetry as it dances through its lines with golden-slippered grace. They may know the stars of the sky the way a man knows the ornamental shells on his lawn. They may know test-tubes and slide-rules, drawing-boards and logarithms. But somehow they never got around to studying—really studying—religion. They have knocked at every door on the Street of Knowledge but God's. They just never got curious. And sometimes they wonder why in their hearts there is an aching, a longing, a hunger that the richest triumph or the gayest party leaves strangely empty!

It may be admitted of course, that other people have been members of the Church, but one day they walked down the aisle, and out into the street, and never looked upon the altar again. But do you suppose that any of these Catholics actually thought their way out of the Church? A few of them may give up the Catholic's "Sign of the Cross" for the agnostic's shrug of the shoulders, but not because any of them had genuine grounds for disbelief. Some of them stopped answering church bells on Sunday morning, not because of the Nicene Creed but simply because it was nicer to stay in bed. Or the fishing was good and the preaching wasn't. Or green fairways called louder than green vestments. Others stopped going because they could not abide all this talk about money; one collection a month was enough. Others found fault with the Church's attitude on Matrimony; one wife a life-time wasn't enough. Some former Catholics are even honest enough to admit that a couple of the Commandments cramped their style, like boxing gloves on a pick-pocket. But whatever it was, you'll find it was not thought or learning or concentrated brainpower that made them walk on the other side of the street from the church.

Then there are grim, honest people, former Catholics too, who have convinced themselves that they hate the Church. This is really a pity, because what they hate is not the Church, but, you might say, the Rectory. You "won't see them inside a church," because somewhere along the line they had a quarrel with a priest. After the passage of years even they themselves are not too clear just what the fight was all about. As a rule, looking back in perspective, the issue was tiny, but the upshot was tremendous. Whoever thought that a whole family might be lost to the Church because Citronella was not chosen for the Second Angel in the Christmas Pageant? Believe me, it can start as insignificantly as that! (No wonder they told us in the Seminary that except where it was a matter of faith or morals, don't try to win an argument; you may end up losing a soul.) And of course in many of these church departments which are only like the fringes of religion, the priest can so easily be wrong, and monumentally wrong! He has had no special training as a choir-master, nor as architect, nor as the miraculous balance wheel between the younger and the older single ladies of the sodality. He isn't a cruise director trained to make everybody happy. He just does his best for God as he sees it, and sometimes his eyesight is terrible.

Now, naturally, these people who think they have been discriminated against, dislike "this domineering priest". That's understandable. (You wouldn't believe it, I know, but there are people who even take a dim view of me.) But why—and here is the whole point—why take it out on the whole Catholic Church, and on God, and on their own soul? To refuse to go to church and listen to the Word of God and receive the Sacraments because you have had a quarrel with a priest is like refusing to receive mail because you have a sniffing disregard for the local postman. For a while

St. Peter and St. Paul didn't get along too well either. But they soon decided that Christ was bigger than either of them. But no matter how you figure it out, it isn't brains that keep people out of church so much as it is a brainstorm.

But, thank God, under the soft white bandage of Time, the open wound closes quietly into a scar. So please, God, for those who have gone away—oh heal their hurts, soften their hearts, open their eyes, take their hand and bring them back to the fireside of the old Faith, where once again they may know the light of Thy Truth and the warmth of Thy Love and feel the snug comfort of being home!

Little Colored Windows

KEEP THE DOOR OPEN

If a man has huge feet and wears a pair of shoes that look like landing barges, it is a phenomenal salesman who will interest him in a pair of shoes, size six and a half A, though they be the finest footwear in the world. Sermons, in one sense, are like shoes. I mean the sermon that fits one group of people neatly and nicely is of absolutely no concern to another group. Why for instance should the girls who are praying fiercely, "Dear St. Anne, get me a man—as quick as you can!" want to be bothered with a thundered warning on the evils of divorce? And why should "the perils of drunkenness" draw anything but a drowsy yawn from the teetotalers who, when they say tea, mean tea. This is what a preacher is up against when it comes to choosing a subject, and he desperately knows it. Sometimes you figure that the Devil would be the only perfect audience because you could presume he was involved in everything. But then you remember (for one exception) the Devil isn't married... though there are some wives who are sure he is.

The answer is probably the elementary distinction between experience and knowledge. There are many themes which may not here and now concern us personally, but about which we should be intelligently informed—know the sound principles of the matter—so that if the situation ever does ring our own personal door-bell, or even if it shyly seeks our advice, we shall know the position to take or the course to counsel.

Anyway today's little talk is about a certain type of letter which is coming in more and more frequently. The words are always heart-broken, the pages often tear-stained, the writer is usually a Catholic mother and the subject a straying daughter. Sometimes the paragraphs are typed and sometimes scribbled, but the mother is generally weeping over her child's bad marriage. "Here I thought I was doing everything I could, to rear her a good Catholic, and now she has run off and married outside the church. For twenty years I tried to do my best, but I guess my best just wasn't enough."

Thousands of mothers have groaned that bitter self-reproach, but it is undeserved, for how could anyone in his senses hold such a mother responsible for such a daughter? Way back in the Scriptures, centuries before the coming of Christ, poor, patient Job winced with that same sick futile feeling. It is the bleak disappointment of having been let down in the tenderest areas of the heart, parenthood and religion. Job packed his reaction into one crushed sentence: "No man can lead another unto God."

And it is true. If anyone really wants to run away from God, there are no ropes that will hold him, not even heart-strings. But how often have I seen it, that eventually the straying sinner is quietly caught and gently drawn back in the loop of a Mother's well-fingered rosary. And this often happens, even after the Mother is dead! Out of her very grave her prayers bloom and bear their fruit!

But what about the particular present case where the Catholic daughter sets her pretty mouth into a grim red line and marries outside the Church? We say she "marries" outside the Church. The sad cold fact is that she has gone through a marriage ceremony, but in the eyes of God's Church, and therefore in the eyes of God, she is not married at all. This may strike some people as high-handed ecclesiastical arrogance, but suppose you look at it this way. Matrimony is a Sacrament; and the laws for validly receiving the Sacraments lie with the Church. The same Christ who gave us the Sacraments, also gave us the Church to administer them. And one law for the Sacrament of Matrimony is that a Catholic must be married in the presence of a priest and two witnesses. For that reason a Catholic can no more go to City Hall to be married than he can go to City Hall to be baptized. He can no more be married by a minister than he can be confirmed or anointed by a minister. If these attitudes seem to be bits of stony arrogance, they are but chips off the central Rock, the doctrine that Our Blessed Lord founded only one true Church, and this is her teaching. In geology all the rocks may be equal; in theology we believe there is only one: Peter, the Rock upon which Christ founded His Church.

Notice though that the Church does not go tinkling its bell and flourishing its book into the domain of the State or into the conscience of the non-Catholic. Since marriage besides being a spiritual Sacrament is also a civil contract, certainly the State has the right to make laws for that contract, like licenses, blood-tests and all the rest. And since the Catholic Church does not make marriage laws for non-Catholics, she respects as valid any marriage of non-Catholics properly contracted whether performed by a minister or any lawful official.

The marriage the Church does not recognize as valid is the marriage entered into by a Catholic without the necessary priest and two witnesses. Such a Catholic would not be meeting a serious requirement for the valid reception of a Sacrament, the Sacrament of Matrimony. Need I add that if Catholic parents attend such a marriage of their child, that is, one performed by a public official or a minister, these parents are cooperatng in something which, according to the Church, is gravely sinful. But, you tell me, the ceremony has already been performed. They (let us say the Catholic girl and the non-Catholic man) are living together as man and wife. What should be done about it, what attitude taken? This is what the Catholic parents want to know ... they and their sisters and their brothers and their cousins and their aunts.

Well, if I were in your place I should try to be kinder than kind. I should try to remember that after all the sin was not committed against me but against God, so what right have I to explode like a volcano? True, your heart may be a dark cave of disappointment, but if you come running out of it waving a club you may drive your daughter away from God forever.

Nobody can approve what is wrong; but a brutal, blistering condemnation of wrong isn't always the best invitation to return to right. Use the blow-torch on a human soul, and instead of burning off the stain, you may just harden it, fix it in deeper.

So to the parents of such a daughter manacled to a bad marriage I would say: "Pity her, pray for her, be kind to her, visit her." Yes, visit her! It is true you cannot approve her situation, but if you act gently and sympathetically (not like someone proudly determined to win an argument, but rather like someone humbly hoping to save a soul) you may be able to persuade her to have the marriage rectified. You would be surprised how often this can be done—and done with no conspicuous church ceremony—as long as neither the girl nor the man is entangled in any previous marriage.

The curling whip of angry words will lash a person, but when you draw it back, the whip returns to you empty and the person is still away. Kindness is the only thin string you have to bring someone back. Violence breaks all ties, even family ties. Don't try to nag her back into the Church or drag her back into the Church. Just build the path by little acts of kindness and more kindness, and prayers and more prayers, and then perhaps at the right mellow moment a simple word of loving suggestion from your heart may work wonders!

After all I cannnot believe that a Catholic girl married outside the Catholic Church walks down any rose-paths of happiness while she is out of the Church. I hold that no matter how luxuriously she seems to live on the outside she is having a hard time on the inside, and if she doesn' come back, it isn't because she is happy in her exile, but only stubborn. One corner of her heart must always be in secret agony. She may of course even scream that she is perfectly contented, but when her loud protest dies down, there is her conscience still ringing like an insistent burglar alarm. Why not? You cannot be a Catholic all your living days, and know it is the only True Faith, and attend its Mass, and receive its Sacraments and say its beads—and then suddenly toss the whole thing into the waste-basket like last year's calendar. The Faith is a tree whose roots are sunk deep in any Catholic heart, and they don't come out easily. As a matter of fact I don't think they ever come out at all. I have talked with more than a few Catholic girls who had snapped their fingers in the face of God and went through the motions of a marriage outside the Church, but who years later quietly slipped through the side-door of the Church and came back. And when they do, when their bad marriage is reset like a broken leg, and blessed by the Church, the first thing they blurt out is that all this time, despite the love and pleasure and everything else, they were never really happy. Because you cannot slip happiness on like a necklace or imprint it like a kiss or wear it like a bridal gown. Happiness must come from within. It starts inside. But if inside, deep down in the heart there is the gnawing knowledge that you have defied God in a serious matter, if over the soul hangs the black shadow of mortal sin, how can there ever be genuine joy?

Turn on all the gay lights of pleasure, beat all the drums of distraction—guilt is still coiled down there like a snake in the shadows. This sense that all is not right goes with the girl on her very honeymoon; and when she is alone, the smile dies and she stares into space. Later this sad sense of living in sin, this longing for something missing that she desperately wants, taps her on the shoulder at the strangest places. She may suddenly feel it, as she sees the crowds hurrying to Midnight Mass at Christmas, or as she looks down into the casket of a close friend killed in an accident, or even as she comes upon the pictures in the newspaper of a wedding in her old church.... The uneasiness is always there, like a dull steady tooth-ache in her conscience, or even a sharp sword in her deepest soul.

Even now as I speak to you someone out there may be churning with the temptation to marry a man outside the Church ... possibly because he is divorced and you cannot marry him in the Church. Well, he may be rich, and he may be handsome, and he may be able to give you everything—everything but happiness. How can you be happy when you will be telling the Almighty (not in words but in deed) that some human being means more to you than your God or your Faith? Doesn't it seem that St. Paul almost had just such a young girl in mind when he wrote to the Galatians: "I am astounded that you are so quick to be a deserter! Who is it that has fascinated you, cast a spell over you, that you refuse obedience to the true Gospel? Are you out of your senses that having begun spiritually you are now wholly taken up with the flesh?"

That was the letter St. Paul wrote, but the girl who is going to marry outside the Church should leave a letter like this: "Dear Mom and Dad ... I'm going to marry him at any cost. I don't care whether I break your hearts. I don't care if I am a disgrace to my Catholic education. I don't care if I'm leaving the Church and the Sacraments. I don't care whether my soul is damned. I don't care if I'm responsible for my children being lost to the faith, or their children. I care for nothing but myself, my will, my pleasure, my happiness!"

There is an answer to that letter. It is that nobody leaves God and finds happiness. And if anyone has lost it, a tortured heart yearning for the Communion Rail, the only way to find it is to come back to Him, the God of mercy and of love.

Little Colored Windows

STUMBLING-BLOCK

OR STEPPING-STONE?

Give a dog a bad name, and he is still trying to live it down the day he dies. Something like that is true about this word "temptation." Suspicions of sinister evil seem to hang about it like the glittering black beadwork of a Mata Hari gown. And yet to prove that temptation cannot possibly be a blood-relative of sin, we have merely to point to one fact in the life of Our Blessed Lord—a fact more startling than any of His miracles: Jesus Christ allowed Himself to be tempted. But why? Satan and forty thousand devils with all hell's hate hot within them, and all the cunning experience of forty centuries behind them, could never cause the slightest flicker in the clear, pure Eyes of Christ. His Sacred Heart was—Sacred, and sin could no more defile it, than you or I could daub mud across the flaming face of the Sun: we would shrivel up into vapor before we got within a hundred thousand miles. So, if Christ allowed Himself to be tempted, it was to teach us that temptation was temptation, and not sin; and furthermore that any temptation can be turned from a stumbling-block into a stepping-stone.

The dictionary is witness that temptation comes from the Latin word "tentare," meaning "to test." Now there is nothing wrong about things being tested, is there? Go to a steel foundry and see how they test a length of railroad track against dangerous flaws. Go to a woolen mill, and see how they test a bolt of cloth for strong fabric and true color. Well, temptation is the laboratory of God where souls are tested for virtue. And why not? After all, if we are going to get Heaven as a prize, shouldn't we first prove that we deserve it? What would be the sense of giving us Heaven as the reward for being good, if we never had any inclination to be bad?

Therefore, temptation is the universal law, the wound-stripe worn by all humanity. There are no exceptions. Let the wind blow, and there is not a leaf on the tree that does not flutter; let temptation come, and there is not man or woman who does not feel its stir. This is true not of nine out of ten; nor of ninety-nine out of a hundred, but of one hundred million out of one hundred million. I do not say that all are attracted equally by the same temptations. Wrong-doing is a varied and fascinating rainbow—you might call it the spectrum of sin—and different colors appeal to different people. This man may meet his test in dishonest green dollars; that one in intoxicating brown liquor. For another it may be the yellow streak of moral cowardice, or the red rage of wild anger, or green-eyed jealousy, or mud-colored impurity. But we cannot escape from temptation, because we cannot escape from ourselves. As long as we have a body with its senses, and therefore a tendency to sensuality; an intellect prone to pride and rash judgment; a heart capable of revenge and hate, well, we are like a cigarette lighter, with the fuel of our passions stored within us and needing only the igniting spark.

But for your comfort, let me remind you of two things. First, these passions, like the fuel, are in themselves good. You have the explosion of sin only when they are misdirected or misused. And secondly, for these people who are constantly complaining that they are always being tempted, isn't it very possible that the devil is ceaselessly pounding on the door of your heart outside, precisely because he is not inside? It is the other people who should be worried—the people who sophisticatedly suppose that the best way to get rid of a temptation is to yield to it; the people who seem to have no qualms of conscience, because they have no conscience—these are the names that are more likely written in Lucifer's beautiful flowing hand on the register of an establishment where the reservations are eternal but where the ice-water and air-conditioning facilities are sadly limited.

But is there any sure, swift way of getting rid of temptations? I heartily wish I could read over this microphone a flash bulletin announcing that science had just discovered a new miracle drug, a kind of moral penicillin or aureomycin: one injection each day for a week and you are immune to any suggestion of sin. However, I'm afraid that's out. But just as even science holds fast to such old reliables as bread and air and water, we have to oppose temptation with the old reliable remedies of 1) pray; 2) get away.

What kind of prayer? Certainly not a polished masterpiece; nothing formal, nothing elaborate. Temptation is war, and the best prayers are crisp, rapid, machine-gun prayers: "My Jesus, help me!" "My God and my All!" "Mary Immaculate, be at my side!"

Then having sent in the call for help, having turned in the fire alarm, get away from the fire. Temptation is fire, and nobody is asbestos. But what happens? So often, instead of abruptly turning away from the temptation, we dilly-dally a bit, we look over the ground, we weigh the pros and cons; we wonder. And we perish. It is somewhat like the case of the man who was contemplating suicide. He walked to the middle of a high bridge, took off his coat, folded it neatly on a bench, climbed to the railing, and was just about to kick back his heels and fling himself out into dizzy space, when he felt a firm hand on his shoulders. There was a burly policeman pulling him down, and saying soothingly: "Now, buddy—what's the big idea anyway? You wouldn't be as foolish as that would you? Come on, let's sit down for a few minutes and talk this over." So they sat down and talked very quietly, and ten minutes later they got up, walked over to the rail of the bridge, and jumped off together.

That is just what will happen every time, if you are foolish enough to debate with the devil! He will put thirty pieces of silver in your hand, and they will clink so merrily and gleam so brightly, that you will be willing even to send Christ to Calvary. "Give us Barrabas, our pleasure, and crucify Christ!" Then when sin is over; when the short false flare of the sky-rocket is out and the darkness is blacker than before; when the eager flame of anticipation has died and left only the cold ashes of disgust—then the reward of your sin, the thirty pieces of silver do not seem so bright. They mock you. Like Judas, you would fling them away. Isn't that the way we feel after yielding to the temptation? Why not be wise and realize it before? Realize that temptation is like a little chunk of cheese in the devil's trap! How the mouse is lured on—spots of yellow cheese dance before his little eyes, the aroma of cheese bombards his little brain. So he puts his head inside the trap. Then everything happens fast. The little teeth sink into the cheese—one delicious nibble—and the next moment down cracks the steel bar. And what good is the cheese to a mouse with a broken back? And what good is all the glittering "come-on" of temptation to us, if the last act is a shattered soul, a conscience soiled, and the Grace of God dead within us? When temptation tugs at your elbow, whispers in your ear, remember that the devil is a smooth swindler who never delivers. He will promise you the world, as long as he can cheat you out of Heaven.

Some of you may be thinking, "But the world is full of temptations. How can we avoid them? What are we supposed to do, knock at the door of a monastery? Hide behind the high walls of a convent? Step off the earth?" Not at all; because the temptations we have to fear most are the temptations we deliberately seek out. Other temptations which come to us in the course of our normal living, and which we cannot avoid, God will help us conquer.

It is like this. Suppose the main aisle of a vast Cathedral were being repaired, and a long narrow plank about twenty-inches wide were laid over the marble floor all the way down the aisle. Any one of us could walk along that plank without any trouble, right down to our bench. But, suppose not the floor but the ceiling were being repaired, and the plank stretched above the aisle, one hundred feet in the air. Could we walk that? Or would we get up there and start to sway, and to slip, and to plunge headlong to the floor? But why? It is the same plank up there as down here; we are the same person. But we have no business up there; it is not our job, not our place. And it is the same with temptations. As you walk along the normal path of your life, you can usually master them fairly easily. But once you deliberately put yourself in danger, you step out on a high, dizzy plank, you are inviting a fall. That plank, for you, can be anything from a parked car to a tavern door. It is all right to say that in itself temptation is no more a sin than an exam is a failure, but you can't put your finger into a bottle of ink and hope and wish and pray that it won't get black. It will.

In other words we are responsible for what happens because we allow it to happen. Like the young girl who has become involved with a married man at the office. Only the way she says it ("she has fallen in love")—it was like getting hay fever, or the hiccups, or athlete's foot. You wouldn't blame her for that, would you? She simply fell in love. But the simple truth is that she did not fall and it was not love. She did not fall, because she walked into it with her eyes wide open. And it was not love, because in her circumstances it was unlawful lust. Oh, soft marshmallow compliments that he handed out; but she swallowed them. A physical attraction that lured her, but she allowed herself to be drawn. And even when her conscience began to whistle like a singing kettle, warning her that passion was at the boiling point—she still ignored it. Prayer, which might have helped her, hung up there like an old unused, unfilled, neglected, fire-extinguisher. Keeping out of his company would have solved everything, but she blithely goes on tap-dancing on the trap-door of temptation, knowing that at any moment it can spring and she will fall—and she does fall!

What good is it for any of us to say, "Lead us not into temptation" in the morning, if we take a running broad jump into temptation that afternoon, or that night? Let's be honest. If the Devil waves at us from across the street, we can fairly easily turn our heads and forget him. But if we deliberately cross the street and shake hands with him—well, "Shake hands with the Devil, and he doesn't let go!"

Shrines Across the Sea

THE SHRINE OF IRELAND

I suppose everyone feels the same about the land of his forbears, and since my mother and father (God rest them!) had been born in Ireland, a curious feeling came across me when for the first time I saw the emerald shore. I caught a glimpse of a green Irish hill, and something inside me, centuries old, sat up and purred. Here we were, a group of pilgrims bent on visiting various shrines of the Madonna across the ocean, and suddenly on this murky dawn off the port bow of the huge liner, Ireland stood up and out of the sea, and some sentimental radar vibrated across the waters and pinged in my heart.

This seemed all the more strange because it wasn't a beautiful morning at all. It rained and it blew, and in the choppy sea below the rail, the little tender "Blarney" drew alongside and hung bobbing like a watch-charm. Ireland that morning was washed by a sea as grey and bitter as her tears, and over her hung a white mist, like the dreamy idealism that often hangs between an Irishman and the hard world of reality. But every now and again the fog that walked like a shrouded leper along the coast vanished for a moment, and you could see high up on a green hill and overlooking the harbor the clear spire of St. Colman's Cathedral, as if it were the dark sleeve of a monk holding up the cross. That cross was the first thing you saw in Ireland that really stood out, and when you left it a week later you felt that after all you had seen, *this* was what Ireland stood for: the Faith held high above crops and cows and war and money and politics and everything else on the little skyline of Irish life. The Cross was highest, the Faith came first!

As soon as we cleared the casual friendly Irish customs, we marched like pilgrims into the cathedral and said our prayers before the same God Whom we had left in America but Who was waiting for us here in Ireland under the same crimson sign of the Altar Light. Two things impressed us in St. Colman's. One was the marble tracery round the arches, so delicately carved it looked like white lace. The other was the "waking" room in the rear. Now, all cathedrals have a baptistry where the child who has just entered the world is brought for his reception into the Church. But this was a room where a man was brought when he was leaving the world, the night before he was buried. And all night long till the morning Mass his friends keep an uninterrupted vigil of prayer. All night long other friends and neighbors drop in and begin a new rosary, so that you can almost imagine against the background music of low murmuring voices, the soul of the deceased climbing to Heaven on the swaying rope-ladder of the beads. Well, your Irishman is a curious fellow. He may have a twinkle in his eye and a quip on his lip and a jig in his heels, but at the same time he is very close to his dead. His sister in Heaven may be a good deal nearer to him than his other sister in Hoboken.

We came out of the cathedral, and it was still pouring rain, which reminds me to remind you that "if you ever cross the sea and go to Ireland, then maybe at the closing of the day" you'll be soaked and sodden unless you bring along a sturdy raincoat. Don't believe it that the Irish rain is practically dry, and only falls in graceful silver harp strings. To them over there, poor amphibious souls, it isn't raining at all unless they are sloshing in water up to their ankles. Otherwise, "It's a soft day, thank God." Hail is a hard day, I guess. When I mentioned the rain to the bus-driver who picked us up at the cathedral he smiled and said, "Sure, Father, that's only a few drops of Holy Water sprinkled on the windshield." In Ireland there is no such thing as bad weather; you just didn't dress right for the day. And many a young gossoon has been fetched a stinging clout on the ear for complaining, "Oh what a miserable day!" "Listen, you! The good God never made a bad day!" And actually what strikes you most is not so much the Irish rain (though that can certainly strike you often enough) as the Irish attitude towards it. All day long the Will of God walks like a banner before the Irishman's thoughts, and the weather is only the robe God happens to be wearing at the moment—golden or grey it makes no great difference, because within it is God. So they will meet you and greet you with, "A fine day, thank God!" or "A touch of wet we're having. Ah, He knows best."

By the time we got to Cork the rain had passed and the day was a blaze of blue and gold, so we went up to the Blarney Castle—and if you are wondering "Did I?" the answer is "I did," though I haven't been able to find out whether it did any good. Then on from Blarney to Killarney—from honeyed charm for your tongue to the most darling Celtic scenery for your eye, and a rolling, dipping countryside that holds the original copyright on the color green. Anything else is diluted and dull. Then our puffing bus began to climb the Kerry hills, and I decided this would be an opportune time to say our daily rosary. We had said it together every day on shipboard and we said it every day in our bus or train for the next month. But we had hardly begun the beads this day when huge grey clouds came rolling overhead like the canvas of covered wagons, the thunder rumbled like wagon-wheels, and the lightning snapped its fiery whip. Soon we were high among the wild and purple peaks of Kerry, under a black, storm-crashing sky, on a circling, slippery narrow road, and when you looked out the bus window you looked down a sheer drop of fifteen hundred feet. I think the place is called Healy's Pass, and when he found it, Mr. Healy must have been chasing one of those black Kerry cows which for altitude records yield only to the cow that jumped over the moon. Anyway, the rosary which we began in almost routine fashion we finished with unexpected fervor.

The next day brought us through the Ireland that everybody knows from technicolor travelogues and the songbook covers ... the land of the white-washed cottage with the tiny red roses along its wall blazing like a stand of vigil lights; the brown thatched roof with swallows landing and leaving like planes at an airport; the jaunty feather of blue smoke curling from the chimney telling you that tea was on over the turf fire. The fields were dotted with great boulders, but these of course were only pebbles from the sling-shot of that Hibernian Paul Bunyan named Finn Macool. We were getting on toward our goal now, which was the Shrine of Our Lady of Knock.

Jokingly, if a man is from County Tipperary, they dub him a stone-thrower; and if he hails from County Roscommon, they call him a sheep-stealer; but if he says he came from County Mayo, they just shake their heads and murmur, "Mayo, God help us!" Well, in all God-help-us Mayo, a bleak, wild-green land then surely, there was no bleaker, poorer spot seventy-five years ago than the village of Knock. It is still only a huddle of houses in the midst of turf bogs brightened here and there by a burst of golden furze. There is a neat rectory, a small school, a guest house run by the Sisters of Charity, a couple of stores where you can buy religious articles, and a church that is a hundred years old. If you were selecting a spot in Ireland to visit, you would hardly choose Knock, but then you might not have chosen Bethlehem either. Doesn't it seem as if Our Lady loves to travel the back roads, to stop at the obscure places, to visit the unimportant people?

The church of Knock is more impressive than you might expect—a squat, square edifice of grey stone with an imposing tower. And the local pastor was the type of elderly priest you see all over Ireland—silvery hair, pink cheeks, and a rich warm voice that would charm a boulder out of the sea. Only once the voice took on a sharp edge—when I remarked that it must be a little wearying for the congregation to sit in these pews that had no backs at all but only a narrow rod for a back, and he answered, "I don't know how it is in America, but here in Ireland people don't come to church to be comfortable."

But his voice was soft and musical again when he stood before the altar of the apparition and told us the touching story. It was on this very spot, he said, because this used to be in the open air and only later they closed it in as a new sanctuary. The time was the night of August 23, 1879, and rain was drenching the roads and drumming on the roofs. The rectory housekeeper was plodding up from the village when she noticed something across the road outside the church. Looked like a group of statues, and as matter of fact His Reverence had ordered some statues, but who was so careless as to leave them in the rain? So she trudged over to investigate. And it turns out that they are not statues, and though it is raining all around them the motionless white figures are perfectly dry and standing in mid air. Down on her knees she falls, crying out with fear and wonder. The colleen with her runs home with the news, and soon fourteen people are gazing at the apparition. In the center stood Our Lady, with her eyes and hands raised as though invoking a blessing; on her right stood St. Joseph, and on her left, with a Gospel Book, St. John the Evangelist.

For about one hour the vision lasted, and then was gone without a word. This was the unique feature: that Mary left no message. Perhaps she felt that the sensitive Irish people would know that simply by her appearing to them at one of Ireland's darkest hours and in one of Ireland's bleakest spots, they

THE SHRINE OF IRELAND

would know that her motherly eyes were upon them. And she brought St. Joseph who had been her support in the poverty of Nazareth, and St. John who had been her support after the tragedy of Calvary, as pledges of her own support and comfort and help. What need of words? Had not Ireland herself been a Mother of Sorrows through the centuries, with the body of a bleeding Faith flung across her lap? No nation deserved more the consoling vision of the Mother of the Crucified. Isn't Ireland's history in the Shamrock—the tiny green Celtic cross?

Each year on the anniversary of the apparition, pilgrims by the tens of thousands from all over Ireland pour into the little village by cars and carts and buses—the railroad still doesn't come near it. In the beginning the clergy were more than conservative, and many were frankly skeptical, so that it was the people who fostered and practically forced the devotion. Now, after extensive investigation, the Archbishop has given approval, there is a Medical Bureau that investigates and checks cures, and the shrine is confidently waiting ultimate sanction of the Holy See.

As for us who straggled out of our bus into the shrine, a chattering group without band or banners, we had no sooner knelt and said our quiet prayers, than the conviction vibrated through all of us: This is holy ground. We have visited a spot that the Mother of God once deigned to visit herself! None of us will ever forget Our Lady of Knock, Consoler of the Poor.

It is all past now, and looking back over our shoulder, Ireland is only a patchquilt of memories. Emerald mountains and golden furze, mealy potatoes and modern power plants, colleens with cheeks like roses and rangy farmers with hands like bunches of bananas, holy wells and square dancing, old ladies with black shawls, the Book of Kells where every page is a tiny stained glass window, the grave of Matt Talbot in which is buried the drunkard who bounced from the gutter to the stars, the jaunting cars and the barefoot children and the gaunt crosses of the Holy Year crowning the remotest hills... they all come back in tender reminiscence. But always underneath any litany of remembered physical details in Eire is the low organ-music of deep, surging faith. And this is the Ireland that really attracts you, the Ireland of the spirit, and the spirit of Ireland. Not that any of our party wanted to live in Ireland—we didn't; America is our country—but we came to love the things that Ireland seemed to stand for: the warm-hearted kindness, the simple piety, the sunny humor, the all-week religion, the lilting speech, the loyalty to the Faith during decades of persecution. And you wonder if, after all, the rain is not just Holy Water falling gently on the great green shrine that is Ireland itself.

Shrines Across the Sea

THE PRIDE OF PORTUGAL

Some years back I had the happiness of being the Chaplain on a pilgrimage for a score or so of "pilgrims." We went bouncing across Europe in a bus and we turned to prayer-books rather than guide-books as a spiritual road map for the various Shrines we visited. On the Continent our first real stop—and our first surprise—was Lisbon. In the fiction and the films of the last war, Lisbon was always the sinister center of international espionage, the neutral airport where secret agents wearing trench coats and snap-brimmed hats and carrying mysterious brief-cases, hurried off the planes, and watched one another with roving, glittering eyes across the smoke-filled cafes. Actually the Lisbon we saw was a bright, airy, colorful city with gaudy flower-beds, gilded balconies, and huge stucco buildings tinted pink or white or buff—like a crisp and clean line of summer wash hanging idly in the sun.

Of course our prime concern was not focused on Lisbon at all, but on a visit to Fatima, but we actually began by hearing Holy Mass in a Lisbon church so old that Columbus could have worshipped there, let alone these brash twentieth-century Americans. When we first stepped into the shadowy church, everything seemed so different from at home. There were no pews, for example; you picked up a straw kneeler from the back of the church and just planted it in front of an altar. There were no stained-glass windows; instead the windows were frosted, but between them hung huge sacred paintings twenty feet high in frames of tropical gold. There was no bookstand; instead the Missal rested on a white silken cushion. There were no altar boys in the strict sense, for the youngest "boy" seemed to be just a little south of sixty, and instead of a cassock they all wore what looked like flaming academic robes. But once you took your chalice and followed the shuffling server out, and bowed before the altar, and began, "In nomine Patris et Filii et Spiritus Sancti" in the universal language of the Church, the age-old idiom of the soul, you felt at home, and the people who were grouped around you, whom you had never seen before (as they had never seen you) were not strangers nor foreigners but brothers and sisters in God, and your heart leaped with the sudden exultant realization that you were a living part of a world-wide Church.

After Mass we piled into our squat brown bus. With the poetic Portuguese touch the bronzed genial chauffeur had arranged, of all things, a vase of flowers in a bracket over the dashboard. More than once, while he was at the wheel, we figured that these flowers would come in handy for our funeral. This driver drove with one hand on the wheel and the other on the horn, and with the illusion that he was a test pilot in a jet, so that to us it will always seem one of the wonders of Fatima that we got there at all. The road arched like a cat's back and rolled like a drunkard between regiments of veteran olive trees; past wind-mills turning their slow Maltese crosses of white canvas against the brilliant blue sky; past furrowed brown farms like patches of corduroy sewed on the land; and where the harvest was already high, you could see the broad straw hats and the flashing sickles of the men and women working in the fields.

At intervals, above the rattle and clatter of the bus, we said our beads in common, and sang some of the old familiar hymns to Our Lady. Finally (after we had been riding almost three hours I think) we were warned it was time now to begin the Stations of the Cross. The Stations are set along the roadway but we never stopped. The bus driver had figured it out neatly that we could go whirling along and still complete the prayers of one Station just before the next would loom up. We had just finished the fourteenth when the road took a sudden swerve and there, as unexpected as a pinnacled iceberg in the shimmering heat, rose the white marble tower of the new Basilica. *Now* you will find it unique and a majestic church, but then the unfinished interior was still ringing with the staccato throb of the workmen's hammers. Frankly, for the mere tourist, neither the Basilica nor Fatima is worth crossing the ocean to see. Viewed from any angle but that of Faith, Fatima is still strictly nothing in the middle of nowhere. I'm afraid that except on occasion of the big pilgrimages the ordinary European traveller might find Fatima a barren, baking disappointment. You have a scrawny countryside of dusty red soil that loses by comparisons with the distant green mountains. You have a few houses that masquerade as hotels and a few stores that sell pious souvenirs. You have the unfinished Basilica, flanked on one side by a retreat house and on the other by a hospital, and stretching out before it is a paved area which looks (if it be not irreverent to say so) like the largest parking space in the world and is supposed to be almost as spacious as the square before St. Peter's in Rome. Yet the day we were there, I doubt whether there were a hundred people there. But it didn't matter. At a corner of this open square you have the heart of Fatima, the sacred spot that gives meaning to everything, that makes your blood tingle as you drop on your knees. This is the tiny chapel (so tiny it is big enough only for altar and priest and altar-boy) that marks the point where the Mother of God appeared to the three children.

To the Catholic world at least that is an old story now: how back in 1917 Mary appeared on the thirteenth of each month from May to October to these three youngsters; how she commanded them to pray the Rosary for the conversion of Russia; how in her last apparition to the children, she promised a sign for all to see. That was October 13th, 1917, and the road from Lisbon to Fatima was clogged with the curious and the devout. At noon seventy thousand people stood or knelt in the dreary rain while the three children said their beads. Then Our Lady said to them, "Look at the sun!" At the sun? But at that moment the clouds parted like curtains on a stage, and the sun hung there a globe of dull silver. The next moment it began to grow brighter and brighter, and to whirl and spin like a giant wheel of colored fire, flinging out shafts of red and green and blue like the spokes of a wheel across the land! Then, suddenly, like a wheel that had slipped its axle, the sun came plunging down toward the people, so much so that the vast throng thought it was the end of the world, and began to pray and to cry and to scream. But just as swiftly the sun went spiralling up again; and the crowd shakily got to its feet, to find its clothes, which had been soaked in the downpour, now were crisply dry!

This is the reason why on the thirteenth of each month, from May to October, the road from Lisbon to Fatima crawls with cars and carts, with peasants and pilgrims. There may be anything from fifty to a hundred thousand people joining in at this hour or at that in a Rosary whose prayers rise up all through the night before the great Monstrance illuminated in the lofty tower of the Basilica.

In the beginning it was nothing like this. There was, in the first place, snarling opposition from the anti-clerical government and the free-thinkers of Lisbon who sternly believed that everybody should be free to think only as the free-thinkers thought. So they boarded off the roads leading to the Shrine; they plastered the neighborhood with scoffing posters; they stole some vestments and crucifixes and banners and staged a mock procession. They even planted a time-bomb that blew the original little chapel to bits. They forget that bombs can destroy only buildings but are useless against the Truth.

At Fatima we met a doctor from Lisbon who told us of a nun he knew in that city who had been bent double with arthritis, and who on one of those pilgrimages on the thirteenth of the month had been instantly and completely cured. When we remarked that it seemed incredible that so obscure and forlorn a spot as Fatima should suddenly have sent its impact to the very ends of the earth, he smiled and said, "Wasn't Bethlehem off that beaten path too? And speaking of Bethlehem, you ought to see where Fatima really started, where the children who saw the vision lived." So our bus rumbled along a road which was little more than a glorified rut. After a jouncing mile we turned off at a dusty barren lane where a half-dozen puny, pallid houses broiled in the sun. This house had been the home of Jacinta and Francesco. By American standards it was more like a garage, or a cellar with a front door. Stone floor, whitewashed walls, shaggy timbers for a ceiling —it did make you think of the Cave of Bethlehem. It was austerely neat with the few possessions of the poor, but somehow it seemed to glitter with the grace of God.

The parents looked as though they were both in their eighties. Like the old ladies in Ireland the mother wore a big black shawl, and her brown wrinkled face reminded you of a walnut, but set in it were the most patient, gentle eyes. Somebody proposed a picture, and the old Dad disappeared only to reappear wearing a coat! You could not say that this poor cotton jacket matched his faded trousers or even any of the patches on them—but apparently he felt that the dignity of the occasion demanded his best. When we left we pushed some money into their hands, and I got to suspecting that everybody must do this, and to wondering where does the money go?

A priest who lives there cleared this up. The money goes, every escudo of it, to the Basilica and the new Seminary at Fatima. And the wrinkled and weakened old father and mother insisted on staying poor and lowly and unchanged, lost at the end of a backwoods road with their primitive houses and their few chickens, content enough with the memory that God's Mother had chosen to speak with their children.

But did she? The people at large were fervidly convinced, but the Church was not throwing its mitre high in the air, dancing down the middle-aisle and shouting, "Miracle." Claim the supernatural, and you will find that the official Catholic Church is about as enthusiastic as an old glacier. So how did the Church react to the first excitement of Fatima? For five years, time enough for all the bubbles of fervor or fanaticism to simmer down, she made no move. Only then the formal investigation began, and with the slow patience of a Church that thinks in centuries and can afford to wait, it took eight more years to examine carefully the witnesses, methodically collect the testimony, scientifically study the alleged cures—because when it comes to apparitions, obviously anyone can say he saw anything and the only proof is a procession of miracles.

It was in 1930 (thirteen years after the event) that the appearance of Our Lady at Fatima was approved for public devotion. Today, years later, as you kneel on the sacred spot where Mary appeared, and say the Rosary that she there enjoined, and pray for the conversion of Russia as she counselled, you suddenly feel that this going to God might be the short cut to straighten out the world after all.

We have tried almost everything else. We have tried the bread and butter of the Marshall Plan. We have tried the diplomatic poker-playing over the tables of the U.N. We have tried the "police action" of the Korean war. We have left no stone unturned in our search for peace, except the altar-stone. We have not really tried God. At Fatima you realize that His Mother is reminding us that if it is peace we seek, how pathetically foolish to ignore Him, the Prince of Peace! And the summit meeting? Let us go up to the Sermon on the Mount!

Shrines Across the Sea

LOURDES THE INCREDIBLE

When you arrive at the station at Lourdes and look around you, your eyes instinctively travel upward out of this valley town toward the huge hulks of the Pyrenees Mountains hunched around in a circle like football players in a huddle. In Portugal most of the mountains seemed grey; in Spain they were a distant carved purple, but here they were so close at hand that they look like tremendous slopes of green moss.

If you start hiking up to your little hotel from the station, you will find yourself grunting up steep cobble-stone streets that make your lungs puff and your imagination wish for an escalator or a ski-tow. But it isn't merely that your legs ache at what you have to climb; your heart aches at what you see. You get the amazed and angry impression that you are walking through the world's largest open-aired religious department store. If ever spirituality was commercialized, if ever piety had a price-tag twisted around it, if ever the sign of the cross was bent and distorted into a dollar sign (or francs—it makes no difference) you have it in the town of Lourdes. Street after street lined with store after store, and every one of them overflowing out to the sidewalks in tables cluttered with "bargains"—each store apparently offering the same religious articles, the almost identical display—how in the world, you wonder, do they all survive?

Thousands and thousands of rosaries, red and blue and white and green and black, hang in gaudy bunches like tobacco leaves or Indian scalps. Medals piled in tiny mounds like potatoes. Shelves upon shelves of little statues in a combination of loud colors like an explosion in a paint factory. And in the same stores you can also buy souvenir canes, kewpie dolls, popcorn, perfume, and in some of them get your pictured snapped. Lourdes is a spiritual Coney Island, with a halo tilted over its ear like a straw hat. And the stores have such sanctimonious names: "The House of St. Genevieve," "At the Roses of St. Therese," "The Flowers of St. Francis," and (to get the Irish vote) one with a bright green awning and large block letters "The House of St. Lawrence O'Toole."

Some of it is probably necessary, but most of it is awfully depressing, so thank God we can and must distinguish between the town of Lourdes and the Shrine of Lourdes. The shrine is as inviolate as a government reservation, and once you walk through its handsome iron gates, you cannot buy anything but Heaven. You find yourself in what looks like a neat baronial park with long lines of symmetrical trees, emerald plots of grass, bright flowers, Stations of the Cross with figures so lifesized and lifelike that they almost scare you; and above all, the Gothic spires of the tripled-tiered church of the Rosary.

Yet even outside the church, the whole Shrine grounds have the atmosphere of an open-air cathedral. There was no sign saying "No Smoking," but nobody was smoking. There was no sign requesting quiet, but all over the place hung an air of reverence. To give you an idea: On one of the days we were at Lourdes a thousand lads from the Belgian Army poured into the Shrine grounds on a pilgrimage, and the next day five thousand from the French Army, and if you don't think the very atmosphere of Lourdes does something to you, you should have seen these young soldiers going from the Grotto to the Stations of the Cross and then on to the Church, and all the time moving with the intent reverence of seminarians.

I have mentioned the French and Belgians, but at Lourdes we met more nationalities than at any other spot in Europe. Here were dark Italians from the Tiber, blond Germans from the Rhine, strapping Irishmen from the Shannon, very reserved Englishmen from the Thames. And I can remember talking with a lanky Scot in his gay kilts, and a young student all the way from Australia, and a colored priest from Africa looking ten feet tall in his long white robes—here was really "The United Nations," representatives from all the countries of the world strung together like beads on a rosary, and the chain that united them was love for the Mother of God—a devotion that encircles the globe.

All pilgrims to Lourdes first strike out for the Grotto, where Our Lady appeared to Bernadette. You look up at a stone hillside and in the lower right corner of this is the natural niche where Mary stood. Now a statue stands there in the pale blue and white of her original garments. On either side instead of the usual vases of flowers are grim racks of crutches, those under the overhang black with candle-smoke, and those in the open bleached with sun and rain. Beneath the statue rises a rather small and simple altar; beyond that, fan out some fifteen or twenty rows of kneeling benches, and then only a few feet away the olive-green river Gave rushing past so rapidly you can hear it swish.

Months before, for the sake of the pilgrims, I had obtained permission in writing to celebrate Holy Mass at the altar of the Grotto on the feast of Saints Peter and Paul. When I tried to present my credentials on the evening of our arrival the sacristy was closed. At eight-fifteen the next morning I silently handed my letter to the grey-haired sacristan. He read it; the next thing I knew he had turned as purple as a monsignor's cassock. He was waving his arms as though he were directing a hundred-piece orchestra and he was exploding in blockbusting French that it was impossible. But impossible!

Well, it didn't vitally matter where I said Mass. It did matter that I obey the ecclesiastical authorities of the place. Of course I was disappointed and I figured the pilgrims would even be more so. Apparently some Bishop or Archbishop had been appointed over my head. So I left the Sacristy, knelt down near the altar and asked Our Lady for help, for just a strictly minor-league miracle.

Do you know that at ten minutes to nine (my scheduled hour) a very polite prelate in a lace rochet and purple cape, bowed to me as though I were a Papal Legate, escorted me to the sacristy, helped me on with the vestments, and murmured his sincere regrets about the unfortunate misunderstanding. To tell the truth I didn't understand one word he said, but from the soft smile and deprecating gestures I knew he was surrendering with honor. Later that morning I found out that the prelate in charge of the shrine who had mailed me my credentials, had taken gravely ill a week before, and the new man had known nothing about previous commitments. Now he led me personally to the altar, and there turned me over to my server, a rugged young Belgian soldier. And oh, it was wonderful to stand beneath the very spot where the Mother of God had stood, and hold up her own Son in the Sacred Host! But the whole atmosphere of Lourdes trembles with the supernatural. You feel that you have but to put out your hand and it will touch the Fingers of God.

In the morning, Lourdes is the baths where the water from St. Bernadette's miraculous spring has been piped into two stone bathhouses, one for the women and the other for the men. Here the pilgrim disrobes and slips into a kind of canvas apron, lies for a minute or so in a trough of flowing cold water, and repeats the prayer that hangs on the wall beneath the little statue of Our Lady. And more than once that Lady, who obtained from Christ at Cana the miracle of changing the water into wine, obtains from Her Son through this water a change from pallid sickness to ruddy health.

In the afternoon, Lourdes is the majestic march of the Monstrance. About four o'clock the bells start swinging in the towers and birds start singing in the trees, and the devout army of pilgrims pours out of houses and hotels, and heads for the open square in front of the church. Already there are assembled there in a heart-breaking crescent, ranks of wheelchairs and stretchers like the grim parade of the world's pain lined up for review. Suddenly the church doors open, and out marches a double file of little girls dressed in the peasant costume and bright kerchief of Bernadette. Then altar boys with twinkling candles leading a canopy of green and gold. Under the canopy a Bishop or Canon is carrying the Monstance with the Blessed Sacrament, and slowly, prayerfully, he raises it in blessing over each silent, pleading invalid.

Meanwhile a young black-robed priest in the center of the cresent is intoning prayers, and the great congregation behind the sick, roar back the responses like thunderous waves crashing against the coast. Most of the miracles of Lourdes take place here. Speaking of miracles, Lourdes is also the Medical Bureau, a solemn temple of Science, side by side with the temple of Sanctity, the church. Here they make it hard for some fraud to fling his crutches into the air and scream "I'm cured!" and then go home to amuse his sophisticated set with the story of how any clever knave can fool these naive clergy at Lourdes. Here you will find that no cure is even considered without first, a preliminary medical record; secondly, an on the spot investigation by a board of doctors who are by no means all Catholics; and thirdly, a thorough double-checking of the patient one year after the event.

In the evening, Lourdes is the March of the Torches. Imagine a mile or more of marching men and women winding in and out about the verdant grounds, each carrying a candle under a tiny lampshade and reciting the rosary, while the whole flickering procession itself looks like a glittering rosary of golden beads. And when they finally draw up in the square in front of the Church, the lights stirring like a vast meadow of yellow flowers, and the spires of the church outlined with soft electric bulbs like ropes of pearls, and the famous pilgrim song of Lourdes, ringing out with its recurring, "Ave! Ave! Ave! Maria!" you suddenly remember that in the New Testament, Mary had predicted, "All generations shall call me blessed," and your heart thrills to realize this is it!

Lourdes at any hour is the brancardiers or voluntary stretcher bearers. You can tell them by the distinctive leather harness looped over their shoulders. This contraption ends in a couple of leather tubes into which they slide the stretcher poles. Who are these men? Anybody! Bakers or barons, lawyers or laborers, they volunteer for anything from a few days to a month. They often put in fourteen hours a day. When the "White Train" rolls into the station with the sick, it is their job to bring to the hospital or hotel the sagging stretchers, the hooded wheel-chairs, or the rolling beds on which people lie like living crucifixes of pain. And that is not all. All day long you can see these men of unassuming, homespun holiness bringing the helpless invalids to the grotto or the baths or wherever they wish to go.

This is what strikes you most about Lourdes: here people really seem to take Christianity seriously. Outside Lourdes, things may be better—towered universities, modern glassed-in factories, skyscrapers, museums, boulevards, and all the rest. But inside Lourdes, people are better. Piety toward God, kindness toward our neighbor hover in the sacred air. Human beings remember for just a little while that their only purpose on this earth is, first to honor God, and second, to help other human beings. Strangely enough they seem to like the experience. It is like the wonderful spirit of Christmas on every day of the year. How else explain it but that the Mother of God once touched this place, and her spirit lingers on?

Shrines Across the Sea

A VISIT TO THE VATICAN

We were standing at the ship's stern, watching its wake flow out like a billowing bridal train of aquamarine trimmed with the lacy foam, and we got to wondering, now that we were drawing away from Europe, what was the high-point of our pilgrimage, its greatest thrill, the moment we would longest remember? Was it Fatima or Lourdes or St. Peter's or the Catacombs or what? We talked it over and we agreed—unanimously—that in our little mountain-range of experience the peak that towered over them all was seeing the Holy Father.

At first our hopes of an audience looked bleak almost to the point of being black. We had rolled into Rome at ten-thirty in the evening, having travelled in our trusty bus ever since eight o'clock that morning. The next day I set out to see some "contacts," some supposedly influential people. But I soon learned that they had long since learned to say "no" in the nicest manner. I got bubbly compliments I didn't deserve on religious broadcasting in America, I got a prelate's autographed book, I got the suavest continental courtesy, but I got no help toward an audience. There was only one seed that still might possibly sprout—because a couple of weeks ago I had written a letter.

So we trooped over to the Redemptorist Church on the Via Merulana where the Fathers live in an unlikely monastery above a row of smart shops. The church itself is on the smallish side, seating not more, I should imagine, than three or four hundred. (This is forgetting the dusty and forgotten gallery.) That is a misleading statement, too, because only half the church has pews, the other half is vacant; so in accordance with the European custom, you can take a straw pre-dieu from the back and plant it where you please. We marched right up to the front pews, took our Novena Booklets, looked up at the original picture of the Mother of Perpetual Help above the main altar, and loudly and proudly said our Novena prayers just as we used to say them every Wednesday at the Mission Church, Boston. Some worshippers looked at us in alarm, as they heard this wild barbaric American tongue, but we went on to the end knowing that Bostonian broad a's were as sweet at least to Our Lady's ears as any liquid Italian vowels.

All this time my worried and pressing intention was that the Mother of God would take us by the hand, children in a foreign land, and lead us somehow to Our Holy Father, the Pope. And that is just what she did. Because we had no sooner streamed out of the church than a priest, an old American school-mate, was bearing down on me with a broad smile and waving a white envelope stamped with the golden seal of the Vatican. I don't say my fingers trembled as I opened the letter, but I'm glad that at that moment I didn't have to thread a needle. "Special audience tomorrow at nine" was the message, and it made us feel that we had done the impossible, like getting into Heaven without dying, or getting from the Cabin Class section to the First Class area on a big liner

At seven-thirty the next morning the pilgrims were gathered round the Altar of the Blessed Sacrament at St. Peter's, and I started out from the sacristy to say the Mass. It seems to me now that the Mass could not have begun just before a quarter to eight, because we walked and walked over the marble floor of St. Peter's (the altar-boy and I) till we finally reached our goal. You never realize the size of St. Peter's till you crawl like a little fly far beneath the vast arches and between the colossal pillars and over the silent stone expanse to some remote altar. Meanwhile the lad was trudging ahead of me, swinging the bottles of water and wine in a kit by his side, like a mechanic carrying his tools. He guided me skillfully through the corps of pietrini who were swishing wide arcs with brooms that looked like bundles of twigs tied to poles. Finally we got to our altar—whose Tabernacle was so high there was a stool to reach it for Communion, and whose altar cards were so massive they rolled back and forth on a brass track.

It was a high privilege to say Mass at the only altar in St. Peter's where the Blessed Sacrament is reserved, and to give Holy Communion to our pilgrim band. After that, somewhere in the depths of the basilica we had a quick cup of coffee and a roll, and then were eagerly off for our visit with the Pope. Here were the same Swiss Guards who yesterday would not let me pass when I wanted to "see somebody." Then they had seemed like haughty, forbidding fellows, outlandish in their bright, wide-striped uniforms that looked like walking awnings. But this morning as the halberds came down and they bowed us in, they seemed like picturesque gentlemen, lending just the right dash of atmosphere and flair. Our excited group was escorted first into one room, then into another, finally into a third, as though we were a ship going from lock to lock in a canal, till finally we came to the wide, open ocean, the vast Throne Room of the Pope.

Throne, ceiling, and walls were done in a scarlet and gold that made the room look like a perpetual sunset. After we looked over the room, we looked around at our neighbors. A "special audience" varies in numbers according to the time of the year, the day of the week, or other circumstances. It might be as few as thirty people and it might be as many as three hundred.

Our special audience was somewhere in between, say about one hundred and fifty people. It may interest the women (having travelled the continent of Europe with seventeen of them, I now know all about women) to know that the black gown and black mantilla that you see so often in newspaper pictures are not obligatory at all. It is protocol of course for celebrities at a private audience, like a princess for example. But the ordinary woman is not expected to buy or even rent a special outfit. All that is asked is ordinary modest attire, so that our party went in just as they were. Two functionaries in full dress lined us up in a hushed and expectant crescent around the three sides of the long chamber and facing the throne.

From some distant part of the palace we now began to hear a series of roaring "Viva's!" and one of the majordomos whispered that the Holy Father was giving an audience to some Italian Alpine troops. We had seen some of these chaps march in just before us, dark handsome lads with green hats and jaunty plumes. The "Viva's!" were their enthusiastic and uninhibited Latin salute to the Pope. To us it sounded like noisy baseball bleachers in a cathedral, but on the other hand to them we probably behaved like a convention of glaciers.

Scarcely had the last "Viva!" rumbled away when His Holiness, slender, erect, intent, came streaking through a door on the right of the throne and across the room. That white cassock of his fairly seemed to fly, so brisk was the stride of this elderly Pontiff. But that was the only rapid thing the Pope did. From then on everything was leisurely, relaxed, easy. He went from group to group, from person to person as though he had all the time in the clock. The throne of course he ignored. That was just a piece of furniture. It was as though we had not come to see the Holy Father, but he had come to see us. So he walked among us and talked with us.

I am afraid my ears were out like television antennae trying to drag in what he was saying to the various visitors, and it is natural that the same questions came up often. His Holiness would ask "Where do you come from?", "Is this your first time in Rome?", "Do you like it?", "You find it pretty warm, don't you?", "Are you a student?" The young folks seemed to get more attention than others. The Pope would ask the name of the school and so on, and always end with a diplomatic, fool-proof "Study hard. Study hard."

Through one of those well-intentioned mishaps that will occur, our group got an interview that resembled a stone skipping across a pond—a quick series of touch-and-go, and it was all over. The kindly priest who had helped engineer the audience in the first place, said, "Holy Father, this is a group of pilgrims all the way from Boston." His Holiness smiled that wonderfully radiant smile, turned to me and said, "Boston?" I kissed his ring and answered, "Yes, Holy Father, Boston."

And that is how it came about that the Holy Father spoke to me and I spoke to the Holy Father!

All along our line he repeated with his warm smile, "Boston?", "Boston?", "Boston?", till he came to Bill Mail. Bill was an Englishman, a Cockney, a non-Catholic, the bus-driver who brought us over two thousand five hundred bouncing miles. I had asked Bill if he would like to come with us and see the Pope, and Bill was delighted. "Extrawdnry!" he said. So when the Pope came to Bill at the end of our band and said, "Boston?", Bill smiled back and said, "No, Your Holiness, London!" "Well, well," said the Pope, "we don't see too many from London. And how are things in London?" And he went on to ask Bill about his wife and family and so on, so that it turned out this good non-Catholic bus-driver got more of the Pope's attention than all the rest of us together.

I saw three American men on the line after us, each of them holding a white silk skull-cap. When the

Holy Father came to them, they asked if he would be good enough to wear each skull-cap for a moment so that they might keep them as souvenirs. For a fleeting moment it seemed to me a shade of annoyance passed over the Pontiff's face, but the next moment he smiled and began putting on each skull-cap in succession. The air was that of a loving father tolerantly doing something he thought foolish, because he loved his children. After all you never know what an American may do or ask next. But if he was very gracious about it all, the situation did seem a little awkward; and a souvenir skull-cap in a closet out in West Thumbtack is a doubtful trophy when its takes advantage of the kindness of a great and lofty figure.

When the last person had been seen, His Holiness turned to us all with that high-powered smile which began in his heart and blossomed out at his lips, and said, "I suppose you would like a photograph taken?" Would we! But the Pope had one stipulation. The children must be in the front. The children on this occasion were two little colored girls, apparently twins, about nine years old, looking very pretty in their plaid dresses and pigtails. When they had arranged themselves right against the cream-colored cassock of the Pope, he nodded to the camera-man, the box clicked, and the next moment His Holiness, still smiling gently, left the room.

We stayed there for a few moments without uttering a word, everybody still under the spell. Some of us were musing that after this morning, nobody would ever seem overwhelmingly important. Because we had seen the man who was the ruler of more than three hundred million people, the man for whom more people would willingly die than for any other on earth, the Vicar of Christ, the Head of His worldwide Church—and we had found him so simple, so unassuming, so humble (a woman drops her rosary, and before she can pick it up he has stooped and picked it up for her) so altogether without pride or pretension or worldly front! Holiness seems to vibrate from him and around him, and the kindly love of a father radiates out of him. Perhaps that sums it up, and that is why they call him just "Holy Father."

Material for Sunday Sermons Based on Epistles or Gospels

Since none of these talks was written with a specific Gospel or Epistle in view, none will fit snugly or smoothly into such a homiletic frame. The following are mere suggestions for the hurried and the harried.

FIRST SUNDAY OF ADVENT	Souls in Pawn and the Redeemer	255
SECOND SUNDAY OF ADVENT	The Long "Night Before Christmas"	347
THIRD SUNDAY OF ADVENT	O Come All Ye Shoppers!	355
FOURTH SUNDAY OF ADVENT	The Stranger in the Manger	377
CHRISTMAS DAY	The Little Lord Jesus	363
SUNDAY WITHIN OCTAVE	Family Fireworks	233
NEW YEAR'S DAY	Ring in the New!	383
FIRST SUNDAY AFTER EPIPHANY *"Loss in the Temple"*	A Church is a Dull Place	461
SECOND SUNDAY AFTER EPIPHANY *"Wedding at Cana"*	Out of Bounds	177
THIRD SUNDAY AFTER EPIPHANY *"Wise in Your Own Conceits"*	Catholics, Excellent and Ex	513
LAST SUNDAY AFTER EPIPHANY *"Till the Whole Was Leavened"*	Queen of the Commonplace	46
SEPTUAGESIMA SUNDAY *"All Drank the Same Spiritual Drink"*	In a Glass, Darkly	291

SEXAGESIMA SUNDAY
"*These Have No Roots*" Novena Mirror 469

QUINQUAGESIMA SUNDAY
"*And They Understood None of These Things*" And They Swallow It 269

FIRST SUNDAY OF LENT
"*Make These Stones into Bread*" Stumbling-Block or Stepping-Stone? 528

SECOND OF LENT
"*Tell the Vision to No Man*" Hands and Holy Water 129

THIRD OF LENT
"*Let Not Obscenity Be Named Among You*" In Praise of St. Blaise 69

FOURTH OF LENT
"*Whence Shall We Buy Bread?*" Worry Is Waste 324

FIRST OF PASSIONTIDE
"*Abraham Is Dead, and the Prophets Are Dead*" A Funeral Is a Sad Sight 490

SECOND OF PASSIONTIDE
"*Obedient Unto Death*" East Side Shrine 422

EASTER
"*You Are Looking for Jesus of Nazareth*" Carpenter and Redeemer 24

LOW SUNDAY
"*Many Other Signs Jesus Worked, Not Written in This Book*" The Book Everybody Claims .. 440

SECOND AFTER EASTER
"*One Fold and One Shepherd*" Man of No Mistakes 505

THIRD AFTER EASTER
"*Abstain From Carnal Desires*" Sin—Original and Otherwise .. 277

FOURTH AFTER EASTER
"*I Go to the Father*" Highway To Heaven 396

FIFTH AFTER EASTER
"*Ask and You Shall Receive*" Outstretched Hands 454

SUNDAY WITHIN OCTAVE OF
   ASCENSION
   "Above all Things Have a Mu-   Hearts are Easily Hurt 184
   tual Love"

PENTECOST
   "Tongues of Fire"   The Box of Kitchen Matches.... 447

TRINITY SUNDAY
   "Go Teach all Nations"   Three Roads to God 403

SECOND AFTER PENTECOST
   "Pray Hold Me Excused"   Patron of Misfits 77

THIRD AFTER PENTECOST
   "The Sheep That Is Lost"   Keep the Door Open 520

FOURTH AFTER PENTECOST
   "Depart From Me, for I Am a   Breathless into Heaven 498
   Sinful Man"

FIFTH AFTER PENTECOST
   "Everyone Who Is Angry with   Festering Hate 134
   His Brother"

SIXTH AFTER PENTECOST
   "I Have Compassion on the   Bronx Express 417
   Crowd"

SEVENTH AFTER PENTECOST
   "Beware of False Prophets"   Strange Gods Before Me 475

EIGHTH AFTER PENTECOST
   "Give an Account of thy Stew-   Honesty is the Only Policy 141
   ardship"

NINTH AFTER PENTECOST
   "He Saw the City and Wept   Tears Over a City 11
   over It"

TENTH AFTER PENTECOST
   "Who Trusted in Themselves as   You Can't Marry an Angel 198
   Just and Despised Others"

ELEVENTH AFTER PENTECOST
   "The Bond of His Tongue was   Red Stabbing Tongues 121
   Loosed"

TWELFTH AFTER PENTECOST "Who is My Neighbor?"	The Other Law 114
THIRTEENTH AFTER PENTECOST "Have Pity on Us"	The Problem of Pain 318
FOURTEENTH AFTER PENTECOST "The Works of the Flesh are Licentiousness, Drunkenness, Carousing"	Saturday Night 298
FIFTEENTH AFTER PENTECOST "And She was a Widow"	Christ and Women 17
SIXTEENTH AFTER PENTECOST "When Thou art Invited to a Wedding Feast"	Recipe for a Wedding Cake .. 171
SEVENTEENTH AFTER PENTECOST "Whose Son is He?"	Sawdust Halo 84
EIGHTEENTH AFTER PENTECOST "Thy Sins are Forgiven Thee"	A Sealed Secret 482
NINETEENTH AFTER PENTECOST "The Marriage Feast Indeed is Ready"	The Good Ship Courtship 149
TWENTIETH AFTER PENTECOST "Come Down Before My Child Dies"	Everybody Has Trouble 307
TWENTY-FIRST AFTER PENTECOST "Put on the Armor of God"	The Flag of Christian Courage 339
TWENTY-SECOND AFTER PENTECOST "The Coin of the Tribute"	Tribute to a Coin 410
TWENTY-THIRD AFTER PENTECOST "Their End is Ruin"	Forest Fire 262
LAST SUNDAY AFTER PENTECOST "Those Who are with Child in Those Days"	The Mothers' Saint 91

TOPICS TREATED

(*Reference is to sermon, not to precise page*)

Advent, 233, 255, 347, 355
Aged, 332
All Souls, 490, 498
America, 39
Angels, 129
Angelus, 426
Anger, 233, 311
Annulment, 205
Apostles, 447
Ash Wednesday, 262, 284
Automobiles, 403

Beckett, St. Thomas, 98
Bells, 426
Bereavement, 318, 490
Bible, 440
Blaise, St., 69

Caesar, 410
Catholics, 530
Character, 311, 410, 447
Charity, 114
Cheerfulness, 311
Christ, 11, 17, 24
Christmas, 233, 347, 355, 363, 370, 377
Church, 403, 461
Coin, 410
Commencement, 513
Confession, 482
Conscience, 284
Courage, 311, 339, 383
Courtship, 149, 156, 163, 171, 177, 191
Cross, 11, 311

Death, 318, 490
Deathbed Repentance, 498
Discouragement, 311, 339, 389
Divorce, 191, 205

Drink, 291, 298

Epiphany, 389, 396, 513
Eternal Truths, 417, 422

Fallen Aways, 513
Family, 184, 198, 233, 240, 248
Father, 227, 332
Fatima, 543
Favors, Novena, 461, 469
Forgiveness, 134
Fortune telling, 475
Funeral, 490, 498

Good Intention, 46
Good Example, 447
Good Samaritan, 114
Gossip, 121, 129
Graft, 141

Hatred, 134
Honesty, 141

Infallibility, 505
Ireland, 535

Jesus Christ, 11, 17, 24
John the Baptist, 347
Joseph, St., 84, 227, 324, 347

Kindness, 114, 184
King, Christ the, 339
Kings, The Three, 389, 396, 513
Knock, Our Lady of, 534

Last Things, 422

Maria Goretti, 106
Marriage, 171, 177, 184, 191, 198, 205, 248

Mary, 32, 39, 46, 53, 61, 298, 535, 543, 551
Misfits, Patron of, 77
Mixed Marriage, 177
Money, 410
Mother, 91, 212, 220
Mother-in-law, 248

Nature, God of, 403
Neighbor, 114, 121, 129, 403
New Year's, 383, 389, 426
Nicholas, St., 255

Obscene Speech, 69
Old Maids, 332

Parents, 332
Passions, 262, 269, 277
Pentecost, 447
Perseverance, 389, 513
Pope, 505, 559
Prayer, 46, 454, 461, 469
Providence, 324
Purity, 69, 106, 149, 156, 269, 277, 284

Rash Judgment, 311, 410
Religion, 403
Resignation, 307, 318
Rosary, 53, 61

Sacraments, 433
Saints, 69, 77, 84, 91, 98, 106, 156, 255
Salvation, 255, 410, 417, 422
Samaritan, 114
Scandal, 121, 129
Science, 513
Seal of Confession, 482
Sin, 11, 262, 269, 277, 284, 291, 298
Soul, 255, 396, 410
Stealing, 141
Suffering, 307, 318, 339
Superstition, 475

Temptation, 262, 284, 528
Thomas a Beckett, 98
Three Kings, 389, 396, 513
Throats, Blessing of, 69
Time, 383
Tolerance, 184, 198

Valentine, St., 156

Women, 17
Worry, 324

Youth, 106, 156, 227, 240

THE DAUGHTERS OF ST. PAUL

In Massachusetts
    50 St. Paul's Ave.
    Jamaica Plain
    BOSTON 30, MASS.
    172 Tremont St.
    BOSTON 11, MASS.
    381 Dorchester St.
    SO. BOSTON 27, MASS.
    325 Main St.
    FITCHBURG, MASS.

In New York
    78 Fort Place
    STATEN ISLAND 1, N.Y.
    39 Erie St.
    BUFFALO 2, N.Y.

In Connecticut
    202 Fairfield Ave.
    BRIDGEPORT, CONN.

In Ohio
    141 West Rayen Ave.
    YOUNGSTOWN 3, OHIO

In Texas
    114 East Main Plaza
    SAN ANTONIO 5, TEXAS

In California
    827 Fifth Ave.
    SAN DIEGO 1, CALIF.

In Louisiana
    86 Bolton Ave.
    ALEXANDRIA, LA.

In Florida
    2700 Biscayne Blvd.
    MIAMI 37, FLORIDA

In Canada
    33 W. Notre Dame
    MONTREAL, CANADA
    1063 St. Clair Ave. West
    TORONTO, CANADA

In England
    29 Beauchamp Place
    LONDON, S.W. 3, ENG.

In India
    Water Field Road—Extension
    PLOT N. 143—BANDRA

In Philippine Islands
    No. 326 Lipa City
    PHILIPPINE ISLANDS

In Australia
    58 Abbotsford Road
HOMEBUSH N.S.W., AUSTRALIA

THE TEACHINGS OF THE DESERT FATHERS

Ancient Christian Writers

THE WORKS OF THE FATHERS IN TRANSLATION

ADVISORY BOARD

Boniface Ramsey, *Chair*
John Dillon
Jeremy Driscoll
Thomas Macy Finn
Thomas L. Knoebel
Joseph Lienhard
John A. McGuckin
Thomas P. Scheck

No. 74

THE TEACHINGS OF THE DESERT FATHERS

TRANSLATED AND INTRODUCED
BY
RICHARD J. GOODRICH

THE NEWMAN PRESS
New York / Mahwah, NJ

COPYRIGHT © 2020 BY RICHARD J. GOODRICH

All rights reserved. No part of this publication may be reproduced, stored in a retrieval system, or transmitted in any form or by any means, electronic, mechanical, photocopying, recording, scanning, or otherwise, without either the prior written permission of the Publisher, or authorization through payment of the appropriate per-copy fee to the Copyright Clearance Center, Inc., www.copyright.com. Requests to the Publisher for permission should be addressed to the Permissions Department, Paulist Press, permissions@paulistpress.com.

Library of Congress Cataloging-in-Publication Data
Names: Goodrich, Richard J., 1962– translator.
Title: The Teachings of the Desert Fathers / translated and introduced by Richard J. Goodrich.
Other titles: Verba seniorum. Selections. English
Description: Mahwah, New Jersey : Paulist Press, 2020. | Series: Ancient Christian writers: the works of the Fathers in translation ; no. 74 | Includes index. | Summary: "An English translation of several Latin collections of the *Apophthegmata partum*, including the *Commonitiones Sanctorum Patrum*, *Vitae partum* 6, Paschasius of Dumium's *Geronticon*, and excerpts from *Vitae partum* 3 and 7"—Provided by publisher
Identifiers: LCCN 2019035980 (print) | LCCN 2019035981 (ebook) | ISBN 9780809106455 (hardcover) | ISBN 9781587687198 (ebook)
Subjects: LCSH: Desert Fathers—Quotations.
Classification: LCC BR63 .V4132 2020 (print) | LCC BR63 (ebook) | DDC 271.009/015—dc23
LC record available at https://lccn.loc.gov/2019035980
LC ebook record available at https://lccn.loc.gov/2019035981

ISBN 978-0-8091-0645-5 (hardcover)
ISBN 978-1-58768-719-8 (e-book)

Published by The Newman Press
an imprint of Paulist Press
997 Macarthur Boulevard
Mahwah, New Jersey 07430
www.paulistpress.com

PRINTED AND BOUND IN CHINA

CONTENTS

Acknowledgments xiii

Introduction 1

PART 1:   *ADMONITIONS OF THE HOLY FATHERS* (AP-CSP)

   Chapter One: The Counsel of the Holy Fathers 17

   Chapter Two: Examples of the Holy Fathers
      against the Spirit of Fornication 24

   Chapter Three: An Exhortation of Saint Macarius
      to the Monks 31

   Chapter Four: The Warnings and Examples of the
      Holy Fathers about the Virtues of Humility
      and Patience 32

   Chapter Five: Concerning Doctrine, to the Monks 52

   Chapter Six: Concerning the Blessed Arsenius 60

PART 2:   *THE SYSTEMATIC COLLECTION OF*
             PELAGIUS AND JOHN (AP-PJ)

   Chapter Eighteen: On Foresight or Contemplation 67

   Chapter Nineteen: Concerning the Holy Elders
      Who Performed Miracles 77

   Chapter Twenty: Concerning the Best Manner of
      Life of Different Holy Men 83

   Chapter Twenty-One: Seven Chapters of the Sayings
      Abba Moses Sent to Abba Poemen 97

PART 3: PASCHASIUS OF DUMIUM, *GERONTICON* (AP-PA)

Prologue 111
Chapter One: How the Solitary Should Live in His Cell 111
Chapter Two: On Breaking One's Fast When a
    Brother Arrives 112
Chapter Three: On Conquering Gluttony 114
Chapter Four: That the Recollection of the Perfect
    Man Takes Away the Desire for Food 115
Chapter Five: On Hiding Abstinence 116
Chapter Six: On Tolerating Destitution 117
Chapter Seven: A Monk Should Not Eat Unless He Works 118
Chapter Eight: Against the Spirit of Blasphemy 119
Chapter Nine: On the Origin of Bodily Suffering 120
Chapter Ten: What One Must Pray in Order to
    Resist Demons 121
Chapter Eleven: About How the Passions Are Defeated
    through the Abstinence of Fasting and Vigils 124
Chapter Twelve: On Fleeing Women 125
Chapter Thirteen: Carnal Passions May Be
    Undermined by Hunger and Thirst 126
Chapter Fourteen: Against the Love of Money;
    Concerning the Perfect Renunciation of Wealth 127
Chapter Fifteen: A Monk Should Not Grieve
    If He Loses Something 130
Chapter Sixteen: Tolerating Poverty Leads to Eternal Rest 130
Chapter Seventeen: One Should Not Be
    Scrupulous When Giving Charity 131
Chapter Eighteen: On Restraining Avarice 131
Chapter Nineteen: On the Utility of Clothing 132
Chapter Twenty: On the Origin of Anger 133
Chapter Twenty-One: On Not Returning Evil for Evil 134
Chapter Twenty-Two: On Returning Good for Evil 135
Chapter Twenty-Three: On Not Resisting One's Enemies 135
Chapter Twenty-Four: On Perfect Patience 136

Contents

Chapter Twenty-Five: On Testing Patience 138
Chapter Twenty-Six: On Not Speaking in Anger 139
Chapter Twenty-Seven: That Envy Is Overcome
  through Patience 140
Chapter Twenty-Eight: A Good Thing Must Be
  Condemned for the Sake of Peace 141
Chapter Twenty-Nine: On Perfect Harmony 142
Chapter Thirty: On Patience When Suffering Accusations 144
Chapter Thirty-One: Against the Spirit of Fear That
  Produces Despair 145
Chapter Thirty-Two: Against the Spirit of *Acedia* 147
Chapter Thirty-Three: Against the Spirit of Vainglory 149
Chapter Thirty-Four: Against the Spirit of Pride 153
Chapter Thirty-Five: That the Perfect Do Not Want to
  Perform Miracles Lest They Be Praised for Them 154
Chapter Thirty-Six: Demons Are Conquered and
  Driven Away by Humility 156
Chapter Thirty-Seven: That a Proud Word Makes a
  Good Man Evil, but a Humble Word
  Produces Good from Evil 157
Chapter Thirty-Eight: That Even the Lowly Are
  Helped by the Humility of the Great 158
Chapter Thirty-Nine: That We Are Often Handed Over
  to Sordid Thoughts Lest We Praise Ourselves 159
Chapter Forty: How Slander May Be Avoided 161
Chapter Forty-One: We Should Never Judge or
  Condemn Anyone on Account of Sin 162
Chapter Forty-Two: On the Obedience of the Monks 165
Chapter Forty-Three: That Obedience Frees a Man
  from Every Danger 167
Chapter Forty-Four: Concerning Charity: That You Should
  Do to Others What You Want Done to Yourself 170
Chapter Forty-Five: On God's Command about a Neighbor:
  That You Do to Him What You Wish Done to Yourself 172
Chapter Forty-Six: On Doing the Will of Your Neighbor 172

Chapter Forty-Seven: Not Doing to Others What
You Don't Want Done to Yourself.. 175
Chapter Forty-Eight: We Should Not Embarrass Our Brother 176
Chapter Forty-Nine: On Not Placing the Affections
of Parents before God 177
Chapter Fifty: On Service for the Sick or the Sickness Itself....... 180
Chapter Fifty-One: That Sickness Is Useful for the Body 181
Chapter Fifty-Two: On the Passing of the Perfect 182
Chapter Fifty-Three: On the Fear of God..................................... 184
Chapter Fifty-Four: On Tears and Sorrow.................................... 185
Chapter Fifty-Five: On Repentance... 186
Chapter Fifty-Six: How, through Repentance, a Man
Is Able to Be Reconciled to God in One Day 187
Chapter Fifty-Seven: That Even the Man Who Dies
While Intending Repentance Will Be Received................... 190
Chapter Fifty-Eight: On Prayer.. 195
Chapter Fifty-Nine: On Preferring Prayer to Work 196
Chapter Sixty: On Coming from Work to Prayer,
as to Rest.. 196
Chapter Sixty-One: Of All the Virtues, Prayer
Requires the Greatest Labor 196
Chapter Sixty-Two: Prayer Must Be Sent Out Everywhere
on Account of Traps, Both a Second and a
Third Time... 197
Chapter Sixty-Three: On Continual Prayer.................................. 197
Chapter Sixty-Four: That Continual Prayer Frustrates
the Purpose of the Devil.. 198
Chapter Sixty-Five: That a Person May Pray While Eating........... 199
Chapter Sixty-Six: How One Prays without Ceasing 199
Chapter Sixty-Seven: One Must Constrain the Wandering Eyes,
Lest They Distract the Senses from Prayer.......................... 200
Chapter Sixty-Eight: On the Faithfulness of the
Perfect in Prayer..201
Chapter Sixty-Nine: That the Prayer of the Perfect
Is Profitable Even for the Dead 202

Chapter Seventy: On Revelations 203
Chapter Seventy-One: On Demonic Assault 203
Chapter Seventy-Two: On the War against Thoughts 204
Chapter Seventy-Three: On Disclosing Thoughts
    with Every Work 207
Chapter Seventy-Four: On Discretion 210
Chapter Seventy-Five: That Certain Things Do Not
    Harm Those Who Have Discretion 210
Chapter Seventy-Six: On Mortification 211
Chapter Seventy-Seven: On Perseverance 211
Chapter Seventy-Eight: On the Work of the Saints 212
Chapter Seventy-Nine: Why Those Working So Hard
    Now Do Not Receive Grace Like Men
    Did in the Past 213
Chapter Eighty: Whether the Holy Men Know When
    the Grace of God Comes upon Them 213
Chapter Eighty-One: On Exhortation and Doctrine 214
Chapter Eighty-Two: That Teaching Can Be Conferred
    through Example Alone, without Words 215
Chapter Eighty-Three: Knowledge Gained through the
    Experience of Work Is Stronger than What
    Is Gained by Reading 216
Chapter Eighty-Four: On the Divine Scriptures 216
Chapter Eighty-Five: On Saying Nothing to Those
    Who Are Curious about Scriptural Questions 217
Chapter Eighty-Six: On Avoiding Curiosity 218
Chapter Eighty-Seven: On Avoiding Disputes 219
Chapter Eighty-Eight: On Silence 219
Chapter Eighty-Nine: On Pilgrimage 221
Chapter Ninety: On Fleeing the Honor of the
    Priesthood 222
Chapter Ninety-One: On the Foolishness of the Perfect 223
Chapter Ninety-Two: On the Quiet Life 223
Chapter Ninety-Three: On the Desert, and Why
    Men Flee to the Desert or into Solitude 224

Chapter Ninety-Four: There Should Be a Great Silence
in Solitude, an Absence of All Noise 229

Chapter Ninety-Five: Concerning the Practices of
the Hermits.. 229

Chapter Ninety-Six: On How One Should Live in
the Monastery... 230

Chapter Ninety-Seven: One Should Not Move from
Monastery to Monastery 232

Chapter Ninety-Eight: Which Brothers Share the Same Merit?..... 232

Chapter Ninety-Nine: What Should Be the General
Life of All...233

Chapter One Hundred: On Not Speaking about the
Holy Scriptures Unless Asked 234

Chapter One Hundred One: The Seven Sentences
That Abba Moses Spoke to Abba Poemen 235

PART 4: *APOPHTHEGMATA PATRUM*, PSEUDO-PASCHASIUS OF DUMIUM (AP-PA)

Chapter Thirteen: Against the Spirit of Pride 239

Chapter Nineteen: On the Indulgences for the Weak,
and on Weakness Itself... 239

Chapter Twenty-One: On the Fear of the Lord 244

Chapter Twenty-Two: On Repentance... 244

Chapter Twenty-Seven: On Perseverance 245

Chapter Thirty-Two: On Silence.. 245

Chapter Thirty-Six: Which Brothers Share the Same Merit?...... 245

Chapter Thirty-Seven: Temporal Profit Is Relinquished
for the Sake of a Love for Charity......................... 246

Chapter Thirty-Eight: How Lamentation and Poverty,
Which Are Done for God, Work............................247

Chapter Thirty-Nine: In This Life, a Man Will Be
Unable to Find Rest...247

Chapter Forty: The Source of Vices... 248

Chapter Forty-One: Which Virtues Should One Obtain? 248

Chapter Forty-Two: How Should One Live in the Monasteries?. 249

Chapter Forty-Three: Which Spiritual Disciplines
    Must Be Observed? 249

Chapter Forty-Four: On the Meditations of the
    Twelve Anchorites 251

PART 5: *APOPHTHEGMATA PATRUM*, PSEUDO-RUFINUS
         (AP-PR)

Abbreviations and Bibliography.. 265

Indexes.. 269

    Subject.. 269

    Stories by Named Monk 276

    Scriptural Citations and Allusions... 278

ACKNOWLEDGMENTS

I am again reminded that no work of scholarship occurs in isolation. Although colleagues and friends may not sit with me as I puzzle over odd Latin syntax, they nevertheless make a great contribution to the work I do. I am privileged to be a member of the History Department at Gonzaga University, which provides a collegial context for my academic endeavors. I also owe a debt that I will never be able to repay to my patient Latin master, David Miller.

This is the third book I have published with Paulist Press, and I am always grateful for the encouragement and guidance I receive from my peerless editor, Nancy de Flon.

Most of all, however, I must acknowledge the daily love and support I receive from my wife, Mary. She is the main reason I would never flee the world to become a desert father.

INTRODUCTION

This volume offers an English translation of three early Latin collections of the sayings (*apophthegmata*) of the Egyptian desert fathers. These collections were compiled in the middle of the fifth century and are some of the earliest examples of the written versions of the *Apophthegmata Patrum* (the *Sayings of the Desert Fathers*).

Background

In AD 407, the Mazices, a people from the western deserts of modern Libya, moved east and attacked the Egyptian monastic settlement in Scetis. Egypt's epicenter of monastic life was devastated, and the surviving monks fled before the marauders.[1]

> When Scetis fell, Arsenius departed weeping, saying, "The world has lost Rome, and the monks have lost Scetis." (AP-G Arsenius 21)

Many of these refugees resumed their ascetic life in the deserts of Palestine. In their new land they shared stories about their illustrious predecessors, men like Anthony, Arsenius, Pambo, and Poemen. Their stories were a living source of doctrine and inspiration, tales intended to ensure continuity with those who had first charted the ascetic lifestyle. They employed the words of their *abbas* (fathers, masters) to instruct those who wished to pursue the monastic way of life. As the century unfolded, anonymous editors began to collect, arrange, and record the sayings and stories of that heroic first generation of Egyptian monks. Collections became books, an ironic development among those who had once doubted the value of the written word:

> A philosopher said to the blessed Anthony, "How do you tolerate, Father, being deprived of the consolation that comes from the volumes of Scripture?"

> Antony replied, "My book is the nature of created things, and it is present whenever I want to read the words of God." (AP-PA 84.3)

Although the process of this codification (and the order in which collections were established) has yet to be fully understood, scholars agree that by the end of the fifth century, several major collections of monastic sayings (the *apophthegmata patrum*) were in circulation. Scholarly monks met Babel's challenge by producing versions in a variety of languages: Greek and Latin, the primary tongues of the Roman Empire, as well as Armenian, Coptic, Ethiopic, and Syriac. These texts, as entire collections, or often subsets, were arranged, rearranged, adapted, and reshaped. Stories were combined to form entirely new *apophthegms*. Stories were reassigned to other monks. Difficult texts were smoothed; theologically suspect material was effaced. This process continued for centuries.

The result is a bewildering morass of material. The collections are clearly interdependent, but (so far) they have resisted modern attempts to understand their transmission history. Short of the discovery of new manuscripts, or the application of computer technology in an innovative manner, it is unlikely that this tangle will ever be resolved.[2]

Despite our inability to make much sense of the origins of our collections, as time passed, several major streams emerged. The best-known collection is the Greek *Alphabetical Collection* (hereafter abbreviated AP-G). This text is arranged in a loose alphabetical order, with *apophthegms* grouped under the names of individual abbas. It contains nearly one thousand stories that are attributed to 130 different monks. It was long assumed that this was the ancestor of all subsequent collections.

In many of the earlier manuscripts, AP-G is accompanied by the Greek *Anonymous Collection* (AP-GN). This was a collection of more than eight hundred *apophthegms* that arranged material in a loose, topical order. For the most part (there are exceptions) these *apophthegms* are not assigned to an abba. The initial collection began life as a supplement to AP-G, a collection of afterthoughts that had not been integrated into the alphabetical series. It was an appendix, and in its original form it probably consisted only of the *apophthegms* found in AP-GN 133–369. As time passed, editors added more stories to the AP-GN until it reached its present form.[3]

The Greek *Systematic Collection* (AP-GS) drew stories from both AP-G and AP-GN and rearranged them thematically. In this collection the *apophthegms* are grouped into twenty-one chapters, each of which is devoted to a single topic: Poverty, Humility, Discretion, and so on. The stories, at least in the early part of each chapter, are arranged alphabetically, which suggests that the AP-GS was created after the AP-G and depended on the earlier Greek collections.[4]

Early twentieth-century scholars assumed that these three Greek collections reflected the earliest stages of the written versions of these works. That is, when the earliest editors began to codify this material, they wrote in Greek. The Latin translations were second-generation works, dependent upon and subsequent to the great Greek collections. In the second half of the twentieth century, scholars such as Jean-Claude Guy challenged this view, and now most scholars believe that our Latin collections are based upon primitive Greek editions that were older than the fully realized Greek collections that are extant today. The Greek collections were not fixed when originally composed, but rather went through several editions. The Latin collections offer a snapshot of the state of the Greek collections at the moment of translation.

An example of this may be found in the relationship between the Greek *Systematic Collection* (AP-GS) and the Latin *Systematic Collection* attributed to Pelagius and John (AP-PJ). Both of these collections are divided into twenty-one chapters.[5] The first twenty chapters treat the topics in the same order; AP-GS 1 and AP-PJ 1 both contain sayings about progress in perfection, AP-GS 2 and AP-PJ 2 discuss silence, and so on. This parallelism continues to AP-GS 20 and AP-PJ 20, chapters that discuss virtuous living.

The stories presented within the parallel chapters also follow the same order. AP-PJ 1.1, a story in which a monk asks Abba Anthony how to please God, is reflected in AP-GS 1.1. The next story (AP-PJ 1.2 and AP-GS 1.2) features an interaction between Abba Pambo and Abba Anthony. The identical sequence of stories persists over the entire collection. The only difference between the two collections is that the Latin AP-PJ does not contain as many stories as the Greek AP-GS. Although the shared stories are arranged in the same order, many of the stories found in AP-GS are not found in AP-PJ.

The fact that the chapters of both collections treat their subjects in the same order, and within those chapters the shared stories follow the same sequence, is certain proof of a relationship between the two works. If one believed in the priority of the Greek collections, then it would be natural to assume that the Latin translators of AP-PJ had used AP-GN as their source text.[6]

When one examines the two texts, however, it quickly becomes evident that this relationship cannot stand. AP-GS contains a number of additions drawn from later monastic history and the later *apophthegms* of AP-GN. An example of this may be found in AP-GS 3.7–14, eight *apophthegms* drawn from the *Spiritual Discourses of Abba Isaiah of Scetis*. *Apophthegms* from this later work are woven throughout AP-GS but are missing in AP-PJ. It is clear that AP-PJ translated an earlier edition of AP-GS. After the Latin translation was created in the middle of the sixth century, additional material was added to AP-GS, expanding the collection until it reached its present form.[7]

This suggests that our Latin collections are far more than derivative translations of more important Greek sources; they are a valuable contribution to our understanding of the textual evolution of these collections. Collections like AP-PJ capture a moment, offer a snapshot of the state of a text at a particular moment in time. Moreover, some of the other Latin collections, such as the *Admonitions of the Holy Fathers* (*Commonitiones Sanctorum Patrum*; hereafter AP-CSP) and Paschasius of Dumium's *Geronticon* (AP-PA), may be some of the oldest collections in existence.

Heribert Rosweyde and the Genesis of This Translation

The Jesuit scholar Heribert Rosweyde was one of the first editors to work on the Latin collections. In the seventeenth century, he gathered and collated ten Latin manuscripts that related to the desert fathers and published them as his *Lives of the Fathers* (*Vitae Patrum*).[8] These ten manuscripts included Latin authors such as Jerome, Rufinus, John Cassian, and Sulpicius Severus, as well as four Latin collections of *apophthegmata*:

VP3: *The Sayings of the Desert Fathers, Attributed to Rufinus*
VP5: *The Systematic Collection of Pelagius and John I*
VP6: *The Systematic Collection of Pelagius and John II*
VP7: *The Geronticon of Paschasius*

Rosweyde's work was reprinted by Migne in volume 73 of the *Patrologia Latina*, and for several centuries, Rosweyde's versions were the only critical editions of these Latin collections.[9] With the exception of VP5/6, these works have received little scholarly attention.

My original plan for this volume was to translate and publish VP3, VP6, and VP7. Since VP5, the first half of the work attributed to Pelagius and John, has been translated into English by Owen Chadwick[10] and Sister Benedicta Ward,[11] it did not seem important to offer a new translation of that text. Oddly enough, neither Chadwick nor Ward chose to translate the second half of this work, VP6. This was a peculiar omission, as the systematic collection of Pelagius and John is incomplete without VP6. Unable to find any English translations of VP6, I chose to translate it for this volume and decided to supplement it with VP3 and VP7. This would ensure that most of Rosweyde's Latin collections were readily accessible in a single volume.[12]

As I studied these works, I became aware of the interrelatedness of the collections. VP3 and VP7 share 159 stories, and many of these are also found in VP5/6. My initial impression was that VP3 represented a development of VP7, although there was enough unique material in the two sources to suggest that both might have drawn upon a common source.

While researching Paschasius of Dumium (the putative author of VP7), I encountered the textual studies of the Portuguese scholar José Freire. In 1971 Freire published a critical edition of Paschasius's *Geronticon* (AP-PA), a Latin translation of a Greek collection of *apophthegms*, made at the monastery of Dumium, in modern day Portugal.[13] Freire was able to show that the collection that Rosweyde had published as VP7 was actually an abbreviated form of Paschasius's longer version. Since it seemed preferable to prepare a translation based on the best (and fullest) critical edition, I used Freire's text as the basis for the translation of Paschasius's *Geronticon* (hereafter abbreviated AP-PA) in this volume. The shortened text, printed by Rosweyde as VP7, is now commonly known as Pseudo-Paschasius's *Geronticon* (AP-Pa). Pseudo-Paschasius's collection does offer twenty-three *apophthegms* and a small collection entitled "The Meditations of the Twelve Anchorites" that are not found in AP-PA. These additions to the collection are printed in part 4.

Vitae Patrum 3 was the final mystery of Rosweyde's text. This collection of 220 *apophthegms*, which Rosweyde credited to Rufinus, shared 159 of its stories with VP6 and AP-PA. The source of the other stories was not clear. Ultimately, Freire's work provided the answer. In 1974, he published a second collection known as the *Commonitiones Sanctorum Patrum* (*Admonitions of the Holy Fathers*; AP-CSP). Freire had discovered this previously unknown collection while preparing his critical edition of Paschasius. This collection is the source of forty-seven stories found in VP3 (hereafter referred to as Pseudo-Rufinus; AP-PR). AP-PR offers fourteen stories (including three taken from the letters of Jerome) that are not found in either AP-PA or AP-CSP. These excerpts are printed in part 5 of this volume.

The Latin Collections

This volume offers translations of three early Latin collections (AP-CSP, AP-PJ, AP-PA), as well as excerpts from Rosweyde's VP3 (AP-PR) and VP7 (AP-Pa) that do not appear in the three collections.

THE ADMONITIONS OF THE HOLY FATHERS (*COMMONITIONES SANCTORUM PATRUM*; AP-CSP)

Although scholars typically regard AP-PJ as the oldest of the Latin collections, it is possible that AP-CSP deserves the prize for antiquity. AP-CSP offers a primitive, systematic arrangement of *apophthegms*. It is divided into six chapters. Chapters 1 and 2 address the topics of abstinence and the battle against lust. Chapter 3 offers a brief exhortation credited to Abba Macarius on the topic of resisting impure thoughts. Chapters 4 and 5 treat humility and a monk's relations with relatives. The final chapter contains six stories about Abba Arsenius.

As a collection, and a guide for monastic life, AP-CSP is of limited value. It does not address the range of topics considered in either AP-PJ or AP-GS. From an evolutionary standpoint, it appears to represent an early attempt to create a systematic arrangement, one in which the full curriculum of topics that might be useful for the monk had yet to be delineated.

Moreover, the internal alphabetical arrangement that gives structure to AP-PJ and AP-GS is not found in AP-CSP. As is well established, the two other systematic collections group their stories thematically (lust, humility, discretion, and so forth) and then within the chapters, the stories tend to follow the order found in the AP-G/AP-GN collections. That is, there is a rough alphabetical arrangement of stories within each systematic chapter. Although AP-CSP shares forty-five of its stories with AP-PJ/AP-GS, it lacks the alphabetical arrangement found in AP-G or the sequence found in AP-GN that creates the sub-ordering of the other systematic collections. As noted above, Guy and others have argued that AP-GN 133–369 represents the earliest core of the anonymous collection. With the exception of one *apophthegm* (AP-CSP 4.12/AP-GN 451), all stories shared with AP-GN are drawn from this primitive core. This would tend to suggest that AP-CSP is an early witness to the state of AP-GN, before subsequent stories were added to its original core.

Another interesting variation may be found in the division of material. With the exception of AP-CSP 2 and AP-PJ/AP-GS 5 (the chapters on lust in the three works), AP-CSP and the two other collections do not agree on how stories should be grouped. To take one example, the stories AP-CSP gathers under one heading (abstinence, chapter 1) are scattered across four chapters of the other two systematic collections (self-control, fortitude, doing nothing for show, and discretion). It seems clear that although AP-CSP shares material with AP-PJ and AP-GS, it represents an independent editorial arrangement.

It should also be noted that although four of the chapters could be regarded as sharing systematic qualities, two chapters reject this pattern. Chapter 3 contains a single story, a lengthy exhortation attributed to Abba Macarius. This exhortation is not found in any of the Greek or Latin collections. Its only parallel is found in the Latin version of Palladius's *Lausiac History*, 9.[14] Chapter 6 forsakes a topical arrangement and instead offers six stories about Abba Arsenius, one of the leading luminaries among the second generation of monks. As noted above, the order of the stories in this chapter does not correspond to the arrangement we find today in AP-G.

In short, the qualities I have mentioned suggest that AP-CSP might be an early collection, a first step on the pathway that led to the better arranged collections we know today. It would not be appropriate to be dogmatic about this proposal, but it is possible that AP-CSP is one of the earliest entries in our corpus.

THE SYSTEMATIC COLLECTION OF PELAGIUS AND JOHN (VITAE PATRUM 6: AP-PJ)

The Latin systematic collection attributed to Pelagius and John is far better known than AP-CSP. Unfortunately, it suffers from the same benign neglect that characterizes the other Latin collections.

We have yet, for instance, to see a modern critical edition for this collection. Apart from the textual notes published by Chadwick,[15] we are still forced to rely on Rosweyde's edition.

Another unfortunate aspect of our reliance on the work of Rosweyde was his division of this material into two separate works (VP5 and VP6). It is clear that this must have been one collection in its earliest form. The division between VP5 and VP6 occurs in the middle of chapter 18, "On Foresight or Contemplation." VP5 contains the first twenty *apophthegms* of chapter 18, and VP6 has seventeen more. Its parallelism with AP-GS suggests a unity that was disturbed at a later time. This makes a modern presentation awkward. I have elected to reunify the collection and to begin the second part of AP-PJ (VP6) with the number 21, continuing the sequence that was abandoned at the end of VP5, rather than 1.1 (the numbering that begins in Rosweyde's VP6).

Tradition suggests that this collection was translated from a Greek manuscript by the Roman deacons Pelagius and John. It is often said, although nowhere proven, that these were the same men who became Pope Pelagius I (556–61) and Pope John III (561–74). If this attribution is accurate, then it would be logical to assume that AP-PJ should be dated to the middle of the sixth century, possibly between the years 538 and 555.[16]

THE GERONTICON OF
PASCHASIUS OF DUMIUM (AP-PA)

The largest collection presented here is attributed to Paschasius of Dumium. Paschasius was a monk at the Abbey of Dumium in northwest Portugal, which was, at that time, in the kingdom of the Suevi.

The monastery was founded by a Gallic missionary named Martin of Braga. Martin had arrived in the country around 550. After winning the favor of the local king, Chararich, he had been granted the right to establish a monastery at Dumium. From 550 to 556 he served as abbot of this monastery and, in 556, was elevated to the bishopric of Braga. He would hold that position until his death in 579.[17]

While serving as abbot, Martin translated a selection of 110 Greek *apophthegms* into Latin. This collection, the *Sayings of the Egyptian Fathers* (AP-M), was based upon a Greek manuscript that Martin had brought with him. It appears to have been written for the purpose of instructing the monks who would spend their lives in the monastery of Dumium.

After this work was completed, Abbot Martin asked one of his monks, Paschasius, to translate a different Greek manuscript into Latin.[18] It would appear that Martin was still the abbot of the monastery at this time, which would place the composition date in a very small window (550–56).[19]

Although late antique attributions always remain open to challenge and revision, there does not seem to be any good reason to believe that these works were not written by Martin and Paschasius. Consequently, we can be confident that the dating is secure, and this represents a fixed point in the history of these manuscripts. In his prologue, Paschasius tells his readers that his translation was based on a single Greek manuscript, and that he had translated it exactly as it had been given to him.[20]

One of the most interesting structural qualities of Paschasius's text is its extreme systematization. The AP-PJ/AP-GS tradition divides its material into twenty-one chapters. AP-PA is divided into 101 chapters. The Greek version behind AP-PA was far more systematic than the Greek manuscripts that underpinned AP-PJ/AP-GS. If AP-PA represents a simple translation of its Greek source, then by the mid-sixth century there were two independent Greek systematic collections.

AP-PA (EXCERPTS)

As noted above, the collection of Paschasius comes down to us in two manuscript traditions. There is the longer (original) work of Paschasius (AP-PA), and a shorter, abbreviated collection (AP-Pa), which Rosweyde published as VP7. The abbreviated collection contains forty-four chapters, as opposed to the 101 of AP-PA. As might be expected, the editor of AP-Pa consolidated the chapters of AP-PA, grouping material from multiple chapters of the AP-PA into single chapters of AP-Pa.[21] There was also a considerable reduction in the total number of stories: the 357 stories of AP-PA have been cut down to 162.

It is rather surprising, in view of the clear desire of an editor to reduce the number of stories in the collection, to find that there are twenty-three *apophthegms* in the AP-Pa that do not appear in AP-PA. Most of the added stories were drawn from Martin of Braga's *Sayings* (AP-M), with the rest coming from the alphabetical and systematic collections, as well as other sources, such as Palladius's *Lausiac History*.

This drastic revision of AP-PA occurred at an early date. Our oldest manuscript evidence for this collection can be dated to 819

(Brussels, 3595 [8216–18]).[22] Consequently, we have two more data points that might be studied to yield insights on the methodology employed by medieval monastic editors.

Since most of the stories found in AP-Pa simply replicate (with subtle differences) the material found in AP-PA, it did not seem useful to reduplicate them in a volume whose length must necessarily be constrained by the economics of publishing. Nevertheless, I have elected to publish the twenty-three *apophthegms* that were added to AP-PA as a short collection of extracts (see part 4).

AP-PR (EXCERPTS)

The collection that Rosweyde published as *Vitae Patrum* 3,[23] hereafter abbreviated AP-PR, contains 220 stories. Of these stories, 190 are found in AP-PA. The first forty stories in this collection are drawn directly from AP-CSP. Rosweyde believed that this was an early collection of stories, and he advanced the possibility that the fourth-century writer Rufinus might have been its author. Modern scholars have rejected that attribution, and it seems clear that AP-PR (*Apopthegmata Patrum Pseudo-Rufinus*) is a later assemblage of stories that is largely drawn from AP-PA and AP-CSP.

To save space and avoid unnecessary repetition, I have not translated the stories from this collection that are found elsewhere in this volume (AP-CSP, AP-PJ, and AP-PA). Twelve stories, drawn from sources such as Rufinus's translation of the *History of the Monks of Egypt* and Jerome's *Epistles*, remain and are printed as excerpts from AP-PR (see part 5).

A Note about the Translation

When rendering an ancient text into a modern language, it is necessary for every translator to find his or her place on a spectrum whose anchor points are literalness and readability. A translation that rigidly adheres to the syntax and arrangement of the original may baffle a modern reader; likewise, the translation that goes too far to recast ancient materials in a modern idiom may lose its value for the scholar.

I have tried to pursue the *via media* in this version; when forced to choose between the two extremes, I have placed readability over original authorial arrangement. There is a considerable amount of interest in this material from a general readership, and it seemed that providing a readable text for nonacademic readers was a desirable goal.

This text has three useful features that will facilitate further research in this field. The first is a complete index that categorizes the material by topic, by the names of the monks mentioned in each *apophthegm*, and by any biblical verses cited in the story.

The second feature is an exhaustive cross-reference for each *apophthegm*. After each story, I have tried to list all of the other places in the major collections where a version of the story may be found. For example, in the following story (AP-PA 1.1), the cross-reference, at the end of the *apophthegm* in square brackets, indicates that a parallel version of the story may also be found in AP-PR and AP-Pa.

> One brother asked Abba Sisoes how he ought to spend the time in his cell. Abba Sisoes replied, "Eat your bread and salt, and let there be no need to cook anything." [AP-PR 44; AP-Pa 1.1]

A key for the abbreviations employed in the cross-references will be found in the bibliography.

Occasionally an *apophthegm* consists of one or more units that have been stitched together by a collection's editor. The final feature is an attempt to deconstruct the *apophthegms* and trace their subunits. For example, this story (AP-CSP 1.3) is made up of three stories that have been combined:

> 3. **(a)** Some of the brothers questioned this same Blessed John about the reason for abstinence, and he replied to them, "As the Prophet Daniel said, *I did not eat bread from desire* (Dan 10:3)."
> **(b)** He said, as a warning for the brothers, "Consider, most beloved, that nothing is stronger among the beasts than the lion, but because of its belly, it falls into a trap and his deadly and great strength is humiliated."
> **(c)** The Blessed John instructed the brothers with another example: "If a general wanted to conquer a city of his adversaries, he would first take away their food. The penitent enemy would be humbled

by hunger and scarcity, and they would surrender themselves to his rule. It is the same for the passions and vices of our bodies: if they are weakened by the hunger of fasting and the work of keeping vigils, then the power of the demons, our adversaries, is humbled, through which they customarily turn the power of our own bodies against us." [**a:** AP-G Sisoes 23; AP-PA 1.2; PLaus 11c; **b.** AP-PR 66b; PLaus 11d; **c.** AP-G John the Dwarf 3; AP-GS 4.20; AP-PR 66a; AP-PJ 4.19; PLaus 11e]

I have added a series of boldface letters in parentheses to denote the boundaries between the stories, and then, in the cross-reference, have indicated the source of the original units. Hopefully these cross-references will allow those who are interested in tracing these stories to find parallels in other collections.

Notes

1. For a brief discussion of the history of Scetis, see William Harmless, *Desert Christians: An Introduction to the Literature of Early Monasticism* (Oxford: Oxford University Press, 2004), 167–80. For the dispersion of monks after the attacks by the Mazices, see Derwas Chitty, "The Books of the Old Men," *Eastern Churches Review* 6 (1974): 16–17. See also below, Paschasius 96.4.

2. For discussions of the state of the problem, see Samuel Rubenson, *The Letters of St. Anthony: Origenist Theology, Monastic Tradition and the Making of a Saint* (Lund, Sweden: Lund University Press, 1990), 145–52; Samuel Rubenson, "The Formation and Reformation of the Sayings of the Desert Fathers," *Studia Patristica* 55 (Leuven: Peeters, 2013), 5–22; Graham Gould, *The Desert Fathers on Monastic Community* (Oxford: Clarendon Press, 1993), 5–25.

3. See discussion at Jean-Claude Guy, *Recherches sur la tradition grecque des apophthemata patrum* (Brussels: Société des Bollandistes, 1962), 79–83. Guy's work is usefully summarized in Gould, *Desert Fathers on Monastic Community*, 6–7.

4. Rubenson has disputed the reliance of AP-GS on AP-G/AP-GN, arguing that a concordance with Syriac versions demonstrates that AP-GS relies on a source that predated AP-G/AP-GN. Moreover, he believes that it would have been more useful if these collections had begun with a systematic arrangement rather than with the less utilitarian alphabetical arrangement. See Rubenson, *Letters of Anthony*, 148–49.

5. In fact the arrangement is a little more complicated than I have described. AP-PJ is divided into two books in Heribert Rosweyde's text, *Vitae Patrum* V (VP5) and *Vitae Patrum* VI (VP6); see Heribert Rosweyde, *Vitae Patrum de Vita et Verbis Seniorum sive Historiae Eremetica Libri X* (Antwerp, 1628) 559–643, 644–61. VP5 has chapters 1—17 in common with AP-GS, and then midway through chapter 18, it comes to an end (VP5 18.20 matches AP-GS 18.26). The second collection (VP6) begins at this point, and VP6 18.1 matches AP-GS 18.27. VP6 and AP-GS continued from that point in parallel, although AP-GS 21 and VP6 4 share no stories. It seems clear that VP5 and VP6 were originally one manuscript. At some point in their transmission history, they were divided, and Rosweyde maintained this separation in his edition.

6. Tradition asserts that the deacons Pelagius and John (later Pope Pelagius (556–61) and Pope John III (561–74) translated their work from a Greek manuscript in the city of Rome.

7. See discussion in John Wortley, ed., *The Book of the Elders: Sayings of the Desert Fathers, Systematic Collection* (Collegeville, MN: Cistercian Publications, 2012), xix–xxi, for a discussion of the transmission history of the collection.

8. Rosweyde, *Vitae Patrum de Vita et Verbis Seniorum sive Historiae Eremetica Libri X.*

9. See J. P. Migne, ed., *Patrologia Cursus Completus*, vol. 73 (Paris, 1879).

10. Owen Chadwick, *Western Asceticism* (Philadelphia: Westminster Press, 1958), 33–189. Chadwick also conducted a full examination of the manuscripts that underpin this collection and offered a series of emendations to Rosweyde's earlier work (338–60) that are useful to anyone studying this collection.

11. Benedicta Ward, *The Desert Fathers: Sayings of the Early Christian Monks* (New York: Penguin Books, 2003).

12. My later work on Paschasius led me to discover that VP7 had been translated into English in Claude Barlow, trans., *Iberian Fathers*, vol. 1, the Fathers of the Church, vol. 62 (Washington DC: Catholic University of America Press, 1969), 117–71.

13. José Geraldes Freire, ed., *A Versão Latina por Pascásio de Dume dos Apophthemata Patrum*, 2nd ed. (Coimbra, Portugal: Coimbra University Press, 2011).

14. *PL* 74, 354–59c.

15. Chadwick, *Western Asceticism*, 338–60.

16. See J.-C. Guy, ed., *Les Apophtegmes des Peres: collection systematique*, vol. 1, Sources Chretiennes, vol. 387 (Paris: Editions du Cerf, 1993), 80.

17. See Claude Barlow, ed., *Martini Episcopi Bracarensis, Opera Omnia*, Papers and Monographs of the American Academy in Rome 12 (New Haven, CT: Yale University Press, 1950), 2–4, for biographical details. The Suevi were a Germanic confederation that occupied what are now parts of Portugal and Spain, and Braga was their capital.

18. Barlow, *Martini*, 3, 12, suggests that the translations of Martin and Paschasius were based upon the same Greek manuscript, but when he advanced that view, he believed that Paschasius was the author of VP7, which shares many *apophthegms* with AP-M. Freire, *Pascásio*, 93, argued that the two texts were based on different manuscripts.

19. Barlow, *Martini*, 3–4.

20. AP-PA, *Prol.*

21. Although the average number of stories per chapter is similar (3.5 in the AP-PA; 3.4 in the AP-Pa), taking the mode of the story counts reveals that the most common arrangement is one story per chapter in AP-PA and two stories per chapter in AP-Pa.

22. Barlow, *Martini*, 24.

23. Reprinted in Migne, *PL* 73:739–814c.

PART 1
Admonitions of the Holy Fathers (AP-CSP)

Chapter One

THE COUNSEL OF THE HOLY FATHERS

1. **(a)** When the monks questioned a certain father, one of the holy elders, about the reason for abstinence, he said, "My dear sons, in this present life we should maintain a hatred toward all relaxation, bodily pleasures, and what is agreeable to the belly. We should not require honor from humans. Then the Lord Jesus will give us heavenly honors, rest in eternal life, and glorious joy with the holy angels."

(b) Now the same elder said, "It is natural for a man to be hungry, but he must take food to support the needs of his body, rather than in passion or to stuff the belly.

"Sleep is also natural for a man, but not in abundance, or with a relaxation of the body that would counter the discipline through which we are able to humble the passions and vices of the flesh. For excessive sleep renders the mind and self-awareness of a man stupid and lazy. On the other hand, vigils produce greater refinement and purity in one's self-awareness and mind. For this reason, the holy fathers said that holy vigils purify and illuminate the mind.

"Anger is also natural in a man: not when he is stirred up in the agitation of passion, but rather when he becomes angry with himself and his vices, so that he is more easily able to improve and separate himself from them. Even if we should see others do what is crooked and against the precepts of God, we should not become angry about their vices; rather, let us take hold of them diligently, reproach and warn them, so that they might be saved through reforming themselves and attain eternal life." [**a:** AP-PR 1; **b:** AP-PR 2]

2. The holy fathers said about John, who was called "the Dwarf," that when he returned from the harvest, greatly fatigued, he presented himself to the holy elders and after making a prayer with them, he proceeded to his own cell. For a long time he was free to attend to his prayers, readings, and meditations on the Holy Scriptures in silence. He did not engage in daily manual labor.

For he said that he had been spread thin by the work done in its proper time. The tautness of his mind had suffered because of this freedom, and now it was distracted by various thoughts. Consequently, he imposed great abstinence on himself, saying, "Because of the work of the harvest, I spent those days eating bread until I was full. Now, because I am inactive in my cell, I must add abstinence and vigils, so that I might compensate and retrieve the practices that were suspended during those days." [PLaus 11a-b]

3. **(a)** Some of the brothers questioned this same blessed John about the reason for abstinence, and he replied to them, "As the Prophet Daniel said, *I did not eat bread from desire* (Dan 10:3)."

(b) He said, as a warning for the brothers, "Consider, most beloved brothers, that nothing is stronger among the beasts than the lion, but because of its belly, it falls into a trap and its deadly and great strength is humiliated."

(c) The blessed John instructed the brothers with another example: "If a general wanted to conquer a city of his adversaries, he would first take away their food. The penitent enemy would be humbled by hunger and scarcity, and they would surrender themselves to his rule. It is the same for the passions and vices of our bodies: if they are weakened by the hunger of fasting and the work of keeping vigils, then the power of our adversaries, the demons, is humbled, for they customarily use the strength of our own bodies against us." [**a:** AP-G Sisoes 23; AP-PA 1.2; PLaus 11c; **b.** AP-PA 13.1b; AP-PR 66b; PLaus 11d; **c.** AP-G John the Dwarf 3; AP-GS 4.20; AP-PJ 4.19; AP-PA 13.1a; AP-PR 66a; PLaus 11e]

4. There was a certain elder in the inner desert who was working vigorously for many years in abstinence and every spiritual work. Certain brothers came to him, and said with admiration, "Father, how are you able to tolerate this place that is so dry and squalid?"

He replied to them, "All the work of the entire time I have spent in this place does not yet measure up to one of the hours of the eternal torment in Gehenna. We must endure work in the short amount of time allotted to our lives, and wear down the passions in our bodies, so that we might find a perpetual rest in that future and eternal age that never ends." [AP-GN 193; AP-GS 7.32; AP-PJ 7.25; AP-PR 3]

5. The holy elders once told us about a certain brother, saying, "There was a time when the demons were attacking him. At the first hour of the day they stirred up a great hunger and exhaustion in his body, so that he was unable to sustain it internally. Nevertheless, that brother said in his heart, 'It would be better for me to wait somehow

until the third hour and then take some food.' When the third hour came, he again said to his thoughts, 'Especially now I should wait more fervently for the sixth hour.'

"When the sixth hour arrived, he placed his bread in water, saying, 'While this bread is soaking, I should also wait until the ninth hour.' When the ninth hour arrived, as was his custom, he completed all the prayers and the psalmody according to the rule, then, taking the bread, he ate.

"He continued this practice for many days.

"One day he carried out this practice in the same way, from the first hour until the ninth. When he sat down to receive his food at the ninth hour, he saw a large smoke cloud rise from the little basket where the bread (that is, the *paximatia*) was kept, and it exited through the window of his cell.

"Consequently, from that day onward, there was never hunger nor weakness in his body; in fact his heart was so greatly strengthened in faith and abstinence that it did not please him to take food, even after a two-day fast. Thus, assisted by God's grace in his battle, the brother, through his patience, extinguished *gastrimargia*, that is, the passion of gluttony and of strong desire." [AP-GN 145; AP-GS 4.71; AP-PJ 4.58; AP-PR 4]

6. The brothers were begging one of the holy elders to stop the great works that, in his zeal for the spiritual life, he had always maintained.

That man replied to them, "Believe me, my sons, that Abraham, Isaac, and Jacob, the holy patriarchs, and all of the saints, will be saddened in that future blessed age when they see those indescribable gifts of God—those great and unutterable good things—that God himself has prepared for the diligent and for those keeping his precepts. For when a person reaches that age, no more good works may be done or added out of a desire for the holy life." [AP-GN 197; AP-GS 7.36; AP-PJ 7.29]

7. The brothers told a story about a certain brother who lived in that place that is called Cells: "It happened that on a feast day, all of the monks had assembled in the church, which is in the desert. A meal of cooked food had been prepared for all of them, so that after the mass, all of the brothers would be able to refresh themselves there.

"Now there was a certain brother who, after he sat at the table, called the serving brother and said, 'Bring me salt, so that I may take it with the bread.'

"Then the serving brother shouted to the other brothers and those who were listening, 'Bring a little salt so that this brother will be able to eat it with his bread, because he does not accept cooked food.'

"One of the elders rose from the table and said to the brother, 'It would have been better for you, brother, to eat meat in your cell today, than to have heard such a word about your abstinence spoken in the presence of all of the brothers. Do you not know that if anyone performs ascetic acts for the sake of public praise or glory, they will lose all of the work of their abstinence and not attain a reward from the Lord? In fact, they will incur even greater blame in his sight.'" [AP-GN 256; AP-GS 8.26; AP-PJ 8.21; AP-PA 6.2; AP-PR 54]

8. The blessed Abba Poemen often explained the Scriptures of the prophets to the brothers, saying, "Unless the leader of Nebuchadnezzar's cooks had come to Jerusalem, fire would not have burned the temple of the Lord (cf. 2 Kgs 25:9)."

He offered a spiritual explanation of this parable, saying "When the spirit of gluttony strikes us (that is the longing of the stomach for delicacies or a fullness of the belly), if anyone heeds and fulfills the delights and desires of the palate, then a fire of pleasure burns the temple of the Lord, that is, our body, as the apostle says, *Do you not know that your body is a temple of God* (1 Cor 3:16)? And so, if anyone violates the temple of God, the Lord will spoil it." [AP-G Poemen 16; AP-GS 4.32; AP-PJ 4.29; AP-PA 3.7; AP-PR 52; PLaus 20.1]

9. **(a)** Abba Benjamin said, "Once, a priest from Cells and I joined a certain old man who was living in the desert of Scetis, and we brought him a small amount of oil. That man said to us, 'Look, here is the little jar that you gave me three years ago, which has remained full to this day.'

(b) "Consequently, we who were listening to him said, 'What is the reason, father, that you do not taste some of that oil on feast days?'

"He replied, 'I do not want to taste it so that it will not become an established habit, and I might require my food to be prepared with savory oil. Because of that pleasant experience, I might feel compelled to go down to the city or the surrounding villages to buy oil and return to the desert. Then I might go down again and return to my cell, and through this need to go back and forth, as I said, my mind and senses might begin to wander, and I would lose the advantage of the solitary life. For the devil takes many shapes, and he weaves various traps so that he might capture the minds of men.'

"Those of us who were listening admired the prudence and manner of life of this holy elder." [**a:** AP-G Benjamin 2; AP-GS 4.12; AP-PJ 4.12; PLaus 6c; **b:** PLaus 6d-e]

10. **(a)** The same Abba Benjamin told us that they had gone out to a certain old man who detained them for a meal and prepared a dish of cooked lentils for them. He put in some seasoned oil, which he made from the seeds of the radishes that grow in those places.

We said to him, "Father, send out some good oil, so that we will be able to eat."

When he heard our words, he made the sign of the cross and said to us, "Is there another oil besides this? I never heard this."

(b) The elder was brought up from infancy in the desert, and he always lived there among the holy elders. He had never once gone into the cities or villages. [**a:** AP-G Benjamin 3; PLaus 6f; **b:** PLaus 6g]

11. Once, brothers had gone out from the monastery to visit those fathers who were living in the desert. When they had come to a certain elderly hermit, he received them with great joy, and, as was his custom, he set food before them. Seeing that they were exhausted from their journey, he made them take food before the ninth hour; he brought whatever he had in his cell so that they might eat, and thus he restored them.

When evening came, they completed the prayers and psalms according to custom, and did the same later that night. Now, the aforementioned elder was lying quietly in another place, separate from his guests, and he heard the monks talking among themselves, saying, "These hermits eat more and better food at their dinners than those who live in the monasteries."

Overhearing these words, the elder remained silent. When the new day dawned, the monks rose early so that they might continue on to another hermit, who was living near this elder. As they left, the elder said to them, "Greet him for me and tell him, 'Pay attention, and do not water the vegetables.'"

When they came to that second elder, they told him what the first had commanded. He quickly grasped the reason, and he took these same brothers and put them to work weaving baskets. Sitting among them, he did not stop working with his hands. In the evening he added more psalms than was customary to the office, and, after completing the prayers, he said to them, "It is not our normal practice to take food daily, but because of your arrival, we should eat today." He placed dried-out bread and salt before them, saying, "Because you are here, we should eat something more than usual." Then he brought out a small amount of vinegar, salt, and oil.

When the monks rose from the table, he again began to recite psalms and continued almost until dawn. Then he said, "We are unable, because of you, to sing the entire Book of Psalms. Therefore, we should take a little rest, for you are tired from your journey."

When the first hour of the morning arrived, and they wanted to leave him, the elder did not permit it, saying, "It will be better if you remain with us for many days. I cannot send you away today, for charity demands that I keep you here another three days."

Now those monks, hearing this, rose during the night, and before dawn came, they secretly fled from that place. [AP-GN 229; AP-GS 10.150; AP-PJ 10.97; AP-PR 5]

12. Some brothers spoke about Abba Niteras, who was a disciple of Abba Silvanus. They said that when he was living in his cell on Mount Sinai, he abstained moderately from every bodily need. Nevertheless, when he was ordained a bishop in Pharan, he constrained himself severely with the most rigorous abstinence, and he was more eager in vigils and more intent in his prayers.

Seeing this change, his disciple said to him, "What is this, Master? When we were living in the desert you did not work so hard in abstinence."

The blessed man replied, "Consider, brother, that we had a secret and poor life in the desert. Now that we have left the desert, we must converse with secular people, and we are offered many different opportunities. I fear that at the end of my life, we will have offended the Lord at some occasion. For if the holy Apostle Paul—who spoke about having Christ in himself, and who possessed such great virtues of the soul that he ascended, while still in the body, to the third heaven—was able to say, *I beat my body and place it in slavery, lest perhaps while preaching to others, I might find myself rejected* (1 Cor 9:27), what should we humble sinners do?" [AP-G Netras 1; AP-GS 10.50; AP-PJ 10.36; PLaus 20.18]

13. An elder making a morning call had come to another elder, who received him with great joy. On account of his arrival, he prepared

a meal of cooked lentils for his visitor's refreshment. They agreed that, in accordance with their custom, they would complete the prayers and psalmody, and then they would have their meal. When they went in, they chanted the psalms, and completed the entire Psalter. They also recited two books of the prophets from the Holy Scriptures, just as if they were reading. By this time the day had departed, and in the same way, night was slipping away. And so, while they were intently praying and chanting the Psalter, a new day dawned, and only then did they realize that the night had passed.

Nevertheless, they continued to converse about the word of the Lord, expounding its spiritual sense to each other. Finally, around the ninth hour, they paid their respects to each other, and the elder who had made the journey returned to his cell.

They had forgotten to eat the meal that had been prepared. When night arrived, the elder discovered the full pot that he had cooked. Gloomily, he said, "Oh! How could we have forgotten this meal?" [AP-GN 150; AP-GS 4.70; AP-PJ 4.57; AP-PR 6]

14. Abba Zeno told us that once, while he was traveling to Palestine, he grew tired from the exertion of his journey and sat down beneath a tree. There was a field full of cucumbers nearby. Zeno thought that he should rise and take some of the cucumbers to refresh himself. "For it is nothing significant," he said, "that I would be taking."

Then, responding to his own thoughts, he said, "Thieves are sent to their punishments by the orders of the judges. I should test myself to see if I am able to bear the punishments that thieves endure."

Clambering to his feet at that hour, he stood in the heat for five days and fried his body.

Finally, he said to his thoughts, "I am unable to endure torments, and therefore I should not become a thief; it would be better, following custom, to work with my hands and refresh myself by my labors. This is what the Holy Scriptures say in the Psalms: *You will eat by the work of your hands; blessed are you and it will be well for you* (Ps 128:2), and we sing these words in sight of the Lord, every day." [AP-G Zeno 6; AP-GS 4.17; AP-PJ 4.17; AP-PA 3.3; AP-PR 7]

15. The priest, Dioscorus, who lived in the desert of Scetis, said, "A monk should not succumb to the desires of the throat and belly. For how will he be different from secular men if he satisfies his pleasures?

"Next, we often see secular men abstain from delights and delicacies because of illness, so that they might secure bodily health.

How much more should a monk pursue abstinence for the health and safety of his soul, in order to attain those true and eternal delicacies found in paradise and the glory of the heavenly kingdom?" [PLaus 4f]

16. **(a)** Some brothers came to Abba Joseph, a perfect man living in Panephysis, and asked him, "How should we receive the strangers or spiritual brothers who arrive to visit us? Should we relax our rule of abstinence for their sake?"

(b) When he heard these words, the elder replied, "When foreign brothers come to us we should receive them with joy, and, for the sake of God, relax our abstinence because of their arrival. Nevertheless, when we are alone in our cells and no one has come, it is necessary that we maintain our abstinence enthusiastically according to our rule."

The brothers received what they had heard like a command from a man of God. Then they gave thanks and returned to their cells. [**a:** AP-G Joseph of Panephysis 1a; AP-GS 13.1a; AP-PJ 13.1a; AP-PA 2.2a; AP-PR 47a]

◦◦◦

Chapter Two

EXAMPLES OF THE HOLY FATHERS AGAINST THE SPIRIT OF FORNICATION

1. A spirit of fornication was attacking a certain disciple of a holy elder, but, assisted by the grace of the Lord, the disciple was resisting manfully the distressing and unclean thoughts of his heart through fasting and prayer and by burdening himself tremendously with manual labor. Now, the blessed elder, seeing his disciple working in this way, said to him, "If you want, my son, I will pray to the Lord, so that he might remove this assault from you."

The disciple responded, "I see, father, that although I must bear this trouble, good fruit is being perfected in me because in the face of these attacks, I fast more and am able to endure longer vigils and prayers. Therefore I pray that you, as you prevail upon the mercy of God on my behalf, would ask that he give strength to me for as long as I am able to stand and struggle properly."

Then the older holy man said to him, "My son, I now perceive that you certainly understand that this spiritual struggle is perfecting you, through patience, for the health of your soul. For this reason the apostle said, *I have fought the good fight, I have accomplished the course, I have kept the faith; for the rest, a crown of righteousness has been preserved for me, but not only on me, but for all who await his arrival* (2 Tim 4:7–8)." [AP-GN 170; AP-GS 5.24; AP-PJ 5.20; AP-PR 8]

2. There was another brother who was violently attacked by an unclean spirit of fornication. Now, getting up during the night, he went out to a certain holy elder who was well-tested in the virtues, and he confessed to him that he was enduring an attack from a spirit of fornication. When the elder heard these words, he consoled him, teaching with spiritual words about the virtue of patience. "As it has been written," he said, "*Be strong, and your heart will be comforted, all you who hope in the Lord* (Ps 31:24)."

After the brother returned to his own cell, he was struck by another attack. He hurried straight back to the elder mentioned above. When he saw him, the elder again taught that he must endure his tribulation patiently and tirelessly, and he said to him, "Believe, my son, that the Lord Jesus Christ will send help to you from his holy heaven, so that you will be able to overcome this suffering."

Comforted by the teaching of the holy elder, the brother returned to his cell, and again his heart was thrown into great confusion by the attack. So once again, at that same hour of the night, he returned to the elder, and begged him to pray intently to the Lord on his behalf.

The elder said to him, "Do not be alarmed, my son. Do not be unnerved; do not conceal your thoughts. Then the confused unclean spirit will leave you. For nothing strikes the power of the demon as much as when someone reveals their secret and unclean thoughts to the holy and blessed fathers. *Now be strong, my son, let your heart be comforted, and wait for the Lord* (Ps 27:14). For where the battle is harder, there will be a more glorious crown. Finally, as the holy prophet Isaiah said, *Is the hand of the Lord too feeble to save people, or has he burdened his ears so that he is unable to hear?* (Isa 59:1).

"And so consider, my little son, that the Lord anticipated your battle, and he prepared an eternal crown for you who are struggling with the devil. For this reason, the Holy Scriptures warn us, saying, *We must enter into the heavenly kingdom through many tribulations* (Acts 14:22)."

Now the brother, after hearing these words, had his heart strengthened in the Lord; he remained near the elder, and never wanted to return to his own cell. [AP-GN 164; AP-GS 5.16a; AP-PJ 5.13a; AP-PR 9]

3. Once, one of the brothers was being attacked by a struggle with fornication, and he was resisting it through constant abstinence so that he would not yield anything to the unclean desires of the flesh. Afterward, on Sunday, he went to the church that is in the desert where the monks live. He threw himself on the floor, and, in tears, publicly confessed before the entire gathering of monks that he was suffering an attack.

When the holy elders and priests heard these words, they ordered the entire gathering of brothers to fast and to keep vigils for an entire week beyond their custom, begging the Lord and our Savior Jesus Christ to drive the demon away from him.

From that time onward, every attack was stilled in that aforementioned brother. [AP-GN 165; AP-GS 5.17; AP-PJ 5.14]

4. Once, while the blessed Abba Moses was living in the place called Petra, the demon of fornication attacked him viciously, so that he was no longer able to sit in his cell. Moses went to the holy Abba Isidore, and told him about the violence of his attack.

Abba Isidore offered testimony from the Holy Scriptures to console him, but when he asked the young monk to return to his cell, Moses did not want to go back. Then Abba Isidore, together with Abba Moses, climbed above his cell, and he said, "Look to the west and see." Isidore looked and he saw a multitude of demons, violently stirred up with fury, and, as if preparing for a battle, they were hurrying to fight.

Then Abba Isidore said to him, "Now look to the east and see." When he looked, he saw an innumerable multitude of holy angels, glorious and shining brighter than the light of the sun, an army of heavenly power.

Abba Isidore said, "Those you saw in the west are those who fight against the holy people of God. But those you saw in the east are the angels the Lord has sent to assist his holy ones. And so understand that *there are many with us*, just as the prophet Elisha said (2 Kgs 6:16). Also the holy apostle John said, *Greater is he who is in us, than he who is in the world* (1 John 4:4)."

Having been comforted by the Lord, the holy Abba Moses returned to his own cell, giving thanks and glorifying the power of our excellent Lord, Jesus Christ. [AP-G Moses 1; AP-GS 18.17; AP-PJ 18.12; AP-PR 10]

5. There was a certain brother in the desert of Scetis who was always ready and eager to participate in the work of the Lord and in spiritual conversation. A demon, an enemy of humans, sent thoughts into this man so that he would recall the beauty of a certain woman at night, and consequently the thoughts of his heart would violently disturb him.

Now it happened that, through the arrangement of the Lord, another brother from Egypt came to visit the first brother in the grace of Christ. While they were talking, a prophecy came, and the brother from Egypt said, "The woman has died."

This was the same woman about whom the above-mentioned brother was suffering. He heard this, and a few days later, he went to that place where the body of the dead woman had been buried. He opened her tomb at night, and with his robe, he wiped some fluid off her rotting body. Then he returned to his cell and, placing the foul mess in his sight, he said to his thoughts, "Behold, you have the thing you desired and were searching for; satisfy yourself with it."

He tortured himself with the offensive smell until that most sordid attack came to an end. [AP-GN 172; AP-GS 5.26; AP-PJ 5.22; AP-PR 11]

6. Two monastic brothers went to a nearby city so that they might sell the work that they had made with their hands during the year. Now one of them went out to purchase certain necessities for himself; the other remained alone in the inn and, prompted by the devil, he fell into fornication.

When the brother who had gone out returned, he said to the second, "Look, we have sold what we needed; now let us return to our cell."

The other brother replied, "I am unable to go back."

The first brother pleaded with the second, saying, "Why don't you want to return to the cell?"

Then the second confessed, and said, "Because I fell into fornication."

Now, wanting to persuade and save his brother's soul, the first monk swore an oath and said, "I also, when I was separated from you, fell in a similar way into fornication. Now, truly, we must return to our cell and undergo penance, *for all things are possible with God* (Luke

1:37). Therefore, once we have repented, he may decide to grant us forgiveness, so that we won't be tortured in the eternal fire of torments and punishments in the underworld of Tartarus—the place where there is no repentance, only eternal fire without an end and awful torments."

After this, they returned to their cell. Then they went to the holy fathers and threw themselves at their feet, lamenting with much howling and tears, and they confessed the temptation and ruin that had overcome them.

They did everything that the holy elders prescribed and taught them to bring about their repentance. For the sake of his sinning brother, the first brother, who had not sinned, made penance, just as if he too had sinned, because he had great charity.

After a short time, the Lord, seeing the work of that monk's charity, revealed what was the reason to the holy fathers: for the sake of charity, the brother had afflicted himself for the spiritual health of his brother. Consequently, the Lord granted forgiveness to the monk who had sinned. Behold, this is an example of what was written: *He laid down his soul for the welfare of his brother* (1 John 3:16). [AP-GN 179; AP-GS 5.31; AP-PJ 5.27; AP-PR 12]

7. There was also another brother who was enduring harassment by a spirit of fornication. He went to a well-tested elder and pleaded with him, saying, "Let me place my problem before you, most blessed Father, and pray for me, because a spirit of fornication is harassing me."

When the elder heard these words, he began praying, day and night, asking God's mercy for the monk. A little later, the same brother returned, and he asked the elder to pray even more intently for him. Again, with great care, the blessed elder prayed for him.

Now the elder, seeing that the younger brother came frequently and begged him to pray, was greatly astonished because the Lord was not listening to his prayer. That same night, the Lord revealed to him that there was a negligent and unproductive laziness in that monk, and his heart was filled with the pleasures of the flesh.

God then granted a vision to the elder: he saw that monk sitting, and the spirit of fornication, in the forms of various women, was tantalizing him, and he was delighted by them. Then the elder saw the angel of the Lord, standing nearby, deeply displeased with that brother because he was neither getting up nor prostrating himself in prayers to God. To the contrary, he preferred his thoughts. God displayed all of these shortcomings to the holy elder, and he understood that because of that monk's fault and negligent behavior, his prayers were not being heard.

Then the elder said to that monk, "This is your fault, brother, because you are delighted by these evil thoughts. For another person, praying and begging God on your behalf, cannot drive this unclean spirit of fornication from you unless you also accept the work of fasting, praying, and many vigils. You must plead with groans that the Lord Jesus Christ might offer the assistance of his grace to you, so that you will be able to resist these evil thoughts. This is true even in the case of doctors, who make and apply medicines to human bodies: even though they do their job with the greatest diligence, if a sick man refuses to abstain from harmful foods, or from other things that customarily damage the weak, he will gain no benefit from the diligence nor the care of the doctors.

"The same applies to the listlessness of the soul, clearly, when the holy fathers, who are spiritual doctors, pray with every effort and their entire hearts for the mercy of Christ, our Lord and Savior, for those who ask help for themselves through the prayers of these elders. Unless those supplicants do what pleases God with every desire of their minds, in both their prayers and every spiritual work, the prayers of the holy men will not profit them; they cannot help the negligent, the unrestrained, or those who care little about the welfare of the soul."

The brother, when he heard these words, felt compunction in his heart. Then with great diligence, following the doctrine of the elders, he afflicted himself with fasting, prayers, and vigils. Ultimately he won the Lord's mercy and the spirit of the unclean passion withdrew from him. [AP-GN 169; AP-GS 5.23; AP-PJ 5.19; AP-PR 13]

8. There was a monk who lived in the desert. Now after many years, a certain woman from his race and family discovered the place in which the above-mentioned monk lived, and, aroused by the devil, she went into the desert to search for him. When she found him, she entered his cell and told him that she was from his people and was a relative, and that she would remain in the cell with him.

Consequently, the monk fell into ruin by sinning with her.

Now there was another monk, also spending time in the desert, and when he came to the hour for eating, the basin that he had filled with drinking water overturned itself and all of the water soaked into the ground. Now this happened for several days: when dinnertime arrived, the basin overturned. The water soaked into the ground, and he was unable to drink. After pondering the situation, he decided that he should go to that other monk and tell him about the bowl that was overturning and spilling all of the water onto the ground.

Evening arrived while he was on his journey, and he slept in an old, ruined temple of idols. In that place, he heard demons speaking with each other, "Tonight we will push that monk into fornication." Hearing these words, the monk marveled. When the next day dawned, he reached the first monk and found him oppressed by an overwhelming sadness.

The visiting monk said to him, "What should I do, brother? At the hour at which I want to refresh myself, the basin that I use to hold water overturns itself and spills the water so that I do not have anything to drink."

The first monk replied, saying, "You have come to question me because your little basin overturns and spills your water? What should I do? Last night I fell into fornication."

The second brother replied, "I already know this."

"From what source are you able to know it?"

The second monk said, "While on my journey, I was resting at night, and I heard the demons speaking to each other and rejoicing about your lapse. I was deeply saddened."

The first monk responded, "Look, I will get up and go back into the secular world."

Hearing these words, the second monk began to beg him, saying, "Do not do this, brother; remain in this place and practice more patience. We can throw out the woman and let her return to her own place, for it is clear that she is a trap devised by the art of the malignant devil. It would be better for you to remain here, afflicted in heart and body, and with the deepest groans of your heart and tears, until the end of your life, beg the kindness of our Lord and Savior, so that you will be able to find mercy on that terrible day of the great judgment of God." [AP-GN 176; AP-GS 5.28; AP-PJ 5.24; AP-PR 14]

9. There was a brother in the desert who was living in that place called Cells. The demons were assaulting him with the temptation of fornication. Thinking about his situation, he said, "Perhaps it would be best to perform more manual labor in order to extinguish my carnal feelings."

Now this brother was a potter by trade. He rose and molded in clay something like the figure of a woman. Then he said to his thoughts, "Behold, your wife! Now it is necessary that, according to custom, you increase your manual labor."

A few days later, in the same way, he made and molded in clay something like a daughter for himself. He said to his thoughts, "Behold, your wife has given birth to your daughter. It is necessary that you work even more so that you will be able to feed and clothe yourself, your wife, and your daughter."

Consequently, he weakened his body even more with labor, to the point where it was unable to tolerate any more work. Then he said to his thoughts, "Since you are unable to sustain any more work, you do not require a woman."

God, seeing the fervor for chastity displayed by the monk's mind, freed him from the annoyance of the attacking demons, and the monk gave glory to God for the magnitude of his grace. [AP-G Olympius 2; AP-GS 5.50; AP-PR 15]

10. A brother questioned the blessed Abba Poemen, saying, "What should I do, Father? The temptation of fornication assaults me, and I am carried away, suffering this madness."

The holy elder replied, "For this reason especially, the prophet David said, *I was striking the lion and often I was strangling the bear* (1 Sam 17:34–36). This passage should be understood to mean 'I was tearing out the madness from my soul and I was countering fornication with many labors.'" [AP-G Poemen 115; AP-GS 5.11; AP-PR 16]

Chapter Three

AN EXHORTATION OF SAINT MACARIUS TO THE MONKS

1. The holy Abba Macarius was often warning and teaching his disciples, saying, "Remember always that we must spend our lives in the sight of God the Omnipotent, who foresees the thoughts of every man and examines the hearts of all. This is attested in the Holy Scriptures as the apostle teaches: *For the word of God is alive and efficacious, sharper than any double-edged sword, extending to the division of soul and spirit, and a judge of the thoughts and intentions of the heart. There is no*

creature that is hidden from its sight, for everything stands exposed and open to its eyes (Heb 4:12–13).

"And so, brothers, if carnal delight and the desire for fornication is not to batter us, we must hurry to repel and push away from our hearts the dirtiest, unclean thoughts, calling most diligently for the help of our Lord Jesus Christ through prayers and fasts, so that he will rescue us by his power, protect us, and grind Satan beneath our feet.

"For we should take hold of ourselves and say to our souls, 'The delight of the body, which amuses you in a bad way, lasts for only a short period. But the torments and tortures of the soul and body in the eternal fire of Gehenna—these punishments will endure forever.'

"Then, after admonishing our souls, we must say, 'If you are embarrassed by the idea that other men, committing sins similar to yours, might see you sinning, why don't you respect and fear the majesty of the Omnipotent God, who considers the secrets of every heart? For as the apostle said, *Everything is uncovered and open to his eyes* (Heb 4:13).'

"And so, if we rebuke ourselves with words like these, the fear of the Lord comes immediately into our heart, and our soul is established in the love for purity. We are stirred up to carry out all of the Lord's precepts, and we are assisted by the grace of our Lord Jesus Christ, who promised to give a heavenly and eternal life in that glorious future age to those who serve him in holiness and purity. They will receive joy with the holy angels in the perpetual light of his splendor." [PLaus 9k]

Chapter Four

THE WARNINGS AND EXAMPLES OF THE HOLY FATHERS ABOUT THE VIRTUES OF HUMILITY AND PATIENCE

1. The holy elder fathers spoke about a certain monk, by that time quite old, who was living in the desert of Scetis. He had once been a servant, and every year he went down from the desert to Alexandria where his masters lived, bringing them the payments that servants customarily turn over to their owners. His masters had great reverence for him on account of their fear of the Lord, and they

always ran out to meet and greet him, asking that he pray to the Lord on their behalf.

The monk poured water into a bowl and hurried to wash the feet of his masters with all humility, wanting to show his subservience to them. They did not wish to allow him to wash their feet, and said, "It is forbidden, most blessed Father, to burden our souls like this."

He replied, "I am your servant, for the Omnipotent God selected you to be my masters. I give thanks to our Lord, that you have consented to allow me to serve the living and true God, Creator and ruler of the heavens and earth, and to bring you the wages of my service."

His masters argued with him, not wishing to accept the payment that he had brought them.

In response, the elder said to them, "If you refuse to accept my payment, then I must resolve not to return to the desert, but rather, I will stay here in this place and serve you."

Hearing these words, his masters agreed to take the payment, both to keep the monk from being saddened and, even more, so that he would return to his cell, that place in the desert. Consequently, he gave what he had collected as a payment to his unwilling masters. As soon as they had received it, they donated it to the poor.

Later, some of the older brothers were questioning that monk, and they said to him, "We implore you, Father, to tell us why you devote such great attention to this payment that you make in exchange for your service, and why you force it on your masters who do not want it and often resist accepting it from you?"

The elder responded to them, "Brothers, I work on account of slavery, because just as I owe a payment to my masters every year to compensate them, so too do I work, with the assistance of the Lord and the help of our Lord Christ, in fasting and prayers, holy vigils, and in every spiritual work. Thus I make progress toward eternal life, and it contributes to the health of my soul. If, perhaps, I did not make this small payment for my service, all of my spiritual labor, which they permit me to devote to the Lord Christ, would be their payment, and they would get the spiritual reward." [AP-G Mius 2; AP-GS 15.47; AP-PJ 15.31; AP-PR 17]

2. There were two brothers who were actually brothers in the flesh. Nevertheless, each was living in the spiritual intention of a monk. The malignant devil laid snares for them, so that he could split them apart. On a certain day when evening came, the younger brother lit an oil lamp, as was the custom, and placed it on the stand.

Then, stirred up by the demon's malice, he overturned the stand and extinguished the lamp. The wicked devil used this event to separate the pair and provoke a quarrel. The older brother stood up and began to strike his younger brother in anger.

The younger brother, lying on the ground, began to beg his brother, saying, "Be magnanimous, Master, and I will relight the lamp."

And so, because the younger brother did not respond to the elder with wild words, the demon was thwarted and he immediately withdrew from them. That night, it made its way straight to the leader of the demons and said, "Because of the humility of that monk, who begged forgiveness from his brother while he lay prostrate on the ground, I was unable to defeat them. When God saw his humility, he poured his grace upon him, and I felt myself to be violently twisted and tortured, so that I was unable to split them apart."

Now a pagan priest, who was staying there, heard all of these words. His heart was struck with compunction in the fear of the Lord and the love of Jesus Christ. Deciding that the cult of idols was intended to mislead and destroy souls, he abandoned all of these practices and immediately hurried to the holy fathers at the monastery. There he told them everything he had heard the wicked demons saying to each other. Then, with salutary counsels, the holy fathers taught him about the doctrine of the Lord and Savior, and they baptized him. Through the holy practices of the monks, he seized life.

Aided by, and cooperating with, the grace of God, he became a highly regarded monk. He was deeply venerated and he was so humble that everyone admired his great humility. He often said, "The application of oneself to humility destroys every power of our demonic adversaries. Through humility, our Lord Jesus Christ triumphed over the devil and destroyed all of his power."

He also added that when he had heard the demons speaking among themselves, they often said, "When we inflame the hearts of men to anger, if anyone endures our jeers with patience, and turning away should continue to ask for those qualities that lead to peace, saying 'I sinned,' then immediately we perceive all of our strength to be weakened, because the grace of divine power draws near to him." [AP-GN 77; AP-GS 15.112; AP-PJ 15.89; AP-PR 18]

3. Once the blessed elder Poemen said to the brothers, "There was a certain new monk in Constantinople, during the time of Emperor Theodosius. He was living in a small cell near the city gates,

in the suburbs that are called the seventh district, where the emperors customarily left the city to spend their time pleasantly.

"Now the emperor, hearing that a hermit who never left his cell was living there, began walking to find the place where the above-mentioned monk lived, and he issued commands to the eunuchs who were accompanying him that none of them should approach the cell of that monk. Only he, by himself, would go forward and knock on the door.

"When the monk arose and opened the door to him, he did not know him, for the emperor had removed the crown from his head so that he would not be recognized. After a prayer, the two sat together, and the emperor questioned the monk, saying, 'How do the holy fathers spend their time in Egypt?'

"The monk replied, 'They all pray to God for your well-being.'

"The emperor, looking around the cell intently, saw nothing in it except for some dried crusts of bread, hanging in a basket. He asked the monk, 'Give me your blessing, Abba, so that we might refresh ourselves.'

"The monk lost no time, and he quickly produced water, salt, and small morsels of food. They ate together. The monk presented a cup of water and the emperor drank.

"Then the emperor said, 'Do you know who I am?'

"The monk replied, 'I do not know. Who are you, Lord?'

"Theodosius said, 'I am Emperor Theodosius, and I came here on account of devotion.'

"When the monk heard this, he prostrated himself before the emperor.

"Theodosius said to him, 'Blessed are you monks who, secure and free from secular duties, enjoy a tranquil and quiet life, and have a responsibility only for the well-being of your soul, so that you are able to enter into eternal life and a heavenly reward. I tell you, in truth, that because I was born to rule, and I now spend my time ruling, I never eat my meal free from worries.' After these words, the emperor paid reverence, very honorably, to the monk, and then he departed.

"Now, the same night, the servant of God began to think to himself, 'Perhaps I should not remain in this place, for many—not only from the common people, but also the prelates and senators—will follow the emperor's example and come to see me, and they will not stop honoring me, a lowly servant of God. Although they will do this in the name of God, I fear that the wicked devil might seize me, and I would begin to receive them gladly, and my heart might take delight in the praise and honor they offer me. Then, through these interactions, I would lose the virtue of humility and come to delight in the praise and honor of men.'

"After thinking all of these thoughts, the man of God fled from his cell that same night, and he made his way to the holy fathers in the Egyptian desert.

"And so we should consider, dearest brothers, with what great concern the servant of God dedicated himself to guard the virtue of humility, so that he would deserve through the work of his holy life, which he carried out on account of the name of the Lord to be known by the Lord Christ in the glory of the eternal, heavenly kingdom." [AP-GN 308; AP-GS 15.85; AP-PJ 15.66; AP-PR 19]

4. Now the other holy elders also spoke about that same holy Poemen, saying, "One time, a provincial judge, who had heard of the holy reputation of the blessed Poemen, had come and wanted to see him. The judge sent a messenger to ask the holy man to receive him.

"The blessed Poemen was deeply saddened and thought to himself, 'If the nobility begin to come to pay their respects and honor me, it is clear that many other people will also crowd around me. This means that my hidden life will be disturbed. My way of life and the grace of humility—which with great effort and the assistance of God, I have worked to maintain from my childhood—will perhaps be lost through the pilfering of the malignant devil, and I will run into the snares of vainglory.'

"Consequently, after considering his thoughts, he decided to excuse himself and he did not receive the judge.

"Now the judge was saddened because the monk would not receive him, and he said to his attendant, 'I believe that my sins are the reason I did not deserve to see the man of God.' Nevertheless, he still hoped to find some occasion to see the holy man. And so, he contrived a reason that would create an opportunity to see him. He arrested the son of the blessed Poemen's sister, and sent him to prison, so that through this affair, the holy man might receive him, or at least he might come to petition the judge for the boy's release.

"The judge told his attendant, so that the holy man would not be saddened, 'Tell him that if he wants to come to me, it is inevitable that we would immediately release his nephew from prison. Otherwise, his crime is so serious that he cannot leave without punishment.'

"Now, hearing this, the boy's mother, that is, Poemen's sister, went into the desert where her brother lived. Standing outside the door of his cell, with many tears and moans, she begged him to go visit the judge and intercede for her son. But the blessed Poemen not only said nothing to her, but he also did not open the door so that she could come in to him.

"Then she began to curse him, saying, 'Oh hardest and most impious man, bearing a heart of iron—how can my weeping and such grief not incline you to mercy, especially when I only have one son, whom I see standing in danger of death?'

"Then Poemen sent a message to her through the brother who attended him, saying, 'Go and say to her, «Poemen has not fathered any sons, and consequently, he does not suffer.»'

"When the judge heard these words, he said to his companions, 'Write to the holy man and say that as soon as he sends me a letter of petition, I will be able to release his nephew.'

"Then, the holy man, prompted by these events, wrote to the judge, saying, 'Your Excellency should diligently investigate this matter, and if the boy admits anything worthy of death, let him be executed, so that in this present age he will be freed of the crime of his sins, and thus will avoid the eternal and perpetual punishments of Gehenna. If, on the other hand, he has done nothing worthy of death, it would seem fair under the laws, that you order him released from the prison.'" [AP-G Poemen 5; AP-GS 8.16; AP-PJ 8.13; AP-PA 49.4; AP-PR 20]

5. Once, many monks came to the holy Poemen. After he had discussed different chapters of the Holy Scriptures with them, he asked them, "Tell me, who sold the holy Joseph?"

They replied, "His brothers sold him."

The blessed elder said to them, "That is not the case; his humility and patience sold him, for he did not want to resist his brothers on account of the humility he bore patiently. If he had wanted to say, 'I am their own brother,' they would have been unable to sell him. But he remained silent and did not oppose them; he committed himself entirely to the judgment of the Omnipotent God. From this it is clearly demonstrated that his humility was responsible for his sale. And again, the same grace of his humility, through the dispensation of divine providence, established him as a king and ruler over all the land of Egypt. Humility brought royal power to him not only in this present age, but he also rules with all the saints in that celestial and perpetual glorious kingdom.

"And so we must, my sons, maintain the virtue of humility with constancy and fortitude, and bear injuries for the sake of justice, so that we will be able to enter into that eternal and celestial glory." [AP-G John the Dwarf 20]

6. Likewise, when the blessed Poemen was still a young man, many people from the village where he had been raised came to him. They asked him to come down and intercede with the judge, for many people from their village were being held in prison. The blessed Poemen said to them, "Give me three days to rest, and then I will come down to meet the judge."

After the people had returned to the village, he went inside his cell and prostrated himself in prayers to the Lord, saying, "Lord God, Creator and Savior of humans, hear me, your sinful servant. You know the many traps of the opposing demons who assault us, those who hurry on various occasions to disturb our secret life so that they might separate our mind from the fear and love of you, Lord. And so I pray for the majesty of your divine power, Lord Christ, our Savior, lest you permit me to have such grace before a judge of this world that he might grant my petition. Rather, let him oppose me and not bestow what I will ask from him. For if he grants what I seek, it is clear that my secret way of life will be disrupted. For men will no longer permit me to rest in this place, but coming one by one, they will beg me to make suggestions to the judges in their cases."

After these words, Poemen came down, went to the judge, and interceded with him on behalf of those who were in prison.

The judge replied to him, saying, "It is not appropriate, Servant of God, for you to intercede on behalf of murderers and grave robbers, because even divine law commands the punishment of such wicked men. And so, consider that I am unable to grant what you ask."

When the blessed Poemen heard these words, he rejoiced greatly because the judge had not granted what he had asked, and he returned to his cell. [AP-G Poemen 9; AP-PJ 21.32; AP-PA 92.3]

7. Now there was a certain elder among the great fathers whose name was Agathon, and he was widely honored for his humility and patience. One time some brothers went out to visit him, for they had heard that he possessed great humility. Wanting to test him to see if he truly possessed the patience of humility, they said, "Many are

scandalized by you, Father, because you possess, in great measure, the vice of pride, and therefore you despise others and regard them as nothing. Moreover, you never stop uttering slanders against the brothers. Also, many people assert that you do these things because you are held by the vice of fornication, and you not only fail to perceive your error, but, because of it, you never stop condemning others."

The old man, responding to these charges, said, "I know that these vices that you have mentioned are present in me; I am unable to deny my many iniquities." Then he threw himself on the ground and began imploring the same brothers, saying, "I pray, brothers, that you will not stop praying to the Lord Christ for me, a man who is wretched and a victim of many sins, so that he may grant a pardon for my many iniquities and evil behaviors."

The aforementioned brothers added more charges to the list, saying, "You must also not hide the fact that many people want to claim that you are a heretic."

When the elder heard this, he said to them, "Although I am at the mercy of many evils and sins, nevertheless, I am not a heretic. Keep that away from my soul."

Then all of the brothers who had come to him, threw themselves on the ground at his feet and implored him, saying, "Abba, we beg you to explain why you were not stirred up when we charged you with such great vices and sins. On the other hand, the word *heretic* disturbed you greatly, and you rejected it and refused to hear the matter."

The elder said to them, "I tolerated those earlier charges of faults and sins on account of humility, since you believed that I am a sinner. For we know that if one guards the great virtue of humility, the soul is healthy. For our Lord and Savior, Jesus Christ, when the Jews attacked him with many insults and jeers, bore all of these attacks with patience, so that he might offer an example of patience to us. False witnesses were suborned, many spoke lies against him, and yet he bore everything patiently, even to his death on the cross. For this reason, the Apostle Peter proclaimed, *Christ suffered on our behalf, leaving us an example, so that we might follow in his footsteps* (1 Pet 2:21). Thus we must endure all adversities patiently and with humility.

"On the other hand, I was unable to endure that conversation when you produced that word, *heresy*, and I rejected it strongly, because heresy is a separation from God. A heretic is separated from God in life and in truth, and he is united with the devil and his angels. Alienated from Christ, he does not have the God to whom he might pray on account of his sins; he has been completely ruined. Nevertheless, if he were to return to the truth and the universal faith of the holy church, he would be received by our good and pious Savior, Christ, and he would be rejoined to the true God, the Creator, and to our Savior, Christ, who is always the Son in the Father, together with the Holy Spirit. To them be glory forever. Amen." [AP-G Agathon 5; AP-GS 10.12; AP-PJ 10.10; AP-PA 25.2; AP-PR 21]

ABOUT HOLY ISAAC'S LOVE OF HUMILITY

8. The older fathers held a council among themselves. All of the monks who were living in the desert of Scetis agreed that the blessed Father Isaac should be ordained a priest for them in the church that was located in that place, where a multitude of monks, who were living in the desert, gathered.

Now, the aforementioned Abba Isaac, after hearing about this council, fled to Egypt, and he hid himself in a certain field among the shrubs, since he judged himself unworthy to be a priest. Many of his brother monks followed, so that they might capture him. When evening came, they settled in that same field, so that the monks, who were tired from the journey, might refresh themselves. They unleashed the donkey that had been carrying their load on the trip to graze.

While the donkey was feeding, it came to the place where Abba Isaac was hiding. When the next day dawned, the monks, needing the donkey, came to the same place where the elder had concealed himself. They marveled at this divine dispensation, and they wanted to bind and tie him so that they might take him back.

But the venerable elder did not permit it, saying, "I am no longer able to oppose you; it seems that it is the will of God that I, although unworthy, must receive ordination as a priest." [AP-G Isaac the Priest of Cells 1; AP-PA 90.2; AP-Pa 33.2; AP-PR 22]

9. Now there were two brother monks who were sharing the same manner of life in a cell, and the holy fathers praised their humility and endurance. Nevertheless, after hearing about them, a certain holy man wanted to test to see if they had a true and perfect humility, and so he went to visit them.

When they had received him joyfully, and completed the prayers and psalms following the custom, he went out through the doors of the cell and saw a small garden where they were growing vegetables for themselves. Seizing his staff, he began to strike with all his might, chopping down all the plants until none remained.

The aforementioned brothers watched and said absolutely nothing; nor were their faces sad or disturbed. Then, after returning to the cell and completing the evening prayers, the two monks entreated him, saying, "If you order it, Master, we will go gather some of the stalks that remain and cook them because it is now the hour at which we take our food."

Then the elder praised them, saying, "I give thanks to our God because I see the Holy Spirit resides in you. Therefore, I encourage and warn you dearest brothers to maintain the virtue of holy humility and patience until the end, so that, in the heavenly kingdom, it will make you great and exalted in the sight of the Lord." [AP-GN 343; AP-GS 16.22; AP-PR 23]

10. There was a certain monk, already old and well tested, who lived in the monastery, and he contracted a very serious disease. Consumed by this great and intolerable weakness, he nevertheless was working in great pain for a long time. The brothers were unable to discover how they might relieve his sickness, because they did not have the medicines in the monastery that were needed to cure his illness.

Now a certain handmaiden of God heard about his sickness, and she implored the abbot of the monastery to allow her to take him to her own cell, so that she might care for him. She justified this because it would be easier to find those medicines in the city that were necessary to treat his illness.

Consequently, the abbot commanded the brothers to carry the old monk to the cell of the handmaiden of God. There she received the elder with deep reverence, and ministered to him on account of the name of the Lord, for the recompense of the eternal reward that she believed she would receive from Christ, our Savior.

For more than three years, she served and ministered to the servant of God. Then men, whose minds had been corrupted by the itch of their thoughts, suspected that the elder did not have a clean conscience about the virgin who cared for him. When the elder heard this, he called upon the divinity of Christ, saying, "You, our Lord God, who alone knows all things, and who sees the many pains caused by my sickness and miseries, and who considers the great affliction of my weakness that has consumed me for such a long time that it was necessary for me to have the service of your handmaiden, who nurses me on behalf of your name—grant to her, my Lord God, a well-deserved reward in the eternal life, that reward you condescended to promise through your goodness to those who on account of your name offer service to the destitute and sick."

Now when his final days approached, many of the holiest elders of the monastery came to him. The elder said to them, "I implore you, lords, fathers, and brothers, that when I am dead, you will take my staff and plant it on my grave, and when it puts down roots and produces fruit, then you will know that my conscience is clean with respect to this handmaiden of God who has nursed me. If, on the other hand, it does not produce foliage, then you will know I am unclean with respect to her."

After the man of God left his body, the holy fathers planted his staff upon his grave in accordance with his command. It produced leaves, and after time passed, bore fruit. Everyone was amazed, and they offered glory to God.

Because of this great miracle, many coming from neighboring regions made much of the Savior's grace, and we also saw the small tree. We bless the Lord who protects, in all circumstances, those who serve him in purity and truth. [AP-G Cassian 2; AP-PR 24]

11. Once they led a certain troubled man, who was being violently tortured by a demon, to Abba Apollo. When those who had brought the demon-possessed man had watched him for three days, they begged the elder to cure the man through prayers poured out to God. The elder replied that he did not possess the merit that would allow him to command demons. Those who had brought the man persisted, pleading, weeping, and begging until finally he acquiesced.

Then, in the name of our Lord and Savior Christ, he commanded the demon, saying, "Depart, unclean spirit, from this creature of God."

The demon responded, "I will go, having been compelled by the strength of Christ; nevertheless, I will ask you a question, and you can answer me. Explain that which was written in the Gospel: Who are the goats and who the sheep? (cf. Matt 25:31–46)."

The elder replied to the demon, "The goats are the unjust, among whom I, a sinner subservient to many sins, am numbered. Nevertheless, God knows who the sheep are."

Then the demon exclaimed in a loud voice, "Because of your humility, I am unable to remain." At once it departed from the man whom it had captured.

Seeing this, all of the people who were gathered around him gave glory to God. [AP-GN 307; AP-GS 15.84; AP-PJ 15.65; AP-PR 25]

12. The holy elders told us that once there was a certain monk who lived in the desert of Scetis. He came to visit the holy fathers who lived in the place that is called Cells, where a multitude of monks resided in separate cells. When he was unable to find a cell where he would be able to stay, a certain elder, who had another cell, gave it to him, saying, "Stay for the moment in this cell, until you find a place where you can remain."

Several brothers gathered in order to pay him a visit. They wanted to hear a word about eternal salvation from him, for he had the spiritual gift of teaching the word of the Lord. Then the elder, who had loaned the cell to the visitor, saw the brothers and was struck in his heart with jealousy. He became indignant and said, "I have lived in this place for such a long time, and the brothers rarely, if ever, visit me, and then only during the feast days. Now see how many brothers go to that impostor every day."

Then he said to his disciple, "Go and tell that monk to leave that cell, because I need it back."

The disciple made his way to the brother, and said, "My abba commands your holiness to order me to bring whatever you need, for he heard you were sick."

Then the visitor replied, "Tell my lord father, 'Pray for me, because I have a great stomach pain.'"

The disciple returned to his abba, and said, "He asks your messenger to grant him a delay of two days, so that he might be able to provide a different cell for himself."

Three days passed, and the old man again sent his disciple, telling him, "Go and tell him to leave my cell. If he delays again, tell him that I am coming immediately, and I will drive him out of my cell by beating him with my staff."

Returning to the abovementioned brother, the disciple said, "Because my abba is deeply concerned about your illness, he has sent me to see if you are better."

The visitor replied, "I give thanks, Master, for your holy charity, because you are concerned about me, and truly I am better because of your prayers."

The disciple returned and said to his abba, "He now prays to your holiness that you wait until Sunday, and then he will leave at once."

When the day of the Lord arrived and the visitor had not left, the old man, inflamed with jealousy and an angry spirit, took a pole and went to expel the man from his cell. His disciple approached and said, "If you command, Father, I will go before you and see if perhaps some other brothers have come to greet him, for they will be scandalized if they see you strike him."

Consequently, the disciple went first and entering the cell, said to the visitor, "Look, my abba is coming to greet you, and so come out quickly and with a display of thanks, run to him, the man who on account of his excessive charity and love is coming to you."

Eagerly, the visitor immediately stood up and ran outside. When he saw the old man, he threw himself on the ground before he could approach, and honoring the elder with a display of thanks, he said, "Let the Lord repay you, most charitable father, with eternal good for your cell, which you offered to me on account of his name, and let the Lord Christ prepare a glorious and splendid mansion for you in the heavenly Jerusalem among his saints."

Hearing these words, the old man was struck to the heart, and casting aside his rod, he returned the visitor's embrace. He kissed him and invited him back to his cell so that they might share a meal as a display of thanks.

Then the old man called the aforementioned disciple and asked, "Tell me, my son, did you tell the brother what I ordered you to say about the cell?"

Then his disciple confessed to him, "Truly, Master, I confess that because of the humility I must show you as father and master, I did not dare speak back to you when you sent me to him, but in fact I told him none of the things you commanded me to say."

After hearing these words, the old man threw himself at the feet of his disciple. "From this day, you will be my father, and I your disciple. Because of your rushing around, restraining us and acting with the fear and the charity of God, the Lord Christ has freed my spirit and the spirit of that brother from the snare of sins."

For this happened because of the faith, holy solicitude, and the exertion of the disciple. That man, who had been perfected in the charity of Christ, valued his abba, and he was afraid that, through the vice of jealousy and anger, something might happen to his spiritual father that would make him lose all of his holy works, which, from the time he had entered into Christ's service, he had performed for the rewards of eternal life. Therefore, the Lord gave his grace, so that they might rejoice together in the peace of Christ. [AP-GN 451; AP-PR 26]

13. The holy elders said about a monk named John, the disciple of Abba Paul, that he possessed great humility and the virtue of obedience, so that even when his abba ordered him to perform difficult tasks, he never contradicted his master, nor did he even grumble lightly. Once, when cow manure was required in the monastery, his abba sent John to a nearby village, so that he could acquire it and quickly bring it back to the monastery.

Now there was a lioness in that village, an evil beast. Obeying the command of his abba, the disciple John immediately set off. But before he left, he had said to the abba, "Master, I heard many monks saying that there is a beast, a lioness, in that place."

Then, joking, the old man replied, "If she attacks you, capture and bind her, then bring her back with you."

Now when the disciple reached that place, it was already evening. Immediately the lioness came out and leapt upon him. The monk, struggling, wanted to capture her, but the animal shook him off and escaped his hands.

He followed her, saying, "My abba ordered me to bind you and bring you to him." At once the beast stood still, and grabbing her, the monk led her back to the monastery.

Since John had been delayed in his journey, his abba became worried about him, and feared the worst. Then the disciple arrived suddenly, bringing the bound lioness. When the elder saw this, he marveled and gave thanks to the Savior, our Lord.

His disciple said, "Look, Master, I have brought the captured lioness, just as you ordered."

But the elder, wanting to disparage his disciple's attitude to keep him from praising himself in his own mind, said, "That beast you have brought here is just as senseless as you are. Release it, send it away, so that it might return to its own place." [AP-G John, Disciple of Paul 1; AP-GS 14.5; AP-PJ 14.4; AP-PA 43.2; AP-PR 27]

14. One of the holy fathers sent his disciple to draw some water. Now, the well was far from the elder's cell, and the disciple had forgotten to take a rope with him to bring up the water. When he reached the well, he was deeply saddened because he was far from their cell. What should he do? He did not know if he should turn back, for he doubted that he should return to the cell without water.

Completely distraught, he threw himself down in prayer, and with many tears, said, "*Lord, have mercy on me, according to your great mercy* (Ps 51:1); you who made the heavens, the earth, and the sea, as well as all things in them; you, who alone performed miraculous works; have mercy on me on account of your servant who sent me."

When he rose from this prayer, he exclaimed, "O Well, O Well, the servant of Christ, my abba, sent me to draw water."

At once, water boiled up as far as the mouth of the well, and after the brother had filled his bottle, he departed, glorifying the power of the Lord Savior. Then the well's water returned to its own place. [AP-GN 27; AP-GS 19.21; AP-PJ 19.17; AP-PR 28]

15. One of the holy men had a disciple named Peter, and he lived alone with him. One day, he became angry, expelled him from the cell, and closed the door behind him. His disciple remained there and did not withdraw to another place, but rather he prayed and wept.

After two days the elder opened his door, found him standing in that place, and was overjoyed when he reflected on his patience and true humility. He embraced his disciple, led him into the cell, and the disciple persevered with the elder until his death. [AP-G Abba of Rome 2; AP-GS 16.26; AP-PJ 16.17]

16. There was a certain brother in the monastery named Eulalius, who was full of grace and well supplied with humility. If it happened that any of the more negligent brothers admitted something blameworthy, then, excusing their faults, he would claim that he was guilty of that fault as well. When he was accused by the elders, he did not deny the charge, but rather, he threw himself down on the ground, begged for their pardon, and said that he had sinned and acted negligently. When they accused him often, and, following the monastic rule, they sentenced him to two and three day fasts, he endured all of these punishments patiently.

Now the brothers were unaware that he was patiently bearing all of this ill treatment on account of the virtue of humility. The monks, and especially the elder brothers, gathered and they said to the father of the monastery, "Consider, Father, what must be done. How long must we tolerate the negligence and the losses that Brother Eulalius causes this monastery? By now nearly all the dishes and utensils in the monastery have been smashed and thrown away because of his carelessness. How can we continue to endure such things?"

The father of the monastery responded, "Let us bear it for a few days more, and then we will learn what should be done about him."

Having spoken these words, he dismissed the brothers. Then entering his own cell, he stretched himself out in prayer and begged for the mercy of God so that he would deign to make it clear to him what to order or decide about the frequently mentioned brother.

Then God revealed to him what he should do. He called a meeting of all the brother abbas, and said to them, "Believe me, brothers, that I prefer the small mat woven by brother Eulalius, with his humility and patience, over all the works of everyone else, who, complaining in their hearts, work in this monastery. Now, so that the Lord may show you what merit this brother has before God, I order you to bring all of the brothers' mats to me."

When the brothers had brought the mats, he ordered them to light a fire and place it in the middle of the brothers' mats. They immediately began to burn, but Eulalius's mat was found to remain intact, for it did not burn.

When all of the brothers saw this, they were terrified and threw themselves on the ground, praying for forgiveness and leniency from Christ. They also praised and greatly admired the patience and humility of Eulalius. From that time on, they honored and made much of him, regarding him as one of the great fathers.

Unfortunately, Eulalius was unable to endure honor and praise, and he said, "Woe to unlucky me! I lost the humility that I had been so anxious to acquire for such a long time with the assistance of the Lord Christ." Then, rising in the night, he slipped out of the monastery and fled into the desert where no one would know him. There he lived in a cave. For he did not want to know the temporal praise of men, but rather the eternal glory that comes from our Savior in the future age. [AP-GN 328; AP-GS 15.109; AP-PJ 15.86; AP-PR 29]

17. We should make a point of learning about the praiseworthy humility and the virtue of patience found in the blessed Abba Athanasius, since by considering his admirable generosity and the tranquility of his spirit, we might imitate his example.

Athanasius had a codex, written on the very best parchment, which was worth eighteen *solidi*, for it had the entire Old and New Testaments written in it. Now when a certain brother came to pay him a visit, he saw the codex in Athanasius's cell. Desiring the book, he stole it from Athanasius and departed.

The aforementioned Abba Athanasius, when, on a certain day he wanted to read his codex but did not find it, understood that the brother had robbed him. He did not want to send after him nor search for him, lest after the theft, perjury might be added to the charges against the brother.

Now the brother went down to a nearby city. He wanted to sell that book, and he was demanding a price of sixteen *solidi* for it. Another brother, who wanted to buy it, said to him, "Give me the codex so that I can determine if it is worth such a high price." And so the monk gave him the codex to assess it. Immediately the second brother proceeded to the holy Athanasius with the codex and said, "I ask you to consider this codex, Father, and determine if it is worth sixteen *solidi*, because the man who wants to sell it is asking this high price."

Abba Athanasius said, "This is a good codex; it is worth such a price."

The brother returned to the monk who wanted to sell it, and said to the thief, "Look, I will accept your price, because I showed the codex to Abba Athanasius and he said to me, 'This is a good codex, and it is worth much.'"

Then the thief asked if the blessed Athanasius said anything else. The brother replied, "Believe me, he said nothing more to me."

When the thief heard this, he said to the brother, "I have thought it over, my brother, and I no longer want to sell this codex."

With a contrite heart, the thief hurried back to Abba Athanasius, threw himself on the ground at his feet, and praying with penitent tears and wailing, he begged to be allowed to return the codex to him. Abba Athanasius would not accept it, and said to him, "Go in peace, my brother. Now you may have the codex with my consent."

The brother persisted, begging him with tears, and saying, "If you don't take the codex, Lord Father, my soul will find no other way to have rest."

After these words, Athanasius took back his codex. The errant brother remained near him, living in his cell until the end of his life. [AP-G Gelasius 1; AP-GS 16.2; AP-PJ 16.1; AP-PR 30]

18. There was a monk who was spending time in the desert. He began to think to himself that he possessed the merits of the virtues, and so he prayed intently, saying, "Lord show me what I lack in this holy manner of life, so that I might attain, with your grace helping me, what is missing in me."

Then our Lord God, who wants every man to be saved and to come to a knowledge of truth in order to humble his opinion and thought, said to him, "Go to the monastery of this abba, and you must do whatever this same father tells you to do."

God also revealed himself to the father of that monastery, saying, "Look, a monk who lives in the desert is coming to you. See that you tell him that he must take a whip, and then send him to care for the pigs."

Now when the elder arrived, he knocked on the door of the monastery and then went in to the abbot. The two men offered the peace to each other. After saying a prayer, the hermit said to the abbot, "Tell me, Father, what I must do to save my soul?"

The abbot replied, "If I told you something, would you listen and obey it?"

The monk said, "I will do whatever you order me to do."

The abbot said, "Take this whip and go tend the pigs."

Now many men, who had considered the monk blessed on account of his holy way of life, saw him tending the pigs and said, "Look at that hermit, about whom there was a great opinion—he has gone mad and must tend the pigs."

When the Lord saw his humility, prompt obedience, and patience—that he endured the disgrace and mockery of men—he poured upon him an abundance of his grace so that the demons were frightened of him. Then the monk returned to his own cell in the desert. [AP-GN 132; AP-GS 15.70; AP-PJ 15.52]

19. (a) Once a certain man came to the blessed Macarius. He wanted to serve Christ in the manner of a monk, and he begged the holy elder to instruct and teach him from the spring of the doctrine of salvation, which abounded in him through the grace of the Holy Spirit. He also asserted that he wanted Macarius to forewarn him as to how he would be able to evade the traps and attacks of the evil one.

Macarius replied to him, "If you truly desire with your whole heart to renounce this world, my son, and to adhere to the Lord, our Savior, as the prophet said in the psalm—*My soul clings to you, your right hand receives me* (Ps 63:8), for the right hand of the Lord is ready to receive all who are fleeing to him—then you must renounce this world and push away all of its acts, just as the apostle wrote to the Colossians: *For you are dead*, he said, *to this world, and your life is hidden with Christ in the Lord, Nevertheless, when Christ appears, then you and your life will also appear with him in glory* (Col 3:3–4)."

The younger man, hearing these words, said, "Believe me, most blessed Father, that I have made my mind a stranger to the world and to all of the things that are in this world, so that I might pass my time as a dead man in this life. For I know that all the things that appear to be good in this world are temporary, transitory, and corruptible."

(b) Then the elder said to him, "Listen to me, son. Go to the tombs of the dead and attack them with many slanders and curses. Throw stones at them, so that, having been provoked, they become annoyed with you."

Having heard these words, the young man immediately hurried to the graveyard. After he had carried out the order of the blessed elder by afflicting the dead with injuries, he returned to the holy Macarius and told him what he had done.

The elder asked him if the dead had offered any response to him.

The young man replied, "They said nothing, Master."

Again the elder commanded him, saying, "Go back tomorrow and praise and glorify them with many loud compliments."

The brother went again to the graveyard, and he began to praise and glorify the dead with respectful words, saying, "You are great and holy and similar to apostolic men. Great is the justice you possess." He praised them with many other words, and then he returned to the cell and said to the elder, "Look, following your command, Lord Father, I praised and glorified the dead, but they said nothing to me."

Then the holy Macarius said to him, "Consider, my son, that you reproached the dead with insults and slanders, but they said nothing to you."

(c) "And so you, also, if you want to be saved, and to please our Savior Christ in the holy purpose, must imitate our Lord and Savior, as the apostle and evangelist John said: *He who says that he remains in Christ, must himself walk in the same way he walked* (1 John 2:6). And in the Gospel, we read that Jews, stirred up by the devil, uttered many insults against our Savior Lord, calling him a Samaritan, saying that he had a demon (cf. John 8:48), and that through Beelzebub, the prince of the demons, he was expelling demons (cf. Matt 12:24). They also dared to say that he was leading the people astray.

"But the Lord, the Creator of heaven and earth, endured all of these words so that he could offer us an example of patience and humility. For if he had wanted to display the power of his majesty and avenge his injuries, he could have immediately thrown the entire world into chaos. Neither the human race nor the world itself would have stood, for in a moment everything would have died. But truly the indescribable piety of the Lord Christ did not wish to do this, he who came not to punish, but rather to save the world. Therefore, he endured all of these insults to show us an example of patience and humility.

"For this reason, he said to the disciples who followed him, *Learn from me, because I am gentle and humble of heart, and you will find rest for your souls* (Matt 11:29). Now all the holy ones in that age, both the prophets and the apostles, steadfastly maintained the virtues of patience and humility in the face of taunts, injuries, and various torments inflicted upon them, and they were never deceived by human praise. Rejecting the vain opinion of empty glory found in this present life, they strove for that single glory that is celestial and eternal, by which they longed to please Christ, the glory that comes from God and remains forever, the glory which no human language is able to explain.

"So, considering these examples of patience and humility, my son, when someone offers you an injury, keep most strongly the virtue of patience and guard your humility. Imitate the prophet who said, *I am a deaf man who does not hear, and like a mute man who does not open his mouth; I have become like a man who does not hear and does not have a complaint in his mouth* (Ps 38:13–14). This is surely sung in our psalmody daily to warn our thoughts.

"Beware lest empty glory and the praise of men delight you, and you lose everything that, through working, you have acquired in your good works—that the fruits of fasting and abstinence, of your vigils and prayers for mercy in the eternal life do not arrive from the Lord. He also spoke in the Gospel of those who seek the praise of men, *Truly I say to you that they have received their reward* (Matt 6:2, 16). There are many places where the Holy Scriptures do not cease to warn us against seeking empty glory.

"And so be warned, my son, and do not let those people inflicting injuries burn in your soul. If your heart is stirred up, curb it through the fear of the Lord so that your soul is kept from anger. Then you will be able to maintain the virtue of humility and patience; then you will really display what you promised when you said, 'I will live as a dead man in this world,' if you make no disturbed response to those who inflict injuries. You will be like those in the graveyard, who offered no reply when you flung many injuries and insults against them.

"We must strongly guard the virtue of humility and patience, so that we will go to a heavenly reward and the glory of eternal life, just as the Lord said in the Apocalypse: *Hold fast to what you have, lest another receive your crown* (Rev 3:11)." [**a:** PLaus 9j; **b:** AP-G Macarius the Great 23; PLaus 9j; **c:** PLaus 9j]

Chapter Five

CONCERNING DOCTRINE, TO THE MONKS

1. The holy and most blessed Anthony, a true father of the monks in Christ, commanded his disciples and often warned them to strip the memory of their parents and relatives from their hearts, and to have no concern for their actions, so that, with a mind that was free and unfettered and without any concern for the body, their soul would be able to cling to God intently, without any interruption. For stability of mind is overturned and exterminated by these kinds of concerns; the light of the heart is greatly obscured, as the soul does not perceive how it is wounded and pulled away by various wandering thoughts.

It must be emphasized that monks should never cease to pray intently to the Lord for the salvation of the souls of their parents and relatives, asking that he might rescue and save them from the coming judgment of this world in eternal fire, and that they would deserve to have a place among the true and eternal light of the just, when Christ, the Son of God, eternal king, should return in the glory of his majesty, with the holy angels, and with all of the spirits and celestial powers, to judge the living and the dead on that day of the great and terrible judgment of God. For monks must intervene and pray to the Lord for their parents, so that they might deserve to receive eternal salvation in the perpetual life, and their lot will place them in the kingdom of Jesus Christ, our Lord.

2. **(a)** There was a certain hermit, named Pior, among the oldest fathers. When he was a young man, the blessed Anthony had taught him about the holy purpose of the monks. He had stayed near the blessed Anthony for a few years. When he was twenty-five years old, he went out to another isolated place in the desert so that he could live alone. The blessed Anthony supported and consented to this arrangement. The holy Anthony said to him, "Go, Pior, and live where you

wish. When the Lord reveals a reasonable occasion to you, come to me."

Now, when this Pior had departed to a place that was located between Nitria and the desert of Scetis, he dug a well, thinking to himself, "Since I will find water here, it will be possible to be content." What actually happened contributed to the growth of his merits. For the water he discovered was so false and bitter that if someone came to visit him, that person had to carry water in their own flask.

He remained in the same place for thirty years, for it is the custom of holy men to fight against their own comforts. *For all things*, as the apostle said, *work to the good for those who love God* (Rom 8:28), for whether they find wealth or sustain loss, let them bear injuries patiently and not be puffed up by honors. For both disgrace and good reputation work together for the good.

But then the brothers began saying that he should leave that spot because of the bitter water. He replied to them, "If we flee bitterness and the work of abstinence, if we wish to have rest in this world, then after our departure from this life we shall not see the eternal and truly sweet good things, nor will we enjoy those perpetual delights of the blessed paradise."

(**b**) The brothers also reported that he only took one biscuit and five olives for a meal, and that he ate while walking around outside.

(**c**) Many of the holy fathers also asserted that for more than thirty years after he had left his parents' home, he had never been persuaded—even when he had heard that his parents had died—to make his way to them in order to search for or visit his relatives.

Now his sister, when she became a widow, had two sons who were teenagers. She sent them to the desert to find her brother, Pior. After they had traveled around the various monasteries looking for him, they suddenly came across him and said, "We are the sons of your sister. She deeply desires to see you before she dies."

Pior did not agree to their request. Then the two teenagers went to the man of God, the blessed Anthony, and explained the reason they had come to him. Anthony sent word to Pior, summoned him, and said, "Why, brother, have you not visited me for such a long time?"

Pior replied, "You ordered me, blessed Father, that I should come to you when God revealed an occasion to me. But look, until now, he has not revealed one to me."

The blessed Anthony said to Pior, "Go and see your sister."

Pior took another monk with him and went to his sister's home. Standing outside the open doorway of the atrium, he stood with closed eyes so that he would not see his sister.

She came out and threw herself at his feet, for she was overcome with great joy.

Pior said to her, "Behold, I am your brother, Pior. Look at me as much as you wish." After this, he immediately returned to his cell in the desert. He did this for the education of the monks, as he did not want to give license to them, when it was agreeable, to visit their parents or relatives. [**a:** Pall. *Hist. Laus.* 39.1; AP-PR 31a; **b:** Pall. *Hist. Laus.* 39.3; AP-PR 31b; **c:** Pall. *Hist. Laus.* 39.2; AP-PR 31c]

3. There was also Abba John, who was dwelling on the mountain that is called Calamus. He had a sister who had maintained a holy manner of life since she had been a child. She had educated and taught her brother John to give up the vanities of the world and enter a monastery. After he entered the monastery, he did not leave it for twenty-four years, nor did he visit his sister, although she strongly desired to see him. Frequently she wrote and sent letters to him, begging him to come to her before he departed from his body, so that, through the charity of Christ, she might rejoice in his presence. Nevertheless, he excused himself because he did not want to leave the monastery.

That revered servant of God, his sister, wrote to him again and said, "Since you do not want to come to me, it will be necessary for me to come to you, since, after such a long time, I deserve to honor your holy charity."

When the above-mentioned John heard these words, he was greatly saddened, and thinking about the matter, he said, "If I permit my sister to pay me a visit, it will give license to the others; all our other parents and relatives will come to visit me." Consequently he decided that it would be better to go and visit his sister. He took two other men, brothers from the monastery, with him.

When he came to the doorway of his sister's monastery, he called out, "Bless and hear the pilgrims."

His sister came out and, along with some other servants of God, opened the door. She did not recognize her brother. He knew his sister, but he did not say a word, in case she recognized his voice.

The monks who were with him said to her, "We ask you, Lord Mother, that you order water to be brought for us so that we might have a drink because we are exhausted from our journey." After they had received the water and drank, they made prayers, gave thanks to God, and then they left, returning to their monastery.

After a few days passed, his sister wrote to him again, saying that she would come and see him before he died, and pray at his monastery. Then he wrote back to her, sending his letter with a monk from his monastery, saying, "Because of the superior grace of Christ, I came to you, but you did not recognize me. You came out to us and gave us water. I accepted it from your hands and drank. After giving thanks to God, I returned to my monastery. It should be enough that you saw me, and you should trouble me no further. Rather, pray constantly for me to our Lord Jesus Christ." [AP-PR 32]

4. We must also mention a similar example, the servant of God, Martin. For his sister, with her son, came to him in the monastery, to visit him after a long time had passed. He did not agree to receive or see his sister, but he did receive her son. The boy begged and implored him to take the tunic and robe that they had brought for him.

Martin did not want to take the clothing, and he said, "From my childhood until this hour, the Lord God has governed me, and right up to my death he provides everything that is necessary." For Martin did not expect or receive gifts from relatives.

Nevertheless, that boy threw himself at Martin's feet and said, "We do not offer these garments to a relative, but to a servant of God and a monk."

The blessed Abba Martin replied, "Through how many monasteries did you come on your journey to us?"

The boy responded, "We passed many monasteries."

"Then why did you not give these garments to those other servants of God and monks?"

He answered, "We gave nothing to anyone."

Martin said, "Look, it is evident that you want to give me these clothes, not as a servant of God or a monk, but rather as a relative and someone close to you. But I do not want to receive them."

Then, after offering a most intent prayer to the Lord for the salvation of their souls, he sent them away. And he ordered them to never come to him again.

5. There was also another monk who went to his sister so that he could visit her, for he had heard that she was sick in her monastery. Now she was a servant of God, celebrated for her holy manner of life.

She refused to receive or see her brother. To prevent him from entering a woman's monastery for her sake, she ordered him, "Go, Lord Brother, and pray for me; for by the excellent grace of God and our Savior, I will see you in the future age, in the kingdom of our Lord Jesus Christ." [AP-GN 153; AP-GS 4.74; AP-PJ 4.61; AP-PA 49.3; AP-PR 33]

6. A brother came to an elder on a stormy night, hoping that he might come out of his monastery for a little while to lift a cow that had fallen into a muddy swamp. He tearfully asked the elder to offer assistance, because he was unable to extricate the cow alone.

Abba Apollo immediately replied to the man making this request, "Why did you not ask our younger brother who lives closer to you than me?"

That man, believing that too much abstinence and the inexhaustible solitude had made Apollo lose control of his mind and forget that their brother had been buried, responded, "How would I be able to call him from the tomb where he has been dead for fifteen years?"

Apollo replied, "Do you forget that I also have been dead to this world for twenty years? Nothing from the tomb of this cell, which pertains to the state of this present life, is able to offer comfort to you. Having been seized by the intention to renounce the world for the sake of Christ, the discipline may not be relaxed even to extract your cow. Christ does not permit, even for the briefest moment, a truce for the disciple who follows him on account of his fathers."

7. We should also mention an example of virtue that concerned the blessed Theodore. Blessed Theodore was a disciple of the holy Pachomius, one of the great fathers, a man who was the father of an infinite multitude of monks and many monasteries in the regions of Thebaid. For when he shone with all the holy virtues and acquired a prophet's grace from God, the Lord revealed many future events to him.

Now once, the sister of the aforementioned Theodore came to the monastery, in which the blessed Theodore was living, so that, after such a long time, she might see her brother. When they announced his sister's arrival to him, he immediately sent two monks, who watched the doorway, and he spoke to his sister through them, saying, "Look, my sister, listen and know that I live. Do not be saddened because you will not see me, but rather, consider the vanity and instability of this present world; change your heart, and seize the holy manner of life, so that you will be able to enter the eternal life and heavenly goods that the Lord has prepared for those who are diligent and keep his commands.

"Take these words to heart, because this is the only true and certain hope: a man must keep the commands of God so that he will deserve to enter into the glorious and eternal promises of our Lord, the Savior, Christ."

Hearing these words, she immediately felt compunction in her heart, and her tears flowed freely in the sight of the Lord. A little later, she entered a convent of nuns, servants of God, that had been built in the same village. As time passed, she grew in the holy life of the servants of Christ.

After their mother heard what had happened, she pleaded with the bishops and they gave her letters written to the above-mentioned holy Pachomius, the father of the monasteries, on behalf of her son.

When the mother arrived, she presented herself at the convent of the servants of God. Then she wrote a letter to the father of the monastery and begged that she might be allowed to see her son. The blessed Pachomius summoned his son, Theodore, and said, "I heard that your mother has come on account of you. Consequently, because of the letters from the bishops, go and see your mother."

Theodore replied, "Do you order me, Master, to see my mother? If I should go to see her after gaining such spiritual knowledge, I am afraid that I would be found guilty before God. It is right to refuse and demonstrate the strength of my spirit as an example to the other brothers. For the sons of Levi did not spare anyone, but they killed their relatives and brothers to placate the anger of the Lord. And so I do not have a mother nor anything from this transitory world. When it had been determined and ordained under the priest and prophet Ezra, that the foreign women should be expelled, and they sent them away with their sons, the priest Ezra said, 'We will do what the law of our Lord God commands, and send away our wives with their sons (cf. 1 Ezra 9:10–12).' For clearly their wives were foreigners. The hearts of the affected men were tormented and their stomachs twisted, but reverence for the law of the Lord prevailed in their souls."

Now his mother heard that he had not agreed to see her. She was ardent in her affection for her son and did not want to return to her home. She remained in the convent, saying, "If I remain in this place, I will often see my son when he goes out with the brothers to perform the necessary duties of the monastery, and through his warnings and exhortations, I will be able to make progress in this holy manner of living. My heart will be conformed to his spiritual doctrines, so that I shall deserve to enter into the eternal rest which our Lord Jesus Christ has promised to the diligent."

God did many great miracles through the holy Pachomius; he frequently cured those who were possessed by demons by calling upon the Lord Christ. God also healed many people with a variety of illnesses and also paralytics, through Pachomius's prayers. [AP-PR 34; *Vita Pach. Gr.*1, 37]

8. For a long time, the blessed Abba Pachomius fought a good fight against the most unclean assaults of the demons, like an athlete of truth, and just as much as the blessed Anthony. In those times, with the most attentive prayers, he begged the Lord to keep him from sleep for a certain length of time, and he would maintain a vigil, through the days and nights, fighting against the opposing demons, until he knocked them down and conquered them, just as it says in the Psalm, *And I will not be turned back until they withdraw* (Ps 18:37). Therefore, he excelled and the Lord granted his petition. For the demons are powerless and weak when any of us struggle against them with complete faith and the full intention of our heart, burning with holy desire and with the strength of our Savior, Christ, helping us.

Now the brothers told us about this same blessed Father Pachomius, who was, as we said, in charge of many monasteries in the region of Tabennesi. They said that he often told the fathers, "As the Lord God is my witness, I often heard the unclean spirits of demons speaking among themselves about the various and diverse arts that they employ against the servants of God and especially against the monks. One of them said, 'I am fighting against a very hard man, and whenever I send perverse thoughts into his mind, he immediately gets up, stretches himself out in prayer, and he prays with much groaning for divine help on his behalf. Then I, with the sensation of a great fire burning me, am driven away in confusion.'

"Then another demon said, 'When I send thoughts into the heart of the monk whom I observe, he agrees, receives, and does them. I often make him flare up in anger, or lead him into contentious brawls, laziness in prayer, and sleep during the psalmody—yet he never opposes me.'

"And so my beloved brothers, it always necessary to guard your mind and spirit, calling on the name of our Lord, Jesus Christ.

Following the precepts of God, let us maintain ourselves in prayers and psalmody, just as the apostle said: *Be established in prayer, and keep watch in them* (Col 4:2).

"Thus, with compunction and fear in our heart, the adversarial and most unclean demons will not succeed in harming us."

Our blessed Father Pachomius taught the brothers to be always mindful of the word of God for the salvation of their souls. But afterward, he sent each of the brothers to their cells to work with their hands and meditate on what they had learned in the Holy Scriptures. It was impossible for one of them to speak an idle word, but rather, they discussed whatever they learned from the Holy Scriptures. They also explained and conferred together about the chapters of the Scriptures, which established them in the fear of the Lord and illuminated their spirits. [AP-PR 35; *Vita Pach. Gr.*1 22]

9. (**a**) There was a great man among the holy elders. Christ had given him such grace, that, through the revelations of the Holy Spirit, he was able to see what others could not see.

(**b**) He spoke to the holy elders, saying, "Once, when many brothers were seated together, they were all talking among themselves, discussing what the Holy Scriptures said that pertained to spiritual health. Now there were holy angels standing among them, rejoicing and considering what they heard with cheerful faces, because conversations about the Lord delighted them.

"However, when certain monks in the group spoke, the holy angels would draw back, indignant with the speakers. Then the most sordid and diseased pigs would approach and roll around among the monks. For the demons, in the guise of pigs, were taking delight in the superfluous and boastful words of the monks."

(**c**) The blessed elder, seeing this interchange, went into his cell and for the entire night, with great weeping and moaning, lamented our miseries. Then he spoke forcefully to the holy fathers throughout the monastery and he warned the brothers, saying, "Be on guard, brothers, against talkativeness, and keep yourself from superfluous speeches containing many words, for this produces an evil death of the spirit. Do we not understand that through our empty words, we become odious to both God and the holy angels? For the Scriptures say, *Because of your many words, you will not escape sin* (Prov 10:19). These words make our mind and spirit weak and empty." [**a**: AP-PR 36a; **b**: AP-GN 359; AP-GS 18.29; AP-PJ 18.23; AP-PR 36b; **c**: AP-PR 36c]

Chapter Six

CONCERNING THE BLESSED ARSENIUS

WHO WAS IN A SUBLIME PALACE DURING THE REIGN OF THE EMPEROR THEODOSIUS. DURING THE REIGN OF HIS SONS, THE *AUGUSTI* ARCADIUS AND HONORIUS, HE RECEIVED BAPTISM.

1. **(a)** This Arsenius, growing in his desire for divine love and relinquishing all of the temporal glory of this life, went to the desert of Scetis so that he might live among the holy fathers, hidden from all the noise of this world. Separated from seductions and bodily delights, he adhered, with the complete determination of his mind, to the Lord Savior, just as it is written, *My spirit clings to you, your right hand supports me* (Ps 63:8).

(b) Consequently, the holy elders said about him, that, just as when he had lived in the world, he wore garments that were more precious than what everyone else wore, afterward, while spending time in the desert of Scetis, he took pains to see that he had the most vile and contemptible garment of all the monks. [**a:** AP-PR 37a; AP-PA 19.2; **b:** AP-G Arsenius 4; AP-GS 15.6; AP-PJ 15.6; AP-PR 37b]

2. Abba Daniel said that the holy Arsenius told the brothers a story, speaking as if he had heard it about another monk, but it was understood that it was Arsenius himself who had seen this great vision: "One of the elders was seated in his cell," said Arsenius, "and suddenly a voice came to him that said, 'Go outside and I will show you the work of men.'

"The monk rose," said Arsenius, "and went outside. The voice led him and showed him a black Ethiopian man cutting wood with an axe; the man made a great bundle of wood and attempted to pick up that bundle. Because of the bundle's size, he was unable to carry it. Then he went, cut more wood, and added it to the bundle.

"Then the monk was shown another man, standing atop a cistern. This man drew water from the cistern and poured it into a bucket. There was a hole in the other side of the bucket, and the water poured through it, back into the cistern.

"Again the voice spoke to the monk, 'Come, follow me, and I will show you something else.' The monk then saw something like a temple building, and two men who were riding horses while carrying a piece of wood over their shoulders—that is, a long pole. They both wanted to go through the door of that temple, but the pole they carried would not allow them to pass because they were carrying it side-by-side. Neither of the pair would humble himself to allow the other to enter first; both wanted to enter first, and they were fighting with each other. Neither prevailed, for neither man humbled himself and gave his place to the other.

"Then the voice explained these visions to the monk. 'Those men who were carrying the pole are those who carry the holy yoke of the monks. Justifying their behavior in their hearts with the exultation of pride, they do not acquire humility. They do not wish to walk in the humble way of our Savior Lord, Jesus Christ, who said, *Learn from me because I am meek and humble in heart, and you will find rest for your souls* (Matt 11:29). And so, because of their prideful hearts, they remain outside, excluded from the reign of Christ, the king of heaven.

"'Now the man who was cutting wood and adding that wood to the bundle, is a man who is oppressed by many sins, and he is always adding another sin to those he has. It would be better if he repented of his earlier sins, but neglecting to make amends for the vices of these earlier sins, he simply adds more on top of his previous sins.

"'The man who was drawing the water from the cistern is the man who performs a good work, but because he performs evil acts through his sins, even the good things he does are lost and destroyed.

"'Consequently, just as the Apostle, said, a man *should work, with fear and trembling, for the salvation of his soul* (Phil 2:12).'" [AP-G Arsenius 33; AP-GS 18.3; AP-PJ 18.2; AP-PA 99.2; AP-Pa 36.3; AP-PR 38]

3. **(a)** The same blessed Arsenius questioned a venerable Egyptian monk about his various thoughts and about the attacks of the demons. One of his old friends met him, and seeing that Arsenius was listening carefully and intently to the monk, he said to him, "I am very amazed, Father. You are a man of great erudition, and you have acquired both Greek and Latin knowledge. So why do you ask this uneducated idiot about the things that must come together for the salvation of your soul?"

The blessed Arsenius replied, "I am learned in the Greek and Latin, as you said. Nevertheless, I have not even learned the alphabet of this Egyptian's true knowledge."

(b) The blessed Arsenius said to the brothers, "The cell of the eager monk, who hurries to possess the virtues of the soul, and to implement all of the precepts of our Savior, the Lord Christ, is similar to that Babylonian furnace where the three young men earned the right to see the Son of God (cf. Dan 3:19–25). It is the column of light, where the Lord spoke to Moses." [**a:** AP-G Arsenius 6; AP-GS 15.7; AP-PJ 15.7; AP-PA 83.1; **b:** AP-GN 206; AP-GS 7.46; AP-PJ 7.38]

4. Now Abba Daniel said about Abba Arsenius, that when he was making baskets from palm fronds, he would pour water into a bowl so that he might soak the palm leaves. When the murky water began to smell, he did not allow anyone to exchange the water, but he added more water to that fetid water, so that it always smelled.

Some of the brothers questioned him, saying, "Why don't you permit your water to be changed, Father? Why do you fill your entire cell with that most disgusting smell?"

The blessed elder replied, "Because I constantly used incense, musk, and a variety of scents during my secular life, it seems fitting to me that now, while I am in this body, I should endure this stench to make amends for that most sweet smell, so that, on the day of judgment, the Lord will free me from that indescribably rank smell of Gehenna, and my spirit will not be condemned with that rich man who was feasting on delicate and splendid foods in this world (cf. Luke 16:19–31)." [AP-G Arsenius 18; AP-GS 4.5; AP-PJ 4.5; AP-PR 39]

5. One of the brothers said to the blessed Arsenius, "Look father, I eagerly meditate on the Holy Scriptures, which I learned, but I do not feel compunction in my heart because I do not understand the virtue of the Divine Scriptures; consequently, my spirit is deeply saddened."

The blessed Arsenius responded, "It is necessary for you, my son, to meditate continuously on the eloquence of the Lord. I heard that the blessed Abba Poemen and many other holy fathers said that those enchanters, who customarily enchant snakes, do not understand the words they speak, but the snakes that hear them understand the power of their words, and they lie quietly and are subdued by them. We should also do the same. Although we may be incapable of understanding the power of the Divine Scriptures, the demons are listening. They are terrified by the power of the divine word and will flee, driven from us because they are unable to bear the utterances of the Holy Scriptures, which were spoken through its servants, the prophets and apostles." [AP-GN 184b; AP-GS 5.37; AP-PJ 5.32; AP-PA 10.2; AP-PR 40]

6. Abba Daniel said, "While the blessed Arsenius was in the desert of Scetis, there was a certain monk who was stealing whatever he could find from the cells of the other monks. Now the blessed Arsenius was hurrying to save his soul, so he compelled him to come into his cell and he said to him, "'If you need anything, I will give it to you. But you must stop, for I do not want you to steal and condemn your soul to the eternal fire of Gehenna after God's judgment.'"

Then he sent to one of his friends and he received money and clothes; he gave them to the thief. Nevertheless, even after these actions, the man was again caught stealing. All of the holy elders, after deciding that the man was not going to stop stealing, expelled him, saying, "'If it was a different vice in this brother, we would be able to sustain him, just as the apostle said: *You stronger men, sustain the weak in faith so that they may be saved* (Rom 15:1). This is something that we must do. Nevertheless, it is not right to sustain a thief, especially when he will not stop after being frequently warned. The man who is like this has lost his soul, and he disturbs all the brothers of the congregation.'" [AP-G Daniel 6; AP-GS 10.23; AP-PJ 10.18]

PART 2

The Systematic Collection of Pelagius and John (AP-PJ)

Chapter Eighteen

ON FORESIGHT OR CONTEMPLATION

21. Once Zacharias went to his abba, Silvanus, and he found him in a trance, with his hands raised toward heaven. When he saw this, he closed the door and departed. When he returned near the sixth hour, and then again at the ninth, he found Silvanus in the same state. At the tenth hour, he knocked on the door of the cell, entered, and found him resting.

Zacharias said to him, "What have you been doing today, Father?" Silvanus replied, "I was ill today, my son."

Then, clasping his feet, Zacharias said, "I will not release you unless you indicate to me what you saw."

The elder responded, "I was snatched up to heaven, and I saw the glory of God. I stood there for a while, and then I was sent away." [AP-G Silvanus 3; AP-GS 18.27]

22. The holy Syncletica said, "Let us become as *prudent as serpents and simple as doves* (Matt 10:16), so that we may astutely perceive the devil's traps. For it was said that the prudent should become like serpents, so that we will not be ignorant of the devil's assault and his arts. For as something similar is overcome by another similar thing, the simplicity of the dove is demonstrated." [AP-G Syncletica 18; AP-GS 18.28]

23. One of the fathers said, "Once, while some elders were sitting and discussing edifying matters, there was one among them having a vision. He saw angels waving their hands and washing them. As the discussion turned to secular matters, the angels were leaving, and stinking pigs were rolling in the middle of the gathering and polluting them. Nevertheless, when they spoke again about edifying matters, the angels returned and resumed washing them." [AP-GN 359; AP-GS 18.29; AP-CSP 5.9b; AP-PR 36b]

24. An elder said, "This is what has been written: *I will turn away from two or three sins of Tyre; on the fourth I will not turn away* (Amos 1:9). This means to think of something evil, to consent to what I have

thought, and to speak of it. But the fourth step is to carry out the evil deed. The wrath of God will not turn away from this." [AP-GN 360; AP-GS 18.30]

25. The monks spoke about a certain great elder in Scetis: "Whenever the brothers were building a cell, he would come out joyfully and, placing the foundation, he would not leave until it was finished.

"Now once when he went to build a cell, he appeared deeply saddened. The brothers asked, 'Why are you sad and gloomy, Abba?'

"He replied, 'This place is forsaken, my sons. For I saw that a fire was lit in Scetis; the brothers, taking cut palm fronds, extinguished it. Again it blazed up, and again the brothers took cut palms and extinguished it. A third time it blazed up, filled all of Scetis, and no one was able to extinguish it. Consequently I am sad and gloomy.'" [AP-GN 361; AP-GS 18.31]

26. An elder said, "It is written, *The righteous will flourish like the palm tree* (Ps 92:12). Now this saying signifies the nourishing, right, and sweet fruit of good actions. There is one heart inside the palm tree, and being white, it is the source of all its action. A similar thing is found in the righteous man. For his heart is one and undivided, gazing only at God. It is also white, having the illumination of faith, and every action of the righteous man is in the heart itself. Also, the sharpness of his thorns is a defense against the devil." [AP-GN 362; AP-GS 18.33]

27. Another elder once said, "The Shunammite woman received Elisha because she did not have a relationship with any other man (cf. 2 Kgs 4:8–17). It is said that the Shunammite woman symbolizes the soul and Elisha symbolizes the Holy Spirit. And so, in whatever hour the soul withdraws from the confusion and disturbance of the world, the Spirit of God will come to it, and then it will be able to produce fruit, even though it is barren." [AP-G Cronius 1; AP-GN 363; AP-GS 18.34; AP-M 16; AP-Pa 37.4b]

28. Another of the fathers said, "The eyes of the pig have a natural formation: by design they are always oriented toward the earth, and are never able to gaze up at the sky. This is also the case for the soul of the person who delights in the sweetness of pleasure; once the soul has fallen into the slime of luxury, it is difficult to look toward God, or to understand anything worthy of God." [AP-GN 364; AP-GS 18.35]

29. There was a certain man who was great among those who foresee events. This man stated, "The power that I saw to be present during a baptism, I also saw upon the robe of a monk when he received the spiritual habit." [AP-GN 365; AP-GS 18.36]

30. A certain elder had been given the grace of seeing what was happening, and he said, "Once I saw a brother meditating in his monastery cell. A demon came and stood outside the cell. While that brother was meditating, the demon was unable to enter the cell; when he stopped meditating, the demon was able to enter." [AP-GN 366; AP-GS 18.38]

31. They said that one of the elders had prayed to God so that he might see demons. He received an answer: "You have no need to see them."

The elder asked again, saying, "Lord, you are able to protect me through your grace."

Then God unveiled his eyes and he saw the demons. They were like bees buzzing around a man and gnashing their teeth over him, but the angels of the Lord were rebuking them. [AP-GN 369; AP-GS 18.39]

32. An elder said, "There were two brothers who lived near each other. One was a foreigner, the other a native. The foreigner had a negligent way of life while the native was very diligent. Now it turned out that the foreigner died peacefully. An elder who lived nearby had a vision about this, and he saw a multitude of angels carrying away the foreigner's soul. When he reached heaven and was about to enter, an investigation of his life was made. Then a voice came from above, saying, 'It is clear that this man lived in a negligent manner, but because he lived as a foreigner, open heaven to him.'

"A little later the native also died, and all of his relatives came to him. The elder discerned that angels did not come to take away his soul, and he was amazed. Falling on his face in the sight of God, he asked, 'Why did the foreigner, who lived more negligently, have such glory, while the man who was so diligent deserve nothing?'

"A voice came to him, saying, 'When the time came that he would die, this diligent man opened his eyes, saw his parents weeping, and his soul was consoled. The foreigner, although he was more negligent, saw none of his family. He wept, and God consoled him.'" [AP-GN 367; AP-GS 18.40]

33. Another of the fathers related that there was a solitary who lived in the desert near Nilopolis; a secular but faithful man served him. There was also, in the same city, a man who was wealthy but impious.

Now it happened that the rich man died, and all the people of the city, together with the bishop, carried his body in a lamp-lit procession. At the same time, that secular man who served the solitary went out, carrying bread for him, as was his custom. There he found that a wild beast had eaten the solitary. He fell on his face before God, saying, "I will not rise from this place until God shows me how it is that an impious man should have such a display for his procession, while this man, who served you day and night should come to this end."

And behold, an angel of the Lord came and said to him, "That impious man had few good works in this world, and he received the reward for his life here; he will find no rest in the next life. Now this solitary, although he was a man distinguished in every virtue, had a small number of human faults. He received his penalty for those here; in the next life he will be found wearing the pure crown of God."

Consoled by these words, the servant departed, glorifying God for his judgments because they are true. [AP-GN 368; AP-GS 18.41]

34. The holy fathers of Scetis prophesied about the last generation, saying, "What have we been able to accomplish?"

One of their number, a man of great life named Ischyrion, said, "We do not keep the commands of God."

The fathers responded to him, "But those who come after us, what will they do?"

Ischyrion answered, "They will be able to do half of our works."

They said to him, "And those who come after them, what will they do?"

He replied, "They will have none of our works in that coming generation. Nevertheless, I see that there will be temptations for them, and those who will be marked out as approved in that time will be better than us and our fathers." [AP-G Ischyrion 1; AP-GS 18.9; AP-PA 95.3; AP-PR 197]

35. A certain elder told a story, saying, "There was a virgin of advanced age who had made progress in the fear of the Lord. When I asked her what practice had brought her to this way of life, she began to weep and said, 'Oh, wonderful man, when I was still young, I had a father who was modest and gentle in his manners although his body

was frail and infirm. He lived a self-absorbed life, and was rarely seen by those who were living in that same neighborhood. He worked his land assiduously, although he was always concerned with his own life. When he felt well, he would carry the fruits of his cultivation to the house; nevertheless, he was often detained in his bed by fevers. He was so taciturn that those who did not know him believed that he was mute.

"'I also had a mother, who, curiously, had a different manner of life: she was more disgraceful than everyone else who lived in that region. Her words went everywhere and it was believed that her entire body was a tongue. She frequently stirred up disputes among everyone; intoxicated with wine, she lingered with dissolute men.

"'She managed the household and those things in the home like the worst prostitute, so that even our ample wealth did not suffice for us. My father had delegated the management of the house to her. Her body was consumed by moral disgrace; few from that neighborhood were able to escape her lust. She never experienced any illness in her body, nor did she feel any pain—not even a little. From her birth until her final day, she had a completely healthy body.

"'During these years, my father, exhausted by a long illness, died. The sky was stirred up. Rain, lightning flashes, and thunder disturbed the air. A storm began and rain fell, day and night, without stopping for three days. We were forced to leave his body upon the bed without a tomb. The men of the neighborhood shook their heads and marveled that such great evil had been hidden from everyone. They said, «This man was the enemy of God, as the earth will not receive him for burial.»

"'Nevertheless, to prevent his rotting body from keeping our family from entering the house, we took him to the tomb. With the sky still confused and the rain falling, we buried him as well as we could.

"'My mother, after these events, became even more licentious. With great wickedness, she misused her body lustfully. She made our house a brothel, and lived in great luxury, surrounded with pleasures. While I was still a child, our money began to run low. Then her death arrived (although she was not afraid of it, or so it seemed to me). She received the good fortune of a funeral, as even the sky seemed to participate in her funeral services.

"'But I, after her death, had reached the age of a young woman; desires and passions were beginning to stir in my body. One evening I began to think, pondering whose life I should choose to imitate.

There was my father, who lived with modesty, gentleness, and sobriety. But on further reflection, I realized that nothing good had come from his life. To the contrary, he had spent his entire time consumed with infirmity and trouble, to the point that when he died, not even the earth would receive his burial. If such a way of life was good in God's sight, why had such evils followed my father, who had chosen to live this way?

"'It is good to live like my mother, my thoughts said, to surrender the body to pleasure, luxury, and lust. For she omitted no disgraceful work; even though she was always drunk, she spent her time unharmed and prosperous.

"'So what should I do? From these examples, it seemed to me that I should live as my mother lived. For it is better to believe those ideas that are clearly seen with one's own eyes, and to go no further.

"'And when it had pleased me to choose the same miserable life for myself, night arrived, and sleep immediately came over me. After my thoughts, a man, with a large body and horrible appearance, stood before me. This man, who frightened me as I looked at him, questioned me with an angry appearance and harsh voice. «Tell me,» he said, «What are the thoughts of your heart?»

"'But I, shaken by his appearance and dress, did not dare look at him. In a louder voice, he again ordered that I tell him those ideas that pleased me. Trembling with fear, and having forgotten all of my ideas, I still said nothing. Then that apparition, with me denying them, recalled to my memory all of the ideas I had been considering in my heart.

"'I was convicted and turned to prayer, begging for forgiveness to follow, and telling him each of my thoughts.

"'Then he said to me, «Come and see your father and mother, and then you will be able to select a life for yourself.» Taking my hand, he drew me away. He led me into a great field that contained many orchards, different fruits, a variety of trees, and an inexpressible sweetness. He took me through that place.

"'My father came running to me; he embraced me, kissed me, and called me his daughter. I returned his embrace and asked to stay there with him. He replied, «You cannot stay now, but if you follow my path, you will come here after a short time.»

"'When I continued praying to remain with him, the one who had led me there took me again by the hand and said, «Come. I will show you also your mother, who is burning in fire, so that you will know which example your life should avoid.»

"'Then I stood in a house that was shadowy and dark, filled with screaming and distress. He showed me a furnace that was blazing with flames and boiling pitch. People with horrible expressions were standing at the furnace. I looked downward and saw my mother in the furnace, immersed to her neck. She was gnashing her teeth, burning with fire, and had taken on the foul smell of many worms. When she saw me, she called with a loud voice, «Oh, my daughter, I am suffering these torments on account of my own works, because all of those works produced by sobriety seemed almost like nonsense. I did not believe that I would be tormented for acts of adultery and fornication, nor intoxication or luxury. But look, because of those small pleasures, I have received Gehenna and I am undergoing punishments; on account of those paltry delights, I am repaid with great torments; I receive great retribution for my contempt toward God. For all the unchanging evils have captured me.

"'«Now is the time for assistance, my daughter. Now is the time to remember the nourishment that you received from me. Now is the time to repay kindness, if you received anything of the good. Have mercy on me as I burn in this fire and am consumed by it. Have mercy on me as I am weakened by the torments of this nature. Have mercy on me, my daughter—stretch out your hand and lead me from this place.»

"'When I refused to do it because of those who were standing nearby, she began calling again with tears, «My daughter, help me. Do not despise the tears of your own mother. Remember my suffering on the day that I gave birth to you. Do not turn away from me, your mother who is lost in the fire of Gehenna.»

"'Now I, stirred by the sound of her weeping, was suffering from human sympathy, and I began to mourn for her, grieving loudly. Those who were in my house, awoke, stoked the fire, and questioned me about the reason for my wailing. I told them what I had seen. Then I resolved this one thing: I must follow the life of my father, having been made certain by the ineffable mercy of God what punishments are stored up for those who wish to live evilly.'

"This blessed virgin acquired understanding from this vision, and she reported that the reward of good works is great, while the evil acts of a wicked life will earn great punishments. Consequently, we should adopt this better counsel for ourselves so that we will become blessed." [AP-GS 18.45]

36. The elder told another story about a certain bishop, so that we, learning about faith especially from this example, might increase our diligence for salvation in God. Some people told the bishop (who was living among us and told us these things himself) that there were two faithful women among the secular wives, who were living shamefully. Now the bishop was disturbed by those who had reported these rumors to him, and, concerned that there might be others living this way, he turned to God in prayer. He asked him to provide some well-deserved certainty about the matter. Then, after that divine and terrible consecration, as individuals approached to partake of the holy mystery, the bishop was able to discern each person's spirit through their faces and tell which sins had suborned them.

He saw that some of the sinful men had black faces, although certain men had faces that appeared to have been burned by the heat, and eyes that were red and bloodshot. Other men had faces that were bright and they wore white robes.

Some, when they received the body of the Lord, were consumed and burned by it; for others, on the other hand, it was as if a light was being produced in them, and after entering the mouth, their entire bodies were illuminated. Among this second group were some who had chosen the solitary life, as well as some who were married, and they were also seen to be illuminated in this manner.

Next the bishop turned and he began to distribute the host to the women, so that he would know what kind of souls they had. He saw, in a similar manner, their faces become black and red with bloodshot eyes, or become white.

The two women—whom the others had accused before the bishop, and on whose account especially he had made his prayer and gained this gift of discernment—approached among the rest of the women. He saw that they had faces that were bright and honorable as they approached the holy mystery, and that they were wrapped in white gowns. After they had participated in the mystery of Christ, they were made to glow with light.

Again the bishop returned to his customary practice of prayer and begged God, wanting to learn the meaning of the revelations that he had seen. Then an angel of the Lord appeared, and he told the bishop to ask questions about each person he had seen. The holy bishop wanted to know about the two women, whether that initial accusation had been true or false.

The angel confirmed that everything that had been said about them was true.

Then the bishop said to the angel, "Then why, as they received the body of Christ, were their faces shining? Why did they wear white robes, and glow with a light that was no less than the others?"

The angel replied, "Because they had come to their senses about their actions, and departing from them through their tears, groans, and acts of mercy toward the poor, they had deserved to be placed in the divine number through their confession. They promised never to walk in these evil ways again, if they could be forgiven for their earlier faults. And so, on account of this, they deserved a divine change, and they were absolved from their crimes. They will live from that time onward, soberly, piously, and righteously."

Nevertheless the bishop said that he was amazed, not so much by the change in those women (for this happened to many), but by the gift of God, which not only spared them the torments, but in fact had deigned to give them grace.

The angel said to him, "You admire this justly, like a man. For our Lord and God, and yours, is good and merciful by nature to those who leave their offenses and come to him through confession. Not only will he prevent them from going into the torments, but also he will soften his anger toward them, and make them worthy of honor. *For God so loved the world that he gave his only begotten Son for it* (John 3:16); *he chose to die for those men who were his enemies* (Rom 5:8). Should he not absolve from penalties those who chose to become his servants and pursued repentance for those things they had done? In fact he will provide good things for the enjoyment of those whom he prepared. So understand this: no human faults are able to defeat the compassion of God. But it is only through repentance that the person who previously had done evil deeds will wash themselves with good acts. For God is merciful: he knows the weakness of your kind, the strength of your passions, the power and cunning of the devil, and although men have fallen into sins, he forgives them like sons and waits for their correction, having patience with them. In fact, he bears the weaknesses of those who are converting, those praying for his goodness. He immediately frees them from their torments and gives them the good rewards prepared for the righteous."

The bishop said to the angel, "I beg you, tell me about the differences in the faces, and which sins each person is subjected to. By recognizing them, I will be freed from all ignorance."

The angel replied, "Those who have a bright and cheerful face live in sobriety, chastity, and righteousness. They are modest, sympathetic, and merciful. But those who have black faces perform the works of fornication and lust, having given themselves to other wicked acts and offenses. Those who appear bloody and red are living in evil and unrighteousness, loving slander; they are blasphemers, cunning, and murderers."

The angel spoke to him again, "Help them, if indeed you desire their salvation. You had your prayer granted so that you might become acquainted with the sins of your disciples by sight. Then, through your admonitions and appeals, you might make them better, through repentance, to him who died for them and rose from the dead, our Lord, Jesus Christ. Consequently your Lord Jesus Christ has given the power, desire, and love to you, to endure seeing all of them in this way, so that they might be converted from their sins to God. You will be able to advise them clearly about the sins that have captured them, in order to prevent them from giving up hope of their salvation because of sin. There will be salvation and a banquet of future good things for the souls of those who repent and turn back to God. There will be great mercies for you, for you will be imitating your Lord, who left heaven and died on earth for the salvation of men." [AP-GN 715; AP-GS 18.46; AP-PA 56.2; AP-Pa 23.1; AP-PR 166]

37. One of the fathers said, "There are three things that are honorable among monks, and we ought to approach them with fear, trembling, and spiritual joy: the sharing of the holy of holies, the dinner with the brothers, and the basin in which the feet of the brothers are washed."

He then offered an example, saying, "There was a certain great elder who had foresight, and it happened that he was eating with many brothers. The elder, while sitting at the table, saw by the spirit, among those eating, that some were eating honey, others bread, but still others, manure. He marveled to himself, and prayed to God, saying, 'Lord, reveal the meaning of this mystery to me, because the same food has been placed before everyone at the table; nevertheless, the food appears to alter when eaten, and some eat honey, some bread, and others manure.'

"Then a voice from above came to him, 'Those who eat honey are those who, with fear, trembling, and an attitude of thanksgiving, eat at the table, and they pray without ceasing. Their prayer, like incense, ascends before God, and so they eat honey.

"'Now those who eat bread are those who give thanks, perceiving what God has given to them.

"'But those who eat manure are those who murmur to themselves and say, «This is good, that is bad.» We ought not think such things, but rather, we should glorify God and offer praises to him, so that he might fulfill in us what was written: *Whether you eat, drink, or do something else, do all things for the glory of God* (1 Cor 10:31).'" [AP-GN 85; AP-GS 18.42]

Chapter Nineteen

CONCERNING THE HOLY ELDERS WHO PERFORMED MIRACLES

1. Abba Doulas, the disciple of Abba Bessarion, said, "Once, when we were walking near the seashore, I became thirsty and said to Abba Bessarion, 'Abba, I am very thirsty.'

"The elder offered a prayer and then said to me, 'Drink from the sea.' The water had become sweet, and I drank. Then I drew out a little and placed it in a flask, in case I became thirsty later.

"When the elder saw this, he said to me, 'Why did you fill that flask with water?'

"I said to him, 'Pardon me, but perhaps I will become thirsty again.'

"And the elder said, 'God, who is in this place, is everywhere.'" [AP-G Bessarion 1; AP-GS 19.1; AP-PA 68.4; AP-PR 215]

2. "Another time, when he had a need, he prayed and then crossed the Chrysoroas River on foot. Amazed, I begged his pardon and then asked, 'How did your feet feel when you walked on the water?'

"The elder answered, 'I felt water up to my ankle, but the rest was solid beneath my feet.'" [AP-G Bessarion 2; AP-GS 19.2]

3. "Again, when we were going to see another elder, the sun approached setting. The elder prayed, 'I beg you Lord, stop the sun

until I reach your servant,' and that is what happened." [AP-G Bessarion 3; AP-GS 19.3]

4. "On another day, a man who had a demon came to Scetis. A prayer was offered in church on his behalf, but the demon would not depart from him because it was tough. Now some of the priests of that place said to each other, 'What will we do about this demon? No one is able to drive him out, except Abba Bessarion, and if we ask him to intervene on this man's behalf, he will not come to church. Therefore, this is what we should do: he comes early before all the others of the church. We will place this man who is tormented in Bessarion's place. When he enters, we will stand to pray, and we will say to Bessarion, «Wake that brother up, Abba.»'

"This is what they did. When Bessarion arrived early, they stood to pray, and said to him, 'Wake that brother up, Abba.'

"The elder said to the suffering man, 'Get up and go outside.' Immediately the demon left the man, and he was restored to health in that hour." [AP-G Bessarion 5; AP-GS 19.4; AP-PA 35.3; AP-Pa 14.2; AP-PR 121]

5. Once, some of the elders spoke about Abba Agathon to Abba Elias in Egypt: "He is a good brother."

The elder said to them, "Compared to his generation he is good."

They replied, "How about compared to the ancient fathers?"

Elias responded, "I already told you that he is good, compared to his generation; but compared to the ancient fathers, well, I saw a man in Scetis who was able to make the sun stand still in the sky, just like Joshua, son of Nun (cf. Josh 10:13)."

All the men listening were amazed and they gave glory to God. [AP-G Elias 2; AP-GS 19.5]

6. They said about Abba Macarius the Great that going up from Scetis, carrying baskets, he became fatigued. He sat down and prayed, "God, you know that I am unable to do this." Then he was taken up, and he found himself beside the river. [AP-G Macarius the Great 14; AP-GS 19.10; AP-PA 68.1; AP-PR 213]

7. A man in Egypt had a paralyzed son. He took him to the cell of the blessed Macarius and left the weeping boy on the doorstep. Then he withdrew to a great distance. When the elder noticed the crying boy, he said to him, "Who brought you here?"

The boy replied, "My father brought me here and left me."

The elder said to him, "Get up and go find him."

The boy was immediately restored to health. Rising, he went and found his father, and the two returned to their own home. [AP-G Macarius the Great 15; AP-GS 19.11; AP-PA 35.4; AP-PR 122]

8. Abba Sisoes said, "When I was in Scetis with Abba Macarius, seven of us would go up to the harvest with him. Once there was a widow collecting ears of grain after us, and she would not stop crying. The elder called the owner of the field and said to him, 'What is wrong with this little old lady who is always crying?'

"The owner said, 'Her husband had a loan, but he died without speaking and did not tell her where he had put the money. Now the master wants to take her and her sons into slavery to satisfy the debt.'

"The elder said to him, 'Tell her to come to us when we rest during the heat of the day.'

"After the woman had come, Macarius said to her, 'Why are you always crying?'

"She replied, 'My husband is dead. He took a loan from a certain man, and before dying, he did not say where he put the money.'

"The elder said to her, 'Come, show us the grave of your husband.' Taking the brothers, Macarius went with her. When they reached the place where he had been placed, the elder said to her, 'Go back to your house.'

"After all the brothers had prayed, Macarius called the dead man, saying to him, 'Where did you put that other man's loan?'

"The dead man responded, 'It is hidden in my house, under the foot of the bed.'

"Macarius said to him, 'Sleep again until the day of the resurrection.'

"Now the brothers, seeing what had happened, fell at his feet. Macarius said to them, 'This was not done on my account, for I am nothing. God did this for the widow and her orphaned children. For this is a great thing: God wants the soul to be without sin, and if anyone should seek this, he will be received.'

"Then returning to the village, he told the widow where the money was hidden. She took it, returned it to the master, and freed her sons. All who heard this story gave glory to God." [AP-G Macarius the Great 7; AP-GS 19.12; AP-PA 35.5]

9. Once Abba Emilis was passing through a place and he saw a monk who had been detained as a murderer. The elder approached,

questioned the brother, and discovered that the people were falsely accusing him. He said to those who were holding him, "Where is the man who was killed?"

They showed him. Then, approaching the dead man, he said to all the people, "Pray." He spread out his arms to God, and the dead man stood up.

Then the abba said to him, in the presence of all the people, "Tell us who it is that killed you."

That man replied, "I was entering the church to entrust some money to the priest, but he got up and killed me, and then, carrying my body, he threw me into the monastery of this abba. Now I beg you to take that money from him and give it to my sons."

Then the elder said to him, "Go. Sleep until the Lord comes and revives you." Immediately he fell asleep again. [AP-G Milesius 1; AP-GS 19.13]

10. Once many brothers came to Abba Pastor. At the same time a relative of Abba Pastor came who had a son, and the face of that boy had been turned backward by an act of the devil. Now when the boy's father saw the great number of the elders, he took his son and sat outside weeping.

It happened that one of the elders went outside. When he saw the man, he said, "Why are you crying, man?"

The father replied, "I am related to Abba Pastor; look at the great attack that was made on this boy. I wanted to present him to the elder so that he might cure him, but I was afraid, for he does not want to see us. Even now, if he should learn that I am here, he will send a pursuer to drive me away from this place. But when I saw that all of you were present, I presumed to come here. Therefore do whatever you wish, Abba; only, have mercy on me: take this boy inside and pray for him."

The elder took the boy, entered, and, acting prudently, he did not immediately present him to Abba Pastor. Rather, beginning with the lesser brothers, he said, "Make the sign of the cross over this boy." When he had made all of the monks make the sign in turn, at last he presented him to Abba Pastor, who did not want to touch him. But the other monks begged him, saying, "You should do what everyone else has done."

Abba Pastor rose, weeping, and prayed, "Lord, save your creature, so that he won't be ruled by the enemy."

Then, making the sign of the cross, he returned the healed boy to his father. [AP-G Poemen 7; AP-GS 19.14; AP-PA 49.5; AP-Pa 14.1; AP-PR 168]

11. A certain father spoke about another Abba Paul, who was living in the lower part of Egypt, near the Thebaid. This Paul was picking up those animals that are called horned serpents, asps, serpents, and scorpions, and tearing them in half. Some brothers, seeing what he was doing, said, "Tell us, what did you do to receive this grace?"

He replied, "Forgive me, brothers. If anyone happens to possess purity, everything will be subject to him, just as it was to Adam in paradise, before the transgression of the divine command." [AP-G Paul 1; AP-GS 19.15]

12. In the times of Emperor Julian the Apostate, after he had gone down to Persia, Julian sent a demon that, traveling quickly into the West, could bring any message from there to him. Now when that demon came to the place where a certain monk lived, it stood there for ten days, immobilized; it was unable to advance any further because that monk was praying without ceasing, night and day.

Finally, the demon returned to the one who had sent it, without completing its mission.

Julian said to it, "Why are you late?"

The demon replied, "I was delayed and returned without performing my task, for I endured ten days with Publius the monk to see if perhaps he would stop praying so that I could pass, but he did not cease, and I was not allowed to proceed. Consequently, I returned, having accomplished nothing."

Then the most impious Julian was indignant, and he said, "When I return, I will punish him."

A few days later, the emperor was killed by the providence of God. Immediately, one of the prefects who had been with Julian went away, sold all that he owned, and gave the money to the poor. Then coming to that elder, he became a great monk, and thus he rested in the Lord. [AP-GN 409; AP-GS 19.16/12.12; AP-PA 64.1]

13. Once, a secular man came to Abba Sisoes on the mountain of Abba Anthony. He brought his son with him, but during the journey, his son died. The man was not disturbed; he carried the son, in faith, to that elder. He prostrated himself with his son, as if he was making a penance in order to be blessed by the elder. Then, rising, the father

of the boy left his son before the feet of the elder, and he went outside the cell.

The elder, believing that the boy was still making his penance before his feet, said to him, "Get up and go outside." The elder did not know that the boy was dead.

Immediately the boy rose and went out. Seeing him, the father became afraid, and returning inside, he worshiped the elder, and told him the reason.

Hearing this, the elder was saddened, for he had not wanted to perform this miracle. Consequently, Sisoes's disciple ordered the father to tell no one what had happened until the elder was dead. [AP-G Sisoes 18; AP-GS 19.17; AP-PA 35.1; AP-PR 120]

14. Once Abraham, the disciple of the same Abba Sisoes, was tempted by a demon. Seeing that Abraham had fallen, the elder rose, stretched out his hands to God, and said, "God, whether you will or don't will it, I will not relax unless you cure him." The brother was cured. [AP-G Sisoes 12; AP-GS 19.18; AP-PA 68.2; AP-PR 214]

15. There was an elder who lived as a solitary near the Jordan River. One day, entering a cave because of the heat, he found a lion. The lion began to growl and roar, gnashing its teeth. The elder said to the animal, "What is bothering you? This place can hold both of us. If you cannot bear it, get up and leave."

Then the lion, unable to endure the monk's presence, went outside. [AP-GN 333; AP-GS 19.19]

16. Once a certain elder went up to Terenuthis in Scetis and he stayed there. Those who saw his work of abstinence brought him a little wine. Some others, hearing about him, brought a demon-possessed man to him.

Now the demon began to curse that elder, saying, "You brought me to this drinker of wine?"

The elder, because of his humility, did not want to expel the demon, but stimulated by its reproach, he said, "I believe in Christ, that before I finish drinking from this cup, you will come out of him."

When the elder began to drink, the demon shouted, "You burn me!" Before he finished drinking, the demon left the man, through the grace of Christ. [AP-G Xanthias 2; AP-GS 19.20]

17. One of the fathers sent his disciple to draw some water. Now the well was quite far from their cell, and the disciple had forgotten to

bring a rope with him. When the brother came to the well and realized that he had not brought a rope, he prayed and then, shouting, said, "O Well, O Well, my abba said that I must fill this bottle with water."

Immediately, water rose to the top of the well, and the brother filled his bottle. Then the water receded to its normal level. [AP-GN 27; AP-GS 19.21; AP-CSP 4.14; AP-PR 28]

Chapter Twenty

CONCERNING THE BEST MANNER OF LIFE OF DIFFERENT HOLY MEN

1. Abba Doulas recounted, "Once, when my abba, Bessarion, and I were walking in the desert, we came to a cave. When we entered, we found a brother there who was sitting and working, weaving palm fronds. He did not want to look at us; he did not greet us, nor did he want to speak with us at all.

"Then my master said to me, 'Let us leave, for perhaps it is not in the mind of this brother to speak with us.'

"After leaving that cave, we walked on to see Abba John. Later, when we were returning, we came to that cave where we had seen the brother. The elder said to me, 'Let us go in to the brother, for God may have shown him that he should speak with us.' When we entered, we discovered that he had died in peace.

"The elder said to me, 'Come, brother, let us gather up his body, for God sent us here to bury him.'

"Now when he picked up his body, we discovered that he was a woman. The elder marveled and said, 'Look! Even women are fighting against the devil in the desert, while we disgrace ourselves in the cities!'

"Then, glorifying the God who protects those who are scrupulous about themselves, we went away." [AP-G Bessarion 4; AP-GS 20.1; AP-PA 93.10; AP-Pa 34.3; AP-PR 194]

2. Abba Vindemius said that Abba Macarius had said, "Once, when I was dwelling in Scetis, two adolescents came down. One of them had just begun to grow a beard, the other had not reached that age. They came to me and said, 'Where is the cell of Macarius?'

"I said to them, 'Why do you want him?'"

"They replied, 'We heard about him and came to Scetis in order to see him.'"

"I said, 'I am he.'"

"After they bowed to me, they said, 'We want to remain here.'"

"Now when I saw they were delicate, like those who are wealthy, I said to them, 'You cannot remain here.'"

"The older brother said, 'If we are unable to remain here then we will go somewhere else.'"

"I thought about it, saying to myself, 'Should I treat them this way and allow them to be scandalized? The work itself will drive them to flee of their own accord.' Then I said to them, 'Come, you must make a cell for yourselves, if you are able.'"

"They replied, 'Show us how, and we will do it.'"

"I gave them an axe and a basket filled with bread, and some salt. I showed them a hard stone and said, 'Take this and bring wood from the swamp for yourselves; when you have built a shelter, remain in that same place.'"

"Now I believed that they would run away because of the work, but they asked me, 'What work should we do here?'"

"I said to them, 'Make ropes of palm leaves.' And taking some leaves of the palms from the swamp, I showed them how to make the beginning of a rope, and how they must stitch it together. I told them, 'Make baskets and give them to the church caretakers, and they will bring bread to you.'"

"After I showed them these practices, I left them. They patiently did everything that I told them to do, and they did not come to me for three years. I delayed and wrestled with my thoughts, saying, 'What do you think they are doing? They do not come to ask me about their thoughts. Those who live at a great distance come to me, but these two, who are nearby, do not come to me. They never go any place, except to church to receive the Eucharist in silence.'"

"Consequently, I fasted for a week and prayed to God that he would show me what they were doing. Rising up after that week, I went to see how they lived. They opened the door to me when I knocked, and they greeted me without speaking. I offered a prayer and sat. The older brother signaled to the younger that he should go out, and then he sat down to make a rope, saying nothing.

"Around the ninth hour, he signaled the time by knocking, and the younger brother came and prepared a modest amount of cooked food. He set the table—when the older brother indicated he should do so—placed three biscuits on top of it, and then stood silently.

"I said, 'Let us get up and eat.' Rising, we ate. Then the younger brother brought a flask and we drank.

"When evening arrived, they said to me, 'Will you leave?'

"I replied, 'No, I will sleep here.'

"Then they spread a straw mat for me in one part of the cell, and one for themselves in another corner. They took off their belts and aprons and lay themselves down to sleep on the mat before me. After they had reclined, I prayed to God to reveal their manner of life to me. Then the roof of the cell was opened, and a great light shone like the light of the day, but they were unable to see that light.

"When they believed that I was sleeping, the elder brother touched the younger on the side. They rose and dressed, and then, raising their hands to heaven, they stood in silence. Although I was watching them, they could not see me. I saw demons, like flies, swarming over the younger brother. Some approached and sat above his mouth, while others were over his eyes.

"Then I saw the angel of the Lord, holding a fiery sword, circling him, and driving the demons away. The demons were unable to approach the older brother.

"When morning arrived, they lay back down. I made it appear that I was just waking up, and they did the same. The older brother said, 'Would you like us to sing the twelve psalms?'

"I said, 'Yes.' Then the younger brother sang five psalms, in six verses and one alleluia. With every word, a fiery torch burst from his mouth and ascended to heaven. A similar thing happened when the elder brother was opening his mouth and singing: something like a fiery vapor came out of his mouth and reached up into heaven. I recited a small amount of the work of God from memory, as they also had done.

"Then, as I departed, I said, 'Pray for me.'

"They bowed to me, silently. Then I understood that the elder brother had been perfected, but the younger was still battling the enemy."

A few days later, the elder brother died, and three days after that, the younger brother died as well. And when the other fathers came to Abba Macarius, he led them to their cell, saying, "Come, see the martyrs' shrine of the young foreigners." [AP-G Macarius the Great 33; AP-GS 20.3; AP-PA 93.11; AP-PR 195]

3. Two of the fathers asked God to show them what standard they had attained in the monastic life. A voice came to them, saying, "In a farmhouse in Egypt there is a secular man named Eucharistius and his wife is called Mary. You have not yet reached their standard."

Getting up, the two elders went to that village. After an investigation, they found the cell of that man and his wife. They asked her, "Where is your husband?"

She said to them, "He is a shepherd of sheep, and he is feeding them." Then she led them into her house.

When it grew late, Eucharistius came with the sheep, and seeing the two elders, he prepared a meal for them. He offered them water in a basin, so that he might wash their feet. They said to him, "We will not taste anything, unless you reveal your manner of life to us."

Then Eucharistius humbly said to them, "I am a herder of sheep, and this is my wife."

When the two elders persevered, questioning him so that he would reveal everything to them, he did not want to speak any more. Then they said to him, "The Lord sent us to you"

Hearing these words, he became frightened and said, "Look, we have these sheep from our relatives, and we divide anything that God gives me from them into three parts. We give one part to the poor, one part is used to receive strangers, and the third is for our own use. Even though I took a wife, I am not polluted, nor is she: she is virgin and we sleep separately, withdrawn from each other. At night we wear sack cloth, but in the day, our own clothes. Until now, no man has known this."

When the two fathers heard these things, they marveled and went away glorifying God. [AP-G Eucharistus the Secular 1; AP-GS 20.2]

4. Once, on the day of the offering, Macarius the Egyptian came from Scetis to the mountain of Nitria, to the monastery of Abba Pambo. The elders of that place said to him, "Speak a word of edification to the brothers, Father."

Macarius said to them, "I have not yet become a monk, but I have seen monks."

Then he said, "Once, when I was sitting in my cell in Scetis, my thoughts were oppressing me, saying, 'Get up, go into the desert, and think about what you see there.'

"I remained for five years, my mind resisting this thought, saying, 'Perhaps this idea comes from a demon.' But when this thought persisted in me, I went into the desert, and I found in that place a lake of water with an island in the middle of it. Various animals of the desert were coming to the lake and drinking from it. Among these creatures I saw two naked men, and my body trembled, for I believed that they were spirits.

"When they saw that I was afraid, they spoke to me, saying, 'Do not fear, for we also are men.'

"I asked them, 'Where are you from, and how did you come to this desert?'

"They replied, 'We are from a monastery, and we agreed that we should come here. We have been here forty years.'

"Now one of them was an Egyptian, and the other a Libyan. They questioned me, asking, 'How is the world? Does the water [of the Nile] rise at the customary time, so that the world has an abundance?'

"I replied, 'Yes.' Then I asked them, 'How can I become a monk?'

"They replied, 'Unless a person renounces everything that is in the world, it is impossible to become a monk.'

"I answered, 'I am weak and unable to live like you.'

"They said, 'If you are unable to be like us, sit in your cell and weep over your sins.'

"Then I asked them, 'In winter, do you not feel the cold? In the summer, does your body not burn in the heat?'

"And they said, 'God made a dispensation for us, so that we do not feel the cold in the winter or the heat in the summer.'

"This is why I said to you that I have not yet become a monk. Forgive me, brothers." [AP-G Macarius the Great 2; AP-GS 20.4]

5. Once, Abba Sisoes was dwelling alone on the mountain of Abba Anthony. Since the man who ministered to him had been delayed, he had not seen a human for ten months. Walking on the mountain, he encountered a Pharanite who was hunting wild animals.

The elder said to him, "Where did you come from? How long have you been here?"

That man replied, "In truth, Abba, I have spent eleven months on this mountain, and I have not seen anyone other than you."

Hearing these words, the elder went into his cell and began striking himself, saying, "Look Sisoes, you were thinking that you had done something extraordinary, but you have not even matched what that secular man has accomplished." [AP-G Sisoes 7; AP-GS 20.5]

6. **(a)** The same Abba Sisoes, when sitting in his cell, always closed his door.

(b) It was said of him that on the day of his death, with the fathers gathered around him, his face glowed like the sun, and he said to them, "Look, Abba Anthony is coming." After a little bit, he spoke again, "Look, a band of prophets is coming." A little later his face glowed brighter, and he said, "Look, a crowd of apostles is coming."

Then his face shone twice as bright, and he was speaking, as if to some others. The elders begged him, saying, "Who are you speaking to, Father?"

He replied, "Look, the angels have come to receive me, and I am asking them for a little more time for repentance."

The elders said to him, "You do not need repentance, Father."

He replied, "Truly, I know that I have only taken the first steps of repentance."

Then everyone understood that he had been perfected.

Once again his face blazed like the sun, and all the fathers were afraid. He said to them, "Look, the Lord comes, saying, 'Bring to me the vase chosen from the desert.'"

Immediately Sisoes gave up his spirit. Something flashed like lightning and the entire cell was filled with a sweet smell. [**a:** AP-G Sisoes 24; AP-GS 20.6; **b:** AP-G Sisoes 14; AP-GS 20.7; AP-PA 52.4; AP-PR 162]

7. They said of Abba Or that he never lied, swore an oath, spoke badly of a person, nor, unless it was necessary, did he speak to anyone. [AP-G Or 2; AP-GS 20.8]

8. The same Abba Or said to his disciple, "Take care that you never introduce an unsuitable word into this cell." [AP-G Or 3; AP-GS 20.9]

9. Two great elders were walking in the desert that is near Scetis, and they heard the murmur of a voice from the ground. They found the entrance to a cave. When they entered, they discovered an old lady there, a holy virgin, enfeebled with age.

They said to her, "When did you come here, old woman? Who takes care of you?" For they found nothing in that cave, apart from the aged woman herself.

She said to them, "I have lived in this desert cave for thirty-eight years, serving Christ with great contentment, and I have not seen a man until today. For God sent you to bury my corpse."

After she had spoken these words, she rested in peace. The fathers glorified God, and once they had buried her body, they returned to their monastery. [AP-GN 132.4; AP-GS 20.12]

10. They tell of a certain solitary who went out into the desert, clothed only in a linen tunic. When he had walked three days, he climbed upon a rock and saw below him, a man eating a green plant like an animal. Climbing down from his concealed position, he grabbed the man. That old man, although he was nude, was unable to bear the smell of men, and with a powerful shove, he managed to evade the brother's hands and escape. The brother pursued, running after him and shouting, "Wait for me! I am following you because of God."

The naked man, turning back, said, "And I am fleeing from you on account of God."

Then the brother threw off the tunic that he wore and followed him. When the elder saw that he had cast off his clothes, he stopped running. When the brother approached him, the elder said to him, "When you threw away the material of the world, then I waited for you."

That brother questioned the elder, saying, "Father, speak a word by which I might be saved."

The elder replied, "Flee men, remain silent, and you will be saved." [AP-GN 132.5; AP-GS 20.13]

11. A certain solitary was addressing the brothers who were in Raithou, where there are seventy palm trees. It is the same place where Moses stayed, along with the people, when he went out from the land of Egypt. The elder said, "Once I thought that I should go into the inner desert, so that perhaps I might find something deeper in myself while I was living in the desert and serving our Lord Jesus Christ. I walked four days and nights, and then I found a cave. When I approached and looked inside, I saw a man sitting there. I knocked, following the monastic custom, so that he would come out and I could greet him.

"That man did not move, for he was resting in peace. Having no doubts, I entered. When I grasped his shoulder, he immediately disintegrated and became dust. Then, looking around, I saw a hanging tunic, but in the same way, when I touched it, it crumbled and was reduced to nothing.

"I was confused by this, and so I went out and walked on through the desert. Then I found another cave and again, the signs of a man. I became eager again. I approached that cave in order to knock, but no one heard me. Entering the cave, I found no one. Then going back outside the cave, I said to myself, 'The servant of God must return here from wherever he might be.'

"After the day had passed, I saw oxen approaching, and the servant of God coming along with them. He was naked, with hair that covered the dishonorable parts of his body. He approached and saw me. He believed that I was a spirit, and he stopped to pray. Later he told me that he was often tempted by spirits.

"Understanding his hesitation, I said to him, 'Servant of God, I am a man. See my footprints! Touch me, because I am flesh and blood.'

"After he concluded his prayer with an 'amen,' he looked at me and was reassured. He took me into his cave and questioned me, asking, 'How did you come here?'

"I said, 'I came for the purpose of searching for the servants of God in this solitude, and God has not cheated me of my desire.'

"I questioned him in turn, 'How did you come here? How long have you been here? What do you eat? Why are you naked? Why don't you put on clothes?'

"He replied, 'I was in a monastery in the Thebaid, and my job was weaving linen. Then a thought entered my mind that I should leave that place and dwell alone. You will be able, the thought said, to be silent, to receive strangers, and to gain a greater reward from this act than from your work. So, to consent to this thought, and to accomplish it, I went out to build a monastery for myself. Then men came there to join me in this work. When we produced a surplus, I hurried to distribute it to the poor and the strangers.

"'But our adversary, the devil, then as always, was envying my future reward, and he was scheming to contrive retribution for me, because I was hurrying to offer my work to God. When he saw one holy virgin place an order with me, which I filled and returned to her, he placed it into her mind that she should place more orders with me. Our frequent contact led to it becoming customary for us to touch hands, smile, and eat together. At last, we conceived the final sorrow and produced iniquity.

"'I remained in that ruined relationship for six months. Finally, I thought that either today, tomorrow, or after many years, I would die and suffer eternal punishment. For if anyone violates a man's wife, he will be subjected to eternal punishment with just cause; how much worthier of torment is the man who has had illicit sex with a bride of Christ?

"'Consequently, I hurried into this desert by night, leaving everything behind for that woman. Coming here, I discovered this cave, this pool of water, and this palm which produces twelve clusters of dates. Every month it gives me one cluster that sustains me for thirty days. After that, a new cluster matures. As time passed, my hair grew long, and since my clothes were ragged, I covered the shameful part of my body with my hair.'

"I questioned him further, asking if he had experienced any difficulty in the beginning. He said to me, 'In the earliest days I was greatly afflicted by a pain in my liver. It threw me to the ground, and I was unable to stand to recite the Psalms; stretched out on the ground, I would call to the Most High. Then, when I was in the cave suffering from pain and exhaustion that was so intense that I could not go out, I saw a man enter the cave. He stood nearby and said to me, «What ails you?»

"'I was comforted a little by his presence and said to him, «I feel pain in the liver.»

"'He asked me, «Where do you hurt?»

"'When I showed him, he joined the fingers of his hands together straight, and he separated that place like a sword. Extracting my liver, he showed me the damaged spot. Then, scraping the liver with his hand, he removed the damage and placed it into a rag. Then he replaced the liver with his hands and closed up the place in my side.

"'Then he said to me, «Behold, you have been made healthy, and thus it is appropriate that you serve our Lord Jesus Christ.»

"'From that day I have been healthy, and have remained here without any trouble.'

"I begged him to allow me to remain in the inner desert, but he said to me, 'You are unable to suffer the attack of demons.'

"Having considered this, I asked him to pray and send me away. Then, after he had prayed, he sent me away. I have told you these stories for the sake of your edification." [AP-GN 132.2; AP-GS 20.15]

12. Another elder, who had been considered worthy to become the bishop of the city of Oxyrhynchus, told a story, although he said that he had heard of these deeds rather than doing them himself. "It seemed right to me," he said, "to enter the inner desert that is

near Oasa, the home of the Mazices people, so that I could see if I might meet anyone serving Christ. So taking a few loaves of bread and enough water for four days in a flask, I began my trip. When four days had passed, and I had consumed my food, I was wondering what I should do. Feeling confident, I decided to continue on. I walked another four days, holding out without food. When my body was no longer able to endure the fasting and the labor of the trip, I became fainthearted and fell to the ground.

"Now a certain person came and touched my lip with his finger, just like a doctor who runs his eyes over what has been spit out. I was immediately strengthened and felt as if I had neither walked nor suffered hunger. When I felt this strength coming into me, I rose and walked on through the desert. Another four days passed, and again, exhausted, I fell down. When I raised my hands to heaven, behold, that same man, who had strengthened me earlier, again placed his finger on my lips and strengthened me.

"He led me on for seventeen days and then I found a hut, a palm tree, and a man standing nearby whose hair was his only clothing. The hair of his elderly head was white all over. He was a forbidding sight. When he saw me, he stood to pray. After he said 'amen,' he recognized that I was a man. Taking my hand, he questioned me, saying, 'How did you come here? Do all the things that are in the world still stand? Are there still persecutions?'

"Now I said to him, 'It is because of you, who serve the Lord Jesus Christ in truth, that I have made my way into this desert. The persecution has ended through the power of Christ. Tell me now, I beg you, how did you come here?'

"Then he, weeping bitterly, began to explain to me, 'I was a bishop, and when the persecution began, many punishments were laid upon me. When I was unable to endure torture, I sacrificed to the gods. Then, later, returning to my senses, I recognized my iniquity, and I sentenced myself to dying in this desert. I have spent forty-nine years here in confession, begging God to forgive my sin. The Lord has supplied nourishment for me from this palm, but I did not receive the comfort of forgiveness for forty-eight years; nevertheless, in this year I have been forgiven.'

"After saying this, he rose quickly and rushed outside, where he stood in prayer for a long time. After he had completed his prayers, he came back to me. I looked intently at his face and became frightened, for it had become like flame. Then he said to me, 'Do not be afraid, for God sent you to give my body a funeral and bury me.'

"After speaking these words, he immediately stretched out his arms and legs, and his life ended. I took off my tunic. I kept half for myself, wrapped his holy body in the other half, and hid him in the earth. The moment he was buried, that palm tree fell violently, and the hut collapsed. I wept bitterly, begging God to revive the palm tree for me, so that I could remain in that place for the rest of my life.

"Since this did not happen, I said to myself, 'This is not the will of God.' Then, praying, I aimed again for the outside world, and behold, that man who had anointed my lips came and appeared to me. He strengthened me, so that I would be able to return to the brothers. I told them these things, begging them to never despair for themselves, but to always seek God through repentance." [AP-GN 132.3; AP-GS 20.16]

13. A brother questioned one of the elders, asking, "Is it one's reputation or the work that saves?"

The elder replied, "The work," and then he continued, "I know a brother who was praying once, and immediately his prayer was heard. For a thought had crept secretly into his mind, that he would like to see how the soul of a sinner and of a righteous man were taken from their bodies.

"God did not want to discourage him in his desires, so while he was seated in his cell, a wolf entered, and taking hold of that brother's robe, it led him outside. The brother rose and followed the animal.

"Now the wolf led him to another city, and, releasing the brother, it departed. Then he stopped at a monastery outside the city in which a man lived who had the name of a great hermit. This hermit was sick and expecting the hour of his death. The brother, who had arrived, saw that a great preparation of candles and lamps was being made around the solitary. It was believed that God had provided bread and water to the people of the city through the hermit and had saved them. The people were saying, 'If this should be his end, then we will all die together.'

"When the hour came for his death, the brother saw a Tartar of hell descending upon that solitary. He was holding a flaming trident, and the brother heard a voice saying, 'Since this soul did not allow me any rest—not even one hour—you should not feel pity for him while I tear his soul out.'

"And so that Tartar, placing the trident of fire that he held into the solitary's heart, twisted it for many hours, and finally extracted his soul.

"After this, the brother entered the city and found a foreign man, diseased and lying in the street; he did not have anyone who could administer medicine to him. The brother stayed with him one day. When the hour of his dormition arrived, the brother saw Michael and Gabriel descending for his soul. One sat on his right, the other on his left, and they were asking his soul to come out. But the soul did not come out, because it did not want to leave its body. Then Gabriel said to Michael, 'Let us take this soul, so that we may leave.'

"Michael responded, 'God has commanded that it should be removed without pain, and so we cannot tear it out by force.'

"Then Michael shouted with a great voice, 'Lord, what do you will about this soul? For it is not agreeing to come out with us.'

"Then a voice came to him, 'Behold, I send David with a lyre, and all who sing to God in Jerusalem. When it hears the Psalms it will come to their voices.'

"When all had descended and stood around the soul singing hymns, that soul left the body, sat in the hands of Michael, and was received with rejoicing." [AP-GN 491; AP-GS 20.17]

14. Again it is said of the same man who was spoken of before, that, once, he went into the city so that he might sell the vases that he had made. He spread out his goods in front of the doorway of a wealthy man who was dying. While sitting there, the elder saw black horses and their riders, also black and terrible, each holding a single rod of fire in their hand.

When they reached that door, they stopped their horses outside, and each quickly entered the house.

The sick man, seeing them, shouted with a great voice, "Lord, help me!"

They said to him, "Now you remember God, when the sun has gone dark for you? Why did you not look for him until this day, while you still had the light of the day? For now, in this hour, you have no share of hope or consolation." [AP-GN 492; AP-GS 20.18/18.51]

15. The fathers said that there had been a certain Macarius who founded the first monastery in Scetis. This is a place in the desert, far from Nitria, with a day and night's journey between them. It is also very dangerous for those who travel there, for if a person strays even

a little, he will wander through the desert in danger of losing his life. All of the men in that place are perfect; no imperfect man can endure the fierce conditions. The place is completely dry, and they have no consolation beyond what is necessary.

This aforementioned Macarius had been a man of the city. One day he joined Macarius the Great. When the pair went to be ferried over the Nile River, they happened to board a large ship, which two tribunes, with much acclaim, had also boarded. These men had also loaded a bronze traveling carriage and horses that wore gold bridles. They were accompanied by soldiers, slaves wearing collars, and others who had gold belts.

The tribunes, seeing those two old monks dressed in rags and sitting in a corner, began praising their poverty. One of the tribunes said to them, "Blessed are you who ridicule this world."

The Macarius from the city responded to them, "We ridicule this world, but this world ridicules you. Nevertheless, I know that you did not want to say that. For we are both called 'blessed,' that is 'Macarius.'"

This statement produced a feeling of compunction in the tribune. Returning to his home, he stripped off his robes, and began to become a monk, performing many acts of charity. [AP-GS 20.19; *Hist. Mon.* 23]

16. They say that while Abba Macarius the Great was once walking in the desert, he found the head of a dead man lying on the ground. When he moved it with the palm rod he carried in his hand, that head spoke to him.

Abba Macarius said to it, "Who are you?"

The head replied to the elder, "I was a priest of the Gentiles who once lived in this place. You are Abba Macarius, a man who possesses the Holy Spirit of God. In whatever hour you choose to pity those who are in torment, and you pray for them, then they are slightly consoled."

The elder said to the skull, "What is this consolation?"

The skull replied, "As far as the sky stands above the earth, so too is the depth of the fires beneath our feet and above our heads. Consequently, we are standing in the middle of fire, and no one is able to see their neighbor face-to-face."

The elder wept and said, "Woe to the day in which a man was born, if this is the consolation one finds in punishment." Then he asked again, "Is there greater punishment in hell?"

The head replied, "There is a greater punishment beneath us."

The elder said, "Who is in it?"

The head said, "We, who did not know God, receive a small amount of mercy; but those who knew God, but denied him and did not do his will, are beneath us."

After these words, the elder took the head and buried it. [AP-G Macarius the Great 38; AP-GS 3.19/20.20; AP-PA 69.1; AP-PR 172]

17. Once, the same Abba Macarius was praying in his cell, and a voice came to him and said, "Macarius, you have not yet achieved the measure of two women who live in the city."

Rising in the morning, Macarius took up his palm staff, and headed for the city. When he arrived and discovered the place, he knocked on the door. One of the women came out and received him into her home. After he had sat down, he called the women. They came and sat with him. The elder said to them, "I have been forced to undertake a great journey because of you. Now tell me about your way of life, and explain what it is."

The women said, "Believe us, that to this night we have not been without our husbands. What way of life are we able to have?"

But the elder, apologetically, continued to question them, so that they would show him their actions.

Then they said to him, "We indeed, in the eyes of the world, are unrelated; nevertheless, it pleased us to marry two men who are brothers according to the flesh. For fifteen years the two of us have lived in the same house, and we do not know if we have ever had an argument, or if one of us has spoken a disgraceful word to the other. We have spent this entire time together in peace and harmony. Now a thought has come into our minds that we should enter a convent. We asked our husbands, but they did not consent. Although we were unable to fulfill our intention, we took an oath between ourselves and God, that until our death, no secular conversation will come out of our mouths."

Hearing these words, Abba Macarius said, "I say truly that it does not matter if you are a nun or a woman living under a husband, a monk or a person of the world; God sends his Holy Spirit to each one, according to their intention." [AP-GN 489; AP-GS 20.21; AP-PA 29.2; AP-PR 97]

18. The fathers spoke of another great elder who, while he was walking in the desert, saw two angels accompanying him, one on his right and the other on his left. While they were walking, they discovered a corpse lying on the road. The elder covered his nostrils because

of the smell. The angels did the same. After going a little further, the elder asked, "Were you also able to smell that?"

They replied, "Not at all, but for your sake, we covered our noses. For we do not smell the uncleanness of this world, nor does it approach us. But we smell the odor of souls that bear the stink of their sins." [AP-GN 19; AP-GS 20.23]

Chapter Twenty-One

SEVEN CHAPTERS OF THE SAYINGS ABBA MOSES SENT TO ABBA POEMEN. THOSE WHO KEEP THEM WILL BE FREE FROM PUNISHMENT.

1. The elder Moses said, "A man ought to be dead to his partner, that is, dead to his friend, so that he will not judge him in any situation." [AP-G Moses S1]

2. He said also, "A man ought to mortify himself from every evil action before he departs the body, so that he will not hurt any man." [AP-G Moses S2]

3. He said again, "Unless a man has it in his heart that he is a sinner, God will not pay attention to him." A father said to him, "What does it mean 'to have it in the heart that he is a sinner?'"

The elder replied, "If anyone bears his own sins, he will not see the sins of his neighbor." [AP-G Moses S3]

4. The elder said again, "Unless a man begins with the act of prayer, he works in vain."

A brother asked him, "What is the relationship between work and prayer?"

The elder replied, "We should no longer do those things against which we pray. For when a man dismisses his own will, then God is reconciled to him and receives his prayers."

A brother asked, "In every work of man, what is it that helps him?"

The elder said to him, "God is the one who helps. For it is written, *God is our refuge and strength, helper in the tribulations that find us often* (Ps 46:1)." [AP-G Moses S4; AP-PR 202; AP-M 35]

5. A brother said, "What do the fasting and vigils that a man performs achieve?"

The elder said to him, "These are the practices that make a soul humble. For it is written, *See my humility and my work; forgive all my sins* (Ps 25:18). And so, if the soul performs these works, then God will have mercy upon it, for the sake of these practices." [AP-G Moses S5]

6. A brother questioned the elder, asking, "What should a man do in the face of every temptation that comes upon him, or with every thought from the enemy?"

The elder replied, "He should weep in the presence of the goodness of God, so that he will help him. He will be consoled quickly if he prays with discernment. For it is written, *The Lord is my helper, and I will not fear what man can do to me* (Ps 118:6)." [AP-G Moses S6]

7. **(a)** A brother questioned him again, saying, "Look, a man struck his servant because of a sin that the servant had committed. What should that servant say?"

The elder replied, "If he is a good servant, he should say, 'I sinned; forgive me.'"

The brother said, "Nothing more?"

The elder said to him, "No. For his master should immediately feel compassion for him, for that action through which he brought blame upon himself, and said, 'I sinned.'

(b) This is not the hour to judge one's neighbor. When the hand of the Lord killed the firstborn in the land of Egypt, *there was not a house in which there was not a death* (Exod 12:30)."

The brother asked, "What is this teaching?"

The elder answered, "If we look at our sins, we will not see the sins of our neighbor. For it is foolish for a man, who has his own death to bear, to ignore that and go and weep over the death of his neighbor. To be dead to your neighbor is to carry your sins, and to refuse to judge any man—this one is good, that one is bad. In order to keep yourself from doing evil to another man, you should not even think evil of another, nor scorn anyone doing evil, nor agree to do evil to your neighbor, and you must refuse to rejoice with the man who does evil to his neighbor. This is what it means to be dead to your neighbor.

"Refuse to gossip about another, but say, 'God knows each one.' Refuse to listen to a detractor, and do not rejoice with him in tearing down another. Do not listen to someone gossiping about his neighbor. This is the meaning of *Do not judge and you will not be judged* (Matt 7:1). You should not hold grudges against any man, nor retain grudges in your heart. You should not be contemptuous of the man who does hold a grudge against his neighbor, and you must not join in this grudge. Do not despise a man who holds a grudge against his neighbor. This is what peace is. Console yourself with this thought: this period of labor will last for a short time, but peace is forever, thanks to God, the Word. Amen." [**a:** AP-G Moses S7a; AP-M 37; **b:** AP-G Moses S7b]

8. Another elder said, "For your sake a man, the Savior, was born. The Son of God came so that you might be saved. He was made human while remaining God. He was made a son. He was made the reader who, receiving the book, read it in the synagogue, saying, *The Spirit of the Lord is upon me, and for this reason he anointed me; to preach to the poor, he sent me* (Luke 4:18).

"He was made a subdeacon. Then, making a whip out of a rope, *he expelled all the sheep, cows, and the others from the temple* (John 2:15). He was made a deacon; tying a linen cloth around himself, he washed the feet of his disciples, and ordered them to wash the feet of the brothers. He was made a priest, and he sat in the middle of the masters, teaching. He was made a bishop, and receiving the bread, he blessed it, broke it, and then gave it to his disciples and the others.

"He was flogged because of you, crucified, and died. On the third day he was resurrected and rose. He did all of these things himself because of you: everything according to the dispensation, everything in sequence, and so, consequently, everything he did was intended to save us. Can you not endure these offices for his sake? Let us be sober, let us be vigilant, let us remain free to attend to prayers, so that we might be saved by doing those things that are pleasing to him.

"Was Joseph not sold in Egypt, in a foreign land? Three boys were captives in Babylon—did they have knowledge of anyone? God was their patron. He supported and glorified them because they feared him. For the man who gives his soul to God no longer follows his own will, but waiting for the decision of God, he does not labor. For if you want to follow your own will, refusing to cooperate with God, you will be worn out quickly." [AP-GN 81]

9. A brother questioned Abba Pastor, "What is the meaning of what has been written, *Do not think about tomorrow* (Matt 6:34)?"

The elder said to him, "This refers to a man who encounters temptation and falls, so that he will not spend a long time thinking about what will happen, but rather he will think about the concerns of the day and his daily tasks, and he will receive the future willingly." [AP-G Poemen 126]

10. A brother questioned Abba John, "How is it that the soul that has its own wounds is not ashamed to slander its neighbor?"

The elder responded to him with a parable: "There was a certain poor man who had a wife. When he saw another, prettier woman, he obtained her also in marriage. Now both women were nude. They stayed in a certain place for nine days, and then they both begged him, saying, 'We want to come with you.' He placed them naked in a barrel, which was loaded on a ship and put in its place. When midday came and the people had withdrawn, one of the women perceived the silence and she jumped to a different place in a nearby earthenware vase. There she discovered some old, torn rags. She tied them to herself, and then, confidently, she was seen walking around.

"The other naked woman, sitting inside the barrel, said to her husband, 'Look, that prostitute is naked and addled.'

"Her husband, grieving, replied, 'What a miracle! She has covered her private parts in one way or the other, but you, completely naked, are not ashamed to condemn her even though she is partly clothed?'

"This is the way of all critics: they do not see their own evil, but are always ready to accuse others." [AP-G, John the Dwarf 15; AP-GS 9.12]

11. Some brothers said to Abba Anthony, "We want to hear a word from you, by which we will be able to be saved."

Then the elder said, "Listen to the Scriptures; that will be sufficient for you."

They replied, "We want to hear something from you, Father."

The elder answered, "You have heard the Lord saying, *If anyone strikes you on the left cheek, turn to him the other* (Matt 5:39)."

They said to Anthony, "We are unable to do this."

Anthony said, "If you are unable to present one cheek and then the other to him, at least offer one patiently."

They replied, "We cannot do this."

Anthony said to them, "If you are unable to do that, then you should not want to strike any more than you want to be struck."

They said, "We are unable to want that."

Then the elder said to his disciple, "Prepare juice for these brothers, because they are extremely weak." Then he said to them, "If you are unable to do this or that, what should I do with you? Prayer alone is necessary for your sake." [AP-G Anthony 19; AP-GS 16.1; AP-PA 21.1; AP-Pa 6.2]

12. Abba John said to some of the brothers, "There were three philosopher friends. One of them died, commending his son to the care of the other two. When the boy reached manhood, he committed adultery with the wife of one of his guardians. When this wickedness was revealed, he was sent away. Then, after he repented, he was not permitted to return. The philosopher said to that teenager, 'Go. Spend three years among the convicts who mine metals in the river. Then I will pardon your fault.'

"After three years, when the boy returned, the philosopher said again, 'Go another three years; give away your pay so that you will suffer injury.' Then the boy did this for another three years.

"Then the philosopher said to him, 'Go now to the city of Athens, so that you might learn philosophy.'

"Now there was an old philosopher at the city gate; he sat there and battered every person who entered with insults. When he attacked the young man, the young man laughed. The old philosopher said to him, 'What is this? I insult you and you laugh?'

"The young man replied, 'You don't want me to laugh? A man who for three years had to give away his wages to be insulted, and here today I suffer insults for free? This is the reason I laughed.'

"The elder said to him, 'Get up and enter the city.'"

When Abba John related this story, he said, "This is the gateway of the Lord, and our fathers, through many injuries, passed through them, rejoicing." [AP-G John the Dwarf 41; AP-PA 24.1; AP-PR 84]

13. Abba John spoke about the soul that desires to repent: "In a certain city there was an incredibly beautiful prostitute who had many lovers. One of the leading citizens came to her and said, 'Pledge your chastity to me, and I will take you as my wife.'

"She promised, and he received her and introduced her into his home. When her other lovers looked for her, unaware that this great man had selected her and made her his wife, they said, 'If we go to the doorway of a man so powerful, and he understands what we are looking for, there is no doubt that we will be punished. So come, behind the house, and we will use only a whisper. When the woman hears that sound of whispering, she will descend to us, and we will not be harmed.'

"When she heard their voices, she sealed her ears, sprang up, and went into the interior of the house and shut herself in."

The elder telling this story said that the prostitute is the soul, her lovers are vices, but the leader and chief man is Christ. His house is the perpetual mansion of heaven, and the whisperers are the evil demons. If the soul is chaste and faithful, it will always run toward God. [AP-G John the Dwarf 16; AP-PA 55.6]

14. Abba Poemen said, "It is written in the Gospel, *let he who has one tunic sell it and buy a sword for himself* (Luke 22:36). Now understand this: he who has rest should send it away so that he can take up the battle." He was speaking about the battle against the devil. [AP-G Poemen 112]

15. The one mentioned above said, "One of the elders in the region of Egypt was living in a cell, and another brother and a virgin were taking care of him. Now it happened one day that both visited the elder, and they arrived at the same time. Since it was already evening, they were unable to leave him, so the elder placed a mat between them so that they could sleep. The brother was unable to endure the battle with his own flesh, and he defiled and corrupted the pitiable virgin. After committing this sin, he departed in the morning.

"Now the elder, when he discerned what had happened, remained silent. The next time they returned to attend to the elder, they showed no sign of distress. When he withdrew from them, one said to the other, 'Do you think this elder knows our crime or not?'

"Led by penitence, they went to him and said, 'Holy Father, do you know how the enemy seduced us?'

"He replied, 'I know, children.'

"They said, 'And what were you thinking in the hour of our death?'

"He replied to them, 'At that hour, my thoughts were in that place where Christ was crucified. I was standing and weeping, as much for me as for you. But because the Lord promised your repentance, let me warn you that you will need to pursue diligently the cure for this wound that you have incurred through pride.'

"Then, having accepted a rule of penitence from him, they each withdrew to fight forcefully, until they were able to become chosen vases." [AP-GN 13]

16. A philosopher asked the holy Anthony, "How are you able to be content, Father? Are you not deprived of the comfort of a book?"

Anthony responded, "My book, O Philosopher, is the nature of created things, which is customarily before me whenever I want to read the words of God." [AP-PA 84.3; Evag. *Prak.* 92]

17. A certain man came to Abba Macarius. He stood in the middle of the day with a great thirst and asked for some water to drink. "Let this shade be enough for you," Macarius said, "which many travelers and voyagers now need but do not enjoy."

18. I was living near an old man who offered words about the practice of continence. "Live faithfully, my son," he said. "For I also for twenty continuous years have not satiated myself with bread, water, or sleep. I am forced to take a certain amount of bread by weight, and water by its measure, but I rejoice that sleep only steals a little from me while I am leaning against a wall."

19. A brother asked an elder whether he ought to eat with brothers when they were leaving. The elder replied, "With a woman, you will not eat."

20. A brother questioned Abba Isidore of Scetis about the thought of fornication. The elder replied to him, "When that thought of fornication comes, it disturbs and occupies the soul, but it does not have the power to make the act happen nor must it make any headway. It does, however, block the path to virtue to a certain degree. Therefore, the temperate man cuts off the thought, and immediately turns to prayer."

21. The elder also said about the same thought, "If we do not have thoughts, we are similar to the animals. But, just as the enemy drives out what is his, we also should do to what is ours. Let us persist in our prayers, and the enemy will flee. Set aside time to meditate on God, and you will defeat the enemy. The perseverance of the good is a victory. It is true, you will win a crown."

22. An elder said, "The man who keeps his death before his eyes in every hour will defeat pettiness of spirit." [AP-M 95]

23. The Abbess Syncletica said, "Our adversary is overcome more easily by those who possess nothing, for he has nothing that he might use to strike them. Many people, mindful of the difficulty of wealth and its temptation to separation from God, have become accustomed to punishing themselves by giving away their money and other material resources."

24. The same woman spoke again, "There are those who collect visible wealth from the many labors and dangers of the seas. While they profit greatly, they long for even more, and they hold the wealth they possess as nothing. But let us refuse to have even necessary things out of our fear of God." [AP-G Syncletica 10; AP-GS 10.101]

25. An elder said, "He who binds a sinful memory in his soul is similar to a fire hiding in the chaff."

26. An elder said, "If you offer a sermon about eternal life, speak the word to those listening with compunction and tears; otherwise, do not speak, lest you devise useless ideas, hurrying to save others with strange words. *For God said to the sinners, Why do you recount my laws, and proclaim my covenant with your mouth?* (Ps 50:16). Therefore say, 'I am a dog, the lowest dog is better than me; the dog loves his master and he will not come to judgment.'"

27. A brother questioned an elder, asking, "Why does the soul like filth?"

The elder said to him, "The soul frequently longs for physical experiences, but the Spirit of God restrains it. Consequently, we should weep and diligently pay attention to our own filthiness. For instance, you saw that when Mary took herself back to the tomb of the Lord and wept, God called her. It will be the same way with the soul." [AP-GS 3.50; AP-M 30]

28. A brother asked an elder, "What are sins?"

The elder said to him, "Sins are when a man who considers his own faults to be nothing attempts to teach others. For this reason, the Lord says, *Hypocrite, remove first the beam from your own eye, and then you will be able to see to remove the mote from your brother's eye* (Matt 7:5)."

29. A brother asked an elder, "What should I do, for my soul wounds me in this little amount of work?"

The elder said to him, "Do we not admire Joseph? When he was a young man in Egypt, in a land that worshiped idols, he manfully endured temptations and God glorified him to the end. We see also Job; he did not let himself relax, fearing God right up to the end, and consequently, nothing was able to move him from his hope in God." [AP-G Poemen 102; AP-GS 7.19]

30. An elder was questioned by a man serving in the military, "Does God accept repentance?"

After teaching the soldier with many words, at last the elder said to him, "Tell me, dear one, if your cloak is torn, do you throw it away?"

The soldier replied, "No, I patch it and continue to use it."

The elder said, "If you spare your own garment, will God not indulge those made in his image?" [AP-G Mius 3; AP-GS 10.176; AP-PA 55.5]

31. There was a brother in a cell who, after the sacred masses had been completed and the priest dismissed the church, would wait until everyone had departed, hoping that someone might take him to eat. On one of those days, with the gathering completed, before everyone went out, this brother hurried away to his cell. When the priest saw the brother leaving, he was amazed. After a week had passed and that brother returned to the church gathering, the priest said to him, "Tell me truthfully, brother, what was the reason that you, who at every gathering of the church, always remains as the last of all, went out before everyone else at last week's gathering?"

The brother replied, "I was holding back from cooking for myself, and I was expecting that someone might take me to eat. But at that gathering, before I came to church, I cooked a few lentils for myself, and so, having consumed the sacred mystery, I went out before everybody."

Hearing these words, the priest gave a command to the church, saying, "Brothers, before you come to the gathering of the church, cook a little something for yourself, so that on account of what you have cooked, you will return to your cell with alacrity."

32. Once a magistrate of some region came into the province of Abba Poemen. Then the inhabitants of that place came and asked the elder to go and intercede with the judge. Poemen said to them, "Allow me three days and then I will go."

The elder prayed to the Lord, saying, "Lord, do not permit this honor to be given to me; otherwise men will not allow me to remain in this place."

Then the elder went and interceded before the judge. That man said, "Are you interceding for a thief, Abba?"

The elder rejoiced, because he had not received the favor that he had asked from the judge, and thus he returned to his cell. [AP-G Poemen 9; AP-PA 92.3; CSP 4.6]

33. The elders said, "When Moses went into the cloud, he spoke with God; when he left the cloud, he spoke with the people. It is the same for a monk: when he is in his cell, he speaks with God; when he leaves his cell, he speaks with demons."

34. A certain young man came to Abba Macarius so that he might be freed from a demon. While he was standing outside, a brother from another monastery arrived and had intercourse with that young man. When the elder came out of his cell, he saw that monk sinning with the young man. He did not scold him, but rather said, "If God, who formed them and now sees them, has patience with them—if God, who, if he chose, could incinerate them—then who am I to find fault with them?"

35. They spoke about another elder, who was living quietly in lower Egypt. A faithful secular man was taking care of him. It happened that the secular man's son was sick, and he asked the elder many times to come and pray over the boy. One day the elder rose and went with him.

The secular man ran ahead, and cheerfully entered his house, saying, "Come out to meet the solitary."

Now the elder, seeing people coming out with torches in the distance, understood that they were coming to meet him. He took off his clothes, threw them in the river, and, standing naked, began to wash them.

His secular servant was ashamed, seeing the elder nude. He said to the men, "Let us go back, for the elder has lost his mind." Then, coming to the elder, he said to him, "Why did you do this? Now everyone will say, 'That elder has a demon.'"

The elder answered, "That is what I wanted to hear." [AP-GN 61; AP-GS 4.35; AP-PA 33.12; AP-Pa 12.7; AP-PR 118]

36. (a) Some of the elders questioned Abba Pastor, saying, "If we see another brother sinning, should we accuse him?"

Abba Pastor replied to them, "If I must go out and I see a man sinning, I will pass by and not accuse him. (b) But because this is written, *bear witness to what your eyes have seen* (Prov 25:7–8), I say to you that if you have not touched it with your own hands, you should not testify. For once a brother was led astray in this way, as it appeared to him that another brother had sinned with a woman. When he was assailed by many thoughts and believed that the brother and woman had come together, he went out and kicked them with his foot, saying, 'Stop already.' And behold, they were sheaves of wheat. Therefore, I say to you, unless you touch it with your own hands, you should not testify." [**a:** AP-G Poemen 113; AP-GS 9.21; **b:** AP-G Poemen 114; AP-GS 9.22]

37. The fathers told a story about a certain brother: while he was living in the desert, the demons led him astray for many years, as he believed that they were angels. His natural father occasionally went out to visit him. One day his father brought a two-edged axe with him, saying, "When I come, I will bring a little wood with me."

One of the demons intervened and said to the son, "Look, the devil comes to you in the guise of your father, concealing an axe in his basket so that he can attack you. You must intervene. Take the axe from him and fight back."

When his father came, according to his custom, the son took the axe from him, struck him, and killed him. Immediately the wicked spirit clung to him and it throttled him. [AP-GN 480]

PART 3

Paschasius of Dumium, *Geronticon* (AP-PA)

PROLOGUE

Had it been permitted, I would have refused this unaccustomed task that you ordered, most holy father, of translating into Latin the lives of the fathers, that were recorded with the studious eloquence of the Greeks, as in other works. For I, inhibited by the knowledge of my embarrassing talent, have never been able to create a work to be recopied or read. I do not dare say that "I know that I know nothing" lest by using this phrase it might appear that I was plagiarizing the sentiment of the most wise Socrates. But I will use it, because I must submit to your command. I will not glory in my cleverness; I will exhibit the trust that I owe you in this work that you have enjoined.

But because there are many of these books written in the Latin language by eloquent men—and I attest that under your guidance I have studied them—if you should discover anything from them inserted here or perhaps expressed less elegantly, I would beg you not to consider it my fault. I have translated exactly what I found written in the codex you gave me, although I do not claim that I did this diligently.

Therefore, what I began, ordered by you, I will complete, assisted by your prayers. Nevertheless, if you decide that this work should be recopied, I would ask that you would deign to polish it with your own words. For it will not be clear to me that this has pleased you, unless I am also made aware of anything that is displeasing.

Chapter One

HOW THE SOLITARY SHOULD LIVE IN HIS CELL

1. One brother asked Abba Sisoes how he ought to spend the time in his cell. Abba Sisoes replied, "Eat your bread and salt, and let there be no need to cook anything." [AP-Pa 1.1a; AP-PR 44]

2. To others asking the same question, he replied, "The prophet Daniel said, *I did not eat the bread of desires* (Dan 10:3)." [AP-G Sisoes 23; AP-CSP 1.3a; AP-Pa 1.1b; PLaus 11c]

3. Two brothers came together to Abba Pambo, and one of them said, "I fast for two days, and then I eat bread. Can I be saved through this practice, or am I deluded?"

The other brother said, "I sell my work every day for two small coins, from which I retain a small amount for my needs; I use the rest for acts of mercy. Can I be saved through this practice, or am I deluded?"

After they asked their questions, which they hoped he would answer, the elder said nothing to them. When they wanted to withdraw, they were stopped by the priests, and hearing that it was the elder's custom not to give an answer quickly, they stayed behind. Then, coming to bid him goodbye, they said, "Pray for us, Father."

That man asked them if they wanted to leave. When they nodded, he recalled the works they performed, writing on the floor, "Pambo, you fast for two days and then eat bread; does this make you a monk? Doesn't Pambo also work daily for two silver coins and then use the money for acts of mercy? On account of these actions, do you hope to be a monk?"

Finally, he added, "These are good works, but if a person maintains a clear conscience about his works, then anyone can attain salvation." [AP-G Pambo 2; AP-GS 10.94; AP-PJ 10.65]

4. When Abba Poemen was questioned about how a person should fast, he replied, "I prefer a monk who eats a little each day, so that he is not satiated. For two- and three-day fasts are not free from vainglory. The elders examined these matters and they discovered that it is good to eat a little every day, so that a person might be hungry every day. They showed that this royal road is easy for us." [AP-G Poemen 31; AP-GS 10.61; AP-PJ 10.44; AP-PR 45]

Chapter Two

ON BREAKING ONE'S FAST WHEN A BROTHER ARRIVES

1. When Abba Silvanus had come to a certain monastery with his disciple, Zacharias, the monks there made them eat a little before they

departed. After they left, his disciple found some water and wanted to drink it. Abba Silvanus said, "Zacharias, today is a fast."

Zacharias replied, "Did we not eat today, Father?"

The elder said to him, "That dish was eaten because of charity. Nevertheless, we must keep our fast." [AP-G Silvanus 1; AP-GS 4.48; AP-PJ 4.40; AP-PR 46]

2. Some of the fathers had gone out to Abba Joseph in Panephysis so that they might question him about receiving brothers—whether it was permitted at that time to share either confidences or joyful conversation with them.

Before they questioned him, he said to his disciples, "Do not marvel at what I will do today." And he put out two chairs for those who came and he said to them, "Sit." He placed one on his right and the other on his left. Then, going into his cell, he donned a disgusting robe. Coming out again, he sat between them. A second time, he got up and went into his cell. He put on a better robe, one that he only wore on a feast day. Coming out, he passed between them. After this, he went in again, and then returned in his normal robe and sat between them.

They were amazed and stupefied by what he had done. He said to them, "Did you perceive what I did?"

When they nodded, he said, "What did I do?"

They replied, "First you used a disgusting robe, and afterward a better robe."

He said, "Was I changed when I wore the shameful robe or the better one?"

"No," they answered.

The elder said, "And so if I am the same in either, I am not changed; the first robe does me no harm, the second does not alter me. Consequently, this is what we must do when we meet the brothers, so that when they are present, we receive them with confidence and joy. When we are alone sorrow must remain in us."

Those who heard what they had believed in their hearts before they had even asked, glorified God and departed happily. [AP-G Joseph of Panephysis 1; AP-GS 13.1; AP-CSP 1.16; AP-PJ 13.1; AP-PR 47]

3. One elder said to another elder, who was charitable and was receiving as many monks as secular visitors, "The lamp gives light to many, nevertheless it will burn its own base." [AP-GN 18; AP-Pa 1.2; PLaus 20.9]

4. One of the fathers said that a man was found who ate much but stopped himself while he was still hungry. Another man was found who ate little and was satisfied. The man who ate much but left himself hungry had a greater reward than the man who ate little and was satisfied. [AP-GN 231; AP-GS 10.154; AP-PJ 10.99; AP-Pa 1.3; AP-PR 48]

Chapter Three

ON CONQUERING GLUTTONY

1. An elder said, "Eat from time to time to keep yourself from desiring food. Nevertheless, when eating what the Lord has sent you, give him thanks." [AP-Pa 1.4; AP-PR 49]

2. The fathers told a story about a certain elder who had desired a cucumber. After he acquired one, he suspended it in front of his eyes. To ensure that he was not conquered by desire, he did not touch the cucumber, but rather, he performed a great penance, punishing himself with the very thing that he desired. [AP-GN 152; AP-GS 4.73; AP-PJ 4.60; AP-PR 50]

3. Abba Zeno became tired while he was walking in Palestine, and he sat down near some plants that were bearing cucumbers in a garden. He wanted to eat one and said to himself, "Take a cucumber and eat. What is this little thing?"

He then replied to his own thought, "Do you know that thieves go down to punishment? Let us see if you are able to bear those torments."

He rose to his feet and stood in the heat for five days. He fried himself, saying, "I am unable to bear the torments. Consequently, if I am unable to stand them, I must not steal and eat." [AP-G Zeno 6; AP-GS 4.17; AP-CSP 1.14; AP-PJ 4.17; AP-PR 7]

4. When the fruit was ripe, Abba Arsenius would order that some be brought to him. Then, tasting only a little from each, he would give thanks to God. [AP-G Arsenius 19; AP-GS 4.6; AP-PJ 4.6]

5. One of the elders had become weak, and for several days he was unable to take any food. His disciple prodded him, saying, "Do you want me to make a little flat-cake for you?" Then he went and did what he said.

Now there was a little vase containing honey, and a similar vase that contained oil extracted from flaxseed. The oil was fetid, and was of no use apart from fueling a lamp. The brother confused the two and poured oil into the elder's food from that vase, thinking that it was honey.

When the elder tasted the food, he said nothing, but ate in silence. He ate a second time, when his disciple urged him. The third time, however, when the disciple gave him food, the elder said, "I am unable to eat, my son."

The disciple, wanting to encourage him, said, "Look, Abba, these flat-cakes are good. I will eat some."

After he tasted the food, he realized what he had done. He fell on his face, saying, "Woe to me, Father, because I have killed you! You have placed this sin upon me because you did not tell me."

The elder said to him, "Do not be afraid because of this, my son. For if God had wanted me to eat honey, you would have sent me honey." [AP-GS 4.72; AP-GN 151; AP-PJ 4.59; AP-PR 51]

6. His disciple, Abraham, asked Abba Sisoes if, on the day of the Sabbath, having participated in the *agape* in the church, a monk must drink three cups of wine. Sisoes replied, "If Satan is not there, then three cups is not much, but if Satan—that is, lust—is present, then this is already too much." [AP-G Sisoes 2b; AP-GS 4.45; AP-PJ 4.37]

7. Abba Poemen said, "Unless Nebuzaradan, the chief cook, had come to Jerusalem, he would not have burned the Temple of the Lord with fire (cf. 2 Kgs 25:9). In the same way, unless gluttonous desire comes into the soul, a man's senses will not be set on fire by the assault of the devil." [AP-G Poemen 16; AP-GS 4.32; AP-CSP 1.8; AP-PJ 4.29; AP-PR 52; PLaus 20.1]

Chapter Four

THAT THE RECOLLECTION OF THE PERFECT MAN TAKES AWAY THE DESIRE FOR FOOD

1. His disciple frequently told Abba Sisoes, "It is time, Father, for us to eat."

The elder would respond, "Why son, have we not eaten yet?" Then, when his disciple shook his head, the elder would say, "Bring the food, so that if we have not eaten already, then we may eat." This was because his desire for God led him to forget food. [AP-G Sisoes 4; AP-GS 4.46; AP-PJ 4.38]

Chapter Five

ON HIDING ABSTINENCE

1. Now Eulogius—a disciple of John, the bishop of Constantinople, and a priest who was very religious—was always fasting for two days, and often he would maintain his fast for a week. Eating only bread and salt, he was praised by men. When he heard of those who lived in Scetis—that their lives were great—he hoped that he might receive some instruction from them, so he traveled to Pelusium. But he became afraid when he saw the desert stretching between Scetis and Mazyces. The brothers said to him, "There is a great elder from Scetis in that place that is called Panephysis. His name is Joseph. Go to him."

Now when he reached Abba Joseph, he hoped to find something harder in their way of life. The elder received him joyfully and said to his disciple, "Put out whatever you have for us today on account of the foreign visitors."

When they sat to eat, those who had accompanied Eulogius said, "Take a little salt," for the priest did not eat any of these things. Nevertheless, Abba Joseph silently drank and ate. Eulogius spent three days in that place, but he did not hear the elder chanting psalms or see him praying. Whatever he did, he did in secret. Consequently, Eulogius departed, having received no help.

Now through God's dispensation there was fog that day. The party went astray and returned to the cell of the elder again near evening. Before they knocked on his door, they heard the monks in the cell chanting psalms for many hours. But when they knocked on the door, the monks fell silent. When the group entered, the elder received them with great joy again. Because the summer night was oppressive, those who were with the priest Eulogius came, took a flask of water, and offered it to him so that he could drink. Now the water itself was seawater mixed with water from the river. When he tasted it, Eulogius could not drink it.

After considering what he had seen, Eulogius went to the elder, fell at his feet, and begged him to explain his way of life, saying, "How is it, Abba, that while we were in this place, you never chanted the psalms, and then after we had left we heard you chanting for such a long time? Or again, when I wanted to drink, I found that the water was salty?"

The elder said to him, "That brother who is with me—I can't believe how foolish he is. He mistakenly sent seawater here."

Eulogius persisted, begging to know the truth.

Then Abba Joseph said to him, "When we drink, we drink a small glass of wine out of our affection for Christ. Nevertheless, the brothers always use this water." Then Joseph taught Eulogius the discernment of all thoughts and said that he must labor in secret if he wanted to accomplish some good, rather than openly before men. Eulogius became remarkable after this, and he was eating everything that was placed before him. He learned to perform his good works in secret. Having been helped, Eulogius left that place with great joy. [AP-G Eulogius 1; AP-GS 8.4; AP-PJ 8.4]

2. Abba Macarius, to restore himself after he had shared a meal with the brothers, had established this rule in his own heart: for each goblet of wine he was given to drink, he would spend the same number of days without drinking any water. If the brothers brought him wine, he drank it with joy, but later he would punish himself with thirst. When his disciple saw this, he disclosed the decision to the elders and conspired to prevent the brothers from bringing him wine, revealing that they were heaping torments rather than cups upon him. [AP-G Macarius the Great 10; AP-GS 4.29; AP-PJ 4.26; AP-PR 53]

Chapter Six

ON TOLERATING DESTITUTION

1. A certain brother said to Abba Theodore, "I would like to not eat bread for a few days." The elder replied, "You do well. For I also remember doing something like this once."

The brother said, "I want to go to the flour mill and make chickpea flour."

The blessed Theodore answered, "If you only want to go to the flour mill once, then make your bread and eat it. For what is the point of others knowing that you do not taste bread?" [AP-G Theodore of Pherme 7; AP-GS 8.10; AP-PJ 8.7]

2. The congregation had gathered in the church on a feast day, and as the others ate, one of the brothers said to the men who were serving, "Because I do not eat anything cooked, hurry and bring me some salt." When the serving brother heard this statement, he ordered the serving monks with a shout heard by all the others, saying, "Because this brother does not eat cooked food, bring him a little salt."

Then the blessed Theodore said, "It would have been better for you to have eaten meat in your cell than to hear these words in the presence of all the brothers." [AP-GN 256; AP-GS 8.26; AP-CSP 1.7; AP-PJ 8.21; AP-PR 54]

Chapter Seven

A MONK SHOULD NOT EAT UNLESS HE WORKS

1. A foreign brother came to Abba Silvanus on Mount Sinai, and he saw that the brothers were working and he said to them, "Why do you *work for food that perishes? For Mary has chosen the good portion* (John 6:27; Luke 10:42)."

Then the elder said to his disciple, Zacharias, "Give that man a book to read and send him into a cell that has nothing in it."

When the ninth hour arrived, that monk began looking around to see if, perhaps, the elder had summoned him to eat. After the ninth hour had passed, he went to the elder and said, "Didn't the brothers eat anything today, Abba?"

When the elder acknowledged that they had eaten, that monk asked, "Why didn't you call me?"

Then Abba Silvanus said to him, "You are a spiritual man, and you do not need this food. Because we are carnal men, we have to eat;

consequently, we must work. You have chosen the good portion, for you read all day, and you do not wish to receive carnal food."

When he heard this, the brother began to repent and to say, "Forgive me."

Silvanus responded, "And so Martha is necessary for Mary, for because of Martha, Mary is praised." [AP-G Silvanus 5; AP-GS 10.99; AP-PJ 10.69; AP-PR 55]

2. Abba John said to his older brother, "I want to be carefree—as the angels are carefree—doing no work, but rather praising the Lord all the time." He then threw off his robe and went out in the desert. After staying there for seven days, he returned to his brother.

When he knocked on the door, his brother did not open it, but said, "Who are you?"

That man said, "I am John."

His brother replied, "John has become an angel and he is no longer among men."

John begged him again, saying, "It's me."

But his brother did not want to open the door, and left him outside while it was growing light.

When morning came, the brother said to John, "You are a man, and it is necessary that you work so that you may eat."

Then John threw himself at his brother's feet and said, "Forgive me, for I am a man and I desire food." [AP-G John the Dwarf 2; AP-GS 10.36; AP-PJ 10.27; AP-PR 56]

Chapter Eight

AGAINST THE SPIRIT OF BLASPHEMY

1. A certain brother was being attacked by the spirit of blasphemy, and he was embarrassed to speak of it. He had heard of some great elders, and he went to them to disclose his condition, but as soon as he arrived, he again became ashamed and did not speak to them.

Consequently, after often visiting Abba Poemen, the elder saw that he was having thoughts, and said to him, "Look, you often come to me, troubled by your thoughts, and then you leave, sad, taking your thoughts with you. Now tell me what problem you have, my son."

That monk replied, "The devil attacks me with blasphemy, and I am too embarrassed to speak of it." As soon as he disclosed the reason, the attack against him appeared to weaken.

The elder said to him, "Do not be sad, my son. When this thought comes to you, say, 'I am not responsible for this thought; let your blasphemy be upon you, Satan, for my soul does not want this responsibility.'"

Now if the soul is not responsible for a thought, the thought will not remain long. Consequently, the brother was restored to health and departed. [AP-G Poemen 93; AP-GS 10.63; AP-Pa 1.5; AP-PR 57]

Chapter Nine

ON THE ORIGIN OF BODILY SUFFERING

1. Abba Moses said, "These four causes produce suffering: an abundance of food and drink; an overabundance of sleep; free time and joking; and appearing in fine clothing." [AP-Pa 1.6; AP-PR 58]

2. The same man said, "There are many passions in the body."

A brother asked him, "What are they?"

That man replied, "As the Apostle Paul says, *Fornication, uncleanliness, and every kind of lust must not be named in us, as befits holy people* (Eph 5:3). Laughter and money-lending also frequently lead to a battle." [AP-GN 427a; AP-GS 5.51a; AP-Pa 1.7]

3. Abba Poemen said, "Just as a member of the imperial bodyguard is armed when he stands by the emperor, the soul should also always be armed in the same way against a demon." [AP-G Poemen 14; AP-GS 5.7; AP-PJ 5.8; AP-PR 59]

Chapter Ten

WHAT ONE MUST PRAY IN ORDER TO RESIST DEMONS

1. An elder said, "Just as poisonous animals are driven away by the stronger herbs or pigments, prayer with fasting repels unclean thoughts." [AP-G Syncletica 3; AP-GS 4.50; AP-PJ 4.42; AP-PR 60]

2. A brother asked one of the fathers, "What should I do? My thoughts disturb me; they do not permit me to rest for even an hour and they sadden my spirit."

The elder replied, "When thoughts come into your heart, do not speak with them. For it is always their nature to suggest, rather than to force. They cannot compel you to do anything. It is in your power to receive them. You know what the Midianites did? They dressed up their daughters and put them on display. They compelled no man to take them, but whoever wanted the girls, fell with them. But others, becoming angry, killed them (cf. Num 25). The same thing is true of thoughts."

The brother said, "What should I do? I am weak and am not strong enough to fight."

The elder answered, "Consider, and when they begin to speak with you, do not respond to them, but rise, pray, and begin to meditate. [Prostrate yourself and say, 'Have mercy on me, Son of God.']"

The brother said, "I do meditate, but there is no compunction in my heart because I do not understand the power of this saying."

The elder responded, "It is essential to meditate, my son. I once heard something that Abba Poemen and many other holy fathers said about this saying: enchanters do not understand the power of the words they speak, but nevertheless the snakes that hear understand the power of their words, and they lie quietly and are subdued by them. The same is true for us. Even if we do not understand the power of these words that we speak, the demons, who are listening, will flee in terror." [AP-GN 184a; AP-GS 5.37; AP-CSP 6.5; AP-PJ 5.32; AP-PR 40]

3. A brother asked one of the elders, "What should I do? My thoughts disturb me."

The elder replied, "When a mother wants to wean a child, she rubs the juice of the sea onion around her nipple. When the child comes, accustomed to receiving a meal, it tastes the bitterness and flees. In the same way, apply sea onion to yourself."

The brother said, "What is this sea onion that I must apply to myself?"

The elder answered, "The recollection of your death and the torments of the age to come." [AP-GN 182; AP-GS 5.35; AP-PJ 5.30]

4. When Abba Macarius lived alone in the desert, the lower part of the desert was full of many brothers. While he was watching the road late at night, he saw a demon approaching in the shape of a man, wearing a perforated linen tunic. A small flask hung from each of the holes.

The elder said to the demon, "Where are you going, great one?"

The demon replied. "I am going to disturb the brothers who are living below."

At this, the elder asked, "Why are you carrying all of those little flasks with you?"

The demon said, "I bring a taste to the brothers, and therefore I must bring many options, so that if one should displease the brother, I put out another, and if that doesn't please him, I offer something else. It is impossible to do anything unless one of my samples pleases them." After saying these words, the demon departed.

The elder remained on the road, watching until the demon returned, and when he did, the elder said, "Be well!"

That demon replied, "What is your greeting to me? All of the monks were against me, and none of them received my counsels."

The elder replied, "And so you have made no friend?"

The demon replied, "I have one friend, or at least one who agrees with me and will see me often. He will be converted quickly."

When the elder asked for the monk's name, the demon said, "Theopentus."

After the demon departed, Abba Macarius quickly rose and descended to the lower desert. When the brothers heard that he had arrived, they went out to meet him. Each monk, hoping that the elder would stay with him, prepared himself.

Macarius asked for the cell of Theopentus, and then made his way to the monk. Theopentus received him with joy, and later, when they were alone together, the elder said, "How are you, my brother?"

Theopentus replied, "It is well, because of your prayers."

The elder asked, "Thoughts do not attack us?"

The monk responded, "I am well," because he was ashamed to speak.

The elder said to him, "Look how many years I have lived in the wilderness, honored by all men. Although I am an elder, even in this state I still find that my thoughts trouble me."

Theopentus replied, "Believe me, Abba, the same thing happens to me."

Then the elder began discussing each of the thoughts, as if they were assaulting him, until Theopentus confessed everything to him.

After this, the elder asked, "How do you fast?"

And Theopentus said, "Until the ninth hour."

Macarius said, "Fast until evening and meditate on the Gospels or other Scriptures without ceasing. Whenever an unclean thought comes upon you, never look down, but rather, look up, and soon the Lord will help you."

Shortly thereafter, Abba Macarius returned to his wilderness. Once again, watching the road, he saw the demon coming, and asked him, "Where are you going?"

The demon replied, "I am going again to stir up the brothers."

When the demon returned, Macarius asked, "How are the brothers?"

"Poor," said the demon. "They have all become savage, and the worst thing is that the one I had as a friend, the monk who was obedient to me, well, I don't know how he has been turned, but it seems to me that he is now more severe toward me than all the rest. I swore that I would not return there for a long time." Having spoken these words, the demon departed. [AP-G Macarius the Great 3; AP-GS 18.13; AP-Pa 1.8; AP-PJ 18.9; AP-PR 61]

Chapter Eleven

ABOUT HOW THE PASSIONS ARE DEFEATED THROUGH THE ABSTINENCE OF FASTING AND VIGILS

1. A brother questioned one of the elders, saying, "What should I do? I am unable to bear my thoughts."

The elder admitted, "I am never attacked in this manner."

The brother was scandalized, and he went to a different elder and said to him, "Look, do you know what that elder said to me? I was scandalized by him, because he spoke like one above human nature."

Then the second elder said to him, "It was not easy for that man of God to tell you this. Now go and bow before him, so that he might explain to you the power of what he said."

Returning, the brother came to the elder and he began to say to him, "Forgive me, Abba, because I acted foolishly. I did not say goodbye to you before I left. Now I beg you, explain to me why you are not attacked."

The elder said to him, "From the time I was made a monk, I have never satiated myself with bread, water, or sleep. My longing for all of these pleasures does not permit me to have the battle that you described."

Then, the brother who had been helped by him departed. [AP-GN 183; AP-GS 5.36; AP-PJ 5.31; AP-PR 62]

2. Having been questioned again about thoughts, Abba Poemen said, "A monk, if he masters his belly and his tongue, and does not accompany those who stroll about, should be confident that he will not die." [AP-G Poemen 62b; AP-GS 5.9b; AP-PJ 5.9b; AP-Pa 1.9; AP-PR 63]

3. Two brothers, who were being attacked by their thoughts, came to Abba Elias. When the elder saw that they were overweight, he smiled at his disciple and said, "Truly brother, I am ashamed on your account, because you feed your body in this way, although you profess yourself to be a monk. Pallor and thinness with humility is the glory of a monk." [AP-Pa 1.10a; AP-PR 64a]

4. He said again, "The monk who eats much and works much should not be trusted. On the other hand, trust a monk who eats little, even if he works little, and he will perform manfully." [AP-PR 64b; AP-Pa 1.10b]

Chapter Twelve

ON FLEEING WOMEN

1. While Abba Arsenius was living in Canopus, a certain woman, a virgin who was wealthy and feared God, came from Rome to Alexandria. Arsenius's fame had spread widely, and she hoped to have an opportunity to see him. After she had been received respectfully by Theophilus, the archbishop of the city, she asked him if he could persuade the blessed Arsenius to extend the honor of receiving her.

And so the archbishop himself went to Arsenius and said, "A certain woman, a Roman, surpassing everyone else in dignity, riches, and reputation, wishes to see you and be blessed. She has come from such a distant region that I insist you meet with her."

When Arsenius refused to meet her, and the woman learned of his refusal, she ordered her horse to be saddled, saying, "I have faith in my God that I will see that man and that I will not be cheated of my opportunity. For I did not come here to see men, who abound in our own city; I want to see a prophet."

When she came to the cell of the blessed Arsenius, she saw him walking outside. Quickly she threw herself down on her face at his feet. Arsenius immediately lifted her up, and rebuked her, saying, "If you desire to see my face so much, then look."

But she, because of her embarrassment, did not dare raise her eyes.

The elder said to her, "Did you not want to learn something about my actions? You should look at them. Why else did you presume to cross such a great sea? Do you not know that you are a woman and it is not permitted for you to go out? Did you come to this place so that later, after you have returned to Rome, you can boast to all the other women that you saw Arsenius, which will result in the sea becoming a highway of women coming to see me?"

She replied, "If God wills, I will permit no women to come here. But I ask that you pray for me and would deign to keep me in your memory."

Arsenius replied, "I pray to my God that he will delete your memory from my heart."

After hearing these words, the woman returned to the city and was struck down by an illness on account of her experience. When the bishop came to pay her a visit and inquire about her problem, she told him the last thing the elder had said about remembering her. Then she confessed that she wanted to die because of her sorrow.

The bishop consoled her with a very reassuring word, "Are you completely unaware that you are a woman? Do you not know that the enemy customarily attacks a man through women? Of course he said that he would delete your face from his heart. Nevertheless he prays to the Lord for your soul."

With these words, the woman was restored. [AP-G Arsenius 28; AP-GS 2.10; AP-PJ 2.7; AP-PR 65]

Chapter Thirteen

CARNAL PASSIONS MAY BE UNDERMINED BY HUNGER AND THIRST

1. **(a)** Abba Moses said, "If a general wanted to overcome some city of his enemies, first he would cut off their food and water, and thus his enemies, compelled by hunger, would submit to his rule. It is the same with the carnal passions; if you decided to live in a state of fasting and hunger, they would be discouraged and would not have power against your soul. **(b)** For who is as powerful as the lion? Nevertheless, he will enter a cage because of his belly, and then his strength is mocked." [**a:** AP-G John the Dwarf 3; AP-GS 4.20; AP-CSP 1.3c; AP-PJ 4.19; AP-PR 66a; **b:** AP-CSP 1.3b; AP-PR 66b; PLaus 11d]

Chapter Fourteen

AGAINST THE LOVE OF MONEY; CONCERNING THE PERFECT RENUNCIATION OF WEALTH

1. A wealthy young man wanted to renounce the world, but as often as he left his home, his thoughts, which involved his various business dealings, called him back. One day they surrounded him as he was going out, and they raised a great cloud of dust before him, so that he might return to his house. That man immediately stripped, and casting his clothing aside, he hurried, naked, to a monastery.

Now God spoke to one of the elders, saying, "Get up and receive my athlete."

The elder went out and met that naked man. When he learned the reason for his nudity, he marveled and gave him the monastic habit to wear.

When someone else would come to that elder to ask him about various thoughts, he would reply, "You should ask this brother about renunciation, because I have yet to attain his level of renunciation." [AP-GN 51; AP-Pa 2.1; AP-PR 67]

2. A certain brother renounced the world. Although he gave his possessions to the poor, he retained a certain amount for his own use. Then he came to Abba Anthony.

When the elder discovered what he had done, he said, "If you want to become a monk, go into the village and buy some meat for yourself. Tie the meat to your naked body and come back to me."

When the brother did this, the dogs and birds began attacking his entire body because of the meat, slashing at him with fangs and claws. When he returned to Anthony, the elder asked if he had done what he had been ordered to do. He showed Anthony his lacerated body. Then the holy Anthony said to him, "Whoever renounces the world, but wishes to still have a little money, will be cut up by the demons in the same manner." [AP-G Anthony 20; AP-GS 6.1; AP-PJ 6.1; AP-PR 68]

3. When a certain magistrate had come to the blessed Arsenius, bringing the will of a relative, which left a very generous inheritance to him, that man hurried to destroy the document. When the magistrate threw himself at Arsenius's feet and begged him not to destroy it lest they cut off his head, Arsenius replied, "I was dead to the world before this man. He has died only recently." Then he quickly returned the will, refusing to learn what had been written in it. [AP-G Arsenius 29; AP-GS 6.2; AP-PJ 6.2]

4. A certain brother questioned an elder, saying, "Do you want me to retain two *solidi* for when my body becomes weak?"

The elder, seeing his thoughts and understanding that he wanted to keep the money, said, "Keep them."

The brother returned to his cell and began to wrestle with his thoughts, saying "Do you believe that the elder spoke truly to me or not?" Then, getting up, he went again to the elder and said, "Before God, tell me the truth, for my thoughts disturb me because of these two *solidi*."

The elder said to him, "Because I saw that your mind wanted to keep them, I said that you should keep them, but it is not good to keep more than is necessary to support the body. Those two *solidi* are your hope, even if it should happen that you lose them. Doesn't God think about us? So direct your thinking toward God, for he cares about us." [AP-GN 262; AP-GS 6.26; AP-PJ 6.22; AP-PR 69]

5. When Abba Theodore was a young man, he had three good spiritual books. He went to Abba Macarius and said, "What should I do, for I own three books? Do you order me to retain them to read and improve myself and also to share them with others for their instruction, or should I sell them and give the money as alms to the poor?"

The elder answered, "Both actions are good, but it is better to possess nothing."

Hearing this, Theodore immediately sold the books and offered the money for alms. [AP-G Theodore of Pherme 1; AP-GS 6.7; AP-PJ 6.6]

6. One of the monks owned a copy of the Gospels. He sold it and gave the proceeds to the hungry, saying something that is worth remembering: "I have sold the very word that was always telling me, *Sell what you own and give to the poor* (Matt 19:21)." [AP-GN 392; AP-GS 6.6; AP-PJ 6.5; AP-PR 70]

7. When one of the fathers was asked if poverty was a perfect good, he responded, "It is a great thing. For the man who endures it of his own will has bodily tribulation but a soul that is at peace. Tribulation and poverty are the tools of the monk." [AP-G Syncletica 5; AP-GS 6.17; AP-PJ 6.13]

8. Once Abba Arsenius became ill. He needed to pay his few coins for medical care. When he did not have any money for food, he accepted alms from another man, and he said, "I thank you, Lord, for you have made me worthy, on account of your name, to receive alms." [AP-G Arsenius 20; AP-GS 6.3; AP-PJ 6.3]

9. When a man asked Abba Agathon to take some money for his own use, Agathon refused, saying, "The work of my hands feeds me."

When that man persisted and said that he should take it on account of the poor, Agathon replied, "That is twice as shameful, because not being poor I would take your money, and by taking responsibility for others, I would fall to vainglory." [AP-GN 258; AP-GS 6.21; AP-PJ 6.17; AP-PR 71]

10. Abba Paul the Galatian said, "If a monk wants to keep some possessions in his cell, then, because of those objects he cannot live without, he will often be compelled to leave his cell and thus will be deceived by a demon." [AP-G Paul the Great 1; AP-GS 7.21; AP-Pa 2.2a; AP-PR 72a]

11. Now Paul himself kept this rule during one forty-day fast in Lent: he endured it with a sixth part of lentils and a small flask of water, and making a straw mat, he wove and unwove it to keep from going outside. [AP-G Paul the Great 3; AP-GS 4.41; AP-Pa 2.2b; AP-PR 72b]

12. A brother questioned an elder, saying, "Be charitable, Abba, and speak a word to me: what am I able to collect in my youth that I will be able to retain in my old age?"

The elder responded, "Either come to Christ and think about yourself, or choose money, so that you won't have to beg." [AP-Pa 2.3]

13. Abba Agathon frequently warned his disciple, saying, "Do not acquire anything for yourself that you would be reluctant to give to a brother who wanted it and, through this, find that you had broken the command of God." [AP-Pa 2.4]

Chapter Fifteen

A MONK SHOULD NOT GRIEVE IF HE LOSES SOMETHING

1. Abba Macarius, when he was living in Egypt, had gone out from his cell, and when he returned, he discovered that he had a thief in his cell. And so he stayed, and like a stranger, loaded the animal with that man, and then led him away with great peace, saying, "*We brought nothing into this world* (1 Tim 6:7). *The Lord gives* (Job 1:21), and whatever he wills, happens. Blessed be the Lord in all things." [AP-G Macarius the Great 18; AP-GS 16.8; AP-PJ 16.6; AP-Pa 3.1; AP-PR 73]

2. A brother lived near the cell of a great elder, and he would enter that cell secretly and steal whatever the elder had. Now when the elder saw this, he did not accuse him, but rather worked even harder, saying, "I believe that this brother is in need."

That elder was suffering a great hardship from his lack of bread. When he was dying and the brothers had gathered around him, he saw the brother who had been stealing his bread, and he said to him, "Come closer to me, brother."

The elder took the brother's hand, kissed it, and then said, "I give thanks for these hands, brothers, for through them, I have been judged worthy to enter the kingdom of heaven."

The thief was overwhelmed by these words. He repented and became the most vigorous of all the monks, conforming to what he had seen the elder do. [AP-GN 339; AP-GS 16.28; AP-PJ 16.19; AP-Pa 3.2; AP-PR 74]

Chapter Sixteen

TOLERATING POVERTY LEADS TO ETERNAL REST

1. One of the elders said, "We find nothing written about that poor man, Lazarus, that would suggest he had done anything virtuous.

The only possibility is that he never grumbled about the wealthy man, although that man offered no mercy to him. He bore the work of his poverty with a measure of grace, and therefore, he was received into the bosom of Abraham." [AP-GN 376; AP-GS 7.47; AP-Pa 4.1]

2. The same man said, "It is not right to think of anything, except our fear of God. For even if a bodily necessity compels us to be anxious, we should never think about its demands before it is time." [AP-Pa 4.2]

Chapter Seventeen

ONE SHOULD NOT BE SCRUPULOUS WHEN GIVING CHARITY

1. A certain priest was performing many acts of mercy. A widow came to him, seeking a little wheat. The priest said to her, "Go, bring a vase, and I will give you some."

The woman returned with a sack. Seeing it, the priest said, "It is large," and he embarrassed the widow.

After he had sent her away, a certain elder said to him, "Didn't you sell wheat to that widow?"

The priest said, "No, but I gave her some for charity."

The elder responded, "You gave that woman a large quantity as charity, even though you appeared to be scrupulous about the small amount that she actually wanted, and you made her feel embarrassed? Do you not know that if anyone performs good works, but the enemy is allowed to introduce any form of scrupulousness, then he will lose the reward for the good works he did?" [AP-GN 282; AP-GS 13.16; AP-PJ 13.14]

Chapter Eighteen

ON RESTRAINING AVARICE

1. While Abba Silvanus was away from his cell, his disciple, Zacharias, with the brothers, moved the fence of Silvanus's garden and

made a larger garden. When the elder returned later, he noticed the change, and put on his sheepskin so that he could go away. His disciples threw themselves at his feet, demanding that he should tell them why he was doing this.

Then the elder said, "I will not enter this cell, unless the fence has been restored to its original position." When this was quickly accomplished, the elder returned. [AP-G Silvanus 8; AP-Pa 5.1]

2. A brother questioned an elder, asking, "If a brother owes me a few coins, do you order that I should remind him about it?"

The elder replied, "Speak to that brother only once, with humility."

The brother said, "What if I speak to him once, and he doesn't give me anything? What should I do?"

Then the elder said, "Say nothing more to him."

The brother replied, "And what shall I do because I will be unable to conquer my thought, unless I have bothered that man?"

The elder said, "Send your thought to rattle about. Only do not sadden your brother, because you are a monk." [AP-G Poemen 169; AP-Pa 5.2; AP-PR 170]

3. (a) Abba Agathon was peaceably selling the work of his hands to those who wanted to buy it. Now 100 coins was the price of a sieve, but a little basket was 250. He stated the price to those wanting to buy, and he quietly received whatever they gave to him, never counting the coins.

(b) He said, "How would it help me to quarrel with them so that they might sin and swear falsely? When I have more coins than I need, I give them to the brothers. Because God does not want alms of this type from me, it would not please him if I permitted someone to sin while making their sacrifice."

A brother asked him, "Where will the bread in your cell come from?"

Agathon replied, "What is the bread of man in the cell?" [**a:** AP-G Agathon 16; AP-Pa 5.3a; **b:** AP-Pa 5.3b]

Chapter Nineteen

ON THE UTILITY OF CLOTHING

1. Abba Agathon managed himself carefully, and he thrived in all things in the work of his hands as well as his clothing—through

discretion. For he wore garments of such a kind that they appeared insufficient to both the good and the wicked. [AP-G Agathon 10; AP-GS 10.14; AP-PR 75]

2. When Abba Arsenius was a secular man and was above nearly every other man, he wore expensive clothing; when he moved to the desert, he hurried to don robes that were worse than what everyone else wore. [AP-G Arsenius 4; AP-GS 15.6; AP-CSP 6.1b; AP-PJ 15.6; AP-PR 37b]

Chapter Twenty

ON THE ORIGIN OF ANGER

1. **(a)** Anger arises from these four causes: through avaricious desire, generated by giving and receiving; when someone loves his own opinion and defends it; when someone wants to magnify himself with honors; and when a person wants to be considered a teacher and hopes to be wiser than everyone else.

Anger from these four causes darkens human perception: if a man holds his neighbor in contempt; if he regards him as worthless; if he envies that man; if he tears him down.

(b) A man's anger manifests itself in four ways: first, from the heart; second, from the face; third from the voice; fourth, from what is done. If anyone wants to remove evil, so that it does not enter his heart, let it not reach his face. If it should come to his face, he should guard his speech so that he does not speak of it. If he does speak of it, he should watch that he does not actually do the evil, but rather, he should quickly dismiss it.

(c) There are three grades of men in the passion of anger: the man who willingly is harmed and injured and shows mercy to his neighbor is a man who is following the nature of Christ. The man who does not want to hurt someone nor want to be hurt is following the nature of Adam. But the man who hurts or injures others, pours out malicious charges, or demands high interest rates, this man follows the nature of the devil. [**a:** AP-Pa 6.1a; AP-PR 76a; **b:** AP-G Poemen 34; AP-GS 18.23; AP-PJ 18.18; AP-Pa 6.1b; AP-PR 76b; **c:** AP-Pa 6.1c; AP-PR 76c]

Chapter Twenty-One

ON NOT RETURNING EVIL FOR EVIL

1. Some brothers came to Abba Anthony, asking to hear a word through which they might be saved. That man said to them, "Do you listen to the Scriptures? Know that these writings should suffice for you."

The brothers continued to insist that he agree to say something to them.

Then he said, "The Gospel says, *If anyone strikes you on the right cheek, turn the other also to that man* (Matt 5:39)."

The brothers responded that it was impossible for them to do this.

The elder replied, "If you are unable to turn the other cheek, then at least offer the same one to be struck again, if he wishes."

Since they swore that they could not do this either, the elder said to them, "If you are unable to do this, at least do not return what you have received."

When they repeated the sentiment they spoke before, Abba Anthony said to his disciple, "Go, prepare food for these brothers so that they can eat, for you can see that they are very weak." Then he said to them, "If you are unable to do one thing, and unwilling to do the other, what do you want from me? As I see it, prayer is necessary for you; your weakness might be healed by this." [AP-G Anthony 19; AP-GS 16.1; AP-PJ 21.11; AP-Pa 6.2]

2. A brother who had been hurt by another came to Abba Sisoes. After explaining the mistreatment, he said, "I want to vindicate myself."

The elder began to beg him to turn the vengeance over to God.

The brother said, "I will not be able to let this go unless I am strongly avenged."

The elder responded to him, "Since you have established this in your soul, we should pray." The elder rose to his feet and began to pray these words, "Lord, you are no longer necessary to us, nor do you need to be troubled on our behalf, because we ourselves, just as this brother said, both want and are able to take revenge."

When that brother heard these words, he begged for forgiveness before the elder's feet, promising that he would never fight with that man who had angered him. [AP-G Sisoes 1; AP-GS 16.13; AP-PJ 16.10; AP-Pa 7.1; AP-PR 77; PLaus 20.14b]

3. **(a)** A brother, when he had been injured by another, came and reported it to an elder. The elder said to him, "Emend your thoughts because your brother did not want to hurt you; your sins have produced this. **(b)** For in every temptation that touches you through a man, do not blame him, but say only, 'These things happen to me on account of my sins.'" [**a:** AP-G Or 12; AP-Pa 7.2a; AP-PR 78a; **b:** AP-GN 305; AP-GS 15.79; AP-PJ 15.61; AP-Pa 7.2b; AP-PR 78b]

Chapter Twenty-Two

ON RETURNING GOOD FOR EVIL

1. Abba Poemen often said, "Malice never overpowers malice; if anyone wrongs you, you must return good to that person, and through goodness, you will conquer malice." [AP-G Poemen 177; AP-GS 10.77; AP-PJ 10.53; AP-Pa 7.3; AP-PR 79]

2. The more someone injured or derided one brother, the more he would run back to him, saying, "These are the people who offer us an opportunity to make progress. On the other hand, those people who bless us, disturb our souls. For it is written, *Those who bless you, deceive you* (Isa 3:12)." [AP-GS 16.16; AP-GN 336; AP-PJ 16.12; AP-Pa 7.4; AP-PR 80]

3. Another elder would hurry to return good to anyone who slandered him, if that person lived nearby. However, if the detractor lived far away, the elder would send him gifts. [AP-Pa 7.5; AP-PR 81]

Chapter Twenty-Three

ON NOT RESISTING ONE'S ENEMIES

1. A brother questioned Abba Sisoes, saying, "If thieves or barbarians rush in, wanting to kill me, and I overcome them, do you command that I should kill them?"

Sisoes replied, "You must not do that. Rather, hand everything over to God. For anything that touches you adversely has come on account of your sins. But if anything good comes, you should ascribe it all to the divine dispensation." [AP-Pa 8.1; AP-PR 82]

2. There was a great hermit on the mountain that is called Athlibeus. One day thieves came upon him. When he gave a shout, the brothers poured out from the surrounding places and captured the thieves. They were sent to the city, and a judge sentenced them to prison. But the brothers became very sad because, on account of them, the thieves had been sent to punishment. Going to Abba Poemen they told him what had happened.

Poemen wrote to the hermit, saying, "Remember where the first betrayal came from, and then you will see the second betrayal. For unless you had produced the first from inside yourself, you would never have perpetrated the second betrayal."

When the hermit heard this word, he felt compunction. Although he was well-known in that region, and for a long time he had not left his cell, he nevertheless rose and went into the city. There he led the thieves from jail and publicly freed them. [AP-G Poemen 90; AP-Pa 8.2; AP-PR 83]

Chapter Twenty-Four

ON PERFECT PATIENCE

1. The disciple of a certain philosopher sinned. When he sought forgiveness, the philosopher, said to him, "I will not forgive you, unless you carry freight for others for three years."

When the disciple returned after three years, after he had done what had been commanded, the philosopher said to him, "I still will not forgive you unless for three years you offer payment to anyone who afflicts you with insults and abuse."

After the disciple had done this he was released from his sin, and his master said to him, "Go and enter the city of the Athenians, so that you may discover wisdom there."

In Athens there was an elder who was devoted to wisdom. He sat at the city gate, heaping abuse on all of the people who were entering for various reasons. When he did this to the young disciple, the youth laughed loudly.

The elder said, "What is it that you are doing? I am insulting you, and you laugh?"

The young man replied, "You don't want me to laugh? For the past three years I paid money so that I might suffer what I receive from you today for free."

Then the elder said, "Enter the city, for you are worthy."

Now Abba John often told this story, but he added the following words: "This is the gate of God, through which our fathers, enduring many tribulations and rejoicing in their injuries, have entered the city of God." [AP-G John the Dwarf 41; AP-PJ 21.12; AP-PR 84]

2. A brother questioned one of the elders, saying, "Give me one rule that I can keep, and through it be saved."

The elder replied, "If you are able to be injured and afflicted with abuse, and yet you endure it and remain silent, this is a great thing that is above all the other commands." [AP-GN 324; AP-GS 15.105; AP-PJ 15.83; AP-PR 85]

3. A certain man, seeing another man laboriously carrying a corpse on a cot, said to him, "Why are you carrying the dead? If you want to do better, carry the living." [AP-GN 335; AP-GS 16.14; AP-PJ 16.11; AP-Pa 9.1]

4. When a group of brothers were asking for a word from Abba Moses, he ordered his disciple, Zacharias, to say something to them. Zacharias placed his robe beneath his feet, trampled it, and then said, "Unless a person has been trampled in this way, he cannot be a monk." [AP-G Zacharias 3b; AP-GS 15.19b; AP-PJ 15.17b; AP-Pa 9.2; AP-PR 86]

5. **(a)** The blessed Anthony prophesied to Abba Ammonas, saying, "You will go far in the fear of God." Then he led him out of the cell and showed him a stone. He said, "Go and injure this stone: strike it!" When Ammonas had done this, the blessed Anthony asked him if the stone had offered any response to him.

Ammonas answered, "No."

Anthony then said, "In the same way, you will reach this standard, so that you will think no injury has been done to you."

(b) Now this Ammonas, during the fourteen years he spent in the desert of Scetis, prayed to God, both day and night, that he might give him the ability to conquer his anger. [**a:** AP-G Ammonas 8a; AP-Pa 9.3; PLaus 20.8a; **b:** AP-G Ammonas 3; AP-GS 7.3; AP-PJ 7.3]

6. Abba Macarius said, "The man who is a true monk conquers himself in all things. For if anyone, while arguing with another person, loses his temper, does he not satisfy his own passion? He must not lose himself in order to save another." [AP-G Macarius the Great 17; AP-GS 4.31; AP-PJ 4.28; AP-PR 87; PLaus 20.17a]

Chapter Twenty-Five

ON TESTING PATIENCE

1. Others were praising a certain brother in the presence of Abba Anthony. But when the elder tested him, he discovered that he would not suffer injury. Consequently, the elder said to him, "You, brother, are like a house that, although the entryway is decorated, has thieves breaking in through the back door." [AP-G Anthony 15; AP-GS 8.2; AP-PJ 8.2; AP-PR 88]

2. Certain people came to Abba Agathon, having heard that he possessed great discretion and never became angry. Wanting to test him, they said, "Are you Agathon, a prideful man and a fornicator?"

Agathon said, "I am."

They added, "You are Agathon, the thief and slanderer?"

He replied again, "I am."

They spoke to him a third time, "You are Agathon, the heretic?"

He responded, "I am not."

They began to question him, asking, "Why did you admit those first faults but reject the last?"

He answered, "I ascribe the earlier faults that you mentioned to myself for the benefit of my soul; nevertheless, to be a heretic is to be separated from God, and I do not want to be separated from him." [AP-G Agathon 5; AP-GS 10.12; AP-CSP 4.7; AP-PJ 10.10; AP-PR 21]

3. When Abba Moses was made a priest in Scetis, the bishop placed a white robe on him during the ordination ceremony. Then the bishop said, "Look, Abba Moses has become all white." Now Moses was a black man.

Moses replied, "You believe, Lord Father, that I am white on the outside, but how am I able to become white on the inside?"

Now the bishop wanted to test him, and so he said to the other clerics, "When he approaches the altar, throw him out, and then one of you follow him to hear what he says."

When Moses entered, they expelled him roughly, saying, "Get out of here, Ethiopian."

As he departed, he said to himself, "They did the right thing to me, a man with skin as black as ashes. For when you are not a man, why should you be allowed to enter with other men?" [AP-G Moses 4; AP-GS 15.43; AP-PJ 15.29]

4. Another time, the fathers in Scetis wanted to test Moses, so they condemned him and said, "Why does this Ethiopian come among us?"

Nevertheless, Moses remained quiet.

Later, after the fathers had left, one monk asked him, "Abba Moses, were you not upset by that statement?"

He replied, "Even if I was disturbed, I did not speak." [AP-G Moses 3; AP-GS 16.9; AP-PJ 16.7]

Chapter Twenty-Six

ON NOT SPEAKING IN ANGER

1. A brother asked Abba Isaac, "Abba, why do the demons fear you?"

The elder replied, "From the time I became a monk, I have established a rule for myself that my anger will never proceed beyond my throat. Consequently, the demons fear me." [AP-G Isidore the Priest 2; AP-GS 4.24; AP-PJ 4.22; AP-PR 89]

2. When one of the fathers came to Abba Achilles, he saw him spitting out blood, and he asked him what it was. Achilles replied, "It was the word of a brother that saddened me. I struggled not to speak it, but rather, I begged the Lord to take it from me. That word became blood in my mouth, and then I spit it out and found rest. Now both that sadness and that word are forgotten." [AP-G Achilles 4; AP-GS 4.9; AP-PJ 4.9; AP-PR 90]

3. Some brothers visited an elder who was living alone in solitude. They discovered, outside his cell, children who were herding calves and speaking nasty words among themselves. After the brothers had each asked the elder about their thoughts and had received his advice, they asked him, "How are you able to bear, Father, the voices of those children? Why don't you order them to stop their joking?"

The elder answered, "Truly, brothers, there are many days when I think about saying something to them, but then I rebuke myself, thinking, 'If I cannot bear this little disturbance, how will I stand it if a great temptation arrives?' Therefore, I say nothing to them, so that I may acquire the custom of enduring them." [AP-GN 338; AP-GS 16.23; AP-PJ 16.14; AP-PR 91A]

4. The same elder said, "He who does not hold his tongue in a time of anger, will never be able to restrain the passions of his flesh." [AP-G Hyperechius 3; AP-GS 4.57; AP-PJ 4.49; AP-PR 91B]

Chapter Twenty-Seven

THAT ENVY IS OVERCOME THROUGH PATIENCE

1. **(a)** Abba John was sitting among the brothers. Each brother was questioning him about his own thoughts, and he gave a response to every monk. Then one of the elders, out of envy, said, "Here is this John, like a woman dressing herself as a prostitute in order to attract lovers to herself."

Abba John responded, "You speak the truth, Abba. There is no other explanation, for God revealed this very fact to you."

(b) The elder spoke again, "Also your cup, John, is full of venom."

John said to that man, "This is just as you said, Abba, and you spoke only about those qualities that you see from the outside. If you were to see those things that are inside me, how much more would you have that you could speak about?"

After this speech, one of his disciples said to him, "Were you not stirred up inside, Abba, by the words of that elder?"

"No," replied John, "for I am the same outside as I am inside."
[**a:** AP-G John the Dwarf 8; AP-PR 92a; **b:** AP-G John the Dwarf 46; AP-GS 16.4; AP-PJ 16.3; AP-PR 92b]

2. There was an elder in Egypt, and before Poemen came to that place, he had enjoyed everyone's greatest veneration. But when Abba Poemen came there from Scetis, many abandoned the elder and went instead to Poemen. Because of this, the elder became jealous and began to attack Poemen's reputation.

Poemen was saddened when he heard this, and he said to his brothers, "What should we do? These people have made us suffer because they abandon such a holy man and consult us, who are nothing. Come brothers! Let us prepare a little food that we can carry straight over to him, and a little wine. Then we can enjoy these gifts together with him. Perhaps through this we will be able to soothe his spirit."

After the brothers had done this, they knocked on the elder's door. When the elder's disciple heard the sound, he asked, "Who is it?"

The monks said, "Tell your abba that Poemen has come, so that he might be blessed by your master."

When the elder heard this from his disciple, he responded, "Go say to them, 'Leave this place, for I have no free time.'"

Nevertheless, the brothers held out in the heat of the summer, saying, "We will not leave here until we become worthy to praise him."

When that man perceived their humility and patience, he felt compunction, opened his door, and they ate together. Then the elder said to them, "In truth there are not only the things that I have heard about you, but also a hundred times more works that I have seen in you."

And from that day, the elder became a friend. [AP-G Poemen 4; AP-GS 17.11; AP-PJ 17.8; AP-PR 93]

Chapter Twenty-Eight

A GOOD THING MUST BE CONDEMNED FOR THE SAKE OF PEACE

1. Abba Motoes built a monastery for himself in a place that is called Heracleona. Many things troubled him while he was there, so

he moved to another place, and in the same way, built a monastery there. But because of the devil's snares, a certain brother was found in this new place who, because of envy, was always angry with Motoes. Therefore he got up and returned to his own village. There he established a monastery and shut himself up in it.

Later, some elders arrived from the place that he had left. They brought with them that brother with whom he had quarreled, since they wanted to ask Motoes to return to his monastery. After they came to that neighborhood, they took off their sheepskins and left that same brother behind. Then they made their way to the elder and knocked on his door. He looked out an open window and recognized them. After offering a prayer, Abba Motoes said to them, "Where are your sheepskins?"

They replied, "Behold, they are nearby with the brother who was always angry with you."

When the elder heard this and the name of that man, he was elated and used an axe to break down the door through which he had entered. Then, going out, he hurried to the place where that brother waited.

Before that man could begin to offer penance, he embraced him. Then he led the monks into his cell. For three days he, a man who had never had the custom of forgoing fasting, celebrated with them. Then he rose and departed with them. [AP-G Motius 2; AP-Pa 10.1; AP-PR 94]

2. A brother questioned Abba Elias, saying, "If I grieve another person, how should I ask for forgiveness?"

The elder replied, "From the bottom of your heart, with sorrow, make penance before that person. Then God, seeing your purpose, will make amends for you." [AP-Pa 10.2; PLaus 20.14a]

3. Abba Agathon often said, "I have never slept if I had a quarrel with someone, nor have I allowed anyone who had a quarrel with me to sleep—as far as it remained in my power—until I had restored peace with that person." [AP-G Agathon 4; AP-GS 17.8; AP-PJ 17.6; AP-PR 95]

Chapter Twenty-Nine

ON PERFECT HARMONY

1. There were two elders living in a cell, and they had never exchanged so much as even a small contentious word between

themselves. Consequently one said to the other, "Let us have a quarrel, just as other men do."

The other monk said, "I do not know how to have a quarrel."

The first responded, "Look, I will place a brick between us, and then I will say, 'This is mine.' Then you say, 'It is not yours, it is mine.' This will produce contention and squabbling."

After they placed the brick between them, the first monk said, "This is mine."

The second monk replied, "I think that it is mine."

Then the first monk said again, "It is not yours, it is mine."

His companion replied, "If it is yours, then take it."

After this was said, they were unable to find something to fight about. [AP-GN 352; AP-GS 17.26; AP-PJ 17.22; AP-PR 96]

2. Once, when the blessed Abba Macarius was praying, a voice came to him from heaven, saying, "Macarius you have not yet attained the standard of two women who live together in a nearby city."

After the elder heard this, he rose, snatched up his staff, and went to the designated city. When he found the door he was seeking and had knocked on it, one of the women came out and welcomed him with great exultation. The elder gathered both women together, and said, "I have undergone a great labor because of you, traveling from the remote wilderness to learn about your work, which you must agree to describe to me."

The women replied to his words, "Believe us, most holy Father, that right up to the present night, we have not been separated from our marital beds. So what kind of work do you look for in us?"

The elder continued to insist that they explain their way of life to him.

Then, having been compelled, they said, "We are not related to each other. Nevertheless, it happened that we were married to brothers, and we have remained with them for fifteen years, living in the same house. Neither of us has said a nasty word to the other, nor have we ever had any quarrels. We have lived thus far in peace and harmony. We both wanted to abandon our husbands and offer ourselves to a religious congregation of virgins, but, despite our many prayers, we were unable to procure a release from our spouses. Since we cannot achieve this goal, we took a vow between ourselves and God that until our death, we will not speak a word about any secular matter."

When the blessed Macarius heard this, he said, "In truth you are not a virgin, wife, monk, nor a secular woman; but God has made this arrangement, and he supplies the spirit of life to all." [AP-GN 489; AP-GS 20.21; AP-PJ 20.17; AP-PR 97]

3. One brother, while he was living in the monastery, was frequently moved to anger, and so he said, "I will go into solitude, and perhaps when I do not have anyone with whom I can quarrel, this passion will die down in me."

He went out and lived alone in a cave. One day, after he had filled his flask with water and placed it on the ground, it suddenly toppled over. He refilled it a second time; again it flipped over. When he had refilled the flask a third time and the same thing happened again, he snatched up the flask and smashed it in his anger.

After he calmed himself, he began to think that he had been deceived by a spirit, and he said, "Look, I am alone, but even so I am defeated by anger. I will return to the monastery, because the battle, patience, and, above all, God's assistance is everywhere."

He then rose and returned to his own place. [AP-GN 201; AP-GS 7.40; AP-PJ 7.33; AP-PR 98]

Chapter Thirty

ON PATIENCE WHEN SUFFERING ACCUSATIONS

1. The blessed Macarius, speaking about himself, said, "When I was a young man and I still resided in a cell, men from the neighborhood seized me and ordained me a priest against my will. I did not want to stay in that place, so I fled to another. There, a certain religious man of the world ministered to me by selling my work.

"At that time, a virgin engaged in premarital sex and became pregnant. When her condition was discovered and she was asked the name of the man, she said, 'That anchorite of yours did this wicked thing to me.'

"Then her parents came, and seizing me, they hung a clay pot around my neck and dragged me through each street in the village, beating me and insulting me with their voices, crying, 'This monk took our daughter by force.'

"After they had beaten me with rods to the point of death, one of the elders said to them, 'Why are you beating this foreign monk?'

"Those who were assaulting me said to the man who had been serving me (for he had followed and was ashamed), 'Look what this man you support has done.'

"Her parents said, 'We will not release him for any reason, unless he agrees to assume the burden of providing for our daughter.'

"When I nodded to the man who was ministering to me, signaling that it would be done, he took charge of me and gave his word. I returned to my cell and found all the little baskets I had made. I gave them to him, so that, after he sold the baskets, he could provide food for my wife and I. Then I said to myself, 'Look Macarius, you have found a wife, and so it is necessary to work harder so that you will be able to feed her.' I began working day and night to provide her daily food.

"But when the time of her misery arrived, she was wracked with pain and unable to give birth for many days. When asked what was the matter, she responded, 'I accused that anchorite of a crime for which he is not guilty. A young man of our neighborhood slept with me.'

"When the man who was ministering to me heard this, he came, overflowing with joy and shouting, 'That unfortunate girl was unable to give birth until she acknowledged that she had woven a lie about you; the entire neighborhood is coming to beg your forgiveness.'

"When I learned this, to keep these men from troubling me anymore, I quickly departed and came to Scetis. That is the reason I came here." [AP-G Macarius the Great 1; AP-GS 15.39; AP-PJ 15.25; AP-PR 99]

Chapter Thirty-One

AGAINST THE SPIRIT OF FEAR THAT PRODUCES DESPAIR

1. Abba Orsisius said, "If an uncooked brick was placed in a foundation near a river, it would not be able to endure for even one day; on the other hand, if it is thoroughly baked, it will hold up like a stone. In the same way will be the man who is not completely cooked nor set ablaze—as was said about Joseph, *The eloquence of the Lord inflamed him*

(Ps 105:19)—but from the beginning he will quickly be dissolved by carnal thoughts." [AP-G Orsisius 1a; AP-GS 15.69a; AP-PJ 15.51a; AP-Pa 11.1]

2. A brother asked Abba Poemen, "What should I do, Father? I am overcome by depression."

The elder said to him, "Regard no one as inconsequential, condemn no one, disparage no one, and the Lord will give you rest." [AP-GS 9.11; AP-M 39; AP-PJ 9.8; AP-Pa 39.2; AP-PR 100]

3. Another brother questioned the same man, saying, "If I sin, even in the smallest sin, my thinking consumes me and accuses me, saying, 'Why did you sin?' What should I do?"

The elder replied, "In whichever hour a man should fall into a fault, and say from the heart, 'Lord God, I have sinned, forgive me!' that consumption by thoughts and fears will quickly end." [AP-G Poemen 99; AP-Pa 11.2; PLaus 20.5a]

4. Abba Poemen, speaking about Abba Isidore, said that only he had understood himself. For whenever a thought said to him, "You are great," he would respond to himself, "As great as Abba Anthony, or at least Abba Pambo, or the rest who were pleasing to God?" Whenever he thought this, he found peace.

When the enemy, disturbing him, suggested despair and punishment to him, saying, "After all your efforts, you will enter into the torments," he replied, "Although I may be sent into the torments, I will nevertheless find you below me." [AP-G Isidore the Priest I 6; AP-PA 11.3; AP-PR 101]

5. Wicked spirits often appeared to Abba Moses, abusing him and saying, "You evade us, Moses, and we are unable to do anything to you. Whenever we want to humiliate you through despair, you are lifted up; and whenever you are lifted up, you humble yourself. Therefore none of us are able to approach you." [AP-Pa 11.4; AP-PR 102]

6. A brother often asked for advice from Abba Sisoes, saying, "What should I do, Father? I have fallen."

Sisoes would reply, "Get up."

The brother would then respond, "I got up."

Again he would confess that he had fallen, and the elder said, "Then get up again."

Now although this brother frequently reported that he had risen and fallen again, the elder continued to employ the same advice, exclaiming, "Do not stop getting up, my son."

The brother responded, "Tell me, Father, how long I must keep getting up."

Then the elder said, "Until you die, snatched up in either a moment of good work, or in an evil work. A man will be judged by the work in which he was caught." [AP-G Sisoes 38; AP-Pa 11.5; AP-PR 103]

7. One of the elders was strongly tempted by his thoughts for ten years, until finally he despaired and said, "I have lost my soul; because I have lost it, once and for all, I will return to the world."

Now when he set out, a voice came to him saying, "You have fought with your thoughts for ten years; they will be your crown. Now return to your place and I will free you from every evil thought."

Consequently, it is not good for anyone to lose hope for themselves on account of their thoughts. For they will provide greater crowns for us if we pass over those thoughts that are leading us astray. [AP-GN 210; AP-GS 7.51; AP-PJ 7.42; AP-PR 104]

Chapter Thirty-Two

AGAINST THE SPIRIT OF *ACEDIA*

1. Once, when the blessed Anthony was living in the desert, tormented by various thoughts and tempted by the spirit of *acedia*, he said to the Lord, "Lord, I wish to be saved, but my various thoughts will not permit it. What should I do in my trouble? How may I prevail to be saved? Please show me."

Rising a short time later, he saw someone similar to himself—sitting down to twist a rope, then rising from his work, and praying. It was an angel, sent for Anthony's emendation. Then Anthony heard these words: "Do these things, Anthony, and you will be saved."

Anthony was filled with great joy, having gained confidence that he was being saved. [AP-G Anthony 1; AP-GS 7.1; AP-PJ 7.1; AP-PR 105]

2. A certain brother questioned Abba Achila, asking, "What should I do, Father? I do none of the works of a monk. Rather, rooted

in negligence, I eat, I drink, I sleep, and I flit from task to task, from thought to thought. Consequently, I am depressed, and I fail."

The elder responded, "Sit in your cell and do what you are capable of without disturbing your soul. I have faith in God that he who sits in his cell for God's sake will be found in the place where Abba Anthony is." [AP-GN 202; AP-GS 7.41; AP-PJ 7.34; AP-PR 106]

3. A brother questioned Abba Arsenius, saying that his thoughts troubled him by suggesting, "Because you are unable to fast or work, go and visit the sick brothers, as this is a charitable work."

The elder, realizing that this thought came from the instigation of the devil, replied, "Go. Eat, drink, sleep, do no work, but don't let your feet carry you outside your cell. For the confinement of a cell is able to lead a monk to a well-ordered life." [AP-G Arsenius 11; AP-GN 195; AP-GS 7.34; AP-PJ 7.27]

4. Another brother asked Abba Achila, "Why do I suffer *acedia* when I am sitting in my cell?"

The elder replied, "Because you have not yet seen the rest for which we hope, nor the torments that we fear. For if you were considering both of these diligently, even if your cell was filled with worms to your neck, you would remain lying among them without *acedia*." [AP-GN 196; AP-GS 7.35; AP-PJ 7.28; AP-PR 107]

5. **(a)** An elder said, "We do not make progress because we do not know our own limits, nor do we have patience in the work we begin, but we want to attain virtue without labor. **(b)** We pass from place to place, disturbed by *acedia*, hoping that we may find a place where the devil is not present.

(c) "In whatever place a man finds himself, if he should try to do something good, but is unable, let him not decide that he would be able to do the good thing if he had gone elsewhere. Without work, no one can attain virtue, and even if it is acquired, it will not remain in the person. For the kingdom of heaven is promised to those who are mourning and fasting." [**a:** AP-GN 297/438a; AP-GS 7.30; AP-PJ 7.23; **b:** AP-GN 438b]

6. A brother, when troubled by thoughts that he should leave his cell, brought this to the abbot. The abbot ordered, "Go and sit in your cell and give your body as a pledge to the wall of your cell, that you will not go out from there. Then release your mind so that it can

think whatever it wants, as long as your body does not leave the cell." [AP-GN 205; AP-GS 7.45; AP-PJ 7.37]

7. **(a)** One brother had asked for a word from Abba Moses, and the elder said to him, "Go and sit in your cell, for your cell is able to teach you all things if you remain in it. **(b)** 'For just as the fish, plucked out of the water, will die, so too will the monk perish if he desires to linger outside his cell.' So said the blessed Anthony.

(c) "For if a monk remains in his cell and remembers his sins, the Lord will be his helper in all things, and he will not suffer tedium." [**a:** AP-G Moses 6; AP-GS 2.19; AP-PJ 2.9; AP-PR 109a; **b:** AP-G Anthony 10; AP-GS 2.1; AP-PJ 2.1; AP-PR 109b]

8. A brother asked Abba Anthony, "Will I please God by the rule I am keeping?"

The elder replied, "Do what I tell you: wherever you go, always have the Lord before your eyes. Whatever work you practice, take your examples from the Holy Scriptures. Do not move quickly from wherever you live, but remain patiently in that place. Keep these three precepts and you will achieve salvation." [AP-G Anthony 3; AP-GS 1.1; AP-PJ 1.1; AP-PR 108]

Chapter Thirty-Three

AGAINST THE SPIRIT OF VAINGLORY

1. A brother asked Abba Poemen if it was better to live apart from others.

The elder responded, "If a man is able to criticize himself, he is able to live anywhere; if, on the other hand, he glorifies himself, he can never stand. A man should never exult in anything good that he has done, because he will quickly lose it." [AP-Pa 12.1; AP-PR 110]

2. If anyone wanted to approach Abba Macarius fearfully or as if he was a holy man, he would learn nothing from the elder. If, however, he acted like one despising him, and addressed him with words such as these—"Abba Macarius, when you were a camel driver or were stealing nitre, were you never flogged by the magistrates after you had been arrested for theft?"—then Macarius would respond freely and joyfully to any question asked. [AP-G Macarius the Great 31; AP-Pa 12.2]

3. Once an Egyptian brother came to Abba Zeno in Syria, and he began to condemn his own thoughts in the elder's presence. The elder heard this, and admiringly said, "The Egyptians hide the virtues they possess, and they reveal vices that they do not have. The Greeks and Syrians proclaim virtues they do not have, and conceal the vices that they do have." [AP-G Zeno 3; AP-Pa 12.4; AP-PR 111]

4. A certain elder said, "Whoever is praised or honored greatly by men will suffer a significant condemnation of the soul; on the other hand, whoever is not honored by men will receive glory from above." [AP-G Or 10; AP-GN 300; AP-GS 15.74; AP-PJ 15.56; AP-Pa 13.1; AP-PR 112]

5. The same man said, "It is impossible to be both plant and seed at the same time. Likewise, it is not possible to have praise and glory from the secular world, while at the same time producing heavenly fruit." [AP-G Syncletica 22; AP-GS 8.25; AP-PJ 8.20; AP-Pa 13.2; AP-PR 113]

6. The same man said, "Just as a treasure that has been revealed diminishes, so too is virtue made public lost. For just as wax melts in front of a fire, the soul, undone by praise, loses its own intensity." [AP-G Syncletica 21; AP-GS 8.24; AP-PJ 8.19; AP-PR 114]

7. The same man said, "When the thought of vainglory or pride attacks you, examine yourself to see if you serve all the commands of God: Do you love your enemies? Do you rejoice in the success of your enemy? Are you saddened when he falls? Do you consider yourself a useless servant, and a worse sinner than all other men?

"Even then you should not think yourself great, even if you have done something good, because you must understand that a haughty thought destroys every good deed." [AP-G Or 11; AP-GN 299; AP-GS 15.72; AP-PJ 15.54; AP-Pa 13.3; AP-PR 115]

8. An elder came to another elder and said to him, "I am already dead to this world."

The other man responded, "Do not place such faith in yourself until you depart this body. For even if you say, 'I am dead,' the devil is not yet dead." [AP-GN 266; AP-GS 11.81; AP-PJ 11.38; AP-Pa 12.5; AP-PR 116]

9. One elder, after he had spent fifty years in the desert, never eating bread or drinking enough water to satisfy himself, said, "I have killed vainglory and avarice."

When Abba Abraham heard this, he went to the elder and asked if he had spoken these words.

After that man confessed, Abraham said to him, "Look, if you walked along a road and saw stones, pieces of brick, and, among this rubble, a lump of gold, would it be possible for your mind to regard all of these as the same?"

The elder replied, "No, but I would fight against my thought so that I did not receive it."

Abba Abraham said, "And so avarice lives, but it is bound." He continued, "You hear about two men; one man esteems and praises you, another despises and criticizes you. If one of these men comes to you, are you able to receive either in the same manner?"

The elder responded, "No, but again, I would fight with my thoughts, so that I might love the man I dread."

Then Abba Abraham said, "Look, the passions still live in you, but they are bound by the holy thoughts that reside powerfully in you on account of your lifestyle." [AP-G Abraham 1; AP-GS 10.19; AP-PJ 10.15; AP-PR 117]

10. One of the brothers questioned an elder, saying, "When I have given bread, water, or anything good that I have made to my brother, the spirit of vainglory suggests that I have only performed these deeds to earn the praise of men."

The elder replied, "Even if you should do good works to earn the praise of men, do not ever refuse those things that your neighbor needs. For two men lived in one village; one sowed seed, but the other did not. The man who sowed produced a small crop, although it was not very nice. The other man produced nothing, because he sowed nothing. Now when a famine struck, which of the two were able to live better?"

The brother answered, "The man who planted would be able to live, even if what he grew was foul."

The elder said, "We must also do little things, even if they seem foul, so that we are not tested by hunger." [AP-G Poemen 51; AP-GS 13.6; AP-PJ 13.6]

11. (a) Abba Sisoes, when he was sitting in the presence of another brother, was overcome by ecstasy, and not knowing that the other brother was listening, he sighed. Then Sisoes began to make penance and said, "Forgive me, brother, I beg you, for I do not think I have yet become a monk, because I sighed in the presence of another who could hear."

(b) Whenever that same elder was in prayer, standing with his hands extended to heaven, he would quickly lower his hands if another person was present, so that it would not seem to that person that he prayed in this manner to win praise. [a: AP-G Tithoes 6; AP-Pa 12.6a; PLaus 20.19; b: AP-G Tithoes 1; AP-GS 12.13; AP-PJ 12.11; AP-Pa 12.6b]

12. An elder lived in the lower parts of the desert. He lived there peacefully, and one of the secular religious men took care of him. Now it happened that the son of the secular man became ill. The secular man begged the elder, with many prayers, to come to his house and pray over the child. The elder got up and went with him.

The secular man ran ahead, and entering his house, said, "Come to meet the anchorite."

When the elder saw the people at a distance, pouring out of their houses with lamps, he discerned that they were coming to him. He immediately stripped off his clothes and threw them in the river. Then, standing naked, he began to wash his garments.

The man who served him saw this and was embarrassed. He said to the other people, "Let us go back, for our elder has lost his senses." Then he approached the elder and said, "Abba, what is it that you have done? For everyone who saw you will say, 'The elder has a demon.'"

The elder replied, "That is what I wanted to hear." [AP-GN 61; AP-PJ 21.35; AP-Pa 12.7; AP-PR 118]

13. A certain provincial magistrate wanted to honor Abba Moses. When Moses heard this, he fled from his place. As it happened, the two men met by chance, and the judge asked Moses, "Tell us, where is the cell of Abba Moses?"

Moses replied, "Why do you want to see that foolish and heretical man?"

The judge went to the church and told the clergy about this encounter, saying, "I heard various things about Abba Moses and wanted a blessing from him. But, in fact, a monk who met me spoke about him and said that he was a heretic."

When the clerics heard this, they were sad. They began to question the judge, asking him about the monk who had spoken these words.

"He was an elder, tall and black, who wore ancient clothing," replied the judge.

When the judge learned from their report that the monk had been Moses himself, he was filled with admiration and departed, satisfied. [AP-G Moses 8; AP-GS 8.13; AP-PJ 8.10; AP-PR 119]

14. A magistrate came to see Abba Simeon. When that man heard this, he immediately went under a palm tree and began to clean it. When the people came to him, they said, "Where is the anchorite?"

He replied, "He is not here; he went away."

Consequently, the people left him. [AP-G Simon 1; AP-GS 8.22; AP-PJ 8.17]

15. Another time, one of the magistrates wanted to see him, so the clerics went out in advance and said to him, "Abba, prepare yourself, because the magistrate has heard of your work and wants to come receive a blessing from you."

That man replied, "I will do this and prepare myself." And so, putting on a patched robe, taking bread and cheese in his hands, and climbing to the gate and stretching out his feet, he sat down and began to eat.

When the magistrate arrived with his officials, he saw him and said, "Is this the anchorite, about whom we have heard so much?" Then cursing him, the magistrate departed. [AP-G Simon 2; AP-GS 8.23; AP-PJ 8.18; AP-Pa 12.8]

Chapter Thirty-Four

AGAINST THE SPIRIT OF PRIDE

1. A brother questioned one of the elders, asking, "What is humility?"

The elder replied, "It is the tree of life, growing to a great height." [AP-GN 699; AP-GS 15.67; AP-PJ 15.49; AP-Pa 13.8]

2. The same man said, "Humility is the ground upon which God ordered sacrifices to be offered to himself." [AP-GN 688; AP-GS 15.55; AP-PJ 15.37; AP-Pa 13.9]

3. (a) An elder, when questioned about how the spirit was able to attain humility, responded, "If it considers itself the worst of all things."

(b) He also said, "Humility is the perfection of man. (c) For a man will be carried toward honor to the same extent that he entrusts himself to humility. Just as pride, if it ascends to heaven, will ultimately be led into the lower world, so too humility, if it should descend to the lower world, is exalted to the heavens." [**a:** AP-M 59; AP-Pa 13.10a; AP-PR 171a; **b:** AP-Pa 13.10b; AP-PR 171b; **c:** AP-M 58; AP-Pa 13.5; AP-PR 171c]

4. Abba Motoes said, "The closer a man comes to God, the more he will see himself as a sinner. For the Prophet Isaiah, seeing God, called himself 'miserable and unclean'" (cf. Isa 6.5). [AP-G Matoes 2; AP-GS 15.41; AP-PJ 15.28; AP-PR 123a]

5. The same man said, "We are not here without anxiety, for Scripture says, *He who stands, let him see that he does not fall* (1 Cor 10:12).

"We navigate this world uncertainly; indeed, we appear to sail a tranquil sea while secular men sail in dangerous places. We sail like those in daylight, lit by the sun of righteousness, while they sail in ignorance, like those in the night.

"But it frequently happens that secular men, although they sail in the darkest night, nevertheless keep watch and, shouting, save their own ship. On the other hand, we who sail in tranquil waters often neglect our safety, and we perish, having relinquished the rudder of humility. For just as it is impossible for a ship to be sound without a rudder, is it likewise impossible for a man to be saved without humility." [AP-G Syncletica S8; AP-GS 11.75; AP-PJ 11.34; AP-PR 123b]

6. The same man said, "Humility is never angry, nor does it allow others to be angry." [AP-Pa 13.11]

7. The same man said, "This is humility: if your brother has sinned against you, you will have forgiven him before he feels repentant." [AP-GN 304; AP-GS 15.78; AP-PJ 15.60; AP-Pa 13.12; PLaus 20.15a]

Chapter Thirty-Five

THAT THE PERFECT DO NOT WANT TO PERFORM MIRACLES LEST THEY BE PRAISED FOR THEM

1. When Abba Sisoes lived on the mountain where Abba Anthony had hidden himself, a certain secular man hurried to him with his small son, for the sake of receiving a blessing. Now it happened that the infant died on the way. The father did not allow any disturbing thoughts into his mind, and he carried his son, with faith, to the elder.

Entering the cell, he threw both himself and the infant on the ground, as is customary for those asking a blessing. Finishing his prayer, the father rose and went outside, leaving the tiny body of his son before the Abba's feet. Then the elder, hoping to order the boy to leave so that he could return to his prayers, said, "Get up, son, and go." He did not know that the child was dead.

Immediately the boy rose and left the cell. When his father saw this, he was astonished. He returned to the cell, praised the elder, and faithfully reported both the story of his son's death as well as his own grief.

But the elder became very despondent, for he did not want anyone to hear such a thing about himself. Through his disciple, he gave an order to the father that nothing should be said of the matter until after his death. [AP-G Sisoes 18; AP-GS 19.17; AP-PJ 19.13; AP-PR 120]

2. Abba Nesteros, while he was walking in the desert with another brother, saw a dragon, and they fled. The brother said to him, "Were you also afraid, Abba?"

The elder replied, "I was not afraid, my son, but it was right for me to flee, for unless I fled the dragon, I would not have destroyed the thought of vainglory." [AP-G Nisterus 1; AP-GS 8.15; AP-PJ 8.12; AP-Pa 12.3]

3. A certain secular man, who was in the grip of an unclean spirit, came into the church. Although everyone offered a prayer, they were unable to expel the unclean spirit. The brothers consulted with each other and said, "What should we do with this spirit? For no one will be able to cast it out except Abba Bessarion. But if we tell him about this man, he will not agree to come to the church. We must do something else. Since he customarily comes to church before everyone else, we must make this suffering man sit here, and later we will say, 'Abba, wake that man who is sleeping.'"

That is what they did. When Abba Bessarion came, everyone stood in prayer, and they said to him, "Abba, wake that man who is asleep."

Bessarion said, "Get up and go outside."

Immediately the unclean spirit went out from his body, and he regained his sanity. [AP-G Bessarion 5; AP-GS 19.4; AP-PJ 19.4; AP-Pa 14.2; AP-PR 121]

4. Now there was a man in Egypt who had a paralyzed son. He brought the boy to the cell of the blessed Bessarion, and he laid the

crying boy before the doorway, and went far away. The infant began to cry. When the elder saw the baby through the window, he said, "Who left you here, son?"

The baby replied, "My father placed me here and then he left."

The elder said, "Get up and go join him."

He was healed immediately and went to his father. [AP-G Macarius the Great 15; AP-GS 19.11; AP-PJ 19.7; AP-PR 122]

5. When the blessed Macarius had revived a certain dead man, so that he might tell him where he had hidden some money that had been loaned to him (to save his widow and son who had been sold into slavery), his disciples threw themselves at Macarius's feet because of their fear. The elder said to them, "You should not presume that this was done for my sake. Nothing was granted to me; God grieved for that widow and her son. For this is the greater thing: God wants our human souls to be without sin, rather than to revive the dead." [AP-G Macarius the Great 7; AP-GS 19.12; AP-PJ 19.8]

6. The same man said, "He who works and judges that he has accomplished something has received his reward here." [AP-Pa 11.6]

Chapter Thirty-Six

DEMONS ARE CONQUERED AND DRIVEN AWAY BY HUMILITY

1. Once, when Abba Macarius was returning to his cell, carrying palm leaves at dawn, the devil met him with a sharpened pruning hook. He attempted to wound Macarius but was unable to do it. Then the devil exclaimed, "I am hindered by your great power, Macarius, for when I want to wound you, it stops me. This is despite the fact that I match whatever you do with a greater work. You fast occasionally, I never refresh myself with food; you often keep vigils, but sleep never overcomes me. Nevertheless, in one practice you defeat me."

When the blessed Macarius asked him about this practice, the devil said, "Your humility alone defeats me."

The blessed Macarius extended his arms in prayer, and the unclean spirit vanished in the breeze. [AP-G Macarius the Great 11; AP-GS 15.40; AP-PJ 15.26; AP-Pa 13.6; AP-PR 124]

2. A man, who had been seized by an evil spirit and was frothing at the mouth, struck one of the elders, a hermit, sharply on the cheek. The elder immediately offered his other cheek to that man, so that he could strike it as well. The devil, unable to bear the heat of the elder's humility, departed at once. [AP-GN 298; AP-GS 15.71; AP-PJ 15.53; AP-PR 125]

3. One of the fathers said, "Every work is in vain without humility. For humility is the precursor of charity. Just as John was the precursor of Jesus, leading all the people to him, so too humility leads to charity—that is, to God himself, for he is charity." [AP-Pa 13.7; AP-PR 126]

4. Abba Theodore was sitting among the other brothers at the table, refreshing himself for the sake of charity. The monks were silently receiving the chalice, but not saying "pardon me." Then that man said, "The monks have lost the sign of humility and their nobility. For in every place, time, or act, to ask forgiveness is the rule of humility. This word, *pardon*, is the glory of the monk." [AP-G Theodore of Pherme 6; AP-GS 15.32; AP-PJ 15.20]

Chapter Thirty-Seven

THAT A PROUD WORD MAKES A GOOD MAN EVIL, BUT A HUMBLE WORD PRODUCES GOOD FROM EVIL

1. **(a)** Once, when Abba Macarius was climbing the mountain of Nitria, he ordered his disciple to go ahead of him. After the disciple had gone ahead, he encountered a priest of the idol worshipers coming toward him who was agitated and carrying a large staff. The disciple said, "Demon, where are you running?"

The priest became irate. He struck the disciple with so many blows that he nearly killed him. Leaving him, the pagan priest started running again. Going a little farther, he encountered the blessed Macarius, who said to him, "Be well, hard worker, be well."

The priest, amazed, said, "What good do you see in me that you would greet me?"

The elder replied, "I see you laboring, but you do not know what you are doing."

The priest responded, "I am moved by your greeting, and recognize you as a great servant of God. But I met another man, who I did not know, a miserable monk, and he insulted me. I beat him on account of his words." Then, seizing the feet of the blessed Macarius, he exclaimed, "I will not let go unless you make me a monk."

Then, going on together, they came to the place where the fallen brother was lying. They both lifted him, because he was unable to walk, and carried him in their hands to the church.

When the other brothers saw that pagan priest accompanying the blessed Macarius, they were amazed, and they made him a monk. Because of him, many pagans became Christians.

(b) Abba Macarius said, "A prideful and evil word will turn even a good man to evil, but a humble and good word will change even a wicked man for the better." [**a:** AP-G Macarius the Great 39a; AP-PR 127a; **b:** AP-G Macarius the Great 39b; AP-GS 10.181; AP-PR 127b]

Chapter Thirty-Eight

THAT EVEN THE LOWLY ARE HELPED BY THE HUMILITY OF THE GREAT

1. Once in Scetis, the fathers had been paid with figs from the vines, but the brothers did not want to give some to Abba Arsenius, fearing that they might seem to injure him by the worthlessness of the gift. When the blessed Arsenius heard this, he did not want to join the congregation in church, saying, "You have excommunicated me. You did not want to send me some of the blessing which God gave to the brothers, because I am unworthy to receive it."

The multitude of brothers learned what he had said, and they were helped by receiving such a great example through the elder's humility. Then a priest went to him and gave him two figs, just like the other brothers, and he joyfully led Arsenius into the congregation. [AP-G Arsenius 16; AP-GS 15.8; AP-PJ 15.8]

Chapter Thirty-Nine

THAT WE ARE OFTEN HANDED OVER TO SORDID THOUGHTS LEST WE PRAISE OURSELVES

1. The blessed Anthony often said, "Unless the miller covers the eyes of the mule grinding the grain, it will eat and receive its wage. In the same way we must accept our own blindfold through the dispensation of God, so that we will not pay attention to the good things we do, lest we should praise ourselves as blessed men, and receive our due wage.

"For the same reason, when we are lost in unclean thoughts, it is essential that we practice this completely: that we condemn ourselves and our opinions, to prevent our unclean ideas from blotting out the small amount of good in us. For a man is never good, even if he desires to be good, unless God lives within him, because *no one is good, except God alone* (Luke 18:19).

"Therefore we must always accuse ourselves truthfully. For the person who blames himself will not lose his own wage." [AP-GN 322; AP-GS 15.100; AP-PJ 15.80; AP-Pa 15.1; AP-PR 128]

2. The same Abba Anthony reported that he had seen all of the enemy's traps spread across the entire earth. Then, sighing, he said, "What quality will allow a person to pass through these traps?"

He heard a voice, speaking to him, "Only humility is able to pass, Anthony, a quality that these traps cannot touch in any way." [AP-G Anthony 7; AP-GS 15.3; AP-PJ 15.3; AP-PR 129]

3. While Anthony was praying in his cell, a voice came to him, saying, "Anthony, you have not yet attained the standard of a leather tanner who lives in Alexandria."

After hearing this, the elder rose the next morning, took up his staff, and hurried to Alexandria. When he reached the designated man, the tanner was amazed by the sight of so great a man. Then Anthony said, "Tell me about your work, because I have left the desert on account of it to come here to you."

That man replied, "I don't think I have ever accomplished anything good. When I rise from my bed in the morning, before I sit down to my work, I say that all the people of this city, from the least to the greatest, will enter the kingdom of God on account of their righteousness, but nevertheless, I, alone, will be consigned to an eternal punishment because of my sins. In the evening, I revisit that same idea in my heart before I go to bed."

When Anthony heard this, he responded, "In truth, my son, as a good craftsman sitting peacefully in your house, you have won the kingdom of God; on the other hand, I, like one lacking all discretion, have spent my time in solitude and have yet to achieve the standard of your words." [AP-GN 490; AP-Pa 15.2; AP-PR 130]

4. A brother came to Abba Sisoes and said that his mind always remained focused on God. The elder replied, "It is not difficult for the mind to remain close to God, but it is a greater thing if you regard yourself as inferior to all of creation." [AP-G Sisoes 13; AP-GS 15.65; AP-PJ 15.47]

5. The same man said, "Manual labor is a guide for humility."

6. A brother asked Abba Poemen, "What does *All things are clean to the clean* (Titus 1:15) mean?"

Poemen said, "If someone is able to grasp this teaching and understand it, he will regard himself as inferior to all of creation."

The brother replied, "How will I be able to see myself as inferior to a man who is a murderer?"

The elder said, "If a man was able to grasp that teaching of the apostle, and he saw a man who murdered, he would say to himself, 'Actually that man committed only this sin, but I commit a homicide every hour, killing myself.'"

When the brother asked how it was possible to do this, Poemen replied, "This alone is righteousness in a man: if he criticizes himself. For a man is righteous when he condemns himself for his own sins." [AP-G Poemen 97; AP-Pa 15.3; AP-PR 131]

7. A brother said to an elder, "My thoughts say to me, 'I am good.'"

The elder replied, "He who does not see his own sins always believes himself to be numbered among the good. But a thousand thoughts are unable to persuade the man who does see his own sins that he is good, for this man knows what he sees. And so every man must work hard to see himself, for negligence and relaxation blind us." [AP-Pa 15.4; PLaus 20.12]

8. A brother said to Abba Poemen, "My thoughts do not allow me to contemplate my sins, but the brothers urge me to think about my faults."

Abba Poemen referred to Abba Isidore in his response: "Abba Isidore was lamenting in his cell, and his disciple was sitting in the other cell. Then the disciple went to the mourning elder, and asked him, 'Why do you grieve, Father?'

"The elder replied, 'I am grieving over my sins, my son.'

"His disciple again spoke to him, 'You do not have any sins, Father.'

"The elder answered, 'Oh son, if God showed my sins to men, three or four men would not be enough to mourn with me; it would require many more.'" [AP-G Dioscorus 2; AP-GS 3.23; AP-Pa 15.5; PLaus 20.5b]

9. Once, when some brothers were sitting near Abba Poemen, one praised one of the other brothers, saying, "He is a good brother because he abhors evil things."

The elder responded, "What does it mean to 'abhor evil things?'"

When the brother did not know what to say to him, he turned the question back on the abba, "Tell me, Abba, what does it mean to abhor evil things?"

The elder replied, "The man who abhors evil, abhors his own sins and blesses all of his brothers." [AP-G Poemen 142; AP-PR 132]

Chapter Forty

HOW SLANDER MAY BE AVOIDED

1. A brother asked Abba Poemen, "How may a man avoid speaking evil about his neighbor?"

The elder replied, "My neighbor and I are two images. Consequently, when I pay attention to my image and criticize myself, the image of my brother seems more respectable than me. When, however, I praise myself, then I regard my brother's image as bad. Therefore I will not tear down another if I always criticize myself." [AP-G Poemen 148; AP-Pa 16.1; AP-PR 133]

2. **(a)** Abba Hyperechius said, "It is better to eat meat and drink wine than to eat the flesh of the brothers through criticism. **(b)** For just as the whispering serpent drove Eve from paradise, so too does anyone who tears down his brother condemn not only his own soul, but all who listen as well." [**a:** AP-G Hyperechius 4; AP-GS 4.59; AP-PJ 4.51; AP-PR 134a; **b:** AP-G Hyperechius 5; AP-GS 60; AP-PJ 4.52; AP-PR 134b]

Chapter Forty-One

WE SHOULD NEVER JUDGE OR CONDEMN ANYONE ON ACCOUNT OF SIN

1. A priest used to come and consecrate the oblation for a certain elder who was living in solitude. Another man, however, came to the elder and accused the priest. So when the priest came to consecrate the oblation, following his custom, the elder was scandalized and would not open the door for him.

After the priest departed, a voice spoke to the elder, saying, "Men have taken judgment away from me."

The elder was immediately thrown into an ecstatic state, and he saw a golden lake, a golden vase, a golden cord, the finest water, and a leper drawing water from the lake and pouring it out.

Now although the elder who saw this wanted to drink, he did not, for the man who was drawing the water was a leper. Then the voice came again to the elder, and said, "Why don't you drink from this water? What sort of problem does he who draws it have? He only draws the water and pours it out."

When the solitary had returned to himself, and he discerned the meaning of his vision, he called the priest and made him consecrate the oblation as he had done in the past. [AP-GN 254; AP-GS 9.16; AP-PJ 9.11]

2. Abba John often said, "We neglect the small burden, which is to criticize ourselves, and we choose to carry the heavy burden: justifying ourselves and condemning others." [AP-G John the Dwarf 21; AP-M 82; AP-PR 135; PLaus 20.5c]

3. A group gathered once in Scetis, and while the fathers were speaking to the crowd about the lives and deeds of many others, Abba

Pior remained silent. Later, going out, he took a sack, filled it with sand, and began carrying it on his back. Then he placed more sand in another small rag and carried it before him.

When the other brothers saw his actions, they asked him what this example signified.

He replied, "This sack, which contains a lot of sand, symbolizes my sins, for I have many iniquities. I have placed my sins on my back because I do not want to see them; if I saw them, I would have to weep and mourn. On the other hand, I have placed the few faults of my brother before my eyes; I am tortured by them as I condemn my brother. It should not be this way. It is better to place my sins before me, to think about them, and to ask God to forgive me."

When the fathers heard this, they said, "In truth, this is the way of salvation." [AP-G Pior 3; AP-GS 9.13; AP-PJ 9.9; AP-PR 136]

4. **(a)** One of the holy fathers, seeing another being negligent, wept bitterly, saying, "Woe to me, for that man sinned today, and tomorrow I will also sin." **(b)** And he warned his disciple saying, "Although someone sins gravely in your presence, do not condemn him. Let yourself think that you sin more than him, even though he is a secular man, unless perhaps he blasphemes God, and then he is a heretic." [**a:** AP-GN 327a; AP-GS 9.17; AP-Pa 16.3a; PLaus 20.10a; **b:** AP-GN 327b; AP-GS 9.19; AP-Pa 16.3b]

5. A brother told Abba Theodore that one of the monks had returned to the world. The elder replied, "You should not be surprised by this small point; rather, be amazed if anyone is able to evade the teeth and snares of the enemy." [AP-G Theodore of Pherme 8; AP-GS 10.34, AP-PJ 10.25]

6. Once Abba Isaac came to the monastery and he saw a negligent brother there. Angered, he ordered the brother to be thrown out of the monastery. While he was returning to the desert, an angel of the Lord came and stood before the door of the cell, saying, "You are not permitted to enter."

Isaac asked the angel to reveal his fault.

The angel replied, "God sent me, saying, 'Go and tell Isaac, «Where do you command us to send that brother who sinned?»'"

Isaac quickly became penitent and said, "I have sinned, O Lord, forgive me."

The angel replied, "Rise, the Lord forgives you. But do not do this again, condemning someone before God judges that person.

'Men have taken my judgment from me, and they do not allow me to have it,' says the Lord."

This story was told so that if it should happen that someone from among the perfect sins, in even the smallest thing, he is quickly revealed. [AP-G Isaac the Theban 1; AP-GS 9.5; AP-PJ 9.3; AP-PR 137]

7. An anchorite, when he learned from the report of his abbot that a certain brother had neglected his duties in his monastery, said to the same abbot, "If he lives as you say, expel that man from the monastery."

When Abba Poemen heard this, he said to that anchorite, "There were two men in one place, and it happened that they both had deaths in their homes. The first man, having suffered a death in his home, did not want to mourn his loss, but having been perfected, he began to weep for the death in his neighbor's home."

When the anchorite heard this, he felt compunction because of Poemen's words and, recalling what he had done, he said, "Forgive me, Abba, for you are of the high places and heaven, while I am from the low places and the earth." [AP-G Poemen 6; AP-GS 9.10; AP-PJ 9.7]

8. A brother who had been living negligently was expelled from his monastery by the other brothers. Consequently, he went to Abba Anthony. After he had remained with Anthony for a while, Anthony sent him back to his monastery. The monks did not want to receive him, and they expelled him again. The man returned to the blessed Anthony and said, "They do not want to receive me, Father."

Then the blessed Anthony sent word to them, saying, "Behold, a ship was shipwrecked in the middle of the sea. It lost its entire cargo and only with the greatest labor did it reach the shore. Nevertheless, you want to cast that which was brought safely back to the shore into the sea again."

When the monks heard these words, they joyfully received the expelled brother. [AP-G Anthony 21; AP-GS 9.1; AP-PJ 9.1]

9. A brother in a monastery was accused of a crime. After he was scolded by the others, he went to Abba Anthony. His brothers followed him, wanting to bring him back, and they began to reproach him. But the brother denied that he had committed the crime. Abba Paphnutius, whose nickname was "the Buffalo," was found there. When he heard the brothers' dispute, he offered a parable: "I saw," he said, "a man on the bank of a river, sunk up to his knees in mud. Certain men

came so that they might pull him out by his outstretched hand, but they pushed him down until he was submerged to his neck."

Then Anthony spoke about the blessed Paphnutius, "Behold the man, who truly is able to save souls."

The brothers felt compunction from this parable, and they took the monk who had run away back to their monastery. [AP-G Anthony 29; AP-PR 138]

10. Abba Poemen said, "If a man should sin, and he denies it, saying that he did not sin, do not argue the point, for you will take away his resolve. Nevertheless, if you should say to him, 'Do not be troubled, brother, but persevere; if you have not sinned, then do not sin,' then you will lead his soul to repentance." [AP-G Poemen 23; AP-GS 10.68; AP-PJ 10.48]

11. One of the elders said, "If you should see another man sinning, do not blame him, but rather, blame the one who is attacking him. Say, 'Woe to me, for that man was unwillingly defeated and the same shall happen to me.' Then lament and search for the comfort of God, for no one wants to sin, but we are all being deceived." [AP-GN 695; AP-GS 11.114; AP-PR 139]

12. A certain anchorite named Timothy heard of another brother's negligence. When the abbot asked Timothy what should be done about that man, he recommended that the monk be expelled from the monastery. After that man had been expelled, temptation came over Timothy. When Timothy wept in the sight of God and cried, "I have sinned. Have mercy on me," a voice came to him and said, "Timothy, this has come to you because you despised your brother in his time of temptation." [AP-G Poemen 70b; AP-Pa 16.4; AP-PR 140]

Chapter Forty-Two

ON THE OBEDIENCE OF THE MONKS

1. One of the elders said, "Obedience is the great ornament of the monk. For whoever shall possess it will be heard and will stand by the Crucified One with faith, for our Lord was obedient even to the point of death." [AP-G Hyperechius 8; AP-GS 14.19; AP-PJ 14.11]

2. One of the fathers, experiencing an ecstatic vision, saw four classes before God. The first consisted of men who were sick yet still gave thanks to God. The second was made up of those who were practicing hospitality, and in that class they were standing and ministering. The third were those who pursued solitude and did not see other men. The fourth were those who, on account of God and obedience, had subordinated themselves to the fathers. This class, which had shown obedience, was superior to the other three classes, and its members each wore a gold necklace and possessed the greatest glory.

When the father explained what he had seen in his vision, an elder asked, "Why does the fourth class possess more glory than the others?"

The father replied, "Because all of the others gain some relief by following their own will, even though they perform good works. The obedient man, on the other hand, relinquishes his own will, and he subordinates himself to what is commanded by the will of the man giving orders. Therefore, he is appointed to a greater glory than the rest." [AP-G Rufus 2; AP-GS 14.29a; AP-PJ 14.19a; AP-PR 141]

3. A certain elder said, "If anyone, with the fear of the Lord and humility, commands his brother to do something, then that command, which was produced for God's sake, compels the brother to obey and do what has been enjoined. If, on the other hand, someone wants to give orders, not according to the fear of the Lord, but rather because he wants to command a brother from his own authority, then God will see the secrets of his heart and he will not permit that brother to hear, nor do, what has been commanded. The work of God—what is done on account of God—is clear, and the authority of man is clear. For commands that originate with God are based in humility; those produced by a desire for authority, anger, or disturbance, come from the enemy." [AP-GN 315; AP-GS 15.93; AP-PJ 15.73; AP-PR 142]

4. Abba Arsenius said to Abba Daniel, "Go and support your father, obeying him so that he will pray for you when he goes to the Lord, and good things will happen for you on account of his prayer." [AP-G Arsenius 35; AP-GS 11.6]

5. Abba Silvanus had a disciple, named Mark, who possessed great obedience. Silvanus valued Mark because of this quality. Nevertheless, he had eleven other disciples who were upset that Silvanus loved Mark more than them. Some of the other elders heard this, and they came sadly to Silvanus to report to him that he had grieved his

other disciples. Before they were able to reveal this, Silvanus took them to each of the brothers' cells, called each by their own name, and said, "Come out, brother, for I have work for you."

None of them wanted to come out.

Then Silvanus and the fathers went to Mark's cell, after all the others. Abba Silvanus knocked on the door and called his name. As soon as Mark heard the voice of the elder, he came outside, and the elder sent him to perform a certain task. Then he said to the other elders, "Where are the other brothers?"

Silvanus entered Mark's cell. Because Mark was a scribe, Silvanus saw the manuscript page that Mark had been copying, and he found that in the moment he had been called, Mark had abandoned the character he had been writing in the middle of the stroke, so that he might fulfill the duty of obedience. He did not want to wait to complete the letter he had begun, once he had heard the voice of the elder. For this reason, all the other elders said to him, "In truth we love this monk, whom you love, because God loves him for his obedience." [AP-G Mark, Disciple of Silvanus 1; AP-GS 14.11; AP-PJ 14.5; AP-PR 143]

6. Another time, while Abba Silvanus was in Scetis with the other elders, he wanted to demonstrate Mark's obedience, for which he cherished him. He saw a wild boar and said to Mark, "Do you see that ox, my son?"

Mark replied, "I see it, Abba."

Then he spoke to him again, "Have you ever seen such fine, straight horns?"

Again Mark asserted the same thing.

The elders admired his obedience. [AP-G Mark, Disciple of Silvanus 2]

Chapter Forty-Three

THAT OBEDIENCE FREES A MAN FROM EVERY DANGER

1. One of the old solitary monks had a man who lived in a nearby village and took care of him. Once that man was delayed for several

days, and the supplies that the elder required ran out. He did not have materials for his work, nor food to eat, and because of this, he began to worry. He said to his disciple, "Are you able to go into the village?"

His disciple replied, "I will do what you ask, Father." Nevertheless, the brother was afraid to go into the village for fear of scandal, but in order to obey his father, he promised to make the trip.

The elder said to him, "Go. I have faith in God, our Father, that he will protect you from every temptation." After offering a prayer, he sent his disciple on his way.

The brother reached the village and asked where the man lived who ministered to his master. He found the home, and when he knocked on the door, he discovered that all of the family was absent, except for one of the daughters of the man who ministered to his master. She opened the door, and the brother questioned her about her father, asking why he had not come for several days. Immediately she begged the brother to come inside the house, and began dragging him in. When the monk did not agree, she grew stronger and pulled him to herself.

Now, when the brother saw that he was being drawn to a sin, and his thoughts were urging him to comply, he groaned and called out to God, "Lord, on account of the prayer of him who sent me, save me in this hour." After speaking these words, he suddenly found himself standing on the bank of the river near his monastery, and he returned to his father without suffering disgrace. [AP-GN 293; AP-GS 14.25; AP-PJ 14.16; AP-PR 144]

2. They said about the monk named John, the disciple of Abba Paul, that he possessed great obedience. Now there was a cave in a certain place and an evil wild beast, a hyena, lived in it. When the abba had seen cow manure in that place, and he needed some, he said to his disciple, "Go and bring some manure to me."

John said, "What should I do about the hyena?"

Then, joking, the elder said to him, "If she attacks you, tie her up and bring her here."

It was already evening when the disciple reached that place. Immediately the hyena came after him, and the monk, obeying the word of the elder, wanted to capture her. When she fled, he followed, saying, "My abba said that I must tie you up." He seized and tied her.

The elder was worried, because his disciple was late, and he sat waiting for him. But then, behold, the disciple arrived, bringing the bound hyena. The elder was amazed when he saw this. Wanting to humble him, to keep him from becoming proud, he struck him and said, "Fool! Why did you bring this miserable dog here?" Then the elder quickly released the animal and sent it away. [AP-G John, Disciple of Paul 1; AP-GS 14.5; AP-CSP 4.13; AP-PJ 14.4; AP-PR 27]

3. Two brothers by birth came to live in a certain monastery. One of them was very religious, and the other possessed great obedience. When his abba commanded him, "Do this," he did it, and when he said, "Do that," he did it. Consequently, he was praised in the monastery because he possessed such great obedience.

His religious brother envied him and said to himself, "I will test my brother to see if he has unwavering obedience." Then he went to the abbot and said, "Send my brother with me, for I am needed in a certain place." The abbot sent him away.

After they had gone out together, the religious brother wanted to test his obedient brother. When they came to a river in which there were many crocodiles, he said, "Descend into the river and cross." The obedient brother went into the river. The crocodiles came and they began to lick his body, but they did not harm him. When the religious brother saw this, he said, "Get out of the river and let us go."

While they were walking, they found the body of a dead man lying on the road. The religious brother said, "If we had some old clothes, we could cover that man."

His brother replied, "We should pray and perhaps God might revive him." After the two stood praying, the dead man was revived, and the religious brother praised himself, saying, "Because of my religiosity, this dead man has been brought back to life."

Nevertheless, God revealed everything to the father of the monastery. He showed him that the religious brother had tempted his brother with crocodiles, and how the dead man had been resuscitated. After they had returned to the monastery, the abba said to the religious brother, "Why did you do these things to your brother? Look, because of his obedience, that dead man revived." [AP-GN 294; AP-GS 14.27; AP-PJ 14.17; AP-PR 145]

Chapter Forty-Four

CONCERNING CHARITY: THAT YOU SHOULD DO TO OTHERS WHAT YOU WANT DONE TO YOURSELF

1. One of the elders of Scetis sent his disciple to lead the camel that carried the baskets he had made to Egypt. Now while he was leading the camel, another elder met the disciple on the way and said, "If I had known when you were going to Egypt, I would have asked you to lead another camel for me."

When the disciple reported this to his own abbot, the elder said to him, "Go, son, take our camel to that man and say to him, 'Because we are unprepared, load your goods.' Then you go with the camel to Egypt, and afterward, return the camel to us, so that we can carry our baskets."

The brother did this; he went to that elder and said, "My abba says, 'Because we are unready, take this camel and load your goods.'" The elder loaded the camel and went to Egypt.

When he had returned again, that brother took back the camel and said, "Pray for me, Father."

When the elder asked where he was going, the disciple replied, "I am going to Scetis, so that I may also bring our baskets here."

When the elder heard this, he felt compunction and began to repent, saying as he wept, "Forgive me, because your charity has taken away my fruit." [AP-GN 344; AP-PR 146]

2. Another elder had completed his baskets and already sewed on their handles, when he heard his neighbor saying, "What shall I do? Market day is at hand, and I do not have handles for my baskets."

Returning to his cell quickly, the first monk removed the handles from his own baskets, and then took them to the brother, saying, "Look, I have extra handles. Take them and put them on your baskets."

He did this on account of his charity, so that the works of his brother would be completed, even though his own remained unfinished. [AP-GN 347; AP-GS 17.20; AP-PJ 17.16; AP-PR 147]

3. Abba John, through the great grace of charity, had forgotten all malice. Once he had borrowed a *solidus* from a brother and bought

the flax he used in his work. Then another brother came seeking a little flax from him, so that he could make a sack for himself. John gave him the flax happily. Later, another monk came looking for some flax, and John gave some to him as well. Many other monks came looking for flax, and John gave joyfully to everyone.

After this, the man who had loaned him the *solidus* came for his money. John said to him, "I will go and bring it to you." Not having any money he could return, John rose and went to Abba Jacob, to ask to borrow money from him so that he might repay the man who had made the initial loan.

While he was walking, he found a *solidus* lying on the road, but he did not take it. Instead, having made a prayer, he returned to his cell. When that brother came looking for his money again, John said to him, "I will deliver it whenever possible."

Going out a second time, he found the *solidus* in the same place it had been before. Having prayed, he again returned to his cell. Again the brother came, troubling him about the *solidus*. Then the elder said, with all earnestness, "I will bring it by whatever means possible."

When he went out a third time, he found the *solidus* lying in the same place. Offering a prayer, he picked it up and went to Abba Jacob and said, "Abba, while coming to you, I found this *solidus* on the road. Perform a charitable deed and announce this in the city, in case someone there lost the money. If its owner is found, return it to him."

Abba Jacob went to the city, and for three days spread the news, but no one was found who had lost a *solidus*. Then John said to Abba Jacob, "If no one lost it, I will give it to that brother, because I owe money to that man. While coming, either to borrow money from you or to take some in charity to repay my debt to that man, I found this coin."

The elder was amazed that, needing money and finding some, John had not taken the coin immediately, but he had left it twice, and on the third occasion, had advertised his find.

This was also an amazing thing about him: if anyone wanted to borrow something from him, he would not give the item with his own hands, but rather, would say to the brother, "Go take what you need." When the thing was returned, he would say, "Go and put it back where you found it." If the item was never returned, he never said anything about it. [AP-G John the Persian 2; AP-GS 6.8; AP-PJ 6.7; AP-PR 148]

Chapter Forty-Five

ON GOD'S COMMAND ABOUT A NEIGHBOR: THAT YOU DO TO HIM WHAT YOU WISH DONE TO YOURSELF

1. A brother asked Abba Poemen, "What is faith?"
The elder replied, "To always live with charity and humility, and to do good to your neighbor." [AP-Pa 17.1]

2. When Abba Theodore was speaking about the work of the spirit and hands, one of the brothers who was listening said to him, "Explain to us the work of the spirit and hands."
The elder replied, "All of the things that we perform to fulfill God's command are regarded as among the works of the spirit; but those things we transact for our own advantage or in any manner we please are recognized as works of the hands." [AP-G Theodore of Pherme 11; AP-GS 10.177; AP-Pa 17.2]

3. Abba Apollo, if any of the brothers asked him to help with their work, would quickly go to him with all joy, saying, "I go, with my king, Christ, to work today for the benefit of my soul. For this is a reward that is credited to my soul." [AP-G Apollo 1; AP-Pa 17.3]

Chapter Forty-Six

ON DOING THE WILL OF YOUR NEIGHBOR

1. Abba Poemen said, "Never carry out your own will, but rather, humble yourself so that you do the will of your neighbor." [AP-G Poemen 158; AP-PR 149A]

2. The same man said, "If anyone does something, submitting his will to another, and the deed itself is not sanctioned by God, but the man, unaware of that, did it anyway, he will still be able to attain the road of God if he is warned by another. On the other hand, the man who follows his own will and chooses not to listen to advice from

someone else, will only attain the road of God with difficulty." [AP-GN 248; AP-GS 10.115; AP-PJ 10.80]

3. Abba Poemen, when he was summoned to eat against his will, went weeping, lest by failing to obey his brother, he might sadden him. Abandoning his own will, he humbly conformed to the will of another. [AP-G Poemen 17; AP-GS 4.33; AP-PJ 4.30; AP-PR 149B]

4. An anchorite was living near a monastery, practicing many virtues. When some monks came to the monastery, they compelled him to eat at a time that was not in accordance with the established rule. Later, the brothers said to him, "Are you saddened, Abba, because you did something against the customary practice?"

The elder responded, "I am only troubled when I do my own will." [AP-GN 284; AP-GS 13.9; AP-PJ 13.8; AP-Pa 18.1; AP-PR 150]

5. Abba Paphnutius never drank wine. Once, while he was walking, he encountered some bandits, and when he met them on the road, they were drinking. The leader of the bandits, who knew that Paphnutius did not drink wine, recognized the monk. Seeing that Paphnutius was exhausted from his journey, the leader filled a large cup with wine, and, holding a sword in his hand, he said to the elder, "Unless you drink this cup, I will kill you."

The elder recognized that the bandit wanted to fulfill God's command, and so, wanting to save him, he took the cup and drank it.

Then the leader of the bandits said to him, "Forgive me, Abba, because I have made you suffer."

The elder responded, "I have confidence in my God that because of this cup of wine, he will show mercy to you in the present age and in the future."

The leader of the bandits said to him, "I also have confidence in God that from this day I will do evil to no one."

Thus, the elder saved the entire group of bandits. [AP-G Paphnutius 2; AP-GS 17.15; AP-PJ 17.12; AP-PR 151]

6. A brother came to Scetis and demanded to see Abba Arsenius. When the other brothers recommended that he should rest a little, he replied, "I will not eat bread until I win the right to see that man."

Then one of the brothers led him to the cell of the blessed Arsenius. Knocking on the door of the cell, they sat down after offering a prayer. When the blessed Arsenius remained silent, the monk who had brought the brother said, "I will go." The monk who had come to fulfill his desire, because Abba Arsenius said nothing to him and was sitting silently out of embarrassment, also said, "I will go with you, brother."

Both men then departed.

The visitor then asked to be taken to see Abba Moses, the man who had been converted after being a thief. Moses received them and was very hospitable before he sent them away.

Then the brother, who had led the visitor to both men, said, "Look, you have seen the two monks you asked about; which of the two pleased you more?"

The visitor replied, "That man who received and fed us well seemed better to me."

After he had spoken this sentiment, one of the fathers prayed to the Lord, saying, "Lord, I entreat you to explain this matter to me, because on account of your name, one monk refuses to see or speak to any men, while the other, on account of your name, is courteous to everybody."

And behold, while in an ecstatic trance, he saw two ships on a river. In one, he saw the Spirit of God sailing together with Abba Arsenius in silence and peace. In the other ship he saw Abba Moses and the angels of God, inserting honey and honeycombs into their mouths. [AP-G Arsenius 38; AP-Pa 18.2]

7. A brother questioned Abba Poemen, saying, "If I happen to see a brother about whom I have heard something wicked, I do not want to let him enter my cell; if I should see a good brother, I rejoice with him. Do you think I am doing what is right?"

The elder replied, "If you do any small good to the good man, do twice as much good to the other man." [AP-G Poemen 70a; AP-GS 17.27; AP-PJ 17.23]

8. There were two brothers; one of them was an elder, who said to the younger, "I think that we should live together, brother."

But the younger responded, "I am a sinner; you will not be able to live with me."

The older monk replied, "We are able to do it."

Now the older monk was pure, and he did not want to hear that a monk was having any unclean thoughts. The younger monk said to him, "Give me this one week, and then we will speak again."

When a week had passed, the elder arrived, and the younger monk, wanting to test him, said, "I fell into a great temptation this week, Abba. I had to go into the village for supplies and I sinned."

The elder said, "Do you wish to repent?"

When the younger monk agreed, the elder said, "I will carry part of this sin with you."

Then the younger monk said, "In this way, we will be able to remain together." They lived together until the time of the elder's death. [AP-GN 346; AP-GS 17.18; AP-PJ 17.14; AP-PR 152]

Chapter Forty-Seven

NOT DOING TO OTHERS WHAT YOU DON'T WANT DONE TO YOURSELF

1. One of the elders used to say, "A man should never do what he dreads to anyone else. Do you fear that someone might tear you down? Do not tear down someone else. Do you fear that someone might spread lies about you, despise you, injure you, or take something from you? Then don't do these things or anything similar to someone else. The person who carries out this word will find that it suffices for salvation." [AP-GN 253; AP-GS 1.31; AP-PJ 1.21; AP-Pa 16.2; AP-PR 153]

2. Abba Isaac said, "I know another brother who was hiding himself in a field, and he wanted to eat a single ear of grain, but unless he asked the owner of the field, saying, 'Do you order me to pick an ear and eat?' he would not taste one. For he was scared, in even this small matter, that he might sin by cheating another." [AP-G Isaac, Priest of Cells 4; AP-GS 4.22; AP-PJ 4.21]

3. Once, when a certain secular man, who was selling onions, had come to Abba Theodore's cell, and he had filled a vase with them, the elder said to his disciple, "Go, fill the same vase with grain and return." There were two vases, one filled with clean grain, and the other dirty grain. The brother returned with the vase that was filled with dirty grain. When the elder noticed, he gave his disciple a harsh look. The disciple tripped on account of his fear and broke the vase. Throwing himself on the floor, he began to repent. Then the elder

said to him, "Rise, brother, for this is not your fault, but I, who gave you the order, sinned." Then, going inside, he filled the fold in his robe with clean grain, and gave it to the vendor for the onions, but he also returned the onions which he had bought, and allowed the man to depart. [AP-G Theodore of Pherme 22]

4. When Abba Or's disciple, Paul, had gone to purchase palm fronds, he discovered that other men, preceding him, had already offered pledges for them, and so he looked elsewhere. Nevertheless, one of the vendors said to him, "Take these for your work, for the man who gave me a pledge to return for them is late." He took them, returned to his elder, and told him what the vendor had said. When the elder heard what had happened, he clapped his hands and said, "Abba Or does not have what is needed for the present year," and he did not permit his disciple to enter the cell until he returned the palm fronds to the place where he had purchased them. [AP-G Or 4]

Chapter Forty-Eight

WE SHOULD NOT EMBARRASS OUR BROTHER

1. A brother asked Abba Sisoes, "If, while we are walking on the road, the guide for our journey makes a mistake, should we not say something to him?"

Sisoes replied, "No."

The brother said, "Should we abandon him, so that he is forced to follow us?"

The elder answered, "What then? Do you want to beat that man with your staffs? I know some brothers who were walking through the night, when the man who was showing them the way became lost. There were eleven brothers, and all of them knew that they had gone astray. Nevertheless they resolved among themselves to say nothing. When it became light and the leader recognized his error, he begged forgiveness for mistakenly leading them away from the route. Nevertheless, all of the monks said, 'We knew we were making a mistake, but we stayed silent to hide your embarrassment.'

"When the guide heard this, he was amazed, because they would have followed him to their deaths without speaking, and he praised the Lord who had bestowed this patience. For they had gone astray by twelve miles." [AP-G Sisoes 30]

∞

Chapter Forty-Nine

ON NOT PLACING THE AFFECTIONS OF PARENTS BEFORE GOD

1. The mother of Abba Poemen and Abba Anub wanted to see them after they came to the desert. She often came to their cell but was never able to see them there. One time, having watched, she met them when they were hurrying to church. Spotting her, the two monks turned around quickly and closed the door of their cell. Then she stood outside, crying and calling for them.

Then Abba Anub, going to the blessed Poemen, asked, "What should we do about that old woman who wails outside our door?"

Abba Poemen rose to his feet and went to the door. Although it was closed, he heard her crying continuously, and he said to her, "Why such a great noise? At your age you should be tired by now, and yet you still pour out your lament?"

The mother, recognizing the voice of her son, exclaimed loudly, "Because I desire to see you, my sons. What is the problem if I see you? Am I not your mother? Did I not nurse you with my breasts? Now I have had enough of the pain caused by all of these delays; after hearing your voice, all of my insides are stirred up by my desire to see you."

Poemen replied, "Would you rather see us now or in the future age?"

She said, "Why? If I do not see you now, how will it be certain that I may see you then?"

The elder answered, "Because if you are able to exercise self-restraint now, so that you don't see us, you will always be able to see us, without a doubt, in that future place."

Then she left them joyfully, saying, "If it is certain that I will see you there, then I no longer want to see you here." [AP-G Poemen 76; AP-GS 4.40; AP-PJ 4.33; AP-PR 154]

2. Mark, the disciple of Abba Silvanus, had a mother, and she came to see him. When the abbot came out, she demanded that he should tell her son to come out and see her. The abbot returned inside and told him, "Go out so that your mother might see you."

Now Mark was dressed in a patched robe, and since he was cooking food, he was covered with soot. Going out quickly for the sake of the obedience he maintained toward the elder, he closed his eyes and said, "Greetings, greetings." He saw none of those people who were looking for him, nor did his mother recognize him.

Once again his mother sent word to the elder, saying, "Abba, make my son come out so that I may see him."

Then the elder said to Mark, "I already told you to go out and see your mother."

Mark replied, "I went out, following your command. Nevertheless, I beg you not to send me out again, for perhaps I will not be able to obey."

Then the elder went out and convinced Mark's mother that he was the monk who had come out a little earlier. Then he sent her away. [AP-G Mark, Disciple of Silvanus 3; AP-GS 14.12; AP-PJ 14.6]

3. A brother set out to visit his sister who was growing weak in a convent of virgins. Nevertheless, she was a faithful woman who never saw a man, and she was unwilling to see even her own brother as he entered with the other women. She commanded him, saying, "Go, brother! Pray for me and I believe that through the grace of Christ, we will see each other in the kingdom of heaven." [AP-GN 153; AP-GS 4.74; AP-CSP 5.5; AP-PJ 4.61; AP-PR 33]

4. There was a certain judge who wanted to see Abba Poemen, but the elder would not consent. The judge wanted to find an opportunity to see him so that Poemen might bless him. Therefore he arrested the son of Poemen's sister, as if he was a thief, saying, "I will not release him unless, perhaps, the elder comes and begs me on the boy's behalf."

The sister came to Abba Poemen's door, weeping for her son. Poemen did not give her any reply.

She began shouting outside his door, saying, "Cruel man, have mercy on me because he is my only son."

Poemen sent word to her, "Poemen did not bear sons."

After hearing this, she departed.

When the judge heard, he sent word, saying, "Even if you only ask me it in a message, I will release the boy."

The elder sent a word and commanded him, "Handle him according to the laws, and execute him if he deserves it; if he doesn't deserve death, do what you will with him." [AP-G Poemen 5; AP-GS 8.16; AP-CSP 4.4; AP-PJ 8.13; AP-PR 20]

5. Abba Joseph had come to Abba Poemen with some of the other elders. At the same time, a man who was related to the aforementioned elder arrived with a child whose face had been disfigured. The father sat with the child outside the monastery, weeping. When one of the elders went out and asked him why he was crying, that man responded, "I am a relative of this Abba Poemen. Do you see this child whom temptation has touched? We are afraid that he does not want to see the child that I have brought here. Even now, if he understood that I was here, he would drive me away. When I saw that you fathers had come to him, I also presumed to come. Now do whatever you will, Abba. Have mercy on me and take this infant inside so that he might pray for him."

When the elder took the child into the cell, he employed the counsel of wisdom: he did not present the child to Abba Poemen first, but beginning with the lesser brothers, he said, "Make the sign of the cross over this child while praying for him." He asked for the same thing from each of the brothers.

After everyone else had prayed, he carried that boy to Abba Poemen. Poemen did not want to touch the child. Nevertheless, when all the monks asked him, because they had all prayed, Poemen groaned, and rising to his feet, prayed, "Lord, make your creation whole, lest the enemy dominate him." After making the sign of the cross over the infant, he was quickly healed and returned to his father. [AP-G Poemen 7; AP-GS 19.14; AP-PJ 10.10; AP-Pa 14.1; AP-PR 168]

6. A brother asked Abba Sisoes, "Because my sister is a beggar, if I were to give her something out of charity, would it not be the same thing as if I had given alms to any of the beggars?"

The elder answered, "It is not the same, because your blood relationship inclines you to do this." [AP-GN 233; AP-GS 10.156; AP-PJ 10.101]

7. The death of a monk's father was reported to him. The monk replied to the man who brought the news, "Stop blaspheming, man! My Father is immortal." [AP-GS 10.194]

Chapter Fifty

ON SERVICE FOR THE SICK OR THE SICKNESS ITSELF

1. One of the elders had liberated a brother when he was suffering from nightmares by ordering the other sick men to keep a fast with him. For nothing, that man said, extinguishes these sufferings like mercy.

2. A brother questioned an elder, saying, "Two brothers live together in a cell. One of them fasts for six complete days, while the other serves the sick. Which of the two performs the greater work before God?"

The elder responded, "Even if that man who fasts six days should hang himself by his eyes, he would still not match the other in the sight of God." [AP-GN 355; AP-GS 17.22; AP-PJ 17.18; AP-Pa 19.1]

3. John the Younger, of Thebes, a disciple of Abba Ammoes, served the old, sick man for twelve years. Despite this, when the elder saw him working, he never spoke a pleasant or agreeable word to him.

Now when the elder was passing from this world, with the other elders sitting around him, he took John's hand, and said to him three times, "Be well, be well, be well."

Then he handed John over to the elders, saying, "This is an angel, not a man; he has served me, a sick man, for so many years without ever hearing a good word." [AP-G John the Theban 1; AP-GS 16.5; AP-PJ 16.4; AP-Pa 19.2; AP-PR 155]

4. Abba Agathon, while entering a city to sell his work, discovered a foreigner lying ill in a doorway because he did not have anyone to take care of him. Consequently, the elder remained in the city. He rented a cell for himself, and from the work of his hands, he took care of that sick man. Agathon remained in that place for four months, until the sick man regained his health. Then he returned to his cell. [AP-G Agathon 27; AP-PR 156]

Chapter Fifty-One

THAT SICKNESS IS USEFUL FOR THE BODY

1. One of the great elders said to his sick disciple, "My son, do not fear infirmity or the blow that strikes your body, for it is the height of religion that someone should offer thanks to God when they are ill. If you are made of steel, you will lose your rust in the fire. But if you are gold and are tested in the fire, you will pass from great to even greater. And so, do not be anxious, brother. For if the Lord wants you to be tortured in your body, who are you who bears this trouble? Hold on and ask him, and he may end the troubles that he wills." [AP-G Syncletica 7; AP-GS 7.23; AP-PJ 7.16; AP-Pa 20.1; AP-PR 157]

2. A certain elder was frequently ill and faint, but one year no illness infected him. When this happened, he began to weep and carry on, saying "You have abandoned me, Lord: you have not wanted to visit me with your presence this year." [AP-GN 209; AP-GS 7.50; AP-PJ 7.41; AP-Pa 20.2; AP-PR 158]

3. One of the elders became sick while he was living alone in his cell. He had no one who was able to serve him, and so rising from his bed, he would find something in his cell and eat it. He remained in this state for several days, and none of the brothers came to visit him. When thirty days had passed, and no one had come, God sent an angel who obeyed him. Seven days later, the other fathers remembered the elder and said, "We must go and see him, in case he has fallen ill."

When they arrived and knocked on his door, the angel vanished. The elder shouted from inside his cell, "Go away from here."

They broke down the door, entered the cell, and asked why he was shouting in that manner.

The elder replied, "For thirty days I was ill and no one visited me. But look, for the past seven days, the angel whom God sent has been serving me. When you came to the door, he left."

After he said these words, he died. [AP-GN 212; AP-GS 7.53; AP-PJ 7.44]

Chapter Fifty-Two

ON THE PASSING OF THE PERFECT

1. An elder was dying in Scetis, and the brothers had encircled his small bed. While those who had joined him were mourning, he opened his eyes and laughed. Then he opened his eyes and laughed again. Then he did the same thing a third time.

The brothers questioned him, saying, "Tell us, Abba, why do you laugh when we are crying?"

He replied, "The first time I laughed was because you are all afraid of death; the second time I laughed was because you are unprepared for it; the third time was because I go to rest from my labor." [AP-GN 279; AP-GS 11.115; AP-PJ 11.52; AP-PR 159]

2. Abba Pambo, when the time came for him to pass from his body, in the hour in which he was departing, said to the holy men standing around him, "From the time I came into this desert place and built this cell for myself, I have never tasted bread that I had not earned by the work of my hands, and I have never done penance for a word that I have spoken, right up to this hour. Therefore I go to God, just as if I had not begun to serve him." [AP-G Pambo 8; AP-GS 1.25; AP-PJ 1.16; AP-PR 160]

3. Abba Agathon, when he was dying, held his eyes open for three days without moving them. The brothers who were attending him said, "Where are you now, Abba?"

He replied, "I am standing in the sight of God, the judge."

The brothers said to him, "Are you afraid?"

He responded, "To the extent it was within my power, I always thought I had kept the commands of God. But I am a man, so how will I know if my works are pleasing to God?"

The brothers asked, "Don't you have faith that your works were done according to God?"

He replied, "I will not have confidence until I come into the sight of God, for the judgment of God is one thing, but the judgment of men is another." [AP-G Agathon 29b; AP-GS 11.9; AP-PJ 11.2; AP-PR 161]

4. The time of Abba Sisoes's dormition had arrived, and when many other elders gathered in his cell, they saw his face glowing with a certain brightness. He said to them, "Look, Abba Anthony is coming to us."

A little later he said, "Look, also the band of prophets."

His face was then flooded with an even brighter light, and he said to them, "The blessed apostles also are present." Then Sisoes seemed to be speaking with some of them.

When the fathers demanded that he tell them whom he was talking to, he said, "Angels, for they have come to carry away my soul, but I am begging them to wait a little longer so that I can make penance."

The fathers said to him, "You do not need to make penance, Abba."

Sisoes replied, "Truthfully, I say to you, that I don't think I've taken hold of the beginning of penance." From what he said, the fathers perceived that he had been perfected in the fear of the Lord.

Then, his face glowing with the splendor of the sun, he said to them, "Look! Look! The Lord comes." Having spoken these words, his spirit departed, and the cell was filled with a pleasing smell. [AP-G Sisoes 14; AP-GS 20.7; AP-PJ 20.6b; AP-PR 162]

5. (a) Blessed Arsenius, as he neared the time when he would leave this world, told his disciples, "Let no one offer charity on my account, except in the Eucharist alone; if I have offered charity, I will find it."

(b) Now his disciples were disturbed, as if his time was at hand, and he said to them, "My hour has not yet come; when it does come, I will not remain silent. Nevertheless you will stand with me in divine judgment before the tribunal of Christ if you hand over anything from this small body of mine as possessions or relics."

His disciples replied to these words, "What must we do, Father, because we do not know how to destroy a body?"

He replied, "Do you know how to tie a rope to my feet and drag me to the mountain?"

(c) Arsenius's eyelashes had fallen out from weeping, (d) for throughout his life, while sitting and working, he had worn a rag on his chest to catch the tears falling from his eyes.

(e) While he was dying, he began to weep. The brothers questioned him, asking, "Why are you crying, Father? Are you afraid?"

He replied, "Truthfully, I am afraid. And this fear that is with me now has always been with me, from the time I became a monk."

(**f**) Nevertheless, when Abba Poemen saw that Arsenius had died, he said, "Blessed are you, Arsenius, because you mourned so much in this world. For the man who does not mourn for himself in this world will lament in the next world, forever. Consequently it is impossible for a person to avoid mourning, either here, out of his own volition, or there, driven by torments." [**a:** AP-G Arsenius 39; AP-GS 10.10; AP-PJ 10.9; AP-PR 163a; **b:** AP-G Arsenius 40a; AP-GS 15.10b; AP-PJ 15.9b; AP-PR 163b; **c:** AP-G Arsenius 42d; AP-GS 15.11c; AP-PR 163c; **d:** AP-GS 3.3; AP-PJ 3.1; AP-PR 163d; **e:** AP-G Arsenius 40c; AP-GS 15.10c; AP-PJ 15.9c; AP-PR 163d; **f:** AP-G Arsenius 41b; AP-GS 15.10e; AP-PJ 15.9e; AP-PR 163e]

Chapter Fifty-Three

ON THE FEAR OF GOD

1. A brother asked Abba Pambo why his soul resisted and did not want to fear God. He replied, "Indeed the soul wants to fear God, but it is not yet time. For fear of the Lord is perfection." [AP-Pa 21.1]

2. A brother asked one of the elders, "How does fear of the Lord enter the soul?"

The elder replied, "If anyone should first possess humility, so that he judges no one and he has nothing, then the fear of the Lord will enter his soul." [AP-G Euprepius 5; AP-GN 137; AP-GS 1.29; AP-PJ 1.19; AP-Pa 21.2]

3. A brother asked Abba Poemen, "What should I do, Father, because my soul is irrational and it does not fear God?"

The elder said to him, "Go and join yourself to a man who fears God, and learn from this man what he fears, and then you, gaining wisdom, will begin to fear." [AP-G Poemen 65; AP-GS 11.59; AP-PJ 11.23]

Chapter Fifty-Four

ON TEARS AND SORROW

1. A brother said to an elder, "Although my soul desires tears, just as I hear the elders produced, they do not come to me and my heart is saddened."

The elder replied, "After forty years, the sons of Israel entered the promised land. Tears are the promised land and the elders passed through many labors to reach it. Once someone has reached that place, he will not fear the battle. Thus, God desires that the soul suffer tribulations and desire to enter that promised land." [AP-GN 142; AP-GS 3.45; AP-PJ 3.27]

2. An elder saw a brother laughing, and he said to him, "In the presence of heaven and earth, we will have to offer an explanation for the entire course of our life, and you laugh? For just as we carry the shadow of our body everywhere, in the same way we must not neglect to carry weeping and compunction wherever we are." [AP-GN 139; AP-GS 3.41; AP-PJ 3.23]

3. When a brother sought to hear a word from Abba Poemen, the elder replied, "In this matter our fathers placed weeping first, for weeping offers a twofold benefit: it not only works, but it protects." [AP-G Poemen 39; AP-GS 3.26; AP-PJ 3.12]

4. (a) The blessed Bishop Athanasius once invited Abba Pambo to descend from the desert to Alexandria. When he was going down with the brothers, he saw some secular people and he said to them, "Get up and greet the monks, so that you may be blessed by them. For these men frequently speak with God and their mouths are holy."

(b) When he saw an actress in the city, Pambo wept deeply. The men standing around him asked why he was crying. The elder replied, "Two things compel my tears: the first is the ruin of this woman; the second is that I do not take as much care to please God as she takes to please men with her obscene practices." [a: AP-G Pambo 7; AP-GS

17.14; AP-PJ 17.11; AP-PR 164a; **b:** AP-G Pambo 4; AP-GS 3.32; AP-PJ 3.14; AP-PR 164b]

Chapter Fifty-Five

ON REPENTANCE

1. A brother asked Abba Poemen, "What is repentance?"

The elder replied, "Repentance from sins is, above all else, not to sin. For this reason, a voice always calls to men, right up to their last breath, 'Convert today!'" [AP-G Poemen 192; AP-Pa 22.1]

2. It was said of one of the elders that as often as his thoughts said to him, "Let it go today and repent tomorrow," he would respond, "No, today we must repent and tomorrow let the will of God be done in us." [AP-GN 271; AP-GS 11.102; AP-PJ 11.44; AP-PR 165]

3. The same man said, "Every evening and every morning, a man ought to examine himself by employing reason, saying, 'Let us see what we did today from those actions that God does not want, and what we did that fulfilled his will.' For in this way a man examining himself throughout his entire life, will be discovered to have made penance and to have adhered to God. Just as no one is able to injure someone who is near an emperor, not even the devil is able to hurt the soul of one who is always near God, because he says, *Draw near to me and I will draw near to you* (Jas 4:8).

"But for the man whose frame of mind is diverted here and there, the enemy will find an opportunity to lead his soul into various passions."

4. **(a)** Abba Poemen said, "I prefer a man who has repented after his sin over a man who has never known or repented of sin. **(b)** For the man who is always saying in his thoughts that he is a sinner, is humble; but the man who has the idea that he is a just man, is not." [**a:** AP-G Sarmatas 1; AP-GS 10-52a; **b:** AP-GS 10-52b]

5. A soldier asked an elder, "Does God receive repentance, Abba?"

The elder replied, "Tell me, dear one, if your cloak had been ripped a little, would you throw it away?"

The soldier answered, "No, I would repair it and use it again."

The elder said to him, "If you would fix and continue to use your garment, do you not think God will not spare his own creation?"

The soldier was encouraged by these words. [AP-G Mius 3; AP-GS 10.176; AP-PJ 21.30]

6. Abba John offered this metaphor about the soul that wished to repent: "There was a prostitute in a certain city who had many lovers. A judge came to her and said, 'Pledge your chastity to me, and I will take you as my wife.'

"She promised, and he received her and took her into his home. When her former lovers were looking for her, they said, 'The judge took her into his home. If we go to his door and are discovered, he will punish us. So come, behind the house, and we will whisper to her. When she recognizes our whispering voice, she will descend to us, and we will not be harmed.'

"Nevertheless, when she heard their voices, she sealed her ears, fled to an inner room, and closed the door." [AP-G John the Dwarf 16; AP-PJ 21.13]

Chapter Fifty-Six

HOW, THROUGH REPENTANCE, A MAN IS ABLE TO BE RECONCILED TO GOD IN ONE DAY

1. (a) Abba Sisoes often offered this word about repentance: "If a man wanted, he would be able to reach the measure of the divine precepts from morning through evening, (b) that is, if he repented through weeping for the sins that he had committed, and, to keep from falling short again, he established a covenant between himself and God." [a: AP-G Alonius 3; AP-GS 11.14; AP-PJ 11.6]

2. One of the fathers spoke about another bishop, who had heard of two men from his congregation who had gone beyond the measure of impurity and were adulterers. The bishop asked God to show him if this was true.

After the offering had been consecrated, and everyone approached for communion, he perceived the faces and souls of every single person. The faces of the sinners appeared black, like carbon, and their eyes were filled with blood. But he saw others with bright faces and wrapped in white robes.

Now when they received the body of the Lord, there seemed to be light in the faces of some, and flames in the faces of the others. He offered communion to them so that he would recognize those who had committed the crimes he had heard about. He saw that one of the men had a clear and respectable face, and he was wrapped in white robes, but the other was black, with a horrible face. After they had taken the gift of the divine mystery, a certain light illuminated the first man, while the other burned, as if with flames.

The bishop prayed for every person who had presented themselves to be instructed by him. An angel of the Lord took a place beside him, and said, "Everything that you heard about them is true. That one remains in his filth and is sinning willingly, and so you see him with a black face, burning with flames. The other man was similar to him, as you heard. But look, you saw that second man illuminated with a bright face, because recalling those things he did earlier, he renounced those evil works, and asked for God's mercy with tears and wailing, promising that if his former sins were forgiven, he would not return to them anymore. With his earlier crimes wiped away, he has come to that grace which you saw."

When the bishop marveled about the grace of God, by which the man was not only taken out of the torments of a life that was so wicked, but also decorated with such great honor, the angel responded, "You do well to be amazed, for you are a man. For our Lord—and yours, naturally—is good and compassionate to those who give up their sins. He not only sends away the sins of those who seek him through confession, but he also creates someone worthy of honor. *For God so loved humans, that he appointed his only begotten Son for the sake of sinners, and he gave him over to death on their behalf* (John 3:16). *And so if he chose to die for them while they were his enemies* (Rom 5:8), how much more will be done when they are his own? Since you know that no human sins can defeat the goodness of God, if only everyone repented of their former deeds, evil would be destroyed. For God is merciful and he knows the weakness of the human species, the strength of passion, and the power and wickedness of the devil. When certain men fall into sins, he indulges them like sons, as he waits for their correction. He suffers with those who are sluggish with respect to repentance, and soon he releases their sins, and bestows the rewards of the righteous on them."

When the bishop heard these things, he was even more amazed. He gave glory to God and told everyone what had happened. [AP-GN 715; AP-GS 18.46; AP-PJ 18.36; AP-Pa 23.1; AP-PR 166]

3. Abba Paul the Simple had this grace: when he saw the elders entering the church, he could perceive whether their thoughts were good or bad, just from their individual faces. When they came to church and were entering, the elder would see them enter with bright faces and rejoicing spirits, and the angels that accompanied them shared their joy. Nevertheless he saw one person was dark, with a misty body, and demons were dragging him here and there, having placed for themselves a bridle in his nose. His holy angel was frightened and followed at a distance.

Sitting in front of the church, the blessed Paul began to weep bitterly and strike his chest on account of the man whom he had seen in such a state. Now all the other elders, when they saw him weeping in this manner, began to ask him to specify whether he had seen something in them or in someone who had entered the congregation.

Paul did not want to enter the church, but he remained outside, weeping for the man he had seen. A little while later, when the congregation was released and the people were leaving, Paul again inspected the faces of each person to see if they were leaving in the same condition in which they had entered. He saw that same man, who before had been dark and misty, leaving the church with a bright face and white body, and the demons were following him at a distance while his holy angel was beside him, merry and rejoicing greatly over him.

Then Paul rose to his feet and shouted with joy, blessing the Lord and saying, "How great is the mercy and kindness of God! How great is his compassion!" Then, climbing to a high place, Paul shouted, "*Come and see the work of the Lord* (Ps 46:8). *Come and see how he wants all men to be saved and to come to the knowledge of truth* (1 Tim 2:4). Come, let us adore him, saying, 'You alone are able to take away our sins.'"

When the people gathered around him, Paul explained what he had seen before they entered the church, and then what he had seen after the service. He found that brother whom he had seen in that condition so that he might reveal his thoughts and deeds and explain how God had granted such a great change to him.

That man began to tell his story in front of everyone, saying, "I am a sinful man, and as often as possible, I committed fornication.

Nevertheless, after I entered the church of God just now, I heard the words of the Prophet Isaiah, the great one of God, speaking about himself, *Wash yourselves, make yourselves clean, and bring all the evils from your souls before the gaze of my eyes. Learn to do well and seek justice. Even if your sins are like scarlet, they will be made as white as snow. If you will be obedient and listen, you will eat the good things of the earth* (Isa 1:16–19).

"Now I, a fornicator, felt compunction from these words of the prophet, and after they entered my heart, I said to God, 'Lord, you are the one who came to save sinners. Now complete in me, an unworthy sinner, these works that you promised through the prophet. For behold, I profess to you from this time forward, and I confess with my entire heart, that I will no longer do evil, but rather, I will renounce all injustice. From this time onward, I will serve you with a clean conscience. And so from today, Lord, from this hour, receive me, a man who is penitent, a worshiper of you, and one who renounces all sins. *I have sworn an oath and determined to serve all your laws set up before me* (Ps 119:106).'

"As a result of this agreement, I left the church determined to have nothing more to do with my earlier sins."

Then all the elders shouted, crying to the Lord, with a great voice, "*How magnificent are your works, Lord. You do all things wisely* (Ps 104:24)." [AP-G Paul the Simple 1; AP-GS 18.26; AP-PJ 18.20; AP-Pa 23.2; AP-PR 167]

Chapter Fifty-Seven

THAT EVEN THE MAN WHO DIES WHILE INTENDING REPENTANCE WILL BE RECEIVED

1. A brother came to Abba Poemen and said that he suffered a great tribulation.

The elder said to him, "Flee from this place; you must walk at least three days and three nights. Then spend an entire year, fasting until nightfall."

The brother replied, "What if I die before the year is completed? What will be done about me?"

Abba Poemen said, "Have faith in God; if you leave me, determined to carry out this plan, even if you die soon, God will receive your repentance." [AP-Pa 24.1]

2. There was a brother living in his cell in Egypt, who was distinguished by his great humility. He had a sister in the city who was a prostitute and the ruin of many souls. The elders were frequently insulting that brother, and they were barely able to persuade him that he should go to her, so that he might admonish her and defeat the sin that she produced.

Now when he came to that place, a certain man who knew her saw him and ran ahead and announced to her, "Look, your brother is coming to you!"

When she heard this, she was filled with joy and abandoned the lovers she had been serving. With her head uncovered, she went out to meet her arriving brother. When she attempted to embrace him, the monk said to her, "My sweetest sister, spare your soul, because many are ruined through you. How will you be able to endure those harsh and eternal torments?"

She, trembling, said to him, "Do you know brother, that there will be salvation for me, even now?"

He replied, "If you desire it, there is salvation."

She threw herself at her brother's feet and begged him to take her with him into the desert.

Her brother said, "Go and cover your head, then follow me."

She said, "Let us go now, for it is better for me to walk with an uncovered head among men, than for me to return to the place of my sin again."

While they were walking together, the brother was urging her toward repentance. Nevertheless, when he saw that some brothers were coming toward them, he said to her, "Because all of the brothers do not yet know that you are my sister, step off the road a little until they pass."

Later, after the brothers had passed, he called her, saying, "Come, sister, we must be on our way."

She did not answer him.

He searched carefully for his sister and found her dead. Her footprints were filled with blood, for she had been walking barefoot.

Now when the brother reported what had happened to the elders, they debated among themselves about her salvation.

Nevertheless, God revealed to one of the elders that—because she had taken no care for her bodily needs, and had even neglected her own wound, and because she had expired in such great suffering—God had accepted her penitence. [AP-GN 43; AP-Pa 24.2; AP-PR 217]

3. One of the brothers spoke about another brother, who, when he wanted to go out into the desert was stopped by his own mother. But that brother said to her, "I want to save my soul." When she was unable to restrain him, she sent him out. That man, after coming to the desert, began wasting his life through his complete negligence.

Later, his mother died. After some time had passed, he became ill and was caught up in ecstasy before the judgment seat; there he discovered his mother among those who were judging him.

When she saw him, she was astonished, and said, "What is this, my son? Are you also condemned in this place? Where are those words that you were accustomed to say, 'I want to save my soul?'"

Her son, embarrassed by the words he was hearing, simply stood there, with nothing to offer in response. Then behold, a voice spoke and this man was recalled. Another brother from the monastery was ordered to take his place. Returning to his senses, the monk related all that he had perceived to those who were standing around him. To confirm the words that he had heard, he asked that someone from those standing around him be sent to the monastery to see if a brother had died who had the same name he had heard. When this was done, it was found to be true.

The monk, after his health had been restored, hid himself and sat thinking about his salvation, weeping and crying over those things he had done in his earlier period of negligence. His sense of compunction was so great that when many begged him to rest a little, lest perhaps he should suffer some harm through his incessant weeping, he refused, saying, "If I cannot bear the reproach of my mother, how, when in the presence of Christ and his angels, will I bear reproaches and punishment on the day of judgment?" [AP-GN 135; AP-GS 3.38; AP-PJ 3.20; AP-PR 216]

4. There was a prostitute named Taisis of such beauty that nearly all men sold their possessions and drove themselves into poverty for her sake. She sowed such jealous discord among them that the entrance to the young woman's house was frequently filled with blood.

When Abba Paphnutius learned of her, he donned the clothing of a secular man, took one *solidus*, and proceeded to her, in that Egyptian city. He gave her the *solidus* as if it was the payment for sin.

She accepted the money and said, "Let us enter the house." When she had invited him to enter so that he might lay on the bed that was draped with expensive covers, he said to her, "If there is an inner room, let us go there."

She said, "There is, but if you fear men, none of them enters this outer room; on the other hand, if you fear God, there is no place that is hidden from his divine eye."

After the elder heard these words, he said, "You know that God exists?"

When she replied that she knew about God and the future eternal kingdom and the torments of the sinners, he said to her, "If you know about these matters, why do you destroy so many souls, so that you will be condemned not only for your actions, but also for leading so many to damnation?"

Having heard these words, Taisis prostrated herself at the elder's feet, and tearfully begged him, saying, "I know there is repentance, Father, and I trust that I could receive remission through your prayers. Let me have three hours, and then I will go wherever you command and do whatever you order."

The Abba established the place where she was to meet him, and then she left. Collecting everything she had received from her sin, she carried it into the center of the city, and with the people watching, she set fire to it, saying, "Let every man come who has sinned with me and see how I am burning what you all gave to me." Now these goods had a value of four hundred pounds of gold.

When everything had burned, she made her way to the place the Abba had established. After she arrived, he shut her up in a small cell in a monastery for women. He sealed the door of her cell with lead, and he left a small window through which food might be slipped in to her. He ordered that the other women should serve her a small amount of bread and water every day.

As he prepared to depart, the door having been sealed, Taisis said to him, "Where do you order, Father, that I pour out my water?"

He replied, "In the cell, as you deserve."

When she asked how she ought to pray, he said to her, "You are not worthy to mention God by name, nor to allow his divine name to pass between your lips, nor to raise your hands to heaven, for your lips are filled with iniquity and your hands with filthy deeds. Instead, sit and face the east, repeating these words only: 'You who formed me, have mercy on me.'"

After she had been sequestered for three years, Abba Paphnutius felt her pain and went to Abba Anthony to ask him if God had restored her or not. When he arrived and carefully related the entire matter to that man, Anthony called his disciple and ordered that on that night, all the monks should maintain a vigil and persist in individual prayer, to see if God might reveal to one of them a decision about the matter that had brought Paphnutius to them.

They all withdrew and began to pray without ceasing. Paul the Great, a disciple of the blessed Anthony, suddenly saw a bed adorned with precious coverings in heaven, which was guarded by three virgins with a shining appearance. He said, "There is no one worthy of this lofty place apart from my father, Anthony."

Then a voice spoke and said, "This is not for your father, Anthony, but for the prostitute Taisis."

Morning arrived. Abba Paul related what he had seen, and having learned the will of God, Paphnutius departed. Going to the monastery where Taisis had been sequestered, he broke down the door that he had sealed. She desired to remain locked up. When he opened her door, he said to her, "Come out, for God has remitted your sins"

She replied, "I call upon God to witness that from the time I entered here, I have placed, like a bundle, all of the sins that I committed before my eyes, and not a breath has escaped from my nostrils for one hour in which my sins have not been before my eyes, but I have been always weeping for what I have seen."

Abba Paphnutius replied to this statement, saying, "God has not redeemed you on account of your penitence, but because you always had this thought in your heart." After he led her out of her cell, she lived only fifteen days, and then she rested in peace.

Chapter Fifty-Eight

ON PRAYER

1. When a certain brother asked Abba Macarius how he should pray, he responded to him, "Superfluous words are unnecessary; rather raise your hands, and say, 'O God, whatever you will. O Lord, whatever pleases you.'

"If conflict comes upon you, say, 'O God, help!' For he knows what things are useful for us, and he provides mercy for us." [AP-G Macarius the Great 19; AP-GS 12.11; AP-PJ 12.10; AP-PR 207]

2. The same man said, "God often usefully defers our request, sometimes doing this, and sometimes doing that. By what he grants, he stimulates the person seeking something to persevere."

3. Abba John said, "A monk ought to be like a man sitting under a great tree who sees the different wild beasts and serpents coming toward him. When he is unable to resist them, he climbs into the tree and is saved. In the same way the monk should sit in his cell, and seeing the depraved thoughts of the enemy coming upon him, when he is unable to resist, he should flee through prayer to God and he will be saved." [AP-G John the Dwarf 12; AP-GS 11.40; AP-PR 208]

4. The same Abba said, "A monk should be like a man who has a fire to his left and water to his right. As often as the fire flares up, he takes some water and extinguishes the flames. It is right for the monk to do this every hour, so that whenever wicked thoughts from the enemy flare up, he will pour out the water of prayer and extinguish them." [AP-G Poemen 146; AP-PR 209]

Chapter Fifty-Nine

ON PREFERRING PRAYER TO WORK

1. When the time for psalmody arrived, Abba Agathon would set aside his work, even if it was still unfinished. For he did not permit the work of his hands to infringe on the order of religion.

Chapter Sixty

ON COMING FROM WORK TO PRAYER, AS TO REST

1. Abba Ammon came to Abba Achilles and found that he had woven a long cord through the night. He asked him, "Father, speak a word to us."

Achilles responded, "I have woven twenty lengths of cord since last evening, and, truthfully, I do not need it, but I work with all my strength so that I may come to prayer as to rest."

And thus Ammon, having been helped, departed. [AP-G Achilles 5]

Chapter Sixty-One

OF ALL THE VIRTUES, PRAYER REQUIRES THE GREATEST LABOR

1. When Abba Agathon was asked which great virtue required the most work in the life of a man, he responded, "I maintain that there is no greater labor than to pray to God. Because as often as a man wants to pray, his enemies hurry to impede him, knowing that nothing confounds them more than prayer. Nevertheless, whenever a man chooses life, and he is able to maintain his decision, he will

possess rest. Of course the demons will struggle to impede prayer to the end of his life, and the work to resist them is difficult.

"For it is not a small battle to pray, with the demons resisting and prohibiting, or to come to prayer with men standing and opposing you on all sides. And so, exert yourselves, my little sons, in your prayers to drive off the contrary and malignant demons." [AP-G Agathon 9; AP-GS 12.2; AP-PJ 12.2]

Chapter Sixty-Two

PRAYER MUST BE SENT OUT EVERYWHERE ON ACCOUNT OF TRAPS, BOTH A SECOND AND A THIRD TIME

1. Abba Zeno, while he was living in Scetis, left his cell one night to walk in the desert. He became lost, walked three days and nights, and finally, exhausted, he fell and was near death.

Behold, a child stood before him, holding bread and a vase of water. The child said to him, "Rise and eat."

Zeno rose and prayed, for he was afraid that this was a ghost.

The child responded, "You do well to pray. Only rise and eat."

Abba Zeno did not agree to this, until he prayed a second and a third time. When that child again praised him, Zeno rose and ate.

After eating, the infant said to him, "You are as far from your cell as you have walked. Now rise and follow me." Immediately Zeno found himself before his cell.

The elder said to the child, "Come into my cell and make a prayer with us." But when the elder went inside the cell, the child did not appear. [AP-G Zeno 5; AP-GS 18.8; AP-PJ 18.7; AP-PR 210]

Chapter Sixty-Three

ON CONTINUAL PRAYER

1. A brother asked an elder to speak about what was needed to attain Christ.

The elder replied, "Work, humility, and prayer without ceasing are able to attain Christ. For all of the holy men, from the beginning until the end, were saved through these three practices. Rest, pleasure, and self-justification are impediments to the soul; nearly all people perish through them." [AP-GS 10.129]

2. A certain abbot, who had a monastery in Palestine, told the blessed Macarius, bishop of Cyprus, "Sustained by your prayers, we do not neglect the rule: we keep the third, sixth, and ninth hours of prayer."

Nevertheless, Macarius criticized him: "You have shown that you neglect and are not engaged in prayers at the other hours; the true monk always maintains, without ceasing, either a prayer or the chanting of a psalm in his heart." [AP-G Epiphanius 3; AP-GS 12.6; AP-PJ 12.6]

Chapter Sixty-Four

THAT CONTINUAL PRAYER FRUSTRATES THE PURPOSE OF THE DEVIL

1. In the time of Emperor Julian, when he had descended into Persia, Julian sent one of the unclean spirits into the West, so that it could bring a message from there. Now when that demon that Julian had sent came to a place where a certain monk named Publius lived, it stood immobilized there for ten days; it was unable to advance any further because that monk was praying without ceasing, day and night.

After returning to Julian without accomplishing its mission, the emperor asked it why it was so late.

The demon replied, "I was delayed, and returned without performing my task, for I remained ten days watching Publius the monk to see if perhaps he would stop praying so that I could pass, but he did not rest, and having been blocked, I returned, having accomplished nothing."

Then impious Julian became angry and said, "When I return, I will punish him."

A few days later, the emperor was killed. One of the men who had descended into Persia with him felt compunction and gave all that he owned to the poor. Then he went to that elder, was made a monk, and he made a worthy end to his life. [AP-GN 409; AP-GS 19.16, 12.12; AP-PJ 19.12]

2. **(a)** Abba Daniel, speaking about the blessed Arsenius, said that on the evening of the Sabbath, he would turn his back to the setting sun. Then, extending his hands to heaven, he would persist in prayer until the rising sun on the following morning had again filled his eyes.

(b) He also conducted vigils on the other nights, and when he wanted to rest a little on account of the fragility of human nature, he would say to sleep, "Come, evil servant." He would quickly sit, close his eyes a little, and then stand back up. [**a:** AP-G Arsenius 30; AP-GS 12.1; AP-PJ 12.1; AP-PR 211a; **b:** AP-G Arsenius 14; AP-GS 4.2; AP-PJ 4.2; AP-PR 211b]

Chapter Sixty-Five

THAT A PERSON MAY PRAY WHILE EATING

1. When the brothers, celebrating an *agape*, were eating in the church and talking among themselves, Abba Isaiah, a priest from the same place, Pelusium, angrily said to them, "Be quiet, brothers. For I know one brother who is eating with you and drinking many glasses with us, and nevertheless, his prayer is ascending into heaven, in the sight of God, like fire." [AP-G Isaiah 4; AP-GS 12.8; AP-PJ 12.7]

2. Another time, when the brothers were eating the *agape*, one laughed at the table. When Abba John saw this, he cried aloud, saying, "What do you believe that brother has in his heart who laughs when he should pray and weep while eating the *agape*?" [AP-G John the Dwarf 9; AP-GS 3.16; AP-PJ 3.6]

Chapter Sixty-Six

HOW ONE PRAYS WITHOUT CEASING

1. When some brothers had come to Abba Lucius, the elder asked them, "What is your customary manual labor?"

They said to him, "We do no work with our hands; rather, following what the apostle said, we *pray without ceasing* (1 Thess 5:17)."

The elder said to them, "Do you not eat?"

The monks admitted it.

Lucius said, "When you eat, who prays for you?" He questioned them again, asking, "Do you never sleep?"

When they admitted that they did sleep, he said to them, "When you sleep, who prays for you?"

Again they found no answer to give him.

Then he said to them, "Forgive me now, but you do not do what you say. Nevertheless, I will tell you how, by working with my hands, I am able to pray without ceasing: I sit down in the morning and I weave a few leaves of the palm tree and I make ropes from them. At the same time, I pray, saying, *Lord, have mercy upon me, according to your great mercy, and according to your great pity, destroy my iniquities* (Ps 51:1). Is that not prayer?"

When they nodded, he continued, "When I have worked through the day while praying, I earn sixteen coins, more or less. From these, I give two coins to the man begging at the door, and I will eat with the rest. In this way, when I eat or sleep, he will pray for me and thus I will perform my prayer without ceasing." [AP-G Lucius 1; AP-GS 12.10; AP-PJ 12.9; AP-PR 212]

Chapter Sixty-Seven

ONE MUST CONSTRAIN THE WANDERING EYES, LEST THEY DISTRACT THE SENSES FROM PRAYER

1. While Abba Silvanus lived on Mount Sinai, his disciple, Zacharias, who was serving him, said to him, "Abba, draw water and water the garden, because I must run an errand."

Silvanus covered his face while he drew water, and he was unable to see anything but his footprints. It happened that a certain brother saw him in the garden while he was far away. Later, when Silvanus had returned to his cell, this brother came to him and began to question him, saying, "Tell me, Abba, why did you cover your face while you watered the garden?"

The elder replied, "Son, it was so that my eyes would not see the trees, and my senses be distracted from the work that I was concentrating on." [AP-G Silvanus 4; AP-GS 11.68; AP-PJ 11.28]

Chapter Sixty-Eight

ON THE FAITHFULNESS OF THE PERFECT IN PRAYER

1. Once Abba Macarius was having a difficult time on the road from Scetis, carrying little baskets that he had woven. He sat down and said, "God, you know that I am unable to walk any further."

He quickly found himself beside the river, which had been a great distance away. [AP-G Macarius the Great 14; AP-GS 19.10; AP-PJ 19.6; AP-PR 213]

2. Once, when Abba Sisoes's disciple, Abraham, had been tempted by a spirit, he extended his hand toward heaven and said, "God, whether you will or do not will, I will not stop praying until you heal him." Immediately, the spirit departed and Abraham was healed. [AP-G Sisoes 12; AP-GS 19.18; AP-PJ 19.14]

3. Abba Ammon came to a lake in the desert and wanted to draw some water. He saw a basilisk, and throwing himself down on his face, he said, "Lord, either I am dead or that beast is."

Quickly, through the power of God, the basilisk was destroyed. [AP-G Ammonas 2; AP-PR 214]

4. Doulas, the disciple of Abba Bessarion told this story about him: "One day while we were walking together along the beach at the sea, I became very thirsty and said to the elder, 'My thirst is tormenting me.'

"He prayed and then ordered me to draw water from the sea and drink. When I did this, I discovered that it was the sweetest water, and I began to fill the small flask I carried with me.

"When Bessarion saw this, he said to me, 'Why are you filling your flask?'

"I replied, 'Forgive me, Abba, for I am afraid that I might become thirsty later.'

"The elder replied, 'Let the Lord forgive you, son, because God is everywhere, and he is able to supply sweet water for you.'" [AP-G Bessarion 1; AP-GS 19.1; AP-PJ 19.1; AP-PR 215]

Chapter Sixty-Nine

THAT THE PRAYER OF THE PERFECT IS PROFITABLE EVEN FOR THE DEAD

1. Abba Macarius, while he was walking in the desert, found the head of a man face down on the ground. When he turned it over with his staff, it seemed to emit a voice. The elder asked who the man had been. The head responded, "I was the leader of the priests of the idols, one of the people who lived in this place. You are Abba Macarius, a man filled with the Divine Spirit. For in whatever hour you feel pity for those who are being punished, and you pray for them, they receive a little comfort."

The elder asked, "Tell me, what is your comfort? What is your punishment? Answer!"

The head, groaning deeply, said, "The height of the fires are as great as the distance between heaven and earth. We are in the middle of the flames, bathed from head to foot on every side, and no one is allowed to see the face of anyone else, for our faces are joined to the back of the person ahead of us. When you pray for us, we can partly see another person, and this is a small comfort for us."

Having heard these words, Macarius shed tears, saying, "Woe to that day on which man transgressed the commands of God."

Then he questioned the head again, asking if there were other, greater punishments in the underworld.

The head replied, "There are greater punishments, for there are others much lower than us."

When Macarius asked who they were, the head answered, "We who did not know God are allowed a little mercy, but those who denied their knowledge of God are tormented in the more painful and inexpressibly awful punishments beneath us."

After hearing these words, the blessed Macarius buried the head deep in the ground and then departed. [AP-G Macarius the Great 38; AP-GS 3.19, 20.20; AP-PJ 20.16; AP-PR 172]

Chapter Seventy

ON REVELATIONS

1. A brother questioned an elder, saying, "Why do some say, 'We see visions of angels?'"

The elder replied, "Blessed is the man who looks at his own sins and sees them." [AP-GN 332; AP-GS 15.110; AP-PJ 15.87]

2. Some brothers came to the blessed Anthony, wanting to ask him if the phantasms they saw were made visible by the impulse of demons. They had brought a donkey, but the animal had died on the road.

When they reached the elder, he said to them, "How did your donkey die on the way?"

They questioned him about how he had known this.

He replied, "The demons showed me."

Then they said, "And we, for this reason, came to ask if the visions we see, and that nearly always happen, are announced by demons?"

The elder was able to satisfy them that those worthless visions were not declared by anything but the demons. [AP-G Anthony 12; AP-GS 10.2; AP-PJ 10.2a]

Chapter Seventy-One

ON DEMONIC ASSAULT

1. A brother asked an elder "Why, Abba, are we assaulted by demons?"

The elder responded, "Because we throw down our weapons: patience, humility, obedience, and penury." [AP-GS 15.76; AP-GN 302; AP-PJ 15.58; AP-Pa 25.1; AP-PR 173]

2. A brother questioned Abba Sisoes, saying, "Do you believe, Abba, that the devil pursues us in the same way he pursued the ancient fathers?"

Sisoes responded, "The men of our age are pursued more vigorously now, because he is upset by the approaching time of punishment. Nevertheless, he does not think it worthy to lay hold of the weak—those whom he can subvert quickly should he want to—but rather he is attacking the strong and great men." [AP-G Sisoes 11; AP-GS 15.63; AP-PJ 15.45; AP-Pa 25.2; AP-PR 174]

3. Abba Abraham asked Abba Poemen how the demons attack us.

The elder said, "Demons do not attack us because we do their will. In fact, our wills have become demons for us, and they trouble us. Now, do you want to know with whom the demons fight? They fight with Abba Moses and others like him; it is the desires of our own hearts that fight us." [AP-G Poemen 67; AP-GS 10.91; AP-PJ 10.62; AP-Pa 25.3]

4. A brother asked Abba Achilles how the demons are able to oppose us.

The elder replied, "Through our wills." Then he added, "The trees of Lebanon said, 'Although we are grand and tall, we are cut down by the smallest iron blade. We should surrender nothing to it from ourselves so that it will be unable to cut us down.' Then the men came, made axe handles from the wood of the trees, and cut them down.

"In this story, the trees are souls, the axe is the devil, and the handles are our wills. Because of our own evil wills, we are cut down." [AP-GS 10.131; AP-Pa 25.4]

Chapter Seventy-Two

ON THE WAR AGAINST THOUGHTS

1. The same man said, "We are not judged based on thoughts that enter us, but rather, because we take action on these thoughts. For it is evil to be shipwrecked on account of thoughts and good to be crowned because of them." [AP-GN 218; AP-GS 10.123; AP-PJ 10.86]

2. A brother said to one of the elders, "I see no battle in my heart."

The elder replied, "You are the portico that runs around the four sides of a square, and whoever wishes may enter and exit through you, although you do not perceive it. If you had a door and closed it, and did not permit evil thoughts to enter through it, then you would see them standing and battling outside it." [AP-GN 270; AP-GS 11.101; AP-PJ 11.43]

3. **(a)** A brother questioned an elder, saying, "What should I do? I have many thoughts and I do not know how to fight against them."

The elder replied, "Do not attempt to fight against all of them, but rather fight against one. For all thoughts have a single leader. It is essential to learn which is the leader. You must fight back against it and the others will be humbled.

(b) "For it often happens in battle that an army is led by a strong man, and the opposition chooses a stronger leader; if the two fight and one man is destroyed, the rest flee and are defeated. In the same way, thoughts have one leader, whether gluttony, avarice, a desire to wander from place to place, or some other idea. If from the beginning you do not recognize the leader and drive it away from you, they will misdirect you into other subsequent thoughts and they will cheat you. When the leader is attacked, it moves the other passions to deceive a man who is mistaking one thought for the others.

"If you want to defeat the passions, always look for the leader of the thoughts, and when you have discerned which it is, fight only against it." [**a:** AP-GN 219; AP-GS 10.125; AP-PJ 10.88]

4. Abba Poemen once questioned Abba Joseph, asking, "What should I do when passions approach me? Should I resist them or allow them to enter my heart?"

The elder replied, "Allow them to enter, and then fight with them."

After Poemen left and returned to his cell, another brother, coming from that same elder Joseph, told Poemen, "I went to Abba Joseph and questioned him about the passions of the heart, whether I should permit them to enter. He told me, 'Do not permit them to enter, but rather, attack them quickly.'"

When Abba Poemen heard that the elder had said something other than what he had told him, he rose, hurried to him, and said, "I trusted you, Abba Joseph, just like God; I told you all of my thoughts, but you gave different advice to another brother and me."

The elder responded, "Do you not know that I love you?" And when it was admitted, the elder continued, "I spoke to you as I would to myself. For once the passions have entered and we begin to fight with them, they make us more worthy. And so I said this to you. But there are others whom the passions must not approach; in their case, they must be repelled quickly." [AP-G Joseph of Panephysis 3; AP-GS 10.38; AP-PJ 10.29]

5. The fathers told a story about a certain elder, who, while he was sitting in his cell, would say, "Get away from me; but you, come, my friend."

When they asked the father whom he was speaking to, he replied, "I was driving off evil thoughts, and welcoming the good." [AP-GN 56]

6. Abba Joseph asked Abba Sisoes, "How long must a man cut the passions out of his heart?"

The elder answered, "You want to know the amount of time?"

When Joseph assented, Sisoes said, "In whatever hour the passions are able to enter your heart, in that same hour, if you are able, you must cut them out." [AP-G Sisoes 22; AP-Pa 39.1; AP-M 26]

7. When some other fathers questioned Abba Silvanus, asking about the lifestyle that had produced his great prudence, he replied, "I never hesitated to drive a thought from my heart that would provoke God to anger." [AP-G Silvanus 6; AP-GS 11.70; AP-PJ 11.30; AP-PR 175]

8. One of the elders, living in a cave in the Thebaid, had a tested disciple. It was the elder's custom to warn his disciple, and after the admonition, to offer a prayer and send him away to sleep. One day some religious laymen came to the elder. The elder instructed them with his sermons and then sent them away. When he sat down again that evening and was warning the brother (as was his custom), he suddenly fell asleep while speaking.

Now the disciple remained until the elder awoke and made, according to custom, his prayer. While he sat for several hours with the sleeping elder, his thoughts urged him to go and rest before he was dismissed. He resisted these thoughts and remained. When the thought came again, he still refused to leave. Seven times the thought pursued him. Nevertheless, he always remained.

After that, when night neared its end, the elder woke and found his disciple sitting near him. He said to him, "Have you not left?"

The disciple replied, "No, because you did not dismiss me."

The elder said, "Why did you not wake me?"

The disciple said, "I did not dare lest I create any trouble for you."

They rose, and offered the office of matins, following their custom, and the elder dismissed him. Now while the elder sat, he fell into an ecstatic vision and saw someone showing him a glorious place, a seat in that place, and on that seat, seven crowns. He asked who owned the crowns. The one showing him the vision answered, "Your disciple. God gave him the place and the seat when he left the world, as well as the seven crowns that he won that night."

When the amazed elder heard this, he was afraid. He called his disciple and asked what he had done that night.

The disciple said, "Forgive me, Abba, but I did nothing."

The elder, thinking that he did not confess out of humility, said, "I will not forgive you unless you tell me what you did or what you thought about this night."

The disciple, unaware of what he had done, did not know what to say. Finally, he said, "I did nothing, Abba, except seven times I was attacked by a thought that encouraged me to leave, but I did not go before you dismissed me."

Then the elder perceived that he had been crowned for each time he had repelled the thought, but he did not tell him this. Nevertheless, he said to the others, "God bestows crowns even for the smallest thoughts." Then, referring to the deed of his disciple, he said, "It is good if someone pushes himself. For it is written, *The violent seize the kingdom of heaven* (Matt 11:12)." [AP-GN 211; AP-GS 7.52; AP-PJ 7.43]

Chapter Seventy-Three

ON DISCLOSING THOUGHTS WITH EVERY WORK

1. **(a)** The blessed Anthony said, "If it is possible, a monk should declare to his elders how many steps he walks, and how many glasses of water he drinks in his cell, so that he would know that he is not going astray in these practices."

(b) He also said, "I saw monks who fell after a great struggle that came though the elation of their heart. For they were placing their hope in their own work rather than in pleasing God, and they exceeded the command of him who said, *Ask your father and he will* *speak to you; your elders will also declare it to you* (Deut 32:7)." [**a:** AP-G Anthony 38; AP-GS 11.2a; AP-PR 176; **b:** AP-G Anthony 37; AP-GS 11.1]

2. It was often told how a certain brother had discovered a place that was quiet and deserted in the wilderness. When he asked his abba to send him there, he said, "I have confidence that, with the support of God and your prayers, I will be able to work in that place."

The elder did not want him to relax and said, "Truthfully, my son, I know that you would work hard there, but because there are no elders in the area to whom you could show your work and ask if it was pleasing to God, and because you believe that you would be able to perform the work of a monk on your own, you would lose both your work and your mind." [AP-GN 370]

3. Abba Poemen said, "The enemy rejoices in no man more than the one who does not want to reveal his thoughts." [AP-G Poemen 101b; AP-PR 177]

4. A brother was assaulted by a thought, and rising in the night, he went out to one of the elders and told him about his thought.

The elder admonished him and sent him away. He returned to his cell, but again the thought began to attack him, and again he went to the elder. After being admonished, he again returned to his cell.

He was attacked again, and returned again to the elder. The tenth time he made this trip to the elder, the elder said to him, "Always come, brother, and tell me what is happening, because there is nothing the attacking demon fears more than to reveal his work, and nothing pleases him more than when his thoughts are kept hidden." [AP-GN 164; AP-GS 5.16a; AP-PJ 5.13a]

5. Abba Poemen, when he was a young man, had gone to a certain elder who lived at a distance to ask him about three of his thoughts. When he reached the elder, he had forgotten one of his thoughts, so he quickly returned to his own cell. After he had taken out the key to open his cell door, he recalled the thought he wanted to ask about, and setting aside the key, he returned to the elder.

The elder asked him, "Why did you return so quickly, brother?"

Poemen replied, "Because after I put the key in my door, I remembered the thought I wanted to ask you about, so I did not open my cell door but returned to you."

Now the distance between their cells was very great. [AP-G Poemen 1; AP-GS 11.55; AP-PJ 11.19]

6. A brother asked an elder, "Which thoughts should I have in my soul?"

The elder replied, "Everything a man thinks, between heaven and earth, is in vain. Only he who dwells in the constant memory of Christ is in truth." [AP-GN 501; AP-GS 12.24b]

7. A brother said to one of the elders, "Look, Abba, I often ask the elders to speak an admonition that will be good for the health of my soul, but I retain nothing of whatever they say. So why should I question them when I do nothing? I am completely unclean."

Now there were two empty vases, and the elder said to the brother, "Go, take one of these vases, bring some water in it, wash it, then pour out the water, and return it to its place."

The brother did this, once, and then again. The elder said to him, "Pick up both vases at the same time." And when he had picked up both vases, the elder asked, "Which is the cleaner of the two?"

The brother responded, "The one I emptied and washed."

Then the elder said, "It is the same with the soul: although it retains nothing from the questions it asks, nevertheless, it is a little cleaner than he who does not ask." [AP-GN 223; AP-GS 10.136; AP-PJ 10.92; AP-PR 178]

8. An elder was living in Scetis who worked hard in the flesh, but he was not so diligent about his thoughts. Therefore he came to Abba John to ask him about his forgetfulness. After hearing a word from him, he forgot what had been said after he had left. He went back to John and asked him again, and in the same way, forgot again. He did this often, and always forgetting what he had heard.

Once, after he had forgotten what Abba John had said to him, he said, "Abba, I forgot what you said, but so that I am not a nuisance to you, I will not come anymore."

John replied, "Go, and light a lamp." After he had lit it, he spoke again, "Take the other lamps and light them from the first."

When he had done that, John said, "Did that first lamp lose any light when you lit the others?" When the elder said no, John said, "John is the same; even if every man in Scetis should come to question me, they would not impede me for the sake of Christ. And so, come as often as you wish, without concern."

Thus, through their patience, God took the forgetfulness away from that elder. [AP-G John the Dwarf 18; AP-GS 11.41; AP-PJ 11.15]

Chapter Seventy-Four

ON DISCRETION

1. One of the elders said, "When a man covers the eyes of an animal, it will walk around the mill. If, however, its eyes are uncovered, it is not easily turned. It is the same with the devil. If he can cover the eyes of a man who lacks discretion, he humiliates him in every sin. If the man's eyes are opened through discretion, he is quickly able to escape the devil." [AP-GN 276; AP-GS 11.108; AP-PJ 11.49]

2. Abba Poemen said, "There is a man who carries an axe all the time, but he is unable to cut down a tree. There is another man who knows how to cut, and with a few blows, he is able to bring down the tree. Discretion is an axe, and if anyone possesses it, he is able to avoid the snares of the enemy." [AP-G Poemen 52; AP-GS 10.88; AP-PJ 10.59]

Chapter Seventy-Five

THAT CERTAIN THINGS DO NOT HARM THOSE WHO HAVE DISCRETION

1. (a) Abba Isaac came to Abba Poemen and saw him pouring water over his feet. Although he had faith, he said to him, "Why have some treated their bodies so harshly?"

Poemen replied, "We do not discipline our bodies, but rather we do it to extinguish the passions."

(b) While he said this, Abba Isaac heard a rooster crow and said, "Are there roosters here, Abba?"

The elder responded, "Why do you compel me to speak? You and those like you have heard them. Nevertheless, he who is wise, hears and thinks nothing about them." [a: AP-G Poemen 184; PLaus 20.4c; b: AP-G Poemen 107]

Chapter Seventy-Six

ON MORTIFICATION

1. A brother questioned Abba Moses, saying, "How can a man mortify himself?"
Moses said to him, "Unless he should decide to live as if he were already three years in the tomb, he will not be able to attain this teaching." [AP-G Moses 12; AP-GS 10.92; AP-PJ 10.63; AP-Pa 26.1]

2. The same man said, "A monk can almost be dead to this world who dreads two things: the relaxation of his body and vainglory." [AP-G Poemen 66; AP-GS 1.24; AP-PJ 1.15; AP-Pa 26.2]

3. An elder said, "The monk will be free from all things when he is strongly focused on a good work. For when he practices a good work, the devil comes, does not find a place in him, and departs. If, however, he does an evil work, the Spirit of God comes often and seeing his evil work, he does not approach, but withdraws. Nevertheless, if he is asked, he will quickly return." [AP-Pa 26.3; AP-PR 179]

4. An elder said, "Dread your belly, the necessities of this secular world, and the longing for evil; steer clear of this world, and you will have rest." [AP-Pa 26.4]

5. The same man said, "A monk must provide rest for himself; that is, he must condemn the world even if he should sustain the loss of his body. For if he still finds fault with others, he will never be able to possess the rest of mortification."

Chapter Seventy-Seven

ON PERSEVERANCE

1. Abba Anthony said, "If a monk worked a few days, and then he relaxed, worked again and then he was negligent, he would achieve

nothing by this, nor will he possess patient perseverance." [AP-GN 444; AP-Pa 27.1]

2. Abba Motoes said, "God desires a light but constant work in a monk, rather than a work that is great in the beginning but is quickly abandoned." [AP-G Matoes 1; AP-GS 7.16; AP-PJ 7.11]

3. One of the brothers asked an elder, "Father, how can we avoid being scandalized or defecting from our belief when we see others returning to the world?"

He replied, "We must consider the hunting dogs; one, seeing a rabbit, gives chase. There are those who are slower, and seeing only the lead dog, want to join him. Some tire and turn back. But the dog who sees the rabbit is not impeded by those who go back; he is not hindered by rocks or brush. He jumps over thorns and although he is often slashed by them, he does not stop.

"It is the same for the person who follows Christ; he endures his cross without stopping; he leaps over every scandal that comes, until he reaches the one who was crucified on our behalf." [AP-GN 203; AP-GS 7.42; AP-PJ 7.35]

Chapter Seventy-Eight

ON THE WORK OF THE SAINTS

1. An elder said, "Until a man possesses Christ, he should work. Once he reaches this point, he will no longer need to work. Nevertheless, he is permitted to work, so that, remembering the tribulation of work, he might guard himself on every side, fearing that he might lose all his labors. For this reason, God led the sons of Israel through the desert for forty years, so that they might remember the suffering of the way, and not want to return again." [AP-Pa 28.1; AP-PR 180]

2. A brother asked one of the elders, "Why is it necessary for the fathers to work?"

The elder replied, "Those who are still working, those asking for a remission of their sins before grace comes over them and takes away their labor, are made pale in their work. But others bloom, those over whom the grace of Christ has come, because of their earlier patience. For the face of their exulting soul is clear. When the sun has no clouds, it shines; when it is covered with clouds, it is pale. This is also true for the soul, when it is obscured by passions and temptations. Nevertheless, the soul is cleaned by God's grace, so that it shines, as it has been written: *Great is his glory in your help* (Ps 21:5)." [AP-Pa 28.2; PLaus 20.6]

3. The same man said, "Although the holy men work like this, they possess another type of rest, because they are free from the thoughts of this world." [AP-GN 235; AP-GS 10.161; AP-Pa 28.3]

Chapter Seventy-Nine

WHY THOSE WORKING SO HARD NOW DO NOT RECEIVE GRACE LIKE MEN DID IN THE PAST

1. A brother questioned an elder, saying, "Why do the people now working in the religious life no longer receive grace like the ancient monks?"

The elder said, "Then there was charity, and each man was drawing his neighbor upward. Now, charity has grown cold, and each man pulls his neighbor down. Therefore, monks no longer receive God's grace." [AP-GN 349; AP-GS 17.23; AP-PJ 17.19; AP-Pa 28.4; AP-PR 181]

Chapter Eighty

WHETHER THE HOLY MEN KNOW WHEN THE GRACE OF GOD COMES UPON THEM

1. A brother questioned an elder, saying, "Do you believe, Abba, that the holy men knew when grace came over them?"

The elder replied, "Not always. For there was a certain disciple of a great elder, and when he had sinned in some way, the angry elder shouted at him, 'Go, and die!'

"At once the disciple fell to the ground and died.

"When the elder saw that, he prayed with fear and great humility, begging God and saying, 'Lord Jesus Christ, revive him, and no longer let me speak such words without consideration.'

"The brother immediately got up." [AP-PR 182]

2. Amma Sarah, when she was walking along a road, had to cross a small river. A certain secular man, seeing her, laughed. But she, knowing that the grace of God would come upon her, said, "Be quiet, or you will be broken."

Turning, she saw his intestines pouring out. In fear she prayed, saying, "My Jesus, restore him, and from now on, I shall not speak such words."

Chapter Eighty-One

ON EXHORTATION AND DOCTRINE

1. Some brothers asked Abba Poemen about hardness of the heart, and the elder replied, "Water, by nature, is soft, and stone is hard. Nevertheless, if the water often drips on the stone, the dripping will perforate it. The word of the Lord is the same, because our heart is hard. A man who often hears the word of the Lord offers a place for the fear of the Lord, so that he might enter him." [AP-Pa 29.1]

2. One of the elders said, "A man who is living according to God, either must be taught with faith what he does not know, or he must show what he does know openly. For if he does neither when he is able, he is insane." [AP-GN 694; AP-GS 10.96; AP-PJ 10.67]

3. One of the fathers said, "It is dangerous if a man who does not live a practical life begins to teach someone else. It is as if he owned a ruined house where he received visitors, and it collapsed and killed them. In the same way, those who have not yet established themselves ruin those who come to them." [AP-G Syncletica 12; AP-GS 10.104]

4. Abba Poemen said, "The man who teaches, but does not practice what he teaches, is similar to a tall fountain that washes the goods

and satiates the thirst of all. Nevertheless, it is unable to care for itself, and has dirt and filth within it." [AP-G Poemen 25; AP-GS 10.72; AP-PJ 10.49b; AP-PR 183a]

5. The same man said, "Teach your soul to practice those things that your tongue teaches others." [AP-GS 8.18; AP-PJ 8.14; AP-PR 183b]

Chapter Eighty-Two

THAT TEACHING CAN BE CONFERRED THROUGH EXAMPLE ALONE, WITHOUT WORDS

1. Abba Isaac, when he was a young man, lived with Abba Cronius, and that man never told him to do anything. He was a frail old man, but he always rose to fetch water for washing or to give a drink to himself or others.

Now this Abba Isaac was also a disciple to Abba Theodore, and Theodore never commanded him to do anything, but when he set out the dinner, he would say, "Brother, if you wish to eat, come and eat."

Isaac would say to him, "Abba, I came to you so that you would help me; why don't you tell me what to do?"

The elder always remained silent.

For this reason, Abba Isaac left and returned to the other fathers. They came and said to Abba Theodore, "That brother came to be taught something from your sanctity. Why didn't you tell him to do something?"

The elder replied to them, "I was never a leader of the monastery; why should I command another man? Meanwhile, I say nothing to him; if he wants, what he sees me do, he should do himself."

From that time Abba Isaac anticipated, and was doing whatever the elder did. Nevertheless, the elder always did everything in silence. Abba Isaac also learned from this so that whatever he did, he did silently. [AP-G Isaac, Priest of Cells, 2]

Chapter Eighty-Three

KNOWLEDGE GAINED THROUGH THE EXPERIENCE OF WORK IS STRONGER THAN WHAT IS GAINED BY READING

1. When Abba Arsenius had questioned an elder about some of his thoughts, another brother said to him, "How can you, a man so erudite in both Greek and Latin literature, not despise asking for advice from this rustic monk?"

Arsenius replied, "I remember having read many Greek and Latin texts, but I have not progressed enough to even master the alphabet of this elder." [AP-G Arsenius 6; AP-GS 15.7; AP-CSP 6.3a; AP-PJ 15.7]

2. Abba Evagrius asked Abba Arsenius, "Why do we gain no benefit from so much reading, when these rustics are able to attain such natural virtue and knowledge?"

The blessed Arsenius replied, "We acquire nothing from secular knowledge, but they have learned virtue and knowledge from their own labors." [AP-G Arsenius 5; AP-GS 10.7; AP-PJ 10.5]

Chapter Eighty-Four

ON THE DIVINE SCRIPTURES

1. The same Abba Arsenius never proposed any question about the Scriptures to the spiritual men; he never wanted to solve any question, although he was certainly able to; nor did he quickly write letters to another man. [AP-G Arsenius 42a; AP-GS 15.11a; AP-PJ 15.10a]

2. A brother asked an elder, "If it happens that I must speak occasionally, what do you order me to speak about—the Scriptures or the teachings of the fathers?"

The elder answered, "If you are unable to keep silent, speak about the teachings of the fathers, for it is dangerous to speak about the Scriptures." [AP-G Amoun of Nitria 2c; AP-GS 11.56c; AP-PJ 11.20c]

3. A philosopher said to the blessed Anthony, "How do you tolerate, Father, being deprived of the consolation that comes from the volumes of Scripture?"

Antony replied, "My book is the nature of created things, and it is present whenever I want to read the words of God." [AP-PJ 21.16; Evag. *Prak.* 92]

Chapter Eighty-Five

ON SAYING NOTHING TO THOSE WHO ARE CURIOUS ABOUT SCRIPTURAL QUESTIONS

1. When a certain anchorite visited Abba Poemen, the elder received him with joy. After they had embraced each other, they sat down and the anchorite began to speak of the Scriptures and heavenly matters. Then the elder turned his face in the other direction and offered no response to him. The anchorite, seeing that the elder would not speak with him, went away sadly, and said to Poemen's disciple, "It is pointless; I have undertaken the labor of such a great journey and come to this elder who cannot bear to speak with me."

The disciple went in to Abba Poemen and said, "This great man came here because of you. He is a man who possesses great glory in his own land, and you don't wish to speak with him?"

Poemen replied, "That man is among the higher beings, and he speaks of heavenly matters. I am from the lower beings, and I speak of terrestrial matters. If he had said anything to me about the struggles of the soul, perhaps I would have replied to him. On the other hand, if he speaks about heavenly matters, I confess that I know nothing about them."

Poemen's disciple went out and said to the anchorite, "Our elder does not want to speak about higher questions, but he will respond if anyone should speak to him about earthly struggles."

The anchorite, convicted by this word, went in to the elder and said, "What should I do, Abba? The struggles of my heart are mastering me."

Then Poemen looked back at him gladly and said, "You have come in the right manner. I will open my mouth and fill it with good things for you."

The anchorite was helped by that word, and said, "This is the true path." Then, after thanking the elder, he returned to his own region. [AP-G Poemen 8; AP-GS 10.54; AP-PJ 10.39; AP-PR 184]

2. A brother came to Abba Theodore. He remained there three days, received no response from Theodore, and left, saddened.

Theodore's disciple said, "Abba, why didn't you say something to that man? See, he went away saddened."

The elder replied, "Truthfully, I said nothing to him because he is a dealer who wants to be glorified by the words of others. [AP-G Theodore of Pherme 3; AP-GS 8.9; AP-PJ 8.6]

Chapter Eighty-Six

ON AVOIDING CURIOSITY

1. An elder said, "It is not right for a monk to ask what sort of a person a man is, or how he is. Through this type of questioning, he will be drawn from his prayers and deflected into slander and long-windedness. Therefore, there is nothing better than to remain silent." [AP-GS 10.128; AP-Pa 30.1; PLaus 20.11]

2. A brother asked an elder, "If another brother should come, bringing news from the outside world to me, what do you order that I should say to this man so that he does not afflict me with this information?"

The elder replied, "Say nothing that we are unable to observe ourselves. Let this be a warning, lest perhaps, speaking to our neighbor, we might say, 'Do not do this,' but later we do the same thing or something worse."

The brother said, "Then what should I do?"

The elder replied, "If we are able to remain silent, that will suffice as an example to our neighbor." [AP-GN 303; AP-GS 15.77; AP-PJ 15.59; AP-Pa 30.2]

Chapter Eighty-Seven

ON AVOIDING DISPUTES

1. **(a)** An elder said, "If anyone should speak with you about either the Scriptures or any other subject, do not argue with him. If he says something good, agree with him. If, however, he speaks evil, say to him, 'You know what you are saying.' Keep this rule and you will possess humility and avoid hatred.

(b) "If you persist in arguing, and you are able to defend your position, it will give offense. Often while you praise another, contention is produced from justification. And so, about any issue whatsoever, unless you stay clear of arguments, you will be unable to possess peace." [**a:** AP-G Matoes 11b; AP-GN 330b; AP-GS 1.34b; AP-PJ 1.23b; AP-Pa 31.1a; AP-PR 185a; **b:** AP-Pa 31.1b; AP-PR 185b]

2. A brother asked Abba Pambo if it was good to praise a neighbor. Pambo replied, "It is better to remain silent." [AP-G Poemen 47; AP-GS 4.37]

Chapter Eighty-Eight

ON SILENCE

1. Abba Agathon, aspiring to silence, placed a stone in his mouth for three years. [AP-G Agathon 15; AP-GS 4.7; AP-PJ 4.7]

2. **(a)** A brother asked an elder, "How long must one dwell in silence?"

The elder replied, "Until you are questioned. For is it written, *Do not speak before you listen* (cf. Jas 1:19). For he who speaks a good word, should not speak it, unless he had first considered whether the word would help him. **(b)** In every place, if you are able to maintain silence, you will possess rest." [**a:** AP-Pa 32.3; AP-PR 186; **b:** AP-G Poemen 84]

3. A brother asked Abba Evagrius for a teaching by which he would be able to be saved.

Evagrius replied, "If you want to be saved, in whatever place you settle, do not speak before another person asks you. Rather, study silence; let nothing worry you; attend to your meditation in the fear of God, rising in the morning and in the evening, and you will fear no attack of the impious."

4. The same Abba Evagrius spoke at a council that had gathered. Then the priest said to him, "We know, Abba Evagrius, that if you were in your own land, you would be a bishop and the leader of many. Nevertheless, now in this place you are a stranger."

At this word, Evagrius felt compunction, yet was not saddened. He bowed his head and looking down at the ground, wrote with a finger, "This is true, *nevertheless I spoke once only* (cf. Job 40:5); Evagrius will not attach this fault to himself again." [AP-G Evagrius 7; AP-GS 16.3; AP-PJ 16.2]

5. Blessed Arsenius frequently repeated this saying: "I have often repented of speaking, but never of remaining silent." [AP-G Arsenius 40b]

6. Blessed Anthony customarily said to his disciple, "If you should strive for silence, do not think that you are demonstrating your virtue, but do it to confess yourself unworthy to speak." [AP-GN 321; AP-GS 15.99; AP-PJ 15.79; AP-Pa 32.1]

7. When a brother said to Abba Sisoes, "I wish to save my soul," Sisoes responded, "How are we are able to save our soul, when our tongue often springs out of our open mouth?" [AP-G Tithoes 3; AP-GS 11.67; AP-PJ 11.27; AP-Pa 32.2]

8. Some brothers, wanting to travel to the blessed Anthony in Scetis, boarded a ship with some people. An unknown elder, who also wanted to make his way to the same father, joined the boat. The brothers, sitting in the boat, spoke among themselves about various topics, both the Scriptures and the teachings of the fathers.

The elder remained silent.

After they reached the blessed Anthony, Anthony said to them, "Brothers, you found this elder; he is a good companion."

Then turning to him, Anthony said, "You also, Father, when you came with them, found these men to be good company."

The elder replied to him, "They are indeed good, but their courtyard does not have a door: anyone may enter the stable, untie their donkey, and lead it wherever they wish."

He said this because these brothers spoke whatever came to their lips. [AP-G Anthony 18; AP-GS 4.1; AP-PJ 4.1]

9. Abba Poemen said, "There is a man who feigns silence, but his heart condemns many; he is like one who speaks much. There is another who speaks from morning to night, and yet, because he does not speak without divine assistance, he pursues the great silence." [AP-G Poemen 27; AP-GS 10.75; AP-PJ 10.51]

Chapter Eighty-Nine

ON PILGRIMAGE

1. An elder said, "A pilgrimage that is made for God's sake is good, if you also maintain silence. For boldness is not a pilgrimage." [AP-Pa 32.5]

2. Abba Arsenius often said, "A foreign monk in an alien land must not become the mediator in any dispute, and then he will be able to attain rest." [AP-G Arsenius 12; AP-GS 10.8; AP-PJ 10.6; AP-Pa 32.6]

3. An elder said, "Just as the bee makes honey wherever it goes, so too the monk, wherever he proceeds, if he goes on account of God's work, is able to produce the sweetness of good deeds." [AP-GN 399; AP-GS 11.86; AP-Pa 32.7; AP-PR 187]

4. The fathers said about Abba Megethios the elder, that one time he left his cell and a thought came to him that he should leave that place. He did not return to the cell because he owned nothing from this world except, perhaps, the single needle he used to split palm leaves. Every day he would make three small cords to provide for his food. [AP-G Megethios 1]

Chapter Ninety

ON FLEEING THE HONOR OF THE PRIESTHOOD

1. Abba Theodore, when he was ordained a deacon in Scetis, did not agree to remain, but he fled to many places. The elders brought him back, saying, "Do not abandon your place."

He replied, "Permit me to pray to the Lord to see if he commands me to minister in my post." He prayed, "Lord, show me if it is your will that I continue in my ordination."

That man saw a column of fire, stretching from earth to heaven, and a voice came to him, "Theodore, if you are able to be like this column, then go and minister."

After hearing this, Theodore did not agree to serve. When he entered the church, the elders suggested that if he would not minister, he could at least hold the chalice. He refused, saying, "If you say anything more about this matter to me, I will leave this place." Thus they left him alone. [AP-G Theodore of Pherme 25; AP-GS 15.33; AP-PJ 15.21; AP-Pa 33.1]

2. Abba Isaac, when he heard that the fathers wanted to make him a priest at Scetis, fled into Egypt, and entering a field, he hid in the grass. Now it happened that the fathers who were pursuing him stopped to rest in that same field, for it was night. They released their donkey so that it could graze. The animal, while feeding, went to where Abba Isaac was hiding.

When morning arrived, the men searching for the donkey came and found the elder. They were amazed. When they wanted to bind Isaac, he said to them, "I will flee no more because I know this is a command from God. No matter where I flee, I will always arrive at this." [AP-G Isaac the Priest of Cells 1; AP-Pa 33.2; AP-PR 22]

3. Abba Motoes came once from the place that is called Raithou, in the lands of Gebalon. Now, his disciple was also with him. Seeing him, the bishop of that place seized him and made him a priest against his will. Later, while they were eating together, the bishop said to him, "Forgive me, Abba, for I know that you did not want this honor, but I, hoping for a blessing from you, presumed to do it."

The elder humbly replied, "My mind wanted it little, but I do not want this duty because I will be separated from the brother who is with me, and alone I will not be able to carry out my prayers."

The bishop said to him, "If you consider him worthy, I will ordain him as well."

Motoes responded, "I do not know whether he is worthy. Nevertheless, I know one thing: he is better than me."

Then the bishop ordained the disciple. Both men remained together until their end, but they never approached the altar to offer the sacrifice. The elder would offer this reason: "I trust in my God that I will not be judged more stringently because of this ordination, for I did not presume to offer the sacrifice. Ordination is for those who are without fault; I, on the other hand, know myself too well." [AP-G Matoes 9; AP-GS 15.42; AP-PJ 15.27; AP-Pa 33.3; AP-PR 188]

Chapter Ninety-One

ON THE FOOLISHNESS OF THE PERFECT

1. When certain people spoke about current affairs to Bishop Ammonas, he paid no attention to their words. Because of this, a woman said to her neighbor, "This elder is a fool."

Ammonas, hearing these words, said, "Woman, how much work have I carried out in solitude so that I might pursue foolishness? Why do you want me to lose it today for your sake?" [AP-G Ammonas 9; AP-GS 15.13; AP-PJ 15.12]

Chapter Ninety-Two

ON THE QUIET LIFE

1. Abba Poemen said, "A man who acts according to any carnal impulse is like a man who is standing beside the deepest lake. For whenever the enemy chooses, he can easily drive him into the lake. On the other hand, the man who is separated from carnal desires is like a man standing far away from the lake; when the enemy wants

to drag him into the lake, he cannot, for it is too far away. Moreover, while he is pulling, God sends his assistance and frees him. Therefore, it is good to flee from carnal conversation." [AP-G Poemen 59; AP-GS 2.25; AP-PJ 2.12b]

2. Abba Motoes said, "If anyone wants to have rest, he must live in the desert. If he does not want to live in the desert, he must live among many brothers. For whoever visits will be received by the others, and he will still have rest. If you are in that place I have named and you do not receive a visitor, your thoughts will make you sad. Nevertheless, among many men, your desire for solitude will be hidden, and it will have rest."

3. Once, a judge from the region in which Abba Poemen lived arrested a man. Men came, seeking the elder, so that he might go to the judge and free the arrested man.

Poemen said, "Grant me three days, and then I will go."

Abba Poemen prayed during these three days, saying, "Lord, do not give me the grace that will permit that man to be released through my intervention, for they will not permit me to remain here in peace."

After three days, he went to the judge to make his demand.

The judge said to him, "Have you come to intercede with me for the sake of a robber, Abba?"

Poemen returned to his cell, rejoicing because his request had not been granted. [AP-G Poemen 9; AP-CSP 4.6; AP-PJ 21.32]

Chapter Ninety-Three

ON THE DESERT, AND WHY MEN FLEE TO THE DESERT OR INTO SOLITUDE

1. The blessed Anthony often said, "The person who flees into the desert is free from three battles: seeing, hearing, and slander; the work of his heart is focused on one thing alone." [AP-G Anthony 11; AP-GS 2.2; AP-PJ 2.2]

2. Abba Aio asked the blessed Macarius to speak a word to him by which he would be able to be saved.

Macarius said to him, "Flee men."

Aio asked, "What does it mean to 'flee men?'"

The elder replied, "To 'flee men' is to sit in your cell, and lament continually over your sins. And, because it is above all the other virtues, it is to restrain your tongue and your stomach." [AP-G Macarius the Great 27; AP-PR 189]

3. **(a)** Abba Arsenius, while he was still a layman living in the palace, prayed to the Lord, saying, "Lord, show me the way by which I might be saved."

He heard a voice say to him, "Arsenius, flee men and you will be saved."

(b) Later, when he had withdrawn into solitude, he prayed the same prayer. Again he heard a voice speaking to him, "Arsenius, flee, remain silent, and rest. These are the beginnings of salvation." [**a:** AP-G Arsenius 1; AP-GS 2.3; AP-PJ 2.3a; AP-PR 190a; **b:** AP-G Arsenius 2; AP-GS 2.4; AP-PJ 2.3b; AP-PR 190b]

4. Once Abba Mark asked the same Abba Arsenius why he fled from men.

He replied, "God knows that I love men, but I am unable to be with both God and men. For the heavenly multitudes and powers possess a single will, but men possess many, varying wills. For this reason, I am unable to relinquish God to be with men." [AP-G Arsenius 13; AP-GS 2.5/17.6; AP-PJ 17.5; AP-Pa 34.1]

5. Some brothers, when they were going to procure flax from the Thebaid, said, "We might have a chance to see the blessed Arsenius."

After they arrived and his disciple, Daniel, announced them to Arsenius, he instructed Daniel to inquire about the reason they had come there from Alexandria. When they replied that they had come to procure flax, Arsenius responded, "That is why they will not see my face; they did not come here on my account, but because of their work. So go, greet them, offer your service, and then send them away, saying, 'The elder is unable to see you.'" [AP-G Arsenius 26; AP-PR 192; AP-Pa 34.2]

6. A monk had come to Abba Arsenius because he wanted to see him. He knocked on his door. Hoping that it was his disciple, Abba Arsenius opened the door. When he saw that it was someone else, Arsenius quickly threw himself, face down, on the ground.

When the visitor insisted that Arsenius get up, Arsenius said, "I will not get up from here until you go away." For many hours the brother begged him to get up, but he would not agree to rise until after the brother departed. [AP-G Arsenius 37; AP-PR 193a]

7. Whenever this same blessed Arsenius attended church with the other brothers, he always sat behind a column, to keep himself from seeing the face of others, as well as to prevent others from seeing his face. [AP-G Arsenius 42b; AP-GS 15.11b; AP-PR 193b]

8. Bishop Theophilus and a judge came from the city of Alexandria to the same blessed Arsenius. The bishop asked to hear a word from him. After remaining silent for a short time, Arsenius said, "Will you do what I tell you?"

When both men assented gratefully, Arsenius continued, "If you hear that Arsenius is in some place, do not go there." [AP-G Arsenius 7; AP-GS 2.6; AP-PJ 2.4a; AP-PR 191a]

9. Again, when the archbishop wanted to honor Arsenius, he sent a message to announce that he was coming. Arsenius sent a message back to him, "If you come, I will open my door to you, but if I open to you, then I must open to everybody. If I open my door to everybody, then Arsenius will not be able to remain here."

When the bishop heard this, he stayed away so that he would not compel the monk to leave that place. [AP-G Arsenius 8; AP-GS 2.7; AP-PJ 2.4b; AP-PR 191b]

10. Abba Bessarion, while he was walking through the desert with his disciple, came to a cave. Entering, they found a brother sitting there, making a rope. The elder did not look at them, greet them, or say anything to them. Consequently, Abba Bessarion said to his disciple, "Let us go, for this elder does not wish to speak with us." Then they went on their way to see Abba John.

Now when they were returning and they came to the same cave, Abba Bessarion said, "Let us go in again to that brother to see if by chance God has persuaded him to speak with us."

When they entered, they found him dead.

Bessarion said to his disciple, "Come brother, let us bury him, because God brought us here for his sake." Now when they buried him they discovered that he was a woman. They marveled and said, "Now women are wrestling with and overcoming demons!"

Then, glorifying God, who is the protector of all, they returned to their own land. [AP-G Bessarion 4; AP-GS 20.1; AP-PJ 20.1; AP-Pa 34.3; AP-PR 194]

11. The blessed Macarius once told a story, saying, "Two young men came to me. One of them was an adult, but the other had just begun to grow a beard. They, not knowing who I was, asked me, 'Where is the cell of Abba Macarius?'

"When I asked why they wanted me, they replied, 'Learning of his great works and way of life, we have hurried to see him with the greatest desire.'

"When I admitted that I was the man they sought, they immediately threw themselves at my feet and asked me to allow them to live with me. Seeing that they were delicate, like those who are wealthy, I responded that it was not possible for them to remain with me.

"Then they said, 'If we cannot live here with you, we will go somewhere else, as we have made up our minds to do it.'

"Having heard their words, I began to think to myself, 'If I drive them away from here, they will feel scandalized. The work itself will encourage them to flee of their own accord; why should they grumble about my will?' Then I said to them, 'Come, you must make a cell for yourselves, if you are able.'

"They asked only to be shown a place for themselves. I gave them a bowl with an axe, a sack of flour, and some salt. I showed them the hardest stone that they might cut to build a dwelling for themselves, and the wood that they could bring from the swamp.

"Now I believed that they would run away because of the work I had set out for them, but they questioned me, saying, 'What work do the other brothers do here?'

"I said to them, 'They make ropes.' Taking some palm leaves, I showed them how to make the beginning of a rope, which I told them could be given to the custodians of the church who would bring bread for them. Then I left them.

"They patiently did everything that I told them to do, and they did not come to me for three years. I was surprised, because other monks came to me from distant lands. They never asked me about anything nor did they approach the other monks. I saw them only in church, taking the oblation in prayerful silence.

"Wanting to know about their manner of life, I fasted for an entire week and prayed to God that he would show me what they were doing. After that, I went to them. I knocked on their door. They opened it and both bowed silently. After offering the customary prayer, I sat. The older brother signaled to the younger that he should go out, and then he sat down to make a rope, saying nothing.

"Around the ninth hour, there was a knock on the door and the younger brother entered. After the older brother nodded, the younger went out again and prepared the food that would refresh us. After receiving another nod, he set three loaves on the table and stood by silently.

"Then I said, 'Rise, let us eat.' After we did this, the younger brother brought a flask filled only with water and we drank.

"After clearing the table, evening arrived and they said to me, 'Will you leave?'

"I replied that I wished to rest there.

"Then they spread a straw mat for me in one corner of the cell, and one for themselves in the other corner. They took off their belts and aprons as if they were preparing for sleep and lay down. Once again I prayed to God that he might reveal their manner of life to me. Then behold, as if the roof of the cell had dissolved, a clear light filled the cell as if it was the middle of the day, but they were unable to see that light.

"When they believed that I was sleeping, they rose, dressed, and extended their hands to heaven. I was able to see what they were doing, although they could not see me. I saw demons, like flies, coming and trying to get into the mouth and eyes of the younger brother. But the angel of the Lord, armed with a fiery sword, circled him and drove the demons away. The demons did not even dare approach the older brother.

"When morning arrived, they lay back down. I pretended that I was just waking up, and they did the same. The older brother said, 'Do you want us to sing the twelve psalms, Father?'

"I said, 'Yes.' Then the younger brother sang five psalms, in six verses and one alleluia. With every single verse, a fiery torch came out from his mouth and ascended to heaven. A similar thing happened when the older brother was opening his mouth and singing: something like a fiery vapor came out of his mouth and reached up into heaven. After them, I also recited a small amount.

"When I departed, I asked them to pray for me.

"They prostrated themselves silently at my feet. Then I understood that the elder brother had been perfected in the fear of the Lord, but the younger was still battling demons.

"A few days later, the elder brother died, and three days after that, the younger brother died as well." [AP-G Macarius the Great 33; AP-GS 20.3; AP-PJ 20.2; AP-PR 195]

Chapter Ninety-Four

THERE SHOULD BE A GREAT SILENCE IN SOLITUDE, AN ABSENCE OF ALL NOISE

1. When Abba Arsenius had come to the other brothers, there was a place where there were many reeds that, when the wind blew, made a noise. Arsenius said, "What is this earthquake?"

"It is the wind," they said, "striking those reeds."

Arsenius told them, "If someone living in solitude and praying to God hears a sparrow singing, he will be unable to keep his mind at rest. Nevertheless, you live near an earthquake; if you are able to remain at rest, then I admire you." [AP-G Arsenius 25; AP-GS 2.8; AP-PJ 2.5]

Chapter Ninety-Five

CONCERNING THE PRACTICES OF THE HERMITS

1. Abba Moses often spoke these thoughts to the solitaries: "There are four principal practices that must be observed: remaining silent, serving the commands of God, humbling yourself, and maintaining poverty. A man may possess three of these virtues with difficulty: that he always mourns, that he always remains mindful of his sins, and in every hour, that he holds his death before his eyes." [AP-Pa 35.1; AP-PR 196]

2. The blessed Anthony often said, "The ancient fathers went into the deserts, and having made themselves healthy, they became physicians. When they returned from the desert, they healed others. Now, if it should happen that one of us goes into the desert, we begin to apply cures to others before we are healed. Our old weaknesses return to us, and, in the end, become worse than they were before. For this reason it was said, *Physician, first heal yourself* (Luke 4:23)." [AP-GN 603; AP-Pa 35.2]

3. Once the holy fathers prophesied about the final generation. One of them, a man with an extraordinary lifestyle named Ischyrion, said, "We still keep the commands of God."

Some of the other fathers asked him, "What about those who will come after us?"

Ischyrion responded, "Perhaps they will fulfill half the commands."

Again they asked, "The generations after them, what will they do?"

He replied, "The men of those generations will not have the work of God's commands. Temptation will come upon them, and those who are found to have been approved in the face of this temptation, will be better than us or our fathers." [AP-G Ischyrion 1; AP-GS 18.9; AP-PJ 18.34; AP-PR 197]

Chapter Ninety-Six

ON HOW ONE SHOULD LIVE IN THE MONASTERY

1. A brother questioned Abba Agathon, "I wish to remain with the brothers; tell me, Father, how may I dwell with them?"

The elder replied, "Observe this, above all other precepts: as you pass through all the days in community, remain as you were on the first day you entered and quietly complete your pilgrimage. Moreover, make sure that you do not assume self-confidence when speaking." [AP-G Agathon 1a; AP-GS 10.11a; AP-PJ 10.8a; AP-Pa 42.1; AP-PR 198]

2. Abba Macarius said to the same Abba Agathon (while Agathon was living with him), "Why do you live with me in this way, like a foreigner?"

Agathon replied, "I am amazed that you said this. For often, when another foreigner is present, I assume confidence when speaking, which is not permitted to me while living with you."

"For confidence is a serious evil: almost the worst, the mother of nearly all other evils. Therefore, a monk should not speak in the presence of others, nor is he permitted to have confidence in his own cell.

"For confidence and laughter are like fires consuming the reeds."

3. When Abba Nesteros was living in the monastery, Abba Poemen asked him, "From where did you attain this virtue, brother, that whenever trouble comes into the monastery, you neither speak nor advance yourself as a mediator?"

Nesteros did not want to answer, but later, having been compelled by the elder, said, "Forgive me, Abba, for in the beginning, when I entered the monastery, I said to myself, 'Look, you and this donkey are equal. For this donkey is beaten and says nothing; when it is injured, it does not respond; you must act the same way.' This is what the psalm says: *I have become a beast of burden before you, and I am always with you* (Ps 73:22–23)." [AP-G Nisterus the Cenobite 2; AP-GS 15.46; AP-PJ 15.30; AP-Pa 42.3]

4. **(a)** Once, when the Mazices invaded Scetis and they had killed many of the fathers, Abba Poemen, together with another abba older than himself named Anub, and five other fathers fled from there and came to the place which is called Terenuthis. There they found an ancient temple that had been deserted, and the seven remained there as equals while each man considered whether they should remain in Egypt.

Abba Anub, who was the oldest, said, "Let each man rest here for seven days, but no one shall speak to anyone else." They agreed to this.

There was a statue in the temple of a certain idol. Abba Anub would rise in the morning and throw stones at it. In the evening he would approach the statue and say to it, "I have sinned, forgive me." He did this for the entire seven-day period.

On the day of the Sabbath, when the monks again came together, Abba Poemen said to him, "What did you want to prove these seven days? What led a man of faith to say to an idol, 'Forgive me'?"

The elder replied to him, "Was the man of faith stoning a statue in its face? I did this for your sake. Tell me, when I threw rocks at this idol, did it speak or become angry? When I sought its forgiveness, did it become confused or praise itself?"

Abba Poemen replied, "No."

Then the elder said, "Look, brothers, we are seven men. If you want to remain together, then each man must become like that idol: when he is injured by another he must not become angry; when someone seeks his pardon, he should not exalt himself. If you do not want to do this, then each man should go where he wishes."

Then the rest of the monks threw themselves on the ground and promised that they would do this. They remained together for many years, with one of their number running the household. The monks ate whatever was placed on the table, with no one saying, "Bring something else to us," or, "I do not want to eat this."

(b) At night they spent four hours sleeping, four hours singing psalms, and four working. During the day they worked to the sixth hour, and then they read and spread out palm leaves until the ninth. After this, they prepared a meal for themselves. [**a:** AP-G Anoub 1; AP-GS 15.12; AP-PJ 15.11; AP-Pa 42.4; AP-PR 199]

Chapter Ninety-Seven

ONE SHOULD NOT MOVE FROM MONASTERY TO MONASTERY

1. An elder said, "If you dwell in a monastery, do not leave that place, for you will harm yourself greatly. Just as the bird sitting on an egg will make that egg rot if it leaves too often, so too will the monk destroy his faith if he moves from place to place.

"Just as the tree will not bear fruit if it is frequently transplanted from place to place, the monk also will not be able to bear heavenly fruit if he often moves from place to place." [AP-G Syncletica 6; AP-GS 7.22; AP-PJ 7.15]

Chapter Ninety-Eight

WHICH BROTHERS SHARE THE SAME MERIT?

1. A brother questioned Abba Poemen, saying, "Which brothers are equal in merit?"

The elder replied, "If there were three men together, one who remained at peace in every word or work, another who was weak, but gave thanks, and a third who, was doing his duty with a clean conscience, these three would share the same merit." [AP-G Poemen 29; AP-GS 10.76; AP-PJ 10.52; AP-Pa 36.1]

Chapter Ninety-Nine

WHAT SHOULD BE THE GENERAL LIFE OF ALL

1. (**a**) Someone asked Abba Poemen, "How should a man live as a Christian?"

He responded, "Like the prophet Daniel, against whom no accusation was made, except that he maintained the purity of his heart, which he demonstrated always in his worship of God.

(**b**) "To injure, to cheat, or to commit perjury is to be a stranger to Christ.

"The soul is stained through these four actions: if someone, desiring carnal pleasures, maintains a friendship with powerful people; if he slanders his neighbor; if, when walking through a city, he does not guard his eyes; and if he has a knowledge of a woman." [**a:** AP-G Poemen 53; AP-GS 1.22; AP-PJ 1.13; **b:** AP-Pa 36.2]

2. The blessed Arsenius related that when he was living in his own cell, he heard a voice saying to him that said he should go outside so that he might contemplate the work of men. Going out, he saw a man drawing water from a well, but the bucket he was using had holes in it, and the water was running back into the well.

Then going a little further, he saw an Ethiopian making a bundle of cut sticks for himself. When he had done this and had realized that it was too heavy to lift, he placed more sticks on the pile. He tried to lift it again, and although he was unable to move the wood, he nevertheless continued to add sticks to the pile.

Going a little further, Arsenius saw two young men sitting on horses before the gates of a city. They were carrying a log sideways and were unable to enter the city. The log, which they carried sideways, did not permit them to pass through the gate, but neither man wanted to follow or come after the other, and so both remained outside the city gate.

Then the one who had showed these things to the blessed Arsenius, said, "The man you saw first—who drew water from the well, but it ran through his perforated bucket back into the well—is similar to a man giving alms; he struggles to do a good work, but because he often does evil things in his other works, he loses his reward through the evil deeds that pollute his few good actions.

"Now that man you saw cutting pieces of wood and adding them to a heavy pile, and then making that pile even heavier, is a man who is established in many sins; after making penance, he adds another sin to his burden.

"Those you saw carrying a log between them, unable to enter the city, are men who bear the miserable yoke of pride—neither wishes to humble himself before the other and follow the humble way of Christ. Consequently, both men remain outside the kingdom of God." [AP-G Arsenius 33; AP-GS 18.3; AP-CSP 6.2; AP-PJ 18.2; AP-Pa 36.3; AP-PR 38]

Chapter One Hundred

ON NOT SPEAKING ABOUT THE HOLY SCRIPTURES UNLESS ASKED

1. A brother asked an elder, "If I read some chapter, do you want me to expound it?"

The elder replied, "It is written, *If anyone responds before he listens, it is foolishness and a shame for him* (Prov 18:13). Therefore, speak if you are questioned, but remain silent if you are not."

2. Abba Alonius served the elders diligently. Each man praised his diligence, but he did not respond to them. One of them said to him, "Why do you not respond to the elders when they praise you?"

Alonius replied, "If I replied to them, I would be like one who was accepting their praise." [AP-G Poemen 55; AP-GS 15.54; AP-PJ 15.39]

3. Once the fathers assembled to discuss Melchizedek, but they forgot to call Abba Copres. Later, they called him and questioned him about that chapter. But he, striking his mouth three times, said, "Woe to you, Copres, because you have not done what God commanded you to do, and because he does not ask you to investigate these matters."

After hearing these words, each father returned to his own place. [AP-G Copres 3; AP-GS 15.38; AP-PJ 15.24]

4. Abba Poemen said, "Withdraw from every person who is contentious in disputes. For the Spirit of God surrounds the soul that

withdraws from human controversies and disturbances." [AP-G Poemen 205]

5. Once, the brothers came to Abba Anthony. Wanting to test them, he questioned them about some words from the Scriptures. Each man offered a response, according to his own understanding. Then Anthony asked Abba Joseph, who was prudent, "What do you say?"

Joseph replied, "I do not know."

Abba Anthony said, "Behold, this man has found the way." He said this to show that one should not presume to say something from his own understanding about the Holy Scriptures. [AP-G Anthony 17; AP-GS 15.4; AP-PJ 15.4]

6. A brother questioned an elder, saying, "What measure do you order me to maintain when speaking?"

He responded, "If your words are superfluous, dismiss them; if, on the other hand, they are good words that edify, give them a good place and speak them. Nevertheless, even if they are good, do not interject pauses in your words; cut them off quickly and you will have rest." [AP-GN 237; AP-GS 10.163]

7. Two brothers had made their way from different cells to a holy elder who was living in Scetis. One of them said to him, "Abba, I have committed the entire Old and New Testament to memory."

The elder replied, "You fill the air with words."

The other brother said, "I copied the Old and New Testament, and I have it with me."

He responded to this brother, "You, likewise, have filled your bookshelves with papers." [AP-GN 385; AP-GS 10.147; AP-PJ 10.94; AP-Pa 41.2]

Chapter One Hundred One

THE SEVEN SENTENCES THAT ABBA MOSES SPOKE TO ABBA POEMEN

1. These are the words that will save anyone—whether in the monastery, solitude, or in the secular world—if they are observed.

First, as it is written, a man ought to love God with all of his heart and all of his mind (cf. Matt 22:37).

Second, a man must *love his neighbor as himself* (Matt 22:39).

Third, a man must separate himself from every evil.

Fourth, a man must not judge his brother in any matter (cf. Matt 7:1; Luke 6:37).

Fifth, a man must not do evil to another for any reason (cf. 1 Pet 3:9).

Sixth, before he dies, a man must cleanse himself from carnal and spiritual evil.

Seventh, a man must have *a heart that is contrite and humble* (Ps 51:17); the man who is able to fulfill this teaching always considers his own sins and not those of his neighbor.

PART 4
Apophthegmata Patrum, Pseudo-Paschasius of Dumium (AP-Pa)

Although the majority of the stories found in Rosewyde's *Vitae Patrum* 7 were drawn from Paschasius's *Geronticon*, this text does contain twenty-three *apophthegms*, plus a small collection entitled *On the Meditations of the Twelve Anchorites* that are not found in that source. These additional stories are printed here.

Chapter Thirteen

AGAINST THE SPIRIT OF PRIDE

4. An elder said, "Do not set your heart against your brother, saying that you are more sober and continent than that man. Rather, put yourself under the grace of God in a spirit of poverty and unfeigned charity, lest you lose your work through the spirit of exaltation." [AP-G Or 13; AP-GN 331; AP-GS 15.73; AP-PJ 15.55]

Chapter Nineteen

ON THE INDULGENCES FOR THE WEAK, AND ON WEAKNESS ITSELF

3. Many brothers, struggling with different needs, came to the holy Anthony. Among them was Eulogius, an Alexandrian monk, and another man who was tormented by elephantiasis. Those who told this story said this was the reason Eulogius had come.

Now this Eulogius was a scholar, learned in the secular texts. Having been captured by a desire for immortality, he had renounced the secular world. He had divided and distributed all of his possessions, but had retained a little of his money, which he was using since he was unable to work.

When he was tormented by a defect of the soul and found that he was unable to patiently pass time with the crowd in the monastery or bear the solitary life, he discovered a man lying in a public street. This man had contracted an illness, as I mentioned above, that made it seem as if he had neither feet nor hands. Only his tongue was immune from his illness, and he was able to use it to beg for help from passersby who were looking upon his sickness.

When Eulogius, standing near, saw the man, he prayed to God. He made a pact with the Lord, speaking these words: "Lord God, in your name I take up the shackle of such a monstrous illness, so that through this work, I will be able to be saved. Be present with me, Jesus Christ, and generously grant me patience for this service."

Then, quickly going to the man who was lying on the street, he said to him, "If you want, brother, I will take you into my home and I will take care of you." When that man willingly agreed, Eulogius said, "I will go and bring my mule to carry you."

The sick man, strongly rejoicing, consented. And so Eulogius quickly did this and transported him to his guest room without delay.

For fifteen continuous years Eulogius served the invalid with care and perpetual concern. During this time, that man, to whom he was offering such care, tolerated his service with thanksgiving; Eulogius looked after him with his hands, medications, foods, and baths, as together they worked toward health.

But after the fifteenth year, the sick man was stirred up by a demon, and forgetting the works of Eulogius and their merits, he began to wish to leave him. He started to berate Eulogius with many insults and reproaches, saying, "Runaway slave, you who devoured your own home and stole another man's wealth, why do you believe you will discover an opportunity for your own salvation by serving me?"

Eulogius questioned him, and satisfying his spirit, he said, "Do not say such things to me, my lord. Tell me how I have saddened you, and I will correct my ways."

Nevertheless, the sick man, suffering from elephantiasis, said in anger, "Go! I do not want your fawning. Cast me out in public; I do not need your nursing."

Eulogius said, "I beg you to be calm and tell me what I have done that has upset you."

The man with elephantiasis, now more bitter in his anger, said to him, "I can no longer bear your fraudulent mockeries; your fawning and mocking gestures I will not tolerate. This arid and frugal life does not please me. I want to stuff myself with meat."

When the most patient Eulogius brought meat to him, the sick man again began to proclaim, "You are unable to satisfy my desires; nor will I live with a solitary. I want to see people, and to go out in public."

Eulogius said to him, "I will bring many brothers to you."

The sick man, more ferocious and in the power of blasphemy, said, "I do not want to see your face, and you would bring me faces that are similar to your own, men who only eat bread?" Then, convulsing, the sick man shouted in a great voice, "I do not want this; I want to go out in public. Oh violence! Throw me out from this place where you have imprisoned me."

The demon had driven the sick man to such a state of insanity and senselessness that if he had had a noose and hands that worked, he would have hanged himself.

Eulogius went to the monks living nearby and said to them, "What should I do? This man with elephantiasis has despaired of me."

They said to him, "For what reason?"

He replied, "Because these are hard things he has tried to impose on me, and I do not know what to do. Should I cast him out? On the other hand, I swore an oath to God, and I am afraid of it. I must not cast him out, but I am unable to bear such abuse day and night again. I do not know what I should do about him."

Then the other monks spoke these words to him: "While the Great One (for that was the title they gave Anthony) still lives and is present go to him. Take the sick man on a ship and wait for Anthony at his monastery. Try to meet him when he leaves his cave. When you see Anthony, tell him what you are enduring, and then ask his advice. Do anything that he tells you to do; you must acquiesce to his warnings, understanding that what he tells you comes from God."

And so, having been gladly instructed by the teachings of the brothers, and overcoming the resistance of the aforementioned sick man with flattering requests, he placed him on a little ship at the coast. Then he left the city by night and made his way to the lodging of the disciples of the holy Anthony. The next day, at the hour of vespers, he encountered that blessed Anthony. Cronius told me that Anthony was dressed in a robe made from skins. It was customary, when he came, that he would call to Macarius and ask him, "Have any brothers come?"

Macarius responded that one had come.

"From Egypt," asked Anthony, "or from Jerusalem?" Anthony had commanded that his disciple give this signal: if any visitors were unworthy to have a discussion with him, Macarius would say they were from Egypt; on the other hand, if they seemed to be spiritual men, he would announce that they were from Jerusalem.

And so, when Anthony arrived, according to his custom, he would ask if there were brothers from Jerusalem or Egypt there. If Macarius responded, "There is someone to see you from Egypt," then the holy Anthony would say to him, "Make them happy, feed them, pray with them, and then order them to depart." When men were said to have come from Jerusalem, Anthony would sit with them through the night and discuss the progress they were making toward their salvation.

On this particular night, they told us, that he had eaten, and one by one, he had called to those who had come to see him. No one had told Anthony that Eulogius was present, but he called that man's name three times with his own voice from the shadows. The above-mentioned scholar did not respond, believing that another man named Eulogius was being summoned.

Anthony then spoke to him again: "I am calling you, Eulogius, you who have come from the city of Alexandria."

Eulogius said to him, "What, I pray, do you command?"

Then Anthony said, "Why did you come here?"

Eulogius replied, "He who has deigned to reveal my name to you, will also, without doubt, reveal the reason that I have come."

Then the elder said, "I know why you have come, but explain your reason before all the brothers, so that they might hear."

Consequently, having been commanded by the great Anthony, Eulogius, the servant of Christ, told his story in front of everyone: "I discovered a man suffering from elephantiasis, lying in a public street, and no man showed any concern for him. I promised God that I would serve the sick man devotedly, as far as I was able, so that I would be saved through him, and he through me. In this state, we lived together for fifteen years, as I believe has already been revealed to your holiness. After many years, during which he had experienced no evil from me, he attacked me with a variety of violent charges and tantrums. Because of this, I thought he wanted to take himself away from me, and so I came to your holiness so that you might condescend to teach me with your counsels what I must do, and to assist me with your prayers. For I am exhausted and tormented by the worst passions."

Anthony then responded to these words with a severe and angry voice, "Would you cast that man out, Eulogius? The one who made him does not cast him out. You would cast him out? God will find a better man than you, and he will choose a man who will look after this destitute man."

When Eulogius, terrified by these words, remained silent, the holy Anthony turned his attention to the sick man and began to assault him with his words. With a great voice he shouted, "You, man with elephantiasis, horrid with mud and slime, worthy of neither earth nor heaven, will you not stop shouting epithets at God? Do you not know that it is Christ who ministers to you? How is it that you have dared to speak such words against Christ? For on account of Christ, this man subjugated himself with this service and duties."

Anthony stopped speaking, leaving the pair lacerated by his stinging words. Then, after offering words to the other brothers, addressing every little matter as the need of each required, he turned his attention back to Eulogius and the sick man. He said to them, "Do not be separated from each other, my sons. Return to where you have lived for such a long time in peace, setting aside every sadness. For even now the Lord God is sending for you. This is the reason that temptation has befallen you, so that you will come to the end of your life together, and each of you will deserve to be crowned. Now do nothing else. For if an angel comes and is unable to find you both in that place about which I spoke, you may be cheated of your crowns."

The two men returned quickly to their cell; they reconciled and restored peace. Eulogius died after forty days, and a few days later, the sick man died as well, his soul decidedly safe.

Now Cronius, who had lived in the Thebaid for a long time, descended to the monastery in Alexandria. It happened that he arrived on the day that the brothers were celebrating the fortieth day for Eulogius and the third for the sick man. When Cronius heard this, he was astounded. He picked up the holy Gospel, placed it in the middle of the brothers, and after the sacrament had been given to all in turn, he said, "I was the translator for the two men you are commemorating. The holy Anthony did not know how to speak Greek. I knew the language of both parties, and I translated between them as they spoke Greek, and Anthony replied in Egyptian." [Pall. *Hist. Laus.* 21.2–15; PLaus 16]

4. Now Cronius told us that Saint Anthony had told him on that same night he sent Eulogius away, that he had prayed for an entire year to see the places of the sinners and of the righteous in a vision. He said that he had seen a tall giant, reaching almost to the clouds, of a foul color, with hands stretching to heaven. A lake spread out like a kind of sea at the feet of the creature. Disturbed souls flew over the lake like birds. Those souls that were flying over the giant's head and hands were saved, but those that were struck by his hands were swallowed up by the lake.

Then a great voice came to Anthony and said, "Know that all of these souls that you see flying, are the souls of the righteous that will find rest in paradise. The other souls will be sent into the fire, where they will suffer, for they followed the will of the flesh, and hanging on to their anger, they tried to seek revenge." [Pall. *Hist. Laus.* 21.16–17]

5. **(a)** Now Cronius, the holy Hierax, and the other brothers from the neighborhood told us this saying: **(b)** A certain elder said, "If a monk knows that there is another man, near whom he would make progress, but he does not go to him because he has bodily needs that he satisfies with his labor—well, a monk of this kind does not believe there is a God." [**a:** Pall. *Hist. Laus.* 22.1; **b:** AP-GN 236; AP-GS 10.162]

6. An elder said, "The man who wants to live in the desert must be a teacher, not a man who needs teaching, or he will come to harm." [AP-GN 221; AP-GS 10.127; AP-PJ 10.93]

Chapter Twenty-One

ON THE FEAR OF THE LORD

3. An elder said, "May fear, humility, and a shortage of food remain with you." [AP-G Euprepius 6; AP-GS 1.30; AP-PJ 1.20]

4. A brother questioned an elder, saying, "Where does my hard heart come from, Abba, and why does it not fear God?"

The elder said to him, "I believe that if a man maintains a reproof in his heart, he will possess a fear of the Lord."

The brother said, "What is this reproof?"

The elder answered, "In every action, a man should reprove his soul, saying to it, 'You must remember that it is necessary for you to meet God.'

"Say this also to your soul: 'What do I want with men?' I believe that if anyone practices this, the fear of God will come to him." [AP-GN 138; AP-GS 3.40; AP-PJ 3.22; AP-M 22]

Chapter Twenty-Two

ON REPENTANCE

2. Abba Pimenius said with a groan, "Every virtue has entered my cell except one virtue, and a man stands based on its work."

The brothers questioned him, "What is this virtue, Abba?"
He replied, "That a man should always criticize himself." [AP-G Poemen 134; AP-M 60; PLaus 20.15d]

Chapter Twenty-Seven

ON PERSEVERANCE

2. An elder said, "What is the point of beginning a work if one does not know how to finish it? What is begun, but remains unfinished, is nothing." [AP-M 103]

Chapter Thirty-Two

ON SILENCE

4. An elder said, "Remaining silent is a pilgrimage." [AP-G Tithoes 2; AP-GS 4.52; AP-PJ 4.44; AP-M 73]

Chapter Thirty-Six

WHICH BROTHERS SHARE THE SAME MERIT?

4. A brother asked Abba Sisoes, "My parents sent me an inheritance. What should I do about it?"
The elder replied, "If I should say, 'Give it to the priests of the church,' they will make banquets for themselves from it. If I should say, 'Give it to your relatives,' you will have no reward. Therefore, if you want to carry out the divine mandate, give it to the poor and the needy, and you will be perfected." [AP-G Poemen 33; AP-GS 10.82; AP-PJ 10.56; AP-M 7]

Chapter Thirty-Seven

TEMPORAL PROFIT IS RELINQUISHED FOR THE SAKE OF A LOVE FOR CHARITY

1. Abba Sisoes said, "One time, when I was in the market selling my baskets to the brothers, I saw that anger was approaching me, and so I scattered my baskets and fled." [AP-G Isidore the Priest I 7; AP-M 11]

2. Abba John said, "Once I had gone up along the desert road through Scetis, weaving a rope. I heard a camel driver speaking vain words, and to keep from becoming angry, I threw away my rope and fled." [AP-G John the Dwarf 5; AP-M 12]

3. A brother asked Abba Pimenius, "Why did the Lord say, *No one has greater charity than someone who lays down his life for his friends* (John 15:13)? How does one do this?"

The elder responded, "If anyone hears an evil word from his neighbor, and although he is able to respond with a similar word, nevertheless he fights in his heart to continue his work, and he restrains himself so that he will not sadden that man—this is the sort of man who lays down his life for his friend." [AP-G Poemen 116; AP-GS 17.13; AP-PJ 17.10; AP-M 14; AP-PR 201]

4. **(a)** Abba Macarius said, "If we remember the evils that we suffer from other people, we will lose our memory of virtue."

Likewise, he said, "Nevertheless, if we cultivate a memory of the evils that the demons have sent to us, we will be without disturbance, knowing that God created good things from the beginning, but the devil planted evils. There will be innumerable destroyers."

(b) He added, "It is a fault in a monk if, having been hurt by the brothers, he does not turn first to charity by purifying his heart. For the only reason that the Shunammite woman deserved to receive the prophet Elisha in her home was that she held a grudge against no one else. The Shunammite is the soul in a person, while Elisha symbolizes the Holy Spirit: unless the soul is pure, it does not deserve to receive the Spirit of God. Thus, long-standing anger blinds the eyes of the heart, and keeps the spirit from prayer." [**a:** AP-G Macarius the Great 36; AP-GS 10.48; AP-PJ 10.34; AP-M 15; PLaus 20.15c; **b:** AP-G Cronius 1; AP-GN 363; AP-GS 18.34; AP-PJ 18.27; AP-M 16]

Chapter Thirty-Eight

HOW LAMENTATION AND POVERTY, WHICH ARE DONE FOR GOD, WORK

1. **(a)** A brother asked the holy Anthony, "What should I do on account of my sins?"

Anthony responded, "The man who wants to be freed from sins will be freed from them through weeping and wailing; whoever wants to be strengthened in the virtues will be strengthened by shedding tears. The psalms themselves commend weeping.

(b) "Remember the example of Hezekiah, the king of Judea, as was written in the prophet Isaiah. Through weeping, he received not only health, but also he was promised a fifteen year extension of his life (cf. Isa 38:5). Through his flowing tears, the power of the Lord stretched out an invading army—185,000 soldiers—in death (cf. 2 Kings 19:35).

"The holy apostle Peter received, through weeping, what he had forfeited by denying Christ. Mary, because she had washed the feet of the Lord with her tears, deserved to select the better part—hearing him. For this is the fear of the Holy Lord, remaining in the age of ages." [**a:** AP-G Poemen 119; AP-GS 3.29; AP-M 33]

2. The blessed Macarius said, "In truth, if contempt becomes like praise for a monk, if poverty like riches, and scarcity like abundance, then he will never die. For it is impossible, while believing correctly and worshiping God dutifully, to fall into unclean passion and the error of demons." [AP-G Macarius the Great 20; AP-M 23]

Chapter Thirty-Nine

IN THIS LIFE, A MAN WILL BE UNABLE TO FIND REST

3. The same elder said, "Flies do not approach a pot on the fire, but they will approach one that is lukewarm, climb into it and produce worms. In the same way, demons flee the monk who is burning with

divine fire, but they delude and mislead a tepid monk." [AP-G Poemen 111; AP-M 42; AP-PR 204]

Chapter Forty

THE SOURCE OF VICES

1. A brother asked the holy Anthony, "Why does God promise good things to the soul through the constant witness of the Scriptures, even though the soul does not want to persist in good things, but it deviates to the transitory, perishable, and unclean pleasures?"

Anthony replied, "To this thought we must join what the Psalmist said: *If I had cherished the iniquity in my heart, God would not have listened* (Ps 66:18). Do you not know that when the belly has eaten its fill, the great vices immediately boil up, just as our Savior predicted through the Gospel: *It is not what enters the mouth that pollutes the soul of a man, but rather those things that come out of the heart that plunge the man into ruin* (Matt 15:11). Look at what is mentioned first: thoughts of evil, homicides, adultery, fornication, thefts, false testimonies, and blasphemies. Whoever has not yet enjoyed heavenly sweetness, so that he wants to search for God wholeheartedly, will revert to unclean things. Who is able to speak rightly? *I became a beast of burden before you and I was always with you* (Ps 73:22–23)." [AP-GS 10.143; AP-M 29]

Chapter Forty-One
WHICH VIRTUES SHOULD ONE OBTAIN?

1. **(a)** A brother said to a certain elder, "Teach me, Father."
(b) The elder said, "Go. Learn to love doing violence to yourself. **(c)** Draw your sword and plunge into the battle."

The brother said to him, "My thoughts do not allow me to do this."

The elder replied, "It is written, *Call upon me in your day of trouble; I will rescue you and you will glorify me* (Ps 50:15). Therefore, call upon the Lord and he will rescue you." [**a:** AP-M 47a; **b:** AP-GS 21.51; AP-M 47b; **c:** AP-GN 25; AP-M 47c]

Chapter Forty-Two

HOW SHOULD ONE LIVE IN THE MONASTERIES?

2. Agathon said again, "If you live with a neighbor, be like a column of stone, which if it is injured, does not become angry. If, on the other hand, it is praised, it does not brag." [AP-G Poemen 198; AP-M 10]

Chapter Forty-Three

WHICH SPIRITUAL DISCIPLINES MUST BE OBSERVED?

1. A brother said to Abba Serapion, who had ten thousand monks under his direction, "Some other brothers from the monastery have elected me to lead them. Show me what you wish me to do."

Serapion replied, "It is hard, perhaps, to have my power. For our Lord Jesus Christ, through his Gospel, instructed, *If you love me, keep my commands* (John 14:15). When the disciples debated among themselves about primacy—who would be the first of their number—he said to them, *If anyone wants to be great among you, let him be your servant, and whoever wants to be first among you, let him be the slave of all* (Mark 10:43–44). The apostle Peter, in his epistles, warns the ministers, *Tend the flock of God that is given to you, caring for them not out of compulsion, but willingly, according to God; do this not for the sake of wicked money, but be an example for the flock. And when the prince of the shepherds appears, you will reap the unfading crown of glory* (1 Pet 5:2–4).

"Thus you must first do what you command, so that you will not just offer commands to them but will be their model as well. Then they will imitate your example. Do not be a hired servant, but rather, a pastor of the sheep, because our Savior called 'blessed' the man he established over his family in order to give them food at the proper time (cf. Matt. 24:45–6)." [AP-M 107]

2. Abba Moses asked Abba Silvanus, "How can a man take hold of the beginning of his conversation every single day?"

Silvanus responded, "One should take control of one thing from all the rest. Rising in the morning, let him take up the beginning of wisdom: in every virtue, in every command of God, in great patience and forbearance, in the charity of God, with humility of spirit and body, in much time spent in the cell, in prayer and pleading, with tears, with purity of heart and eyes, with control of the tongue and speech, in the renunciation of all material things and the desires of the flesh, having a suffering in battle, in the continence of spirit and the contest of the battle, in penitence and weeping, in the simplicity of the soul and silence, in fasting and nightly vigils, in the work of the hands, according to what the Apostle Paul said: *working with my hands, in hunger and thirst, in coldness and nudity, in works both majestic and in persecutions, in pits, caves, and caverns* (2 Cor 11:27). *Be a doer of the word, and not just a hearer* (Jas 1:22), producing a talent in a double measure, having a wedding garment, grounded upon the solid rock.

"Do not let mercy and faith depart from you. Continue thinking that every day brings you closer to death, and like one enclosed in a tomb, have no care for anything in this secular world, because secular concerns and the desire for wealth are the thorns the Lord warned about in the Gospel, *those that suffocate the good seed* (Luke 8:14). Do not let fasting from meals, humility, and weeping recede from you, *because the Lord scatters the bones of the men who are pleasing themselves* (Ps 53:5).

"Let fear dwell in you every hour, just as it was written, *On account of your fear, Lord, we conceived in the womb, we grieved, and we brought forth a spirit of salvation* (Isa 26:18).

"If anyone is strong, let him watch out for these things. Do not compare yourself to the great or judge yourself righteous. Rather, believe yourself to be inferior to all creatures, the worst sinner among men anywhere. *For whoever deems himself to be something, when he is nothing, leads himself astray* (Gal 6:3). Do not judge your neighbor, nor look down on the foreigner who falls short, but weep over your sins, and pay no attention to the deeds of other men.

"Be gentle in spirit and avoid anger. Hold nothing in your heart—neither hatred nor something against an enemy—without reason. Do not despise your enemy in his tribulations, nor return evil for evil, but be at peace with all; this is the bond of perfection. Do not give yourself to someone doing evil, nor rejoice with the man who does evil to his neighbor.

"Do not slander anyone because God is the judge and witness in all matters. Do not hate anyone on account of their sin, for it is written, *Do not judge, lest you be judged* (Matt 7:1). When you argue something, watch that you do not perjure yourself. Do not despise the man who is sinning, but pray for him, so that God will turn that man to penitence. If you hear of someone who does iniquity, respond by saying, 'Am I their judge? I am a sinful man, I am dead in my sins.' For a dead man does not have a reason to care about anything.

"He who attends to and thinks about all these things is a worker of all righteousness, as the prophet declared about our redeemer, Christ, *I am a worm and not a man* (Ps 22:6). Another prophet, Habakkuk said, *A stone from the wall will shout, and a beam of wood will speak* (Hab 2:11); but we, while we praise ourselves in many things, will be made to stumble in many things.

"But the person who has kept these things, lives under the grace and strength of our Lord, Jesus Christ." [AP-G John the Dwarf 34; AP-GS 1.13; AP-PJ 1.8; AP-M 109]

Chapter Forty-Four

ON THE MEDITATIONS OF THE TWELVE ANCHORITES

Once, twelve wise anchorites, holy and spiritual men, gathered together and began to ask each other to say something that a person could work on in their cell and could reflect upon spiritually.

1. The first monk, who was also the oldest among them, said, "I, brothers, from the time when I began to find peace, have crucified myself completely from those actions that are from the outside, remembering what was written, *Let us break their chains and cast aside their yoke* (Ps 2:3). Like one building a wall between the soul and the bodily actions, I said in my mind, 'In the same way one who is inside a wall does not see what is standing outside, you also will not look upon the exterior actions, but gaze at yourself, supporting daily the hope of God. In this way you will regard malicious thoughts and evil desires as the offspring of serpents and scorpions.' Whenever I perceive these thoughts springing up in my heart, I attend to them with a violent

threat and I dry them up with anger. I never cease being angry in my body and mind, lest something bad happen."

2. The second monk said, "I said, at that time when I renounced the earth, 'Today you are reborn; today you began to serve God; today you began to live here. Thus, be a pilgrim every day, and tomorrow you will be liberated.'

"This is how I counsel myself every day."

3. The third said, "I ascend to my God at daybreak. Adoring him, I throw myself on my face and confess my faults. Then, descending, I adore the angels of God and beg them to intercede with God for me and every creature. When I have finished this, I go to the abyss, and what the Jews do when they enter Jerusalem—weeping and wailing over the situation of their fathers—I do also, circling and waiting. I weaken my body with torments and I wail with those who are lamenting."

4. The fourth said, "I imagine that I am sitting on the Mount of Olives with the Lord and his disciples. I say to myself, 'Know nothing according to the flesh, but, with these men, always be an imitator of heavenly conversations, like the good Mary Magdalene, sitting at the feet of Jesus and listening to his words. *Let us make ourselves holy and perfect, just as our Father, who is in heaven* (Matt 5:48). And, *Learn from me for I am gentle and humble of heart* (Matt 11:29).'"

5. The fifth said, "I see the angels, ascending and descending to call souls, and I am always waiting for my end, saying, *My heart is ready, God, my heart is ready* (Ps 108:1)."

6. The sixth said, "I, through every single day, have established my words to be heard by God, believing that he says to me, 'Work for my sake and I will give you rest. Fight a little more and you will see my glory and will greet me. If you esteem me, if you will be my sons, turn back, asking for the Father. If you are my brothers, be ashamed on account of the many things I suffered for your sake. If you are my sheep, follow the passion of the Lord.'"

7. The seventh said, "I meditate on these things assiduously, and, without ceasing, I speak to myself about faith, hope, and charity. Consequently, I rejoice with hope; for the sake of love, I never discourage anyone and I strengthen my faith."

8. The eighth said, "I watch for the determined devil, who is seeking someone to devour. Whenever he comes, I wait for him with my inner eyes, and I call upon the Lord God against him, so that he will be ineffectual, and prevail in nothing, especially among those fearing God."

9. The ninth said, "Every day I wait for the gathering of intellectual powers, and I see the Lord of glory in the middle of them, shining upon all. When I depart from him I ascend to heaven, expecting to regard with wonder the beauty of the angels, those who sing hymns incessantly to God, and their sweet songs.

"I am carried away by the sounds and voices and pleasantness, so that it is agreeable to remember what is written, *The heavens proclaim the glory of God and the earth announces the work of his hands* (Ps 19:1). I regard everything that is upon the earth as ash and manure."

10. The tenth said, "I wait for the angel who assists me to be nearby. I guard myself by remembering what is written: *I kept the Lord in my sight always, and because he is at my right, I will not be moved* (Ps 16:8). Consequently, I fear him as the one who guards my ways and ascends daily to God to report my acts and words."

11. The eleventh said, "I am imposing virtues on my person, acting as if I possessed abstinence, chastity, kindness, and love. I surround myself with these qualities, so that wherever I might go, I say these words to myself, 'Where are your followers?' Do not be fainthearted, do not give up, but keep these qualities near you always. Dedicate yourself to speak about virtue to everyone, so that after death, they will testify before God, that they found rest in you."

12. The twelfth monk said, "You Fathers who have a heavenly way of life possess heaven and wisdom. Let no one marvel. I see that you have been elevated by your works and you are pursuing higher things. By your virtue you have been removed from the earth; you have separated yourselves from it in all things. What may I say? I would not be wrong if I called you earthly angels or heavenly men. But I judge myself to be unworthy of these matters, because I see my sins; everywhere I go, they precede me on the right and on the left. I have conceded myself to the inferno, saying, 'You will live with those of whom you are worthy; you will be numbered among them after a short time.'

"I see that both tears and incessant crying will be present in that place; nothing will stop them. I see a certain gnashing of teeth, the salting down of the entire body, and people shaking from head to foot. Then, throwing myself on the ground and grasping ashes, I pray to God that I might never undergo these experiences.

"I see also an immense sea, boiling with fire, and waves of fire—crashing and bellowing so that someone might believe they could touch heaven. In that awe-inspiring sea there are innumerable men, cast down by their savage practices. With one voice, they scream and howl together, with a sort of howling and voices that no one has ever heard on the earth. They burn like dry brush, for God has turned his mercy away from them on account of their injustice.

"Then I lament for the human race because a man must dare to speak or pay attention to something, with so many evils in the world. I keep my mind on these things, reflecting with sorrow on what the Lord said, because I judge myself unworthy of heaven and earth, and I think about what was written: *My tears have become my bread, day and night* (Ps 42:3)."

These are the responses of the wise and spiritual fathers. Let what is worthy of remembrance come among us, so that we will be able to display a version of this way of life in our work, and that by becoming blameless, perfect, and irreproachable, we might please our Savior.

To him be the honor and glory forever. Amen. [AP-GN 487]

PART 5
Apophthegmata Patrum, Pseudo-Rufinus (AP-PR)

As noted in the introduction, the collection that Rosewyde labeled *Vitae Patrum* 3 was a fusion of *apophthegms* from the *Geronticon* of Paschasius (AP-PA) and the *Commonitiones sanctorum patrum* (AP-CSP). Nevertheless, the collection does contain twelve unique stories that are offered here.

41. Once there was a homicide near the blessed Macarius, and the crime was attributed to an innocent man. This man who was enduring the false accusation got up and fled to the cell of the blessed Macarius. Now those who were present, and those who were harassing the man, detained him, saying they would be in danger unless they arrested and handed the murderer over, according to the laws. But the man who was charged with the crime swore on the sacraments that his conscience was free of the dead man's blood.

After the struggle about which course to adopt had raged all day, the holy Macarius asked for the location of the murdered man's grave. After they revealed the location to him, he went with them to the tomb, and planting his knees on the site, he invoked the name of Christ and said to those who were assisting, "Now the Lord will show if this man you are hounding is truly guilty."

Raising his voice, he called upon the dead man by name. When a voice from the tomb responded to him, the holy Macarius said to him, "By the faith of Christ, I implore you to tell us now if you were killed by this man who is charged because of you."

Then, in a clear voice, the dead man answered from the tomb that the accused had not killed him.

With great astonishment, everyone fell to the ground. Then, forming a circle around his feet, they began to beg Macarius to ask the dead man who had killed him.

The holy man replied, "I will not ask this; it is enough for me that an innocent man has been set free. It is not my business to reveal the guilty man. Perhaps he will feel compunction for the wicked act he has committed and seek repentance so that his soul may be saved." [Ruf. *Hist. Mon.* 21.1]

42. In the same way, at another time, when a brother brought the holy Macarius a bunch of grapes, he, who on account of charity, *was not looking out for himself, but thought of others* (Phil 2:4), took the grapes to another brother, who was weaker because of an illness. The sick man gave thanks to God because of the dutifulness of his brother, and he took the grapes. But this man also, thinking no less about others than himself, gave the grapes to another sick brother. Next,

that brother handed them on to another, and so on. The grapes were passed around all of the cells, which are scattered at a great distance from each other. Since the monks did not know who had initially sent the grapes, they were finally brought to that very man who had passed them on.

The holy Macarius, rejoicing that he had witnessed such great abstinence and charity among the brothers, increased the harsher disciplines of the spiritual life for himself. [AP-GN 494; *Hist. Mon.* 21.13–14]

43. Now this story about Macarius was corroborated for our faith by those who heard it from his mouth: at a certain time of the night, a demon, who appeared to be a monk, knocked on the door of his cell and said, "Rise, Abba Macarius, and let us go to the meeting where the brothers have gathered for vigils."

But that man, full of God's grace, could not be deceived, for he knew this was a trick of the devil. He said, "Oh liar and enemy of truth, what relationship do you have with the gathering and assembly of the holy men?"

That demon replied, "Is it hidden from you, Macarius, that without us, there is no gathering or assembly of monks? Come then, and you will see our work there."

However, Macarius said, "*Let the Lord command you, unclean demon* (Jude 9)." Then, turning to prayer, he implored the Lord to show him if what the demon had boasted about was true.

He went to the gathering where the brothers were celebrating the vigils, and a second time he petitioned the Lord in prayer to reveal the truth of the demon's words to him. Then he saw, like certain small boys, black Ethiopians scampering about the entire church, here and there, wherever they wanted to go. Now these scampering Ethiopian boys were making sport with individual monks and with those brothers who were stretched out in prayer and psalmody. If one of the boys touched a monk's eyes with two fingers, the monk immediately fell asleep. If they placed a finger in a monk's mouth, they made him yawn.

Likewise, after the psalms, when the brothers had prostrated themselves for prayer, the demons went running between the individual monks. Standing in front of a certain monk who was prostrate in prayer, a demon transformed itself into the shape of a woman; before another, they appeared like men who were building and carrying something. All of the demons were doing different things. Whatever form the demons adopted, like children playing, those monks who were praying were turned to that thought in their hearts.

Nevertheless, when the demons attempted to do something among some of the brothers, they were thrown aside, as if violently repelled. Therefore, the demons did not dare to stand before or pass among those monks; they played upon the necks and backs of the others.

When the blessed Macarius saw this, he groaned deeply, and shedding tears to God, he said, "Look, O Lord, *and do not remain silent nor overlook it* (Ps 83:1). Rise up, and let your enemies be scattered and send them into flight before your face, *because our spirits are filled with these deceptions* (Ps 88:3)."

Now after this prayer, in order to discover the truth, he summoned those brothers before whose faces he had seen the demons playing in different guises and various images. He compelled each of them to reveal whether they had pursued edifying thoughts in prayer or had been distracted by the actions and images that the prompting of the demons had produced.

Each of them confessed that there had been thoughts in their hearts, just as he was charging. Then the monks truly understood that all evil, superfluous, and vain thoughts that are conceived in a person's heart either during psalmody, or at the time of a dream or prayer, are produced through the deception and inspiration of demons. However, those shadowy Ethiopians, and those who produce thoughts, are driven away from every man who guards his heart and serves in the fear and love of the Lord. For having joined his mind to Christ, and becoming especially attentive at the time of prayer, the monk receives nothing evil or superfluous. [Ruf. *Hist. Mon.* 29.4]

200. There were also another seven well-tested men who were living in the desert that is contiguous with the land of the Saracens. Their cells were not separated by a great distance, and they were bound by the chain of charity. One of them was called Peter, the second Stephen, the third John, the fourth George, the fifth Theodore, the sixth Felix, and the seventh Lawrence.

They lived in that empty and most desolate wilderness, almost uninhabitable by men, and only showed themselves to each other one time a week. For on the day of the Sabbath, they gathered at the ninth hour, each coming from his own place to the place they had arranged together, each bringing what he had been able to find. One brought nuts, another *lactorones*, another dates, another figs, another the common herbs (that is, charlock, carrots, papayas, and rock parsley). These items were their principal foods, for they regarded bread, oil, or a beverage as something outside their customary use. They were sustained by the aforementioned herbs and fruits. Their clothing was made of the palm leaves they gathered.

Their scarce water was what they could find in those places. There was no way to procure water other than by going out early and shaking the various herbs, collecting the dew that fell abundantly upon them. This was their only source of drinking water.

When, as we said, they gathered in one place, after giving thanks to God, they ate the food. After dinner, they remained sitting until nightfall, meditating on the Holy Scriptures. Secular gossip did not spread among them, nor the concerns of the world or accounts of earthly deeds, but only spiritual conversation: a reminder of the desirable kingdom of heaven, the future blessing, the glory of the just, the penalties in store for sinners, and the repose of the saints. Having recalled these things, they breathed in from the bottom of their chests and wept most copiously.

When they had maintained their vigil through the entire night, offering praises to the Lord, on the day of the Lord, at the ninth hour, they came to the end of the time for visiting and speaking with each other. Each man returned to his own cell, in which he, alone, was devoting himself to the only God, day and night.

Consequently, they were engaged in their devotions when the Saracens overran the wilderness and discovered them. Bursting in upon them, they ejected the monks from the desert. The Saracens suspended them upside down from tied feet and inflicted many injuries on the monks. Finally, they heaped up the bitterest of the herbs beneath them and tortured their eyes with the smoke emitted by burning these bitter herbs.

After the Saracens had afflicted them with many tortures, they sent them away, barely alive. We know this from one of them who, afterward, lived in this place; but the others, where they went, we do not know.

201. A brother asked Abba Poemen, "What did the Lord mean when he said in the Gospel, *No one has greater charity than the person who lays down his soul for his friend* (John 15:13)? How may this be done?"

The elder responded, "If anyone hears an evil word from his neighbor, and he is able to respond in the same manner, but rather than doing so he endures it in his heart, and he restrains himself with his power and work to avoid responding with a bad word to that neighbor and saddening the man—this man lays down his soul for his friend." [AP-G Poemen 116; AP-GS 17.13; AP-PJ 17.10; AP-Pa 37.3; AP-M 14]

203. A brother asked an elder, "What should a man do in every temptation that comes upon him, and in every thought that the enemy sends to him?"

The elder replied, "He ought to wail in the sight of the benevolent God, so that God will hurry and assist him. For it is written, *The Lord is my helper, and I will despise my enemies* (Ps 118:7)." [AP-M 36]

204. A certain elder said, "Flies do not approach a boiling pot, but if it is cool, they will penetrate it and produce worms. In the same way, demons will flee the monk who is burning with the flame of divine love, but they will ridicule and pursue the tepid monk." [AP-G Poemen 111; AP-Pa 39.3; AP-M 42]

205. Abba Silvanus, while he was living in a cave, fell into an ecstatic trance and lay face down. After many hours, he rose to his feet and began weeping violently. His disciple, standing nearby, said, "What are you doing, Father?"

But Silvanus continued to weep silently.

When his disciple compelled him to speak about the reason he was weeping, Silvanus said, "I was snatched up to the judgment, my son, and saw many from our monastic way of life going into punishment, and many laypeople entering the kingdom of God."

After saying these things, the elder mourned deeply. [AP-G Silvanus 2; AP-GS 3.33; AP-PJ 3.15]

206. An elder said to the brothers, "Every day, reflect upon the fact that death is near you, and, as if you were already sealed in a tomb, have no care about this world. Let the fear of God abide in you continually, in every hour. Believe that you are inferior to all men. Do not tear anyone down, for God knows all things. Be at peace with all, and the Lord will give you rest always."

218. One time, when the blessed Anthony had been brought into the city by the holy Bishop Athanasius of Alexandria to refute the heretics, a most erudite blind man named Didymus came to him. They spoke about many points in the Holy Scriptures, among the other discourses they had about the holy volumes. Anthony admired Didymus's

mind and praised the acumen of his spirit. He asked Didymus, "Are you not sad that you are without eyes of the flesh?"

When Didymus was embarrassed and remained silent, Anthony questioned him a second and a third time, until he elicited the acknowledgment that it made the defense of the soul simpler.

Anthony responded, "I am amazed that a prudent man mourns the pain of loss of something that the ants, flies, and gnats possess. Is it not better to rejoice at the possession of a gift that only the saints and apostles deserved? For it is much better to see by the spirit than by the flesh and to possess those eyes through which the rod of sin is unable to strike, than to possess eyes that are able to send a man into the ruin of Gehenna, through the desire for what was seen by sight alone." [Hier. *Ep.* 68.2]

219. A certain father from Nitria, more thrifty than avaricious, and unaware that the Lord Jesus had been sold for thirty pieces of silver, left one hundred *solidi* when he died, money that he had earned from weaving linen. Now a council of monks met (for in that place five thousand monks live, divided into cells) to decide what should be done with the money. Some thought it should be distributed to the poor, others that it should be given to the church, and some that it should be sent to the monk's parents.

But Macarius, Pambo, Isidore, and other old men, with the Holy Spirit speaking in them, decreed that the money should be buried with its owner, saying, *May your money be in hell with you* (Acts 8:20).

Now in case someone should think this was done cruelly, such a great terror and fear invaded all of the monks of Egypt, that today they would consider it a great crime to leave behind even one *solidus*. [Hier. *Ep.* 22.33]

220. There was a Greek youth who had been established in an Egyptian monastery. Neither continence nor heavy labors were able to extinguish the flames of his flesh. When his struggle with temptation was brought before the father of the monastery, that man saved him through this art: he ordered a certain man, who was hard and bitter, to pursue the young man with reproaches and jeers. After inflicting this injury, the man was required to make complaints about the youth. When he had done what had been commanded, witnesses were called who, also on his behalf, told lies against the youth.

That youth began to weep against the lies. Every day he wept; every day his tears flowed. Sitting alone, because he had been filled with bitterness and abandoned by all assistance, he cast himself at the feet of Jesus. What more is there? He was treated this way for an entire year. When that time was finished, the boy was questioned about his earlier thoughts: did he still suffer from them? He answered, "Father, I am not permitted to live, how would I be allowed to fornicate?"

Thus having been looked after by his spiritual father, the young man was saved by conquering lust. [Hier. *Ep.* 125.13]

ABBREVIATIONS AND BIBLIOGRAPHY

Primary Sources and Abbreviations

AP-CSP *Admonitions of the Holy Fathers*
Freire, José Geraldes, ed. *Commonitiones Sanctorum Patrum: Uma nova colecção de apotegmas*. Coimbra, Portugal: Coimbra University Press, 1974.

AP-G *Greek Alphabetical Collection*
Cotelier, J.-B., ed. *Ecclesiae graeca monumenta*. Vol. 1. Paris 1677. Reprinted in J.-P. Migne, *Patrologia graeca*. Vol. 65. Paris, 1864.
Translations:
Ward, Benedicta, trans. *The Sayings of the Desert Fathers*. Kalamazoo, MI: Cistercian Publications, 1975.

AP-GN *Greek Anonymous Collection*
Nau, Frederick, ed. *Revue de l'Orient Chretien*. Vols. 12–14 (1907–9), 17–18 (1912–13).
Translations:
Wortley, John, trans. *The Anonymous Sayings of the Desert Fathers: A Select Edition and Complete English Translation*. Cambridge: Cambridge University Press, 2013.

AP-GS *Greek Systematic Collection*
Guy, Jean-Claude, ed. *Les Apophtegmes des Peres: collection systematique*. Sources Chretiennes 387, 474, 498. Paris: Editions du Cerf, 1993, 2003, 2005.
Translations:
Wortley, John, trans. *The Book of the Elders: Sayings of the Desert Fathers. The Systematic Collection*. Collegeville, MN: Liturgical Press, 2012.

AP-M Martin of Braga, *Sayings of the Egyptian Fathers*
Barlow, Claude, ed. *Martini Episcopi Bracarensis, Opera Omnia*. Papers and Monographs of the American Academy in Rome, 12. New Haven, CT: Yale University Press, 1950.
Translations:
Martin of Braga. "The Sayings of the Egyptian Fathers." In *The Iberian Fathers*, vol. 1, *Martin of Braga, Paschasius of Dumium, Leander of Seville*. Translated by Claude Barlow, 17–34. Washington DC: Catholic University of America Press, 1969.

AP-PA Paschasius of Dumium, *Geronticon*
> Freire, José Geraldes, ed. *A Versão Latina por Pascásio de Dume dos Apophthemata Patrum.* 2nd ed. Coimbra, Portugal: Coimbra University Press, 2011.
> Translations:
> Regnault, Lucien, trans. *Livre des anciens: recueil d'apophtegmes des Pères du désert.* Foi vivante. Classiques; 365. Paris: Éd. du Cerf, 1995.

AP-Pa Pseudo-Paschasius, *Geronticon*
> Rosweyde, Heribert, ed. *Vitae patrum 7.* Anvers, 1615. Reprinted in J. P. Migne, ed. *Patrologia cursus completus, series latina,* 73. Paris, 1860: 513–31.
> Translation:
> Pseudo-Paschasius of Dumium. "Questions and Answers of the Greek Fathers." In *The Iberian Fathers,* vol. 1, *Martin of Braga, Paschasius of Dumium, Leander of Seville,* 117–71. Translated by Claude Barlow. Washington, DC: Catholic University of America Press, 1969.

AP-PJ *The Systematic Collection of Pelagius and John*
> Rosweyde, Heribert, ed. *Vitae patrum 5 & 6.* Anvers, 1615. Reprinted in Migne, J. P., ed. *Patrologia cursus completus, series latina.* Vol. 73. Paris, 1860.
> Translations:
> Chadwick, Owen, trans. *Western Asceticism.* Philadelphia: Westminster Press, 1958.
> Regnault, Lucien, Jean Dion, and Guy Marie Oury, eds. *Les Sentences des Pères du désert: recueil de Pélage & Jean.* Solesmes: Éditions de Solesmes, 1976.
> Ward, Benedicta, trans. *The Desert Fathers: Sayings of the Early Christian Monks.* London: Penguin Books, 2003.

AP-PR Pseudo-Rufinus, *Sayings of the Egyptian Fathers*
> Rosweyde, Heribert, ed. *Vitae patrum 3.* Anvers, 1615. Reprinted in Migne, J. P., ed. *Patrologia cursus completus, series latina.* Vol. 73. Paris, 1860.

Evag. Prak. Evagrius of Pontus, *Praktikos*
> Guillaumont, A., and C. Guillaumont, eds. *Évagre le Pontique, traité pratique ou le moine.* Sources Chretiennes 170 and 171. Paris: Editions du Cerf, 1971.
> Translation:
> Bamberger, John, trans. *Evagrius Ponticus: The Pratikos and Chapters on Prayer.* Kalamazoo, MI: Cistercian Publications, 1981.

Hier. Ep. Jerome, *Epistles*
> Hilberg, Isidore, ed. *Hieronymus Epistularum Pars I, III.* Vienna: Verlag der Österreichischen Akademie der Wissenschafter, 1996.

Translations:
Fremantle, W. H., trans. *Jerome, Epistles.* The Nicene and Post-Nicene Fathers, Second Series. Vol. 6. Edinburgh: T&T Clark, 1892.

Hist. Mon. *History of the Monks in Egypt*
Festugière, A. J., ed. *Historia monachorum in Aegypto.* Subsidia Hagiographica 34. Brussels, 1961.
Translation:
Russell, Norman, and Benedicta Ward. *The Lives of the Desert Fathers: The Historia Monachorum in Aegypto.* Kalamazoo, MI: Cistercian Publications, 1980.

Pall. Hist. Laus. Palladius, *The Lausiac History*
Butler, Cuthbert, ed. *The Lausiac History of Palladius.* Vol. 2. Cambridge: Cambridge University Press, 1898.
Translation:
Meyer, Robert. *Palladius: The Lausiac History.* Ancient Christian Writers 34. New York: Newman Press, 1964.

PLaus. *The Lausiac History* **(Latin)**
Migne. J. P., ed. *Patrologia cursus completus, series latina.* Vol. 74, 343–82. Paris, 1860.

Ruf. Hist. Mon. Rufinus, *History of the Monks in Egypt* **(Latin)**
Flugel, Eva Schulz, ed. *Tyrannius Rufinus, Historia Monachorum Sive de Vita Sanctorum Patrum.* New York: Walter de Gruyter, 1990.
Translation:
Russell, Norman, and Benedicta Ward. *The Lives of the Desert Fathers: The Historia Monachorum in Aegypto.* Kalamazoo, MI: Cistercian Publications, 1980.

Vita Pach. Gr.1, *The First Greek Life of Pachomius*
Halkin, F., ed. *Sancti Pachomii Vitae Graeca.* Subsidia hagiographica 19. Brussels, 1932.
Translation:
Veilleux, Armand, trans. *Pachomian Koinonia,* vol. 1, *The Life of Saint Pachomius and his Disciples.* Kalamazoo, MI: Cistercian Publications, 1980.

Secondary Sources

Bartelink, G. J. M. "Les Apophtegmes des Pères: A propos de deux études récentes." *Vigiliae Christianae* 47, no. 4 (1993): 390–97.
Burton-Christie, Douglas. *The Word in the Desert: Scripture and the Quest for Holiness in Early Christian Monasticism.* New York: Oxford University Press, 1993.

Chitty, Derwas. "The Books of the Old Men." *Eastern Churches Review* 6 (1974): 15–21.

Gould, Graham. "The Collection of *Apophthegmata Patrum* in *Palladii Lausiaca* 20 (PL 74, 377–82)." *Studia Patristica* 45:27–33. Leuven: Peeters, 2010.

———. *The Desert Fathers on Monastic Community*. Oxford: Clarendon Press, 1993.

Guy, Jean-Claude. *Recherches sur la tradition grecques des Apophthegmata Patrum*. Brussels: Société des Bollandistes, 1962.

Haines-Eitzen, Kim. *Guardians of Letters: Literacy, Power, and the Transmitters of Early Christian Literature*. New York: Oxford University Press, 2000.

Harmless, William. *Desert Christians: An Introduction to the Literature of Early Monasticism*. Oxford: Oxford University Press, 2004.

———. "Remembering Poemen Remembering: The Desert Fathers and the Spirituality of Memory." *Church History* 69, no. 3 (2000): 483–518.

Jordan, Mark, and Kent Emery, eds. *Ad litteram: Authoritative Texts and Their Medieval Readers*. Notre Dame, IN: University of Notre Dame Press, 1992.

Mantello, Frank, and A. G. Rigg, eds. *Medieval Latin: An Introduction and Bibliographical Guide*. Washington, DC: Catholic University of America Press, 1996.

Ponesse, Matthew. "Standing Distant from the Fathers: Smaragdus of Saint-Mihiel and the Reception of Early Medieval Learning." *Traditio* 67 (2012): 71–99.

Rubenson, Samuel. "The Formation and Reformation of the Sayings of the Desert Fathers." *Studia Patristica* 55:5–22. Leuven: Peeters, 2013.

———. *The Letters of St. Anthony: Origenist Theology, Monastic Tradition and the Making of a Saint*. Lund, Sweden: Lund University Press, 1990.

INDEXES

Subject

abstinence, AP-CSP 1.1, 1.2, 1.3, 1.4, 1.9, 1.12, 1.15, 1.16; AP-PJ 21.18; AP-PA 5.2; against revealing practices, AP-CSP 1.7; AP-PA 5.1
acedia, AP-PA 32.1, 32.4, 32.5, 32.6
actress, AP-PA 54.4
advice, different for individual monks, AP-PA 72.4
agape, AP-PA 65.1; proper respect for, AP-PA 3.6, 65.2
angels, care for sick monks, AP-PA 51.3; guardian, AP-PJ 20.18; AP-PA 56.3; monitor conversations, AP-CSP 5.9; AP-PJ 18.23; on the side of monks, AP-PJ 20.2; AP-PA 93.11; smell sins, AP-PJ 20.18; visions of, AP-PA 70.1; AP-Pa 44.5
anger, AP-PA 20.1, 24.6, 28.3, 29.3, 34.6; against sins, AP-Pa 44.1; avoiding, AP-PA 26.1; AP-Pa 37.1, 37.2, 37.4, 42.2
arguments, avoiding, AP-PA 29.1, 87.1
animals, monks living as, AP-PJ 20.4, 20.10
ascetic disciplines, downplayed, AP-PJ 20.5, 50.2; to be performed in secret, AP-CSP 1.7; AP-PA 5.1, 6.1, 6.2; value of, AP-PJ 21.5
attitude, controls value of work, AP-PA 98.1
authority, commanding others, AP-PA 42.3

baptism, AP-PJ 18.29
basilisk, AP-PA 68.3
bearing with the weak, AP-PA 15.2
Bible, reading will repel demons, AP-CSP 6.5; AP-PA 10.2, 10.4; softens hard hearts, AP-PA 81.1; sold to provide money for the hungry, AP-PA 14.5, 14.6; teaching about is dangerous, AP-PA 84.2, 100.3
blessing, people seeking from the elders, AP-PA 33.13, 35.1
blindness, a blessing, AP-PR 218

cell, AP-CSP 6.3; AP-PJ 21.31; AP-PA 32.2, 32.3, 32.4, 32.6, 32.7, 93.2; the place where the monk speaks with God, AP-PJ 21.33
charity, AP-PA 5.2, 27.2, 36.3, 44.1, 44.2, 44.3, 49.6, 52.5; AP-Pa 37.3, 44.7; AP-PR 201; bearing another's sins, AP-PA 46.8; caution against being too charitable, AP-PA 2.3; more important than fasting, AP-PA 2.1; offering freely, AP-PA 17.1; receiving AP-PA 14.8
clothing, AP-PA 19.1; fine clothing leads to pollution, AP-PA 9.1; vile and disgusting, AP-CSP 6.1; AP-PA 19.2
community, models for living together, AP-PA 96.4; AP-PR 200

confidence, AP-PA 96.1, 96.2
conflict, AP-PA 28.3
consolation, of God better than family, AP-PJ 18.32
conversation, a battleground between angels and demons, AP-CSP 5.9; AP-PJ 18.23
criticism, avoiding, AP-PJ 21.10; AP-PA 3.5, 40.2, 41.2, 41.4; responding to, AP-PA 21.3, 25.4, 27.1; self-criticism, AP-PA 40.1
cucumber. AP-PA 3.2, 3.3
curiosity, avoiding, AP-PA 85.1, 86.1; not satisfying about others, AP-PA 85.2

David, king, AP-PJ 20.13
dead, child raised from, AP-PJ 19.13; AP-PA 35.1; speaking with, AP-PJ 19.8, 19.9; AP-PR 41
death, AP-PJ 18.32, 20.6; AP-PA 24.3, 52.1–5; the dead sleep until the resurrection, AP-PJ 19.8, 19.9; meditation upon as spiritual discipline, AP-PJ 21.22; souls taken from the body, AP-PJ 20.13, 20.14
decline, of the monks, AP-PJ 18.34, 19.5; AP-PA 95.3
deferring the work of a monk (not), AP-CSP 1.6; AP-PA 55.2
demons, expelled, AP-PJ 19.4, 19.16; AP-PA 35.3; attacking monks, AP-CSP 2.1, 2.2, 2.3, 2.4, 2.5, 4.2; AP-PJ 20.2, 21.37; AP-PA 8.1, 10.4, 31.4, 31.5, 36.2, 56.3, 73.4, 93.11; AP-Pa 44.8; AP-PR 43 conversations of overheard, AP-CSP 2.8; do not tempt those who do their own will, AP-PA 71.3, 71.4; expelled by humility, AP-CSP 4.2; AP-PA 36.2; expelled by the power of the Scriptures, AP-CSP 6.5; AP-PA 10.2; in the form of bees, AP-PJ 18.31; in the form of pigs, AP-CSP 5.9; AP-PJ 18.23; offering visions, AP-PA 70.2; used as messengers, AP-PJ 19.12; AP-PA 64.1; war against, AP-CSP 5.8; AP-PJ 21.14; weapons against, AP-PJ 18.30; AP-PA 71.1; AP-Pa 44.8
depression, overcoming, AP-PA 31.2
desert, advantages of, AP-CSP 1.4; AP-PA 93.1
desires, dangers of, AP-PJ 21.25, 92.1; mastering, AP-PJ 21.20, 21.21, 21.27; AP-PA 10.4, 11.1, 11.2, 31.4, 31.7, 32.1, 32.2, 33.9; produced by overeating, AP-PA 11.3
disaster, predicted for Scetis, AP-PJ 18.25
discretion, AP-CSP 1.11; AP-PA 2.4, 5.1, 19.1, 74.1, 74.2, 75.1, 85.1
disputes, avoiding, AP-PA 89.2
distractions, avoiding, AP-PA 67.1
doing unto others, AP-PA 46.7, 47.1, 47.3, 47.4

education, AP-CSP 6.3; AP-PA 83.1, 83.2, 84.1
Egyptian monasticism, superiority of, AP-CSP 6.3; AP-PA 33.3
Elisha, Prophet, AP-PJ 18.27; AP-Pa 37.4
encouragement, AP-PA 41.10
envy, AP-PA 27.1, 27.2
Eucharist, reveals sins of congregation, AP-PJ 18.36; women and men receive it separately, AP-PJ 18.36
evil, deeds will not be overlooked, AP-PJ 18.24; intended as corrective for sins, AP-PA

23.1; not returning, AP-PJ 21.11; AP-PA 21.1; returning good for, AP-PA 22.1, 22.3

faith, AP-PA 45.1; AP-Pa 44.7
false accusations, AP-PA 30.1
family, relationships with, AP-CSP 4.4, 5.3, 5.4, 5.5, 5.6, 5.7; AP-PA 49.1–6, 49.7
fasting, AP-CSP 1.3, 1.5, 2.3; AP-PA 1.4, 2.1, 10.1, 13.1, 14.11, 50.1, 50.2; AP-Pa 21.3
fear of the Lord, AP-PA 53.1, 53.2, 53.3; AP-Pa 21.3, 21.4
fire, divine, AP-Pa 39.3; AP-PR 204
flight, from humans, AP-PA 93.2, 93.4
food, bread, salt, and water, AP-PA 1.1, 1.2; cooked before mass, AP-PJ 21.31; forgetting AP-PA 4.1
foresight, AP-PJ 18.22
forgetfulness, AP-PA 73.8
forgiveness, AP-PA 21.2; of God, AP-PJ 20.12, 21.30; AP-PA 31.3, 34.7
fornication, AP-PJ 21.20; AP-CSP 2.6, 2.8; temptation from the demon of, AP-CSP 2.1, 2.2, 2.3, 2.4, 2.5, 2.7, 2.8, 2.9, 2.10

Gabriel, archangel, AP-PJ 20.13
gluttony, AP-CSP 1.3, 1.5, 1.8; AP-PA 2.4, 3.1, 3.2, 3.4, 3.6, 3.7, 9.1, 11.3, 11.4
good, versus evil, AP-Pa 40.1
Good Samaritan, emulating, AP-PA 50.4
grace (of God), as an aid to overcoming temptation, AP-CSP 2.1, 2.5; as a corrective for sin, AP-PJ 18.36; AP-PA 56.2; comes upon the monk unexpectedly, AP-PA 80.1; linked to charity, AP-PA 79.1; linked to work, AP-PA 78.2
guidelines, for the monastic life, AP-PA 1.3, 101.1; AP-Pa 43.2, 44.1–12

harm, as a corrective, AP-PR 220; done to us by others, AP-PA 21.2, 21.3, 22.1, 22.2, 22.3
harmony, in living together, AP-PA 29.1, 29.2
healing, AP-PJ 19.7, 19.10, 20.11; AP-PA 35.4, 49.5, 95.2
Heaven, AP-CSP 3.1; AP-PJ 18.35
Hell, layers of, AP-PJ 20.16; AP-PA 69.1; perils of, AP-PJ 18.35, 18.42; AP-Pa 44.12
heresy, AP-CSP 4.7
hermits, eaten by wild animals, AP-PJ 18.33; must be properly trained AP-Pa 19.6; not the best lifestyle for some monks, AP-PA 73.2
Hezekiah, king, AP-Pa 38.1
hospitality, AP-PA 46.4, 46.6
humans, avoiding, AP-PJ 20.10
humility, AP-CSP 4.2, 4.5, 4.8, 4.9, 4.16, 4.18, 4.19, 6.3; AP-PJ 19.13, 20.3, 20.5, 21.12; AP-PA 24.4, 25.2, 25.3, 27.1, 31.5, 33.12, 33.13, 34.1–7, 35.1, 35.6, 36.4, 37.1, 38.1, 39.2, 39.4, 39.5, 39.6, 39.7, 46.1, 46.3, 83.1, 96.1, 100.3, 100.5; AP-Pa 21.3; a defense against satanic traps, AP-PA 39.2; guarding, AP-CSP 4.3, 4.4; overcomes demons, AP-CSP 4.2; AP-PA 36.1, 36.2; a precondition for developing charity, AP-PA 36.3
hyena, AP-PA 43.2
hypocrisy, AP-PJ 21.28

illness, care of the sick, AP-CSP 4.10, 4.12; AP-PA 42.2, 50.2, 50.4, 51.1; AP-Pa 19.3; AP-PR 42; a spiritual discipline, AP-PA 51.2
inheritances, AP-PA 14.3; AP-Pa 36.4
inner desert, AP-PJ 20.11
insults and injuries, bearing, AP-CSP 4.19; AP-PJ 21.12; AP-PA 24.1, 24.2, 24.5, 25.1

Job, prophet, AP-PJ 21.29
John, the Baptist, AP-PA 36.3
Joseph, patriarch, AP-CSP 4.5; AP-PJ 21.29; AP-PA 31.1
Joshua, son of Nun, AP-PJ 19.5
judges, intervening with, AP-CSP 4.6; AP-PJ 21.32; AP-PA 49.4, 92.3
judgment, of others brings similar temptations on ourselves, AP-PA 41.12; refusal to condemn others AP-PJ 21.1, 21.3, 21.7, 21.10, 21.34, 21.36; AP-PA 41.1, 41.3, 41.4, 41.6, 41.7, 41.8, 41.9, 41.10, 41.11, 48.1; of self leads to spiritual progress, AP-Pa 22.2, 39.3, 39.6, 39.7, 39.9
Julian, emperor, AP-PJ 19.12; AP-PA 64.1

kindness, leads to conversion, AP-PA 37.1

Last Judgment, AP-PA 31.6, 52.3, 57.3; AP-PR 205
laughing, AP-PA 52.1, 54.2, 65.2
Lazarus, beggar, AP-PA 16.1
leisure, produces suffering, AP-PA 9.1
lions, AP-CSP 4.13; AP-PJ 19.15; AP-PA 13.1
lust, AP-CSP 2.5

luxurious food, avoiding, AP-CSP 1.9, 1.10

manual labor, a defense against temptation, AP-CSP 2.9, 2.10; produces humility, AP-PA 39.5
Mary Magdalene, AP-PJ 21.27; AP-Pa 38.1
Mazices, AP-PA 96.4
Melchizedek, AP-PA 100.3
Michael, archangel, AP-PJ 20.13
miracles, AP-PJ 19.1; AP-PA 68.3, 68.4; control of natural elements, AP-CSP 4.14; AP-PJ 19.17; divine transport across great distances, AP-PJ 19.6; AP-PA 62.1, 68.1; freezing the sun in place, AP-PJ 19.3, 19.5; inadvertent, AP-PJ 19.4, 19.7, 19.13; AP-PA 35.1, 35.3, 35.4; raising the dead, AP-PA 43.3, 80.1; reluctance to perform, AP-PA 49.5; speaking with the dead, AP-PJ 19.8, 19.9; AP-PA 35.5; AP-PR 41; stopping the sun, AP-PJ 19.3, 19.5; walking on water, AP-PJ 19.2
monastery, advice for leading, AP-Pa 43.1; expulsion from, AP-CSP 6.6; rules for living in, AP-PA 96.3
money, forgiving debts, AP-PA 18.2; hoarding, AP-PR 219; no concern for, AP-PA 18.3; unnecessary for a monk, AP-PA 14.4
mortification, AP-PA 76.1, 76.2, 76.5
Moses, AP-PJ 20.11, 21.33
murder, AP-PJ 21.37, AP-PR 41

nature, reveals God, AP-PJ 21.16; AP-PA 84.3
ninth hour, as time to eat, AP-PA 7.1, 10.4, 93.11, 96.4

obedience, AP-CSP 4.13; AP-PA 42.1, 42.2, 42.5, 42.6, 43.2, 46.1, 46.3, 72.8; better than religiosity, AP-PA 43.3, 46.5; commands based in God's will must be obeyed, AP-PA 42.3
odor, pleasant when God is present, AP-PJ 20.6; AP-PA 52.4; sinful souls smell bad, AP-PJ 20.18
ordination, forced, AP-CSP 4.8; AP-PA 90.3; resistance to, AP-PA 30.1, 90.1, 90.2
overconfidence, AP-PA 33.8

passions, AP-PA 9.2, 72.3, 72.4, 72.6
peace, AP-PA 76.4, 92.2; maintained through silence, AP-PA 87.1, 88.2
penitence, AP-PA 55.1
perseverance, AP-CSP 1.6; AP-PA 32.1, 32.3, 77.1, 77.2, 77.3; AP-Pa 27.2; against thoughts, AP-PA 31.7, 33.9; AP-Pa 41.1; in the face of demonic temptation, AP-CSP 2.1, 2.2, 2.3, 2.4, 2.7; AP-PA 31.6; in trying circumstances, AP-PA 50.3, 51.1
Peter, apostle, AP-CSP 4.7; AP-Pa 38.1
philosophers, AP-PJ 21.12, 21.16; AP-PA 24.1, 84.3
pigs, AP-CSP 4.18; AP-PJ 18.28; demons in the form of, AP-CSP 5.9; AP-PJ 18.23
pilgrimage, AP-PA 89.3, 89.1; AP-Pa 32.4
pleasing God, AP-PA 54.4
possessions, AP-PJ 21.24; AP-PA 14.10, 18.1; giving away, AP-PJ 21.23; AP-PA 14.5, 14.6, 14.13, 15.1; owning nothing, AP-PA 89.4

poverty, value of, AP-PJ 21.23; AP-PA 14.7; AP-Pa 38.2
practices, evil, AP-PA 99.1
praise, heavenly vs. worldly, AP-PA 33.4, 33.5, 33.6, 39.1; indifference to, AP-PA 100.2; AP-Pa 42.2
praxis, life in the cell, AP-PA 1.3
prayer, antidote to thoughts and temptations, AP-PJ 19.14; AP-PA 10.1, 58.3, 58.4, 68.2; on behalf of others, AP-PA 42.4; on behalf of relatives, AP-CSP 5.1; better than food, AP-CSP 1.13; brings relief to those in Hell, AP-PJ 20.16, 69.1; a difficult discipline, AP-PA 61.1; essential before work, AP-PJ 21.4; persistence in, AP-PA 58.2, 68.2; possible while eating, AP-PA 65.1; practice of, AP-PA 33.11, 58.1, 64.2; AP-Pa 44.3, 44.4; preferable to work, AP-PA 59.1; without ceasing, AP-PA 63.1, 63.2, 66.1
pride, AP-PA 33.6, 73.1, 99.2; AP-Pa 13.4
prostitution, AP-PJ 21.13; AP-PA 55.6, 57.2, 57.4
providential care, AP-PJ 19.1; AP-PA 68.4
punishment, more severe in Hell for those who reject God, AP-PA 69.1
purity, AP-PJ 19.11

reconciliation, AP-PA 28.1, 28.2
reflection, on deeds of the day, AP-PA 55.3
relatives, separating from, AP-CSP 5.1, 5.2, 5.4, 5.5, 5.6, 5.7
renunciation, AP-PJ 21.2; AP-PA 14.1, 14.2, 14.2, 14.4, 14.10

repentance, AP-PJ 20.6; AP-PA 15.2, 31.6, 55.1, 55.2, 55.4, 56.1, 56.2, 56.3, 57.2, 57.3, 57.4; even the plan to repent is acceptable to God, AP-PA 57.1; for failure during persecution, AP-PJ 20.12; God accepts, AP-PJ 21.30; AP-PA 55.5; should be accomplished before it is too late, AP-PJ 20.14

reputation, scorning, AP-CSP 4.6; AP-PJ 21.32, 21.35; AP-PA 33.13, 33.14, 33.15, 92.3

revealing, practices to elders, AP-PJ 21.15

rewards, heavenly vs. earthly, AP-PJ 18.33

righteousness, AP-PJ 18.26

sacraments, do not depend on worthiness of priest, AP-PA 41.1

salvation, attaining, AP-PA 32.1, 32.8, 63.1, 93.3

Saracens, attacking monks, AP-PR 200

Satan, war against monks, AP-PA 3.6, 71.2

Scetis, AP-PJ 20.15; devastation of, AP-PJ 18.25; AP-PA 96.4

secular vs. monastic models of life, AP-PJ 18.33, 20.3, 20.5; AP-PA 29.2, 34.5, 39.3

self-accusation, AP-PA 33.7; AP-Pa 22.2

self-aggrandizement (against), AP-PA 31.4, 70.1

self-control, AP-CSP 1.5, 1.9, 1.15; AP-PA 3.4, 3.6, 26.1, 26.2, 93.2, 96.4; AP-Pa 37.3; AP-PR 201

self-justification, resisting, AP-PA 21.3

service, offered to the infirm, AP-CSP 4.10; AP-PA 50.3, 50.4

sex, AP-PJ 20.11, 21.15

Shunammite woman, AP-PJ 18.27; AP-Pa 37.4

silence, AP-PA 25.4, 88.1, 88.3, 88.4, 88.6, 88.7, 88.8, 94.1, 100.1; better than praise, AP-PA 87.2; better than speech, AP-PA 88.2, 88.5, 88.1; equated to pilgrimage, AP-Pa 32.4; essential for pilgrimage, AP-PA 89.1; more than not speaking, AP-PA 88.9; preferred to curiosity, AP-PA 86.1, 86.2; to protect the spirit, AP-CSP 5.9

sins, acknowledging, AP-PJ 21.3; AP-PA 39.8; avoiding, AP-PA 47.2; burden of, AP-PA 99.2

slander, repaying with good, AP-PA 22.3

slaves, former as monks, AP-CSP 4.1

sleep, an abundance produces suffering, AP-PA 9.1; as an ascetic discipline, AP-PA 64.2

solitude, AP-PA 93.5, 93.8, 93.9; not a certain antidote for spiritual struggles, AP-PA 29.3, 73.2

speech, control of, AP-PJ 20.7, 20.8; AP-PA 26.1, 26.2, 26.3, 26.4, 93.2

spiritual direction, AP-Pa 43.1

spiritual progress, AP-PA 73.7, 95.1

stability, AP-PA 97.1

steadfastness, AP-CSP 4.14; AP-PJ 21.29; AP-PA 31.1, 32.1

strife, avoiding, AP-PA 100.4

suffering (deprivation/tribulation) to thwart perils of Hell, AP-CSP 6.4; AP-PJ 21.17; AP-PA 14.7

sun, stopped in the sky by a monk's prayer, AP-PJ 19.3, 19.5

Taisis, prostitute, AP-PA 57.4
Tartar, rips souls out of bodies, AP-PJ 20.13
teachers, must practice what they teach, AP-PA 81.2, 81.4; must speak briefly, AP-PA 100.6; must understand what they teach, AP-PJ 21.26, 21.28; AP-PA 81.3, 95.2; AP-Pa 19.6
temptations, AP-PR 203; a danger until death, AP-PA 33.8; overcoming through abuse, AP-PR 220; resisting, AP-PJ 21.9, 21.13; AP-PA 47.2, 55.6; resisting through prayer, AP-PJ 19.14, 21.6; AP-PA 43.1, 58.4, 68.2
tepid monks, AP-PJ 21.11; AP-PA 21.1; AP-PR 204
thankfulness, AP-PJ 18.37
theft, AP-CSP 1.14; AP-PA 3.3; tolerating for the good of the thief, AP-CSP 4.17; AP-PA 15.1, 15.2
theodicy, AP-PJ 18.33, 18.35, 18.41; AP-PA 23.1
Theodosius, emperor, AP-CSP 4.3
Theophilus, archbishop of Alexandria, AP-PA 12.1, 93.8, 93.9
thief, AP-CSP 6.6
thoughts, driven away by prayer and fasting, AP-PA 10.1; driven away by recollection of death, AP-PA 10.3; rejecting evil, AP-PA 72.1, 72.2, 72.3, 72.5, 72.7; revealing thoughts to elders, AP-CSP 2.2; AP-PA 8.1, 33.3, 73.1, 73.2, 73.3, 73.4, 73.5, 73.6

tongue, control of, AP-PJ 20.7, 20.8; AP-PA 26.1, 26.2, 26.3, 26.4, 93.2
training, by example, AP-PA 82.1

unconventional models of holiness/ vocations, AP-CSP 4.1; AP-PJ 20.3, 20.4, 20.17; AP-PA 29.2, 39.3; AP-PR 205

vainglory, AP-PA 14.9, 33.3, 33.6, 33.10, 33.11, 35.2, 95.2; resisting, AP-PA 31.4, 33.1, 33.2, 33.4, 33.7, 33.12, 33.13, 33.14, 33.15
vengeance, to be left to God, AP-PA 21.2
vigilance, AP-PA 9.3
vigils, AP-PA 36.1, 64.2
visions, AP-PA 72.8; of demons, AP-PJ 18.31; of heaven, AP-PJ 18.21; of heaven and hell, AP-Pa 19.4; AP-PR 205; of heavenly visitors, AP-PA 62.1, 70.1; offered by demons, AP-PA 70.2; of the spiritual condition of humans, AP-PJ 18.36; AP-PA 56.2, 99.2
visitors, receiving, AP-CSP 1.16; reluctance to receive, AP-PA 46.6, 93.5, 93.6, 93.8, 93.9
vocation, abandoning, AP-PA 41.5
vows, daily of the monk, AP-Pa 44.2

wealth, AP-PA 14.2, 14.3
weeping, AP-PJ 21.27; AP-PA 52.5, 54.1, 54.2, 54.3; AP-Pa 38.1
will, subordinating to another, AP-PA 42.2, 46.1, 46.2, 46.3, 46.4
wine, AP-PJ 19.16; AP-PA 3.6, 5.2, 27.2, 40.2, 46.5
wolf, as divine guide, AP-PJ 20.13

women, a danger to monks, AP-PJ 21.19; AP-PA 12.1; living as ascetics, AP-PJ 20.1, 20.9, 20.17; AP-PA 29.2, 93.10; saved from life of prostitution, AP-PA 57.2

work, an antidote against the devil, AP-PA 76.3; for the good of the soul, AP-PA 45.3; frees a person from thinking of the world, AP-PA 78.3; futile when a monk is mired in sin, AP-CSP 6.2; AP-PA 99.2; good work, AP-PA 89.3; leads to grace, AP-PA 78.2; leads to prayer, AP-PA 60.1; a means of attaining Christ, AP-PA 32.5, 78.1; necessary to support a monk, AP-PA 7.1, 7.2, 66.1; of the spirit vs. the hands, AP-PA 45.2

world, rejection of, AP-PJ 20.15; AP-PA 93.3; AP-PR 206

wrongs, enduring as a spiritual discipline, AP-CSP 4.16, 4.17; AP-PJ 21.12, 23.2, 24.1, 24.2, 25.4, 27.1, 30.1; AP-PR 220

Stories by Named Monk

Abraham, AP-PJ 19.14; AP-PA 3.6, 33.9, 68.2, 71.3
Achila, AP-PA 32.2, 32.4
Achilles, AP-PA 26.2, 60.1, 71.4
Agathon, AP-PJ 19.5; AP-PA 14.9, 14.13, 18.3, 19.1, 25.2, 28.3, 50.4, 52.3, 59.1, 61.1, 88.1, 96.1, 96.2; AP-Pa 42.2,
Aio, AP-CSP 4.8; AP-PA 93.2
Alonius, AP-PA 100.2
Ammonas [Ammoes, Ammon], AP-PA 24.5, 50.3, 60.1, 68.3, 91.1
Anoub [Nub, Nuph], AP-PA 49.1, 96.4
Anthony, AP-CSP 5.1, 5.2; AP-PJ 21.11, 21.16; AP-PA 14.2, 21.1, 24.5, 25.1, 32.1, 32.2, 32.7, 32.8, 39.1, 39.2, 39.3, 41.8, 41.9, 57.4, 70.3, 73.1, 77.1, 84.3, 88.6, 88.8, 93.1, 95.2, 100.5; AP-Pa 19.3, 19.4, 38.1, 40.1; AP-PR 218
Apollo, AP-CSP 5.6; AP-PA 45.3
Arsenius, AP-CSP 6.1–6; AP-PA 3.4, 12.1, 14.3, 14.8, 19.2, 32.3, 38.1, 42.4, 46.6, 52.5, 64.2, 83.1, 83.2, 84.1, 88.5, 89.2, 93.3–9, 94.1, 99.2
Athanasius, AP-CSP 4.17
Athanasius, bishop of Alexandria, AP-PA 54.4

Benjamin, AP-CSP 1.9, 1.10
Bessarion, AP-PJ 19.1–4, 20.1; AP-PA 35.3, 35.4, 68.4, 93.10

Copres, AP-PA 100.3
Cronius, AP-PA 82.1; AP-Pa 19.3–5

Daniel, disciple of Arsenius, AP-CSP 6.2, 6.4, 6.6; AP-PA 42.4, 64.2
Didymus, the Blind, AP-PR 218
Dioscorus, AP-CSP 1.15
Doulas, disciple of Bessarion, AP-PJ 19.1–4, 20.1; AP-PA 68.4

Elias, AP-PJ 19.5; AP-PA 11.3, 11.4, 28.2

Emilis [Milesius], AP-PJ 19.9
Eucharistius, AP-PJ 20.3
Eulalius, AP-CSP 4.16
Eulogius, AP-PA 5.1; AP-Pa 19.3
Evagrius, AP-PA 83.2, 88.3, 88.4

Hierax, AP-Pa 19.5
Hyperechius, AP-PA 40.2

Isaac, AP-PA 47.2, 75.1, 82.1
Isaac, priest of Cells, AP-CSP 4.8; AP-PA 26.1, 90.2
Isaac of Thebes, AP-PA 41.6
Isaiah, AP-PA 65.1
Ischyrion, AP-PJ 18.34; AP-PA 95.3
Isidore, AP-CSP 2.4; AP-PA 31.4, 39.8; AP-PR 219
Isidore of Scetis, AP-PJ 21.20, 21.21

Jacob, AP-PA 44.3
John, disciple of Abba Paul, AP-CSP 4.13; AP-PA 43.2
John of Calamus, AP-CSP 5.3
John of Thebes, disciple of Ammonas, AP-PA 50.3
John the Dwarf, AP-CSP 1.2, 1.3; AP-PJ 21.10, 21.12, 21.13; AP-PA 7.2, 24.1, 27.1, 41.2, 55.6, 58.3, 58.4, 65.2, 73.8, AP-Pa 37.2
John the Persian, AP-PA 44.3
Joseph, AP-PA 49.5, 72.6, 100.5
Joseph of Panephysis, AP-CSP 1.16; AP-PA 2.2, 5.1, 72.4

Lucius, AP-PA 66.1

Macarius, bishop of Cyprus, AP-PA 63.2
Macarius of Alexandria, AP-PJ 20.15
Macarius the Great, AP-CSP 3.1; AP-PJ 19.6, 19.7, 19.8, 20.2, 20.4, 20.15, 20.16, 20.17, 21.17, 21.34; AP-PA 5.2, 10.4, 14.5, 15.1, 24.6, 29.2, 30.1, 33.2, 35.5, 35.6, 36.1, 37.1, 58.1, 58.2, 68.1, 69.1, 93.2, 93.11, 96.2; AP-Pa 37.4, 38.2; AP-PR 41, 42, 43, 219
Mark, AP-PA 93.4
Mark, disciple of Silvanus, AP-PA 42.5, 42.6, 49.2
Martin, AP-CSP 5.4
Mary, wife of Eucharistius, AP-PJ 20.3
Matoes [Motoes], AP-PA 34.4, 34.5, 34.6, 34.7
Megethios, AP-PA 89.4
Moses, AP-CSP 2.4; AP-PJ 21.1–7; AP-PA 9.1, 9.2, 13.1, 24.4, 25.3, 25.4, 31.5, 32.7, 33.13, 46.6, 71.3, 76.1, 76.2, 95.1, 101.1; AP-Pa 43.2
Motoes, AP-PA 28.1, 77.2, 90.3, 92.2

Nesteros, AP-PA 35.2, 96.3
Niteras, AP-CSP 1.12

Or, AP-PJ 20.7, 20.8; AP-PA 47.4
Orsisius, AP-PA 31.1

Pachomius, AP-CSP 5.7, 5.8
Pambo [Pammon, Piamon], AP-PA 1.3, 52.2, 53.1, 54.4, 87.2; AP-PR 219
Paphnutius, AP-PA 41.9, 46.5, 57.4
Paul, AP-CSP 4.13; AP-PJ 19.11; AP-PA 43.2
Paul, disciple of Or, AP-PA 47.4
Paul the Great [Galatian], AP-PA 14.10, 14.11, 57.4
Paul the Simple, AP-PA 56.3
Peter, AP-CSP 4.14
Pior, AP-CSP 5.2; AP-PA 41.3
Poemen [Pastor, Pimenius], AP-CSP 1.8, 4.3, 4.4, 4.5, 4.6, 6.5; AP-PJ 19.10, 21.9, 21.14, 21.15, 21.32, 21.36; AP-PA 1.4, 3.7, 8.1, 9.3,

11.2, 22.1. 23.2, 27.2, 31.2, 31.3, 31.4, 33.1, 39.6, 39.8, 39.9, 40.1, 41.7, 41.10, 45.1, 46.1, 46.2, 46.3, 46.7, 49.1, 49.4, 49.5, 53.3, 54.3, 55.1, 55.4, 57.1, 71.3, 72.4, 73.3, 73.5, 74.2, 75.1, 81.1, 81.4, 81.5, 85.1, 88.9, 92.1, 92.3, 96.3, 96.4, 98.1, 99.1, 100.4, 101.1; AP-Pa 22.2, 37.3, 39.3; AP-PR 201
Publius, AP-PJ 19.12; AP-PA 64.1

Sarah, AP-PA 80.2
Serapion, AP-Pa 43.1
Silvanus, AP-PJ 18.21; AP-PA 2.1, 7.1, 18.1, 42.5, 42.6, 49.2, 67.1, 72.7; AP-Pa 43.2; AP-PR 205
Simeon, AP-PA 33.14, 33.15
Sisoes [Tithoes], AP-PJ 19.8, 19.13, 19.14, 20.5, 20.6; AP-PA 1.1, 1.2, 3.6, 4.1, 21.2, 23.1, 31.6, 33.11, 35.1, 39.4, 39.5, 48.1, 49.6, 52.4, 56.1, 68.2, 71.2, 72.6, 88.7; AP-Pa 36.4, 37.1
Syncletica, AP-PJ 18.22, 21.23, 21.24

Theodore, AP-CSP 5.7; AP-PA 45.2, 47.3, 82.1, 85.2, 90.1
Theodore of Pherme, AP-PA 6.1, 6.2, 14.5, 36.4, 41.5
Timothy, AP-PA 41.12

Vindemius, AP-PJ 20.2

Xanthias, VP-PJ 19.16

Zacharias, disciple of Moses, AP-PA 24.4
Zacharias, disciple of Silvanus, AP-PJ 18.21; AP-PA 2.1, 7.1, 18.1, 67.1
Zeno, AP-CSP 1.14; AP-PA 3.3, 33.3, 62.1

Scriptural Citations and Allusions

OLD TESTAMENT

Exod 12:30, AP-PJ 21.7
Num 25, AP-PA 10.2
Deut 32:7, AP-PA 73.1
Josh 10:13, AP-PJ 19.5
1 Sam 17:34–6, AP-CSP 2.10
2 Kgs 4.8–17, AP-PJ 18.27
2 Kgs 6:16, AP-CSP 2.4
2 Kgs 25:9, AP-CSP 1.8; AP-PA 3.7
Ezra 9:10–12, AP-CSP 5.7
Job 1:21, AP-PA 15.1
Job 40.5, AP-PA 88.4
Ps 2:3, AP-Pa 44.1
Ps 16:8, AP-Pa 44.10
Ps 18:37, AP-CSP 5.8
Ps 19:1, AP-Pa 44.9
Ps 21:5, AP-PA 78.2
Ps 22:6, AP-Pa 43.2
Ps 25:18, AP-PJ 21.5
Ps 27:14, AP-CSP 2.2
Ps 31.24, AP-CSP 2.2
Ps 38:13–14, AP-CSP 4.19
Ps 42:3, AP-Pa 44.12
Ps 46:1, AP-PJ 21.4
Ps 46:8, AP-PA 56.3
Ps 50:15, AP-Pa 41.1
Ps 50:16, AP-PJ 21.26
Ps 51.1, AP-CSP 4.14; AP-PA 66.1
Ps 51:17, AP-PA 101.1

Ps 53:5, AP-Pa 43.2
Ps 63:8, AP-CSP 4.19
Ps 66:18, AP-Pa 40.1
Ps 73:22–23, AP-PA 96.3;
   AP-Pa 40.1
Ps 83:1, AP-PR 43
Ps 88:3, AP-PR 43
Ps 92:12, AP-PJ 18.26
Ps 104:24, AP-PA 56.3
Ps 105:19, AP-PA 31.1
Ps 108:1, AP-Pa 44.5
Ps 118:6, AP-PJ 21.6
Ps 118.7, AP-PR 203
Ps 119:106, AP-PA 56.3
Ps 128:2, AP-CSP 1.14
Prov 10:19, AP-CSP 5.9
Prov 18:13, AP-PA 100.1
Prov 25:7–8, AP-PJ 21.36
Isa 1:16–19, AP-PA 56.3
Isa 3:12, AP-PA 22.2
Isa 6:5, AP-PA 34.4
Isa 26:18, AP-Pa 43.2
Isa 59:1, AP-CSP 2.2
Dan 3:19–25, AP-CSP 6.3
Dan 10:3, AP-CSP 1.3; AP-PA 1.2
Amos 1:9, AP-PJ 18.24
Hab 2:11, AP-Pa 43.2

NEW TESTAMENT

Matt 5:39, AP-PJ 21.11, AP-PA 21.1
Matt 5:48, AP-Pa 44.4
Matt 6:2, 16, AP-CSP 4.19
Matt 6:34, AP-PJ 21.9
Matt 7:1, AP-PJ 21.7; AP-PA 101.1;
   AP-Pa 43.2
Matt 7:5, AP-PJ 21.28
Matt 10:16, AP-PJ 18.22
Matt 11:12, AP-PA 72.8
Matt 11:29, AP-CSP 4.19, 6.2;
   AP-Pa 44.4
Matt 12:24, AP-CSP 4.19
Matt 15:11, AP-Pa 40.1
Matt 19:21, AP-PA 14.6
Matt 22:37, AP-PA 101.1
Matt 22:39, AP-PA 101.1
Matt 24:45–46, AP-Pa 43.1
Matt 25:31–46, AP-CSP 4.11
Mark 10:43–44, AP-Pa 43.1
Luke 1:37, AP-CSP 2.6
Luke 4:18, AP-PJ 21.8
Luke 4:23, AP-PA 95.2
Luke 6:37, AP-PA 101.1
Luke 8:14, AP-Pa 43.2
Luke 10:42, AP-PA 7.1
Luke 16:19–31, AP-CSP 6.4
Luke 18:19, AP-PA 39.1
Luke 22:36, AP-PJ 21.14
John 2:15, AP-PJ 21.8
John 3:16, AP-PJ 18.36, AP-PA 56.2
John 6:27, AP-PA 7.1
John 8:48, AP-CSP 4.19
John 14:15, AP-Pa 43.1
John 15:13, AP-Pa 37.3;
   AP-PR 201
Acts 8:20, AP-PR 219
Acts 14:22, AP-CSP 2.2
Rom 5:8, AP-PJ 18.36,
   AP-PA 56.2
Rom 8:28, AP-CSP 5.2
Rom 15:1, AP-CSP 6.1
1 Cor 3:16, AP-CSP 1.8
1 Cor 9:27, AP-CSP 1.12
1 Cor 10:12, AP-PA 34.5
1 Cor 10:31, AP-PJ 18.37
2 Cor 11:27, AP-Pa 43.2
Gal 6:3, AP-Pa 43.2
Eph 5:3, AP-PA 9.2
Phil 2:4, AP-PR 42
Phil 2:12, AP-CSP 6.2
Col 3:3–4, AP-CSP 4.19
Col 4:2, AP-CSP 5.8

1 Thess 5:17, AP-PA 66.1
1 Tim 2:4, AP-PA 56.3
1 Tim 6:7, AP-PA 15.1
2 Tim 4:7–8, AP-CSP 2.1
Titus 1:15, AP-PA 39.6
Heb 4:12–13, AP-CSP 3.1
Heb 4:13, AP-CSP 3.1
Jas 1:19, AP-PA 88.2
Jas 1:22, AP-Pa 43.2

Jas 4:8, AP-PA 55.3
1 Pet 2:21, AP-CSP 4.7
1 Pet 3:9, AP-PA 101.1
1 Pet 5:2–4, AP-Pa 43.1
1 John 2:6, AP-CSP 4.19
1 John 3:16, AP-CSP 2.6
1 John 4:4, AP-CSP 2.4
Jude 9, AP-PR 43
Rev 3:11, AP-CSP 4.19

Ancient Christian Writers

1. The Epistles of St. Clement of Rome and St. Ignatius of Antioch
2. St. Augustine: The First Catechetical Instruction
3. St. Augustine: Faith, Hope and Charity
4. Julianus Pomerius: The Contemplative Life
5. St. Augustine: The Lord's Sermon on the Mount
6. The Didache, The Epistle of Barnabas, The Epistles and the Martyrdom of St. Polycarp, The Fragments of Papias, The Epistle to Diognetus
7. Arnobius of Sicca: The Case Against the Pagans, Vol. 1
8. Arnobius of Sicca: The Case Against the Pagans, Vol. 2
9. St. Augustine: The Greatness of the Soul, The Teacher
10. St. Athanasius: The Life of St. Antony
11. St. Gregory the Great, Pastoral Care
12. St. Augustine: Against the Academics
13. Tertullian: Treatises on Marriage and Remarriage: To His Wife, An Exhortation to Chastity, Monogamy
14. St. Prosper of Aquitaine: The Call of All Nations
15. St. Augustine: Sermons for Christmas and Epiphany
16. St. Irenaeus: Proof of the Apostolic Preaching
17. The Works of St. Patrick; St. Secundinus, Hymn on St. Patrick
18. St. Gregory of Nyssa: The Lord's Prayer, The Beatitudes
19. Origen: Prayer, Exhortation to Martyrdom
20. Rufinus: A Commentary on the Apostles' Creed
21. St. Maximus the Confessor: The Ascetic Life, The Four Centuries on Charity
22. St. Augustine: The Problem of Free Choice
23. Athenagoras: Embassy for the Christians, The Resurrection of the Dead
24. Tertullian: The Treatise against Hermogenes
25. St. Cyprian: The Lapsed, The Unity of the Catholic Church
26. Origen: The Song of Songs, Commentary and Homilies
27. St. Methodius: The Symposium: A Treatise on Chastity
28. Tertullian: Treatises on Penance: On Penitence and On Purity
29. St. Augustine on the Psalms, Vol. 1
30. St. Augustine on the Psalms, Vol. 2
31. St. John Chrysostom: Baptismal Instruction
32. St. Prosper of Aquitaine: Defense of St. Augustine
33. Letters of St. Jerome, Vol. 1
34. Palladius: The Lausiac History
35. Letters of St. Paulinus of Nola, Vol. 1
36. Letters of St. Paulinus of Nola, Vol. 2
37. Firmicus Maternus: The Error of the Pagan Religions
38. Egeria: Diary of a Pilgrimage
39. The Octavius of Marcus Minucius Felix
40. The Poems of St. Paulinus of Nola
41. St. Augustine: The Literal Meaning of Genesis, Vol. 1
42. St. Augustine, The Literal Meaning of Genesis, Vol. 2
43. The Letters of St. Cyprian of Carthage, Vol. 1

44. The Letters of St. Cyprian of Carthage, Vol. 2
45. Palladius: Dialogue on the Life of St. John Chrysostom
46. The Letters of St. Cyprian of Carthage, Vol. 3
47. The Letters of St. Cyprian of Carthage, Vol. 4
48. St. Augustine on Faith and Works
49. Theodoret of Cyrus: On Divine Providence
50. Sermons of St. Maximus of Turin
51. Cassiodorus: Explanation of the Psalms, Vol. 1
52. Cassiodorus: Explanation of the Psalms, Vol. 2
53. Cassiodorus: Explanation of the Psalms, Vol. 3
54. Origen: Treatise on the Passover and Dialogue with Heraclides
55. St. Irenaeus of Lyons: Against the Heresies (Book 1)
56. St. Justin Martyr: The First and Second Apologies
57. John Cassian: The Conferences
58. John Cassian: The Institutes
59. Evagrius Ponticus: Ad Monachos
60. Quodvultdeus of Carthage: The Creedal Homilies
61. Isidore of Seville: De Ecclesiasticis Officiis
62. Origen: Homilies 1–14 on Ezekiel
63. Julian of Toledo: Prognosticum futuri saeculi
64. St. Irenaeus of Lyons: Against the Heresies (Book 3)
65. St. Irenaeus of Lyons: Against the Heresies (Book 2)
66. St. Jerome: Commentary on Ecclesiastes
67. Theodoret of Cyrus: A Cure for Pagan Maladies
68. St. Jerome: Commentary on Isaiah; Origen: Homilies 1–9 on Isaiah
69. Theodore the Studite: Writings on Iconoclasm
70. Sulpicius Severus: The Complete Works
71. St. Jerome: Commentary on Ezekiel
72. St. Irenaeus of Lyons: Against the Heresies (Books 4 and 5) *forthcoming*
73. Isidore of Seville: Sententiae
74. The Teachings of the Desert Fathers
75. Chromatius of Aquileia: Sermons and Tractates on Matthew
76. Pelagius: Commentaries on Paul's Epistles (tentative) *forthcoming*